Documents of

AMERICAN
BROADCASTING

Documents of

AMERICAN

BROADCASTING

Edited by **FRANK J. KAHN**
Herbert H. Lehman College
City University of New York

APPLETON-CENTURY-CROFTS
Division of Meredith Corporation/New York

Dedicated to the memory
of my father,
Ernest L. Kahn

PREFACE

The germinal idea for this book occurred to me several years ago, shortly after I began teaching. As an instructor of broadcasting I considered it advisable for my students to read certain laws, decisions, reports, and other documents in their original form. Although some excellent textbooks on broadcasting referred to such materials, and others included selected extracts or, in all too few instances, a document or two in their entirety, no collection of primary sources was available. Thus, I either duplicated certain documents for classroom distribution, referred students to law books they were untrained to use or, as was most often the case, dropped the idea simply because of the difficulty in gaining access to such sources. Other instructors shared the same problem of inconvenient accessibility. *Documents of American Broadcasting* should satisfy the obvious need for a collection of primary reference sources in the field of broadcasting.

Although it is a supplementary text and reference work for various broadcasting courses, the book can be used as a primary text in courses such as "History of Broadcasting," "Radio-TV Law," or "Freedom of Speech in Broadcasting." It should also be helpful to radio and television practitioners.

Undoubtedly, had this work been edited by someone else its contents would have been somewhat, if not very substantially, different. The selections are functions of my particular orientation to broadcasting and broadcasting education, as well as the era during which the selections were made. The bibliographical entries in the lists of "Related Reading" have been chosen on the basis of their ease of access and their historical or contemporary significance.

Individual documents have been grouped into five sections. Many of them become doubly valuable when read in conjunction with documents in other sections. For example, the "Network" case (*National Broadcasting Co., Inc. et al. v. United States et al.,* 319 U.S. 190 (1943)) which appears in Part IV, "Regulation of Competition," is also highly relevant to Part II, "Freedom of Expression: Regulation of Programming," since the decision has much to say regarding freedom of speech in broadcasting. Instructors are urged not to misconstrue an organizational convenience as didactic necessity.

Every effort has been made to include as much of each document as readers are likely to find useful. Most documents appear in their entirety;

v

others have been edited so as to remove irrelevancies. Too much is preferable to too little. Any reader can skip over what he deems of little consequence.

Variant footnote styles and forms of legal citation have not been brought into conformity. Such attempts at consistency would modify documents whose formal and substantive integrity are of paramount concern.

I am indebted to Giraud Chester, Bob Crawford, Frank P. Fogarty, Eugene S. Foster, Garnet R. Garrison, Lawrence Myers, Jr., Charles A. Siepmann, and Edgar E. Willis, all of whom commented on the concept, contents, and organization of this book, and all of whom gave advice that tested and often improved my original conception. I, of course, am solely responsible for any of this work's shortcomings.

While acknowledgements to copyright holders are included in the text, special thanks are due to Jonah Gitlitz of the Code Authority, National Association of Broadcasters, C. Wrede Petersmeyer and Charles H. Tower of the Corinthian Broadcasting Company, and McGeorge Bundy of the Ford Foundation. These gentlemen made available documents without which this collection would have been incomplete.

.F.J.K.

CONTENTS

PART THREE

FREEDOM OF EXPRESSION:
BROADCAST JOURNALISM   341

PART FOUR

REGULATION OF COMPETITION   479

INTRODUCTION

Broadcasting in the United States has progressed from its fumbling, almost accidental beginnings to accepted institutional status. Today radio and television are properly regarded as popular entertainment media, as well as powerful economic, educational, journalistic, and political instruments in American society.

The basic system of U.S. broadcasting is an amalgam of commercial free enterprise and limited governmental regulation. This structure is augmented by a similarly regulated noncommercial, educational system. Yet, the present organization of the broadcast media in this country did not simply happen. Rather, it is the product of particular American values and needs, as well as of unique democratic methods of applying values to implement needs.

The documents in this volume cast light on shifting values and needs, and are fundamental to a full understanding of the development and significance of broadcasting in America. They have been selected and arranged so as to focus on the history and recurrent issues in the field. The editor's interpretation of the documents has been minimized in order that the reader may analyze and judge the materials for himself. For those who wish to consider these documents in a more complete historical and interpretive context, the following sources are recommended:

> CHESTER, Giraud, Garnet R. GARRISON, and Edgar E. WILLIS. *Television and Radio,* 3rd ed. New York: Appleton-Century-Crofts, 1963.
>
> HEAD, Sydney W. *Broadcasting in America.* Boston: Houghton Mifflin, 1956.
>
> SIEPMANN, Charles A. *Radio, Television, and Society.* New York: Oxford University Press, 1950.

More specific bibliographic entries appear throughout the book.

Legal Citation

Since legal citation may pose some problem for those unfamiliar with legal research, an explanation is necessary for readers who wish to explore sources cited in many of these documents.

Judicial and quasi-judicial citations follow the form, 36 FCC 147,

with the name of the case preceding and the year (in parentheses) following, thus: *In re Pacifica Foundation,* 36 FCC 147 (1964). "FCC" means
that the decision is found in *Federal Communications Commission Reports.*
The number immediately preceding "FCC" indicates the volume (36) in
which the decision is located, while the number directly following "FCC"
denotes the page (147) on which the decision begins. An entry such as 33
FCC 250, 255 refers to page 255 of a decision that begins on page 250 of
volume 33 of *Federal Communications Commission Reports.*

The following source abbreviations are the most frequently encountered in broadcast law citations:

App. D.C.	*Appeals Cases, District of Columbia*
C.F.R.	*Code of Federal Regulations*
F.	*Federal Reporter*
FCC	*Federal Communications Commission Reports*
Fed. Reg.	*Federal Register*
F. Supp.	*Federal Supplement*
Ops. Att'y Gen.	*Opinions of the Attorney General*
R.R.	*Radio Regulation* (Pike and Fischer)
U.S.	*United States Supreme Court Reports*

Any citation followed by the notation "2d," e.g., 62 F.2d 850, means that
the decision is found in the second series of the indicated source. *Federal
Communications Commission Reports, Federal Reporter,* and Pike and
Fischer's *Radio Regulation* are currently in their second series.

"FCC 63-734" and similar entries refer to Federal Communications
Commission mimeographed notices. The first two numerals are the last two
digits of the year in which the notice was published, while the following
numbers specify the sequential order of notices within that year. Thus, the
above example is the 734th notice published by the Federal Communications Commission in 1963.

Federal legislative materials such as enacted laws, debates, reports and
messages, and hearings, are found in *United States Code* and *Statutes at
Large, Congressional Record,* Senate and House documents serial sets, and
separately published volumes of hearing transcripts, respectively.

For further guidance concerning legal notation, consult the most recent
edition of *A Uniform System of Citation,* published by the Harvard Law
Review Association, Cambridge, Massachusetts. Any good law dictionary
(*Blackstone's,* for example) will serve to define legal terms.

PART | ONE

DEVELOPMENT OF
BROADCAST REGULATION

THE GROWTH of communications law generally parallels the startling evolution of communications technology. Since technology usually precedes the regulation of its economic and social effects, radio regulation has never quite kept pace with technical developments in the field. Broadcasting assumed its familiar structure of support by advertisers under the archaic provisions of the Radio Act of 1912. Similarly, developments such as community antenna television or Pay-TV were never contemplated in the Communications Act of 1934, and the Communications Satellite Act of 1962 is silent concerning regulation of direct satellite-to-home broadcast transmission, a technical feat that seems to be just around the corner.

Congress enacted effective broadcast regulation in 1927 only when it became painfully apparent that the absence of such legislation would result in the misuse of a potentially valuable national resource—the radio spectrum. Unable to oversee the fine points of broadcast regulation itself, the Congress established an expert body (first the Federal Radio Commission, then the Federal Communications Commission) to act as its regulatory instrument. The basic Congressional mandate was that broadcasting must serve the public interest; the definition and application of that criterion were left to the Commission, which was entrusted with broad discretionary powers.

Whatever criticisms may be made regarding the development of broadcast law in the United States (and these range from charges of laxity to complaints of stringency), it is clear that American broadcasting could never have achieved its amazing accomplishments without the regulatory scheme that took shape in the last half century. Both the prescriptive and proscriptive provisions of our laws serve to give credence to the contention

3

that America's unique amalgam of private enterprise and the public interest in broadcasting is consistent with public policy as enunciated by the people's elected representatives. Whether broadcasting shaped the law or the law shaped broadcasting then becomes as unanswerable a question as the old, familiar one about chickens and eggs. One suggested answer: "A chicken is what an egg makes in order to reproduce itself."[1]

[1] David K. Berlo, *The Process of Communication* (New York: Holt, Rinehart and Winston, 1960), p. 38.

1 THE U.S. CONSTITUTION 1787-1868

Federal broadcast regulation springs from that source of all Federal law, the Constitution. The commerce clause, Article I, Section 8, was subsequently interpreted by the Supreme Court to include the regulation of interstate communication, of which broadcasting is an example. The First Amendment to the Constitution is echoed by Section 29 of the Radio Act of 1927 and Section 326 of the Communications Act of 1934.

Article I, Section 8. The Congress shall have Power . . . To regulate Commerce with foreign Nations, and among the several States, and with the Indian Tribes . . .

First Amendment. Congress shall make no law respecting an establishment of religion, or prohibiting the free exercise thereof; or abridging the freedom of speech, or of the press; or the right of the people peaceably to assemble, and to petition the government for a redress of grievances.

Fifth Amendment. No person shall . . . be deprived of life, liberty, or property, without due process of law; nor shall private property be taken for public use, without just compensation.

Sixth Amendment. In all criminal prosecutions, the accused shall enjoy the right to a speedy and public trial, by an impartial jury of the State and district wherein the crime shall have been committed, which district shall have been previously ascertained by law, and to be informed of the nature and cause of the accusation; to be confronted with the witnesses against him; to have compulsory process for obtaining witnesses in his favor, and to have the Assistance of Counsel for his defence.

Fourteenth Amendment. Sec. 1. . . . No State shall make or enforce any law which shall abridge the privileges or immunities of citizens of the United States; nor shall any State deprive any person of life, liberty, or property, without due process of law; nor deny to any person within its jurisdiction the equal protection of the laws. . . .

2 | THE WIRELESS SHIP ACT OF 1910

Public Law 262, 61st Congress
June 24, 1910

This first American radio law, enacted ten years before the advent of broadcasting, was limited to the use of radio as a lifesaving device at sea.

Be it enacted by the Senate and House of Representatives of the United States of America in Congress assembled, That from and after the first day of July, nineteen hundred and eleven, it shall be unlawful for any ocean-going steamer of the United States, or of any foreign country, carrying passengers and carrying fifty or more persons, including passengers and crew, to leave or attempt to leave any port of the United States unless such steamer shall be equipped with an efficient apparatus for radio-communication, in good working order, in charge of a person skilled in the use of such apparatus, which apparatus shall be capable of transmitting and receiving messages over a distance of at least one hundred miles, night or day: *Provided,* That the provisions of this act shall not apply to steamers plying only between ports less than two hundred miles apart.

SEC. 2. That for the purpose of this act apparatus for radio-communication shall not be deemed to be efficient unless the company installing it shall contract in writing to exchange, and shall, in fact, exchange, as far as may be physically practicable, to be determined by the master of the vessel, messages with shore or ship stations using other systems of radio-communication.

SEC. 3. That the master or other person being in charge of any such vessel which leaves or attempts to leave any port of the United States in violation of any of the provisions of this act shall, upon conviction, be fined in a sum not more than five thousand dollars, and any such fine shall be a lien upon such vessel, and such vessel may be libeled therefor in any district court of the United States within the jurisdiction of which such vessel shall

6

arrive or depart, and the leaving or attempting to leave each and every port of the United States shall constitute a separate offense.

Sec. 4. That the Secretary of Commerce and Labor shall make such regulations as may be necessary to secure the proper execution of this act by collectors of customs and other officers of the Government.

3 | THE RADIO ACT OF 1912

Public Law 264, 62d Congress
August 13, 1912

This first comprehensive piece of radio legislation made it illegal to operate a radio station without a license from the Secretary of Commerce, but failed to provide sufficient discretionary standards for the effective regulation of broadcasting, which was still not envisioned at the time of enactment.

Be it enacted by the Senate and House of Representatives of the United States of America in Congress assembled, That a person, company, or corporation within the jurisdiction of the United States shall not use or operate any apparatus for radio communication as a means of commercial intercourse among the several States, or with foreign nations, or upon any vessel of the United States engaged in interstate or foreign commerce, or for the transmission of radiograms or signals the effect of which extends beyond the jurisdiction of the State or Territory in which the same are made, or where interference would be caused thereby with the receipt of messages or signals from beyond the jurisdiction of the said State or Territory, except under and in accordance with a license, revocable for cause, in that behalf granted by the Secretary of Commerce and Labor upon application therefor; but nothing in this Act shall be construed to apply to the transmission and exchange of radiograms or signals between points situated in the same State: *Provided,* That the effect thereof shall not extend beyond the jurisdiction of the said State or interfere with the reception of radiograms or signals from beyond said jurisdiction; and a license shall not be required for the transmission or exchange of radiograms or signals by or on behalf of the Government of the United States, but every Government station on land or sea shall have special call letters designated and published in the list of radio stations of the United States by the Department of Commerce and Labor. Any person, company, or corporation that shall use or operate any

8

apparatus for radio communication in violation of this section, or knowingly aid or abet another person, company, or corporation in so doing, shall be deemed guilty of a misdemeanor, and on conviction thereof shall be punished by a fine not exceeding five hundred dollars, and the apparatus or device so unlawfully used and operated may be adjudged forfeited to the United States.

SEC. 2. That every such license shall be in such form as the Secretary of Commerce and Labor shall determine and shall contain the restrictions, pursuant to this Act, on and subject to which the license is granted; that every such license shall be issued only to citizens of the United States or Porto Rico or to a company incorporated under the laws of some State or Territory or of the United States or Porto Rico, and shall specify the ownership and location of the station in which said apparatus shall be used and other particulars for its identification and to enable its range to be estimated; shall state the purpose of the station, and, in case of a station in actual operation at the date of passage of this Act, shall contain the statement that satisfactory proof has been furnished that it was actually operating on the above-mentioned date; shall state the wave length or the wave lengths authorized for use by the station for the prevention of interference and the hours for which the station is licensed for work; and shall not be construed to authorize the use of any apparatus for radio communication in any other station than that specified. Every such license shall be subject to the regulations contained herein, and such regulations as may be established from time to time by authority of this act or subsequent acts and treaties of the United States. Every such license shall provide that the President of the United States in time of war or public peril or disaster may cause the closing of any station for radio communication and the removal therefrom of all radio apparatus, or may authorize the use or control of any such station or apparatus by any department of the Government, upon just compensation to the owners.

SEC. 3. That every such apparatus shall at all times while in use and operation as aforesaid be in charge or under the supervision of a person or persons licensed for that purpose by the Secretary of Commerce and Labor. Every person so licensed who in the operation of any radio apparatus shall fail to observe and obey regulations contained in or made pursuant to this act or subsequent acts or treaties of the United States, or any one of them, or who shall fail to enforce obedience thereto by an unlicensed person while serving under his supervision, in addition to the punishments and penalties herein prescribed, may suffer the suspension of the said license for a period to be fixed by the Secretary of Commerce and Labor not exceeding one year. It shall be unlawful to employ any unlicensed person or for any unlicensed person to serve in charge or in supervision of the use and operation of such apparatus, and any person violating this provision shall be guilty of a misdemeanor, and on conviction thereof shall be punished by a fine of not more than one hundred dollars or imprisonment for not more than two months; or both, in the discretion of the court, for each and every such offense: *Provided,* That in case of emergency the Secretary of Commerce and Labor may authorize a collector of customs to issue a temporary permit, in lieu of a license, to the operator on a vessel subject to the radio ship act of June twenty-fourth, nineteen hundred and ten.

SEC. 4. That for the purpose of preventing or minimizing interference with communication between stations in which such apparatus is operated, to facilitate radio communication, and to further the prompt receipt of distress signals, said private and commercial stations shall be subject to the regulations of this section. These regulations shall be enforced by the Secretary of Commerce and Labor through the collectors of customs and other officers of the Government as other regulations herein provided for.

The Secretary of Commerce and Labor may, in his discretion, waive the provisions of any or all of these regulations when no interference of the character above mentioned can ensue.

The Secretary of Commerce and Labor may grant special temporary licenses to stations actually engaged in conducting experiments for the development of the science of radio communication, or the apparatus pertaining thereto, to carry on special tests, using any amount of power or any wave lengths, at such hours and under such conditions as will insure the least interference with the sending or receipt of commercial or Government radiograms, of distress signals and radiograms, or with the work of other stations.

In these regulations the naval and military stations shall be understood to be stations on land.

REGULATIONS

Normal wave length

First. Every station shall be required to designate a certain definite wave length as the normal sending and receiving wave length of the station. This wave length shall not exceed six hundred meters or it shall exceed one thousand six hundred meters. Every coastal station open to general public service shall at all times be ready to receive messages of such wave lengths as are required by the Berlin convention. Every ship station, except as hereinafter provided, and every coast station open to general public service shall be prepared to use two sending wave lengths, one of three hundred meters and one of six hundred meters, as required by the international convention in force: *Provided,* That the Secretary of Commerce and Labor may, in his discretion, change the limit of wave length reservation made by regulations first and second to accord with any international agreement to which the United States is a party.

Other wave lengths

Second. In addition to the normal sending wave length all stations, except as provided hereinafter in these regulations, may use other sending wave lengths: *Provided,* That they do not exceed six hundred meters or that they do exceed one thousand six hundred meters: *Provided further,* That the character of the waves emitted conforms to the requirements of regulations third and fourth following.

Use of a "pure wave"

Third. At all stations if the sending apparatus, to be referred to hereinafter as the "transmitter," is of such a character that the energy is radiated in two or more wave lengths, more or less sharply defined, as indicated by a sensitive wave meter, the energy in no one of the lesser waves shall exceed ten per centum of that in the greatest.

Use of a "sharp wave"

Fourth. At all stations the logarithmic decrement per complete oscillation in the wave trains emitted by the transmitter shall not exceed two-tenths, except when sending distress signals or signals and messages relating thereto.

Use of "standard distress wave"

Fifth. Every station on shipboard shall be prepared to send distress calls on the normal wave length designated by the international convention in force, except on vessels of small tonnage unable to have plants insuring that wave length.

Signal of distress

Sixth. The distress call used shall be the international signal of distress
• • • — — — • • •

Use of "broad interfering wave" for distress signals

Seventh. When sending distress signals, the transmitter of a station on shipboard may be tuned in such a manner as to create a maximum of interference with a maximum of radiation.

Distance requirements for distress signals

Eighth. Every station on shipboard, wherever practicable, shall be prepared to send distress signals of the character specified in regulations fifth and sixth with sufficient power to enable them to be received by day over sea a distance of one hundred nautical miles by a shipboard station equipped with apparatus for both sending and receiving equal in all essential particulars to that of the station first mentioned.

"Right of way" for distress signals

Ninth. All stations are required to give absolute priority to signals and radiograms relating to ships in distress; to cease all sending on hearing a distress signal; and, except when engaged in answering or aiding the ship in distress, to refrain from sending until all signals and radiograms relating thereto are completed.

Reduced power for ships near a government station

Tenth. No station on shipboard, when within fifteen nautical miles of a naval or military station, shall use a transformer input exceeding one kilowatt, nor, when within five nautical miles of such a station, a transformer input exceeding one-half kilowatt, except for sending signals of distress, or signals or radiograms relating thereto.

Intercommunication

Eleventh. Each shore station open to general public service between the coast and vessels at sea shall be bound to exchange radiograms with any similar shore station and with any ship station without distinction of the radio system adopted by such stations, respectively, and each station on shipboard shall be bound to exchange radiograms with any other station on shipboard without distinction of the radio systems adopted by each station, respectively.

It shall be the duty of each such shore station, during the hours it is in operation, to listen in at intervals of not less than fifteen minutes and for a period not less than two minutes, with the receiver tuned to receive messages of three hundred-meter wave lengths.

Division of time

Twelfth. At important seaports and at all other places where naval or military and private commercial shore stations operate in such close proximity that interference with the work of naval and military stations can not be avoided by the enforcement of the regulations contained in the foregoing regulations concerning wave lengths and character of signals emitted, such private or commercial shore stations as do interfere with the reception of signals by the naval and military stations concerned shall not use their transmitters during the first fifteen minutes of each hour, local standard time. The Secretary of Commerce and Labor may, on the recommendation of the department concerned, designate the station or stations which may be required to observe this division of time.

Government stations to observe division of time

Thirteenth. The naval or military stations for which the above-mentioned division of time may be established shall transmit signals or radiograms only during the first fifteen minutes of each hour, local standard time, except in case of signals or radiograms relating to vessels in distress, as hereinbefore provided.

Use of unnecessary power

Fourteenth. In all circumstances, except in case of signals or radiograms relating to vessels in distress, all stations shall use the minimum amount of energy necessary to carry out any communication desired.

General restrictions on private stations

Fifteenth. No private or commercial station not engaged in the transaction of bona fide commercial business by radio communication or in experimentation in connection with the development and manufacture of radio apparatus for commercial purposes shall use a transmitting wave length exceeding two hundred meters, or a transformer input exceeding one kilowatt, except by special authority of the Secretary of Commerce and Labor contained in the license of the station: *Provided,* That the owner or operator of a station of the character mentioned in this regulation shall not be liable for a violation of the requirements of the third or fourth regulations to the penalties of one hundred dollars or twenty-five dollars, respectively, provided in this section unless the person maintaining or operating such station shall have been notified in writing that the said transmitter has been found, upon tests conducted by the Government, to be so adjusted as to violate the third and fourth regulations, and opportunity has been given to said owner or operator to adjust said transmitter in conformity with said regulations.

Special restrictions in the vicinities of government stations

Sixteenth. No station of the character mentioned in regulation fifteenth situated within five nautical miles of a naval or military station shall use a transmitting wave length exceeding two hundred meters or a transformer input exceeding one-half kilowatt.

Ship stations to communicate with nearest shore stations

Seventeenth. In general, the shipboard stations shall transmit their radiograms to the nearest shore station. A sender on board a vessel shall, however, have the right to designate the shore station through which he desires to have his radiograms transmitted. If this can not be done, the wishes of the sender are to be complied with only if the transmission can be effected without interfering with the service of other stations.

Limitations for future installations in vicinities of government stations

Eighteenth. No station on shore not in actual operation at the date of the passage of this act shall be licensed for the transaction of commercial business by radio communication within fifteen nautical miles of the following naval or military stations, to wit: Arlington, Virginia; Key West, Florida; San Juan, Porto Rico; North Head and Tatoosh Island, Washington; San Diego, California; and those established or which may be established in Alaska and in the Canal Zone; and the head of the department having control of such Government stations shall, so far as is consistent with the transaction of governmental business, arrange for the transmission and receipt of commercial radiograms under the provisions of the Berlin convention of nineteen hundred and six and future international conventions or treaties to which the United States may be a party, at each of the stations above referred to, and shall fix the rates therefor, subject to control of such rates by Congress. At such stations and wherever and whenever shore stations open for general public business between the coast and vessels at sea under the provisions of the Berlin convention of nineteen hundred and six and future international conventions and treaties to which the United States may be a party shall not be so established as to insure a constant service day and night without interruption, and in all localities wherever or whenever such service shall not be maintained by a commercial shore station within one hundred nautical miles of a naval radio station, the Secretary of the Navy shall, so far as is consistent with the transaction of Government business, open naval radio stations to the general public business described above, and shall fix rates for such service, subject to control of such rates by Congress. The receipts from such radiograms shall be covered into the Treasury as miscellaneous receipts.

Secrecy of messages

Nineteenth. No person or persons engaged in or having knowledge of the operation of any station or stations shall divulge or publish the contents of any messages transmitted or received by such station, except to the person or persons to whom the same may be directed, or their authorized agent, or to another station employed to forward such message to its destination, unless legally required so to do by the court of competent jurisdiction or other competent authority. Any person guilty of divulging or publishing any message, except as herein provided, shall, on conviction thereof, be punishable by a fine of not more than two hundred and fifty dollars or imprisonment for a period of not exceeding three months, or both fine and imprisonment, in the discretion of the court.

Penalties

For violation of any of these regulations, subject to which a license under sections one and two of this act may be issued, the owner of the apparatus shall be liable to a penalty of one hundred dollars, which may be reduced or remitted by the Secretary of Commerce and Labor, and for repeated violations of any of such regulations the license may be revoked.

For violation of any of these regulations, except as provided in regulation nineteenth, subject to which a license under section three of this act may be issued, the operator shall be subject to a penalty of twenty-five dollars, which may be reduced or remitted by the Secretary of Commerce and Labor, and for repeated violations of any such regulations, the license shall be suspended or revoked.

SEC. 5. That every license granted under the provisions of this act for the operation or use of apparatus for radio communication shall prescribe that the operator thereof shall not willfully or maliciously interfere with any other radio communication. Such interference shall be deemed a misdemeanor, and upon conviction thereof the owner or operator, or both, shall be punishable by a fine of not to exceed five hundred dollars or imprisonment for not to exceed one year, or both.

SEC. 6. That the expression "radio communication" as used in this act means any system of electrical communication by telegraphy or telephony without the aid of any wire connecting the points from and at which the radiograms, signals, or other communications are sent or received.

SEC. 7. That a person, company, or corporation within the jurisdiction of the United States shall not knowingly utter or transmit, or cause to be uttered or transmitted, any false or fraudulent distress signal or call or false or fraudulent signal, call, or other radiogram of any kind. The penalty for so uttering or transmitting a false or fraudulent distress signal or call shall be a fine of not more than two thousand five hundred dollars or imprisonment for not more than five years, or both, in the discretion of the court, for each and every such offense, and the penalty for so uttering or transmitting, or causing to be uttered or transmitted, any other false or fraudulent signal, call, or other radiogram shall be a fine of not more than one thousand dollars or imprisonment for not more than two years, or both, in the discretion of the court, for each and every such offense.

SEC. 8. That a person, company, or corporation shall not use or operate any apparatus for radio communication on a foreign ship in territorial waters of the United States otherwise than in accordance with the provisions of sections four and seven of this act and so much of section five as imposes a penalty for interference. Save as aforesaid, nothing in this act shall apply to apparatus for radio communication on any foreign ship.

SEC. 9. That the trial of any offense under this act shall be in the district in which it is committed, or if the offense is committed upon the high seas or out of the jurisdiction of any particular State or district the trial shall be in the district where the offender may be found or into which he shall be first brought.

SEC. 10. That this act shall not apply to the Philippine Islands.

SEC. 11. That this act shall take effect and be in force on and after four months from its passage.

4 BREAKDOWN OF THE ACT OF 1912

Broadcasting in the United States began in 1920, when station KDKA in Pittsburgh, Pennsylvania, reported the Harding-Cox election returns to a widely dispersed audience. By early 1923 some 576 stations were licensed for broadcasting. The public's investment in receiving apparatus had increased by leaps and bounds as more stations came on the air.

Secretary of Commerce Herbert Hoover valiantly tried to minimize interference problems under the Act of 1912. The three legal decisions, below, vitiated the discretionary powers the Secretary had been exercising, and pointed out the need for more effective broadcast regulation.

A HOOVER v. INTERCITY RADIO CO., INC.*

286 F. 1003 (D.C. Cir.)
February 5, 1923

VAN ORSDEL, Associate Justice.   This appeal is from an order of the Supreme Court of the District of Columbia, directing the issuance of a writ of mandamus requiring appellant, Secretary of Commerce, to issue to plaintiff company, a license to operate a radio station in the city of New York.

The plaintiff alleged that it has been engaged in the business of wireless telegraphy between New York and other cities of the United States since January 16, 1920, under licenses issued from time to time by defendant, pursuant to the Act of Congress approved August 13, 1912, 37 Stat. 302 (Comp. St. § 10100–10109). It was further alleged that the last license ex-

* Opinion taken with permission from Vol. 286, *Federal Reporter.*

pired on November 12, 1921; that defendant refused to grant plaintiff a new license for the operation of its station; that appellee, in all respects, complied with the requirements of the act of Congress and of the regulations contained therein; and that the duty imposed upon defendant of granting licenses is purely a ministerial one.

Defendant answered, admitting the refusal of the license, but defending on the ground that he had been unable to ascertain a wave length for use by plaintiff, which would not interfere with government and private stations, and that under the provisions of the act of Congress the issuance or refusal of a license is a matter wholly within his discretion.

Section 1 of the act (Comp. St. § 10100) forbids the operation of radio apparatus, where interferences would be caused with receipt of messages or signals from beyond the jurisdiction of the state or territory in which it is situated, "except under and in accordance with a license, revocable for cause, in that behalf granted by the Secretary of Commerce and Labor upon application therefor." The license shall be in form prescribed by the Secretary, containing the restrictions pursuant to the act "on and subject to which the license is granted." Section 2 (Comp. St. § 10101). The license also "shall state the wave length or the wave lengths authorized for use by the station for the prevention of interference and the hours for which the station is licensed for work." The license is further made subject to the regulations of the act and such regulations as may be made by the authority of the act.

The Secretary of Commerce is given authority, for the purpose of preventing or minimizing interference with communication between stations, to enforce the regulations established by the act through the collectors of customs and other officers of the government, with power, however, in his discretion, to waive the provisions of the regulations when no interference obtains.

The act further provides as follows:

All stations are required to give absolute priority to signals and radiograms relating to ships in distress; to cease all sending on hearing a distress signal; and, except when engaged in answering or aiding the ship in distress, to refrain from sending until all signals and radiograms relating thereto are completed. Section 4 (Comp. St. § 10103).

Private or commercial shore stations, so situated that their operation interferes with naval and military stations, are forbidden to "use their transmitters during the first fifteen minutes of each hour, local standard time," during which time the military and naval stations shall transmit signals or radiograms, "except in case of signals or radiograms relating to vessels in distress." The Secretary is forbidden to license private or commercial stations to adopt a wave length between 600 meters and 1,600 meters, the wave lengths between these figures being reserved for governmental agencies. Penalties are prescribed for violations of the act.

Congress seems to have legislated on the subject of radio telegraphy with reference to the undeveloped state of the art. Interference in operation is conceded; hence the act undertakes to prescribe regulations by which the interference may be minimized rather than prevented. It regulates the preferences to be accorded distress signals and government business. It specifically subjects private and commercial stations to the regulations prescribed by the act, the enforcement of which is imposed upon the Secretary of Commerce, acting "through the collectors of customs and other officers of the government." Indeed, the impossibility of totally eliminating interference was recognized internationally by the London Convention which resulted in the Treaty of July 8, 1913 (38 Stat. 1672).

Complete control of the whole subject was reserved by Congress in the provision of section 2 (Comp. St. § 10101) that "such license shall be subject to the regulations contained herein, and such regulations as may be established from time to time by authority of this act or subsequent acts or treaties of the United States," and the further provision that "such license shall provide that the President of the United States in time of war or public peril or disaster may cause the closing of any station for radio communication and the removal therefrom of all radio apparatus, or may authorize the use or control of any such station or apparatus by any department of the government, upon just compensation to the owners."

We are in accord with the construction placed upon the act by the Attorney General on October 24, 1912 (29 Op. Atty. Gen. 579), in response to an inquiry from the Secretary of Commerce and Labor, as follows:

> The language of the act, the nature of the subject-matter regulated, as well as the general scope of the statute, negative the idea that Congress intended to repose any such discretion in you in the matter of licenses. It is apparent from the act as a whole that Congress determined thereby to put the subject of radio communication under federal supervision, so far as it was interstate or foreign in its nature. It is also apparent therefrom that that supervision and control is taken by Congress upon itself, and that the Secretary of Commerce and Labor is only authorized to deal with the matter as provided in the act, and is given no general regulative power in respect thereto. The act prescribes the conditions under which the licensees shall operate, containing a set of regulations, with penalties for their violation.

That Congress intended to fully regulate the business of radio telegraphy, without leaving it to the discretion of an executive officer, is apparent from the report of the House committee in recommending the passage of the bill to the House of Representatives, as follows:

The first section of the bill defines its scope within the commerce clause of the Constitution, and requires all wireless stations, ship and shore, public and private, to be licensed by the Secretary of Commerce and Labor. This section does not give the head of that department discretionary power over the issue of licenses, but in fact provides for an enumeration of the wireless stations of the United States and on vessels under the American flag. The license system proposed is substantially the same as that in use for the documenting upward of 25,000 merchant vessels.

It was further stated by the chairman of the committee on commerce in the Senate, when the bill was under consideration, that "it is compulsory with the Secretary of Commerce and Labor that upon application these licenses shall be issued."

While committee reports are not binding upon the courts in interpreting statutes, they are indicative of the legislative intention, and will be followed when the statements so made accord with the reasonable interpretation to be drawn from the language of the act itself.

We are not unmindful of the strict rule forbidding interference with the exercise of official discretion by the extraordinary processes of the courts. The rule that mandamus will not lie to control the action of an official of the executive department, in the exercise of discretionary power, is too well settled to require discussion. But where the duty imposed is purely ministerial, and there is no discretion reposed in the officer, the courts will not hesitate to require the performance of the duty as prescribed.

In the present case the duty of naming a wave length is mandatory upon the Secretary. The only discretionary act is in selecting a wave length, within the limitations prescribed in the statute, which, in his judgment, will result in the least possible interference. The issuing of a license is not dependent upon the fixing of a wave length. It is a restriction entering into the license. The wave length named by the Secretary merely measures the extent of the privilege granted to the licensee.

It logically follows that the duty of issuing licenses to persons or corporations coming within the classification designated in the act reposes no discretion whatever in the Secretary of Commerce. The duty is mandatory; hence the courts will not hesitate to require its performance.

The judgment is affirmed, with costs.

B | UNITED STATES v. ZENITH RADIO CORPORATION et al.*

12 F.2d 614 (N.D. Ill.)
April 16, 1926

WILKERSON, District Judge. The information charges violations of section 1 of the Act of August 13, 1912, c. 287 (37 Stat. 302 [Comp. St. § 10100]).

The first count alleges that on December 19, 1925, defendant Zenith Radio Corporation used and operated certain apparatus for radio communication, as a means of commercial intercourse among several states of the United States, to wit, from Mt. Prospect, Ill., to Seattle, Wash.; which apparatus was so used and operated not under and in accordance with a license such as described in the act; and that defendant McDonald aided, abetted, and procured the commission of the offense. The second, third, and fourth counts charges offenses on other dates in the same language as count 1.

The fifth, sixth, seventh, and eighth counts are the same as the first four counts, except that it is charged that the corporation "used and operated certain apparatus for radio communication for the transmission of radiograms and signals, the effect of which then and there extended beyond the jurisdiction of the state in which the same were then and there made."

Section 1 of the act in question prohibits the use of apparatus for radio communication as a means of commercial intercourse among the several states, or with foreign nations, or upon any vessel of the United States engaged in interstate or foreign commerce, or for the transmission of radiograms or signals the effect of which extends beyond the jurisdiction of the state or territory in which the same are made, or where interference would be caused thereby with the receipt of messages or signals from beyond the jurisdiction of said state or territory, except under and in accordance with a license, revocable for cause, granted by the Secretary of Commerce upon application therefor. It is provided:

Any person, company, or corporation that shall use or operate any apparatus for radio communication in violation of this section, or knowingly aid

* Opinion taken with permission from Vol. 12, *Federal Reporter,* second series.

or abet another person, company, or corporation in so doing, shall be deemed guilty of a misdemeanor. . . .

Section 2 of the act (Comp. St. § 10101) provides:

Every such license shall be in such form as the Secretary of Commerce (and Labor) shall determine and shall contain the restrictions, pursuant to this act, on and subject to which the license is granted; every such license shall be issued only to citizens of the United States or Porto Rico or to a company incorporated under the laws of some state or territory or of the United States or Porto Rico, and shall specify the ownership and location of the station in which said apparatus shall be used and other particulars for its identification and to enable its range to be estimated; shall state the purpose of the station, and, in case of a station in actual operation at the date of passage of this act, shall contain the statement that satisfactory proof has been furnished that it was actually operating on the above-mentioned date; shall state the wave length or the wave lengths authorized for use by the station for the prevention of interference and the hours for which the station is licensed for work; and shall not be construed to authorize the use of any apparatus for radio communication in any other station than that specified. Every such license shall be subject to the regulations contained herein and such regulations as may be established from time to time by authority of this act or subsequent acts and treaties of the United States. Every such license shall provide that the President of the United States in time of war or public peril or disaster may cause the closing of any station for radio communication and the removal therefrom of all radio apparatus, or may authorize the use or control of any such station or apparatus by any department of the government, upon just compensation to the owners.

Section 4 of the act (Comp. St. § 10103) provides:

For the purpose of preventing or minimizing interference with communication between stations in which such apparatus is operated, to facilitate radio communication, and to further the prompt receipt of distress signals, said private and commercial stations shall be subject to the regulations of the section. These regulations shall be enforced by the Secretary of Commerce (and Labor) through the collectors of customs and other officers of the government as other regulations herein provided for.

The Secretary of Commerce (and Labor) may, in his discretion, waive the provisions of any or all of these regulations when no interference of the character above mentioned can ensue.

Among the regulations prescribed in section 4 are the following:

Normal wave length

First. Every station shall be required to designate a certain definite wave length as the normal sending and receiving wave length of the station. This wave length shall not exceed six hundred meters or it shall exceed one thousand six hundred meters. Every coastal station open to general public service shall at all times be ready to receive messages of such wave lengths as are required by the Berlin convention. Every ship station, except as hereinafter provided, and every coast station open to general public service shall be prepared to use two sending wave lengths, one of three hundred meters and one of six hundred meters, as required by the international convention in force: Provided, that the Secretary of Commerce (and Labor) may, in his discretion, change the limit of wave length reservation made by regulations first and second to accord with any international agreement to which the United States is a party.

Other wave lengths

Second. In addition to the normal sending wave length all stations, except as provided hereinafter in these regulations, may use other sending wave lengths: Provided, that they do not exceed six hundred meters or that they do exceed one thousand six hundred meters: Provided further, that the character of the waves emitted conforms to the requirements of regulations third and fourth following. . . .

Division of time

Twelfth. At important seaports and at all other places where naval or military and private or commercial shore stations operate in such close proximity that interference with the work of naval and military stations cannot be avoided by the enforcement of the regulations contained in the foregoing regulations concerning wave lengths and character of signals emitted, such private or commercial shore stations as do interfere with the reception of signals by the naval and military stations concerned shall not use their transmitters during the first fifteen minutes of each hour, local standard time. The Secretary of Commerce (and Labor) may, on the recommendation of the department concerned, designate the station or stations which may be required to observe this division of time. . . .

General restrictions on private stations

Fifteenth. No private or commercial station not engaged in the transaction of bona fide commercial business by radio communication or in experimentation in connection with the development and manufacture of radio apparatus for commercial purposes shall use a transmitting wave length exceeding two hundred meters, or a transformer input exceeding one kilowatt, except by special authority of the Secretary of Commerce (and Labor) contained in the license of the station: Provided, that the owner or operator of a station of the character mentioned in this regulation shall not be liable for a violation of the requirements of the third or fourth regulations to the penalties of one hundred dollars or twenty-five dollars, respectively, provided in this section unless the person maintaining or operating such station shall have been notified in writing that the said transmitter has been found, upon tests conducted by the government, to be so adjusted as to violate the said third and fourth regulations, and opportunity has been given to said owner or operator to adjust said transmitter in conformity with said regulations. . . .

Penalties

For violation of any of these regulations, subject to which a license under sections one and two of this act may be issued, the owner of the apparatus shall be liable to a penalty of one hundred dollars, which may be reduced or remitted by the Secretary of Commerce (and Labor), and for repeated violations of any of such regulations, the license may be revoked.

For violation of any of these regulations, except as provided in regulation nineteenth, subject to which a license under section three of this act may be issued, the operator shall be subject to a penalty of twenty-five dollars, which may be reduced or remitted by the Secretary of Commerce (and Labor), and for repeated violations of any such regulations, the license shall be suspended or revoked.

The Secretary of Commerce granted a license on September 21, 1925, to defendant corporation, and that license was in effect at the times of the alleged offenses charged in the information. . . .

Among the provisions of the license, the following are to be noted particularly:

This station to be operated only on Thursday nights from 10 to 12 p. m., Central Standard time, and then only when the use of this period is not desired by the General Electric Company's Denver station. This license is also issued conditionally upon the avoidance of interference with other stations.

In view of special conditions the station is authorized to use for communication exclusively with stations licensed by the United States the following additional wave lengths under 600 or over 1,600 meters: Meters, 332.4.

The material facts are not in dispute. It is agreed that defendant corporation, on the dates charged in the information, operated its station on a wave length and at times which were not authorized.

The broad provisions of section 1 of the act prohibits the use of the radio apparatus except *under and in accordance* with a license granted by the Secretary of Commerce. The use of the apparatus in violation of this provision is made a misdemeanor, punishable by fine up to $500 and forfeiture of the apparatus.

Section 2 of the act provides that the license shall contain the restrictions, *pursuant to the act,* on and subject to which the license is granted. It is provided in section 2 that the license "shall state the wave length or the wave lengths authorized for use by the station for the prevention of interference and the hours for which the station is licensed for work." It is further provided: "Every such license shall be subject to the regulations contained herein and such regulations as may be established from time to time by authority of this act or subsequent acts and treaties of the United States."

There is no express grant of power in the act to the Secretary of Commerce to establish regulations. The regulations subject to which the license is granted are contained in the fourth section of the act.

The fifteenth regulation prohibits a private or commercial station not engaged in the transaction of bona fide commercial business by radio communication or in experimentation in connection with the development and manufacture of radio apparatus for commercial purposes from using a wave length exceeding 200 meters except by special authority of the Secretary of Commerce. Defendant's license authorizes the use of a wave length of 332.4 meters on Thursday night from 10 to 12 p. m. *when the use of this period is not desired by the General Electric Company's Denver Station.*

Each of the acts of the defendant, relied upon by the United States as the basis of prosecution, is within the prohibition of the fifteenth regulation. Each count of the information covers broadcasting on a wave length of 329.5 meters at a time not covered by the authority in the license. Section 4 contains a special provision for penalties for violations of the regulations as follows:

For violation of any of these regulations, subject to which a license under sections one and two of this act may be issued, the owner of the apparatus shall be liable to a penalty of one hundred dollars, which may be reduced or remitted by the Secretary of Commerce, . . . and for repeated violations . . . the license may be revoked.

Does the operation of the station upon any wave length at any other time than from 10 to 12 p. m. on Thursday constitute a violation of section 1? The license provides:

This station to be operated only on Thursday nights from 10 to 12 p. m. Central Standard time and then only when the use of this period is not desired by the General Electric Company's Denver Station.

The provision in section 2 as to stating in the license the hours for which the station is licensed must be read and interpreted in its relation to the entire act.

The Secretary of Commerce is required to issue the license subject to the regulations in the act. The Congress has withheld from him the power to prescribe additional regulations. If there is a conflict between a provision in the license and the regulations established by Congress, the latter must control. Division of time is covered by the twelfth regulation. The provision in section 2 as to hours appears, in view of the references in that section to the regulations, to refer to the regulation as to the division of time. At least, the statute is ambiguous in this respect, and, while it should be given a reasonable construction, ambiguities are not to be solved so as to embrace offenses not clearly within the law. Krichman v. U. S., 256 U. S. 363, 367, 41 S. Ct. 514, 65 L. Ed. 992.

Furthermore, we must remember, in considering an act of Congress, that a construction which might render it unconstitutional is to be avoided. A statute must be construed, if fairly possible, so as to avoid not only the conclusion that it is unconstitutional but grave doubts upon that score. U. S. v. Standard Brewery, 251 U. S. 210, 220, 40 S. Ct. 139, 64 L. Ed. 229; U. S. v. Jin Fuey Moy, 241 U. S. 394, 401, 36 S. Ct. 658, 60 L. Ed. 1061, Ann. Cas. 1917D, 854.

If section 2 is construed to give to the Secretary of Commerce power to restrict the operation of a station as the United States contends is done by this license, what is the test or standard established by Congress, by which the discretion of the Secretary is to be controlled? In other words, what rule has Congress laid down for his guidance in determining division of time between the defendant and the General Electric Company? U. S. v. Grimaud, 220 U. S. 506, 519, 31 S. Ct. 480, 55 L. Ed. 563; Union Bridge Co. v. U. S., 204 U. S. 364, 27 S. Ct. 367, 51 L. Ed. 523; Field v. Clark, 143 U. S. 649, 692, 12 S. Ct. 495, 36 L. Ed. 294. No language is more worthy of frequent and thoughtful consideration than these words of Mr. Justice Matthews, speaking for the Supreme Court in Yick Wo v. Hopkins, 118 U. S. 356, 369, 6 S. Ct. 1064, 1071 (30 L. Ed. 220):

When we consider the nature and the theory of our institutions of government, the principles upon which they are supposed to rest, and review the history of their development, we are constrained to conclude that they do not mean to leave room for the play and action of purely personal and arbitrary power.

Congress cannot delegate its power to make a law, but it can make a law to delegate a power to determine some fact or state of facts upon which the law makes or intends to make its own action depend. Has Congress prescribed the rule or standard which is to control the Secretary of Commerce in the exercise of his discretion with the degree of certainty required in criminal statutes? It is axiomatic that statutes creating and defining crimes cannot be extended by intendment, and that no act, however wrongful, can be punished under such a statute, unless clearly within its terms. There can be no constructive offenses, and, before a man can be punished, his case must be plainly and unmistakably within the statute. U. S. v. Weitzel, 246 U. S. 533, 543, 38 S. Ct. 381, 62 L. Ed. 872; U. S. v. Harris, 177 U. S. 305, 310, 20 S. Ct. 609, 44 L. Ed. 780; Todd v. U. S., 158 U. S. 278, 282, 15 S. Ct. 889, 39 L. Ed. 982.

If we view the acts of the defendant corporation as violations of the fifteenth regulation, and admit for the present purpose the validity of that regulation, do they constitute a violation of section 1 also because the restrictions imposed under the regulation are included in the license? It is elementary that where there is, in an act, a specific provision relating to a particular subject, that provision must govern in respect to the subject as against general provisions in the act, although the latter, standing alone, would be broad enough to include the subject to which the more particular provision relates. Endlich, Interpretation of Statutes, § 216; Swiss National Insurance Co. v. Miller, 53 App. D. C. 173, 289 F. 571, 576; Washington v. Miller, 235 U. S. 422, 428, 35 S. Ct. 119, 59 L. Ed. 295; U. S. v. Nix, 189 U. S. 199, 205, 23 S. Ct. 495, 47 L. Ed. 775; Townsend v. Little, 109 U. S. 504, 519, 3 S. Ct. 357, 27 L. Ed. 1012. This rule is particularly applicable to criminal statutes in which the specific provisions relating to particular subjects carry smaller penalties than the general provision. Congress, when it inserted the regulations in the statute, provided especially for their violation. That provision should control, in my opinion, against the general, indefinite, and ambiguous provisions of sections 1 and 2.

My conclusion is that, under the rules applicable to criminal statutes, sections 1 and 2 cannot be construed to cover the acts of the defendant upon which this prosecution is based. Other questions have been argued which it is unnecessary to decide.

Reference has been made to the rule of practical construction. It is sufficient to say that administrative rulings cannot add to the terms of an act of Congress and make conduct criminal which such laws leave untouched. U. S. v. Standard Brewery, 251 U. S. 210, 220, 40 S. Ct. 139, 64 L. Ed. 229.

Finding for defendants.

 ATTORNEY GENERAL'S OPINION

35 Ops. Att'y Gen. 126
July 8, 1926

DEPARTMENT OF JUSTICE
July 8, 1926.

SIR: Receipt is acknowledged of your letter of June 4, 1926, in which you ask for a definition of your powers and duties with respect to the regulation of radio broadcasting under the Act of August 13, 1912, c. 287 (37 Stat.

302). Specifically, you request my opinion upon the following five questions:

(1) Does the 1912 Act require broadcasting stations to obtain licenses, and is the operation of such a station without a license an offense under that Act?

(2) Has the Secretary of Commerce authority under the 1912 Act to assign wave lengths and times of operation and limit the power of stations?

(3) Has a station, whose license stipulates a wave length for its use, the right to use any other wave length, and if it does operate on a different wave length, it is in violation of the law and does it become subject to the penalties of the Act?

(4) If a station, whose license stipulates a period during which only the station may operate and limits its power, transmits at different times, or with excessive power, is it in violation of the Act and does it become subject to the penalties of the Act?

(5) Has the Secretary of Commerce power to fix the duration of the licenses which he issues or should they be indeterminate, continuing in effect until revoked or until Congress otherwise provides?

With respect to the first question, my answer to both its parts is in the affirmative. Section 1 of the Act of 1912 provides—

That a person, company, or corporation within the jurisdiction of the United States shall not use or operate any apparatus for radio communication as a means of commercial intercourse among the several States, or with foreign nations, or upon any vessel of the United States engaged in interstate or foreign commerce, or for the transmission of radiograms or signals the effect of which extends beyond the jurisdiction of the State or Territory in which the same are made, or where interference would be caused thereby with the receipt of messages or signals from beyond the jurisdiction of the said State or Territory, except under and in accordance with a license, revocable for cause, in that behalf granted by the Secretary of Commerce (and Labor) upon application therefor; but nothing in this Act shall be construed to apply to the transmission and exchange of radiograms or signals between points situated in the same State: *Provided,* That the effect thereof shall not extend beyond the jurisdiction of the said State or interfere with the reception of radiograms or signals from beyond said jurisdiction. . . .

Violation of this section is declared to be a misdemeanor.

There is no doubt whatever that radio communication is a proper subject for Federal regulation under the commerce clause of the Constitution. *Pensacola Telegraph Company* v. *Western Union Telegraph Company,* 96 U. S. 1, 9, 24 Op. 100. And it may be noticed in passing that even purely intrastate transmission of radio waves may fall within the scope of Federal power when it disturbs the air in such a manner as to interfere with interstate communication, a situation recognized and provided for in the Act. Cf. *Minnesota Rate Cases,* 230 U. S. 352.

While the Act of 1912 was originally drafted to apply primarily to wireless telegraphy, its language is broad enough to cover wireless telephony as well; and this was clearly the intention of its framers (62nd Cong., 2nd Sess., S. Rept. 698). Whether the transmission is for profit is immaterial so far as the commerce clause is concerned. *American Express Company* v. *United States,* 212 U. S. 522; *Caminetti* v. *United States,* 242 U. S. 470.

For these reasons I am of the opinion that broadcasting is within the terms of the 1912 Act; that a license must be obtained before a broadcasting station may be lawfully operated; and that the penalties of section 1 of the Act may be imposed upon any person or corporation who operates such a station without a license.

Your second question involves three separate problems:

(a) The assignment of wave lengths.

(b) The assignment of hours of operation.

(c) The limitation of power.

(a) As to the assignment of wave lengths, section 2 of the Act provides—

That every such license shall be in such form as the Secretary of Commerce (and Labor) shall determine and shall contain the restrictions, pursuant to this Act, on and subject to which the license is granted; . . . shall state the wave length or the wave lengths authorized for use by the station for the prevention of interference and the hours for which the station is licensed for work. . . . Every such license shall be subject to the regulations contained herein and such regulations as may be established from time to time by authority of this Act or subsequent Acts and treaties of the United States.

The power to make general regulations is nowhere granted by specific language to the Secretary. On the contrary, it seems clear from section 4 of the Act that Congress intended to cover the entire field itself, and that, with minor exceptions, Congress left very little to the discretion of any administrative officer. This fact is made additionally plain by the reports which accompanied the Act in both Houses. 62d Cong. 2d Sess., S. Rept. 698; *ibid.,* H. R. Rept. 582. Cf. 29 Op. 579.

The first regulation in section 4 provides that the station shall be required to designate a definite wave length, outside of the band between 600 and 1,600 meters (reserved for Government stations), and that ship stations shall be prepared to use 300 and 600 meters.

The second regulation provides that in addition to the normal sending wave length, all stations, except as otherwise provided in the regulations, may use "other sending wave lengths," again excluding the band from 600 to 1,600 meters.

These two regulations constitute a direct legislative regulation of the use of wave lengths. They preclude the possibility of administrative discretion in the same field. In *Hoover* v. *Intercity Radio Company,* 286 Fed.

1003, it was held that it was mandatory upon the Secretary under the Act to grant licenses to all applicants complying with its provisions. The court added in that case these remarks:

> In the present case the duty of naming a wave length is mandatory upon the Secretary. The only discretionary act is in selecting a wave length, within the limitations prescribed in the statute, which, in his judgment, will result in the least possible interference. The issuing of a license is not dependent upon the fixing of a wave length. It is a restriction entering into the license. The wave length named by the Secretary merely measures the extent of the privilege granted to the licensee.

You have advised me that following this decision you have assumed that you had discretionary authority in assigning wave lengths for the use of particular stations, and have made such assignments to the individual broadcasting stations.

However, in my opinion, these remarks of the Court of Appeals are to be construed as applying only to the *normal* sending and receiving wave length which every station is required to designate under the first regulation. But under the second regulation, any station is at liberty to use "other wave lengths" at will, provided only that they do not trespass upon the band from 600 to 1,600 meters. This conclusion appears to be in accord with the opinion of the District Court for the Northern District of Illinois in the case . . . of *United States* v. *Zenith Radio Corporation.*

But it is suggested that under the fifteenth regulation broadcasting stations may not, without special authority from the Secretary, use wave lengths over 200 meters or power exceeding one kilowatt. This regulation is applicable only to "private and commercial stations not engaged in the transaction of bona fide commercial business by radio communication." I am of opinion that broadcasting is "the transaction of bona fide commercial business" (*Witmark* v. *Bamberger, 291* Fed. 776; *Remick* v. *American Automobile Accessories Co., 298* Fed. 628), and that it is conducted "by radio communication." Broadcasting stations, therefore, do not fall within the scope of the fifteenth regulation; and the Secretary is without power to impose on them the restrictions provided therein.

From the foregoing consideration I am forced to conclude that you have no general authority under the Act to assign wave lengths to broadcasting stations, except for the purpose of designating normal wave lengths under regulation 1.

(b) As to the assignment of hours of operation:

The second section of the Act, already quoted, provides that the license shall state "the hours for which the station is licensed for work." By the twelfth and thirteenth regulations the Secretary, on the recommendation of the Department concerned, may designate stations which must refrain from operating during the first 15 minutes of each hour—a period to be reserved in designated localities for Government stations. These two regulations are the only ones in which a division of time is mentioned; and it is to them that the second section of the Act refers. I therefore conclude that you have no general authority to fix the times at which broadcasting stations may operate, apart from the limitations of regulations 12 and 13.

(c) As to the limitation of power:

The only provisions concerning this are to be found in regulation 14, which requires all stations to use "the minimum amount of energy necessary to carry out any communication desired." It does not appear that the Secretary is given power to determine in advance what this minimum amount shall be for every case; and I therefore conclude that you have no authority to insert such a determination as a part of any license.

What I have said above with respect to your second question necessarily serves also as an answer to your third. While a station may not lawfully operate without a license, yet under the decision in the *Intercity Co.* case and under 29 Op. 579 you are required to issue such a license on request. And while a normal wave length must be designated under regulation 1, any station is free to operate on other wave lengths under regulation 2.

The same considerations cover your fourth question. Since the Act confers upon you no general authority to fix hours of operation or to limit power, any station may with impunity operate at hours and with powers other than those fixed in its license, subject only to regulations 12 and 13 and to the penalties against malicious interference contained in section 5.

With respect to your fifth question, I can find no authority in the Act for the issuance of licenses of limited duration.

It is apparent from the answers contained in this opinion that the present legislation is inadequate to cover the art of broadcasting, which has been almost entirely developed since the passage of the 1912 Act. If the present situation requires control, I can only suggest that it be sought in new legislation, carefully adapted to meet the needs of both the present and the future.

Respectfully,

WILLIAM J. DONOVAN,
Acting Attorney General.

To the SECRETARY OF COMMERCE.

5 PRESIDENT COOLIDGE'S MESSAGE TO CONGRESS

H. Doc. 483, 69th Congress, 2d Session
December 7, 1926

During the period subsequent to the Attorney General's Opinion of July 8, 1926, chaos ruled the airwaves. Stations switched their frequencies and increased their power at will, as Secretary Hoover abandoned his attempts to minimize interference. In short order 200 new stations crowded on the air. Broadcast reception was jumbled and sporadic.

President Coolidge, in the following excerpt from his Congressional message, recommended that new radio legislation be enacted.

RADIO LEGISLATION

The Department of Commerce has for some years urgently presented the necessity for further legislation in order to protect radio listeners from interference between broadcasting stations and to carry out other regulatory functions. Both branches of Congress at the last session passed enactments intended to effect such regulation, but the two bills yet remain to be brought into agreement and final passage.

Due to decisions of the courts, the authority of the department under the law of 1912 has broken down; many more stations have been operating than can be accommodated within the limited number of wave lengths available; further stations are in course of construction; many stations have departed from the scheme of allocation set down by the department, and the whole service of this most important public function has drifted into such chaos as seems likely, if not remedied, to destroy its great value. I most urgently recommend that this legislation should be speedily enacted.

I do not believe it is desirable to set up further independent agencies in the Government. Rather I believe it advisable to entrust the important functions of deciding who shall exercise the privilege of radio transmission and under what conditions, the assigning of wave lengths and determination of power, to a board to be assembled whenever action on such questions becomes necessary. There should be right of appeal to the courts from the decisions of such board. The administration of the decisions of the board and the other features of regulation and promotion of radio in the public interest, together with scientific research, should remain in the Department of Commerce. Such an arrangement makes for more expert, more efficient, and more economical administration than an independent agency or board, whose duties, after initial stages, require but little attention, in which administrative functions are confused with semijudicial functions and from which of necessity there must be greatly increased personnel and expenditure.

6 SENATE JOINT RESOLUTION 125

Public Resolution 47, 69th Congress
December 8, 1926

On March 15, 1926, the House of Representatives passed a radio bill introduced by Congressman Wallace White, Jr., and based on recommendations of the Fourth National Radio Conference. On July 2, 1926, the Senate passed a similar bill introduced by Senator Clarence Dill. Senate-House conferees reported one day later that they could not reconcile the differences in the two versions prior to the session's end. They suggested passage of a Senate Joint Resolution that would preserve the status quo of all radio by limiting licensing periods and by requiring licensees to sign a waiver of claim to ownership of frequencies. This Resolution, although swiftly passed by the Senate and House, was delayed by the impending close of the session. The Resolution was thus not signed by the President until December 8, 1926.

Resolved by the Senate and House of Representatives of the United States of America in Congress assembled, That until otherwise provided by law, no original license for the operation of any radio broadcasting station and no renewal of a license of an existing broadcasting station, shall be granted for longer periods than ninety days and no original license for the operation of any other class of radio station and no renewal of the license for an existing station of any other class than a broadcasting station, shall be granted for longer periods than two years; and that no original radio license or the renewal of an existing license shall be granted after the date of the passage of this resolution unless the applicant therefor shall execute in writing a waiver of any right or of any claim to any right, as against the United States, to any wave length or to the use of the ether in radio transmission because of previous license to use the same or because of the use thereof.

34

7 | THE RADIO ACT OF 1927

Public Law 632, 69th Congress
February 23, 1927

The Senate-House conferees presented their compromise bill on January 27, 1927. It was passed by the House on January 29; the Senate approved it on February 18. Five days later President Coolidge signed the Radio Act of 1927 into law.

The five-member Federal Radio Commission, created as a temporary body by the Act, remained in power from year to year through various acts of Congress until the 1927 Act was supplanted by the Communications Act of 1934, which gave rise to a permanent body.

The 1927 Act established "public interest, convenience, and necessity," a phrase borrowed from public utility legislation, as the discretionary licensing standard. This and other features of the Act were substantially re-enacted in the 1934 law. The Radio Act of 1927 may, therefore, be regarded as the basis of current broadcast regulation.

Be it enacted by the Senate and House of Representatives of the United States of America in Congress assembled, That this Act is intended to regulate all forms of interstate and foreign radio transmissions and communications within the United States, its Territories and possessions; to maintain the control of the United States over all the channels of interstate and foreign radio transmission; and to provide for the use of such channels, but not the ownership thereof, by individuals, firms, or corporations, for limited periods of time, under licenses granted by Federal authority, and no such license shall be construed to create any right, beyond the terms, conditions, and periods of the license. That no person, firm, company, or corporation shall use or operate any apparatus for the transmission of energy or communications or signals by radio (a) from one place in any Territory or possession of the United States or in the District of Columbia to another place in the same Territory, possession, or District; or (b) from any State, Territory, or possession of the United States, or from the District of Columbia to any other State, Territory, or possession of the United States; or (c) from any place in any State, Territory, or possession of the United States, or in the District of Columbia, to any place in any foreign country or to any vessel; or (d) within any State when the effects of such use extend beyond the borders of said State, or when interference is caused by such use or operation with the transmission of such energy, communications, or signals from within said State to any place beyond its borders, or from any place beyond its borders to any place within said State, or with the transmission or reception of such energy, communications, or signals from and/or to places beyond the borders of said State; or (e) upon any vessel of the United States; or (f) upon any aircraft or other mobile stations within the United States, except under and in accordance with this Act and with a license in that behalf granted under the provisions of this Act.

SEC. 2. For the purposes of this Act, the United States is divided into five zones, as follows: The first zone shall embrace the States of Maine, New Hampshire, Vermont, Massachusetts, Connecticut, Rhode Island, New York, New Jersey, Delaware, Maryland, the District of Columbia, Porto Rico, and the Virgin Islands; the second zone shall embrace the States of Pennsylvania, Virginia, West Virginia, Ohio, Michigan, and Kentucky; the third zone shall embrace the States of North Carolina, South Carolina, Georgia, Florida, Alabama, Tennessee, Mississippi, Arkansas, Louisiana, Texas, and Oklahoma; the fourth zone shall embrace the States of Indiana, Illinois, Wisconsin, Minnesota, North Dakota, South Dakota, Iowa, Nebraska, Kansas, and Missouri; and the fifth zone shall embrace the States of Montana, Idaho, Wyoming, Colorado, New Mexico, Arizona, Utah, Nevada, Washington, Oregon, California, the Territory of Hawaii, and Alaska.

SEC. 3. That a commission is hereby created and established to be known as the Federal Radio Commission, hereinafter referred to as the commission, which shall be composed of five commissioners appointed by the President, by and with the advice and consent of the Senate, and one of whom the President shall designate as chairman: *Provided,* That chairmen thereafter elected shall be chosen by the commission itself.

Each member of the commission shall be a citizen of the United States and an actual resident citizen of a State within the zone from which appointed at the time of said appointment. Not more than one commissioner shall be appointed from any zone. No member of the commission shall be financially interested in the manufacture or sale of radio apparatus or in the transmission or operation of radiotelegraphy, radiotelephony, or radio broadcasting. Not more than three commissioners shall be members of the same political party.

The first commissioners shall be appointed for the terms of two, three, four, five, and six years, respectively, from the date of the taking effect of this Act, the term of each to be designated by the President, but their successors shall be appointed for terms of six years, except that any person chosen to fill a vacancy shall be appointed only for the unexpired term of the commissioner whom he shall succeed.

The first meeting of the commission shall be held in the city of Washington at such time and place as the chairman of the commission may fix. The commission shall convene thereafter at such times and places as a majority of the commission may determine, or upon call of the chairman thereof.

The commission may appoint a secretary, and such clerks, special counsel, experts, examiners, and other employees as it may from time to time find necessary for the proper performance of its duties and as from time to time may be appropriated for by Congress.

The commission shall have an official seal and shall annually make a full report of its operations to the Congress.

The members of the commission shall receive a compensation of $10,000 for the first year of their service, said year to date from the first meeting of said commission, and thereafter a compensation of $30 per day for each day's attendance upon sessions of the commission or while engaged upon work of the commission and while traveling to and from such sessions, and also their necessary traveling expenses.

SEC. 4. Except as otherwise provided in this Act, the commission, from time to time, as public convenience, interest, or necessity requires, shall—

(a) Classify radio stations;

(b) Prescribe the nature of the service to be rendered by each class of licensed stations and each station within any class;

(c) Assign bands of frequencies or wave lengths to the various classes of stations, and assign frequencies or wave lengths for each individual station and determine the power which each station shall use and the time during which it may operate;

(d) Determine the location of classes of stations or individual stations;

(e) Regulate the kind of apparatus to be used with respect to its external effects and the purity and sharpness of the emissions from each station and from the apparatus therein;

(f) Make such regulations not inconsistent with law as it may deem necessary to prevent interference between stations and to carry out the provisions of this Act: *Provided, however,* That changes in the wave lengths, authorized power, in the character of emitted signals, or in the times of operation of any station, shall not be made without the consent of the station licensee unless, in the judgment of the commission, such changes will promote public convenience or interest or will serve public necessity or the provisions of this Act will be more fully complied with;

(g) Have authority to establish areas or zones to be served by any station;

(h) Have authority to make special regulations applicable to radio stations engaged in chain broadcasting;

(i) Have authority to make general rules and regulations requiring stations to keep such records of programs, transmissions of energy, communications, or signals as it may deem desirable;

(j) Have authority to exclude from the requirements of any regulations in whole or in part any radio station upon railroad rolling stock, or to modify such regulations in its discretion;

(k) Have authority to hold hearings, summon witnesses, administer oaths, compel the production of books, documents, and papers and to make such investigations as may be necessary in the performance of its duties. The commission may make such expenditures (including expenditures for rent and personal services at the seat of government and elsewhere, for law books, periodicals, and books of reference, and for printing and binding) as may be necessary for the execution of the functions vested in the commission and, as from time to time may be appropriated for by Congress. All expenditures of the commission shall be allowed and paid upon the presentation of itemized vouchers therefor approved by the chairman.

SEC. 5. From and after one year after the first meeting of the commission created by this Act, all the powers and authority vested in the commission under the terms of this Act, except as to the revocation of licenses, shall be vested in and exercised by the Secretary of Commerce; except that thereafter the commission shall have power and jurisdiction to act upon and determine any and all matters brought before it under the terms of this section.

It shall also be the duty of the Secretary of Commerce—

(A) For and during a period of one year from the first meeting of the commission created by this Act, to immediately refer to the commission all applications for station licenses or for the renewal or modification of existing station licenses.

(B) From and after one year from the first meeting of the commission created by this Act, to refer to the commission for its action any application for a station license or for the renewal or modification of any existing station license as to the granting of which dispute, controversy, or conflict arises or against the granting of which protest is filed within ten days after the date of filing said application by any party in interest and any application as to which such reference is requested by the applicant at the time of filing said application.

(C) To prescribe the qualifications of station operators, to classify them according to the duties to be performed, to fix the forms of such licenses, and to issue them to such persons as he finds qualified.

(D) To suspend the license of any operator for a period not exceeding two years upon proof sufficient to satisfy him that the licensee (a) has violated any provision of any Act or treaty binding on the United States which the Secretary of Commerce or the commission is authorized by this Act to administer or by any regulation made by the commission or the Secretary of Commerce under any such Act or treaty; or (b) has failed to carry out the lawful orders of the master of the vessel on which he is employed; or (c) has willfully damaged or permitted radio apparatus to be damaged; or (d) has transmitted superfluous radio communications or signals or radio communications containing profane or obscene words or language; or (e) has willfully or maliciously interfered with any other radio communications or signals.

(E) To inspect all transmitting apparatus to ascertain whether in construction and operation it conforms to the requirements of this Act, the rules and regulations of the licensing authority, and the license under which it is constructed or operated.

(F) To report to the commission from time to time any violations of this Act, the rules, regulations, or orders of the commission, or of the terms or conditions of any license.

(G) To designate call letters of all stations.

(H) To cause to be published such call letters and such other announcements and data as in his judgment may be required for the efficient operation of radio stations subject to the jurisdiction of the United States and for the proper enforcement of this Act.

The Secretary may refer to the commission at any time any matter the determination of which is vested in him by the terms of this Act.

Any person, firm, company, or corporation, any State or political division thereof aggrieved or whose interests are adversely affected by any decision, determination, or regulation of the Secretary of Commerce may appeal therefrom to the commission by filing with the Secretary of Commerce notice of such appeal within thirty days after such decision or determination or promulgation of such regulation. All papers, documents, and other records pertaining to such application on file with the Secretary shall thereupon be transferred by him to the commission. The commission shall hear such appeal de novo under such rules and regulations as it may determine.

Decisions by the commission as to matters so appealed and as to all other matters over which it has jurisdiction shall be final, subject to the right of appeal herein given.

No station license shall be granted by the commission or the Secretary of Commerce until the applicant therefor shall have signed a waiver of any claim to the use of any particular frequency or wave length or of the ether as against the regulatory power of the United States because of the previous use of the same, whether by license or otherwise.

SEC. 6. Radio stations belonging to and operated by the United States shall not be subject to the provisions of sections 1, 4, and 5 of this Act. All such Government stations shall use such frequencies or wave lengths as shall be assigned to each or to each class by the President. All such stations, except stations on board naval and other Government vessels while at sea or beyond the limits of the continental United States, when transmitting any radio communication or signal other than a communication or signal relating to Government business shall conform to such rules and regulations designed to prevent interference with other radio stations and the rights of others as the licensing authority may prescribe. Upon proclamation by the President that there exists war or a threat of war or a state of public peril or disaster or other national emergency, or in order to preserve the neutrality of the United States, the President may suspend or amend, for such time as he may see fit, the rules and regulations applicable to any or all stations within the jurisdiction of the United States as prescribed by the licensing authority, and may cause the closing of any station for radio communication and the removal therefrom of its apparatus and equipment, or he may authorize the use or control of any such station and/or its apparatus and equipment by any department of the Government under such regulations as he may prescribe, upon just compensation to the owners. Radio stations on board vessels of the United States Shipping Board or the United States Shipping Board Emergency Fleet Corporation or the Inland and Coastwise Waterways Service shall be subject to the provisions of this Act.

SEC. 7. The President shall ascertain the just compensation for such use or control and certify the amount ascertained to Congress for appropriation and payment to the person entitled thereto. If the amount so certified is unsatisfactory to the person entitled thereto, such person shall be paid only 75 per centum of the amount and shall be entitled to sue the United States to recover such further sum as added to such payment of 75 per centum which will make such amount as will be just compensation for the use and control. Such suit shall be brought in the manner provided by paragraph 20 of section 24, or by section 145 of the Judicial Code, as amended.

SEC. 8. All stations owned and operated by the United States, except mobile stations of the Army of t\ie United States, and all other stations on land and sea, shall have special call letters designated by the Secretary of Commerce.

Section 1 of this Act shall not apply to any person, firm, company, or corporation sending radio communications or signals on a foreign ship while the same is within the jurisdiction of the United States, but such communications or signals shall be transmitted only in accordance with such regulations designed to prevent interference as may be promulgated under the authority of this Act.

SEC. 9. The licensing authority, if public convenience, interest, or necessity will be served thereby, subject to the limitations of this Act, shall grant to any applicant therefor a station license provided for by this Act.

In considering applications for licenses and renewals of licenses, when and in so far as there is a demand for the same, the licensing authority shall make such a distribution of licenses, bands of frequency of wave lengths, periods of time for operation, and of power among the different States and communities as to give fair, efficient, and equitable radio service to each of the same.

No license granted for the operation of a broadcasting station shall be for a longer term than three years and no license so granted for any other class of station shall be for a longer term than five years, and any license granted may be revoked as hereinafter provided. Upon the expiration of any license, upon application therefor, a renewal of such license may be granted from time to time for a term of not to exceed three years in the case of broadcasting licenses and not to exceed five years in the case of other licenses.

No renewal of an existing station license shall be granted more than thirty days prior to the expiration of the original license.

SEC. 10. The licensing authority may grant station licenses only upon written application therefor addressed to it. All applications shall be filed with the Secretary of Commerce. All such applications shall set forth such facts as the licensing authority by regulation may prescribe as to the citizenship, character, and financial, technical, and other qualifications of the applicant to operate the station; the ownership and location of the proposed station and of the stations, if any, with which it is proposed to communicate; the frequencies or wave lengths and the power desired to be used; the hours of the day or other periods of time during which it is proposed to operate the station; the purposes for which the station is to be used; and such other information as it may require. The licensing authority at any time after the filing of such original application and during the term of any such license may require from an applicant or licensee further written statements of fact to enable it to determine whether such original application should be granted or denied or such license revoked. Such application and/or such statement of fact shall be signed by the applicant and/or licensee under oath or affirmation.

The licensing authority in granting any license for a station intended or used for commercial communication between the United States or any Territory or possession, continental or insular, subject to the jurisdiction of the United States, and any foreign country, may impose any terms, conditions, or restrictions authorized to be imposed with respect to submarine-cable licenses by section 2 of an Act entitled "An Act relating to the landing and the operation of submarine cables in the United States," approved May 24, 1921.

SEC. 11. If upon examination of any application for a station license or for the renewal or modification of a station license the licensing authority shall determine that public interest, convenience, or necessity would be served by the granting thereof, it shall authorize the issuance, renewal, or modification thereof in accordance with said finding. In the event the licensing authority upon examination of any such application does not reach such decision with respect thereto, it shall notify the applicant thereof, shall fix and give notice of a time and place for hearing thereon, and shall afford such applicant an opportunity to be heard under such rules and regulations as it may prescribe.

Such station licenses as the licensing authority may grant shall be in such general form as it may prescribe, but each license shall contain, in addition to other provisions, a statement of the following conditions to which such license shall be subject:

(A) The station license shall not vest in the licensee any right to operate the station nor any right in the use of the frequencies or wave length designated in the license beyond the term thereof nor in any other manner than authorized therein.

(B) Neither the license nor the right granted thereunder shall be assigned or otherwise transferred in violation of this Act.

(C) Every license issued under this Act shall be subject in terms to the right of use or control conferred by section 6 hereof.

In cases of emergency arising during the period of one year from and after the first meeting of the commission created hereby, or on applications filed during said time for temporary changes in terms of licenses when the commission is not in session and prompt action is deemed necessary, the Secretary of Commerce shall have authority to exercise the powers and duties of the commission, except as to revocation of licenses, but all such exercise of powers shall be promptly reported to the members of the commission, and any action by the Secretary authorized under this paragraph shall continue in force and have effect only until such time as the commission shall act thereon.

SEC. 12. The station license required hereby shall not be granted to, or after the granting thereof such license shall not be transferred in any manner, either voluntarily or involuntarily, to (a) any alien or the representative of any alien; (b) to any foreign government, or the representative thereof; (c) to any company, corporation, or association organized under the laws of any foreign government; (d) to any company, corporation, or association of which any officer or director is an alien, or of which more than one-fifth of the capital stock may be voted by aliens or their representatives or by a foreign government or representative thereof, or by any company, corporation, or association organized under the laws of a foreign country.

The station license required hereby, the frequencies or wave length or lengths authorized to be used by the licensee, and the rights therein granted shall not be transferred, assigned, or in any manner, either voluntarily or involuntarily, disposed of to any person, firm, company, or corporation without the consent in writing of the licensing authority.

SEC. 13. The licensing authority is hereby directed to refuse a station license and/or the permit hereinafter required for the construction of a station to any person, firm, company, or corporation, or any subsidiary thereof, which has been finally adjudged guilty by a Federal court of unlawfully monopolizing or attempting unlawfully to monopolize, after this Act takes effect, radio communication, directly or indirectly, through the control of the manufacture or sale of radio apparatus, through exclusive traffic arrangements, or by any other means or to have been using unfair methods of competition. The granting of a license shall not estop the United States or any person aggrieved from proceeding against such person, firm, company, or corporation for violating the law against unfair methods of competition or for a violation of the law against unlawful restraints and monopolies and/or combinations, contracts, or agreements in restraint of trade, or from instituting proceedings for the dissolution of such firm, company, or corporation.

SEC. 14. Any station license shall be revocable by the commission for false statements either in the application or in the statement of fact which may be required by section 10 hereof, or because of conditions revealed by such statements of fact as may be required from time to time which would warrant the licensing authority in refusing to grant a license on an original application, or for failure to operate substantially as set forth in the license, for violation of or failure to observe any of the restrictions and conditions of this Act, or of any regulation of the licensing authority authorized by this Act or by a treaty ratified by the United States, or whenever the Interstate Commerce Commission, or any other Federal body in the exercise of authority conferred upon it by law, shall find and shall certify to the commission that any licensee bound so to do, has failed to provide reasonable facilities for the transmission of radio communications, or that any licensee has made any unjust and unreasonable charge, or has been guilty of any discrimination, either as to charge or as to service or has made or prescribed any unjust and unreasonable classification, regulation, or practice with respect to the transmission of radio communications or service: *Provided,* That no such order of revocation shall take effect until thirty days' notice in writing thereof, stating the cause for the proposed revocation, has been given to the parties known by the commission to be interested in such license. Any person in interest aggrieved by said order may make written application to the commission at any time within said thirty days for a hearing upon such order, and upon the filing of such written application said order of revocation shall stand suspended until the conclusion of the hearing herein directed. Notice in writing of said hearing shall be given by the commission to all the parties known to it to be interested in such license twenty days prior to the time of said hearing. Said hearing shall be conducted under such rules and in such manner as the commission may prescribe. Upon the conclusion hereof the commission may affirm, modify, or revoke said orders of revocation.

SEC. 15. All laws of the United States relating to unlawful restraints and monopolies and to combinations, contracts, or agreements in restraint of trade are hereby declared to be applicable to the manufacture and sale of and to trade in radio apparatus and devices entering into or affecting interstate or foreign commerce and to interstate or foreign radio communications. Whenever in any suit, action, or proceeding, civil or criminal, brought under the provisions of any of said laws or in any proceeding brought to enforce or to review findings and orders of the Federal Trade Commission or other governmental agency in respect of any matters as to which said commission or other governmental agency is by law authorized to act, any licensee shall be found guilty of the violation of the provisions of such laws or any of them, the court, in addition to the penalties imposed by said laws, may adjudge, order, and/or decree that the license of such licensee shall, as of the date the decree or judgment becomes finally effective or as of such other date as the said decree shall fix, be revoked and that all rights under such license shall thereupon cease: *Provided, however,* That such licensee shall have the same right of appeal or review as is provided by law in respect of other decrees and judgments of said court.

SEC. 16. Any applicant for a construction permit, for a station license, or for the renewal or modification of an existing station license whose application is refused by the licensing authority shall have the right to appeal from said decision to the Court of Appeals of the District of Columbia; and any licensee whose license is revoked by the commission shall have the right to appeal from such decision of revocation to said Court of Appeals of the District of Columbia or to the district court of the United States in which the apparatus licensed is operated, by filing with said court, within twenty days after the decision complained of is effective, notice in writing of said appeal and of the reasons therefor.

The licensing authority from whose decision an appeal is taken shall be notified of said appeal by service upon it, prior to the filing thereof, of a certified copy of said appeal and of the reasons therefor. Within twenty days after the filing of said appeal the licensing authority shall file with the court the originals or certified copies of all papers and evidence presented to it upon the original application for a permit or license or in the hearing upon said order of revocation, and also a like copy of its decision thereon and a full statement in writing of the facts and the grounds for its decision as found and given by it. Within twenty days after the filing of said statement by the licensing authority either party may give notice to the court of his desire to adduce additional evidence. Said notice shall be in the form of a verified petition stating the nature and character of said additional evidence, and the court may thereupon order such evidence to be taken in such manner and upon such terms and conditions as it may deem proper.

At the earliest convenient time the court shall hear, review, and determine the appeal upon said record and evidence, and may alter or revise the decision appealed from and enter such judgment as to it may seem just. The revision by the court shall be confined to the points set forth in the reasons of appeal.

SEC. 17. After the passage of this Act no person, firm, company, or corporation now or hereafter directly or indirectly through any subsidiary, associated, or affiliated person, firm, company, corporation, or agent, or otherwise, in the business of transmitting and/or receiving for hire energy, communications, or signals by radio in accordance with the terms of the license issued under this Act, shall by purchase, lease, construction, or otherwise, directly or indirectly, acquire, own, control, or operate any cable or wire telegraph or telephone line or system between any place in any State, Territory, or possession of the United States or in the District of Columbia, and any place in any foreign country, or shall acquire, own, or control any part of the stock or other capital share of any interest in the physical property and/or other assets of any such cable, wire, telegraph, or telephone line or system, if in either case the purpose is and/or the effect thereof may be to substantially lessen competition or to restrain commerce between any place in any State, Territory, or possession of the United States or in the District of Columbia and any place in any foreign country, or unlawfully to create monopoly in any line of commerce; nor shall any person, firm, company, or corporation now or hereafter engaged directly or indirectly through any subsidiary, associated, or affiliated person, company, corporation, or agent, or otherwise, in the business of transmitting and/or receiving for hire messages by any cable, wire, telegraph, or telephone line or system (a) between any place in any State, Territory, or possession of the United States or in the District of Columbia, and any place in any other State, Territory, or possession of the United States; or (b) between any place in any State, Territory, or possession of the United States, or the District of Columbia, and any place in any foreign country, by purchase, lease, construction, or otherwise, directly or indirectly acquire, own, control, or operate any station or the apparatus therein, or any system for transmitting and/or receiving radio communications or signals between any place in any State, Territory, or possession of the United States or in the District of Columbia, and any place in any foreign country, or shall acquire, own, or control any part of the stock or other capital share or any interest in the physical property and/or other assets of any such radio station, apparatus, or system, if in either case the purpose is and/or the effect thereof may be to substantially lessen competition or to restrain commerce between any place in any State, Territory, or possession of the United States or in the District of Columbia, and any place in any foreign country, or unlawfully to create monopoly in any line of commerce.

SEC. 18. If any licensee shall permit any person who is a legally qualified candidate for any public office to use a broadcasting station, he shall afford equal opportunities to all other such candidates for that office in the use of such broadcasting station, and the licensing authority shall make rules and regulations to carry this provision into effect: *Provided,* That such licensee shall have no power of censorship over the material broadcast under the provisions of this paragraph. No obligation is hereby imposed upon any licensee to allow the use of its station by any such candidate.

SEC. 19. All matter broadcast by any radio station for which service, money, or any other valuable consideration is directly or indirectly paid, or promised to or charged or accepted by, the station so broadcasting, from any person, firm, company, or corporation, shall, at the time the same is so broadcast, be announced as paid for or furnished, as the case may be, by such person, firm, company, or corporation.

SEC. 20. The actual operation of all transmitting apparatus in any radio station for which a station license is required by this Act shall be carried on only by a person holding an operator's license issued hereunder. No person shall operate any such apparatus in such station except under and in accordance with an operator's license issued to him by the Secretary of Commerce.

SEC. 21. No license shall be issued under the authority of this Act for the operation of any station the construction of which is begun or is continued after this Act takes effect, unless a permit for its construction has been granted by the licensing authority upon written application therefor. The licensing auhority may grant such permit if public convenience, interest, or necessity will be served by the construction of the station. This application shall set forth such facts as the licensing authority by regulation may prescribe as to the citizenship, character, and the financial, technical, and other ability of the applicant to construct and operate the station, the ownership and location of the proposed station and of the station or stations with which it is proposed to communicate, the frequencies and wave length or wave lengths desired to be used, the hours of the day or other periods of time during which it is proposed to operate the station, the purpose for which the station is to be used, the type of transmitting apparatus to be used, the power to be used, the date upon which the station is expected to be completed and in operation, and such other information as the licensing authority may require. Such application shall be signed by the applicant under oath or affirmation.

Such permit for construction shall show specifically the earliest and latest dates between which the actual operation of such station is expected to begin, and shall provide that said permit will be automatically forfeited if the station is not ready for operation within the time specified or within such further time as the licensing authority may allow, unless prevented by causes not under the control of the grantee. The rights under any such permit shall not be assigned or otherwise transferred to any person, firm, company, or corporation without the approval of the licensing authority. A permit for construction shall not be required for Government stations, amateur stations, or stations upon mobile vessels, railroad rolling stock, or aircraft. Upon the completion of any station for the construction or continued construction for which a permit has been granted, and upon it being made to appear to the licensing authority that all the terms, conditions, and obligations set forth in the application and permit have been fully met, and that no cause or circumstance arising or first coming to the knowledge of the licensing authority since the granting of the permit would, in the judgment of the licensing authority, make the operation of such station against the public interest, the licensing authority shall issue a license to the lawful holder of said permit for the operation of said station. Said license shall conform generally to the terms of said permit.

SEC. 22. The licensing authority is authorized to designate from time to time radio stations the communications or signals of which, in its opinion, are liable to interfere with the transmission or with respect thereto which the Commission may by order require, to keep a licensed radio operator listening in on the wave lengths designated for signals of distress and radio communications relating thereto during the entire period the transmitter of such station is in operation.

SEC. 23. Every radio station on shipboard shall be equipped to transmit radio communications or signals of distress on the frequency or wave length specified by the licensing authority, with apparatus capable of transmitting and receiving messages over a distance of at least one hundred miles by day or night. When sending radio communications or signals of distress and radio communications relating thereto the transmitting set may be adjusted in such a manner as to produce a maximum of radiation irrespective of the amount of interference which may thus be caused.

All radio stations, including Government stations and stations on board foreign vessels when within the territorial waters of the United States, shall give absolute priority to radio communications or signals relating to ships in distress; shall cease all sending on frequencies or wave lengths which will interfere with hearing a radio communication or signal of distress, and, except when engaged in answering or aiding the ship in distress, shall refrain from sending any radio communications or signals until there is assurance that no interference will be caused with the radio communications or signals relating thereto, and shall assist the vessel in distress, so far as possible, by complying with its instructions.

SEC. 24. Every shore station open to general public service between the coast and vessels at sea shall be bound to exchange radio communications or signals with any ship station without distinction as to radio systems or instrument adopted by such stations, respectively, and each station on shipboard shall be bound to exchange radio communications or signals with any other station on shipboard without distinction as to radio systems or instruments adopted by each station.

SEC. 25. At all places where Government and private or commercial radio stations on land operate in such close proximity that interference with the work of Government stations can not be avoided when they are operating simultaneously such private or commercial stations as do interfere with the transmission or reception of radio communications or signals by the Government stations concerned shall not use their transmitters during the first fifteen minutes of each hour, local standard time.

The Government stations for which the above-mentioned division of time is established shall transmit radio communications or signals only during the first fifteen minutes of each hour, local standard time, except in case of signals or radio communications relating to vessels in distress and vessel requests for information as to course, location, or compass direction.

SEC. 26. In all circumstances, except in case of radio communications or signals relating to vessels in distress, all radio stations, including those owned and operated by the United States, shall use the minimum amount of power necessary to carry out the communication desired.

SEC. 27. No person receiving or assisting in receiving any radio communication shall divulge or publish the contents, substance, purport, effect, or meaning thereof except through authorized channels of transmission or reception to any person other than the addressee, his agent, or attorney, or to a telephone, telegraph, cable, or radio station employed or authorized to forward such radio communication to its destination, or to proper accounting or distributing officers of the various communicating centers over which the radio communication may be passed, or to the master of a ship under whom he is serving, or in response to a subpœna issued by a court of competent jurisdiction, or on demand of other lawful authority; and no person not being authorized by the sender shall intercept any message and divulge or publish the contents, substance, purport, effect, or meaning of such intercepted message to any person; and no person not being entitled thereto shall receive or assist in receiving any radio communication and use the same or any information therein contained for his own benefit or for the benefit of another not entitled thereto; and no person having received such intercepted radio communication or having become acquainted with the contents, substance, purport, effect, or meaning of the same or any part thereof, knowing that such information was so obtained, shall divulge or publish the contents, substance, purport, effect, or meaning of the same or any part thereof, or use the same or any information therein contained for his own benefit or for the benefit of another not entitled thereto: *Provided,* That this section shall not apply to the receiving, divulging, publishing, or utilizing the contents of any radio communication broadcasted or transmitted by amateurs or others for the use of the general public or relating to ships in distress.

SEC. 28. No person, firm, company, or corporation within the jurisdiction of the United States shall knowingly utter or transmit, or cause to be uttered or transmitted, any false or fraudulent signal of distress, or communication relating thereto, nor shall any broadcasting station rebroadcast the program or any part thereof of another broadcasting station without the express authority of the originating station.

SEC. 29. Nothing in this Act shall be understood or construed to give the licensing authority the power of censorship over the radio communications or signals transmitted by any radio station, and no regulation or condition shall be promulgated or fixed by the licensing authority which shall interfere with the right of free speech by means of radio communications. No person within the jurisdiction of the United States shall utter any obscene, indecent, or profane language by means of radio communication.

SEC. 30. The Secretary of the Navy is hereby authorized unless restrained by international agreement, under the terms and conditions and at rates prescribed by him, which rates shall be just and reasonable, and which, upon complaint, shall be subject to review and revision by the Interstate Commerce Commission, to use all radio stations and apparatus, wherever located, owned by the United States and under the control of the Navy Department (a) for the reception and transmission of press messages offered by any newspaper published in the United States, its Territories or possessions, or published by citizens of the United States in foreign countries, or by any press association of the United States, and (b) for the reception and transmission of private commercial messages between ships, between ship and shore, between localities in Alaska and between Alaska and the continental United States: *Provided,* That the rates fixed for the reception and transmission of all such messages, other than press messages between the Pacific coast of the United States, Hawaii, Alaska, the Philippine Islands, and the Orient, and between the United States and the Virgin Islands, shall not be less than the rates charged by privately owned and operated stations for like messages and service: *Provided further,* That the right to use such stations for any of the purposes named in this section shall terminate and cease as between any countries or localities or between any locality and privately operated ships whenever privately owned and operated stations are capable of meeting the normal communication requirements between such countries or localities or between any locality and privately operated ships, and the licensing authority shall have notified the Secretary of the Navy thereof.

SEC. 31. The expression "radio communication" or "radio communications" wherever used in this Act means any intelligence, message, signal, power, pictures, or communication of any nature transferred by electrical energy from one point to another without the aid of any wire connecting the points from and at which the electrical energy is sent or received and any system by means of which such transfer of energy is effected.

SEC. 32. Any person, firm, company, or corporation failing or refusing to observe or violating any rule, regulation, restriction, or condition made or imposed by the licensing authority under the authority of this Act or of any international radio convention or treaty ratified or adhered to by the United States, in addition to any other penalties provided by law, upon conviction thereof by a court of competent jurisdiction, shall be punished by a fine of not more than $500 for each and every offense.

SEC. 33. Any person, firm, company, or corporation who shall violate any provision of this Act, or shall knowingly make any false oath or affirmation in any affidavit required or authorized by this Act, or shall knowingly swear falsely to a material matter in any hearing authorized by this Act, upon conviction thereof in any court of competent jurisdiction shall be punished by a fine of not more than $5,000 or by imprisonment for a term of not more than five years or both for each and every such offense.

SEC. 34. The trial of any offense under this Act shall be in the district in which it is committed; or if the offense is committed upon the high seas, or out of the jurisdiction of any particular State or district, the trial shall be in the district where the offender may be found or into which he shall be first brought.

SEC. 35. This Act shall not apply to the Philippine Islands or to the Canal Zone. In international radio matters the Philippine Islands and the Canal Zone shall be represented by the Secretary of State.

SEC. 36. The licensing authority is authorized to designate any officer or employee of any other department of the Government on duty in any Territory or possession of the United States other than the Philippine Islands and the Canal Zone, to render therein such services in connection with the administration of the radio laws of the United States as such authority may prescribe: *Provided,* That such designation shall be approved by the head of the department in which such person is employed.

SEC. 37. The unexpended balance of the moneys appropriated in the item for "wireless communication laws," under the caption "Bureau of Navigation" in Title III of the Act entitled "An Act making appropriations for the Departments of State and Justice and for the judiciary, and for the Departments of Commerce and Labor, for the fiscal year ending June 30, 1927, and for other purposes," approved April 29, 1926, and the appropriation for the same purposes for the fiscal year ending June 30, 1928, shall be available both for expenditures incurred in the administration of this Act and for expenditures for the purposes specified in such items. There is hereby authorized to be appropriated for each fiscal year such sums as may be necessary for the administration of this Act and for the purposes specified in such item.

SEC. 38. If any provision of this Act or the application thereof to any person, firm, company, or corporation, or to any circumstances, is held invalid, the remainder of the Act and the application of such provision to other persons, firms, companies, or corporations, or to other circumstances, shall not be affected thereby.

SEC. 39. The Act entitled "An Act to regulate radio communication," approved August 13, 1912, the joint resolution to authorize the operation of Government-owned radio stations for the general public, and for other purposes, approved June 5, 1920, as amended, and the joint resolution entitled "Joint resolution limiting the time for which licenses for radio transmission may be granted, and for other purposes," approved December 8, 1926, are hereby repealed.

Such repeal, however, shall not affect any act done or any right accrued or any suit or proceeding had or commenced in any civil cause prior to said repeal, but all liabilities under said laws shall continue and may be enforced in the same manner as if committed; and all penalties, forfeitures, or liabilities incurred prior to taking effect hereof, under any law embraced in, changed, modified, or repealed by this Act, may be prosecuted and punished in the same manner and with the same effect as if this Act had not been passed.

Nothing in this section shall be construed as authorizing any person now using or operating any apparatus for the transmission of radio energy or radio communications or signals to continue such use except under and in accordance with this Act and with a license granted in accordance with the authority hereinbefore conferred.

SEC. 40. This Act shall take effect and be in force upon its passage and approval, except that for and during a period of sixty days after such approval no holder of a license or an extension thereof issued by the Secretary of Commerce under said Act of August 13, 1912, shall be subject to the penalties provided herein for operating a station without the license herein required.

SEC. 41. This Act may be referred to and cited as the Radio Act of 1927.

8 PRESIDENT ROOSEVELT'S MESSAGE TO CONGRESS

S. Doc. 144, 73d Congress, 2d Session
February 26, 1934

Various proposals to unify and consolidate Federal regulation of interstate communications media had been considered since 1929. President Roosevelt made the following legislative recommendation after an Interdepartmental Committee conducted a study of the problem. Congress responded with the Communications Act of 1934.

To the Congress:

I have long felt that for the sake of clarity and effectiveness the relationship of the Federal Government to certain services known as utilities should be divided into three fields: Transportation, power, and communications. The problems of transportation are vested in the Interstate Commerce Commission, and the problems of power, its development, transmission, and distribution, in the Federal Power Commission.

In the field of communications, however, there is today no single Government agency charged with broad authority.

The Congress has vested certain authority over certain forms of communications in the Interstate Commerce Commission, and there is in addition the agency known as the Federal Radio Commission.

I recommend that the Congress create a new agency to be known as the Federal Communications Commission, such agency to be vested with the authority now lying in the Federal Radio Commission and with such authority over communications as now lies with the Interstate Commerce Commission—the services affected to be all of those which rely on wires, cables, or radio as a medium of transmission.

It is my thought that a new commission such as I suggest might well be organized this year by transferring the present authority for the control of communications of the Radio Commission and the Interstate Commerce Commission. The new body should, in addition, be given full power to investigate and study the business of existing companies and make recommendations to the Congress for additional legislation at the next session.

FRANKLIN D. ROOSEVELT

THE WHITE HOUSE
February 26, 1934

9 | THE COMMUNICATIONS ACT OF 1934

Public Law 416, 73d Congress
June 19, 1934 (Amended to December, 1964)

This Act is the statute through which Congress currently exercises its jurisdiction over interstate communications by wire and radio. Although the Act has been frequently amended, the substance of the broadcasting provisions of the 1934 version, based largely on the Radio Act of 1927, has remained intact.

Only those sections most relevant to broadcasting appear in this edited version; Titles II and VI, dealing with "Common Carriers" and "Miscellaneous Provisions," respectively, are completely omitted.

TITLE I—GENERAL PROVISIONS

Purposes of Act; Creation of Federal Communications Commission

SEC. 1. For the purpose of regulating interstate and foreign commerce in communication by wire and radio so as to make available, so far as possible, to all the people of the United States a rapid, efficient, Nation-wide, and world-wide wire and radio communication service with adequate facilities at reasonable charges, for the purpose of the national defense, for the purpose of promoting safety of life and property through the use of wire and radio communication, and for the purpose of securing a more effective execution of this policy by centralizing authority heretofore granted by law to several agencies and by granting additional authority with respect to interstate and foreign commerce in wire and radio communication, there is hereby created a commission to be known as the "Federal Communications Commission," which shall be constituted as hereinafter provided, and which shall execute and enforce the provisions of this Act.

Application of Act

SEC. 2. (a) The provisions of this Act shall apply to all interstate and foreign communication by wire or radio and all interstate and foreign transmission of energy by radio, which originates and/or is received within the United States, and to all persons engaged within the United States in such communication or such transmission of energy by radio, and to the licensing and regulating of all radio stations as hereinafter provided; but it shall not apply to persons engaged in wire or radio communication or transmission in the Canal Zone, or to wire or radio communication or transmission wholly within the Canal Zone.

(b) Subject to the provisions of section 301, nothing in this Act shall be construed to apply or to give the Commission jurisdiction with respect to (1) charges, classifications, practices, services, facilities, or regulations for or in connection with intrastate communication service by wire or radio of any carrier, or (2) any carrier engaged in interstate or foreign communication solely through physical connection with the facilities of another carrier not directly or indirectly controlling or controlled by, or under direct or indirect common control with such carrier, or (3) any carrier engaged in interstate or foreign communication solely through connection by radio, or by wire and radio, with facilities, located in an adjoining State or in Canada or Mexico (where they adjoin the State in which the carrier is doing business), of another carrier not directly or indirectly controlling or controlled by, or under direct or indirect common control with such carrier, or (4) any carrier to which clause (2) or clause (3) would be applicable except for furnishing interstate mobile radio communication service or radio communication service to mobile stations on land vehicles in Canada or Mexico; except that sections 201 through 205 of this Act, both inclusive, shall, except as otherwise provided therein, apply to carriers described in clauses (2), (3), and (4).

Definitions

SEC. 3. For the purposes of this Act, unless the context otherwise requires—

(a) "Wire communication" or "communication by wire" means the transmission of writing, signs, signals, pictures, and sounds of all kinds by aid of wire, cable, or other like connection between the points of origin and reception of such transmission, including all instrumentalities, facilities, apparatus, and services (among other things, the receipt, forwarding, and delivery of communications) incidental to such transmission.

(b) "Radio communication" or "communication by radio" means the transmission by radio of writing, signs, signals, pictures, and sounds of all kinds, including all instrumentalities, facilities, apparatus, and services (among other things, the receipt, forwarding, and delivery of communications) incidental to such transmission.

(c) "Licensee" means the holder of a radio station license granted or continued in force under authority of this Act.

(d) "Transmission of energy by radio" or "radio transmission of energy" includes both such transmission and all instrumentalities, facilities, and services incidental to such transmission.

(e) "Interstate communication" or "interstate transmission" means communication or transmission (1) from any State, Territory, or possession of the United States (other than the Canal Zone), or the District of Columbia, to any other State, Territory, or possession of the United States (other than the Canal Zone), or the District of Columbia, (2) from or to the United States to or from the Canal Zone, insofar as such communication or transmission takes place within the United States, or (3) between points within the United States but through a foreign country; but shall not, with respect to the provisions of title II of this Act, include wire or radio communication between points in the same State, Territory, or possession of the United States, or the District of Columbia, through any place outside thereof, if such communication is regulated by a State commission.

(f) "Foreign communication" or "foreign transmission" means communication or transmission from or to any place in the United States to or from a foreign country, or between a station in the United States and a mobile station located outside the United States.

(g) "United States" means the several States and Territories, the District of Columbia, and the possessions of the United States, but does not include the Canal Zone.

(h) "Common carrier" or "carrier" means any person engaged as a common carrier for hire, in interstate or foreign communication by wire or radio or in interstate or foreign radio transmission of energy, except where reference is made to common carriers not subject to this Act; but a person engaged in radio broadcasting shall not, insofar as such person is so engaged, be deemed a common carrier.

(i) "Person" includes an individual, partnership, association, joint-stock company, trust, or corporation.

(j) "Corporation" includes any corporation, joint-stock company, or association.

(k) "Radio station" or "station" means a station equipped to engage in radio communication or radio transmission of energy.

(l) "Mobile station" means a radio-communication station capable of being moved and which ordinarily does move.

(m) "Land station" means a station, other than a mobile station, used for radio communication with mobile stations.

(n) "Mobile service" means the radio-communication service carried on between mobile stations and land stations, and by mobile stations communicating among themselves.

(o) "Broadcasting" means the dissemination of radio communications intended to be received by the public, directly or by the intermediary of relay stations.

(p) "Chain broadcasting" means simultaneous broadcasting of an identical program by two or more connected stations.

(q) "Amateur station" means a radio station operated by a duly authorized person interested in radio technique solely with a personal aim and without pecuniary interest. . . .

(bb) "Station license," "radio station license," or "license" means that instrument of authorization required by this Act or the rules and regulations of the Commission made pursuant to this Act, for the use or operation of apparatus for transmission of energy, or communications, or signals by radio by whatever name the instrument may be designated by the Commission.

(cc) "Broadcast station," "broadcasting station," or "radio broadcast station" means a radio station equipped to engage in broadcasting as herein defined.

(dd) "Construction permit" or "permit for construction" means that instrument of authorization required by this Act or the rules and regulations of the Commission made pursuant to this Act for the construction of a station, or the installation of apparatus, for the transmission of energy, or communications, or signals by radio, by whatever name the instrument may be designated by the Commission. . . .

Provisions relating to the Commission

SEC. 4. (a) The Federal Communications Commission (in this Act referred to as the "Commission") shall be composed of seven commissioners appointed by the President, by and with the advice and consent of the Senate, one of whom the President shall designate as chairman.

(b) Each member of the Commission shall be a citizen of the United States. No member of the Commission or person in its employ shall be financially interested in the manufacture or sale of radio apparatus or of apparatus for wire or radio communication; in communication by wire or radio or in radio transmission of energy; in any company furnishing services or such apparatus to any company engaged in communication by wire or radio or to any company manufacturing or selling apparatus used for communication by wire or radio; or in any company owning stocks, bonds, or other securities of any such company; nor be in the employ of or hold any official relation to any person subject to any of the provisions of this Act, nor own stocks, bonds, or other securities of any corporation subject to any of the provisions of this Act. Such commissioners shall not engage in any other business, vocation, profession, or employment. Any such commissioner serving as such after one year from the date of enactment of the Communications Act Amendments, 1952, shall not for a period of one year following the termination of his service as a commissioner represent any person before the Commission in a professional capacity, except that this restriction shall not apply to any commissioner who has served the full term for which he was appointed. Not more than four members of the Commission shall be members of the same political party.

(c) The Commissioners first appointed under this Act shall continue in office for the terms of one, two, three, four, five, six, and seven years, respectively, from the date of the taking effect of this Act, the term of each to be designated by the President, but their successors shall be appointed for terms of seven years and until their successors are appointed and have qualified, except that they shall not continue to serve beyond the expiration of the next session of Congress subsequent to the expiration of said fixed term of office; except that any person chosen to fill a vacancy shall be appointed only for the unexpired term of the Commissioner whom he succeeds. No vacancy in the Commission shall impair the right of the remaining commissioners to exercise all the powers of the Commission.

(d) Each commissioner shall receive an annual salary of $20,000, payable in monthly installments, and the chairman during the period of his service as chairman, shall receive an annual salary of $20,500.*

(e) The principal office of the Commission shall be in the District of Columbia, where its general sessions shall be held; but whenever the convenience of the public or of the parties may be promoted or delay or expense prevented thereby, the Commission may hold special sessions in any part of the United States.

(f) (1) The Commission shall have authority, subject to the provisions of the civil-service laws and the Classification Act of 1949, as amended, to appoint such officers, engineers, accountants, attorneys, inspectors, examiners, and other employees as are necessary in the exercise of its functions.

(2) Without regard to the civil-service laws, but subject to the Classification Act of 1949, each commissioner may appoint a legal assistant, an engineering assistant, and a secretary, each of whom shall perform such duties as such commissioner shall direct. In addition, the chairman of the Commission may appoint, without regard to the civil-service laws, but subject to the Classification Act of 1949, an administrative assistant who shall perform such duties as the chairman shall direct.

(3) The Commission shall fix a reasonable rate of extra compensation for overtime services of engineers in charge and radio engineers of

---

* Commissioners currently receive $28,750 annually; the Chairman receives $29,500. [Ed.]

the Field Engineering and Monitoring Bureau of the Federal Communications Commission, who may be required to remain on duty between the hours of 5 o'clock postmeridian and 8 o'clock antemeridian or on Sundays or holidays to perform services in connection with the inspection of ship radio equipment and apparatus for the purposes of part II of title III of this Act or the Great Lakes Agreement, on the basis of one-half day's additional pay for each two hours or fraction thereof of at least one hour that the overtime exceeds [extends] beyond 5 o'clock postmeridian (but not to exceed two and one-half days' pay for the full period from 5 o'clock postmeridian to 8 o'clock antemeridian) and two additional days' pay for Sunday or holiday duty. The said extra compensation for overtime services shall be paid by the master, owner, or agent of such vessel to the local United States collector of customs or his representative, who shall deposit such collection into the Treasury of the United States to an appropriately designated receipt account: *Provided,* That the amounts of such collections received by the said collector of customs or his representatives shall be covered into the Treasury as miscellaneous receipts; and the payments of such extra compensation to the several employees entitled thereto shall be made from the annual appropriations for salaries and expenses of the Commission: *Provided further,* That to the extent that the annual appropriations which are hereby authorized to be made from the general fund of the Treasury are insufficient, there are hereby authorized to be appropriated from the general fund of the Treasury such additional amounts as may be necessary to the extent that the amounts of such receipts are in excess of the amounts appropriated: *Provided further,* That such extra compensation shall be paid if such field employees have been ordered to report for duty and have so reported whether the actual inspection of the radio equipment or apparatus takes place or not: *And provided further,* That in those ports where customary working hours are other than those hereinabove mentioned, the engineers in charge are vested with authority to regulate the hours of such employees so as to agree with prevailing working hours in said ports where inspections are to be made, but nothing contained in this proviso shall be construed in any manner to alter the length of a working day for the engineers in charge and radio engineers or the overtime pay herein fixed.

(g) The Commission may make such expenditures (including expenditures for rent and personal services at the seat of government and elsewhere, for office supplies, law books, periodicals, and books of reference, for printing and binding, for land for use as sites for radio monitoring stations and related facilities, including living quarters where necessary in remote areas, for the construction of such stations and facilities, and for the improvement, furnishing, equipping, and repairing of such stations and facilities and of laboratories and other related facilities (including construction of minor subsidiary buildings and structures not exceeding $25,000 in any one instance) used in connection with technical research activities), as may be necessary for the execution of the functions vested in the Commission and as from time to time may be appropriated for by Congress. All expenditures of the Commission, including all necessary expenses for transportation incurred by the commissioners or by their employees, under their orders, in making any investigation or upon any official business in any other places than in the city of Washington, shall be allowed and paid on the presentation of itemized vouchers therefor approved by the chairman of the Commission or by such other members or officer thereof as may be designated by the Commission for that purpose.

(h) Four members of the Commission shall constitute a quorum thereof. The Commission shall have an official seal which shall be judicially noticed.

(i) The Commission may perform any and all acts, make such rules and regulations, and issue such orders, not inconsistent with this Act, as may be necessary in the execution of its functions.

(j) The Commission may conduct its proceedings in such manner as will best conduce to the proper dispatch of business and to the ends of justice. No commissioner shall participate in any hearing or proceeding in which he has a pecuniary interest. Any party may appear before the Commission and be heard in person or by attorney. Every vote and official act of the Commission shall be entered of record, and its proceedings shall be public upon the request of any party interested. The Commission is authorized to withhold publication of records or proceedings containing secret information affecting the national defense.

(k) The Commission shall make an annual report to Congress, copies of which shall be distributed as are other reports transmitted to Congress. Such reports shall contain—

(1) such information and data collected by the Commission as may be considered of value in the determination of questions connected with the regulation of interstate and foreign wire and radio communication and radio transmission of energy;

(2) such information and data concerning the functioning of the Commission as will be of value to Congress in appraising the amount and character of the work and accomplishments of the Commission and the adequacy of its staff and equipment: *Provided,* That the first and second annual reports following the date of enactment of the Communications Act Amendments, 1952, shall set forth in detail the number and caption of pending applications requesting approval of transfer of control or assignment of a broadcasting station license, or construction permits for new broadcasting stations, or for increases in power, or for changes of frequency of existing broadcasting stations at the beginning and end of the period covered by such reports;

(4) an itemized statement of all funds expended during the preceding year by the Commission, of the sources of such funds, and of the

authority in this Act or elsewhere under which such expenditures were made; and

(5) specific recommendations to Congress as to additional legislation which the Commission deems necessary or desirable, including all legislative proposals submitted for approval to the Director of the Bureau of the Budget.

(1) All reports of investigations made by the Commission shall be entered of record, and a copy thereof shall be furnished to the party who may have complained, and to any common carrier or licensee that may have been complained of.

(m) The Commission shall provide for the publication of its reports and decisions in such form and manner as may be best adapted for public information and use, and such authorized publications shall be competent evidence of the reports and decisions of the Commission therein contained in all courts of the United States and of the several States without any further proof or authentication thereof.

(n) Rates of compensation of persons appointed under this section shall be subject to the reduction applicable to officers and employees of the Federal Government generally.

(o) For the purpose of obtaining maximum effectiveness from the use of radio and wire communications in connection with safety of life and property, the Commission shall investigate and study all phases of the problem and the best methods of obtaining the cooperation and coordination of these systems.

Organization and functioning of the Commission

SEC. 5. (a) The member of the Commission designated by the President as chairman shall be the chief executive officer of the Commission. It shall be his duty to preside at all meetings and sessions of the Commission, to represent the Commission in all matters relating to legislation and legislative reports, except that any commissioner may present his own or minority views or supplemental reports, to represent the Commission in all matters requiring conferences or communications with other governmental officers, departments or agencies, and generally to coordinate and organize the work of the Commission in such manner as to promote prompt and efficient disposition of all matters within the jurisdiction of the Commission. In the case of a vacancy in the office of the chairman of the Commission, or the absence or inability of the chairman to serve, the Commission may temporarily designate one of its members to act as chairman until the cause or circumstance requiring such designation shall have been eliminated or corrected.

(b) Within six months after the enactment of the Communications Act Amendments, 1952, and from time to time thereafter as the Commission may find necessary, the Commission shall organize its staff into (1) integrated bureaus, to function on the basis of the Commission's principal workload operations, and (2) such other divisional organizations as the Commission may deem necessary. Each such integrated bureau shall include such legal, engineering, accounting, administrative, clerical, and other personnel as the Commission may determine to be necessary to perform its functions.*

(d) (1) When necessary to the proper functioning of the Commission and the prompt and orderly conduct of its business, the Commission may, by published rule or by order, delegate any of its functions (except functions granted to the Commission by this paragraph and by paragraphs (4), (5), and (6) of this subsection) to a panel of commissioners, an individual commissioner, an employee board, or an individual employee, including functions with respect to hearing, determining, ordering, certifying, reporting, or otherwise acting as to any work, business, or matter; except that in delegating review functions to employees in cases of adjudication (as defined in the Administrative Procedure Act), the delegation in any such case may be made only to an employee board consisting of three or more employees referred to in paragraph (8). Any such rule or order may be adopted, amended, or rescinded only by a vote of a majority of the members of the Commission then holding office. Nothing in this paragraph shall authorize the Commission to provide for the conduct, by any person or persons other than persons referred to in clauses (2) and (3) of section 7(a) of the Administrative Procedure Act, of any hearing to which such section 7(a) applies.

(2) As used in this subsection (d) the term "order, decision, report, or action" does not include an initial, tentative, or recommended decision to which exceptions may be filed as provided in section 409(b).

(3) Any order, decision, report, or action made or taken pursuant to any such delegation, unless reviewed as provided in paragraph (4), shall have the same force and effect, and shall be made, evidenced, and enforced in the same manner, as orders, decisions, reports, or other actions of the Commission.

(4) Any person aggrieved by any such order, decision, report or action may file an application for review by the Commission within such time and in such manner as the Commission shall prescribe, and every such application shall be passed upon by the Commission. The Commission, on its own initiative, may review in whole or in part, at such time and in such manner as it shall determine, any order, decision, report, or action made or taken pursuant to any delegation under paragraph (1).

(5) In passing upon applications for review, the Commission may grant, in whole or in part, or deny such applications without specifying

---

* Subsection 5(c) was repealed by Public Law 87–192, approved August 31, 1961. [Ed.]

any reasons therefor. No such application for review shall rely on questions of fact or law upon which the panel of commissioners, individual commissioner, employee board, or individual employee has been afforded no opportunity to pass.

(6) If the Commission grants the application for review, it may affirm, modify, or set aside the order, decision, report, or action, or it may order a rehearing upon such order, decision, report, or action in accordance with section 405.

(7) The filing of an application for review under this subsection shall be a condition precedent to judicial review of any order, decision, report, or action made or taken pursuant to a delegation under paragraph (1). The time within which a petition for review must be filed in a proceeding to which section 402(a) applies, or within which an appeal must be taken under section 402(b), shall be computed from the date upon which public notice is given of orders disposing of all applications for review filed in any case.

(8) The employees to whom the Commission may delegate review functions in any case of adjudication (as defined in the Administrative Procedure Act) shall be qualified, by reason of their training, experience, and competence, to perform such review functions, and shall perform no duties inconsistent with such review functions. Such employees shall be in a grade classification or salary level commensurate with their important duties, and in no event less than the grade classification or salary level of the employee or employees whose actions are to be reviewed. In the performance of such review functions such employees shall be assigned to cases in rotation so far as practicable and shall not be responsible to or subject to the supervision or direction of any officer, employee, or agent engaged in the performance of investigative or prosecuting functions for any agency.

(9) The secretary and seal of the Commission shall be the secretary and seal of each panel of the Commission, each individual commissioner, and each employee board or individual employee exercising functions delegated pursuant to paragraph (1) of this subsection.

(e) Meetings of the Commission shall be held at regular intervals, not less frequently than once each calendar month, at which times the functioning of the Commission and the handling of its work load shall be reviewed and such orders shall be entered and other action taken as may be necessary or appropriate to expedite the prompt and orderly conduct of the business of the Commission with the objective of rendering a final decision (1) within three months from the date of filing in all original application, renewal, and transfer cases in which it will not be necessary to hold a hearing, and (2) within six months from the final date of the hearing in all hearing cases; and the Commission shall promptly report to the Congress each such case which has been pending before it more than such three- or six-month period, respectively, stating the reasons therefor.

TITLE III—PROVISIONS RELATING TO RADIO

PART I—GENERAL PROVISIONS

License for radio communication or transmission of energy

SEC. 301. It is the purpose of this Act, among other things, to maintain the control of the United States over all the channels of interstate and foreign radio transmission; and to provide for the use of such channels, but not the ownership thereof, by persons for limited periods of time, under licenses granted by Federal authority, and no such license shall be construed to create any right, beyond the terms, conditions, and periods of the license. No person shall use or operate any apparatus for the transmission of energy or communications or signals by radio (a) from one place in any Territory or possession of the United States or in the District of Columbia to another place in the same Territory, possession, or district; or (b) from any State, Territory, or possession of the United States, or from the District of Columbia to any other State, Territory, or possession of the United States; or (c) from any place in any State, Territory, or possession of the United States, or in the District of Columbia, to any place in any foreign country or to any vessel; or (d) within any State when the effects of such use extend beyond the borders of said State, or when interference is caused by such use or operation with the transmission of such energy, communications, or signals from within said State to any place beyond its borders, or from any place beyond its borders to any place within said State, or with the transmission or reception of such energy, communications, or signals from and/or to places beyond the borders of said State; or (e) upon any vessel or aircraft of the United States; or (f) upon any other mobile stations within the jurisdiction of the United States, except under and in accordance with this Act and with a license in that behalf granted under the provisions of this Act.

General powers of the Commission

SEC. 303. Except as otherwise provided in this Act, the Commission from time to time, as public convenience, interest, or necessity requires shall—

(a) Classify radio stations;

(b) Prescribe the nature of the service to be rendered by each class of licensed stations and each station within any class;

(c) Assign bands of frequencies to the various classes of stations, and assign frequencies for each individual station and determine the power which each station shall use and the time during which it may operate;

(d) Determine the location of classes of stations or individual stations;

(e) Regulate the kind of apparatus to be used with respect to its external effects and the purity and sharpness of the emissions from each station and from the apparatus therein;

(f) Make such regulations not inconsistent with law as it may deem necessary to prevent interference between stations and to carry out the provisions of this Act: *Provided, however,* that changes in the frequencies, authorized power, or in the times of operation of any station, shall not be made without the consent of the station licensee unless, after a public hearing, the Commission shall determine that such changes will promote public convenience or interest or will serve public necessity, or the provisions of this Act will be more fully complied with;

(g) Study new uses for radio, provide for experimental uses of frequencies, and generally encourage the larger and more effective use of radio in the public interest;

(h) Have authority to establish areas or zones to be served by any station;

(i) Have authority to make special regulations applicable to radio stations engaged in chain broadcasting;

(j) Have authority to make general rules and regulations requiring stations to keep such records of programs, transmissions of energy, communications, or signals as it may deem desirable;

(k) Have authority to exclude from the requirements of any regulations in whole or in part any radio station upon railroad rolling stock, or to modify such regulations in its discretion;

(l) (1) Have authority to prescribe the qualifications of station operators, to classify them according to the duties to be performed, to fix the forms of such licenses, and to issue them to such citizens or nationals of the United States as the Commission finds qualified, except that in issuing licenses for the operation of radio stations on aircraft the Commission may, if it finds that the public interest will be served thereby, waive the requirement of citizenship in the case of persons holding United States pilot certificates or in the case of persons holding foreign aircraft pilot certificates which are valid in the United States on the basis of reciprocal agreements entered into with foreign governments;

(2) Notwithstanding section 301 of this Act and paragraph (1) of this subsection, the Commission may issue authorizations, under such conditions and terms as it may prescribe, to permit an alien licensed by his government as an amateur radio operator to operate his amateur radio station licensed by his government in the United States, its possessions, and the Commonwealth of Puerto Rico provided there is in effect a bilateral agreement between the United States and the alien's government for such operation on a reciprocal basis by United States amateur radio operators: *Provided,* That when an application for an authorization is received by the Commission, it shall notify the appropriate agencies of the Government of

such fact, and such agencies shall forthwith furnish to the Commission such information in their possession as bears upon the compatibility of the request with the national security: *And provided further,* That the requested authorization may then be granted unless the Commission shall determine that information received from such agencies necessitates denial of the request. Other provisions of this Act and of the Administrative Procedure Act shall not be applicable to any request or application for or modification, suspension, or cancellation of any such authorization.

(m) (1) Have authority to suspend the license of any operator upon proof sufficient to satisfy the Commission that the licensee—

(A) Has violated any provision of any Act, treaty, or convention binding on the United States, which the Commission is authorized to administer, or any regulation made by the Commission under any such Act, treaty, or convention; or

(B) Has failed to carry out a lawful order of the master or person lawfully in charge of the ship or aircraft on which he is employed; or

(C) Has willfully damaged or permitted radio apparatus or installations to be damaged; or

(D) Has transmitted superfluous radio communications or signals or communications containing profane or obscene words, language, or meaning, or has knowingly transmitted—

(1) False or deceptive signals or communications, or

(2) A call signal or letter which has not been assigned by proper authority to the station he is operating; or

(E) Has willfully or maliciously interfered with any other radio communications or signals; or

(F) Has obtained or attempted to obtain, or has assisted another to obtain or attempt to obtain, an operator's license by fraudulent means.

(2) No order of suspension of any operator's license shall take effect until fifteen days' notice in writing thereof, stating the cause for the proposed suspension, has been given to the operator licensee who may make written application to the Commission at any time within said fifteen days for a hearing upon such order. The notice to the operator licensee shall not be effective until actually received by him, and from that time he shall have fifteen days in which to mail the said application. In the event that physical conditions prevent mailing of the application at the expiration of the fifteen-day period, the application shall then be mailed as soon as possible thereafter, accompanied by a satisfactory explanation of the delay. Upon receipt by the Commission of such application for hearing, said order of suspension shall be held in abeyance until the conclusion of the hearing which shall be conducted under such rules as the Commission may prescribe. Upon the conclusion of said hearing the Commission may affirm, modify, or revoke said order of suspension.

(n) Have authority to inspect all radio installations associated with stations required to be licensed by any Act or which are subject to the provisions of any Act, treaty, or convention binding on the United States, to ascertain whether in construction, installation, and operation they conform to the requirements of the rules and regulations of the Commission, the provisions of any Act, the terms of any treaty or convention binding on the United States, and the conditions of the license or other instrument of authorization under which they are constructed, installed, or operated.

(o) Have authority to designate call letters of all stations;

(p) Have authority to cause to be published such call letters and such other announcements and data as in the judgment of the Commission may be required for the efficient operation of radio stations subject to the jurisdiction of the United States and for the proper enforcement of this Act:

(q) Have authority to require the painting and/or illumination of radio towers if and when in its judgment such towers constitute, or there is a reasonable possibility that they may constitute, a menace to air navigation.

(r) Make such rules and regulations and prescribe such restrictions and conditions, not inconsistent with law, as may be necessary to carry out the provisions of this Act, or any international radio or wire communications treaty or convention, or regulations annexed thereto, including any treaty or convention insofar as it relates to the use of radio, to which the United States is or may hereafter become a party.

(s) Have authority to require that apparatus designed to receive television pictures broadcast simultaneously with sound be capable of adequately receiving all frequencies allocated by the Commission to television broadcasting when such apparatus is shipped in interstate commerce, or is imported from any foreign country into the United States, for sale or resale to the public.

Waiver by licensee

SEC. 304. No station license shall be granted by the Commission until the applicant therefore shall have signed a waiver of any claim to the use of any particular frequency or of the ether as against the regulatory power of the United States because of the previous use of the same, whether by license or otherwise.

Government-owned stations

SEC. 305. (a) Radio stations belonging to and operated by the United States shall not be subject to the provisions of sections 301 and 303 of this Act. All such Government stations shall use such frequencies as shall be assigned to each or to each class by the President. All such stations, except stations on board naval and other Government vessels while at sea or beyond the limits of the continental United States, when transmitting any radio communication or signal other than a communication or signal relating to Government business, shall conform to such rules and regulations designed to prevent interference with other radio stations and the rights of others as the Commission may prescribe.

(b) Radio stations on board vessels of the United States Maritime Commission or the Inland and Coastwise Waterways Service shall be subject to the provisions of this title.

(c) All stations owned and operated by the United States, except mobile stations of the Army of the United States, and all other stations on land and sea, shall have special call letters designated by the Commission.

(d) The provisions of sections 301 and 303 of this Act notwithstanding, the President may, provided he determines it to be consistent with and in the interest of national security, authorize a foreign government, under such terms and conditions as he may prescribe, to construct and operate at the seat of government of the United States a low-power radio station in the fixed service at or near the site of the embassy or legation of such foreign government for transmission of its messages to points outside the United States, but only (1) where he determines that the authorization would be consistent with the national interest of the United States and (2) where such foreign government has provided reciprocal privileges to the United States to construct and operate radio stations within territories subject to its jurisdiction. Foreign government stations authorized pursuant to the provisions of this subsection shall conform to such rules and regulations as the President may prescribe. The authorization of such stations, and the renewal, modification, suspension, revocation, or other termination of such authority shall be in accordance with such procedures as may be established by the President and shall not be subject to the other provisions of this Act or of the Administrative Procedure Act.

Foreign ships

SEC. 306. Section 301 of this Act shall not apply to any person sending radio communications or signals on a foreign ship while the same is within the jurisdiction of the United States, but such communications or signals shall be transmitted only in accordance with such regulations designed to prevent interference as may be promulgated under the authority of this Act.

Allocation of facilities; Term of licenses

SEC. 307. (a) The Commission, if public convenience, interest, or necessity will be served thereby, subject to the limitations of this Act, shall grant to any applicant therefor a station license provided for by this Act.

(b) In considering applications for licenses, and modifications and renewals thereof, when and insofar as there is demand for the same, the Commission shall make such distribution of licenses, frequencies, hours of operation, and of power among the several States and communities as to provide a fair, efficient, and equitable distribution of radio service to each of the same.

(c) The Commission shall study the proposal that Congress by statute allocate fixed percentages of radio broadcasting facilities to particular types or kinds of non-profit radio programs or to persons identified with particular types or kinds of non-profit activities, and shall report to Congress, not later than February 1, 1935, its recommendations together with the reasons for the same.

(d) No license granted for the operation of a broadcasting station shall be for a longer term than three years and no license so granted for any other class of station shall be for a longer term than five years, and any license granted may be revoked as hereinafter provided. Upon the expiration of any license, upon application therefor, a renewal of such license may be granted from time to time for a term of not to exceed three years in the case of broadcasting licenses, and not to exceed five years in the case of other licenses, if the Commission finds that public interest, convenience, and necessity would be served thereby. In order to expedite action on applications for renewal of broadcasting station licenses and in order to avoid needless expense to applicants for such renewals, the Commission shall not require any such applicant to file any information which previously has been furnished to the Commission or which is not directly material to the considerations that affect the granting or denial of such application, but the Commission may require any new or additional facts it deems necessary to make its findings. Pending any hearing and final decision on such an application and the disposition of any petition for rehearing pursuant to section 405, the Commission shall continue such license in effect. Consistently with the foregoing provisions of this subsection, the Commission may by rule prescribe the period or periods for which licenses shall be granted and renewed for particular classes of stations, but the Commission may not adopt or follow any rule which would preclude it, in any case involving a station of a particular class, from granting or renewing a license for a shorter period than that prescribed for stations of such class if, in its judgment, public interest, convenience, or necessity would be served by such action.

(e) No renewal of an existing station license in the broadcast or the common carrier services shall be granted more than thirty days prior to the expiration of the original license.

Applications for licenses; Conditions in license for foreign communication

SEC. 308. (a) The Commission may grant construction permits and station licenses, or modifications or renewals thereof, only upon written application therefor received by it: *Provided,* That (1) in cases of emergency found by the Commission involving danger to life or property or due to damage to equipment, or (2) during a national emergency proclaimed by the President or declared by the Congress and during the continuance of any war in which the United States is engaged and when such action is necessary for the national defense or security or otherwise in furtherance of the war effort, or (3) in cases of emergency where the Commission finds, in the nonbroadcast services, that it would not be feasible to secure renewal applications from existing licensees or otherwise to follow normal licensing procedure, the Commission may grant construction permits and station licenses, or modifications or renewals thereof, during the emergency so found by the Commission or during the continuance of any such national emergency or war, in such manner and upon such terms and conditions as the Commission shall by regulation prescribe, and without the filing of a formal application, but no authorization so granted shall continue in effect beyond the period of the emergency or war requiring it: *Provided further,* That the Commission may issue by cable, telegraph, or radio a permit for the operation of a station on a vessel of the United States at sea, effective in lieu of a license until said vessel shall return to a port of the continental United States.

(b) All applications for station licenses, or modifications or renewals thereof, shall set forth such facts as the Commission by regulation may prescribe as to the citizenship, character, and financial, technical, and other qualifications of the applicant to operate the station; the ownership and location of the proposed station and of the stations, if any, with which it is proposed to communicate; the frequencies and the power desired to be used; the hours of the day or other periods of time during which it is proposed to operate the station; the purposes for which the station is to be used; and such other information as it may require. The Commission, at any time after the filing of such original application and during the term of any such license, may require from an applicant or licensee further written statements of fact to enable it to determine whether such original application should be granted or denied or such license revoked. Such application and/or such statement of fact shall be signed by the applicant and/or licensee.

(c) The Commission in granting any license for a station intended or used for commercial communication between the United States or any Territory or possession, continental or insular, subject to the jurisdiction of the United States, and any foreign country, may impose any terms, conditions, or restrictions authorized to be imposed with respect to submarine-cable licenses by section 2 of an Act entitled "An Act relating to the landing and the operation of submarine cables in the United States," approved May 24, 1921.

Action upon applications; Form of and conditions
attached to licenses

SEC. 309. (a) Subject to the provisions of this section, the Commission shall determine, in the case of each application filed with it to which section

308 applies, whether the public interest, convenience, and necessity will be served by the granting of such application, and, if the Commission, upon examination of such application and upon consideration of such other matters as the Commission may officially notice, shall find that public interest, convenience, and necessity would be served by the granting thereof, it shall grant such application.

(b) Except as provided in subsection (c) of this section, no such application—

> (1) for an instrument of authorization in the case of a station in the broadcasting or common carrier services, or
>
> (2) for an instrument of authorization in the case of a station in any of the following categories:
>
>> (A) fixed point-to-point microwave stations (exclusive of control and relay stations used as integral parts of mobile radio systems),
>>
>> (B) industrial radio positioning stations for which frequencies are assigned on an exclusive basis,
>>
>> (C) aeronautical en route stations,
>>
>> (D) aeronautical advisory stations,
>>
>> (E) airdrome control stations,
>>
>> (F) aeronautical fixed stations, and
>>
>> (G) such other stations or classes of stations, not in the broadcasting or common carrier services, as the Commission shall by rule prescribe,

shall be granted by the Commission earlier than thirty days following issuance of public notice by the Commission of the acceptance for filing of such application or of any substantial amendment thereof.

(c) Subsection (b) of this section shall not apply—

> (1) to any minor amendment of an application to which such subsection is applicable, or
>
> (2) to any application for—
>
>> (A) a minor change in the facilities of an authorized station,
>>
>> (B) consent to an involuntary assignment or transfer under section 310 (b) or to an assignment or transfer thereunder which does not involve a substantial change in ownership or control,
>>
>> (C) a license under section 319(c) or, pending application for or grant of such license, any special or temporary authorization to permit interim operation to facilitate completion of authorized construction or to provide substantially the same service as would be authorized by such license,
>>
>> (D) extension of time to complete construction of authorized facilities,
>>
>> (E) an authorization of facilities for remote pickups, studio

links and similar facilities for use in the operation of a broadcast station,

(F) authorizations pursuant to section 325(b) where the programs to be transmitted are special events not of a continuing nature,

(G) a special temporary authorization for nonbroadcast operation not to exceed thirty days where no application for regular operation is contemplated to be filed or not to exceed sixty days pending the filing of an application for such regular operation, or

(H) an authorization under any of the proviso clauses of section 308(a).

(d) (1) Any party in interest may file with the Commission a petition to deny any application (whether as originally filed or as amended) to which subsection (b) of this section applies at any time prior to the day of Commission grant thereof without hearing or the day of formal designation thereof for hearing; except that with respect to any classification of applications, the Commission from time to time by rule may specify a shorter period (no less than thirty days following the issuance of public notice by the Commission of the acceptance for filing of such application or of any substantial amendment thereof), which shorter period shall be reasonably related to the time when the applications would normally be reached for processing. The petitioner shall serve a copy of such petition on the applicant. The petition shall contain specific allegations of fact sufficient to show that the petitioner is a party in interest and that a grant of the application would be prima facie inconsistent with subsection (a). Such allegations of fact shall, except for those of which official notice may be taken, be supported by affidavit of a person or persons with personal knowledge thereof. The applicant shall be given the opportunity to file a reply in which allegations of fact or denials thereof shall similarly be supported by affidavit.

(2) If the Commission finds on the basis of the application, the pleadings filed, or other matters which it may officially notice that there are no substantial and material questions of fact and that a grant of the application would be consistent with subsection (a), it shall make the grant, deny the petition, and issue a concise statement of the reasons for denying the petition, which statement shall dispose of all substantial issues raised by the petition. If a substantial and material question of fact is presented or if the Commission for any reason is unable to find that grant of the application would be consistent with subsection (a), it shall proceed as provided in subsection (e).

(e) If, in the case of any application to which subsection (a) of this section applies, a substantial and material question of fact is presented or the Commission for any reason is unable to make the finding specified in such subsection, it shall formally designate the application for hearing on the ground or reasons then obtaining and shall forthwith notify the applicant and all other known parties in interest of such action and the grounds and reasons therefor, specifying with particularity the matters and things in issue but not including issues or requirements phrased generally. When the Commission has so designated an application for hearing, the parties in interest, if any, who are not notified by the Commission of such action may acquire the status of a party to the proceeding thereon by filing a petition for intervention showing the basis for their interest not more than thirty days after publication of the hearing issues or any substantial amendment thereto in the Federal Register. Any hearing subsequently held upon such application shall be a full hearing in which the applicant and all other parties in interest shall be permitted to participate. The burden of proceeding with the introduction of evidence and the burden of proof shall be upon the applicant, except that with respect to any issue presented by a petition to deny or a petition to enlarge the issues, such burdens shall be as determined by the Commission.

(f) When an application subject to subsection (b) has been filed, the Commission, notwithstanding the requirements of such subsection, may, if the grant of such application is otherwise authorized by law and if it finds that there are extraordinary circumstances requiring emergency operations in the public interest and that delay in the institution of such emergency operations would seriously prejudice the public interest, grant a temporary authorization, accompanied by a statement of its reasons therefor, to permit such emergency operations for a period not exceeding ninety days, and upon making like findings may extend such temporary authorization for one additional period not to exceed ninety days. When any such grant of a temporary authorization is made, the Commission shall give expeditious treatment to any timely filed petition to deny such application and to any petition for rehearing of such grant filed under section 405.

(g) The Commission is authorized to adopt reasonable classifications of applications and amendments in order to effectuate the purposes of this section.

(h) Such station licenses as the Commission may grant shall be in such general form as it may prescribe, but each license shall contain, in addition to other provisions, a statement of the following conditions to which such license shall be subject: (1) The station license shall not vest in the licensee any right to operate the station nor any right in the use of the frequencies designated in the license beyond the term thereof nor in any other manner than authorized therein; (2) neither the license nor the right granted thereunder shall be assigned or otherwise transferred in violation of this Act; (3) every license issued under this Act shall be subject in terms to the right of use or control conferred by section 606 of this Act.

Limitation on holding and transfer of licenses

Sec. 310. (a) The station license required hereby shall not be granted to or held by—

(1) Any alien or the representative of any alien;

(2) Any foreign government or the representative thereof;

(3) Any corporation organized under the laws of any foreign government;

(4) Any corporation of which any officer or director is an alien or of which more than one-fifth of the capital stock is owned of record or voted by aliens or their representatives or by a foreign government or representative thereof or by any corporation organized under the laws of a foreign country;

(5) Any corporation directly or indirectly controlled by any other corporation of which any officer or more than one-fourth of the directors are aliens, or of which more than one-fourth of the capital stock is owned of record or voted after June 1, 1935, by aliens, their representative, or by a foreign government or representative thereof, or by any corporation organized under the laws of a foreign country, if the Commission finds that the public interest will be served by the refusal or the revocation of such license.

Nothing in this subsection shall prevent the licensing of radio apparatus on board any vessel, aircraft, or other mobile station of the United States when the installation and use of such apparatus is required by Act of Congress or any treaty to which the United States is a party.

Notwithstanding paragraph (1) of this subsection, a license for a radio station on an aircraft may be granted to and held by a person who is an alien or a representative of an alien if such person holds a United States pilot certificate or a foreign aircraft pilot certificate which is valid in the United States on the basis of reciprocal agreements entered into with foreign governments.

Notwithstanding section 301 of this Act and paragraphs (1) and (2) of this subsection, the Commission may issue authorizations, under such conditions and terms as it may prescribe, to permit an alien licensed by his government as an amateur radio operator to operate his amateur radio station licensed by his government in the United States, its possessions, and the Commonwealth of Puerto Rico provided there is in effect a bilateral agreement between the United States and the alien's government for such operation on a reciprocal basis by United States amateur radio operators: *Provided,* That when an application for an authorization is received by the Commission, it shall notify the appropriate agencies of the Government of such fact, and such agencies shall forthwith furnish to the Commission such information in their possession as bears upon the compatibility of the request with the national security: *And provided further,* That the requested authorization may then be granted unless the Commission shall determine that information received from such agencies necessitates denial of the request. Other provisions of this Act and of the Administrative Procedure Act shall not be applicable to any request or application for or modification, suspension, or cancellation of any such authorization.

(b) No construction permit or station license, or any rights thereunder, shall be transferred, assigned, or disposed of in any manner, voluntarily or involuntarily, directly or indirectly, or by transfer of control of any corporation holding such permit or license, to any person except upon application to the Commission and upon finding by the Commission that the public interest, convenience, and necessity will be served thereby. Any such application shall be disposed of as if the proposed transferee or assignee were making application under section 308 for the permit or license in question; but in acting thereon the Commission may not consider whether the public interest, convenience, and necessity might be served by the transfer, assignment, or disposal of the permit or license to a person other than the proposed transferee or assignee.

Special requirements with respect to certain applications in the broadcasting service

Sec. 311. (a) When there is filed with the Commission any application to which section 309(b)(1) applies, for an instrument of authorization for a station in the broadcasting service, the applicant—

(1) shall give notice of such filing in the principal area which is served or is to be served by the station; and

(2) if the application is formally designated for hearing in accordance with section 309, shall give notice of such hearing in such area at least ten days before commencement of such hearing.

The Commission shall by rule prescribe the form and content of the notices to be given in compliance with this subsection, and the manner and frequency with which such notices shall be given.

(b) Hearings referred to in subsection (a) may be held at such places as the Commission shall determine to be appropriate, and in making such determination in any case the Commission shall consider whether the public interest, convenience, or necessity will be served by conducting the hearing at a place in, or in the vicinity of, the principal area to be served by the station involved.

(c) (1) If there are pending before the Commission two or more applications for a permit for construction of a broadcasting station, only one of which can be granted, it shall be unlawful, without approval of the Commission, for the applicants or any of them to effectuate an agreement whereby one or more of such applicants withdraws his or their application or applications.

(2) The request for Commission approval in any such case shall be made in writing jointly by all the parties to the agreement. Such request shall contain or be accompanied by full information with respect to the agreement, set forth in such detail, form, and manner as the Commission shall by rule require.

(3) The Commission shall approve the agreement only if it determines that the agreement is consistent with the public interest, convenience, or necessity. If the agreement does not contemplate a merger, but contemplates the making of any direct or indirect payment to any party thereto in consideration of his withdrawal of his application, the Commission may determine the agreement to be consistent with the public interest, convenience, or necessity only if the amount or value of such payment, as determined by the Commission, is not in excess of the aggregate amount determined by the Commission to have been legitimately and prudently expended and to be expended by such applicant in connection with preparing, filing, and advocating the granting of his application.

(4) For the purposes of this subsection an application shall be deemed to be "pending" before the Commission from the time such application is filed with the Commission until an order of the Commission granting or denying it is no longer subject to rehearing by the Commission or to review by any court.

Administrative sanctions

SEC. 312. (a) The Commission may revoke any station license or construction permit—

(1) for false statements knowingly made either in the application or in any statement of fact which may be required pursuant to section 308;

(2) because of conditions coming to the attention of the Commission which would warrant it in refusing to grant a license or permit on an original application;

(3) for willful or repeated failure to operate substantially as set forth in the license;

(4) for willful or repeated violation of, or willful or repeated failure to observe any provision of this Act or any rule or regulation of the Commission authorized by this Act or by a treaty ratified by the United States;

(5) for violation of or failure to observe any final cease and desist order issued by the Commission under this section; or

(6) for violation of section 1304, 1343, or 1464 of title 18 of the United States Code.

(b) Where any person (1) has failed to operate substantially as set forth in a license, (2) has violated or failed to observe any of the provisions of this Act, or section 1304, 1343, or 1464 of title 18 of the United States Code, or (3) has violated or failed to observe any rule or regulation of the Commission authorized by this Act or by a treaty ratified by the United States, the Commission may order such person to cease and desist from such action.

(c) Before revoking a license or permit pursuant to subsection (a), or issuing a cease and desist order pursuant to subsection (b), the Commission shall serve upon the licensee, permittee, or person involved an order to show cause why an order of revocation or a cease and desist order should not be issued. Any such order to show cause shall contain a statement of the matters with respect to which the Commission is inquiring and shall call upon said licensee, permittee, or person to appear before the Commission at a time and place stated in the order, but in no event less than thirty days after the receipt of such order, and give evidence upon the matter specified therein; except that where safety of life or property is involved, the Commission may provide in the order for a shorter period. If after hearing, or a waiver thereof, the Commission determines that an order of revocation or a cease and desist order should issue, it shall issue such order, which shall include a statement of the findings of the Commission and the grounds and reasons therefor and specify the effective date of the order, and shall cause the same to be served on said licensee, permittee, or person.

(d) In any case where a hearing is conducted pursuant to the provisions of this section, both the burden of proceeding with the introduction of evidence and the burden of proof shall be upon the Commission.

(e) The provisions of section 9(b) of the Administrative Procedure Act which apply with respect to the institution of any proceeding for the revocation of a license or permit shall apply also with respect to the institution, under this section, of any proceeding for the issuance of a cease and desist order.

Application of antitrust laws; Refusal of licenses and permits in certain cases

SEC. 313. (a) All laws of the United States relating to unlawful restraints and monopolies and to combinations, contracts, or agreements in restraint of trade are hereby declared to be applicable to the manufacture and sale of and to trade in radio apparatus and devices entering into or affecting interstate or foreign commerce and to interstate or foreign radio communications. Whenever in any suit, action, or proceeding, civil or criminal, brought under the provisions of any of said laws or in any proceedings brought to enforce or to review findings and orders of the Federal Trade Commission or other governmental agency in respect of any matters as to which said Commission or other governmental agency is by law authorized to act, any licensee shall be found guilty of the violation of the provisions of such laws or any of them, the court, in addition to the penalties imposed by said laws, may adjudge, order, and/or decree that the license of such licensee shall, as of the date the decree or judgment becomes finally effective or as of such other date as the said decree shall fix, be revoked and that all rights under such license shall thereupon cease: *Provided, however,* That such licensee shall have the same right of appeal or review, as is provided by law in respect of other decrees and judgments of said court.

(b) The Commission is hereby directed to refuse a station license and/or the permit hereinafter required for the construction of a station to any person (or to any person directly or indirectly controlled by such person) whose license has been revoked by a court under this section.

Preservation of competition in commerce

SEC. 314. After the effective date of this Act no person engaged directly, or indirectly through any person directly or indirectly controlling or controlled by, or under direct or indirect common control with, such person, or through an agent, or otherwise, in the business of transmitting and/or receiving for hire energy, communications, or signals by radio in accordance with the terms of the license issued under this Act, shall by purchase, lease, construction, or otherwise, directly or indirectly, acquire, own, control, or operate any cable or wire telegraph or telephone line or system between any place in any State, Territory, or possession of the United States or in the District of Columbia, and any place in any foreign country, or shall acquire, own, or control any part of the stock or other capital share or any interest in the physical property and/or other assets of any such cable, wire, telegraph, or telephone line or system, if in either case the purpose is and/or the effect thereof may be to substantially lessen competition or to restrain commerce between any place in any State, Territory, or possession of the United States, or in the District of Columbia, and any place in any foreign country, or unlawfully to create monopoly in any line of commerce; nor shall any person engaged directly, or indirectly through any person directly or indirectly controlling or controlled by, or under direct or indirect common control with, such person, or through an agent, or otherwise, in the business of transmitting and/or receiving for hire messages by any cable, wire, telegraph, or telephone line or system (a) between any place in any State, Territory, or possession of the United States, or in the District of Columbia, and any place in any other State, Territory, or possession of the United States; or (b) between any place in any State, Territory, or possession of the United States, or the District of Columbia, and any place in any foreign country, by purchase, lease, construction, or otherwise, directly or indirectly acquire, own, control, or operate any station or the apparatus therein, or any system for transmitting and/or receiving radio communications or signals between any place in any State, Territory, or possession of the United States, or in the District of Columbia, and any place in any foreign country, or shall acquire, own, or control any part of the stock or other capital share of any interest in the physical property and/or other assets of any such radio station, apparatus, or system, if in either case, the purpose is and/or the effect thereof may be to substantially lessen competition or to restrain commerce between any place in any State, Territory, or possession of the United States, or in the District of Columbia, and any place in any foreign country, or unlawfully to create monopoly in any line of commerce.

Facilities for candidates for public office

SEC. 315. (a) If any licensee shall permit any person who is a legally qualified candidate for any public office to use a broadcasting station, he shall afford equal opportunities to all other such candidates for that office in the use of such broadcasting station: *Provided,* That such licensee shall have no power of censorship over the material broadcast under the provisions of this section. No obligation is hereby imposed upon any licensee to allow the use of its station by any such candidate. Appearance by a legally qualified candidate on any—

  (1) bona fide newscast,

  (2) bona fide news interview,

  (3) bona fide news documentary (if the appearance of the candidate is incidental to the presentation of the subject or subjects covered by the news documentary), or

  (4) on-the-spot coverage of bona fide news events (including but not limited to political conventions and activities incidental thereto),

shall not be deemed to be use of a broadcasting station within the meaning of this subsection. Nothing in the foregoing sentence shall be construed as relieving broadcasters, in connection with the presentation of newscasts, news interviews, news documentaries, and on-the-spot coverage of news events, from the obligation imposed upon them under this Act to operate in the public interest and to afford reasonable opportunity for the discussion of conflicting views on issues of public importance.

  (b) The charges made for the use of any broadcasting station for any of the purposes set forth in this section shall not exceed the charges made for comparable use of such station for other purposes.

  (c) The Commission shall prescribe appropriate rules and regulations to carry out the provisions of this section.

Modification by Commission of construction permits or licenses

SEC. 316. (a) Any station license or construction permit may be modified by the Commission either for a limited time or for the duration of the term thereof, if in the judgment of the Commission such action will promote the public interest, convenience, and necessity, or the provisions of this Act or of any treaty ratified by the United States will be more fully complied with. No such order of modification shall become final until the holder of the license or permit shall have been notified in writing of the proposed action and the grounds and reasons therefor, and shall have been given reasonable opportunity, in no event less than thirty days, to show cause by public hearing, if requested, why such order of modification should not issue: *Provided,* That where safety of life or property is involved, the Commission may by order provide for a shorter period of notice.

(b) In any case where a hearing is conducted pursuant to the provisions of this section, both the burden of proceeding with the introduction of evidence and the burden of proof shall be upon the Commission.

Announcement with respect to certain matter broadcast

SEC. 317. (a)(1) All matter broadcast by any radio station for which any money, service or other valuable consideration is directly or indirectly paid, or promised to or charged or accepted by, the station so broadcasting, from any person, shall, at the time the same is so broadcast, be announced as paid for or furnished, as the case may be, by such person: *Provided,* That "service or other valuable consideration" shall not include any service or property furnished without charge or at a nominal charge for use on, or in connection with, a broadcast unless it is so furnished in consideration for an identification in a broadcast of any person, product, service, trademark, or brand name beyond an identification which is reasonably related to the use of such service or property on the broadcast.

(2) Nothing in this section shall preclude the Commission from requiring that an appropriate announcement shall be made at the time of the broadcast in the case of any political program or any program involving the discussion of any controversial issue for which any films, records, transcriptions, talent, scripts, or other material or service of any kind have been furnished, without charge or at a nominal charge, directly or indirectly, as an inducement to the broadcast of such program.

(b) In any case where a report has been made to a radio station, as required by section 508 of this Act, of circumstances which would have required an announcement under this section had the consideration been received by such radio station, an appropriate announcement shall be made by such radio station.

(c) The licensee of each radio station shall exercise reasonable diligence to obtain from its employees, and from other persons with whom it deals directly in connection with any program or program matter for broadcast, information to enable such licensee to make the announcement required by this section.

(d) The Commission may waive the requirement of an announcement as provided in this section in any case or class of cases with respect to which it determines that the public interest, convenience, or necessity does not require the broadcasting of such announcement.

(e) The Commission shall prescribe appropriate rules and regulations to carry out the provisions of this section.

Operation of transmitting apparatus

SEC. 318. The actual operation of all transmitting apparatus in any radio station for which a station license is required by this Act shall be carried on only by a person holding an operator's license issued hereunder, and no person shall operate any such apparatus in such station except under and in accordance with an operator's license issued to him by the Commission: *Provided, however,* That the Commission if it shall find that the public interest, convenience, or necessity will be served thereby may waive or modify the foregoing provisions of this section for the operation of any station except (1) stations for which licensed operators are required by international agreement, (2) stations for which licensed operators are required for safety purposes, (3) stations engaged in broadcasting (other than those engaged solely in the function of rebroadcasting the signals of television broadcast stations) and (4) stations operated as common carriers on frequencies below thirty thousand kilocycles: *Provided further,* That the Commission shall have power to make special regulations governing the granting of licenses for the use of automatic radio devices and for the operation of such devices.

Construction permits

SEC. 319. (a) No license shall be issued under the authority of this Act for the operation of any station the construction of which is begun or is continued after this Act takes effect, unless a permit for its construction has been granted by the Commission. The application for a construction permit shall set forth such facts as the Commission by regulation may prescribe as to the citizenship, character, and the financial, technical, and other ability of the applicant to construct and operate the station, the ownership and location of the proposed station and of the station or stations with which it is proposed to communicate, the frequencies desired to be used, the hours of the day or other periods of time during which it is proposed to operate the station, the purpose for which the station is to be used, the type of transmitting apparatus to be used, the power to be used, the date upon which the station is expected to be completed and in operation, and such other information as the Commission may require. Such application shall be signed by the applicant.

(b) Such permit for construction shall show specifically the earliest and latest dates between which the actual operation of such station is expected to begin, and shall provide that said permit will be automatically forfeited if the station is not ready for operation within the time specified or within such further time as the Commission may allow, unless prevented by causes not under the control of the grantee.

(c) Upon the completion of any station for the construction or continued construction of which a permit has been granted, and upon it being made to appear to the Commission that all the terms, conditions, and obligations set forth in the application and permit have been fully met, and that no cause or circumstance arising or first coming to the knowledge of the Commission since the granting of the permit would, in the judgment of the Commission, make the operation of such station against the public interest, the Commission shall issue a license to the lawful holder of said permit for the operation of said station. Said license shall conform generally to the terms of said permit. The provisions of section 309 (a), (b), (c), (d), (e), (f), and (g) shall not apply with respect to any station license the issuance of which is provided for and governed by the provisions of this subsection.

(d) A permit for construction shall not be required for Government stations, amateur stations, or mobile stations. With respect to stations or classes of stations other than Government stations, amateur stations, mobile stations, and broadcasting stations, the Commission may waive the requirement of a permit for construction if it finds that the public interest, convenience, or necessity would be served thereby: *Provided, however,* That such waiver shall apply only to stations whose construction is begun subsequent to the effective date of the waiver. If the Commission finds that the public interest, convenience, and necessity would be served thereby, it may waive the requirement of a permit for construction of a station that is engaged solely in rebroadcasting television signals if such station was constructed on or before the date of enactment of this sentence.

False distress signals; Rebroadcasting; Studios of foreign stations

SEC. 325. (a) No person within the jurisdiction of the United States shall knowingly utter or transmit, or cause to be uttered or transmitted, any false or fraudulent signal of distress, or communication relating thereto, nor shall any broadcasting station rebroadcast the program or any part thereof of another broadcasting station without the express authority of the originating station.

(b) No person shall be permitted to locate, use, or maintain a radio broadcast studio or other place or apparatus from which or whereby sound waves are converted into electrical energy, or mechanical or physical reproduction of sound waves produced, and caused to be transmitted or delivered to a radio station in a foreign country for the purpose of being broadcast from any radio station there having a power output of sufficient intensity and/or being so located geographically that its emissions may be received consistently in the United States, without first obtaining a permit from the Commission upon proper application therefor.

(c) Such application shall contain such information as the Commission may by regulation prescribe, and the granting or refusal thereof shall be subject to the requirements of section 309 hereof with respect to applications for station licenses or renewal or modification thereof, and the license or permission so granted shall be revocable for false statements in the application so required or when the Commission, after hearings, shall find its continuation no longer in the public interest.

Censorship; Indecent language

SEC. 326. Nothing in this Act shall be understood or construed to give the Commission the power of censorship over the radio communications or signals transmitted by any radio station, and no regulation or condition shall be promulgated or fixed by the Commission which shall interfere with the right of free speech by means of radio communication.

Prohibition against shipment of certain television receivers

SEC. 330. (a) No person shall ship in interstate commerce, or import from any foreign country into the United States, for sale or resale to the public, apparatus described in paragraph (s) of section 303 unless it complies with rules prescribed by the Commission pursuant to the authority granted by that paragraph: *Provided,* That this section shall not apply to carriers transporting such apparatus without trading in it.

(b) For the purposes of this section and section 303(s) —

(1) The term "interstate commerce" means (A) commerce between any State, the District of Columbia, the Commonwealth of Puerto Rico, or any possession of the United States and any place outside thereof which is within the United States, (B) commerce between points in the same State, the District of Columbia, the Commonwealth of Puerto Rico, or any possession of the United States but through any place outside thereof, or (C) commerce wholly within the District of Columbia or any possession of the United States.

(2) The term "United States" means the several States, the District of Columbia, the Commonwealth of Puerto Rico, and the possessions of the United States, but does not include the Canal Zone.*

* See pp. 565–569 and 585–596 for Sections 390–399 contained in the ETV Facilities Act of 1962 and the Public Broadcasting Act of 1967. [Ed.]

TITLE IV—PROCEDURAL AND ADMINISTRATIVE PROVISIONS

Jurisdiction to enforce Act and orders of Commission

Sec. 401. (a) The district courts of the United States shall have jurisdiction, upon application of the Attorney General of the United States at the request of the Commission, alleging a failure to comply with or a violation of any of the provisions of this Act by any person, to issue a writ or writs of mandamus commanding such person to comply with the provisions of this Act.

(b) If any person fails or neglects to obey any order of the Commission other than for the payment of money, while the same is in effect, the Commission or any party injured thereby, or the United States, by its Attorney General, may apply to the appropriate district court of the United States for the enforcement of such order. If, after hearing, that court determines that the order was regularly made and duly served, and that the person is in disobedience of the same, the court shall enforce obedience to such order by a writ of injunction or other proper process, mandatory or otherwise, to restrain such person or the officers, agents, or representatives of such person, from further disobedience of such order, or to enjoin upon it or them obedience to the same.

(c) Upon the request of the Commission it shall be the duty of any district attorney of the United States to whom the Commission may apply to institute in the proper court and to prosecute under the direction of the Attorney General of the United States all necessary proceedings for the enforcement of the provisions of this Act and for the punishment of all violations thereof, and the costs and expenses of such prosecutions shall be paid out of the appropriations for the expenses of the courts of the United States.

(d) The provisions of the Expediting Act, approved February 11, 1903, as amended, and of section 238(1) of the Judicial Code, as amended, shall be held to apply to any suit in equity arising under Title II of this Act, wherein the United States is complainant.

Proceedings to enjoin, set aside, annul, or suspend orders of the Commission

Sec. 402. (a) Any proceeding to enjoin, set aside, annul, or suspend any order of the Commission under this Act (except those appealable under subsection (b) of this section) shall be brought as provided by and in the manner prescribed in Public Law 901, Eighty-first Congress, approved December 29, 1950.

(b) Appeals may be taken from decisions and orders of the Commission to the United States Court of Appeals for the District of Columbia in any of the following cases:

(1) By any applicant for a construction permit or station license, whose application is denied by the Commission.

(2) By any applicant for the renewal or modification of any such instrument of authorization whose application is denied by the Commission.

(3) By any party to an application for authority to transfer, assign, or dispose of any such instrument of authorization, or any rights thereunder, whose application is denied by the Commission.

(4) By any applicant for the permit required by section 325 of this Act whose application has been denied by the Commission, or by any permittee under said section whose permit has been revoked by the Commission.

(5) By the holder of any construction permit or station license which has been modified or revoked by the Commission.

(6) By any other person who is aggrieved or whose interests are adversely affected by any order of the Commission granting or denying any application described in paragraphs (1), (2), (3), and (4) hereof.

(7) By any person upon whom an order to cease and desist has been served under section 312 of this Act.

(8) By any radio operator whose license has been suspended by the Commission.

(c) Such appeal shall be taken by filing a notice of appeal with the court within thirty days from the date upon which public notice is given of the decision or order complained of. Such notice of appeal shall contain a concise statement of the nature of the proceedings as to which the appeal is taken; a concise statement of the reasons on which the applicant intends to rely, separately stated and numbered; and proof of service of a true copy of said notice and statement upon the Commission. Upon filing of such notice, the court shall have jurisdiction of the proceedings and of the questions determined therein and shall have power, by order, directed to the Commission or any other party to the appeal, to grant such temporary relief as it may deem just and proper. Orders granting temporary relief may be either affirmative or negative in their scope and application so as to permit either the maintenance of the status quo in the matter in which the appeal is taken or the restoration of a position or status terminated or adversely affected by the order appealed from and shall, unless otherwise ordered by the court, be effective pending hearing and determination of said appeal and compliance by the Commission with the final judgment of the court rendered in said appeal.

(d) Upon the filing of any such notice of appeal the Commission shall, not later than five days after the date of service upon it, notify each person shown by the records of the Commission to be interested in said appeal of the filing and pendency of the same and shall thereafter permit any such person to inspect and make copies of said notice and statement of reasons therefor at the office of the Commission in the city of Washington. Within thirty days after the filing of an appeal, the Commission shall file with the court the record upon which the order complained of was entered, as provided in Section 2112 of Title 28, United States Code.

(e) Within thirty days after the filing of any such appeal any interested person may intervene and participate in the proceedings had upon said appeal by filing with the court a notice of intention to intervene and a verified statement showing the nature of the interest of such party, together with proof of service of true copies of said notice and statement, both upon appellant and upon the Commission. Any person who would be aggrieved or whose interest would be adversely affected by a reversal or modification of the order of the Commission complained of shall be considered an interested party.

(f) The record and briefs upon which any such appeal shall be heard and determined by the court shall contain such information and material, and shall be prepared within such time and in such manner as the court may by rule prescribe.

(g) At the earliest convenient time the court shall hear and determine the appeal upon the record before it in the manner prescribed by section 10(e) of the Administrative Procedure Act.

(h) In the event that the court shall render a decision and enter an order reversing the order of the Commission, it shall remand the case to the Commission to carry out the judgment of the court and it shall be the duty of the Commission, in the absence of the proceedings to review such judgment, to forthwith give effect thereto, and unless otherwise ordered by the court, to do so upon the basis of the proceedings already had and the record upon which said appeal was heard and determined.

(i) The court may, in its discretion, enter judgment for costs in favor of or against an appellant, or other interested parties intervening in said appeal, but not against the Commission, depending upon the nature of the issues involved upon said appeal and the outcome thereof.

(j) The court's judgment shall be final, subject, however, to review by the Supreme Court of the United States upon writ of certiorari on petition therefor under section 1254 of title 28 of the United States Code, by the appellant, by the Commission, or by any interested party intervening in the appeal, or by certification by the court pursuant to the provisions of that section.

Inquiry by Commission on its own motion

SEC. 403. The Commission shall have full authority and power at any time to institute an inquiry, on its own motion, in any case and as to any matter or thing concerning which complaint is authorized to be made, to or before the Commission by any provision of this Act, or concerning which any question may arise under any of the provisions of this Act, or relating to the enforcement of any of the provisions of this Act. The Commission shall have the same powers and authority to proceed with any inquiry instituted on its own motion as though it had been appealed to by complaint or petition under any of the provisions of this Act, including the power to make and enforce any order or orders in the case, or relating to the matter or thing concerning which the inquiry is had, excepting orders for the payment of money.

Reports of investigations

SEC. 404. Whenever an investigation shall be made by the Commission it shall be its duty to make a report in writing in respect thereto, which shall state the conclusions of the Commission, together with its decision, order, or requirements in the premises; and in case damages are awarded such report shall include the findings of fact on which the award is made.

Rehearings

SEC. 405. After an order, decision, report, or action has been made or taken in any proceeding by the Commission, or by any designated authority within the Commission pursuant to a delegation under section 5(d)(1), any party thereto, or any other person aggrieved or whose interests are adversely affected thereby, may petition for rehearing only to the authority making or taking the order, decision, report, or action; and it shall be lawful for such authority, whether it be the Commission or other authority designated under section 5 (d)(1), in its discretion, to grant such a rehearing if sufficient reason therefor be made to appear. A petition for rehearing must be filed within thirty days from the date upon which public notice is given of the order, decision, report, or action complained of. No such application shall excuse any person from complying with or obeying any order, decision, report, or action of the Commission, or operate in any manner to stay or postpone the enforcement thereof, without the special order of the Commission. The filing of a petition for rehearing shall not be a condition precedent to judicial review of any such order, decision, report, or action, except where the party seeking such review (1) was not a party to the proceedings resulting in such order, decision, report, or action, or (2) relies on questions of fact or law upon which the Commission, or designated authority within the Commission, has been afforded no opportunity to pass. The Commission, or designated authority within the Commission, shall enter an order, with a concise statement of the reasons therefor, denying a petition for rehearing or granting such petition, in whole or in part, and ordering such further proceedings as may be appropriate: *Provided,* That in any case where such petition relates to an instrument of authorization granted without a hearing, the Commission, or designated authority within the Commission, shall take such action within ninety days of the filing of such petition. Rehearings shall be governed by such general rules as the Commission may establish, except that no evidence other than newly discovered evidence, evidence which has become available only since the original taking of evidence, or evidence which the Commission or designated authority within the Commission believes should have been taken in the original proceeding shall be taken on any rehearing. The time within which a petition for review must be filed in a proceeding to which section 402(a) applies, or within which an appeal must be taken under section 402(b) in any case, shall be computed from the date upon which public notice is given of orders disposing of all petitions for rehearing filed with the Commission in such proceeding or case, but any order, decision, report, or action made or taken after such rehearing reversing, changing, or modifying the original order shall be subject to the same provisions with respect to rehearing as an original order.

TITLE V—PENAL PROVISIONS—FORFEITURES

General penalty

SEC. 501. Any person who willfully and knowingly does or causes or suffers to be done any act, matter, or thing, in this Act prohibited or declared to be unlawful, or who willfully or knowingly omits or fails to do any act, matter, or thing in this Act required to be done, or willfully and knowingly causes or suffers such omission or failure, shall, upon conviction thereof, be punished for such offense, for which no penalty (other than a forfeiture) is provided in this Act, by a fine of not more than $10,000 or by imprisonment for a term not exceeding one year, or both; except that any person, having been once convicted of an offense punishable under this section, who is subsequently convicted of violating any provision of this Act punishable under this section, shall be punished by a fine of not more than $10,000 or by imprisonment for a term not exceeding two years, or both.

SEC. 502. Any person who willfully and knowingly violates any rule, regulation, restriction, or condition made or imposed by the Commission under authority of this Act, or any rule, regulation, restriction, or condition made or imposed by any international radio or wire communications treaty or convention, or regulations annexed thereto, to which the United States is or may hereafter become a party, shall, in addition to any other penalties provided by law, be punished, upon conviction thereof, by a fine of not more than $500 for each and every day during which such offense occurs.

SEC. 503. (a) Any person who shall deliver messages for interstate or foreign transmission to any carrier, or for whom, as sender or receiver, any such carrier shall transmit any interstate or foreign wire or radio communication, who shall knowingly by employee, agent, officer, or otherwise, directly or indirectly, by or through any means or device whatsoever, receive or accept from such common carrier any sum of money or any other valuable consideration as a rebate or offset against the regular charges for transmission of such messages as fixed by the schedules of charges provided for in this Act, shall in addition to any other penalty provided by this Act forfeit to the United States a sum of money three times the amount of money so received or accepted and three times the value of any other consideration so received or accepted, to be ascertained by the trial court; and in the trial of said action all such rebates or other considerations so received or accepted, for a period of six years prior to the commencement of the action, may be included therein, and the amount recovered shall be three times the total amount of money, or three times the total value of such consideration, so received or accepted, or both, as the case may be.

(b) (1) Any licensee or permittee of a broadcast station who—

(A) willfully or repeatedly fails to operate such station substantially as set forth in his license or permit,

(B) willfully or repeatedly fails to observe any of the provisions of this Act or of any rule or regulation of the Commission prescribed under authority of this Act or under authority of any treaty ratified by the United States,

(C) fails to observe any final cease and desist order issued by the Commission,

(D) violates section 317(c) or section 509(a)(4) of this Act, or

(E) violates section 1304, 1343, or 1464 of title 18 of the United States Code,

shall forfeit to the United States a sum not to exceed $1,000. Each day during which such violation occurs shall constitute a separate offense. Such forfeiture shall be in addition to any other penalty provided by this Act.

(2) No forfeiture liability under paragraph (1) of this subsection (b) shall attach unless a written notice of apparent liability shall have been issued by the Commission and such notice has been received by the licensee or permittee or the Commission shall have sent such notice by registered or certified mail to the last known address of the licensee or permittee. A licensee or permittee so notified shall be granted an opportunity to show in writing, within such reasonable period as the Commission shall by regulations prescribe, why he should not be held liable. A notice issued under this paragraph shall not be valid unless it sets forth the date, facts, and nature of the act or omission with which the licensee or permittee is charged and specifically identifies the particular provision or provisions of the law,

rule, or regulation or the license, permit, or cease and desist order involved.

(3) No forfeiture liability under paragraph (1) of this subsection (b) shall attach for any violation occurring more than one year prior to the date of issuance of the notice of apparent liability and in no event shall the forfeiture imposed for the acts or omission set forth in any notice of apparent liability exceed $10,000.

Provisions relating to forfeitures

SEC. 504. (a) The forfeitures provided for in this Act shall be payable into the Treasury of the United States, and shall be recoverable in a civil suit in the name of the United States brought in the district where the person or carrier has its principal operating office or in any district through which the line or system of the carrier runs: *Provided,* That any suit for the recovery of a forfeiture imposed pursuant to the provisions of this Act shall be a trial de novo: *Provided further,* That in the case of forfeiture by a ship, said forfeiture may also be recoverable by way of libel in any district in which such ship shall arrive or depart. Such forfeitures shall be in addition to any other general or specific penalties herein provided. It shall be the duty of the various district attorneys, under the direction of the Attorney General of the United States, to prosecute for the recovery of forfeitures under this Act. The costs and expenses of such prosecutions shall be paid from the appropriation for the expenses of the courts of the United States.

(b) The forfeitures imposed by parts II and III of title III and sections 503(b) and 507 of this Act shall be subject to remission or mitigation by the Commission, upon application therefor, under such regulations and methods of ascertaining the facts as may seem to it advisable, and, if suit has been instituted, the Attorney General, upon request of the Commission, shall direct the discontinuance of any prosecution to recover such forfeitures: *Provided, however,* That no forfeiture shall be remitted or mitigated after determination by a court of competent jurisdiction.

(c) In any case where the Commission issues a notice of apparent liability looking toward the imposition of a forfeiture under this Act, that fact shall not be used, in any other proceeding before the Commission, to the prejudice of the person to whom such notice was issued, unless (i) the forfeiture has been paid, or (ii) a court of competent jurisdiction has ordered payment of such forfeiture, and such order has become final.

Venue of offenses

SEC. 505. The trial of any offense under this Act shall be in the district in which it is committed; or if the offense is committed upon the high seas, or out of the jurisdiction of any particular State or district, the trial shall be in the district where the offender may be found or into which he shall be first brought. Whenever the offense is begun in one jurisdiction and completed in another it may be dealt with, inquired of, tried, determined, and punished in either jurisdiction in the same manner as if the offense had been actually and wholly committed therein.

Coercive practices affecting broadcasting

SEC. 506. (a) It shall be unlawful, by the use or express or implied threat of the use of force, violence, intimidation, or duress, or by the use or express or implied threat of the use of other means, to coerce, compel or constrain or attempt to coerce, compel, or constrain a licensee—

(1) to employ or agree to employ, in connection with the conduct of the broadcasting business of such licensee, any person or persons in excess of the number of employees needed by such licensee to perform actual services; or

(2) to pay or give or agree to pay or give any money or other thing of value in lieu of giving, or on account of failure to give, employment to any person or persons, in connection with the conduct of the broadcasting business of such licensee, in excess of the number of employees needed by such licensee to perform actual services; or

(3) to pay or agree to pay more than once for services performed in connection with the conduct of the broadcasting business of such licensee; or

(4) to pay or give or agree to pay or give any money or other thing of value for services, in connection with the conduct of the broadcasting business of such licensee, which are not to be performed; or

(5) to refrain, or agree to refrain, from broadcasting or from permitting the broadcasting of a noncommercial educational or cultural program in connection with which the participants receive no money or other thing of value for their services, other than their actual expenses, and such licensee neither pays nor gives any money or other thing of value for the privilege of broadcasting such program nor receives any money or other thing of value on account of the broadcasting of such program; or

(6) to refrain, or agree to refrain, from broadcasting or permitting the broadcasting of any radio communication originating outside the United States.

(b) It shall be unlawful, by the use or express or implied threat of the use of force, violence, intimidation or duress, or by the use or express or implied threat of the use of other means, to coerce, compel or constrain or attempt to coerce, compel or constrain a licensee or any other person—

(1) to pay or agree to pay any exaction for the privilege of, or on account of, producing, preparing, manufacturing, selling, buying, renting, operating, using, or maintaining recordings, transcriptions, or mechanical, chemical, or electrical reproductions, or any other articles, equipment,

machines, or materials, used or intended to be used in broadcasting or in the production, preparation, performance, or presentation of a program or programs for broadcasting; or

(2) to accede to or impose any restriction upon such production, preparation, manufacture, sale, purchase, rental, operation, use, or maintenance, if such restriction is for the purpose of preventing or limiting the use of such articles, equipment, machines, or materials in broadcasting or in the production, preparation, performance, or presentation of a program or programs for broadcasting; or

(3) to pay or agree to pay any exaction on account of the broadcasting, by means of recordings or transcriptions, of a program previously broadcast, payment having been made, or agreed to be made, for the services actually rendered in the performance of such program.

(c) The provisions of subsection (a) or (b) of this section shall not be held to make unlawful the enforcement or attempted enforcement, by means lawfully employed, of any contract right heretofore or hereafter existing or of any legal obligation heretofore or hereafter incurred or assumed.

(d) Whoever willfully violates any provision of subsection (a) or (b) of this section shall, upon conviction thereof, be punished by imprisonment for not more than one year or by a fine of not more than $1,000, or both.

(e) As used in this section the term "licensee" includes the owner or owners, and the person or persons having control or management, of the radio station in respect of which a station license was granted.

Disclosure of certain payments

Sec. 508. (a) Subject to subsection (d), any employee of a radio station who accepts or agrees to accept from any person (other than such station), or any person (other than such station) who pays or agrees to pay such employee, any money, service or other valuable consideration for the broadcast of any matter over such station shall, in advance of such broadcast, disclose the fact of such acceptance or agreement to such station.

(b) Subject to subsection (d), any person who, in connection with the production or preparation of any program or program matter which is intended for broadcasting over any radio station, accepts or agrees to accept, or pays or agrees to pay, any money, service or other valuable consideration for the inclusion of any matter as a part of such program or program matter, shall, in advance of such broadcast, disclose the fact of such acceptance or payment or agreement to the payee's employer, or to the person for whom such program or program matter is being produced, or to the licensee of such station over which such program is broadcast.

(c) Subject to subsection (d), any person who supplies to any other person any program or program matter which is intended for broadcasting over any radio station shall, in advance of such broadcast, disclose to such other person any information of which he has knowledge, or which has been disclosed to him, as to any money, service or other valuable consideration which any person has paid or accepted, or has agreed to pay or accept, for the inclusion of any matter as a part of such program or program matter.

(d) The provisions of this section requiring the disclosure of information shall not apply in any case where, because of a waiver made by the Commission under section 317(d), an announcement is not required to be made under section 317.

(e) The inclusion in the program of the announcement required by section 317 shall constitute the disclosure required by this section.

(f) The term "service or other valuable consideration" as used in this section shall not include any service or property furnished without charge or at a nominal charge for use on, or in connection with, a broadcast, or for use on a program which is intended for broadcasting over any radio station, unless it is so furnished in consideration for an identification in such broadcast or in such program of any person, product, service, trademark, or brand name beyond an identification which is reasonably related to the use of such service or property in such broadcast or such program.

(g) Any person who violates any provision of this section shall, for each such violation, be fined not more than $10,000 or imprisoned not more than one year, or both.

Prohibited practices in case of contests of intellectual knowledge, intellectual skill, or chance

SEC. 509. (a) It shall be unlawful for any person, with intent to deceive the listening or viewing public—

(1) To supply to any contestant in a purportedly bona fide contest of intellectual knowledge or intellectual skill any special and secret assistance whereby the outcome of such contest will be in whole or in part prearranged or predetermined.

(2) By means of persuasion, bribery, intimidation, or otherwise, to induce or cause any contestant in a purportedly bona fide contest of intellectual knowledge or intellectual skill to refrain in any manner from using or displaying his knowledge or skill in such contest, whereby the outcome thereof will be in whole or in part prearranged or predetermined.

(3) To engage in any artifice or scheme for the purpose of prearranging or predetermining in whole or in part the outcome of a purportedly bona fide contest of intellectual knowledge, intellectual skill, or chance.

(4) To produce or participate in the production for broadcasting of, to broadcast or participate in the broadcasting of, to offer to a licensee for broadcasting, or to sponsor, any radio program, knowing or having reasonable ground for believing that, in connection with a purportedly bona fide contest of intellectual knowledge, intellectual skill, or chance constituting

any part of such program, any person has done or is going to do any act or thing referred to in paragraph (1), (2), or (3) of this subsection.

(5) To conspire with any other person or persons to do any act or thing prohibited by paragraph (1), (2), (3), or (4) of this subsection, if one or more of such persons do any act to effect the object of such conspiracy.

(b) for the purposes of this section—

(1) The term "contest" means any contest broadcast by a radio station in connection with which any money or any other thing of value is offered as a prize or prizes to be paid or presented by the program sponsor or by any other person or persons, as announced in the course of the broadcast.

(2) The term "the listening or viewing public" means those members of the public who, with the aid of radio receiving sets, listen to or view programs broadcast by radio stations.

(c) Whoever violates subsection (a) shall be fined not more than $10,000 or imprisoned not more than one year, or both.

10 THE CRIMINAL CODE

Title 18, U.S.C.
(1958 Edition)

These selected sections of the Criminal Code pertaining to broadcasting supplement the provisions of the Communications Act of 1934, as amended. Sections 1304 and 1464 of the Code, below, originally appeared in modified form in the Act as Sections 316 and 326, respectively.

§ 1304. *Broadcasting lottery information*

Whoever broadcasts by means of any radio station for which a license is required by any law of the United States, or whoever, operating any such station, knowingly permits the broadcasting of, any advertisement of or information concerning any lottery, gift enterprise, or similar scheme, offering prizes dependent in whole or in part upon lot or chance, or any list of the prizes drawn or awarded by means of any such lottery, gift enterprise, or scheme, whether said list contains any part or all of such prizes, shall be fined not more than $1,000 or imprisoned not more than one year, or both.

Each day's broadcasting shall constitute a separate offense.

(Codified June 25, 1948, Ch. 645, 62 stat. 763.)

§ 1343. *Fraud by wire, radio, or television*

Whoever, having devised or intending to devise any scheme or artifice to defraud, or for obtaining money or property by means of false or fraudulent pretenses, representations, or promises, transmits or causes to be transmitted by means of wire, radio, or television communication in interstate or foreign commerce, any writings, signs, signals, pictures, or sounds for the purpose of executing such scheme or artifice, shall be fined not more than $1,000 or imprisoned not more than five years, or both.

(Added July 16, 1952, Ch. 879, sec. 18(a), 66 stat. 722, amended July 11, 1956, Ch. 561, 70 stat. 523.)

§ 1464. *Broadcasting obscene language*

Whoever utters any obscene, indecent, or profane language by means of radio communications shall be fined not more than $10,000 or imprisoned not more than two years, or both.

(Codified June 25, 1948, Ch. 645, 62 stat. 769.)

11 | THE COMMUNICATIONS SATELLITE ACT OF 1962

Public Law 624, 87th Congress, 2d Session
August 31, 1962

The National Aeronautics and Space Administration launched its first experimental communications satellite, Echo I, on August 12, 1960. Telstar, Relay, and Syncom followed to herald the arrival of the age of intercontinental television communication.

Comsat, the Communications Satellite Corporation, authorized by the Act of 1962 to own and operate commercial communications satellites, was incorporated on February 1, 1963.

TITLE I—SHORT TITLE, DECLARATION OF POLICY AND DEFINITIONS

Short title

SEC. 101. This Act may be cited as the "Communications Satellite Act of 1962."

Declaration of policy and purpose

SEC. 102. (a) The Congress hereby declares that it is the policy of the United States to establish, in conjunction and in cooperation with other countries, as expeditiously as practicable a commercial communications satellite system, as part of an improved global communications network, which will be responsive to public needs and national objectives, which will serve the communication needs of the United States and other countries, and which will contribute to world peace and understanding.

(b) The new and expanded telecommunication services are to be made available as promptly as possible and are to be extended to provide global coverage at the earliest practicable date. In effectuating this program, care and attention will be directed toward providing such services to economically less developed countries and areas as well as those more highly

97

developed, toward efficient and economical use of the electromagnetic frequency spectrum, and toward the reflection of the benefits of this new technology in both quality of services and charges for such services.

(c) In order to facilitate this development and to provide for the widest possible participation by private enterprise, United States participation in the global system shall be in the form of a private corporation, subject to appropriate governmental regulation. It is the intent of Congress that all authorized users shall have nondiscriminatory access to the system; that maximum competition be maintained in the provision of equipment and services utilized by the system; that the corporation created under this Act be so organized and operated as to maintain and strengthen competition in the provision of communications services to the public; and that the activities of the corporation created under this Act and of the persons or companies participating in the ownership of the corporation shall be consistent with the Federal antitrust laws.

(d) It is not the intent of Congress by this Act to preclude the use of the communications satellite system for domestic communication services where consistent with the provisions of this Act nor to preclude the creation of additional communications satellite systems, if required to meet unique governmental needs or if otherwise required in the national interest.

Definitions

SEC. 103. As used in this Act, and unless the context otherwise requires—

(1) the term "communications satellite system" refers to a system of communications satellites in space whose purpose is to relay telecommunication information between satellite terminal stations, together with such associated equipment and facilities for tracking, guidance, control, and command functions as are not part of the generalized launching, tracking, control, and command facilities for all space purposes;

(2) the term "satellite terminal station" refers to a complex of communication equipment located on the earth's surface, operationally connected with one or more terrestrial communication systems, and capable of transmitting telecommunications to or receiving telecommunications from a communications satellite system.

(3) the term "communications satellite" means an earth satellite which is intentionally used to relay telecommunication information;

(4) the term "associated equipment and facilities" refers to facilities other than satellite terminal stations and communications satellites, to be constructed, and operated for the primary purpose of a communications satellite system, whether for administration and management, for research and development, or for direct support of space operations;

(5) the term "research and development" refers to the conception, design, and first creation of experimental or prototype operational devices

for the operation of a communications satellite system, including the assembly of separate components into a working whole, as distinguished from the term "production" which relates to the construction of such devices to fixed specifications compatible with repetitive duplication for operational applications; and

(6) the term "telecommunication" means any transmission, emission or reception of signs, signals, writings, images, and sounds or intelligence of any nature by wire, radio, optical, or other electromagnetic systems.

(7) the term "communications common carrier" has the same meaning as the term "common carrier" has when used in the Communications Act of 1934, as amended, and in addition includes, but only for purposes of sections 303 and 304, any individual, partnership, association, joint-stock company, trust, corporation, or other entity which owns or controls, directly or indirectly, or is under direct or indirect common control with, any such carrier; and the term "authorized carrier," except as otherwise provided for purposes of section 304 by section 304(b)(1), means a communications common carrier which has been authorized by the Federal Communications Commission under the Communications Act of 1934, as amended, to provide services by means of communications satellites;

(8) the term "corporation" means the corporation authorized by title III of this Act.

(9) the term "Administration" means the National Aeronautics and Space Administration; and

(10) the term "Commission" means the Federal Communications Commission.

TITLE II—FEDERAL COORDINATION, PLANNING, AND REGULATION

Implementation of policy

SEC. 201. In order to achieve the objectives and to carry out the purposes of this Act—

(a) the President shall—

(1) aid in the planning and development and foster the execution of a national program for the establishment and operation, as expeditiously as possible, of a commercial communications satellite system;

(2) provide for continuous review of all phases of the development and operation of such a system, including the activities of a communications satellite corporation authorized under title III of this Act;

(3) coordinate the activities of governmental agencies with responsibilities in the field of telecommunication, so as to insure that there is

full and effective compliance at all times with the policies set forth in this Act;

(4) exercise such supervision over relationships of the corporation with foreign governments or entities or with international bodies as may be appropriate to assure that such relationships shall be consistent with the national interest and foreign policy of the United States;

(5) insure that timely arrangements are made under which there can be foreign participation in the establishment and use of a communications satellite system;

(6) take all necessary steps to insure the availability and appropriate utilization of the communications satellite system for general governmental purposes except where a separate communications satellite system is required to meet unique governmental needs, or is otherwise required in the national interest; and

(7) so exercise his authority as to help attain coordinated and efficient use of the electromagnetic spectrum and the technical compatibility of the system with existing communications facilities both in the United States and abroad.

(b) the National Aeronautics and Space Administration shall—

(1) advise the Commission on technical characteristics of the communications satellite system;

(2) cooperate with the corporation in research and development to the extent deemed appropriate by the Administration in the public interest;

(3) assist the corporation in the conduct of its research and development program by furnishing to the corporation, when requested, on a reimbursable basis, such satellite launching and associated services as the Administration deems necessary for the most expeditious and economical development of the communications satellite system;

(4) consult with the corporation with respect to the technical characteristics of the communications satellite system;

(5) furnish to the corporation, on request and on a reimbursable basis, satellite launching and associated services required for the establishment, operation, and maintenance of the communications satellite system approved by the Commission; and

(6) to the extent feasible, furnish other services, on a reimbursable basis, to the corporation in connection with the establishment and operation of the system.

(c) the Federal Communications Commission, in its administration of the provisions of the Communications Act of 1934, as amended, and as supplemented by this Act, shall—

(1) insure effective competition, including the use of competitive bidding where appropriate, in the procurement by the corporation and communications common carriers of apparatus, equipment, and services re-

quired for the establishment and operation of the communications satellite system and satellite terminal stations; and the Commission shall consult with the Small Business Administration and solicit its recommendations on measures and procedures which will insure that small business concerns are given an equitable opportunity to share in the procurement program of the corporation for property and services, including but not limited to research, development, construction, maintenance, and repair.

(2) insure that all present and future authorized carriers shall have nondiscriminatory use of, and equitable access to, the communications satellite system and satellite terminal stations under just and reasonable charges, classifications, practices, regulations, and other terms and conditions and regulate the manner in which available facilities of the system and stations are allocated among such users thereof;

(3) in any case where the Secretary of State, after obtaining the advice of the Administration as to technical feasibility, has advised that commercial communication to a particular foreign point by means of the communications satellite system and satellite terminal stations should be established in the national interest, institute forthwith appropriate proceedings under section 214(d) of the Communications Act of 1934, as amended, to require the establishment of such communication by the corporation and the appropriate common carrier or carriers;

(4) insure that facilities of the communications satellite system and satellite terminal stations are technically compatible and interconnected operationally with each other and with existing communications facilities;

(5) prescribe such accounting regulations and systems and engage in such ratemaking procedures as will insure that any economies made possible by a communications satellite system are appropriately reflected in rates for public communication services;

(6) approve technical characteristics of the operational communications satellite system to be employed by the corporation and of the satellite terminal stations; and

(7) grant appropriate authorizations for the construction and operation of each satellite terminal station, either to the corporation or to one or more authorized carriers or to the corporation and one or more such carriers jointly, as will best serve the public interest, convenience, and necessity. In determining the public interest, convenience, and necessity the Commission shall authorize the construction and operation of such stations by communications common carriers or the corporation, without preference to either;

(8) authorize the corporation to issue any shares of capital stock, except the initial issue of capital stock referred to in section 304(a), or to borrow any moneys, or to assume any obligation in respect of the securities of any other person, upon a finding that such issuance, borrowing, or assumption is compatible with the public interest, convenience, and necessity

and is necessary or appropriate for or consistent with carrying out the purposes and objectives of this Act by the corporation;

(9) insure that no substantial additions are made by the corporation or carriers with respect to facilities of the system or satellite terminal stations unless such additions are required by the public interest, convenience, and necessity;

(10) require, in accordance with the procedural requirements of section 214 of the Communications Act of 1934, as amended, that additions be made by the corporation or carriers with respect to facilities of the system or satellite terminal stations where such additions would serve the public interest, convenience, and necessity; and

(11) make rules and regulations to carry out the provisions of this Act.

TITLE III—CREATION OF A COMMUNICATIONS SATELLITE CORPORATION

Creation of corporation

SEC. 301. There is hereby authorized to be created a communications satellite corporation for profit which will not be an agency or establishment of the United States Government. The corporation shall be subject to the provisions of this Act and, to the extent consistent with this Act, to the District of Columbia Business Corporation Act. The right to repeal, alter, or amend this Act at any time is expressly reserved.

Process of organization

SEC. 302. The President of the United States shall appoint incorporators, by and with the advice and consent of the Senate, who shall serve as the initial board of directors until the first annual meeting of stockholders or until their successors are elected and qualified. Such incorporators shall arrange for an initial stock offering and take whatever other actions are necessary to establish the corporation, including the filing of articles of incorporation, as approved by the President.

Directors and officers

SEC. 303. (a) The corporation shall have a board of directors consisting of individuals who are citizens of the United States, of whom one shall be elected annually by the board to serve as chairman. Three members of the board shall be appointed by the President of the United States, by and with the advice and consent of the Senate, effective the date on which the other members are elected, and for terms of three years or until their successors have been appointed and qualified, except that the first three members of the board so appointed shall continue in office for terms of one, two, and three years, respectively, and any member so appointed to fill a vacancy shall be appointed only for the unexpired term of the director whom he succeeds. Six members of the board shall be elected annually by those stockholders who are communications common carriers and six shall be elected annually by the other stockholders of the corporation. No stockholder who is a communications common carrier and no trustee for such a stockholder shall vote, either directly or indirectly, through the votes of subsidiaries or affiliated companies, nominees, or any persons subject to his direction or control, for more than three candidates for membership on the board. Subject to such limitation, the articles of incorporation to be filed by the incorporators designated under section 302 shall provide for cumulative voting under section 27(d) of the District of Columbia Business Corporation Act (D.C. Code, sec. 29–911(d)).

(b) The corporation shall have a president, and such other officers as may be named and appointed by the board, at rates of compensation fixed by the board, and serving at the pleasure of the board. No individual other than a citizen of the United States may be an officer of the corporation. No officer of the corporation shall receive any salary from any source other than the corporation during the period of his employment by the corporation.

Financing of the corporation

SEC. 304. (a) The corporation is authorized to issue and have outstanding, in such amounts as it shall determine, shares of capital stock, without par value, which shall carry voting rights and be eligible for dividends. The shares of such stock initially offered shall be sold at a price not in excess of $100 for each share and in a manner to encourage the widest distribution to the American public. Subject to the provisions of subsections (b) and (d) of this section, shares of stock offered under this subsection may be issued to and held by any person.

(b) (1) For the purposes of this section the term "authorized carrier" shall mean a communications common carrier which is specifically authorized or which is a member of a class of carriers authorized by the Commission to own shares of stock in the corporation upon a finding that such ownership will be consistent with the public interest, convenience, and necessity.

(2) Only those communications common carriers which are authorized carriers shall own shares of stock in the corporation at any time, and no other communications common carrier shall own shares either di-

rectly or indirectly through subsidiaries or affiliated companies, nominees, or any persons subject to its direction or control. Fifty per centum of the shares of stock authorized for issuance at any time by the corporation shall be reserved for purchase by authorized carriers and such carriers shall in the aggregate be entitled to make purchases of the reserved shares in a total number not exceeding the total number of the nonreserved shares of any issue purchased by other persons. At no time after the initial issue is completed shall the aggregate of the shares of voting stock of the corporation owned by authorized carriers directly or indirectly through subsidiaries or affiliated companies, nominees, or any persons subject to their direction or control exceed 50 per centum of such shares issued and outstanding.

(3) At no time shall any stockholder who is not an authorized carrier, or any syndicate or affiliated group of such stockholders, own more than 10 per centum of the shares of voting stock of the corporation issued and outstanding.

(c) The corporation is authorized to issue, in addition to the stock authorized by subsection (a) of this section, nonvoting securities, bonds, debentures, and other certificates of indebtedness as it may determine. Such nonvoting securities, bonds, debentures, or other certificates of indebtedness of the corporation as a communications common carrier may own shall be eligible for inclusion in the rate base of the carrier to the extent allowed by the Commission. The voting stock of the corporation shall not be eligible for inclusion in the rate base of the carrier.

(d) Not more than an aggregate of 20 per centum of the shares of stock of the corporation authorized by subsection (a) of this section which are held by holders other than authorized carriers may be held by persons of the classes described in paragraphs (1), (2), (3), (4), and (5) of section 310(a) of the Communications Act of 1934, as amended (47 U.S.C. 310).

(e) The requirement of section 45(b) of the District of Columbia Business Corporation Act (D.C. Code, sec. 29–920(b)) as to the percentage of stock which a stockholder must hold in order to have the rights of inspection and copying set forth in that subsection shall not be applicable in the case of holders of the stock of the corporation, and they may exercise such rights without regard to the percentage of stock they hold.

(f) Upon application to the Commission by any authorized carrier and after notice and hearing, the Commission may compel any other authorized carrier which owns shares of stock in the corporation to transfer to the applicant, for a fair and reasonable consideration, a number of such shares as the Commission determines will advance the public interest and the purposes of this Act. In its determination with respect to ownership of shares of stock in the corporation, the Commission, whenever consistent with the public interest, shall promote the widest possible distribution of stock among the authorized carriers.

Purposes and powers of the corporation

SEC. 305. (a) In order to achieve the objectives and to carry out the purposes of this Act, the corporation is authorized to—

(1) plan, initiate, construct, own, manage, and operate itself or in conjunction with foreign governments or business entities a commercial communications satellite system;

(2) furnish, for hire, channels of communication to United States communications common carriers and to other authorized entities, foreign and domestic; and

(3) own and operate satellite terminal stations when licensed by the Commission under section 201(c)(7).

(b) Included in the activities authorized to the corporation for accomplishment of the purposes indicated in subsection (a) of this section, are, among others not specifically named—

(1) to conduct or contract for research and development related to its mission;

(2) to acquire the physical facilities, equipment and devices necessary to its operations, including communications satellites and associated equipment and facilities, whether by construction, purchase, or gift;

(3) to purchase satellite launching and related services from the United States Government;

(4) to contract with authorized users, including the United States Government, for the services of the communications satellite system; and

(5) to develop plans for the technical specifications of all elements of the communications satellite system.

(c) To carry out the foregoing purposes, the corporation shall have the usual powers conferred upon a stock corporation by the District of Columbia Business Corporation Act.

TITLE IV—MISCELLANEOUS

Applicability of Communications Act of 1934

SEC. 401. The corporation shall be deemed to be a common carrier within the meaning of section 3(h) of the Communications Act of 1934, as amended, and as such shall be fully subject to the provisions of title II and title III of that Act. The provision of satellite terminal station facilities by one communication common carrier to one or more other communications common carriers shall be deemed to be a common carrier activity fully subject to the Communications Act. Whenever the application of the provisions of this Act shall be inconsistent with the application of the provisions of the Communications Act, the provisions of this Act shall govern.

Notice of foreign business negotiations

Sec. 402. Whenever the corporation shall enter into business negotiations with respect to facilities, operations, or services authorized by this Act with any international or foreign entity, it shall notify the Department of State of the negotiations, and the Department of State shall advise the corporation of relevant foreign policy considerations. Throughout such negotiations the corporation shall keep the Department of State informed with respect to such considerations. The corporation may request the Department of State to assist in the negotiations, and that Department shall render such assistance as may be appropriate.

Sanctions

Sec. 403. (a) If the corporation created pursuant to this Act shall engage in or adhere to any action, practices, or policies inconsistent with the policy and purposes declared in section 102 of this Act, or if the corporation or any other person shall violate any provision of this Act, or shall obstruct or interfere with any activities authorized by this Act, or shall refuse, fail, or neglect to discharge his duties and responsibilities under this Act, or shall threaten any such violation, obstruction, interference, refusal, failure, or neglect, the district court of the United States for any district in which such corporation or other person resides or may be found shall have jurisdiction, except as otherwise prohibited by law, upon petition of the Attorney General of the United States, to grant such equitable relief as may be necessary or appropriate to prevent or terminate such conduct or threat.

(b) Nothing contained in this section shall be construed as relieving any person of any punishment, liability, or sanction which may be imposed otherwise than under this Act.

(c) It shall be the duty of the corporation and all communications common carriers to comply, insofar as applicable, with all provisions of this Act and all rules and regulations promulgated thereunder.

Reports to the Congress

Sec. 404. (a) The President shall transmit to the Congress in January of each year a report which shall include a comprehensive description of the activities and accomplishments during the preceding calendar year under the national program referred to in section 201(a)(1), together with an evaluation of such activities and accomplishments in terms of the attainment of the objectives of this Act and any recommendations for additional legislative or other action which the President may consider necessary or desirable for the attainment of such objectives.

(b) The corporation shall transmit to the President and the Congress, annually and at such other times as it deems desirable, a comprehensive and detailed report of its operations, activities, and accomplishments under this Act.

(c) The Commission shall transmit to the Congress, annually and at such other times as it deems desirable, (i) a report of its activities and actions on anticompetitive practices as they apply to the communications satellite programs; (ii) an evaluation of such activities and actions taken by it within the scope of its authority with a view to recommending such additional legislation which the Commission may consider necessary in the public interest; and (iii) an evaluation of the capital structure of the corporation so as to assure the Congress that such structure is consistent with the most efficient and economical operation of the corporation.

RELATED READING

ARCHER, Gleason L. *History of Radio to 1926.* New York: The American Historical Society, 1938.

BARNOUW, Erik. *A Tower in Babel.* New York: Oxford University Press, 1966.

CHAFEE, Zechariah, Jr. *Government and Mass Communications.* 2 vols. Chicago: University of Chicago Press, 1947.

Code of Federal Regulations, Title 47 (Revised as of January 1, 1968). Washington: Government Printing Office, 1968. (Published annually.)

DAVIS, Stephen. *The Law of Radio Communication.* New York: McGraw-Hill, 1927.

DAVIS, Stephen B. "The Law of the Air," *The Radio Industry.* New York: A. W. Shaw, 1928.

DUNLAP, Orrin E., Jr. *Communications in Space: From Wireless to Satellite Relay.* New York: Harper and Brothers, 1962.

EMERY, Walter B. "The FCC: Its Powers, Functions, and Personnel," *Journal of Broadcasting,* II (Summer, 1958), 225–239.

——. *Broadcasting and Government: Responsibilities and Regulations.* East Lansing: Michigan State University Press, 1961.

EYDE, Kay. "Satellites and International Television," *NAEB Journal,* XXIV (March–April, 1965), 51–60.

FEDERAL COMMUNICATIONS COMMISSION. *The Communications Act of 1934 with Amendments and Index Thereto.* Washington: Government Printing Office, 1961. (Supplementary Packets 1 through 3, published from 1961 to 1965, are available from the Government Printing Office.)

——. *Silver Anniversary Report for Fiscal Year 1959.* Washington: Government Printing Office, 1959.

FORD, Frederick W. "The Meaning of the 'Public Interest, Convenience or Necessity,'" *Journal of Broadcasting,* V (Summer, 1961), 205–218.

GELMAN, Morris J. "The Future of Television: The Invisible Shield," *Television,* XXIII (February, 1966), 44–48, 55–60.

HERRING, James M., and Gerald C. GROSS. *Telecommunications: Economics and Regulation.* New York: McGraw-Hill, 1936.

HETTINGER, Herman S., ed. *The Annals—Radio: The Fifth Estate.* Philadelphia: The American Academy of Political and Social Science, 1935.

HOLT, Darrel. "The Origin of 'Public Interest' in Broadcasting," *Educational Broadcasting Review,* I (October, 1967), 15–19.

"Interpreting the FCC Rules and Regulations: The Commission's Position on 'Lotteries,'" *Broadcast Management/Engineering,* I (May, 1965), 13–15.

JANSKY, C. M., Jr. "The Contribution of Herbert Hoover to Broadcasting," *Journal of Broadcasting,* I (Summer, 1957), 241–249.

LICHTY, Lawrence W. "The Impact of FRC and FCC Commissioners' Backgrounds on the Regulation of Broadcasting," *Journal of Broadcasting,* VI (Spring, 1962), 97–110.

————. "Members of the Federal Radio Commission and Federal Communications Commission, 1927–1961," *Journal of Broadcasting,* VI (Winter, 1961–62), 23–34.

MARKS, Leonard H. "Communication Satellites: New Horizons for Broadcasters," *Journal of Broadcasting,* IX (Spring, 1965), 97–101.

PAGLIN, Max D. "Some Regulatory and International Problems Facing the Establishment of Communication Satellite Systems," *Journal of Broadcasting,* VI (Fall, 1962), 285–294.

PRESIDENT'S COMMUNICATIONS POLICY BOARD. *Telecommunications: A Program for Progress.* Washington: Government Printing Office, 1951.

ROSENBLOOM, Joel. "Authority of the Federal Communications Commission," in *Freedom and Responsibility in Broadcasting,* John E. Coons, ed. Evanston, Ill.: Northwestern University Press, 1961.

SCHMECKEBIER, Laurence F. *The Federal Radio Commission: Its History, Activities and Organization.* Washington: Brookings Institute, 1932.

SHIPLEY, Carl L. "Radio and Television Law," *Journal of Broadcasting,* I (Winter, 1956–57), 57–69.

SPALDING, John W. "1928: Radio Becomes a Mass Advertising Medium," *Journal of Broadcasting,* VIII (Winter, 1963–64), 31–44.

SPERRY, Robert. "A Selected Bibliography of Works on the Federal Communications Commission, *Journal of Broadcasting,* XII (Winter, 1967–68), 83–93.

STRASSBURG, Bernard, and Claude M. BLAIR. "Space Communications—A Symposium," *Television Quarterly,* II (Winter, 1963), 48–63.

UDELL, Gilman G. (comp.). *Radio Laws of the United States.* Washington: Government Printing Office, 1962.

UNITED STATES CONGRESS, HOUSE, COMMITTEE ON INTERSTATE AND FOREIGN COMMERCE. *Regulation of Broadcasting: Half a Century of Government Regulation of Broadcasting and the Need for Further Legislative Action,* Study for the Committee [by Robert S. McMahon], 85th Congress, 2d Session, on H. Res. 99. Washington: Government Printing Office, 1958.

WARNER, Harry P. *Radio and Television Law,* rev. ed. Albany: Matthew Bender, 1953.

YANKWICH, Leon R. "Federal and State Control Conflicts in Broadcasting," *Journal of Broadcasting,* I (Winter, 1956–57), 70–74.

ZEIDENBERG, Leonard. "Is the FCC Obsolete?," *Television,* XXIII (October, 1966), 27–31, 51–57.

PART TWO

FREEDOM OF EXPRESSION: REGULATION OF PROGRAMMING

GOVERNMENTAL censorship of broadcast content is expressly forbidden by Section 326 of the Communications Act, which reinforces the First Amendment to the Constitution. Yet, the Federal Communications Commission is charged with the task of regulating broadcasting in the "public interest, convenience, and necessity." Accordingly, the Commission has found it necessary to exercise some control over programming, however obliquely.

The FCC's stance in the area of program regulation is that of an acrobat trying to balance himself on a slack rope suspended between the public interest at one end and Section 326 at the other. To impose prior restraints on programming is contrary to the philosophical and legal underpinnings of freedom of speech. To exercise absolutely no influence over broadcast content seems inimical to the concept of the public interest.

With the exception of blatantly offensive programming, e.g., defamation and obscenity, the FCC has generally allowed licensees complete freedom in deciding what to include in their program schedules, on the condition that such freedom be exercised with conjoint responsibility. The broadcaster, then, is given the responsibility to determine what programs will serve the public interest. The Commission accepts the licensee's well-considered judgment in this area, unless there is evidence to indicate that the programs broadcast by the licensee are clearly contrary to the public interest.

Governmental regulation of programming is not confined to such tangible material as court cases and policy statements. On occasion a commissioner's speech or a proposed (but not enacted) FCC rule will stimulate program decisions in the industry. This phenomenon is known as "regulation by raised eyebrow," and is often as imprecise as it is subtle.

Nor are governmental pressures the only ones that affect the output of radio and television stations. Audience ratings, sponsor needs, and the temper of the times all exert their influences on what is broadcast. The codes of the National Association of Broadcasters, together with the program policy statements and continuity acceptance standards of stations and networks, are self-regulatory devices which are more palatable to the industry as instruments of content control than government decrees.

Federal regulation of programming has been criticized for being ineffectual by some, an abridgment of free speech by others. Self-regulation has similarly been attacked on two contradictory fronts—for encouraging only "bland" programming, and for being overly permissive by not clearly prohibiting that which is "daring" or "risqué." Both forms of regulation evolve only so long as such healthy debate continues.

1 | THE BRINKLEY CASE

KFKB Broadcasting Association, Inc., *v.*
Federal Radio Commission*
47 F.2d 670 (D.C. Cir.)
February 2, 1931

> *Dr. John R. Brinkley was hardly the only malpractitioner, medical
> or other, who gained access to the airwaves during radio's forma-
> tive era. His station, KFKB, was among the most popular in the
> country for several years.*
>
> *This Court of Appeals decision affirmed the Federal Radio
> Commission's denial of Brinkley's application for license renewal.
> The famed purveyor of the "goat gland" operation subsequently
> broadcast to his American audience from a Mexican station. The
> Brinkley case stands, nevertheless, as the first judicial affirmation of
> the Commission's right to consider a station's past programming
> with relation to the "public interest, convenience, and necessity"
> when license renewal is sought.*

ROBB, Associate Justice.

Appeal from a decision of the Federal Radio Commission denying appellant's application for the renewal of its station license.

The station is located at Milford, Kan., is operating on a frequency of
1,050 kilocycles with 5,000 watts power and is known by the call letters
KFKB. The station was first licensed by the Secretary of Commerce on September 20, 1923, in the name of the Brinkley-Jones Hospital Association,
and intermittently operated until June 3, 1925. On October 23, 1926, it was
relicensed to Dr. J. R. Brinkley with the same call letters and continued to
be so licensed until November 26, 1929, when an assignment was made to
appellant corporation.

On March 20, 1930, appellant filed its application for renewal of
license (Radio Act of 1927, c. 169, 44 Stat. 1162, U. S. C. Supp. 3, tit. 47,

* Opinion taken with permission from Vol. 47, *Federal Reporter*, second series.

§ 81, et seq. [47 USCA § 81 et seq.]). The commission, failing to find that public interest, convenience, or necessity would be served thereby, accorded appellant opportunity to be heard. Hearings were had on May 21, 22, and 23, 1930, at which appellant appeared by counsel and introduced evidence on the question whether the granting of the application would be in the public interest, convenience, or necessity. Evidence also was introduced in behalf of the commission. Upon consideration of the evidence and arguments, the commission found that public interest, convenience, or necessity would not be served by granting the application and, therefore, ordered that it be denied, effective June 13, 1930. A stay order was allowed by this court, and appellant has since been operating thereunder.

The evidence tends to show that Dr. J. R. Brinkley established Station KFKB, the Brinkley Hospital, and the Brinkley Pharmaceutical Association, and that these institutions are operated in a common interest. While the record shows that only 3 of the 1,000 shares of the capital stock of appellant are in Dr. Brinkley's name and that his wife owns 381 shares, it is quite apparent that the doctor actually dictates and controls the policy of the station. The Brinkley Hospital, located at Milford, is advertised over Station KFKB. For this advertising the hospital pays the station from $5,000 to $7,000 per month.

The Brinkley Pharmaceutical Association, formed by Dr. Brinkley, is composed of druggists who dispense to the public medical preparations prepared according to formulas of Dr. Brinkley and known to the public only by numerical designations. Members of the association pay a fee upon each sale of certain of those preparations. The amounts thus received are paid the station, presumably for advertising the preparations. It appears that the income of the station for the period February, March, and April, 1930, was as follows:

Brinkley Pharmaceutical Association	$27,856.40
Brinkley Hospital	6,500.00
All other sources	3,544.93
Total	$37,901.33

Dr. Brinkley personally broadcasts during three one-half hour periods daily over the station, the broadcast being referred to as the "medical question box," and is devoted to diagnosing and prescribing treatment of cases from symptoms given in letters addressed either to Dr. Brinkley or to the station. Patients are not known to the doctor except by means of their letters, each letter containing a code signature, which is used in making answer through the broadcasting station. The doctor usually advises that the writer of the letter is suffering from a certain ailment, and recommends the procurement from one of the members of the Brinkley Pharmaceutical Association, of one or more of Dr. Brinkley's prescriptions, designated by numbers. In Dr. Brinkley's broadcast for April 1, 1930, presumably representative of all, he prescribed for forty-four different patients and in all, save ten, he advised the procurement of from one to four of his own prescriptions. We reproduce two as typical:

Here's one from Tillie. She says she had an operation, had some trouble 10 years ago. I think the operation was unnecessary, and it isn't very good sense to have an ovary removed with the expectation of motherhood resulting therefrom. My advice to you is to use Women's Tonic No. 50, 67, and 61. This combination will do for you what you desire if any combination will, after three months' persistent use.

Sunflower State, from Dresden Kans. Probably he has gall stones. No, I don't mean that, I mean kidney stones. My advice to you is to put him on Prescription No. 80 and 50 for men, also 64. I think that he will be a whole lot better. Also drink a lot of water.

In its "Facts and Grounds for Decision," the commission held "that the practice of a physician prescribing treatment for a patient whom he has never seen, and bases his diagnosis upon what symptoms may be recited by the patient in a letter addressed to him, is inimical to the public health and safety, and for that reason is not in the public interest"; that "the testimony in this case shows conclusively that the operation of Station KFKB is conducted only in the personal interest of Dr. John R. Brinkley. While it is to be expected that a licensee of a radio broadcasting station will receive some remuneration for serving the public with radio programs, at the same time the interest of the listening public is paramount, and may not be subordinated to the interests of the station licensee."

This being an application for the renewal of a license, the burden is upon the applicant to establish that such renewal would be in the public interest, convenience, or necessity (Technical Radio Lab. v. Fed. Radio Comm., 59 App. D. C. 125, 36 F.(2d) 111, 114, 66 A. L. R. 1355; Campbell v. Galeno Chem. Co., 281 U. S. 599, 609, 50 S. Ct. 412, 74 L. Ed. 1063), and the court will sustain the findings of fact of the commission unless "manifestly against the evidence." Ansley v. Fed. Radio Comm., 60 App. D. C. 19, 46 F.(2d) 600.

We have held that the business of broadcasting, being a species of interstate commerce, is subject to the reasonable regulation of Congress. Technical Radio Lab. v. Fed. Radio Comm., 59 App. D. C. 125, 36 F.(2d) 111, 66 A. L. R. 1355; City of New York v. Fed. Radio Comm., 59 App. D. C. 129, 36 F.(2d) 115; Chicago Federation of Labor v. Fed. Radio Comm., 59 App. D. C. 333, 41 F.(2d) 422. It is apparent, we think, that the business is impressed with a public interest and that, because the number of available broadcasting frequencies is limited, the commission is necessarily called upon to consider the character and quality of the service to be rendered. In considering an application for a renewal of the license, an important consideration is the past conduct of the applicant, for "by their fruits ye shall know them." Matt. VII:20. Especially is this true in a case like the present, where the evidence clearly justifies the conclusion that the future conduct of the station will not differ from the past.

In its Second Annual Report (1928), p. 169, the commission cautioned broadcasters "who consume much of the valuable time allotted to them under their licenses in matters of a distinctly private nature which are not only uninteresting, but also distasteful to the listening public." When Congress provided that the question whether a license should be issued or renewed should be dependent upon a finding of public interest, convenience, or necessity, it very evidently had in mind that broadcasting should not be a mere adjunct of a particular business but should be of a public character. Obviously, there is no room in the broadcast band for every business or school of thought.

In the present case, while the evidence shows that much of appellant's programs is entertaining and unobjectionable in character, the finding of the commission that the station "is conducted only in the personal interest of Dr. John R. Brinkley" is not "manifestly against the evidence." We are further of the view that there is substantial evidence in support of the finding of the Commission that the "medical question box" as conducted by Dr. Brinkley "is inimical to the public health and safety, and for that reason is not in the public interest."

Appellant contends that the attitude of the commission amounts to a censorship of the station contrary to the provisions of section 29 of the Radio Act of 1927 (47 USCA § 109). This contention is without merit. There has been no attempt on the part of the commission to subject any part of appellant's broadcasting matter to scrutiny prior to its release. In considering the question whether the public interest, convenience, or necessity will be served by a renewal of appellant's license, the commission has merely exercised its undoubted right to take note of appellant's past conduct, which is not censorship.

As already indicated, Congress has imposed upon the commission the administrative function of determining whether or not a station license should be renewed, and the commission in the present case has in the exercise of judgment and discretion ruled against the applicant. We are asked upon the record and evidence before the commission to substitute our judgment and discretion for that of the commission. While section 16 of the Radio Act of 1927 (44 Stat. 1162, 1169, U. S. C., Supp. 3, tit. 47, § 96) authorized an appeal to this court, we do not think it was the intent of Congress that we should disturb the action of the commission in a case like the present. Support is found for this view in the Act of July 1, 1930 (46 Stat. 844 [47 USCA § 96]), amending section 16 of the 1927 Act. The amendment specifically provides "that the review by the court shall be limited to questions of law and that findings of fact by the commission, if supported by substantial evidence, shall be conclusive unless it shall clearly appear that the findings of the commission are arbitrary or capricious." As to the interpretation that should be placed upon such provision, see Ma-King v. Blair, 271 U. S. 479, 483, 46 S. Ct. 544, 70 L. Ed. 1046.

We are therefore constrained, upon a careful review of the record, to affirm the decision.

Affirmed.

2 | THE SHULER CASE

Trinity Methodist Church, South, v.
Federal Radio Commission*
62 F.2d 850 (D.C. Cir.)
November 28, 1932

This Court of Appeals decision, building on the prior Brinkley *case, held that the Federal Radio Commission's refusal to renew the license of Reverend Shuler's radio station, KGEF, because of his defamatory and otherwise objectionable utterances over the station, violated neither the First nor the Fifth Amendments to the Constitution. The Supreme Court declined to review this decision (288 U.S. 599 (1933)).*

GRONER, Associate Justice.

Appellant, Trinity Methodist Church, South, was the lessee and operator of a radio-broadcasting station at Los Angeles, Cal., known by the call letters KGEF. The station had been in operation for several years. The Commission, in its findings, shows that, though in the name of the church, the station was in fact owned by the Reverend Doctor Shuler and its operation dominated by him. Dr. Shuler is the minister in charge of Trinity Church. The station was operated for a total of 23¼ hours each week.

In September, 1930, appellant filed an application for renewal of station license. Numerous citizens of Los Angeles protested, and the Commission, being unable to determine that public interest, convenience, and necessity would be served, set the application down for hearing before an examiner. In January, 1931, the matter was heard, and the testimony of ninety witnesses taken. The examiner recommended renewal of the license. Exceptions were filed by one of the objectors, and oral argument requested. This was had before the Commission, sitting in banc, and, upon consideration of the evidence, the examiner's report, the exceptions, etc., the Commission denied the application for renewal upon the ground that the public interest,

---

* Opinion taken with permission from Vol. 62, *Federal Reporter*, second series.

convenience, and/or necessity would not be served by the granting of the application. Some of the things urging it to this conclusion were that the station had been used to attack a religious organization, meaning the Roman Catholic Church; that the broadcasts by Dr. Shuler were sensational rather than instructive; and that in two instances Shuler had been convicted of attempting in his radio talks to obstruct the orderly administration of public justice.

This court denied a motion for a stay order, and this appeal was taken. The basis of the appeal is that the Commission's decision is unconstitutional, in that it violates the guaranty of free speech, and also that it deprives appellant of his property without due process of law. It is further insisted that the decision violates the Radio Act because not supported by substantial evidence, and therefore is arbitrary and capricious.

We have been at great pains to examine carefully the record of a thousand pages, and have reached the conclusion that none of these assignments is well taken.

We need not stop to review the cases construing the depth and breadth of the first amendment. The subject in its more general outlook has been the source of much writing since Milton's *Areopagitica,* the emancipation of the English press by the withdrawal of the licensing act in the reign of William the Third, and the *Letters* of Junius. It is enough now to say that the universal trend of decisions has recognized the guaranty of the amendment to prevent previous restraints upon publications, as well as immunity of censorship, leaving to correction by subsequent punishment those utterances or publications contrary to the public welfare. In this aspect it is generally regarded that freedom of speech and press cannot be infringed by legislative, executive, or judicial action, and that the constitutional guaranty should be given liberal and comprehensive construction. It may therefore be set down as a fundamental principle that under these constitutional guaranties the citizen has in the first instance the right to utter or publish his sentiments, though, of course, upon condition that he is responsible for any abuse of that right. Near v. Minnesota ex rel. Olson, 283 U. S. 697, 51 S. Ct. 625, 75 L. Ed. 1357. "Every freeman has an undoubted right to lay what sentiments he pleases before the public; to forbid this is to destroy the freedom of the press; but if he publishes what is improper, mischievous, or illegal, he must take the consequences of his own temerity." 4th Bl. Com. 151, 152. But this does not mean that the government, through agencies established by Congress, may not refuse a renewal of license to one who has abused it to broadcast defamatory and untrue matter. In that case there is not a denial of the freedom of speech, but merely the application of the regulatory power of Congress in a field within the scope of its legislative authority. See KFKB Broadcasting Ass'n v. Federal Radio Commission, 60 App. D. C. 79, 47 F.(2d) 670.

Section 1 of the Radio Act of 1927 (44 Stat. 1162, title 47, USCA,

§ 81) specifically declares the purpose of the act to be to regulate all forms of interstate and foreign radio transmissions and communications within the United States, its territories and possessions; to maintain the control of the United States over all the channels of interstate and foreign radio transmissions; and to provide for the use of such channels for limited periods of time, under licenses granted by federal authority. The federal authority set up by the act to carry out its terms is the Federal Radio Commission, and the Commission is given power, and required, upon examination of an application for a station license, or for a renewal or modification, to determine whether "public interest, convenience, or necessity" will be served by the granting thereof, and any applicant for a renewal of license whose application is refused may of right appeal from such decision to this court.

We have already held that radio communication, in the sense contemplated by the act, constituted interstate commerce, KFKB Broadcasting Ass'n v. Federal Radio Commission, supra; General Elec. Co. v. Federal Radio Commission, 58 App. D. C. 386, 31 F.(2d) 630, and in this respect we are supported by many decisions of the Supreme Court, Pensacola Telegraph Co. v. Western Union Tel. Co., 96 U. S. 1, 9, 24 L. Ed. 708; International Text-Book Co. v. Pigg, 217 U. S. 91, 106, 107, 30 S. Ct. 481, 54 L. Ed. 678, 27 L. R. A. (N. S.) 493, 18 Ann. Cas. 1103; Western Union Teleg. Co. v. Pendelton, 122 U. S. 347, 356, 7 S. Ct. 1126, 30 L. Ed. 1187. And we do not understand it is contended that where, as in the case before us, there is no physical substance between the transmitting and the receiving apparatus, the broadcasting of programs across state lines is not interstate commerce, and, if this be true, it is equally true that the power of Congress to regulate interstate commerce, complete in itself, may be exercised to its utmost extent, and acknowledges no limitation, other than such as prescribed in the Constitution (Gibbons v. Ogden, 9 Wheat. 1, 6 L. Ed. 23), and these powers, as was said by the Supreme Court in Pensacola Tel. Co. v. Western Union Tel. Co., supra, "keep pace with the progress of the country, and adapt themselves to the new developments of time and circumstances."

In recent years the power under the commerce clause has been extended to legislation against interstate commerce in stolen automobiles, Brooks v. United States, 267 U. S. 432, 45 S. Ct. 345, 69 L. Ed. 699, 37 A. L. R. 1407; to transportation of adulterated foods, Hipolite Egg Co. v. United States, 220 U. S. 45, 31 S. Ct. 364, 55 L. Ed. 364; in the suppression of interstate commerce for immoral purposes, Hoke v. United States, 227 U. S. 308, 33 S. Ct. 281, 57 L. Ed. 523, 43 L. R. A. (N. S.) 906, Ann. Cas. 1913E, 905; and in a variety of other subjects never contemplated by the framers of the Constitution. It is too late now to contend that Congress may not regulate, and, in some instances, deny, the facilities of interstate commerce to a business or occupation which it deems inimical to the public welfare or contrary to the public interest. Lottery Cases, 188 U. S. 321,

352, 23 S. Ct. 321, 47 L. Ed. 492. Everyone interested in radio legislation approved the principle of limiting the number of broadcasting stations, or, perhaps, it would be more nearly correct to say, recognized the inevitable necessity. In these circumstances Congress intervened and asserted its paramount authority, and, if it be admitted, as we think it must be, that, in the present condition of the science with its limited facilities, the regulatory provisions of the Radio Act are a reasonable exercise by Congress of its powers, the exercise of these powers is no more restricted by the First Amendment than are the police powers of the States under the Fourteenth Amendment. See In re Kemmler, 136 U. S. 436, 448, 449, 10 S. Ct. 930, 34 L. Ed. 519; Hamilton v. Kentucky, etc., Co., 251 U. S. 146, at page 156, 40 S. Ct. 106, 64 L. Ed. 194. In either case the answer depends upon whether the statute is a reasonable exercise of governmental control for the public good.

In the case under consideration, the evidence abundantly sustains the conclusion of the Commission that the continuance of the broadcasting programs of appellant is not in the public interest. In a proceeding for contempt against Dr. Shuler, on appeal to the Supreme Court of California, that court said (In re Shuler, 210 Cal. 377, 292 P. 481, 492) that the broadcast utterances of Dr. Shuler disclosed throughout the determination on his part to impose on the trial courts his own will and views with respect to certain causes then pending or on trial, and amounted to contempt of court. Appellant, not satisfied with attacking the judges of the courts in cases then pending before them, attacked the bar association for its activities in recommending judges, charging it with ulterior and sinister purposes. With no more justification, he charged particular judges with sundry immoral acts. He made defamatory statements against the board of health. He charged that the labor temple in Los Angeles was a bootlegging and gambling joint. In none of these matters, when called on to explain or justify his statements, was he able to do more than declare that the statements expressed his own sentiments. On one occasion he announced over the radio that he had certain damaging information against a prominent unnamed man which, unless a contribution (presumably to the church) of a hundred dollars was forthcoming, he would disclose. As a result, he received contributions from several persons. He freely spoke of "pimps" and prostitutes. He alluded slightingly to the Jews as a race, and made frequent and bitter attacks on the Roman Catholic religion and its relations to government. However inspired Dr. Shuler may have been by what he regarded as patriotic zeal, however sincere in denouncing conditions he did not approve, it is manifest, we think, that it is not narrowing the ordinary conception of "public interest" in declaring his broadcasts—without facts to sustain or to justify them—not within that term, and, since that is the test the Commission is required to apply, we think it was its duty in considering the application for renewal to take notice of appellant's conduct in his previous use of the permit, and, in the circumstances, the refusal, we think, was neither arbitrary nor capricious.

If it be considered that one in possession of a permit to broadcast in interstate commerce may, without let or hindrance from any source, use these facilities, reaching out, as they do, from one corner of the country to the other, to obstruct the administration of justice, offend the religious susceptibilities of thousands, inspire political distrust and civic discord, or offend youth and innocence by the free use of words suggestive of sexual immorality, and be answerable for slander only at the instance of the one offended, then this great science, instead of a boon, will become a scourge, and the nation a theater for the display of individual passions and the collision of personal interests. This is neither censorship nor previous restraint, nor is it a whittling away of the rights guaranteed by the First Amendment, or an impairment of their free exercise. Appellant may continue to indulge his strictures upon the characters of men in public office. He may just as freely as ever criticize religious practices of which he does not approve. He may even indulge private malice or personal slander—subject, of course, to be required to answer for the abuse thereof—but he may not, as we think, demand, of right, the continued use of an instrumentality of commerce for such purposes, or any other, except in subordination to all reasonable rules and regulations Congress, acting through the Commission, may prescribe.

Nor are we any more impressed with the argument that the refusal to renew a license is a taking of property within the Fifth Amendment. There is a marked difference between the destruction of physical property, as in Pennsylvania Coal Co. v. Mahon, 260 U. S. 393, 43 S. Ct. 158, 67 L. Ed. 322, 28 A. L. R. 1321, and the denial of a permit to use the limited channels of the air. As was pointed out in American Bond & Mtg. Co. v. United States (C. C. A.) 52 F.(2d) 318, 320, the former is vested, the latter permissive, and, as was said by the Supreme Court in Chicago, B. & Q. R. Co. v. Illinois, 200 U. S. 561, 593, 26 S. Ct. 341, 350, 50 L. Ed. 596, 4 Ann. Cas. 1175: "If the injury complained of is only incidental to the legitimate exercise of governmental powers for the public good, then there is no taking of property for the public use, and a right to compensation, on account of such injury, does not attach under the Constitution." When Congress imposes restrictions in a field falling within the scope of its legislative authority and a taking of property without compensation is alleged, the test is whether the restrictive measures are reasonably adapted to secure the purposes and objects of regulation. If this test is satisfied, then "the enforcement of uncompensated obedience" to such regulation "is not an unconstitutional taking of property without compensation or without due process of law." Atlantic Coast Line R. Co. v. Goldsboro, 232 U. S. 548, 558, 34 S. Ct. 364, 368, 58 L. Ed. 721.

A case which illustrates this principle is Greenleaf-Johnson Lumber Co. v. Garrison, 237 U. S. 251, 35 S. Ct. 551, 59 L. Ed. 939. In that case the state of Virginia had established lines of navigability in the harbor of Norfolk. The lumber company applied for and obtained permission from the state to build a wharf from its upland into the river to the line of navigability. Some twenty years later the government, in the exercise of its control of the navigable waters and in the interest of commerce and navigation, adopted the lines of navigability formerly established by the state of Virginia, but a few years prior to the commencement of the suit the Secretary of War, by authority conferred on him by the Congress, re-established the lines, as a result of which the riparian proprietor's wharf extended some two hundred feet within the new lines of navigability. The Secretary of War asserted the right to require the demolition of the wharf as an obstruction to navigation. The owner insisted that, having received a grant of privilege from the state of Virginia prior to the exercise by the government of its power over the river, and subsequently acquiesced in by its adoption of the state lines, the property right thus acquired became as stable as any other property, and the privilege so granted irrevocable, and that it could be taken for public use only upon the payment of just compensation. The contention was rejected on the principle that the control of Congress over the navigable streams of the country is conclusive, and its judgment and determination the exercise of a legislative power in respect of a subject wholly within its control. To the same effect is Gibson v. United States, 166 U. S. 269, 17 S. Ct. 578, 41 L. Ed. 996, in which a work of public improvement in the Ohio river diminished greatly the value of the riparian owner's property by destroying his access to navigable water; and Union Bridge Co. v. United States, 204 U. S. 364, 27 S. Ct. 367, 51 L. Ed. 523, where the owner of a bridge was required to remodel the same as an obstruction to navigation, though erected under authority of the state when it was not an obstruction to navigation; and Louisville Bridge Co. v. United States, 242 U. S. 409, 37 S. Ct. 158, 61 L. Ed. 395, in which the same rule was applied in the case of a bridge erected expressly pursuant to an act of Congress. So also in United States v. Chandler-Dunbar Water Power Co., 229 U. S. 53, 33 S. Ct. 667, 57 L. Ed. 1063, the right of the government to destroy the water power of a riparian owner was upheld; and in Lewis Blue Point Oyster Cultivation Co. v. Briggs, 229 U. S. 82, 33 S. Ct. 679, 57 L. Ed. 1083, the right of compensation for the destruction of privately owned oyster beds was denied. All of these cases indubitably show adherence to the principle that one who applies for and obtains a grant or permit from a state, or the United States, to make use of a medium of interstate commerce, under the control and subject to the dominant power of the government, takes such grant or right subject to the exercise of the power of government, in the public interest, to withdraw it without compensation.

Appellant was duly notified by the Commission of the hearing which it ordered to be held to determine if the public interest, convenience, or necessity would be served by granting a renewal of its license. Due notice of this hearing was given and opportunity extended to furnish proof to establish the right under the provisions of the act for a renewal of the grant. There was, therefore, no lack of due process, and, considered from every point of view, the action of the Commission in refusing to renew was in all respects right, and should be, and is, affirmed.

Affirmed.

VAN ORSDEL, Associate Justice, concurs in the result.

3 | THE BLUE BOOK

Public Service Responsibility of Broadcast Licensees
March 7, 1946

*The "Blue Book," so called because of the color of its cover, is the
most thoroughly substantiated and reasoned expression of FCC programming policy yet issued. Largely the work of Charles A. Siepmann, then a consultant to the Commission, this document elicited
cries of protest from the broadcasting industry on the ground that
freedom of speech was being abridged. Neither vigorously enforced
nor officially repudiated by the Commission, the "Blue Book" remains a more forceful potential instrument of program regulation
in the public interest than has hitherto been promulgated.*

PART I. THE COMMISSION'S CONCERN
WITH PROGRAM SERVICE

On April 10, 1945, the Federal Communications Commission
announced "a policy of a more detailed review of broadcast station performance when passing upon applications for license renewals."[1]

The need for such a policy had earlier been set forth by Chairman Paul
A. Porter in an address to the National Association of Broadcasters March
12, 1945. The Chairman stated:

. . . Briefly the facts are these: an applicant seeks a construction permit for
a new station and in his application makes the usual representations as to the
type of service he proposes. These representations include specific pledges that
time will be made available for civic, educational, agricultural and other public
service programs. The station is constructed and begins operations. Subsequently
the licensee asks for a three-year renewal and the record clearly shows that he
has not fulfilled the promises made to the Commission when he received the
original grant. The Commission in the past has, for a variety of reasons, including limitations of staff, automatically renewed these licenses even in cases
where there is a vast disparity between promises and performance.

We have under consideration at the present time, however, a procedure

[1] FCC Mimeograph No. 81575, April 10, 1945.

whereby promises will be compared with performance. I think the industry is entitled to know of our concern in this matter and should be informed that there is pending before the Commission staff proposals which are designed to strengthen renewal procedures and give the Commission a more definite picture of the station's overall operation when licenses come up for renewal.

A procedure involving more detailed review of renewal applications was instituted experimentally in April 1945; and this report is based in part upon experience since then with renewal applications.

The need for detailed review on renewal can best be illustrated by a series of specific instances. The cases which follow are *not* presented for any substantive light they may throw on policy with respect to program service. Part III of this report will deal with substantive program service matters. The following cases are set forth to show various occasions for detailed review on renewal rather than the principles in terms of which such review should proceed.

A. Comparison of promise and performance: Station KIEV

The KIEV case (8 F.C.C. 207) illustrates primarily the need for sound procedures to compare promises with performance when acting on renewal of licenses.

Under date of January 27, 1932, the Cannon System, Ltd., applied for a construction permit for a new standard broadcast station at Glendale, California. Because the quota[2] for the zone in which California was located had been filled, the Cannon System, Ltd., further requested that the facilities assigned to Station KGIX, Las Vegas, Nevada, be withdrawn, in order to make possible a grant of its application.

In prosecuting its application (Docket No. 1595), Cannon System, Ltd., represented that it proposed to operate the station as a civic project; that the central location of its proposed studios would be convenient for the program talent to be broadcast; that the applicant proposed to cooperate with the Glendale Chamber of Commerce and all the local civic, educational, fraternal and religious institutions in donating to them, without charge, periods of time for broadcasting programs of special interest to Glendale listeners; that one-third of the broadcasting time would be devoted to educational and semi-educational matters; that agricultural features would be presented and that programs would include local, state and national news items; that special features would be presented for the large

[2] Under Section 9 of the Radio Act of 1927, as amended March 28, 1928, each zone and each state in the United States was assigned a quota, and new applications could not be granted, with certain exceptions, in a zone or state whose quota was already filled. Since the Fifth Zone quota was filled, KIEV was of the opinion that its application would be granted only at the expense of some other station, and hence requested the withdrawal of the facilities assigned to KGIX. A subsequent change in California quota facilities rendered this question moot. (*In re Cannon System, Ltd.,* F.R.C. Docket 1595, decided Sept. 23, 1932.)

Spanish population in the Glendale area; that 20 percent of all its broadcast hours would be devoted to sustaining programs of an agricultural nature; etc. It further represented that the lack of a broadcast station in Glendale discriminated against "the use of Glendale's excellent talent."

On the basis of such representations, the renewal application of Station KGIX was designated for hearing jointly with the application of the Cannon System, Ltd., for a new station. Following this hearing, the Federal Radio Commission found that "although the Glendale area now receives service from a number of stations situated elsewhere, there appears to be a need in that city for the purely local service, largely civic and educational in character, proposed to be rendered therein by applicant, Cannon System, Ltd."

With respect to Station KGIX, the Commission found that cutting its hours from unlimited to limited would permit the station "to render any substantial service theretofore rendered or proposed to be rendered." Accordingly, the application of the Cannon System, Ltd., was granted, and the authorized time of Station KGIX was cut in half in its renewed license.

On May 22, 1939, Station KIEV filed an application for renewal of its license and the Commission was unable to determine from an examination of the application that a renewal would be in the public interest. Accordingly, the application was designated for hearing[3] and was heard beginning December 7, 1939.

Commission inspectors had made recordings of the programs broadcast by the applicant on December 15, 21, and 27, 1938. On the basis of these recordings, the Commission found:

. . . On the first of these days the programs consisted of 143 popular records and 9 semi-classical records. There were 264 commercial announcements and 3 minutes of announcements concerning lost and found pets. On December 21, 1938, the programs were made up of 156 popular and 10 semi-classical records and were accompanied by 258 commercial announcements. Ten minutes were devoted to the lost and found pet column. On December 27, 1938, 165 popular, 12 semi-classical records, 10 minutes of the lost and found pet column and 199 commercial announcements made up the day's schedule. During these 3 days, which represented a total of 36 hours of broadcast time, only 23 minutes were devoted to programs other than records and commercial announcements.[4] The alleged policy of the station had been to limit commercial announcements to

[3] The issues in the hearing included the following:
  "1. To determine the nature and character of the program service rendered by the applicant;
  "2. To determine whether the station's program service has been and is now in conformity with the representations made to the Commission in support of the original application for construction permit or license, and all subsequent applications by the licensee. . . ."

[4] In originally urging that its own application be granted and that the renewal application of Station KGIX be denied, Cannon Systems, Ltd., had called attention to the fact that the KGIX programs were 75 percent transcribed or recorded, and had characterized this as "reprehensible and inexcusable." It appears, however, that the Cannon System programs on the three days monitored were more than 98 percent recorded.

160 announcements for each 10-hour day but it appears that the manager, employed on a commission basis, permitted a greater number to be broadcast. Even if the station's definition of a "commercial," which excludes time signals and introductions in the name of the sponsor, is accepted, the number of commercial programs on the dates recorded would be far in excess of those originally proposed.

Further examples of the divergence between promise and performance are found in the following record facts. For a period of over a year no regular news was broadcast over the station. Little effort was made to promote any programs other than those characterized by purely commercial continuity. The musical portions were composed almost entirely of popular records. Each 5-minute program contains at least one commercial announcement and some recorded music. While the licensee made its station available free of charge to civic, charitable, fraternal, and educational organizations, it expended no substantial effort actively to assist and aid such organizations in the preparation and production of programs. As a result, programs of this character became in most instances mere announcements for such organizations. (8 F.C.C. 207, 208-209.)

The Commission's decision, dated September 25, 1940, set forth at some length its views with respect to "the disparity between the proposed service and the programs actually broadcast." It stated:

In the Commission's view the licensee of Station KIEV did not make a reasonable effort to make its programs conform to its representations. The disparity between the proposed service and the programs actually broadcast indicates such a disregard of the representations made as to cast doubt on their sincerity in the first instance, and, therefore, on the qualifications of the licensee. Furthermore, false statements of talent expenditures were made in successive renewal applications. The Commission, in the allocation of frequencies to the various communities, must rely upon the testimony of applicants and upon the representations made in original and renewal applications, to determine whether the public interest will be served by a grant of such applications. Faced here by such a disregard for representations so made, particularly upon the question of service to the public, the Commission is satisfied that a denial of the renewal application might well be justified. It should be noted that the emphasis is here placed upon the question of the truth of representations made to the Commission as a basis for the grant and renewal of a broadcast license. No adverse criticism is directed at the use of a proper proportion of high quality records or electrical transcriptions.

Upon all the facts, however, it has been concluded not to deny the pending application. The record shows that attempts to improve programs have been made. An additional member has been placed on the staff with the duty of arranging programs of a civic, educational and charitable nature. The percentage of time devoted to recorded music and to commercialization has been much reduced, and the remainder of the program schedule dedicated to diversified nonrecorded program material. News programs have been added and a 5-year contract entered into with the United Press. Religious programs are being prepared by the Ministerial Association. Local civic and fraternal organizations are being more actively assisted in the preparation of programs. To a substantial extent the public has come to utilize the transmitting facilities and the broadcast service.

There is, therefore, ground for urging that we may expect the present trend of improvement in program service to be carried forward. With some reluctance the Commission concludes that this application may be granted. The facts developed in this proceeding will, however, be given cumulative weight in dealing with any future questions involving the conduct of this station. (8 F.C.C. 207, 209-210.)

Despite the additional representations made in connection with its 1940 renewal, the KIEV logs for the week beginning April 23, 1944, show that more than 88 percent of its program time was still being devoted to mechanically reproduced music. Less than 3.7 percent of its program time —or 30 minutes a day—was devoted to the "talent" which the applicant assured the Commission was available in the community. This consisted of one singer who sang for 15 minutes 6 times a week, one pianist for 15 minutes on Saturday, one 15-minute school program, and a devotional program daily except Sunday from 6:30 to 6:45 a.m., when audiences, of course, are small. U.P. news was broadcast. The station's programs were still being interspersed with spot announcements on an average of one every 5.5 minutes. A total of 1042 spot announcements were broadcast during the week, of which 1034 were commercial and 8 were broadcast as a public service. A search of the week's logs fails to disclose any "duets, quartets, excerpts from operas, cuttings from great poems," or other special features originally promised when the Cannon System, Ltd., was seeking a license at the expense of Station KGIX. Nor does it reveal an adherence to the representations made in connection with its renewal granted in January 1940.

B. Competing applications: Station WSNY

In the *Cannon System* case (KIEV), there was an element of competition between applicants, since the Cannon System proposed that the license of an existing station not be renewed. In the *Western Gateway* case (9 F.C.C. 92), the issue of two competing applications for a single available assignment was squarely raised.[1]

On December 8, 1939, the Van Curler Broadcasting Corporation filed an application for a new station to operate in Schenectady, New York, on a frequency of 1210 kilocycles, with power of 250 watts. A month later the Western Gateway Broadcasting Corporation filed a competing application

---

[1] This need to decide between competing applicants is a commonplace in the standard broadcast band. It may be somewhat less frequent in the new FM band because of the possibility of a larger number of stations in most communities; but competing applications for FM along the Eastern seaboard and in other metropolitan areas are already on file with the Commission. Television will also in all probability give rise to competing applications for identical facilities.

for a new station in the same city, utilizing the same power on the same frequency. The two mutually exclusive applications were jointly heard.

Since both applicants specified similar or identical equipment and both appeared initially to be qualified financially and legally, the hearings were primarily concerned with the program representations of the two applicants. The Van Curler Broadcasting Corporation, for example, represented that it would regularly broadcast programs of the American Legion, the Schenectady Municipal Housing Authority, the Schenectady Council of Churches, etc.; that school programs for the city school system would be broadcast from 1:30 to 2 p. m. daily; that a local town-meeting program, patterned after the "American Town Meeting of the Air," would be broadcast Tuesday evenings from 8 to 9 p. m.; that a special line and studios would be installed at Union College for the broadcasting of its educational programs; etc.[2]

The other applicant, Western Gateway, also made detailed program representations—for example, that it would broadcast book reviews; a music appreciation series; a local "Radio Workshop" patterned after the CBS program of the same title; round table religious discussions embracing all religious faiths; programs of various local civic organizations, etc. The percentage of time to be devoted to each type of program was explicitly set forth.[3]

[2] "The Schenectady Municipal Housing Authority would broadcast a weekly one-quarter hour program, publicizing its activities. The Council of Churches of Schenectady would cooperate with the applicant in presenting religious programs. The proposed religious programs consist of: A one-quarter hour morning devotional program, presented 5 days a week by local ministers; a one-quarter hour Jewish program on Saturday afternoons; morning church services, presented from local churches for 1 hour on Sundays; and Vesper services for one-half hour on Sunday afternoons. Definite arrangements have been made with the city superintendent of schools for the broadcasting of school programs from 1:30 to 2 p.m. daily. Arrangements have been made with the State Forum Counselor, assigned by the United States Office of Education, to the New York Council of School Superintendents to broadcast programs in connection with this group's work in promoting adult civic education. The broadcasts to be presented would consist of: A local town meeting program (patterned after the well-known program, "American Town Meeting of the Air"), which would be carried on Tuesday evenings from 8 to 9 p.m.; and three one-quarter hour programs each week. The Federation of Women's Clubs of Schenectady, representing some 38 clubs, would broadcast a one-half hour program each week during the seasons of the year when the clubs are most active. Definite arrangements have already been made for the presentation of some 43 programs by affiliates of the Federation. A one-quarter hour book review would be presented each week in cooperation with the city public library; and the applicant has also agreed to broadcast special announcements concerning the library. The City of Scotia would broadcast a weekly program devoted to matters of local interest to the listeners living in that community. The applicant has agreed to contribute to these groups the use of the facilities of the projected station, as well as professional production assistance, and to reserve specific periods of time on an immovable-sustaining basis for their regular programs." (9 F.C.C. 92, 100-101.)

[3] "The proposed station would be operated on the average of about 17 hours daily. According to the applicant's proposed program plans, time would be devoted as follows: Entertainment (51.41 percent), includes various types of music (presented by local and professional talent, records and transcriptions), drama, quiz programs,

On the basis in part of these program service representations, the Commission on February 24, 1942, granted the application of Western Gateway and denied the application of Van Curler. With respect to the successful applicant, the Commission concluded:

Western Gateway Broadcasting Corporation is qualified in every respect to construct and operate the station proposed; it proposes to render a balanced program service comparable to that normally provided by local broadcast stations; and its proposed station would provide a satisfactory technical service throughout the City of Schenectady and the rural areas contiguous thereto. (9 F.C.C. 92, 101.)

With respect to the unsuccessful applicant, Van Curler Broadcasting Corporation, the Commission found that, "while this applicant has made a showing of the public-service programs, newscasts, transcribed features, musical clock programs, and time and other reports, it expects to broadcast, it has not adduced evidence as to its other program plans." Moreover, the Commission raised the question of credibility with respect to the representations made by the unsuccessful applicant. It noted that one of the directors had first testified that $5,000 which he had invested in the company was his own, and subsequently testified instead that it had been borrowed from a brother-in-law. Said the Commission:

In the performance of our duties we must, among other things, determine whether the operation of proposed stations, or the continued operation of existing stations, would serve public interest, and in so doing we are, of necessity, required to rely to a large extent upon statements made by station licensees, or those connected therewith. Caution must, therefore, be exercised to grant station licenses only to those persons whose statements are trustworthy. (9 F.C.C. 92, 102)

---

and programs designed especially for the women (such as shopping and household hints, fashion comments, and advice on the care of children); educational (16.53 percent), includes safety programs, book reviews, a music appreciation series, a program entitled "Radio Workshop" (a local version of CBS program of the same title), patriotic broadcasts, dramatized historical events, local round table discussions, and others; religious (6 percent), includes a morning program of religious hymns (presented by talent furnished by local churches and schools), a daily devotional program conducted by local clergymen, round table discussions embracing all religious faiths, and Sunday services from local churches; agricultural (1.27 percent), includes market and other reports, Farm Bureau topics, Grange notices, and others; news (16.95 percent), includes during each day, 5-minute newscasts every hour, a 10-minute sports review, a one-quarter hour news commentary presented by James T. Healey, two five-minute local newscasts, and two one-quarter hour news digests; civic (7.84 percent), includes programs concerning the activities of various local organizations and institutions, discussions of governmental and civic problems, and programs designed to promote interest in the community, state and nation. Programs presented by means of mechanical reproduction would be broadcast for about 20 percent of the time. Material for newscasts would be obtained from a well-known news service and local newspapers," etc. (9 F.C.C. 92, 96.)

Examination of the logs of Station WSNY, the Western Gateway station, for the week beginning January 18, 1945, and a consideration of the statement concerning the public service rendered by Station WSNY filed by the licensee under date of May 24, 1945, in connection with its license renewal, warrant the conclusion that while a very genuine effort is being made by the licensee to serve the Schnectady area,[4] nevertheless, the station's present operations clearly fall short of the extreme representations made when Western Gateway was competitively seeking approval of a new station as against Van Curler. For example, Station WSNY represented that approximately 20 percent of its time would be devoted to programs presented by means of mechanical reproduction. An examination of the WSNY logs for the week beginning January 18, 1945, shows in contrast, that 78 percent of the program time of the station is devoted to mechanically reproduced programs. At least some of the types of programs specifically set forth in the original representations do not appear on the program schedules less than 3 years after the station went on the air.

C. Applications for increased facilities: Station WTOL

The relation between the Commission's renewal procedures and its actions in connection with applications for increased facilities for existing broadcast stations is illustrated in the case of Station WTOL, Toledo. (7 F.C.C. 194.)

Station WTOL was originally licensed to operate daytime only; but in 1938 it applied for authority to broadcast unlimited time. In the hearing on its application, the station relied heavily on the need for added evening hours in order to serve local organizations in Toledo, and to make use of the live talent in Toledo after 6 p. m. The applicant represented, for example, that after 6 p. m., 84 percent of its time would be devoted to live-talent broadcasts; that the Toledo Council of Churches, the American Legion, the YMCA and "other worthwhile organizations" desired time over the station *at night,* and that the only other station in Toledo was unable to clear sufficient time for such programs because it was affiliated with a national network.[1]

---

[4] With respect to its statements filed May 24, 1945, Station WSNY declares: "WE BE-
LIEVE THAT NO OTHER STATION IN AMERICA CAN MATCH THE RECORD OF COMMUNITY
INTEREST AND PUBLIC SERVICE BROADCASTING INDICATED IN THESE VARIOUS STATE-
MENTS."

[1] "The applicant's proposed weekly program schedule was admitted in evidence, and
shows, among other things, that approximately 35.5 percent of the station's time will
be devoted to news, drama, education, religious, civic, and sports broadcasts, and the
remaining 64.5 percent will be devoted to musical entertainment, approximately
one-half of which will be commercial broadcasts. The program service proposed
appears somewhat similar in character to its existing service, except that a greater
percentage of the total time will be devoted to the use of live talent broadcasts.
Approximately 62 percent of the station's time will be devoted to broadcasts using
live talent and after 6 p.m. live talent will be used approximately 84 percent of the
time. . . .
     "The policy of the station has been, and will continue to be, to give free time

The president of the licensee corporation testified as follows on direct examination:

Q. What is the purpose of this application for night-time hours?

A. It is to give the people of Toledo an opportunity to have a station which can broadcast a great many events which can not at the present time be broadcast, because the only other station there is a regional station with a chain hook-up. For instance, we had during the summer civic opera which, by special permission of the Federal Communications Commision was broadcast. We have had a great many other musical occasions which could not be broadcast, although request was made by the managers of musical organizations for broadcasts. We have many important and interesting speakers who come to Toledo for dinner meetings, and other occasions, where there is a demand made for broadcasting, and these and other educational features can be carried if we have full time operation (F.C.C. Docket 5320, Tr. 81-82.)

In granting the WTOL application for unlimited time, the Commission concluded:

Station WTOL is rendering a satisfactory local program service to the Toledo, Ohio, audience during daytime hours and a similar program service is proposed for the evening hours which is not now available from any radio broadcast station serving this area. The other existing station (WSPD) in Toledo is of a regional classification and does not adequately meet the local needs of the Toledo area during the evening hours. There is a need in the Toledo, Ohio, area for the service proposed by the applicant. (7 F.C.C. 194, 198.)

The WTOL application was granted on April 17, 1939, and eight months later Station WTOL, like the only other station in Toledo, became affiliated with a national network. By 1944 the "local" programs upon which WTOL had relied were conspicuous by their absence. During the week beginning November 13, 1944, for example, approximately 15 percent of the station's time was devoted to "live" broadcasts rather than the 62 percent originally represented. After 6 p. m., instead of devoting 84 percent of the time to local live broadcasts, as represented, Station WTOL devoted only 13.7 percent of its time to such programs. Nearly half of the "live" programs, moreover, were wire news involving no live talent other than the voice of a news announcer.[2]

---

to the Toledo Council of Churches for religious broadcasts. This organization desires time at night over Station WTOL. The station has also cooperated with the municipal and county governments and the various agencies of both the State and Federal Governments in giving free time on the station and this policy will continue. The station has given free time to the Toledo Post of the American Legion, the Y.M.C.A., Boy Scouts of America, and other worthwhile organizations. These organizations desire time over the station at night and will cooperate in furnishing program material for broadcasts. Station WSPD is at the present time affiliated with the National Broadcasting Company and has been unable to give sufficient time to these organizations at night." (7 F.C.C. 194, 196-7.)

[2] For discussion of "wire programs" as distinguished from "local live" programs, see "Uniform Definitions and Program Logs."

In contrast to its allegations that time after 6 p. m. was sought for local public service, the station broadcast only 20 minutes of local live sustaining programs after 6 p. m. during the entire week—10 minutes of bowling scores and 10 minutes of sports news.

Throughout the week, 91.8 percent of the broadcast time was commercial. No evening time whatever during the week was given to the Toledo American Legion, YMCA, Boy Scouts, or any other local organizations which, according to the representations, desired time over the station at night.

Nor was the time after 6 p. m. filled with commercial programs of such outstanding merit as to leave no room for local service. From 6:15 to 6:30 p. m. on Tuesday, for example, a 15-minute program of transcribed music was interrupted by seven spot announcements—at 6:18, 6:19, 6:22, 6:24½, 6:25½, 6:26½, and 6:29 p. m. From 10:10 to 10:30 the same evening, a transcribed musical program entitled "Music Hall" was interrupted by 10 spot announcements in 20 minutes—at 10:15, 10:16, 10:20, 10:21, 10:22, 10:23, 10:25, 10:26, 10:27, and 10:29½ p. m.

D. Transfer of Control: Station WBAL

In recent years, the purchase of an existing standard broadcast station has become a more common means of entering broadcasting than the erection of a new station.[1] The case of Station WBAL, Baltimore, illustrates the extent to which the service rendered by a station may be affected by a transfer or assignment of license to a purchaser, and the need for integrating Commission transfer and renewal procedures.

Station WBAL was originally licensed to the Consolidated Gas, Electric Light and Power Company of Baltimore, by the Department of Commerce. It began operations November 2, 1925.[2]

When the Federal Radio Commission was established in 1927, Station WBAL was one of many stations which sought to procure a "cleared chan-

---

[1] During the four years 1941 through 1944, inclusive, 98 new standard broadcast stations were licensed, while 110 were assigned or transferred in toto, excluding merely formal transfers or assignments involving no actual change of control.

[2] The station began broadcasting with the following statement by the president of the then licensee corporation:

"It is my privilege on this, our opening night, to dedicate this new radio station to Baltimore and Maryland, and to the service of their people in such ways as may be found most useful to them. This station is to be known as 'Baltimore,' and it will be so designated and referred to in the future announcing and operation. The company which has financed its construction and will operate it now dedicates it to the public service of this city and Commonwealth. It will be satisfied to participate along with all others in this great community in such progress and advantage as its operation may bring forth. After tonight the name of this company may not be heard in the announcements of this station, nor is it proposed to commercialize its operation."

nel," 25 of which were then being proposed. In support of its claim to a cleared channel, the station submitted "A Description of WBAL, Baltimore," prepared for the information of the Federal Radio Commission, August 1927. The "Description" stated: "Although WBAL is owned by a private corporation, its operation closely approximates that of a public enterprise." The Station's program policy was described as follows:

WBAL has endeavored to be a distinctive personality among broadcasting stations. To attain this end its programs have maintained high musical and artistic standards. The Station's "No Jazz" policy is indicative.

The Station Director is also head of the Baltimore Municipal Department of Music. The direct connections which the Director and various members of the musical staff have with the private and public musical activities of the City make possible a selection of the best artistic personnel, and provides a means of coordination which is seldom found possible. The Station has maintained its own features to a unique degree, until quite recently, over ninety percent of its programs being rendered by its own studio organizations.

In addition to the regular features of the Studio, the programs of the Station have included as a regular feature during the winter months, semi-weekly organ recitals from the Peabody Conservatory of Music, at which institution is located the largest single pipe organ south of New York. The Station has also broadcast each season, a number of the most important musical services from various churches throughout the city. During the summer these features were supplanted by outdoor programs from a permanent pick-up point in one of the public parks of the city, featuring two programs each week, one by the Baltimore Municipal Band, the other by the Baltimore City Park Orchestra. Programs of the Baltimore Symphony Orchestra and other orchestral and choral programs of city-wide interest have also been included in the station's broadcasting each season.

The station also employed regular musical organizations:

The following staff organizations which, in line with the policy of not referring to the Gas and Electric Company, are designated simply by the call letters of the Station, have been retained as regular features to insure a uniformly high standard of program. Some appear daily, others semi-weekly, or weekly.

WBAL Concert Orchestra	WBAL String Quartet
WBAL Opera Company	WBAL Dance Orchestra
WBAL Salon Orchestra	WBAL Male Quartet
WBAL Ensemble	WBAL Mixed Quartet
WBAL Dinner Orchestra	WBAL Trio

From the personnel of the various organizations is also drawn talent for special presentations, such as continuity programs, musical scenarios and programs for special events.

The competition among the several hundred stations then on the air for the 25 proposed clear channels was very strenuous, and the Commission made it clear that "superior programs" would be one test, or perhaps the principal test, of eligibility.[3]

On November 20, 1934, application was made for transfer of control of the WBAL Broadcasting Company from the Consolidated Gas, Electric Light and Power Company to American Radio News Corporation, an absentee holding company. An amended application was filed December 1, 1934, and the transfer was approved, without a hearing, on January 8, 1935. At that time, no representations concerning program service were required of transferees, so that the purchasers were able to enter broadcasting without the representations which would have been required had they applied for a new station. Currently, transferees are required to state whether the transfer will affect the service, and if so, in what respects.

An examination of the program logs of Station WBAL for the week beginning Sunday, April 23, 1944, shows that its present mode of operation is in marked contrast to its operation described above under the previous licensee.

Thus, during the week beginning Sunday, April 23, 1944, only 12.5 percent of the program time between 8 a. m. and 11 p. m. was sustaining. On Monday through Friday of that week, less than 6 percent of the program time between 8 a. m. and 11 p. m. was sustaining, and no sustaining programs whatever were broadcast on those days between 2 p. m. and 11 p. m.—a total of 45 hours.[4]

Between 8 a. m. and 11 p. m. of the week beginning April 23, 1944, Station WBAL broadcast 507 spot announcements, of which 6 were sustaining public service announcements. An example—not unique—of the piling up of spot announcements is found in the 45-minute period from

---

[3] Thus on December 5, 1927, Commissioner O. H. Caldwell wrote to the Mayor of Baltimore:

"The members of the Commission have asked me to acknowledge yours of December 1st., and to assure you that *the Commission desires to facilitate in every way the presentation of good programs* to the people of Baltimore through the local stations.

"If there are any channels now in use by other stations to which any Baltimore station feels better entitled, *by reason of superior programs,* the Baltimore station has but to make application, and after a hearing has been held, at which both sides will be given an opportunity to present full testimony, the members of the Commission will endeavor to assign the channel in the best public interest." (Emphasis supplied.)

[4] As used in this paragraph a "commercial" program is any program which is either paid for by a sponsor, or interrupted more than once per 15 minutes by commercial spot announcements. A 15-minute program preceded, followed, and interrupted once by commercial spot announcements is nevertheless classified as sustaining. For the Commission's proposed future definitions of "commercial" and "sustaining" programs, see "Uniform Definitions and Program Logs." For a discussion of the importance of and need for sustaining programs, see below, pp. 147–171.

8:15 a. m. to 9:00 a. m. on Monday, April 24, 1944, during which 16 spot announcements were broadcast or one every 2.8 minutes.

Less than 2.5 percent of the station's time between 8 a. m. and 11 p. m. during the week was devoted to sustaining programs of local live origin. The only live sustaining programs carried during the entire week, 8 a. m. to 11 p. m., were as follows:

News at various time	95 minutes
"Gif-Ted Children," by remote control, Saturday, 9:45–10:00 a.m.	15 minutes
"The Family Hour," Saturday, 10:15–10:30 a. m.	15 minutes
"Musical Maneuvers," Saturday, 2:00–2:30 p. m.	30 minutes
Total live sustaining for the week	155 minutes

Station WBAL devoted 9 hours and 50 minutes to religious programs during the week—only 30 minutes of which was on a sustaining basis. The remaining 9 hours and 20 minutes were paid for by the religious organizations involved.

Station WBAL carried one forum or round table discussion-type program, either local or of network origin, during the week. The University of Chicago Round Table was made available to WBAL by NBC; but WBAL carried instead two transcribed commercial music programs and two 5-minute commercial talk programs.

The extent to which Baltimore has long been a world-renowned music center is noted above. During the entire week in question, the only local live music broadcast by Station WBAL between 8 a. m. and 11 p. m. was as follows:

A 10-minute "Music Award" commercial program.

"Musical Maneuvers," Saturday, 2:00–2:30 p. m.

"Songs of Romance," commercial, at various times, totalling 50 minutes for the week.

The National Broadcasting Company designates certain of its outstanding sustaining programs as "Public Service Programs": These programs were until 1945 marked with an American shield on its program schedules. During the week beginning April 23, 1944, NBC designated 19 programs as "Public Service Programs." Of these, Station WBAL carried five[5] and failed to carry 14. The 14 NBC "Public Service Programs" not carried and the programs carried by WBAL in lieu thereof are shown below:

[5] "Here's to Youth," "Doctors at War," "American Story," "Army Hour," and "Catholic Hour," all half-hour programs.

Time	NBC Public Service Program	WBAL Program
SUNDAY		
9:15–9:30 a.m.	"Commando Mary"—War Work for Women.	"Good Tidings Hour." Reverend Peters, commercial program.
10–10:30 a.m.	"National Radio Pulpit"—Reverend John Milton Phillips of the Grand Avenue Baptist Church in Omaha, Guest Speaker; Radio Choriters. Direction George Shackley. (From WOW, Omaha, and New York.)	10–10:05, News; 10:05–10:30, "Sunday Morning Round-up," transcribed music with four spot announcements for Anderson Motors, Fava Fruit Co., Four Besske Brothers, and Cactus Pills.
1:15–1:30 p.m.	"Labor for Victory"—Congress of Industrial Organizations; guest speakers.	"Willis Jones," commercial program sponsored by the Willis Jones committee.
1:30–2:00 p.m.	"University of Chicago Round Table Discussion"—guest speakers.	1:30–1:45, transcribed commercial music; 1:45–1:50, commercial talk, "Listen, Motorist"; 1:50–1:55, transcribed commercial music, 1:55–2:00, "Stay Out of Court," commercial talk.
4:30–4:55 p.m.	"Land of the Free", "Indians of the North." Drama: Inter-American University of the Air; guest speaker (from Canada).	"Women of the Week," local commercial, drama, sponsored by the Schleisner Company.
11:30–12:00 mid.	"The Pacific Story—Hirohito: Eclipse of the Son of Heaven." Dramatization. (From Hollywood.)	"The Open Bible," commercial program sponsored by the Hamilton Baptist Church.
MONDAY		
12:30–1:00 p.m.	"U. S. Navy Band" (from Washington).	12:30–12:45, "Masters of Rhythm," transcribed music with six spot announcements; 12:45–1, "Treasury Salute," transcribed music.

TUESDAY

12:30–1:00 p.m.   "U. S. Coast Guard on Parade" (from WTIC, Hartford).

12:30–12:45, "Masters of Rhythm," transcribed music with six spot announcements; 12:45–1, "Treasury Salute," transcribed music.

11:30–12:00 mid.   "Words at War"–dramatized stories.

11:30–11:45, "Open Bible," commercial transcribed program sponsored by Hamilton Baptist Church; 11:45–12, "Treasury Salute," transcribed music.

WEDNESDAY

12:30–1:00 p.m.   "U. S. Air Force Band"–Capt. George S. Howard, Conductor (from Washington).

12:30–12:45, "Masters of Rhythm," transcribed music with six spot announcements; 12:45–1, "Treasury Salute," transcribed music.

FRIDAY

12:30–1:00 p.m.   "U. S. Marine Band" (from Washington).

12:30–12:45, "Masters of Rhythm," transcribed music with six spot announcements; 12:45–1, "Treasury Salute," transcribed music.

SATURDAY

1:30–1:45 p.m.   "The Baxters Invest in Health," drama; National Congress of Parent and Teachers Associations.

1:30–1:35, "Latest News"; spot announcement for Arrid deodorant; 1:35–1:45, "Behind the News."

1:45–2:00 p.m.   "War Telescope"–John MacVane from London via shortwave.

"Front-Page Drama," electrical transcription, commercial program sponsored by Sunday *American*.

6:00–6:30 p.m.   "I Sustain the Wings"–Army Air Force Band, Capt. Glenn Miller conducting.

6–6:05, "Esso News," sponsored by Standard Oil Co.; 6:05–6:15, "National Sports," sponsored by National Beer Co.; transcribed spot announcement for "Whiz Candy"; 6:15–6:30, "Paul Robertson Talk," political speech.

E. Representations made in court: Station KHMO

The *KHMO* case (4 F.C.C. 505; 70 App. D. C. 80) is of interest because it involves an element of judicial review, and a comparison of representations made in court with present performance.

The Courier Post Publishing Company of Hannibal, Missouri, now the licensee of Station KHMO, originally applied for a new station at Hannibal in 1936, as did a competing applicant. The Commission, after a hearing, was unable to find that a need existed for a local station in Hannibal and accordingly both applications were denied.

On appeal to the U. S. Court of Appeals for the District of Columbia (70 App. D.C. 80, 104 F.(2d) 213), the Court found that the Commission was in error, and that a need did exist for a local broadcast station to serve the particular local interests of the Hannibal community. Speaking through Judge Vinson, the Court noted (pp. 82-83) that service was available from other stations, but that "none of these stations provide for the local needs of Hannibal." The Court cited a Commission definition of a local station as one which would serve "to present programs of local interest to the residents of that community; to utilize and develop local entertainment talent which the record indicates is available; to serve local, religious, educational, civic, patriotic, and other organizations; to broadcast local news; and to generally provide a means of local public expression and a local broadcast service to listeners in that area."[1]

The Court cited in detail the programs which the applicant proposed to broadcast[2] and relied in particular on the applicant's representations that it "planned to use local talent—an abundance of which was shown to be available—and in this manner serve public interest of that area. Thus, it appears that the petition for a construction permit is supported by overwhelming evidence showing *the local need for a local station to serve in the manner set out.*" (Emphasis supplied.)

[1] *Okmulgee Broadcasting Corporation,* 4 FCC 302.
[2] Thus the Court noted that the applicant "proposed to give portions of its time, without charge, to the various local civic, educational, athletic, farming, fraternal, religious, and charitable organizations. Its proposed program consists of: Entertainment 42%, educational 20%, news 9%, religious 9%, agriculture 10%, fraternal 5%, and civic activities 5%. The tentative program contemplated, particularly, the use of the facilities of the station to aid education in supplementing classroom work, and in broadcasting from a secondary studio located at Hannibal La Grange College subjects of scholastic interest and athletic events; the use by the Hannibal Chamber of Commerce to further business relations; the use by the County Agriculture Agent to bring before farmers and farm clubs the subject matter that is offered through the United States Department of Agriculture and Missouri College of Agriculture on farm problems; the use by the County Health Department to give information concerning maternity and child health, public health problems, particularly prevention of disease, food and milk control, and general sanitation; the use of the station by business in advertising; the promotion of literary and philanthropic activities; the promotion of better civic spirit; the furtherance of physical culture, and social activities of the Y.M.C.A. and Boy Scouts; and the broadcasting of daily religious services of the several Hannibal churches." (70 App. D.C. 80, 82-3.)

Pursuant to this decision of the Court of Appeals, the Commission granted a license. It appears, however, that the program service rendered is markedly different from the representations upon which the Court relied. For example, only 14.2 percent of the station's time for the week beginning April 22, 1945, was devoted to the "local talent"[3] said to be so abundant in the area. More than 85.8 percent of its time, in contrast, was devoted to network programs and transcriptions. Instead of giving its time "without charge" to local religious organizations, as represented, Station KHMO sold 4¾ hours of time during the week to such organizations on a commercial basis, and provided no time for local religious programs without charge.

PART II. COMMISSION JURISDICTION WITH RESPECT TO PROGRAM SERVICE

The contention has at times been made that Section 326 of the Communications Act, which prohibits censorship or interference with free speech by the Commission, precludes any concern on the part of the Commission with the program service of licensees. This contention overlooks the legislative history of the Radio Act of 1927, the consistent administrative practice of the Federal Radio Commission, the re-enactment of identical provisions in the Communications Act of 1934 with full knowledge by the Congress that the language covered a Commission concern with program service, the relevant court decisions, and this Commission's concern with program service since 1934.

The Communications Act, like the Radio Act of 1927, directs the Commission to grant licenses and renewals of licenses only if public interest, convenience and necessity will be served thereby. The first duty of the Federal Radio Commission, created by the Act of 1927, was to give concrete meaning to the phrase "public interest" by formulating standards to be applied in granting licenses for the use of practically all the then available radio frequencies. From the beginning it assumed that program service was a prime factor to be taken into consideration. The renewal forms prepared by it in 1927 included the following questions:

(11) Attach printed program for the last week.
(12) *Why will the operation of the station be in the public convenience, interest and necessity?*
  (a) Average amount of time weekly devoted to the following services (1) entertainment (2) religious (3) commercial (4) educational (5) agricultural (6) fraternal.
  (b) Is direct advertising conducted in the interest of the applicant or others?

Copies of this form were submitted for Congressional consideration.[1]

---

[3] Including news programs read off the ticker by a local announcer.

[1] *Hearings on Jurisdiction of Radio Commission,* House Committee on Merchant Marine and Fisheries, 1928, p. 26.

In its Annual Report to Congress for 1928, the Commission stated (p. 161):

The Commission believes it is entitled to consider the program service rendered by the various applicants, to compare them, and to favor those which render the best service.

The Federal Radio Commission was first created for a term of one year only. In 1928 a bill was introduced to extend this term and extensive hearings were held before the House Committee on Merchant Marine and Fisheries. The Commissioners appeared before the Committee and were questioned at length as to their administration of the Act. At that time Commissioner Caldwell reported that the Commission had taken the position that

. . . each station occupying a desirable channel should be kept on its toes to produce and present the best programs possible and, if any station slips from that high standard, another station which is putting on programs of a better standard should have the right to contest the first station's position and after hearing the full testimony, to replace it. (Hearings on Jurisdiction, p. 188.)

The Commissioner also reported that he had concluded, after 18 months' experience, that station selections should not be made on the basis of priority in use and stated that he had found that a policy—

. . . of hearings, by which there is presented full testimony on the demonstrated capacity of the station to render service, is a much better test of who is entitled to those channels. (Ibid.)

By 1929 the Commission had formulated its standard of the program service which would meet, in fair proportion, "the tastes, needs and desires of all substantial groups among the listening public." A well-rounded program service, it said, should consist of

entertainment, consisting of music of both classical and lighter grades, religion, education, and instruction, important public events, discussion of public questions, weather, market reports, and news and matters of interest to all members of the family. (Great Lakes Broadcasting Co., reported in F.R.C., 3d Annual Report, pp. 33–35.)

By the time Congress had under consideration replacing the Radio Act of 1927 with a new regulatory statute, there no longer existed any doubt that the Commission did possess the power to take over-all program service into account. The broadcasting industry itself recognized the "manifest duty" of the Commission to consider program service. In 1934, at hearings before the House Committee on Interstate Commerce on one of the bills which finally culminated in the Communications Act of 1934, the National Association of Broadcasters submitted a statement which contained the following (*Hearings on H. R. 8301,* 73rd Cong., p. 117):

It is the manifest duty of the licensing authority, in passing upon applications for licenses or the renewal thereof, to determine whether or not the applicant is rendering or can render an adequate public service. *Such service necessarily includes* broadcasting of a considerable proportion of programs devoted to education, religion, labor, agricultural and similar activities concerned with human betterment. In actual practice over a period of 7 years, as the records of the Federal Radio Commission amply prove, this has been *the principal test* which the Commission has applied in dealing with broadcasting applications. (Emphasis supplied.)

In hearings before the same committee on the same bill (*H. R. 8301, 73rd Cong.*) Chairman Sykes of the Federal Radio Commission testified (pp. 350–352):

That act puts upon the individual licensee of a broadcast station the private initiative to see that those programs that he broadcasts are in the public interest. . . . Then that act makes those individual licensees responsible to the licensing authority to see that their operations are in the public interest.

Our licenses to broadcasting stations last for 6 months. *The law says that they must operate in the public interest, convenience, and necessity.* When the time for a renewal of those station licenses comes up, *it is the duty of the Commission in passing on whether or not that station should be relicensed for another licensing period, to say whether or not their past performance during the last license period has been in the public interest.* (Emphasis supplied.)

Under the law, of course, we cannot refuse a renewal until there is a hearing before the Commission. We would have to have a hearing before the Commission, to go thoroughly into the nature of all of the broadcasts of those stations, consider all of those broadcasts, and then say whether or not it was operating in the public interest.

In the full knowledge of this established procedure of the Federal Radio Commission, the Congress thereupon re-enacted the relevant provisions in the Communications Act of 1934.

In the course of the discussion of the 1934 Act, an amendment to the Senate bill was introduced which required the Commission to allocate 25 percent of all broadcasting facilities for the use of educational, religious, agricultural, labor, cooperative and similar non-profit-making organizations. Senator Dill, who was the sponsor in the Senate of both the 1927 and 1934 Acts, spoke against the amendment, stating that the Commission already had the power to reach the desired ends (78 *Cong. Rec.* 8843):

The difficulty probably is in the failure of the present Commission to take the steps that it ought to take to see to it that a larger use is made of radio facilities for education and religious purposes.

I may say, however, that the owners of large radio stations now operating have suggested to me that it might be well to provide in the license that a certain percentage of the time of a radio station shall be allotted to religious, educational, or non-profit users.

Senator Hatfield, a sponsor of the amendment, had also taken the position that the Commission's power was adequate, saying (78 *Cong. Rec.* 8835):

I have no criticism to make of the personnel of the Radio Commission, except that *their refusal literally to carry out the law of the land warrants the Congress of the United States writing into legislation the desire of Congress that educational institutions be given a specified portion of the radio facilities of our country.* (Emphasis supplied.)

The amendment was defeated and Section 307(c) of the Act was substituted which required the Commission to study the question and to report to Congress its recommendations.

The Commission made such a study and in 1935 issued a report advising against the enactment of legislation. The report stated:

Commercial stations are now responsible under the law, to render a public service, and the tendency of the proposal would be to lessen this responsibility.

The Commission feels that present legislation has the flexibility essential to attain the desired ends without necessitating at this time any changes in the law.

There is no need for a change in the existing law to accomplish the helpful purposes of the proposal.

In order for non-profit organizations to obtain the maximum service possible, cooperation in good faith by the broadcasters is required. *Such cooperation should, therefore, be under the direction and supervision of the Commission.* (Report of the Federal Communications Commission to Congress Pursuant to Sec. 307(c) of the Communications Act of 1934, Jan. 22, 1935.) (Emphasis supplied.)

On the basis of the foregoing legislative history there can be no doubt that Congress intended the Commission to consider overall program service in passing on applications. The Federal Communications Commission from the beginning accepted the doctrine that its public interest determinations, like those of its predecessor, must be based in part at least on grounds of program service. Thus early in 1935 it designated for joint hearing the renewal applications of Stations KGFJ, KFWB, KMPC, KRKD, and KIEV, in part "to determine the nature and character of the program service rendered . . ." *In re McGlasham et al.,* 2 F.C.C. 145, 149. In its decision, the Commission set forth the basis of its authority as follows:

Section 309(a) of the Communications Act of 1934 is an exact restatement of Section 11 of the Radio Act of 1927. This section provides that subject to the limitations of the Act the Commission may grant licenses if the public interest, convenience, and necessity will be served thereby. The United States Court of Appeals for the District of Columbia in the case of *KFKB Broadcasting Association, Inc.* v. *Federal Radio Commission,* 60 App. D.C. 79, held that under Section 11 of the Radio Act of 1927 the Radio Commission was necessarily called upon to consider the character and quality of the service to be rendered and that in considering an application for renewal an important consideration is the past conduct of the applicant. (2 F.C.C. 145, 149.)

The courts have agreed that the Commission may consider program service of a licensee in passing on its renewal application. In the first case in which an applicant appealed from a Commission decision denying the renewal of a station license in part because of its program service, the court simply assumed that program service should be considered in determining the question of public interest and summarized and adopted the Commission's findings concerning program service as a factor in its own decision.[2] In 1931, however, the question was squarely presented to the Court of Appeals when the KFKB Broadcasting Association contended that the action of the Commission in denying a renewal of its license because of the type of program material and advertising which it had broadcast, constituted censorship by the Commission. The Court sustained the Commission, saying:

It is apparent, we think, that the business is impressed with a public interest and that, because the number of available broadcasting frequencies is limited, *the Commission is necessarily called upon to consider the character and quality of the service to be rendered.* In considering an application for a renewal of a license, an important consideration is the past conduct of the applicant, for "by their fruits shall ye know them." Matt. VII: 20. Especially is this true in a case like the present, where the evidence clearly justifies the conclusion that the future conduct of the station will not differ from the past. (*KFKB Broadcasting Association v. Federal Radio Commission,* 47 F. 2d 670.) (Emphasis supplied.)

In 1932, the Court affirmed this position in *Trinity Methodist Church v. Federal Radio Commission,* 62 F. (2d) 850, and went on to say that it is the "duty" of the Commission "to take notice of the appellant's conduct in his previous use of the permit."

The question of the nature of the Commission's power was presented to the Supreme Court in the *network* case. The contention was then made that the Commission's power was limited to technological matters only. The Court rejected this, saying (*National Broadcasting Company v. United States,* 319 U.S. 190, 216–217):

The Commission's licensing function cannot be discharged, therefore, merely by finding that there are no technological objections to the granting of a license. If the criterion of "public interest" were limited to such matters, how could the Commission choose between two applicants for the same facilities, each of whom is financially and technically qualified to operate a station? Since the very inception of federal regulation by radio, comparative considerations as to the service to be rendered have governed the application of the standard of "public interest, convenience, or necessity."

[2] *Technical Radio Laboratory* v. *Federal Radio Commission,* 59 App. D.C. 125, 36 F. (2d) 111.

The foregoing discussion should make it clear not only that the Commission has the authority to concern itself with program service, but that it is under an affirmative duty, in its public interest determinations, to give full consideration to program service. Part III of this Report will consider some particular aspects of program service as they bear upon the public interest.

PART III. SOME ASPECTS OF "PUBLIC INTEREST" IN PROGRAM SERVICE

As has been noted, the Commission must determine, with respect to each application granted or denied or renewed, whether or not the program service proposed is "in the public interest, convenience, and necessity."

The Federal Radio Commission was faced with this problem from the very beginning, and in 1928 it laid down a broad definition which may still be cited in part:

Broadcasting stations are licensed to serve the public and not for the purpose of furthering the private or selfish interests of individuals or groups of individuals. The standard of public interest, convenience, or necessity means nothing if it does not mean this. . . . The emphasis should be on the *receiving* of service and the standard of public interest, convenience, or necessity should be construed accordingly. . . . The *entire* listening public within the service area of a station, or of a group of stations in one community, is entitled to service from that station or stations. . . . In a sense a broadcasting station may be regarded as a sort of mouthpiece on the air for the community it serves, over which its public events of general interest, its political campaigns, its election results, its athletic contests, its orchestras and artists, and discussion of its public issues may be broadcast. *If . . . the station performs its duty in furnishing a well rounded program, the rights of the community* have been achieved. (In re Great Lakes Broadcasting Co., F.R.C. Docket No. 4900; cf. 3rd Annual Report of the F.R.C., pp. 32–36.) (Emphasis supplied.)

Commission policy with respect to public interest determinations is for the most part set by opinions in particular cases. (See, for example, cases indexed under "Program Service" in Volumes 1 through 9 of the Commission's Decisions.) A useful purpose is served, however, by occasional overall reviews of Commission policy. This Part will discuss four major issues currently involved in the application of the "public interest" standard to program service policy; namely, (A) the carrying of sustaining programs, (B) the carrying of local live programs, (C) the carrying of programs devoted to public discussion, and (D) the elimination of commercial advertising excesses.

A. The carrying of sustaining programs

The commercial program, paid for and in many instances also selected, written, casted, and produced by advertisers and advertising agencies, is the staple fare of American listening. More than half of all broadcast time is devoted to commercial programs; the most popular programs on the air are commercial. The evidence is overwhelming that the popularity of American broadcasting as we know it is based in no small part upon its commercial programs.

Nevertheless, since the early days of broadcasting, broadcasters and the Commission alike have recognized that sustaining programs also play an integral and irreplaceable part in the American system of broadcasting. The sustaining program has five distinctive and outstanding functions.

1. To secure for the station or network a means by which in the overall structure of its program service, it can achieve a *balanced* interpretation of public needs.
2. To provide programs which by their very nature may not be sponsored with propriety.
3. To provide programs for significant minority tastes and interests.
4. To provide programs devoted to the needs and purposes of nonprofit organizations.
5. To provide a field for experiment in new types of programs, secure from the restrictions that obtain with reference to programs in which the advertiser's interest in selling goods predominates.

(1) Balance-wheel function of the sustaining program

The sustaining program is the balance-wheel by means of which the imbalance of a station's or network's program structure, which might otherwise result from commercial decisions concerning program structure, can be redressed.

Dr. Frank N. Stanton, then Director of Research and now vice-president of the Columbia Broadcasting System, explained this function to the House Committee on Interstate and Foreign Commerce (*Hearings on H. R. 4597,* 77th Cong., 2nd Sess., May 7, 1942, page 289):

> One use Columbia makes of sustaining programs is to supplement commercial offerings in such ways as to achieve, so far as possible, a full and balanced network service. For example, if the commercial programs should be preponderantly musical, Columbia endeavors to restore program balance with drama or the like in its sustaining service.

The Commission, as well as broadcasters themselves, has always insisted that a "well-balanced program structure" is an essential part of broadcasting in the public interest. At least since 1928, and continuing to the present, stations have been asked, on renewal, to set forth the average amount of time, or percentage of time, devoted to entertainment programs, religious programs, educational programs, agricultural programs, fraternal programs, etc.; and the Commission has from time to time relied upon the data thus set forth in determining whether a station has maintained a well-balanced program structure.[1]

In metropolitan areas where the listener has his choice of several stations, balanced service to listeners can be achieved either by means of a balanced program structure for each station or by means of a number of comparatively specialized stations which, considered together, offer a balanced service to the community. In New York City, a considerable degree of specialization on the part of particular stations has already arisen—one station featuring a preponderance of classical music, another a preponderance of dance music, etc. With the larger number of stations which FM will make possible, such specialization may arise in other cities. To make possible this development on a sound community basis, the Commission proposes in its application forms hereafter to afford applicants an opportunity to state whether they propose a balanced program structure or special emphasis on program service of a particular type or types.

Experience has shown that in general advertisers prefer to sponsor programs of news and entertainment. There are exceptions; but they do not alter the fact that if decisions today were left solely or predominantly to advertisers, news and entertainment would occupy substantially all of the time. The concept of a well-rounded structure can obviously not be maintained if the decision is left wholly or preponderantly in the hands of advertisers in search of a market, each concerned with his particular half hour,

---

[1] The question asked on renewal in recent years is as follows:
"State the average percentage of time per month (combined total should equal 100%) devoted to—

"Commercial Programs

"1. Entertainment
2. Educational
3. Religious
4. Agricultural
5. Civic (include in this item fraternal, Chamber of Commerce, charitable, and other civic but non-governmental programs)
6. Governmental (include in this item all municipal, state, and federal programs, including political or controversial broadcasts by public officials, or candidates for public office, and regardless of whether or not the programs included under this item are entertainment, educational, agricultural, etc., in character)
7. News
8. —
9. Total"

"Sustaining Programs

[The categories specified under this column are the same as those in the adjacent column.—Ed.]

rather than in the hands of stations and networks responsible under the statute for overall program balance in the public interest.

A device by which some networks and stations are seeking to prevent program imbalance is the "package" program, selected, written, casted and produced by the network or station itself, and sold to the advertiser as a ready-built package, with the time specified by the station or network. In order to get a particular period of time, the advertiser must take the package program which occupies that period. This practice, still far from general, appears to be a step in the direction of returning control of programs to those licensed to operate in the public interest. The commercial "package" program is not a substitute for the sustaining program, however, for reasons set forth in subsections (2) through (5) of this section.

What happens when the balance-wheel function of the sustaining program is neglected can be illustrated by the case of the "soap opera," defined as "a continuing serial in dramatic form, in which an understanding of today's episode is dependent upon previous listening."

In January 1940, the four networks provided listeners with 59½ daytime hours of sponsored programs weekly. Of these, 55 hours were devoted to soap operas. *Only 4½ sponsored daytime hours a week on the four networks were devoted to any other type of program.* Advertisers, in short, were permitted to destroy overall program balance by concentration on one type of program. The number of soap operas subsequently increased, reaching in April 1941 a total of some 50 commercially sponsored network soap operas a day.[2] Since then, there has been some decline, and the introduction of some sustaining programs in daytime hours has begun to modify the picture.

The extent of program imbalance still prevalent is indicated by the fact that in September 1945 the National Broadcasting Company was still devoting 4¾ hours per day, Monday through Friday, to 19 soap operas, and the Columbia Broadcasting System was similarly devoting 4¼ hours daily, Monday through Friday, to 17 such programs.

The following table presents data concerning soap operas during the period December 1944–April 1945.[2a] Column 1 shows the "rating" of the 19 soap operas broadcast by NBC and the 17 broadcast by CBS—that is, the percentage of telephone homes in 32 large cities where a respondent stated that the radio was tuned to the program in question or the station carrying the program. Column 2 shows the size of the available audience as determined by the same telephone calls—that is, the percentage of telephone homes in which someone was at home and awake to answer the telephone. Column 3, which is the "resultant" of columns 1 and 2, thus shows the recruiting power of the program—that is, the percentage of the available audience actually tuned to each soap opera. It will be noted that the most

[2] C. E. Hooper, Inc., "Year End Review of 1943 Daytime Radio Listening."
[2a] See *Fortune,* March 1946, p. 119, "Soap Opera."

NBC SOAP OPERAS

		Program Rating	Available Audience	Recruiting Efficiency
Mon.–Fri. 10:15 a.m.	Lora Lawton	3.3	75.3	4.4
10:30 a.m.	Road of Life	3.0	75.4	4.0
10:45 a.m.	Joyce Jordan	3.0	73.6	4.1
11:45 a.m.	David Harum	2.9	72.2	4.0
2:00 p.m.	Guiding Light	5.5	68.2	8.1
2:15 p.m.	Today's Children	6.0	67.1	8.9
2:30 p.m.	Woman in White	5.6	66.0	8.5
3:00 p.m.	A Woman of America	4.6	66.1	7.0
3:15 p.m.	Oxydol's Own Ma Perkins	6.1	66.2	9.2
3:30 p.m.	Pepper Young's Family	7.1	65.9	10.7
3:45 p.m.	Right to Happiness	7.0	66.4	10.5
4:00 p.m.	Backstage Wife	6.7	67.6	9.9
4:15 p.m.	Stella Dallas	6.9	67.4	10.2
4:30 p.m.	Lorenzo Jones	6.7	68.7	9.8
4:45 p.m.	Young Widder Brown	7.5	69.6	10.7
5:00 p.m.	When a Girl Marries	8.9	71.1	12.5
5:15 p.m.	Portia Faces Life	7.9	71.6	11.0
5:30 p.m.	Just Plain Bill	6.5	73.4	8.9
5:45 p.m.	Front Page Farrell	5.6	74.7	7.5

CBS SOAP OPERAS

Mon.–Fri. 10:00 a.m.	Valiant Lady	2.9	76.1	3.8
10:15 a.m.	Light of the World	3.7	75.3	4.9
10:30 a.m.	The Strange Romance of Evelyn Winters	3.4	75.4	4.5
10:45 a.m.	Bachelor's Children	4.3	73.6	5.8
11:00 a.m.	Amanda of Honeymoon Hill	2.8	74.5	3.8
11:15 a.m.	Second Husband	3.3	73.3	4.5
11:30 a.m.	Bright Horizon	4.5	73.1	6.2
12:15 p.m.	Big Sister	6.7	72.1	9.3
12:30 p.m.	The Romance of Helen Trent	7.0	72.1	9.7
12:45 p.m.	Our Gal Sunday	6.8	70.8	9.6
1:00 p.m.	Life Can Be Beautiful	7.2	70.4	10.2
1:15 p.m.	Ma Perkins	7.7	69.7	11.0
1:45 p.m.	Young Dr. Malone	5.1	68.2	7.5
2:00 p.m.	Two On a Clue	4.3	68.2	6.3
2:15 p.m.	Rosemary	4.1	67.1	6.1
2:30 p.m.	Perry Mason	3.8	66.0	5.8
2:45 p.m.	Tena & Tim	3.8	66.1	5.7

Source: "Sectional" Hooperatings, Dec. 1944–April 1945, Winter-Spring.

popular soap opera on the air during the period in question recruited 12.5 percent of the available audience. The average NBC soap opera recruited 8.4 percent of the available audience, and the average CBS soap opera recruited 6.7 percent of the available audience. In contrast, approximately 76.8 percent of the available audience answering the telephone during the soap opera hours reported that they had their radios turned off altogether.

The "ratings" of the NBC and CBS soap operas must be considered in the light of the dominant position in the spectrum occupied by the stations concerned. Thus in the 32 cities in which the surveys in question were made, the power of the stations affiliated with each network was as follows:

	Total power	*Average power per station*
32 CBS stations	925,000 w	28,906 w
32 NBC stations	835,000 w	26,093 w
32 ABC stations	222,250 w	6,945 w
32 Mutual stations	200,000 w	6,250 w

Several reasons may be suggested for the popularity of soap operas among advertisers.[3] First, the soap opera is among the cheapest of all network shows to produce. The weekly production costs of the ordinary soap opera are reported to be less, for five 15-minute periods, than some advertisers spend on a one-minute transcribed spot announcement. Second, advertisers are not interested merely or primarily in the size of the audience which they achieve. They are interested also, and perhaps primarily, in two other indices of program effectiveness. One is the "sponsor identification index" which is defined as "the percent of listeners to a specific program which knows the name of the program's advertiser, or of any of his products." The other is the "product use index," defined as "the use of a sponsor's brand of product and that of his competitors among listeners to his program compared with non-listeners." An advertiser relying on the sponsor identification index, for example, may prefer a soap opera which appeals to only one million listeners and indelibly impresses the name of his product on two-thirds of them, rather than a non-soap opera program which appeals to two million listeners but impresses the sponsor's name on less than one-

---

[3] According to the Cooperative Analysis of Broadcasting (CAB), network commercial time during the day from October 1943 to April 1944 was divided as follows:

Serial drama	57.4%
News and talks	10.7%
Variety	8.7%
Drama	6.8%
Children's Programs	4.7%
Classical and Semi-Classical	4.5%
Audience Participation	2.8%
Popular Music	2.2%
Familiar Music	1.3%
Hymns	0.9%
	100 %

third. Similarly, an advertiser may prefer a soap opera which, as in an actual instance, results in the use of his product by 46.5 percent of those who listen (as compared with 25.1 percent of use among non-listeners), even though the program in question appeals to comparatively few listeners.

Mr. Duane Jones, head of an advertising agency reputed to be one of the five largest in New York, clearly was considering the special interests of advertisers rather than the public interest, when he declared:

> The best radio program is the one that sells the most goods, not necessarily the one that holds the highest Hooper or Crossley rating.[4]

Whether or not the reasons cited for the popularity of soap operas among advertisers are the decisive ones, it is clear that the result on many stations has been a marked imbalance of program structure during the daytime hours; and it is significant that the first steps recently taken to redress this imbalance have been the addition of sustaining programs. It is by means of the sustaining program that program imbalance, consequent upon sponsor domination of excessive blocks of time, can be redressed by those responsible for program structure—balance—the licensees, including the networks.

(2) *Programs inappropriate for commercial sponsorship*

A second role of the sustaining program is to provide time for broadcasts which by their very nature may not be appropriate for sponsorship. As early as 1930, Mr. Merlin H. Aylesworth, then president of the National Broadcasting Company, recognized this role of the sustaining program in testimony before the Senate Committee on Interstate Commerce, even proposing that college football games were by their nature inappropriate for commercial sponsorship.[5] More recently, in 1941, Mr. Niles Trammell, president of the National Broadcasting Co., has stated:

> Another reason for the use of sustaining programs was the voluntary recognition on the part of broadcasters that programs of certain types, such as religious programs, informative programs furnished by various governmental

---

[4] The advertiser view cited may be contrasted with one of the "basic principles" in the interpretation of the phrase "public interest, convenience or necessity" laid down by the Federal Radio Commission in 1928:

"While it is true that broadcasting stations in this country are for the most part supported or partially supported by advertisers, broadcasters are not given these great privileges by the United States Government for the primary benefit of advertisers. *Such benefit as is derived by advertisers must be incidental and entirely secondary to the interest of the public."* (Emphasis in original.)

[5] *"Mr. Aylesworth. . . .* We have refused to permit from our system the sponsoring of football games by commercial institutions. That may be a wrong policy; I do not know; but I have assumed that with all these youngsters in their management boards and with all of the commercialism that is talked about, and so forth, that I just did not quite like to see the Yale-Harvard game announced 'through the courtesy of so and so.' " (*Hearings on S. 6,* 1930, p. 1711.)

agencies and certain programs involving discussions of political principles and other controversial issues, were not suited to advertising sponsorship. The use of high types of sustaining programs also creates goodwill for the station and induces people to become accustomed to listening to certain stations in preference to others.[6]

The *Code of the National Association of Broadcasters* similarly recognized, until 1945, that the presentation of controversial issues (except forums) should be exclusively in sustaining programs. While the Commission has recently held that an absolute ban on the sale of time for the discussion of public issues may under certain circumstances not serve the public interest,[7] it is nevertheless clear that such broadcasts should be primarily of a sustaining nature.

The Commission has never set forth and does not now propose to set forth the particular types of program which, for one reason or another, must remain free from commercial sponsorship. It does, however, recognize along with the stations and networks themselves that there are such programs.[8] Self-regulation consonant with public sentiment, and a responsible concern for the public interest, can best insure a suitable interpretation of the basic principle which the industry itself has always recognized, that some programs are by their nature unsuitable for commercial sponsorship. Public interest requires that sustaining time be kept available for such broadcasts.

(3) *Significant minority tastes and interests*

It has long been an established policy of broadcasters themselves and of the Commission that the American system of broadcasting must serve significant minorities among our population, and the less dominant needs and tastes which most listeners have from time to time. Dr. Frank Stanton, in his testimony before the House Committee on Interstate and Foreign Commerce in 1942, previously cited, set forth this function of the sustaining programs as follows:

[6] Affidavit of Niles Trammel, in *National Broadcasting Co.* v. *United States* in the Supreme Court of the U.S., October Term, 1941, No. 1025, Transcript of Record, p. 228.

[7] *In the Matter of United Broadcasting Co. (WHKC)*, decided June 26, 1945.

[8] For example, one station has recently stated its refusal to exploit the problems of returning veterans on commercial programs, preferring programs devoted to veteran problems on a sustaining basis. *Variety,* for March 14, 1945, reports:

"WMCA FEELS VETS WOULD RESENT COM'L EXPLOITATION OF REHABILITATION SHOW.

"Plans for the production of a new program helping returning GIs rehabilitate themselves, and to aid their families in the readjustment period, are being planned by WMCA, N.Y. Move further reflects the industry-wide consciousness of the vital issue. . . .

"Show will not be for sale, station feeling vets would resent having solution of their problems made the subject of commercial exploitation. As result it's going on as a public service show."

There is another feature of sustaining service which differentiates it from commercial programs. While the CBS sustaining service recognizes the broad popular tastes, it also gives attention to smaller groups. It is known that the New York Philharmonic Symphony Orchestra, the Columbia Work Shop, Invitation to Learning, Columbia Broadcasting Symphony, and many other ambitious classical programs never reach the largest audience, but Columbia, nonetheless, puts them on year after year for minorities which are growing steadily.

Many sustaining programs, originally designed for comparatively small audiences, have proved so popular that they have subsequently acquired commercial sponsorship. "Of Men and Books," for example, was a sustaining feature of a literary nature for more than seven years, from May 26, 1938 to September 8, 1945, before a sponsor was obtained. When such a program becomes sponsored, the way is open for devoting sustaining time to still other types of programs having less than maximum audience appeal.

But even if they may not be able to compete, initially or ever, with Fibber McGee and Molly in size of audience, "sponsor identification index," and "product use index," such programs are essential to a well-balanced program structure. It is no doubt partly due to recognition of this fact that time has always been reserved from sponsorship for the carrying of such programs on a sustaining basis.

(4) *Service to non-profit organizations*

A well-balanced program structure has always been deemed to include programs devoted to the needs and purposes of non-profit organizations.

Sections 307(c) of the Communications Act of 1934 specifically directed the Commission to "study the proposal that Congress by statute allocate fixed percentages of radio broadcasting facilities to particular types or kinds of non-profit activities," and to report to Congress its recommendations. The Commission undertook prolonged hearings on the question, at which witnesses for non-profit organizations, networks and stations were heard at length. Such organizations as the National Committee on Education by Radio, individual educational institutions, representatives of many religious organizations, the American Federation of Labor, the Women's National Radio Committee, the Farmers' Union, and many others testified concerning the importance of broadcasting to their organizations and the services which their organizations could render to the public through broadcasting. Networks and stations, in turn, testified without hesitation to their willingness to assist and to supply time for the non-profit organizations.[9]

---

[9] Merlin A. Aylesworth, then president of the National Broadcasting Company, testified in particular: "We know if we do not render a public service, the Commission will give the license to others who will render better public service." (*Hearings* pursuant to Sec. 307(c), p. A23.)

William S. Paley, until recently president of the Columbia Broadcasting System, similarly testified: "We hold our license by serving the public interest, con-

The Commission, in its report to Congress pursuant to Section 307(c) of the Communications Act, recommended that specific percentages of facilities *not* be reserved by statute for non-profit organizations, specifically on the ground that existing commercial stations were ready and willing to carry programs of non-profit organizations and that non-profit organizations would benefit thereby. Said the Commission:

It would appear that the interests of the non-profit organizations may be better served by the use of the existing facilities, thus giving them access to costly and efficient equipment and to established audiences, than by the establishment of new stations for their peculiar needs. In order for non-profit organizations to obtain the maximum service possible, cooperation in good faith by the broadcasters is required. *Such cooperation should, therefore, be under the direction and supervision of the Commission. . . . It is our firm intention to assist the non-profit organizations to obtain the fullest* opportunities for expression. (Pp. 6, 9-10; emphasis supplied.)

Cooperation between networks, stations, and non-profit organizations has always been present in greater or less degree, and it may be noted that many outstanding programs, both network and local, have resulted from such cooperation. Among the programs honored at the 9th Annual Exhibition of Educational Radio Programs, 1945 (the Ohio State University Awards), for example, were the following:

Group I—Regional web, regional or clear-channel station

RELIGIOUS BROADCASTS: First Award, "Salute to Valor" series, planned and produced by National Council of Catholic Men, WEAF, New York, and NBC. Honorable Mention: "Victorious Living" series, planned and produced by International Council of Religious Education, widely used over regional and clear-channel stations.

CULTURAL PROGRAMS: Honorable Mention: "Words at War" series, planned by Council on Books in Wartime, WEAF, New York, and NBC.

PUBLIC DISCUSSION PROGRAMS: First Award, "University of Chicago Round Table" series, planned and produced by U. of Chicago, WMAQ, Chicago, and NBC.

PERSONAL AND FAMILY LIFE PROGRAMS: Honorable Mention: "The Baxters" series, planned by National Congress of Parents-Teachers, WMAQ, Chicago, and NBC. Special Mention: "Alcoholics Anonymous" series, WWJ, Detroit.

PROGRAMS FURTHERING WAR, PEACE: First Award: "The March of Minnesota" series, planned and produced by Minnesota Resources Committee, WCCO, Minneapolis, and special state network. First Award, "Russian War Relief Presents" series, planned and produced by Russian War Relief, Inc.;

---

venience, and necessity. And only by adequate cooperation with all public spirited groups can we be deemed to perform the conditions of our contract." (*Ibid.,* p. 11151.)

produced by members of Radio Directors Guild of New York City; released to many stations.

CHILDREN'S PROGRAM, OUT-OF-SCHOOL: First Award, "Books Bring Adventure" series, planned and produced by Association of Junior Leagues of America.

IN SCHOOL PROGRAMS, PRIMARY CHILDREN: First Award, "Your Story Parade" series, planned and produced by Texas State Department of Education, WBAP, Fort Worth, and Texas Quality web.

Group II—Local station or organization

CULTURAL PROGRAMS: Special Mention: "New World A-Coming" series, planned and produced by station WMCA in cooperation with Citywide Citizens Committee on Harlem; WMCA, New York.

PUBLIC DISCUSSION PROGRAMS: First Award, "Free Speech Forum" series, planned and produced by WMCA and New York Newspaper Guild; WMCA, New York.

NEWS INTERPRETATION: First Award, "History in the Making" series, planned and produced by University of Colorado and Rocky Mountain Radio Council; KVOD, Denver.

CHILDREN'S PROGRAMS, OUT-OF-SCHOOL: First Award, "Story Time" series, planned and produced by Colorado State College of Education and Rocky Mountain Radio Council; KLZ, Denver.

IN SCHOOL PROGRAMS, ELEMENTARY CHILDREN: Honorable Mention: "News Today—History Tomorrow" series, planned and produced by Rochester Public Schools, WHAM, Rochester, N. Y.

IN SCHOOL PROGRAMS, JUNIOR-SENIOR HIGHS: First Award, "Our America" series, planned and produced by Radio Council of Chicago Public Schools; WBEZ, Chicago Public Schools.

The *Peabody* and *Variety* awards similarly feature such programs as the WTIC temperance series prepared in cooperation with Alcoholics Anonymous, "Worcester and the World," broadcast by station WTAG in cooperation with the United Nations Information Office; programs of the American Jewish Committee; "Assignment Home," produced by CBS in cooperation with Army Service Forces, etc.

Such programs as these have done much to enrich American broadcasting. It may well be that they have kept in the radio audience many whose tastes and interests would otherwise cause them to turn to other media. Radio might easily deteriorate into a means of amusing only one cultural stratum of the American public if commercially sponsored entertainment were not leavened by programs having a different cultural appeal. Just as the programs of non-profit organizations benefit from being aired along with the mass-appeal programs of advertisers, so, it may be, the programs of the advertisers reach a larger and more varied audience by reason of the serious sustaining programs produced in cooperation with non-profit organizations. The furnishing of time and assistance to non-profit organizations is thus not merely a responsibility of networks and stations, but also an opportunity.

Special problems are involved in connection with program service designed especially for farmers—market reports, crop reports, weather reports, talks on farming, and other broadcasts specifically intended for rural listeners. The question of programs particularly adapted to the needs of rural listeners has been made an issue in the Commission's forthcoming Clear Channel Hearings (Docket No. 6741) and surveys of rural listeners have been made for the Commission by the Division of Program Surveys, Bureau of Agricultural Economics, Department of Agriculture, and by the Bureau of the Census.[10]

(5) *Program experimentation*

Dr. Stanton, in his testimony previously cited, has described still another role of the sustaining program in the American system of broadcasting:

. . . It is through the sustaining or noncommercial program service that Columbia has developed its greatest contributions to network radio broadcasting. On its own time and at its own expense, Columbia has pioneered in such experimental fields as that of original radio drama through the Columbia Workshop Series. Further, it was the first to originate news broadcasts involving on-the-spot reports from correspondents located over all the world. The Columbia School of the Air, now in its thirteenth year, is another example of the use to which Columbia puts its sustaining time by providing a balanced curriculum of broadcasts, 5 days a week throughout the school year, suitable for use in the classrooms. Columbia has also taken the leadership in the matter of new program content in adult education, music and public debate.

Various advertisers and advertising agencies have frankly stated the extent to which their commercial requirements make necessary a special tailoring of commercial programs. The president of the American Tobacco Company, a sponsor of many network commercial programs, has been quoted to this effect:

We have some funny things here about radio, and we have been criticized for it. Taking 100% as the total radio value, we give 90% to commercials, to what's said about the product, and we give 10% to the show.

We are commercial and we cannot afford to be anything else. I don't have the right to spend the stockholder's money just to entertain the public. In particular, sponsors are naturally loath to sponsor any program which may offend even a minority of listeners. . . . The last thing I could afford to do is to offend the public.

Similarly Procter & Gamble, probably the largest sponsor in American broadcasting, has been described as having "a policy never to offend a single listener."

---

[10] *Attitudes of Rural People Toward Radio Service,* Bureau of Agricultural Economics, U.S. Department of Agriculture, January 1946.

In 1935, to take an extreme example, Alexander Woollcott's "Town Crier" broadcasts were discontinued when the sponsor complained Mr. Woollcott had criticized Hitler and Mussolini, and might thus offend some listeners.

In the field of creative and dramatic writing for radio, the sponsor's understandable desire to please, to avoid offense to anyone, and to integrate the tone and content of his program with his sales appeal, may exert an especially restrictive influence on artistic self-expression, and on the development of the radio art. Not a few distinguished writers are known to be unwilling to accept sponsorship because of restraints and stereotypes imposed which reflect the commercial as against the artistic preoccupations of the sponsor. *Variety* comments on this situation in its issue of June 20, 1945:

> Radio script writers are turning in increasing numbers to the legit field. . . . What is particularly significant, however, is the motive behind the wholesale transfer of allegiance of the scripters from radio to Broadway. For some time the feeling has been mounting among many of the serious writers for radio that they've been retarded by a lack of freedom of expression . . . and that as long as radio remains more or less of a "duplicating machine" without encouraging creative expression and without establishing an identity of its own, it's inevitable that the guy who has something to say will seek other outlets.

Norman Rosten, himself a writer of commercial programs and winner of a grant from the American Academy of Arts and Letters for his radio writing, has stated the point of view of some radio writers in part as follows:

> The sponsor and the advertising agency have taken over radio quietly in this matter of writing. Except for sustaining shows (often worthy, such as "Assignment Home") or special public service programs magnanimously aired after 11:30 p.m., the broadcasting company sells Time. It owns the air. It will sell you a piece. Period.

> By "non-commercial radio" I do not mean simply any sustaining series. I mean a non-format show, an experimental show, one which does not have limitations of content or form. Something like the old Columbia Workshop. I mean a half hour each week on each network for a program of original radio plays. With or without love in a cottage. In poetry or prose. Any way we please. No commercial and no strings. All we want is a piece of wavelength and your good auspices. Not a seasonal replacement, but an all-year-round proposition. The present hit-or-miss, one-shot system is a phony. Nor does a new "Thirteen by Corwin" mean the millennium. Mr. Corwin's triumph has not saved his fellow-writers. How about a "Thirteen by Thirteen?" or "Twenty-six by Twenty-six?" The writers are here and some good ones. How about setting the Saga of Lux or the creaking door aside one half hour per week per network? It might well usher in a renaissance in radio drama. How about it NBC, CBS, American and Mutual? Put up or, as the saying quaintly goes, shut up. Prove it, or forever

hold your pronouncements about radio coming of age. We are nearing the middle of the 20th century. Shall the singing commercial and the Lone Ranger inherit the earth?

There is no reason to believe that the present boundaries of program service are the ultimate boundaries. If broadcasting is to explore new fields, to devise new types of programs for the American listener, it is clear that the sustaining program must continue as a means by which experimentation and innovation may have the fullest scope, undeterred by the need for immediate financial success or the imposition on writers of restraints deriving from the natural, but limiting, preoccupations of the advertiser.

It is especially important that some sustaining programs be reserved from commercial restraints in view of the degree of concentration of control currently existing among advertisers and advertising agencies. In 1944, for example:

26% of CBS business came from 4 advertisers.
38% of CBS business was handled by 4 advertising agencies.
25% of ABC (Blue Network) business came from 4 advertisers.
37% of ABC (Blue Network) business was handled by 4 advertising agencies.
23% of MBS business came from 4 advertisers.
31% of MBS business was handled by 4 advertising agencies.[11]

One advertiser, Procter & Gamble, is reputed to have spent $22,000,-000 on radio advertising in 1944. It purchased approximately 2,000 hours a week of station time—equivalent to the entire weekly time, from sign-on to sign-off, of more than 18 broadcast stations. Procter & Gamble, of course, produces many of its own shows through its own advertising agencies and has control over all its shows. This control is exercised, naturally enough, for the purpose of selling soap. It may incidentally have profound effects on the manners, mores, and opinions of the millions who listen. That is an inevitable feature of the American system of broadcasting; but it is not inevitable that only programs so produced and so controlled shall reach the ear of American listeners. The sustaining program is the necessary makeweight.

(6) *Statistics of sustaining programs*

But while networks and stations alike have traditionally recognized the importance of the sustaining program as an integral part of the American system of broadcasting, there is evidence to suggest that such programs are disappearing from the program service of some stations, especially during the best listening hours.

No accurate statistical series has yet been established to determine the

[11] *Broadcasting Yearbook,* 1945, pp. 30, 32. Comparable data for NBC not available.

proportion of time devoted to sustaining programs, or the trends from year to year. In the most recent annual reports of stations and networks to the Commission, however, station licensees have analyzed their program structure for the month of January 1945. Since no definition of "sustaining" has heretofore been promulgated, these figures must be approached with caution. Some stations, for example, classify a 15-minute "participating" program as sustaining, even though it is interrupted by three, four, or five spot announcements. Some "bonus" stations which carry network programs without direct remuneration from the network classify all their network commercial programs as "sustaining." The returns to the Commission are in some cases carelessly prepared; some stations, for example, report more than 5 hours of programs daily between 6 and 11 p. m. Some of the returns are wholly unusable. Nevertheless, the returns of 703 stations for the month of January 1945 appeared sufficiently complete to warrant tabulation.

These 703 stations were on the air an average of 16 hours and 5 minutes daily. Of this time, they reported 8 hours and 40 minutes, or 53.9 percent, as commercial, and the remaining 7 hours and 25 minutes, or 46.1 percent, as sustaining.

These overall figures suggest that the sustaining program remains a major part of broadcasting today. On closer analysis, however, certain questions arise.

First, it should be noted that in general, the larger stations carried a considerably smaller percentage of sustaining programs than the smaller stations, as shown on the following table:

AVERAGE HOURS PER DAY AND PERCENTAGE OF TIME ON THE AIR DEVOTED TO COMMERCIAL AND SUSTAINING PROGRAMS BY CLASS OF STATION FOR MONTH OF JANUARY, 1945

	Commercial		Sustaining	
	Hours per day	% of time on air	Hours per day	% of time on air
50 kw stations (41)	12:50	67.3	6:14	32.7
500 w—50 kw stations (214)	10.41	61.3	6:45	38.7
250 w or less stations (376)	7:37	47.6	8:23	52.4
Part time stations (72)	5:46	53.3	5:30	46.7
All stations (703)	8:40	53.9	7:25	46.1

Source: Annual Financial Reports, 1944.

Second, the proportion of time devoted to sustaining programs during the best listening hours from 6 to 11 p.m. was lower than during other hours:

AVERAGE HOURS AND PERCENTAGE OF TIME ON THE AIR,
6 TO 11 P. M., DEVOTED TO COMMERCIAL AND
SUSTAINING PROGRAMS BY CLASS OF STATION
FOR MONTH OF JANUARY, 1945

	Commercial		*Sustaining*	
	Hours per day	% of time on air	Hours per day	% of time on air
6 P.M. to 11 P.M. only				
50 kw stations (41)	4:16	84.7	:46	15.3
500 w—50 kw stations (214)	3:38	72.9	1:21	27.1
250 w or less stations (376)	2:38	53.9	2:16	46.1
Part time stations (72)	:46	60.5	:31	39.5
All stations (703)	2:51	62.4	1:43	37.6

Source: Annual Financial Reports, 1944.

The above statistics are, of course, averages, and hence do not illustrate the paucity of sustaining programs on particular stations. The four following charts* show in black the commercial programs, and in white the sustaining programs, of Stations WLW, WBAL, WCAU, and WSIX for a random week. Especially noteworthy is the tendency to crowd sustaining programs into the Saturday afternoon and Sunday morning segments, and to crowd them out of the best listening hours from 6 to 11 p.m.

The following eight charts† similarly illustrate the paucity of sustaining programs during the best listening hours on the stations designated as "basic affiliates" by the four major networks. . . . It will be noted that on Sunday, April 23, 1944, the following stations carried no sustaining programs whatever between the hours of 6 and 11 p.m.:

WHO	WIRE	WCED	WXZY
WSYR	WTMJ	KOIL	WING
WSPD	WDEL	KMBC	WMAL
WAVE	WHT	WCKY	WEMP

Similarly on Monday, April 24, 1944, the following stations carried no sustaining programs whatever between the hours of 6 and 11 p.m.:

WAGE	WSAI	WFBL	WSPD
WAKR	WNBH	WTOP	WBAL
WXYZ	WEMP	WTAG	WAVE
WING	WTOL	WBBM	WIRE
WENR–WLS	WABC	WADC	WTMJ
WISH	WJR	WMT	WOW
		WHAS	WMAQ

* The four charts are omitted. [Ed.]
† The eight charts are omitted. [Ed.]

(7) *Statistics of network sustaining programs*

More striking even than the dearth on some stations and during some hours of sustaining programs generally, is the dearth of *network* sustaining programs.

The five-fold function of sustaining programs, earlier outlined, has particular significance as it applies to network sustaining programs. These are unique in character. They command resources of talent, of writers, actors, producers, beyond the capacity of all or at least most local stations to offer. They cover many issues and subjects, treatment of which can best be given in the great metropolitan centers where network headquarters are situated. Even more important, the network sustaining program is the primary channel through which a nation-wide audience can be reached for treatment of the subjects earlier referred to as the peculiar province of sustaining programs. It is the very essence of network service that it should reach a nation-wide audience. Any factor intervening to prevent this militates against the principle of network operations.

The failure of American broadcasters to provide nation-wide distribution for even outstanding network sustaining programs can be illustrated by a few examples.

The Columbia Broadcasting System describes "Invitation to Learning" in these terms:

> Distinguished scholars, authors, and critics meet informally on this series to discuss the outstanding classics of literature. The summer and fall schedules include a series of 31 great books to bring the total number discussed on the program to 285.

On Sunday, April 2, 1944, the most recent date for which data are available, 39 CBS stations carried this program, while 97 rejected it.

"Transatlantic Call: People to People" is described by CBS as follows:

> On alternate Sundays the British Broadcasting Corporation and the Columbia Broadcasting System shake hands across the ocean. In this half-hour program, British and American audiences are presented with a picture of the national characteristics and attitudes of the two countries. The audiences of the two nations learn the reasons for the apparent differences between them, at the same time realizing the basic similarity of their attitudes and behavior.

This program was carried on Sunday, April 2, 1944, by 50 CBS stations and rejected by 86.

"Columbia's Country Journal" is described by CBS as follows:

> The farmer's role in war time, his "food for victory" campaign, and his daily problems form the weekly theme of Charles ("Chuck") Worcester's

"radio farm magazine." Originating in Washington for national farm news, it frequently switches to various farm regions of the country highlighting local problems. Occasional reports from abroad and native folk music are regular features.

On April 8, 1944, this program was carried by 53 and rejected by 83 CBS affiliates.

"Words at War" is described by NBC as follows:

WORDS AT WAR, a weekly series of dramatizations of current books relating to the war, is presented by NBC in cooperation with the Council on Books in Wartime. This series served as the summer replacement for "Fibber McGee and Molly," and four times in eight months was cited by the Writers' War Board for its programs. Among the outstanding books dramatized on "Words at War" were "Der Fuehrer," by Konrad Heiden; "The Veteran Comes Back," by Dr. William Waller; "Assignment U. S. A.," by Seldon Menefee; "War Crimes and Punishment," by George Creel; . . .

This program was carried on Tuesday, May 2, 1944, the last date for which data are available, by 52 NBC stations and rejected by 61. It was broadcast over the network at 11:30 p.m., E.W.T., when listeners are comparatively few, and has since been discontinued altogether.

"The NBC Inter-American University of the Air" is described by NBC as:

presenting an integrated schedule of programs of high educational and cultural value . . . Its 1943 schedule included Lands of the Free, Music of the New World, For This We Fight, The Editors Speak, and Music at War—each a series of stimulating programs that proved the worth of radio as an educational medium. Programs of the NBC University of the Air are now "assigned listening" in more than 100 colleges and universities throughout the United States. School teachers taking the "in-service" training courses of the Board of Education of the City of New York receive credits and promotion based upon their study of Lands of the Free and Music of the New World.

The only two programs of the Inter-American University of the Air noted during the week beginning Sunday, April 30, 1944, were "Lands of the Free," broadcast from 4:30 to 4:55 p.m. on Sunday, April 30, and "Music of the New World," broadcast from 11:30 to midnight on Thursday, May 4. *"Lands of the Free" was carried by 24 NBC stations and refused by 114; "Music of the New World" was carried by 66 and refused by 60.*[12]

The NBC labor program was described by the network as follows:

---

[12] One station broadcast only the second half of "Music of the New World." For the first half it substituted a participating program of spot announcements interspersed with transcribed music.

Labor for Victory brought authoritative speakers to discuss labor's role in the war effort, in programs produced by the American Federation of Labor alternating with the Congress of Industrial Organizations.

This program was carried on Sunday, April 30, 1944 by 35 NBC stations and rejected by 104.

"The Reviewing Stand" is an MBS program described by the network as follows:

Roundtable discussion of current problems under auspices of Northwestern University

It was made available by MBS on Sunday, April 23, 1944 to its full network of 216 stations. Of these, only 40 MBS affiliates carried it.

"Halls of Montezuma," a Marine Corps series from the U. S. Marine Corps base at San Diego, featured the "Sea Soldiers' Chorus" and the "Marine Symphony Orchestra." *It was carried by 50 of the 215 MBS affiliates to which it was made available on Wednesday, April 26, 1944.*

"Mutual's Radio Chapel," a sustaining religious program, was made available to all MBS affiliates. *On Sunday, April 23, 1944, thirteen MBS stations carried it.*

No comparable figures were available from the Blue Network (now the American Broadcasting Company). The extent to which network sustaining programs have been neglected is well illustrated by this failure of the Blue Network even to determine whether or not its sustaining programs were being carried. It is difficult to see how a network can maintain a well-balanced program structure or can determine which of its network sustaining programs to continue and which to replace, if it has not even determined the extent to which such programs are being carried by its affiliates.

The eight charts . . . show the rarity of network sustaining programs from 6 to 11 p.m. on the "basic affiliate" stations of the four major networks. Network sustaining programs are shown by a white "S" superimposed on a black square. It will be noted that the following "basic affiliates" carried no network sustaining programs whatever from 6 to 11 p.m. on Sunday, April 23, 1944:

WXYZ	WTOL	WPRO	WLW
WING	WMT	WJR	WAVE
WHDH	WGAR	WBBM	WCSH
WMAL	WCED	WKRC	WHAM
WISH	KOIL	WIBC	WIRE
WTCN	KMBC	WHO	WTMJ
WCOL	WKBW	WSYR	WDEL
WEMP	WCKY	WSPD	WTIC

Similarly, the following "basic affiliates" carried no network sustaining programs whatever on Monday, April 24, 1944 from 6 to 11 p.m.:

WELI	WISH	WCED	WCKY	WBZA
WAGE	WFIL	WDRC	KMOX	WTIC
WWVA	WEBR	WCAU	WGAR	WDEL
WAKR	WOWO	WPRO	WMT	WRC
WJW	WSAI	WFBL	WHAS	WWJ
WXYZ	WNBH	WTOP	WFBM	WLW
WING	WEMP	WTAG	KDKA	WAVE
WENR–WLS	WTOL	WJAS	KYW	WIRE
KCMO	WABC	KRNT	WSPD	WTMJ
WHDH	WEEI	WBBM	WBAL	KSTP
WMAL	WJR	KMBC	WHAM	WOW
		WADC	WBZ	WMAQ

The paucity of network sustaining programs . . . results from two factors: first, the failure of the networks to supply sustaining programs in quantity during the best listening hours and second, the failure of some stations to carry even those network sustaining programs which are offered.

The mere fact that a station does not carry an outstanding network sustaining program does not mean, of course, that it has sacrificed public interest for private gain. In any particular case, the decision to cancel a network sustaining program may be a wise one, reached on the basis of the availability of a local program of still greater public interest. To determine whether this is the case, it is necessary to compare the network sustaining program rejected with the program scheduled in its stead, and to view the network sustaining program as part of a particular station's schedule.

An example of this technique may be supplied with respect to Station WCAU. This is a 50,000-watt station, occupying an entire clear channel by itself. Station WCAU is affiliated with the Columbia Broadcasting System and is owned by the group which also controls CBS. Hence WCAU might be expected to make available to its listeners at least the outstanding CBS sustaining programs. Indeed, one of the grounds relied on by the Federal Radio Commission when awarding a clear channel to Station WCAU as against competing applicants for such assignments was that WCAU would carry the programs of the Columbia Broadcasting System. (F. R. C. Docket No. 880, decided November 17, 1931.)

Of the 3,165 minutes of network sustaining programs made available to Station WCAU by CBS during the week beginning February 8, 1945, Station WCAU broadcast 1,285 minutes, or 40.6%. From 6 p.m. to 11 p.m. throughout the week, however, Station WCAU broadcast only 55 minutes of network sustaining programs, or 20.8% of the network sustaining programs available to it during this time. On Mondays, Wednesdays, and Thursdays,

WCAU broadcast no network sustaining programs whatever from 9:45 a.m. to 11 p. m. The full schedule of network sustaining programs carried by Station WCAU was as follows:

	8 a.m.– *1 p.m.*	*1 p.m.–* *6 p.m.*	*6 p.m.–* *11 p.m.*	*11 p.m.–* *1:02 a.m.*	*Total*
Sunday	180	30	none	95	305
Monday	45	none	none	65	110
Tuesday	45	none	30	65	140
Wednesday	45	none	none	65	110
Thursday	45	none	none	100	145
Friday	45	none	15	65	125
Saturday	45	200	10	95	350
Total	450	230	55	550	1,285

More than 63% of all network sustaining programs carried by WCAU between the hours of 8 a.m. and 11 p.m. were on Saturday and Sunday. Network sustaining programs from 8 a.m. to 11 p.m., by days, were broadcast as follows:

Sunday	210 minutes
Monday	45 minutes
Tuesday	75 minutes
Wednesday	45 minutes
Thursday	45 minutes
Friday	60 minutes
Saturday	255 minutes
Total	735 minutes

Among the CBS sustaining programs not carried by WCAU, and the WCAU programs substituted therefor, were the following:

SOME NETWORK SUSTAINING PROGRAMS AVAILABLE TO BUT REFUSED BY STATION WCAU

Name of CBS *Sustaining Program*	*Description*[13]	*WCAU Program* *Substituted*
FEATURE STORY 4:30–4:45 p.m. Monday through Friday	"Members of CBS' world-wide staff of news correspondents bring to the microphone the many human interest stories that lie under the surface of the latest military and political events and usually miss being told."	"Rhona Lloyd," local talk sponsored by Aristocrat.

[13] Quoted from "CBS Program Book—Winter, 1945."

Name of CBS Sustaining Program	*Description*	*WCAU Program Substituted*
TRANS-ATLANTIC CALL: PEOPLE TO PEOPLE 12:30–1 p.m. Sunday	"On alternate Sundays, the British Broadcasting Corporation and the Columbia Broadcasting System shake hands across the ocean. In this half hour program, British and American audiences are presented with a picture of the national characteristics and attitudes of the two countries. The audiences of the two nations learn the reasons for the apparent differences between them, at the same time realizing the basic similarity in their attitudes and behavior."	"Ranger Joe," transcribed music sponsored by Ranger Joe, Inc.; "Perry Coll," music sponsored by Western Savings Fund.
CALLING PAN-AMERICA 6:15–6:45 p.m. Thursday	"CBS draws the Americas closer together with this weekly program shortwaved from Latin-American capitals. The series 'calls' a different nation to the microphone each Saturday, and presents a vivid radio picture of its life, culture and music."	"Ask Washington," commercial talk sponsored by Hollingshead, 15 minutes; transcribed commercial spot announcement for movie, "National Velvet," sponsored by Metro-Goldwyn-Mayer; phonograph records, "Songs of the Stars" sposored by Breitenbach, 15 minutes.
SERVICE TIME 5:00–5:30 p.m. Monday through Friday	"Presented in cooperation with the fighting forces, this program devotes itself to the branches of the armed service, spotlighting the activities of a different branch each day. Various service bands and glee clubs are featured, and high ranking officials make personal appearances. There are also interviews with personnel returned from combat zones." Monday — Waves	*"Monday*–Phonograph records interspersed with spot announcements for Household Finance Company (5:03:30–5:04:30); Panther Panco Bilt Rite (5:07:30–5:08:30); National Biscuit Premium Crackers (5:11:40–5:12:40); Cuticura-Potter Chemical Company (5:16:00–5:17:00); Glenwood Range (5:19:50–5:20:50); Civil Service (Sustaining) (5:24:15–5:24:35); and

Name of CBS Sustaining Program	*Description*	*WCAU Program Substituted*
	on Parade. Tuesday—It's Maritime. Wednesday — Wacs on Parade. Thursday —Marines in the Making. Friday—First in The Air.	weather report (5:29:00– 5:29:35). *Tuesday through Friday*—similar phonograph records interspersed with similar spot announcements.
SALT LAKE TABERNACLE CHOIR AND ORGAN 12 noon–12:30 p.m. Sunday	"This is the oldest consecutively presented public-service series in radio, having celebrated its 785th network broadcast on July 30, 1944. The Tabernacle Choir is conducted by J. Spencer Cornwall and Richard P. Condie, assistant. Organists are Alexander Schreiner, Dr. Frank Asper and Wade M. Stephens."	"Children's Hour," sponsored by Horn & Hardart, 11:30–12:20: news comment by Carroll Alcott, sponsored by Horn & Hardart 12:20–12:30.
SALLY MOORE AND THE COLUMBIA CONCERT ORCHESTRA 6:30–6:45 p.m. Monday and Friday	"The young American contralto, CBS' most recent discovery, presents distinctive song recitals of semi-classical music accompanied by the Columbia Concert Orchestra."	Phonograph records sponsored by Groves Laxative Bromo Quinine.
ENCORE APPEARANCE 6:30–6:45 p.m. Wednesday	"The program offers further opportunity to the new singers who have given outstanding performance on CBS' 'New Voices in Song.' They are accompanied by the Columbia Concert Orchestra."	Phonograph records sponsored by Groves Laxative Bromo Quinine.
WILDERNESS ROAD 5:45–6:00 p.m. Monday through Friday	"A dramatic serial of a pioneering American family that went through the hazardous Cumberland Gap in 1783 with Daniel Boone as their guide. The story recreates that adventure-filled period in American history when every frontier presented a challenge to the New World settlers."	*Monday*—Music by Eliot Lawrence interspersed with commercial spot announcements for Rinso (5:48:20–5:49:20); Bell Telephone (5:51:15– 5:52:15); and Household Finance Company (5:55: 40–5:56:40). *Tuesday through Friday*—similar music interspersed with spot announcements.

Name of CBS Sustaining Program	Description	WCAU Program Substituted
INVITATION TO LEARNING 11:30–12 noon Sunday	"Distinguished scholars, authors, and critics meet informally on this series to discuss the outstanding classics of literature. The winter schedule includes a new series of 30 great books to bring the total number discussed on the program to 254."	"Children's Hour," local commercial program sponsored by Horn & Hardart.
THE PEOPLE'S PLATFORM 6:15–6:45 p.m. Saturday	"The vital issues of today and the postwar world are analyzed weekly on this program, one of radio's most interesting forums. Four eminent guests and Lyman Bryson, CBS Director of Education, who acts as moderator gather informally for these sessions."	"Listen to Lawrence," local commercial music program sponsored by Sun Ship Company.

A special case of failure to carry a network sustaining program is to be noted on Sunday from 2:55 to 3:00 p.m. Beginning at 3 p.m., Station WCAU carries the New York Philharmonic program sponsored by U. S. Rubber. This program is preceded over CBS by a 5-minute introductory talk by Olin Downes, the well-known music critic, on a sustaining basis. WCAU carried the symphony for which it is paid, but rejected the sustaining introduction to the symphony in favor of a five-minute commercial program, "Norman Jay Postscript," sponsored by the Yellow Cab Company.

For a similar analysis of network sustaining programs not carried by Station WBAL, an NBC affiliate, see pp. 138–139.

It has been urged that the network sustaining program is doomed by reason of the fact that a network affiliate can carry local programs only during network sustaining periods, and that station owners quite properly reject network sustaining programs in order to leave some time available for local programs of great public interest. Station owners, on this view, should be praised for eliminating network sustaining programs from their schedules, since in this way they make possible local service to their own communities.

Prior to the enactment of Regulation 3.104, when many stations had all or substantially all of their time under option to the networks, this viewpoint had some cogency. Chain broadcasting Regulation 3.104, however, allows each station freedom to reject network *commercial* programs for two hours out of each five. Thus the individual station licensee's choice is not between broadcasting local live programs during network sustaining hours and not broadcasting them at all. On the contrary, a licensee is free to present during each segment of the broadcast day a well-balanced schedule of network and local, commercial and sustaining programs alike (except to the extent, that the network fails to deliver a reasonable proportion of network sustaining programs). The choice is not between network sustaining programs and local programs; rather it is between a balanced program structure and one which lacks such balance.

In recent months, the Commission before renewing the license of a broadcast station has compared the percentage of commercial programs actually broadcast during a sample week with the percentage which the station stated that it would broadcast in its original application. Where a serious discrepancy was noted, and where the proportion of sustaining programs appeared to be so low as to raise a question concerning the station's operation in the public interest, the station's comments were requested. The replies received indicate several widespread misconceptions concerning the basis of Commission policy respecting commercial and sustaining programs.

First, many station licensees stated that they saw no differences between a commercial and a sustaining program, and a few even stated their belief that a station could operate in the public interest with no sustaining programs. (The need for sustaining programs as a balance-wheel to make possible a well-balanced program structure, as a means of broadcasting programs inappropriate for commercial sponsorship, as a service for significant minority tastes and interests, as a service to non-profit organizations, and as a vehicle for program experimentation has been set forth on pp. 147–170).

Second, a number of stations pointed out that many of their commercial programs were clearly in the public interest. The Commission is in full accord with this view. The fact that some advertisers are broadcasting programs which serve an important public interest, however, does not relieve a station of its responsibility in the public interest. Broadcast licensees properly consider their status to be very different from the status of a common carrier, merely providing physical facilities for the carrying of matter paid for and produced by others. Broadcasters rightly insist that their function in the community and the nation is of a higher order. The maintenance of this independent status and significance, however, is inconsistent with the abnegation of independent responsibility, whether to a network or to advertisers. The conceded merit of many or most programs broadcast during periods which a broadcaster has sold to others does not relieve him of the responsibility for broadcasting his own programs during periods which he has reserved from sponsorship for public service.

Third, a few licensees have alleged that they are unable to estimate the amount of time which they will devote to sustaining programs hereafter because they cannot predict how much demand for time there will be from commercial advertisers. Such licensees have obviously abdicated to advertisers the control over their stations. The requirement of a well-balanced program structure, firmly founded in the public interest provisions of the

Communications Act, is a responsibility of the station licensee. To permit advertisers to dictate either the proportion of time which the station shall devote to sustaining programs or any other major policy decision is inconsistent with the basic principles of licensee responsibility on which American broadcasting has always rested.

In their replies, many licensees have pointed out that a comparison of promise and performance with respect to sustaining programs and other categories is difficult or impossible without uniform definitions of what constitutes a commercial program, a sustaining program, etc. To meet this difficulty, the Commission is promulgating herewith uniform definitions of various program categories. (See "Uniform Definitions and Program Logs.")

B. *The carrying of local live programs*

All or substantially all programs currently broadcast are of four kinds: (1) network programs, including programs furnished to a station by telephone circuit from another station; (2) recorded (including transcribed) programs; (3) wire programs (chiefly wire news, syndicated to many stations by telegraph or teletype and read off the wire by a local announcer); and (4) local live programs, including remote broadcasts. For definitions of these four main classes, see "Uniform Definitions and Program Logs."

Network programs. The merit of network programs is universally recognized; indeed, the Commission's Chain Broadcasting Regulations 3.101 and 3.102 were designed in considerable part to insure a freer flow of network programs to the listener. In January 1945, approximately 47.9% of all the time of standard broadcast stations was devoted to network programs.

Transcriptions. The transcribed or recorded program has not had similar recognition. As early as 1922, the Department of Commerce by regulation prohibited the playing of phonograph records by stations having the better (Class B) channel assignments except in emergencies or to fill in between program periods; and later in the year it amended the regulation to prohibit even such use of records by Class B stations. Through the years the phonograph record, and to a lesser extent the transcription, have been considered inferior program sources.

No good reason appears, however, for not recognizing today the significant role which the transcription and the record, like the network, can play in radio programming. Five particular advantages may be cited:

(a) Transcriptions are a means of disposing of radio's most ironic anomaly—the dissipation during a single broadcast, in most cases for all time, of all the skill and labor of writer, director, producer, and cast. Transcriptions make possible the compilation of a permanent archive of the best in radio, comparable in other types of programs to the recorded symphony or chamber music. Good programs with timeless interest can thus be repeated not once but many times.

(b) Transcriptions make possible the placing of programs at convenient hours. For example, a network broadcast may either be inconvenient in time for listeners in a given time zone or may conflict with a station's commitment to its locality. By transcribing the program at the station as it comes in on the network line, the program can be made available at another and still convenient hour.[1]

(c) Transcriptions make possible the sharing of programs among stations not directly connected by wire lines. Several New York stations, for example, are currently making their outstanding programs available via transcription to stations throughout the country. Similarly, non-radio organizations can produce and distribute programs via transcription, as in the case of the award-winning children's transcription series of the Junior League.

(d) Transcriptions offer to the writer, director, and producer of programs the same technical advantages that the moving picture industry achieves through cutting-room techniques. Imperfections can be smoothed out; material recorded at different times and places can be blended into a single program, etc. While the basic advantages of this more plastic technique may not yet be fully utilized, recent developments in the transcription field, including those pioneered by the armed forces and the introduction of wire recorders, suggest a significant role for such programs in the future.

(e) Portable recorders make it possible to present to the listener the event as it occurs rather than a subsequent re-creation of it. The recording of actual press conferences, for example, and the actual battlefront recordings by the Marine Corps and Army Signal Corps point the way to an expansion of recording techniques as a means of radio reporting.

In January, 1945, approximately 32.3% of all the time of standard broadcast stations was devoted to transcriptions and recordings.

Wire Programs. The wire service, by which spot news and sometimes also other program texts are telegraphically distributed to stations, has in recent years assumed a role of increasing importance.[2] By means of wire service for news and other texts of a timely nature, plus transcriptions for programs of less urgent timeliness, the unaffiliated station can very nearly achieve the breadth of service attained through network affiliation. No statistics are currently available concerning the proportion of time devoted to wire service programs.

Local Live Programs. There remains for discussion the local live program, for which also, no precise statistics are available. It is known, how-

---

[1] Conversely, however, some stations appear to use the transcription technique for shifting an outstanding network public service program from a good hour to an off hour when listeners are few and commercial programs not available.

[2] For a proposed definition of "wire" programs, see "Uniform Definitions and Program Logs."

ever, that in January, 1945, approximately 19.7% of all the time of standard broadcast stations was devoted to local live *and* wire service programs; and that during the best listening hours from 6 to 11 p.m., approximately 15.7% of all the time was devoted to these two classes of programs combined.

In granting and renewing licenses, the Commission has given repeated and explicit recognition to the need for adequate reflection in programs of local interests, activities and talent. Assurances by the applicant that "local talent will be available"; that there will be "a reasonable portion of time for programs which include religious, educational, and civic matters"; that "time will be devoted to local news at frequent intervals, to market reports, agricultural topics and to various civic and political activities that occur in the city" have contributed to favorable decision on many applications. As the Commission noted in its *Supplemental Report on Chain Broadcasting* (1941):

It has been the consistent intention of the Commission to assure that an adequate amount of time *during the good listening hours* shall be made available to meet the needs of the community in terms of public expression and of local interest. If these regulations do not accomplish this objective, the subject will be given further consideration. (Emphasis supplied.)

The networks themselves have recognized the importance of local live programs. Under date of October 9, 1944, the National Broadcasting Company, when requesting the Commission to amend Chain Broadcasting Regulation 3.104, stated:

Over the years our affiliated stations have been producing highly important local programs in these three open hours of the morning segment. From 8 a.m. to 10 a.m. N.Y.T., most of the stations have developed variety or "morning clock" programs which have met popular acceptance. These periods are not only profitable to the individual station but are sought for use by civic, patriotic and religious groups for special appeals because of their local listening audience appeal. Likewise, from 12 noon to 1 p.m. they have developed highly important farm news programs or other local interest shows. *To interfere with local program schedules of many years' standing would deprive our stations of their full opportunity to render a desirable local public service.* (Emphasis supplied.)

The Commission's reply, released December 20, 1944, as Mimeograph No. 79574, stated in part:

One purpose of Regulation 3.104 was to leave 14 of the 35 evening hours in each week free of network option, *in order to foster the development of local programs.*[3] . . . The Commission . . . concurs fully in your statement that interference with local programs which have met with public acceptance and

[3] The failure of Regulation 3.104 to achieve this purpose is illustrated by the eight charts . . . showing many stations which carried no non-network programs whatever during the evening hours on the two days analyzed.

which are sought for use by local civic, patriotic and religious groups, local church services, and other highly important local program schedules of years' standing is to be avoided. (Emphasis supplied.)

The courts have also supported the position taken by the Commission that the interests of the whole listening public require that provision be made for local program service. Where the record showed that of the two stations already functioning in an area, one carried 50 percent network programs and the other 85 percent, the court stated: "In view of this situation it is not difficult to see why the Commission decided that public interest would be served by the construction of a local non-network station."[4]

But the soundness of a local program policy does not rest solely on the consistent Commission policy of encouraging a reasonable proportion of local programs as part of a well-balanced program service. Three examples will serve to suggest that local programming may also be good business policy and may contribute to the popularity of the station. These examples were noted by Professor C. H. Sandage of the Harvard School of Business Administration, during a survey of radio advertising possibilities for retailers financed by the Columbia Broadcasting System.

(a) One 250-watt station located in the Middle West had struggled along for 4 years and lost money each year until a reorganization was forced in 1942.

The former management had attempted to compete directly with outside stations whose signals were strong in the local community. Good entertainment was provided, but no attempt was made to establish the station as a local institution interested in the life of the community. Neither local listeners nor local businessmen supported the station.

The new management reversed this policy completely. All attempts at copying outside stations were eliminated. Management not only studied the activities peculiar to that community but also took a personal interest in them. Station facilities were made available on a free basis to civic institutions such as the Chamber of Commerce, women's clubs, parent-teacher association, public schools, and Community Chest. School sports contests were broadcast, and other programs of distinctly local interest were developed. In a relatively short time an audience of more than 50 percent of all local radio listeners had been attracted to the station . . . At the time the new management came in, gross monthly income was $2,400 and at the end of 12 months this amount has been increased to $6,000. *The new manager attributed all improvement to the policy of making the station a real local institution and a true voice of the community.*[5]

---

[4] *Great Western Broadcasting Association* v. *F.C.C.,* 94 F. 2d 244, 248. In the KHMO case, the court ordered the Commission to issue a license to an applicant for a local station in an area where three stations were already operating, none of which gave genuine local service. The court expressed approval of the Commission's findings in similar cases, that "under the direct provisions of the statute the *rights of the citizens to enjoy local broadcasting privileges were being denied." (Courier Post Broadcasting Co.* v. *F.C.C.,* 104 F. 2d 213, 218) (Emphasis supplied).

[5] Sandage, *Radio Advertising for Retailers,* p. 210. (Emphasis supplied.)

(b) Amateur shows have been used effectively in developing local talent.

An Illinois retailer has used this type of show for a number of years and has built an audience which in 1942 surpassed in size the audience for any other radio program broadcast at the same time . . . It was competing with John Charles Thomas, New York Philharmonic, and the Army Hour. Only the John Charles Thomas program approached the rating for the local program. As in all programs which make use of local talent of fair quality, a considerable audience was attracted because of an interest in local people.[6]

(c) A feed mill in Missouri developed a quartet called the "Happy Millers" which sang hillbilly and western music.

Public acceptance has been phenomenal, partly *because of the interest of rural people in the type of entertainment afforded but also because the entertainers are all local people and well known in the community*.[7]

These few examples can no doubt be supplemented from their own experience by many alert station managers throughout the country.

While parallels between broadcast stations and newspapers must be approached with caution, their common elements with respect to local interest may be significant. The local newspaper achieves world-wide news coverage through the great press associations, taps the country's foremost writers and cartoonists through the feature syndicates, and from the picture services procures photographs from everywhere in abundant quantity. But the local newspaper editor, faced with such abundant incoming material, does not therefore discharge his local reporters and photographers, nor does he seek to reproduce locally the New York *Times* or *Daily News*. He appreciates the keen interest in local material and makes the most of that material—especially on the front page. The hours from 6 to 11 p.m. are the "front page" of the broadcast station. The statistics of local programming during these hours, or generally, are not impressive.

Extent of local live program service

No reliable statistics are currently available concerning the time devoted to local live programs, partly because there has heretofore been no accepted definition of "local live," partly because "wire" programs of news syndicated to many stations have been included in the local live classification, and partly because programs of phonograph records have been classified as "local live" by some stations if a live announcer intersperses advertising comments among the records. The paucity of local live, and especially local live sustaining programs, is indicated, however, by the following table which shows the time reported by 703 stations as having been devoted to local live

[6] *Ibid.*, pp. 166–167.
[7] *Ibid.*, p. 161. (Emphasis supplied.)

programs in January, 1945. The table can perhaps be best interpreted as showing the time devoted to non-network, non-transcribed programs:

AVERAGE HOURS PER DAY AND PERCENTAGE OF TIME ON THE AIR DEVOTED TO LOCAL LIVE PROGRAMS BY CLASS OF STATION
FOR MONTH OF JANUARY, 1945

	Commercial		Sustaining	
	Hours per day	% of time on air	Hours per day	% of time on air
50 kw stations (41)	3:02	15.9	1:52	9.8
500 w—50 kw stations (214)	2:23	13.6	1:11	6.8
250 w or less stations (376)	1:43	10.7	1:00	6.3
Part time stations (72)	2:11	20.3	1:09	10.7
All stations (703)	2:02	12.7	1:07	7.0

Source: Annual Financial Reports, 1944.

From 6 to 11 p.m., moreover, non-network, non-transcribed programs are considerably rarer, amounting on the average to only 42 minutes in five hours for all stations. *Sustaining* programs of this type average only 13 minutes in five hours.

AVERAGE HOURS AND PERCENTAGE OF TIME ON THE AIR, 6–11 P. M., DEVOTED TO LOCAL LIVE PROGRAMS BY CLASS OF STATION
FOR MONTH OF JANUARY, 1945

	Commercial		Sustaining	
	Hours per day	% of time on air	Hours per day	% of time on air
6 p.m. to 11 p.m. only				
50 kw stations (41)	:36	12.0	:12	3.9
500 w—50 kw stations (214)	:34	11.4	:14	4.7
250 w or less stations (376)	:29	9.8	:15	4.9
Part time stations (72)	:11	15.0	:07	8.7
All stations (703)	:29	10.6	:13	4.9

Source: Annual Financial Reports, 1944.

On particular stations, of course, the picture is even more extreme. The eight charts . . . for example, show in white the time devoted to non-network programs by the "basic affiliates" of the four major networks. It will be noted that on Sunday, April 23, 1944, the following stations carried no non-network programs whatever—and hence no local live programs—during the best listening hours from 6 to 11 p.m.:

WORC	WAGE	WMT	WCAU	KDB	WGY
WFCI	KQV	WDRC	WJAS	WBZ	WTAM
WNBC	WADC	WFBM	WTOP	WBZA	WMAQ
WCBM	WCAO	KFAB	WHBF	WJAR	WOW
WTRY	WEEI	WHAS	KWK	WRC	

In the face of this progressive blackout of non-network programs during the best listening hours on many stations, it has been proposed that some stations be licensed exclusively for non-network broadcasting, and that the Commission regulations prohibit the carrying of network programs by stations so licensed. This proposal appears impracticable. In communities where the number of stations does not exceed the number of networks, the result would be to deprive listeners of regular network service from one or more of the networks. In communities where the number of stations exceeds the number of networks, moreover, the regulation would be of little practical value since in such communities one or more of the stations will remain without a network affiliation in any event. The solution to network monopolization of a station's time, accordingly, must be found in terms of a balance of network and non-network programs, rather than in a distinction between network and non-network stations.

The most immediately profitable way to run a station, may be to procure a network affiliation, plug into the network line in the morning, and broadcast network programs throughout the day—interrupting the network output only to insert commercial spot announcements, and to substitute spot announcements and phonograph records for outstanding network sustaining programs. The record on renewal since April, 1945, of standard broadcast stations shows that some stations are approaching perilously close to this extreme. Indeed, it is difficult to see how some stations can do otherwise with the minimal staffs currently employed in programming.

For every three writers employed by 834 broadcast stations in October, 1944, there were four salesmen employed. For every dollar paid to the average writer, the average salesman was paid $2.39. And in terms of total compensation paid to writers and salesmen, the stations paid $3.30 for salesmen for every $1.00 paid for writers. The comparable relationship for 415 local stations is even more unbalanced.[8]

The average local station employed less than $\frac{1}{3}$ of a full time musician and less than $\frac{1}{6}$ of a full time actor.[9]

---

[8] In the week of October 15, 1944, 834 stations employed 863 writers at an average compensation of $40.14, totalling $34,641; and 1195 salesmen at an average compensation of $95.92, totalling $114,624. The 415 local stations employed 259 writers full time at an average salary of $31.87 but employed 409 salesmen at an average of $68.85.

[9] Many or most stations are financially able to employ far larger program staffs than at present. . . .

Such figures suggest, particularly at the local station level, that few stations are staffed adequately to meet their responsibilities in serving the community. A positive responsibility rests upon local stations to make articulate the voice of the community. Unless time is earmarked for such a purpose, unless talent is positively sought and given at least some degree of expert assistance, radio stations have abdicated their local responsibilities and have become mere common carriers of program material piped in from outside the community.

C. Discussion of public issues

American broadcasters have always recognized that broadcasting is not merely a means of entertainment, but also an unequaled medium for the dissemination of news, information, and opinion, and for the discussion of public issues. Radio's role in broadcasting the election returns of November 1920 is one of which broadcasters are justly proud; and during the quarter of a century which has since elapsed, broadcasting has continued to include news, information, opinion and public discussion in its regular budget of program material.

Especially in recent years, such information programs as news and news commentaries have achieved a popularity exceeding the popularity of any other single type of program. The war, of course, tremendously increased listener interest in such programs; but if broadcasters face the crucial problems of the post-war era with skill, fairness, and courage, there is no reason why broadcasting cannot play as important a role in our democracy hereafter as it has achieved during the war years.

The use of broadcasting as an instrument for the dissemination of news, ideas, and opinions raises a multitude of problems of a complex and sometimes delicate nature, which do not arise in connection with purely entertainment programs. A few such problems may be briefly noted, without any attempt to present an exhaustive list:

(1) Shall time for the presentation of one point of view on a public issue be sold, or shall all such presentations of points of view be on sustaining time only?

(2) If presentations of points of view are to be limited only to sustaining time, what measures can be taken to insure that adequate sustaining time during good listening hours is made available for such presentations, and that such time is equitably distributed?

(3) If time is also on occasion to be sold for presentation of a point of view, what precautions are necessary to insure that the most time shall not gravitate to the side prepared to spend the most money?

(4) Are forums, town meetings, and round-table type broadcasts, in

which two or more points of view are aired together, intrinsically superior to the separate presentation of points of view at various times?

(5) Should such programs be sponsored?

(6) What measures will insure that such programs be indeed fair and well-balanced among opposing points of view?

(7) Should locally originated discussion programs, in which residents of a community can themselves discuss issues of local, national, or international importance be encouraged, and if so, how?

(8) How can an unbiased presentation of the news be achieved?

(9) Should news be sponsored, and if so, to what extent should the advertiser influence or control the presentation of the news?

(10) How and by whom should commentators be selected?

(11) Should commentators be forbidden, permitted, or encouraged to express their own personal opinions?

(12) Is a denial of free speech involved when a commentator is discharged or his program discontinued because something which he has said has offended (a) the advertiser, (b) the station, (c) a minority of his listeners, or (d) a majority of his listeners?

(13) What provisions, over and above Section 315 of the Communications Act of 1934,[10] are necessary or desirable in connection with the operation of broadcast stations during a political campaign?

(14) Does a station operate in the public interest which charges a higher rate for political broadcasts than for commercial programs?

(15) The Federal Communications Commission is forbidden by law to censor broadcasts. Should station licensees have the absolute right of censorship, or should their review of broadcasts be limited to protection against libel, dissemination of criminal matter, etc.?

(16) Should broadcasters be relieved of responsibility for libel with respect to broadcasts over which they exercise no control?

(17) Should the "right to reply" to broadcasts be afforded; and if so, to whom should the right be afforded, and under what circumstances?

(18) When a station refuses time on the air requested for the discussion of public issues, should it be required to state in writing its reasons for refusal? Should it be required to maintain a record of all such requests for time, and of the disposal made of them?

(19) What measures can be taken to open broadcasting to types of

---

[10] "Sec. 315. If any licensee shall permit any person who is a legally qualified candidate for any public office to use a broadcasting station, he shall afford equal opportunities to all other such candidates for that office in the use of such broadcasting station, and the Commission shall make rules and regulations to carry this provision into effect: *Provided,* That such licensee shall have no power of censorship over the material broadcast under the provisions of this section. No obligation is hereby imposed upon any licensee to allow the use of its station by any such candidate."

informational programs which contravene the interests of large advertisers—for example, news of the reports and decisions of the Federal Trade Commission concerning unfair advertising; reports of the American Medical Association concerning the effects of cigarette-smoking; temperance broadcasts; etc?

These are only a few of the many questions which are raised in complaints to the Commission from day to day. The future of American broadcasting as an instrument of democracy depends in no small part upon the establishment of sound solutions to such problems, and on the fair and impartial application of general solutions to particular cases.

Under the Communications Act, primary responsibility for solving these and similar issues rests upon the licensees of broadcast stations themselves. Probably no other type of problem in the entire broadcasting industry is as important, or requires of the broadcaster a greater sense of objectivity, responsibility, and fair play.

While primary responsibility in such matters rests with the individual broadcaster, the Commission is required by the statute to review periodically the station's operation, in order to determine whether the station has in fact been operated in the public interest. Certainly, the establishment of sound station policy with respect to news, information, and the discussion of public issues is a major factor in operation in the public interest.

The Commission has never laid down, and does not now propose to lay down, any categorical answers to such questions as those raised above. Rather than enunciating general policies, the Commission reaches decisions on such matters in the crucible of particular cases.[11]

One matter of primary concern, however, can be met by an over-all statement of policy, and must be met as part of the general problem of over-all program balance. This is the question of the *quantity* of time which should be made available for the discussion of public issues.

The problems involved in making time available for the discussion of public issues are admittedly complex. Any vigorous presentation of a point of view will of necessity annoy or offend at least some listeners. There may be a temptation, accordingly, for broadcasters to avoid as much as possible any discussion over their stations, and to limit their broadcasts to entertainment programs which offend no one.

To operate in this manner, obviously, is to thwart the effectiveness of broadcasting in a democracy.

A test case may illustrate the problem here raised. At the request of the Senate Committee on Interstate Commerce, the Commission undertook a study of all network and local programs broadcast from January 1, 1941 through May 31, 1941, relative to the foreign policy issue then before the

---

[11] See, for example, the *Mayflower* case, 8 F.C.C. 333, and *United Broadcasting Company (WHKC)* case, decided June 26, 1945.

country, that of isolationism versus intervention in the world conflict. The period reviewed was one of great crisis. The issue at stake would affect the history and even the survival of our country and its institutions. Five major questions of foreign policy were involved—lend-lease, the convoying of ships to Britain, the acquisition of foreign bases, the acquisition of foreign ships, and the maintenance of the British blockade. From this study the following facts emerged.

The four major networks submitted 532 programs. Upon analysis only 203 scripts were deemed relevant; 14 scripts were unobtainable.

Assuming all 14 of these scripts to have been relevant, this means that 217 scripts during a 5-month period dealt with the 5 major issues of foreign policy listed above. Put another way, each network broadcast a program devoted to one or more of these issues every third day.

But while the networks made these programs available, not all affiliated stations carried them. Of 120 CBS affiliates, 59.3% carried the average lend-lease program. Of 165 MBS affiliates, 45.5% carried it. Of the approximately 200 NBC stations on both Red and Blue networks of NBC, 69 stations carried the average NBC program on lend-lease.

Even more significant are the figures relating to non-network programs. Of 742 stations reporting, only 288 claimed to have originated even one program on any subject relevant to this study. The remaining 454 denied having broadcast a single non-network program on foreign policy during the entire 5-month period. While subject to possible sampling error, the study indicates that station time devoted to discussion programs distributed by the four networks exceeded station time devoted to discussion programs originated by the stations in the ratio of 30 to 1.

The carrying of any particular public discussion, of course, is a problem for the individual broadcaster. But the public interest clearly requires that an adequate amount of time be made available for the discussion of public issues; and the Commission, in determining whether a station has served the public interest, will take into consideration the amount of time which has been or will be devoted to the discussion of public issues.

D. *Advertising excesses*

(1) *Value of advertising*

Advertising represents the only source of revenue for most American broadcasting stations, and is therefore an indispensable part of our system of broadcasting. In return for spending some 397 million dollars per year[1] on American broadcasting, the advertiser can expect that his name and wares will be effectively made known to the public.

---

[1] See p. . . . . [This footnote refers to a table, omitted here, comparing annual expenditures for broadcast advertising and listeners' costs for receiver acquisition, operation, and maintenance.—Ed.]

Advertising in general, moreover, and radio advertising in particular, plays an essential role in the distribution of goods and services within our economy. During the postwar era if manufacturers are to dispose of the tremendous output of which our postwar industry will be capable, they must keep their products before the public.

Finally, informative advertising which gives reliable factual data concerning available goods and services is itself of direct benefit to the listener in his role as consumer. Consumer knowledge of the new and improved products which contribute to a higher standard of living is one of the steps toward achieving that higher standard of living.

However, the fact that advertisers have a legitimate interest and place in the American system of broadcasting does not mean that broadcasting should be run solely in the interest of the advertisers rather than that of the listeners. Throughout the history of broadcasting, a limitation on the amount and character of advertising has been one element of "public interest." A brief review will illustrate this point.

(2) Historic background

Commercial broadcasting began in 1920 or 1921, and by 1922 the dangers of excessive advertising had already been noted. Thus at the First Annual Radio Conference in 1922, Secretary of Commerce Herbert Hoover declared:

It is inconceivable that we should allow so great a possibility for service, for news, for entertainment, for education and for vital commercial purposes to be drowned in advertising chatter. . . .

The Conference itself took heed of Secretary Hoover's warning and recommended:

. . . that direct advertising in radio broadcasting service be absolutely prohibited and that indirect advertising be limited to the announcements of the call letters of the station and of the name of the concern responsible for the matter broadcasted, subject to such regulations as the Secretary of Commerce may impose.

In 1927, following the passage of the Radio Act, advertising abuses were among the first topics to engage the attention of the newly established Federal Radio Commission. Thus, in its first formal statement of the "broad underlying principles which . . . must control its decisions on controversies arising between stations in their competition for favorable assignments," one of the "broad underlying principles" set forth was that "the amount and character of advertising must be rigidly confined within the limits consistent with the public service expected of the nation." To quote further:

. . . The Commission must . . . recognize that without advertising, broadcasting would not exist, and *must confine itself to limiting this advertisement in amount and in character* so as to preserve the largest possible amount of service to the public. Advertising must be accepted for the present as the sole means of support of broadcasting, and *regulation must be relied upon to prevent the abuse and over use of the privilege.*[2] (Emphasis supplied.)

This general principle was applied in particular cases, especially in connection with actions on renewal of station licenses. Thus in announcing, on August 23, 1928, its decision not to renew the license of Station WCRW, the Commission stated:

It is clear that a large part of the program is distinctly commercial in character, consisting of advertisers' announcements and of direct advertising, including the quoting of prices. An attempt was made to show a very limited amount of educational and community civic service, but the amount of time thus employed is negligible and evidence of its value to the community is not convincing. Manifestly this station is one which exists chiefly for the purpose of deriving an income from the sale of advertising of a character which must be objectionable to the listening public and without making much, if any, endeavor to render any real service to the public.

The station's license was not renewed.

It was urged in some quarters, then as now, that the Commission need not concern itself with program service because whenever the public found a broadcast irksome, listeners would shift to other stations and the situation would thus automatically correct itself. The Federal Radio Commission, in announcing on August 29, 1928 its decision to place Stations WRAK, WABF, WBRE, and WMBS "on probation" by renewing their license for 30 days only, rather than for the customary 90 days, gave short shrift to this argument. It stated:

Listeners are given no protection unless it is given to them by this Commission, for they are powerless to prevent the ether waves carrying the unwelcome messages from entering the walls of their homes. Their only alternative, which is not to tune in on the station, is not satisfactory, particularly when in a city such as Erie only the local stations can be received during a large part of the year. When a station is misused for such a private purpose the entire listening public is deprived of the use of a station for a service in the public interest.

Despite the Federal Radio Commission's concern with excessive advertising, there is reason to believe that substantial Congressional sentiment considered the Commission too lax in the exercise of its functions with respect to advertising. Thus on January 12, 1932, the Senate passed Senate Resolution 129, introduced by Senator Couzens, then chairman of the Senate Committee on Interstate Commerce, which provided in part as follows:

[2] *In re Great Lakes Broadcasting Co.,* F.R.C. Docket No. 4900.

Whereas there is growing dissatisfaction with the present use of radio facilities for purposes of commercial advertising: Be it

Resolved, That the Federal Radio Commission is hereby authorized and instructed to make a survey and to report to the Senate on the following questions:

1. What information there is available on the feasibility of Government ownership and operation of broadcasting facilities.
2. To what extent the facilities of a representative group of broadcasting stations are used for commercial advertising purposes.
3. To what extent the use of radio facilities for purposes of commercial advertising varies as between stations having power of one hundred watts, five hundred watts, one thousand watts, five thousand watts, and all in excess of five thousand watts.
4. What plans might be adopted to reduce, to limit, to control, and perhaps, to eliminate the use of radio facilities for commercial advertising purposes.
5. What rules or regulations have been adopted by other countries to control or to eliminate the use of radio facilities for commercial advertising purposes.
6. Whether it would be practicable and satisfactory to permit only the announcement of sponsorship of programs by persons or corporations.[3]

(3) Evolution of industry standards

(a) *Commercials in sponsored programs.*   Broadcasters and advertisers themselves have always recognized the basic doctrine that advertising must be limited and abuses avoided. Thus, Mr. Herbert Wilson Smith, of the National Carbon Company, sponsors of the Ever-Ready Hour, testified before the House Merchant Marine and Fisheries Committee concerning radio legislation on January 7, 1926:

. . . When these musical and semi-dramatic programs are given, we precede the program by some such announcement as this one, for example, on December 15, 1925.

Tuesday evening means the Ever-Ready Hour, for it is on this day and at this time each week that the National Carbon Company, makers of Ever-Ready flashlights and radio batteries, engages the facilities of these 14 radio stations to present its artists in original radio creations. Tonight the sponsors of the hour have included in the program, etc.

Now, that is the extent of the advertising, direct or indirect, of any character which we do in connection with our program. . . . The statement of the name of your company or the sponsorship of the program must be delicately handled so that the listener will not feel that he is having advertising pushed over on him; then throughout the rest of the entertainment, there is given a very high-class program, a musical program, entirely for the pleasure of the listeners. (*Hearings on H. R. 5589*, 69th Cong., 1st sess., pp. 81-82.)

---

[3] The Commission's study made pursuant to this Resolution was published as Senate Document 137, 72nd Cong. 1st sess.

On March 25, 1929 the National Association of Broadcasters, composed at that time of 147 broadcast stations throughout the country, adopted "Standards of Commercial Practice" which specifically provided:

Commercial announcements, as the term is generally understood, shall not be broadcast between 7 and 11 p.m.

In 1930 Mr. William S. Hedges of Station WMAQ, then president of the National Association of Broadcasters and now vice-president of the National Broadcasting Company, testified before the Senate Committee on Interstate Commerce concerning the quantitative limits on advertising which he then enforced.[4]

The Chairman (Senator Couzens). What portion of a 30-minute program would you say should be devoted to advertising?
Mr. Hedges. It all depends on the way you do it. Our rule, however, in our station is that no more than one minute out of the 30 minutes is devoted to advertising sponsorship. In other words, the radio listener gets 29 minutes of corking good entertainment, and all he has to do is to learn the name of the organization that has brought to him this fine program.
The Chairman. Do all of the advertisers on your station confine themselves to 1 minute of advertising out of thirty minutes?
Mr. Hedges. Some of them do not use as much as that.
The Chairman. And some use more?
Mr. Hedges. Very few. (pp. 1752-3)

Mr. William S. Paley, until recently president of the Columbia Broadcasting System, testified in the same hearings that only 22 percent of the time of CBS, or 23 hours per week out of 109½ hours of operation, was devoted to commercial programs; the remaining 78 percent of the time was sustaining (pp. 1796–9). He cited the "CBS Credo" on advertising:

No overloading of a program with advertising matter, either through announcements that are too long or by too frequent mention of a trade name or product. (p. 1801).

Mr. Paley testified further:

Senator Dill. How much of the hour do you allow for advertising in a program of an hour, or how much in a program of half an hour?
Mr. Paley. Well, that varies, Senator Dill. I do not know how many seconds or how many minutes during an hour we actually give for the advertising time, but a few weeks ago our research department told me that of all the time used on the air during a particular week, that the actual time taken for advertising mention was seven-tenths of 1 percent of all our time. (p. 1802).

Since 1930, there has been a progressive relaxation of industry standards, so that the NAB standards at present permit as much as one and three-

[4] Senate Committee on Interstate Commerce, *Hearings on S. 6,* 71st. Cong., 2d sess.

quarter minutes of advertising in a five-minute period, and do not even require this limit on participating programs, "musical clocks," etc. The *NAB
Code* provisions in effect from 1937 to 1945 were as follows:

Member stations shall hold the length of commercial copy, including that
devoted to contests and offers, to the following number of minutes and seconds:

Daytime

Five-minute programs	2:00
Five-minute news programs*	1:45
Ten-minute programs	2:30
Fifteen-minute programs	3:15
Twenty-five minute programs	4:15
Thirty-minute programs	4:30
Sixty-minute programs	9:00

Nighttime

Five-minute programs	1:45
Five-minute news programs*	1:30
Ten-minute programs	2:00
Fifteen-minute programs	2:30
Twenty-five minute programs	2:45
Thirty-minute programs	3:00
Sixty-minute programs	6:00

* Further restriction by individual stations is recommended.

Exceptions:
   The above limitations do not apply to participation programs, announcement programs, "musical clocks," shoppers' guide and local programs falling
within these general classifications.
   Because of the varying economic and social conditions throughout the
United States, members of the NAB shall have the right to present to the NAB
for special ruling local situations which in the opinion of the member may justify exceptions to the above prescribed limitations.

In August 1945 these standards were further amended to eliminate the day-
night differential, and to apply the former nighttime maxima to all hours.
   (b) *Spot Announcements.* In addition to the commercials within sponsored programs, there are, of course, commercial spot announcements
within or between programs. No standard appears to be generally accepted
for limiting spot announcements—though one network has recently announced with respect to its owned stations that commercial spot announcements must be limited to 1 minute or 125 words, that not more than three
may be broadcast in any quarter-hour, that "station-break" spot announcements must be limited to 12 seconds or 25 words, and that these must not
be more frequent than one each quarter-hour. The result is to permit 12
minutes and 48 seconds of spot announcements per hour. The NAB standards place no limitation whatever on spot announcements.

(4) *Present practices: time devoted to commercials*

In addition to the general relaxation of advertising standards in recent years, there is abundant evidence that even the present NAB standards are being flouted by some stations and networks.

As a rough index to contemporary advertising practices, the Commission recorded the programs of the six Washington, D. C., stations for Friday, July 6, 1945, and analyzed the recordings and station logs for that day. The Washington stations comprise:

WRC—a 5,000-watt regional station, owned by the National Broadcasting Company.

WTOP—a 50,000-watt clear-channel station, owned and operated by the Columbia Broadcasting System.

WMAL—a 5,000-watt regional station, owned by the Washington *Evening Star,* affiliated with the American Broadcasting Company (Blue Network).

WOL—a 1,000-watt regional station licensed to the Cowles Broadcasting Company and affiliated with the Mutual Broadcasting System.

WINX—a 250-watt local station licensed to the Washington Post.

WWDC—a 250-watt local station licensed to the Capital Broadcasting Company.

It seems reasonable to suppose that these six stations, operating in a major metropolitan area and the capital of the country, including two stations owned by major networks and two others affiliated with major networks would represent practices superior to the practices of stations generally.

Frequent examples of commercial advertising in excess of NAB standards were noted on all four networks and all six stations. The results of the study suggest that on networks and stations alike, the NAB standards are as honored in the breach as in the observance.

(5) *Other advertising problems*

The proportion of overall time devoted to advertising commercials, discussed above, is only one of a series of problems raised by present network and station policies. No thorough study has been made of these other advertising problems, and accordingly, the following paragraphs should be considered as suggestive only, and designed to stimulate further research in this field. More light is needed both on the nature of existing practices and on their effect. A partial list of advertising problems other than the proportion of time devoted to advertising includes:

(a) *Length of individual commercials.* One commercial recorded by the Commission ran for just five minutes, without program interruption of any kind.

That many advertisers are content with spot announcements of reasonable length is indicated by the following table showing the scheduled length of 70 commercial spot announcements broadcast over Station WCAU on Monday, February 12, 1945, between 8 a.m. and 11 p.m.:

No. of 15-second commercial spot announcements			2
No. of 20-second " " "			2
No. of 25-second " " "			36
No. of 30-second " " "			2
No. of 45-second " " "			1
No. of 60-second " " "			26
No. of 95-second " " "			1
			70

On the other hand, some advertisers are frankly of the opinion that the longer the commercial plug, the more effective the program. Mr. Duane Jones, president of an advertising agency said to be one of the five largest in New York, placing more than 2,000 commercials a week for 26 clients, has given forceful expression to this view:

In dealing with advertising on the air, we in the Duane Jones Co. have found that, when we increase the length and number of commercials on the air to test our programs, invariably their Crossley ratings go up. . . . When making these tests, we load the programs to the limit under NAB rulings with commercials that precede, interrupt, and follow these broadcasts. And we know from the results that any arbitrary curtailment of commercials would seriously impair the audience value of these shows.

This view does not appear to be universally held; and evidence is available that lengthy commercials result in listeners tuning out a program. Thus *Variety* for May 2, 1945, reported:

TOO MANY PLUGS COOL "ROMANCE"

Colgate's "Theatre of Romance" is going way overboard on commercial spiels each week, CBS execs pointed out to Sherman, Marquette agency chiefs on Friday (27)—and it must stop immediately for the good of the program and the web's rating, they added.

A chart-check over a two-month period shows that the commercials on "Romance" run anywhere from three minutes and 15 seconds to four and one-half minutes. CBS' ruling on the commercial's time-limit for 30-minute sponsored shows, proved over the years, is three minutes. Over that, according to researchers at the network, listeners become restless, continuity is uneven and the stanza suffers in rating.

Charts show that the drama picks up rating shortly after going on the air, and that every time a commercial is spieled, the rating sags. On "Romance," too, for a full two minutes before it goes off each week during which the surveys were taken, ratings drop as much as three points. And on many shows, besides the Colgate blurbs, the announcer pitches in with a government-agency plug as well.

Sherman, Marquette will have to hold the commercials within the three-minute limit, or less, from here on in, CBS has informed them.[5]

A study of the six Washington stations for Friday, July 6, 1945, from 8 a.m. to 11 p.m. suggests that commercials one minute or more in length are quite common. More than 150 such announcements were noted on the six Washington stations during that period.

(b) *Number of commercials.* The extreme case of an excessive *number* of spots noted to date is Station KMAC, which broadcast 2215 commercial announcements in 133 hours on the air during the week beginning January 21, 1945. This was an average of 16.7 spots per hour. Spot announcements in excess of 1,000 per week have been noted on a number of stations.

(c) *Piling up of commercials.* The listener who has heard one program and wants to hear another has come to expect a commercial plug to intervene. Conversely, the listener who has heard one or more commercial announcements may reasonably expect a program to intervene. Listed below is a series of commercial spot announcements broadcast by Station WTOL in Toledo, on November 14, 1944, during the dinner hour, without program interruption:

6:39:30 p.m.	Transcribed spot announcement.
6:40:00	Live spot announcement.
6:41:00	Transcribed spot announcement.
6:42:00	" " "
6:43:00	" " "
6:44:00	" " "

This programless period occurred each weekday dinner hour during the week of November 13, 1945, except on Thursday, when Station WTOL interrupted its spots to broadcast one minute of transcribed music.

Such series are not unique. The "hitch-hiker" and "cowcatcher" on network programs, now rarer but not yet exterminated, have at times meant

[5] Television may bring still longer commercials. *Variety* for March 14, 1945, reports:
"A new venture in video experimentation, as far as a Chicago station is concerned, will be tried Tuesday (20) when a 3½-minute commercial is aired over WBKB, Balaban & Katz station here. Designed to fill in the air time between studio programs, the package is completely canned and is composed of slide film, synchronized to a recorded musical background and narration with the video part entirely cartooned.
"Set up as a Red Heart dog food commercial, it was produced by David W. Doyle, associate radio director of the Henri, Hurst & McDonald, Inc., agency; written by Betty Babcock and narrated by Ray Suber. Following tests here it may later be used on WNBT (NBC) and WABD (DuMont), New York."

that a listener desiring to hear two consecutive network programs must survive five intervening commercial plugs—the closing plug of the first program, a "hitch-hiker" plug for another product of the same sponsor, a local plug in the station break between programs, a "cowcatcher" for a minor product of the sponsor of the second network program, and finally the opening commercial of the second program.

Professor C. H. Sandage, in his survey of radio advertising by retailers, has pointed out that excessive spot announcements may even destroy advertiser confidence in broadcasting:

> There is real danger that excessive use of spots will drive not only listeners away from a station but also a number of advertisers whom some refer to as the more respectable. A Midwest jeweler who operated a first-class, noninstallment credit store reported that he had cancelled his use of radio because he felt that radio management in his city had allowed the air to become too crowded with spot announcements. He also believed that many announcements were purchased by firms selling cheap and shoddy merchandise. Another advertiser reported: "Radio announcements are O. K. for loan sharks but not for me." Similar comments were sufficiently frequent to indicate that this factor had kept a number of retailers from using the facilities of radio.[6]

(d) *Time between commercials.* Listener satisfaction may depend in part upon the length of the intervals between commercials. The National Association of Broadcasters may have been recognizing this feature of the commercial when in 1929 it banned commercial announcements between 7 and 11 p.m., thus affording four hours of listening uninterrupted by commercial advertising—as distinguished from announcement of the name of the advertiser and of his product.

Some stations and some advertisers are becoming aware of the value of uninterrupted listening. Thus the WOL program on July 9, 1945 from 7:30 to 7:58 p.m. made a point of announcing that the four movements of a symphony would be played "without interruption."

(e) *The middle commercial.* The Radio Council of Greater Cleveland, composed of representatives of 112 organizations having a total membership of 155,000, conducted a questionnaire survey in 1945 with respect to the "middle commercial" and related problems. The study, while perhaps subject to considerable sampling error, nevertheless indicates roughly the extent of listener dissatisfaction. More than 95 percent of those responding stated that they preferred commercials only at the beginning and end.

Canadian regulations prohibit the middle commercial on newscasts altogether. Canadian Regulation 13(2), adopted November 17, 1941, provides in part:

> The only announcement of sponsorship for news . . . shall be two in number, one at the beginning and one at the end, and shall be as follows:

[6] Sandage, *Radio Advertising for Retailers,* p. 186.

"Through the courtesy of (name and business of sponsor) Station _____ presents (presented) the news of the day furnished by (name of news service)."

The Association of Radio News Analysts, a group whose own livelihood depends upon commercial newscasts, has been among those who believe the middle commercial to be an unhealthy growth. Article IV of the *ARNA Code* of Ethics states:

> The association deplores the interruption of a news analysis by commercial announcements.

Many members of the ARNA, which includes outstanding news analysts and commentators throughout the country, refuse to appear on a program which is interrupted by a middle commercial. Raymond Swing, in a telegram to the St. Louis *Post-Dispatch* published February 5, 1945, described his own experience with the middle commercial:

> I made my own rebellion against them on May 10, 1940, when writing my broadcast reporting German violation of French, Belgian, Dutch and Luxembourg neutrality in launching the Western offensive. It seemed hideous to have this account interrupted by a sales talk, and I balked.
>
> To the credit of Mutual officials, for whom I was then broadcasting, and the advertising agency handling the program, they supported my stand. Since then my contracts for broadcasts on the Blue network have specified that my program not be interrupted by middle commercials.
>
> Listeners are entitled to hear the news without jarring interruptions, and I feel confident it is sound advertising policy to recognize the right.

Despite the successful revolt of Mr. Swing and some others, it should be noted that as late as Friday, July 6, 1945, recording of broadcasts on the six Washington stations showed some news and analysis programs being interrupted by commercials on all four networks and all six stations.

The St. Louis *Post-Dispatch* has carried on for some months a concerted campaign against the middle commercial in newscasts, and has been followed by newspapers throughout the country. Leaders in the campaign have been other newspapers which, like the *Post-Dispatch,* are themselves the licensees of standard broadcast stations.

Judge Justin Miller, then of the United States Circuit Court of Appeals and now president of the National Association of Broadcasters, commented on the middle commercial and the *Post-Dispatch* campaign in a letter to the editor published April 20, 1945:

> I have just read in *Broadcasting* a reprint of your editorial of April 10, "In the Interest of Radio." Let me add my voice to that of others who have commended you for the position which you have taken.
>
> There is no more reason why a newscast should be interrupted for a plug-ugly than that such ads should be inserted in the middle of news stories or editorials in a newspaper; especially when the interruption—deliberately or un-

consciously, whichever it may be—is in nauseating contrast to the subject under discussion by the commentator.

It is particularly encouraging that this insistence upon higher professional standards should come from a newspaper—a representative of the profession which has most intelligently through the years defended the guarantees of the first amendment. Only by intelligent anticipation of public reaction and by equally intelligent self-discipline can we prevent legislative intemperance.

While many stations and some sponsors deleted the middle commercial on newscasts following the *Post-Dispatch* campaign, others adopted measures which fall short of elimination. One network, for example, divides 15 minutes of news and comment into a 10-minute program for one sponsor and a 5-minute program for another—with a station-break announcement between. The result is to move the middle commercial from the precise mid-point to the two-thirds point of the quarter-hour—and to subject the listener to two or even three interrupting impacts. Another network claims to have eliminated the middle commercial, but actually it requires that commercials be limited to the first two and the last three minutes of the 15-minute period —as a result of which the news is interrupted twice instead of once. It is clear that such devices, while they eliminate the commercial at the exact middle, fail to meet the chief listener complaint—which is that the news is *interrupted*. Some sponsors, in contrast, have made a sound asset of actual elimination of the middle commercial; their opening announcement ends with some such phrase as: "We bring you now the news—*uninterrupted*." It may well be that such emphasis upon the essentials of good programming, made explicit to listeners by appropriate announcement over the air, will do much to eliminate inferior procedures indulged in by other networks, stations, or sponsors.

(f) *The patriotic appeal.* Patriotism, especially in time of war, is an emotion near the forefront of the minds of most listeners. To misuse the listener's deepest patriotic feelings for the sale of commercial products over the air is a violation of a public trust. It is well established that the American flag shall not be used in visual advertising;[7] and the aural symbols of our national life should be similarly immune from commercialization. An example of the patriotic appeal to buy headache remedies is the following announcement over Station WBT, Charlotte, on September 4, 1944:

As every one of you well knows, the United States is face to face with a great challenge. People everywhere are seriously concerned about the Nation's all-out effort. Regardless of how or where you serve, you first duty is to keep well. Get adequate rest. Follow a reasonable diet. Exercise properly. Avoid unnecessary exposures or excesses. When a simple headache develops, or the pain of neuralgia strikes, try a BC Headache Powder. The quick-acting, prescription-type ingredients in the BC formula usually work fast and relieve in a

[7] Public Law 623, approved June 22, 1942, provides: "The flag should never be used for advertising purposes in any manner whatsoever."

hurry. Remember this. Get one of the 25-cent packages of BC today. You'll like the way BC eases tantalizing headaches and soothes nerves ruffled or upset by pain. USE ONLY ACCORDING TO DIRECTIONS, and consult a physician when pains persist or recur frequently.

Another announcement over the same station said in part:

All of us have a big job on our hands if we want to keep America the land of the free and the home of the brave. The all-out effort means hard work, and lots of it. Production must move forward—fast! . . . Get one of the 10 or 25-cent packages of BC today. . . .

(g) *The physiological commercial.* Appeals to listeners to "take an internal bath," inquiring of the listener whether he has the common ailment known as "American stomach," discussions of body odors, sluggish bile, etc., are a distinguishing characteristic of American broadcasting.

Various networks and stations impose various restrictions on such physiological advertising. Mr. Lewis Gannett, well-known book critic, sums up listener reaction thus in the New York *Herald Tribune* for February 28, 1945:

The aspect of home-front life which most disgusted me on return was the radio. BBC programs may be dull and army radio programs may be shallow, but if the soldier in Europe has had a chance to hear the radio at all, he has heard it straight, without the neurotic advertising twaddle which punctuates virtually every American program. . . . The first evening that I sat by a radio at home, I heard one long parade of headaches, coughs, aching muscles, stained teeth, "unpleasant full feeling," and gastric hyperacidity. . . . Our radio evenings are a sick parade of sicknesses and if they haven't yet made us a sick nation, I wonder why.

According to data compiled by the Publisher's Information Bureau, more money is spent for network advertising of drugs and toilet goods than for any other products; 27.9% of all network gross billings is for such products. Drug and cosmetic advertising is said to have trebled between 1939 and 1944. The increasing identification of radio as a purveyor of patent medicines and proprietary remedies raises serious problems which warrant careful consideration by the broadcasting industry.

Professor Sandage's survey, cited above, asked various advertisers who did not use radio advertising the reason for their refraining. His study states:

A common reason for nonuse in a few communities was the character of advertising carried by local stations. Leading merchants commented that radio messages carried on these stations were too much like the patent medicine advertisements of pre-Federal Trade Commission days. These merchants did not wish to be associated on the air with such advertisers.[8]

[8] Sandage, *Radio Advertising for Retailers*, p. 73.

(h) *Propaganda in commercials.* The commercial announcement is sometimes used to propagandize for a point of view or one side of a debated issue rather than to sell goods and services. An example is the following announcement over Station KWBU, Corpus Christi, Texas, on August 1, 1944:

When you see a C[entral] P[ower and] L[ight Company] lineman hanging on a pole with one foot in heaven so to speak and hear him holler "headache," you better start running. He is not telling you how he feels but giving warning that he dropped a wrench or hammer and everyone had better look out below. The C[entral] P[ower and] L[ight Company] lineman has a tough job of keeping the electricity flowing to your home. They work night and day to keep headaches from you—to keep your lamps lit and your radio running despite lightning, floods, and storms. Only carefully trained and experienced men could do this job, but there are some in this country who think that the Government should own and operate the light and power industry. Then a lineman might hold his job for political reasons rather than for his ability to render good service to you. Business management under public regulation has brought you good reliable electric service at low prewar prices. That is the American way—let's keep it.

A second example is the following, broadcast over 12 Michigan stations in 1944:

American Medicine, the private practice of which represents the cumulative knowledge of decades, the heritage of centuries, the sacrifices and discoveries of countless individuals, has made the United States the healthiest country in the world. Spinal meningitis, diphtheria, smallpox, typhoid fever and other fatal diseases, scourges of yesteryear, are today either preventable or curable, a credit to the tireless efforts of the American medical profession. Thirty-seven states now have voluntary prepayment medical or hospital plans developed by the medical profession and the hospitals. *No theoretical plan, government controlled and operated, and paid for by you, should replace the tried and proved system of the private practice of medicine now in use.*[9]

On January 10, 1944, four days after the U. S. Department of Justice filed suit against the DuPont Company in connection with an alleged cartel agreement, DuPont used its commercial advertising period on the well-known "Cavalcade of America" program over NBC to explain one side of a controversial issue. To quote:

I want to talk to you tonight about an agreement current in the news and of wide public interest. This is the agreement which the DuPont Company has had for years with a British chemical company, Imperial Chemical Industries, Ltd. It provides for a mutual opportunity to acquire patent licenses and technical and scientific information relating to important chemical developments.

[9] *Journal of the American Medical Association,* Vol. 127, No. 5, p. 283 (February 3, 1945). Emphasis supplied.

It has been a matter of public record and known to our government for ten years.

Literally hundreds of transfers of technical and scientific information have occurred for the advancement of chemical science and the benefit of the American people in peace and war. Agreements of a similar character, but limited to specific chemical fields have been made from time to time with continental European companies for the use of scientific data obtained from abroad. Many valuable products have resulted for the use of the American public and necessary to our armed forces. In this war, DuPont chemists have materially improved and have further developed the scientific data flowing from these contractual arrangements.

The scientific and technical information gained has contributed substantially to American progress and to the success of American arms. Many important products have resulted from these agreements to which reference may be made without disclosing military secrets. Developments were made incident to synthetic ammonia manufactured from nitrogen extracted from the air. Without this we could not have smokeless powder and TNT in anything like the quantities needed. The development of Methyl Methacrylate plastic used for the transparent enclosures to be found on every combat airplane stems from these agreements. A new process vital to quantity production of aircraft engines and a new plastic polythene, which has gone into the production of new electrical items urgently needed by the Army and Navy. Also high in this last are rayon, dyes, celophane, zelan,—water repellent for military apparel, as well as many other chemical products. All have been improved and perfected here but they came originally from abroad.

These agreements have been of the greatest benefit in giving to the American public products and processes which in the past have materially raised the standard of living, products and processes which are a part of the promise for the future of "Better Things for Better Living Through Chemistry."

(i) *Intermixture of program and advertising.* A listener is entitled to know when the program ends and the advertisement begins. The *New York Times* comment on this and related topics is here in point:

The virtual subordination of radio's standards to the philosophy of advertising inevitably has led the networks into an unhealthy and untenable position. It has permitted Gabriel Heatter to shift without emphasis from a discussion of the war to the merits of hair tonic. It has forced the nation's best entertainers to act as candy butchers and debase their integrity as artists. It has permitted screeching voices to yell at our children to eat this or that if they want to be as efficient as some fictional character. . . . The broadcaster often has argued that it is not his function to "reform" the public taste, but, be that as it may, it certainly is the broadcaster's responsibility not to lower it.

The Association of Radio News Analysts has particularly inveighed against the practice of having the announcements read by the same voice as the news analysis. Article IV of the ARNA Code of Ethics provides:

The association believes the reading of commercial announcements by radio news analysts is against the best interests of broadcasting.

According to the president of the ARNA, John W. Vandercook:

> ARNA has . . . consistently arrayed itself in opposition to the reading of such commercial announcements by news analysts. It is our belief that the major networks and all of the more reputable American advertising agencies are in substantial agreement with us and support our stand.
>
> We, however, recognize and applaud the necessity for perpetual vigilance and unremitting efforts to extirpate the all-too-common breaches of these principles. (St. Louis *Post-Dispatch*, Feb. 5, 1945.)

The above is not to be taken as an exhaustive list of advertising excesses. Since it is not the intention of the Commission to concern itself with advertising excesses other than an excessive ratio of advertising time to program time, no exhaustive study has been undertaken. There is need, however, for a thorough review by the industry itself of current advertising practices, with a view towards the establishment and enforcement of sound standards by the industry itself.

PART IV. ECONOMIC ASPECTS

The problem of program service is intimately related to economic factors. A prosperous broadcasting industry is obviously in a position to render a better program service to the public than an industry which must pinch and scrape to make ends meet. Since the revenues of American broadcasting come primarily from advertisers, the terms and conditions of program service must not be such as to block the flow of advertising revenues into broadcasting. Finally, the public benefits when the economic foundations of broadcasting are sufficiently firm to insure a flow of new capital into the industry, especially at present when the development of FM and television is imminent.

A review of the economic aspects of broadcasting during recent years indicates that there are no economic considerations to prevent the rendering of a considerably broader program service than the public is currently afforded.*

PART V. SUMMARY AND CONCLUSIONS— PROPOSALS FOR FUTURE COMMISSION POLICY

A. Role of the public

Primary responsibility for the American system of broadcasting rests with the licensee of broadcast stations, including the network organizations. It is to the stations and networks rather than to federal regulation that listeners

---

* Sixteen tables of economic data supporting this view are omitted. [Ed.]

must primarily turn for improved standards of program service. The Commission, as the licensing agency established by Congress, has a responsibility to consider overall program service in its public interest determinations, but affirmative improvement of program service must be the result primarily of other forces.

One such force is self-regulation by the industry itself, through its trade associations.

Licensees acting individually can also do much to raise program service standards, and some progress has indeed been made. Here and there across the country, some stations have evidenced an increased awareness of the importance of sustaining programs, live programs, and discussion programs. Other stations have eliminated from their own program service the middle commercial, the transcribed commercial, the piling up of commercials, etc. This trend toward self-improvement, if continued, may further buttress the industry against the rising tide of informed and responsible criticism.

Forces outside the broadcasting industry similarly have a role to play in improved program service. There is need, for example, for professional radio critics, who will play in this field the role which literary and dramatic critics have long assumed in the older forms of artistic expression. It is, indeed, a curious instance of the time lag in our adjustment to changed circumstances that while plays and concerts performed to comparatively small audiences in the "legitimate" theater or concert hall are regularly reviewed in the press, radio's best productions performed before an audience of millions receive only occasional and limited critical consideration. *Publicity* for radio programs is useful, but limited in the function it performs. Responsible criticism can do much more than mere promotion; it can raise the standards of public appreciation and stimulate the free and unfettered development of radio as a new medium of artistic expression. The independent radio critic, assuming the same role long occupied by the dramatic critic and the literary critic, can bring to bear an objective judgment on questions of good taste and of artistic merit which lie outside the purview of this Commission. The reviews and critiques published weekly in *Variety* afford an illustration of the role that independent criticism can play; newspapers and periodicals might well consider the institution of similar independent critiques for the general public.

Radio listener councils can also do much to improve the quality of program service. Such councils, notably in Cleveland, Ohio, and Madison, Wisconsin, have already shown the possibilities of independent listener organization. First, they can provide a much needed channel through which listeners can convey to broadcasters the wishes of the vast but not generally articulate radio audience. Second, listener councils can engage in much needed research concerning public tastes and attitudes. Third, listener councils can check on the failure of network affiliates to carry outstanding network sustaining programs, and on the local programs substituted for outstanding network sustaining programs. Fourth, they can serve to publicize and to promote outstanding programs—especially sustaining programs which at present suffer a serious handicap for lack of the vast promotional enterprise which goes to publicize many commercial programs. Other useful functions would also no doubt result from an increase in the number and an extension of the range of activities of listener councils, cooperating with the broadcasting industry but speaking solely for the interest of listeners themselves.

Colleges and universities, some of them already active in the field, have a like distinctive role to play. Together with the public schools, they have it in their power to raise a new generation of listeners with higher standards and expectations of what radio can offer.

In radio workshops, knowledge may be acquired of the techniques of radio production. There are already many examples of students graduating from such work who have found their way into the industry, carrying with them standards and conceptions of radio's role, as well as talents, by which radio service cannot fail to be enriched.

Even more important, however, is the role of colleges and universities in the field of radio research. There is room for a vast expansion of studies of the commercial, artistic and social aspects of radio. The cultural aspects of radio's influence provide in themselves a vast and fascinating field of research.

It is hoped that the facts emerging from this report and the recommendations which follow will be of interest to the groups mentioned. With them rather than with the Commission rests much of the hope for improved broadcasting quality.

B. Role of the Commission

While much of the responsibility for improved program service lies with the broadcasting industry and with the public, the Commission has a statutory responsibility for the public interest, of which it cannot divest itself. The Commission's experience with the detailed review of broadcast renewal applications since April 1945, together with the facts set forth in this report, indicate some current trends in broadcasting which, with reference to licensing procedure, require its particular attention.

In issuing and in renewing the licenses of broadcast stations the Commission proposes to give particular consideration to four program service factors relevant to the public interest. These are: (1) the carrying of sustaining programs, including network sustaining programs, with particular reference to the retention by licensees of a proper discretion and responsibility for maintaining a well-balanced program structure; (2) the carrying of local live programs; (3) the carrying of programs devoted to the discussion of public issues, and (4) the elimination of advertising excesses.

(1) *Sustaining programs.* The carrying of sustaining programs has always been deemed one aspect of broadcast operation in the public interest. Sustaining programs, as noted above (pp. 147–159), perform a five-fold function in (a) maintaining an overall program balance, (b) providing time for programs inappropriate for sponsorship, (c) providing time for programs serving particular minority tastes and interests, (d) providing time for non-profit organizations—religious, civic, agricultural, labor, educational, etc., and (e) providing time for experiment and for unfettered artistic self-expression.

Accordingly, the Commission concludes that one standard of operation in the public interest is a reasonable proportion of time devoted to sustaining programs.

Moreover, if sustaining programs are to perform their traditional functions in the American system of broadcasting, they must be broadcast at hours when the public is awake and listening. The time devoted to sustaining programs, accordingly, should be reasonably distributed among the various segments of the broadcast day.

For the reasons set forth on pages 162–171, the Commission, in considering overall program balance, will also take note of network sustaining programs available to but not carried by a station, and of the programs which the station substitutes therefor.

(2) *Local live programs.* The Commission has always placed a marked emphasis, and in some cases perhaps an undue emphasis, on the carrying of local live programs as a standard of public interest. The development of network, transcription, and wire news services is such that no sound public interest appears to be served by continuing to stress local live programs exclusively at the expense of these other categories. Nevertheless, reasonable provision for local self-expression still remains an essential function of a station's operation (pp. 171–178), and will continue to be so regarded by the Commission. In particular, public interest requires that such programs should not be crowded out of the best listening hours.

(3) *Programs devoted to the discussion of public issues.* The crucial need for discussion programs, at the local, national, and international levels alike is universally realized, as set forth on pp. 178–181. Accordingly, the carrying of such programs in reasonable sufficiency, and during good listening hours, is a factor to be considered in any finding of public interest.

(4) *Advertising excesses.* The evidence set forth above (pp. 181–196), warrants the conclusion that some stations during some or many portions of the broadcast day have engaged in advertising excesses which are incompatible with their public responsibilities, and which threaten the good name of broadcasting itself.

As the broadcasting industry itself has insisted, the public interest clearly requires that the amount of time devoted to advertising matter shall bear a reasonable relationship to the amount of time devoted to programs.

Accordingly, in its application forms the Commission will request the applicant to state how much time he proposes to devote to advertising matter in any one hour.

This by itself will not, of course, result in the elimination of some of the particular excesses described on pp. 187–196. This is a matter in which self-regulation by the industry may properly be sought and indeed expected. The Commission has no desire to concern itself with the particular length, content, or irritating qualities of particular commercial plugs.

C. Procedural proposals

In carrying out the above objectives, the Commission proposes to continue substantially unchanged its present basic licensing procedures—namely, the requiring of a written application setting forth the proposed program service of the station, the consideration of that application on its merits, and subsequently the comparison of promise and performance when an application is received for a renewal of the station license. The ends sought can best be achieved, so far as presently appears, by appropriate modification of the particular forms and procedures currently in use and by a generally more careful consideration of renewal applications.

The particular procedural changes proposed are set forth below. They will not be introduced immediately or simultaneously, but rather from time to time as circumstances warrant. Meanwhile, the Commission invites comment from licensees and from the public.

1. Uniform definitions and program logs

The Commission has always recognized certain basic categories of programs —e.g., commercial and sustaining, network, transcribed, recorded, local, live, etc. Such classifications must, under Regulation 3.404, be shown upon the face of the program log required to be kept by each standard broadcast station; and the Commission, like its predecessor, has always required data concerning such program classifications in its application forms.

Examination of logs shows, however, that there is no uniformity or agreement concerning what constitutes a "commercial" program, a "sustaining" program, a "network" program, etc. Accordingly, the Commission will adopt uniform definitions of basic program terms and classes, which are to be used in all presentations to the Commission. The proposed definitions are set forth below.

A *commercial program* (C) is any program the time for which is paid for by a sponsor *or* any program which is interrupted by a spot announcement (as defined below), at intervals of less than 15 minutes. A network program shall be classified as "commercial" if it is commercially sponsored on the network, even though the particular station is not paid for carrying it—unless all commercial announcements have been deleted from the program by the station.

(It will be noted that any program which is *interrupted* by a commercial announcement is classified as a commercial program, even though the purchaser of the interrupting announcement has not also purchased the time preceding and following. The result is to classify so-called "participating" programs as commercial. Without such a rule, a 15-minute program may contain 5 or even more minutes of advertising and still be classified as "sustaining." Under the proposed definition, a program may be classified as "sustaining" although preceded and followed by spot announcements, but if a spot announcement *interrupts* a program, the program must be classified as "commercial.")

A *sustaining* program (S) is any program which is *neither* paid for by a sponsor *nor* interrupted by a spot announcement (as defined below).

A *network* program (N) is any program furnished to the station by a network or another station. Transcribed delayed broadcasts of network programs are classified as "network," not "recorded." Programs are classified as network whether furnished by a nationwide, regional, or special network or by another station.

A *recorded* program (R) is any program which uses phonograph records, electrical transcriptions, or other means of mechanical reproduction in whole or in part—except where the recording is wholly incidental to the program and is limited to background sounds, sound effects, identifying themes, musical "bridges," etc. A program part transcribed or recorded and part live is classified as "recorded" unless the recordings are wholly incidental, as above. A transcribed delayed broadcast of a network program, however, is not classified as "recorded" but as "network."

A *wire* program (W) is any program the text of which is distributed to a number of stations by telegraph, teletype, or similar means, and read in whole or in part by a local announcer. Programs distributed by the wire news services are "wire" programs. A new program which is part wire and in part of local non-syndicated origin is classified as "wire" if more than half of the program is usually devoted to the reading verbatim of the syndicated wire text, but is classified as "live" if more than half is usually devoted to local news or comment.

(The above is a new program category. Programs in this category resemble network and transcribed programs in the respect that they are syndicated to scores or hundreds of stations. They resemble local live programs only in the respect that the words are vocalized by a local voice; the text is not local but syndicated. Such programs have an important role in broadcasting, especially in the dissemination of news. With respect to stations not affiliated with a network, the wire program for timely matter, plus the transcription for less urgent broadcasts affords a close approach to the services of a regular network. The only difficulty is that with respect to program classifications heretofore, the wire program has been merged with the local live program, which it resembles only superficially, preventing a statistical analysis of either. By establishing definitions for "wire commercial" and "wire sustaining," the Commission expects to make possible statistical studies with respect to such programs, and also to make more significant the statistical studies with respect to the "local live commercial" and "local live sustaining" categories.)

A *local live* program (L) is any local program which uses live talent exclusively, whether originating in the station's studios or by remote control. Programs furnished to a station by a network or another station, however, are not classified as "live" but as "network." A program which uses recordings in whole or in part, except in a wholly incidental manner, should not be classified as "live" but as "recorded." Wire programs, as defined above, should likewise not be classified as "live."

A *sustaining-public service announcement* (PSA) is an announcement which is not paid for by a sponsor and which is devoted to a non-profit cause —e.g., war bonds, Red Cross, public health, civic announcements, etc. Promotional, "courtesy," participating announcements, etc. should not be classified as "sustaining public service announcements" but as "spot announcements." War Bond, Red Cross, civic and similar announcements for which the station receives remuneration should not be classified as "sustaining public service announcements" but as "spot announcements."

A *spot announcement* (SA) is any announcement which is neither a sustaining public service announcement (as above defined) nor a station identification announcement (call letters and location). An announcement should be classified as a "spot announcement," whether or not the station receives remuneration, unless it is devoted to a nonprofit cause. Sponsored time signals, sponsored weather announcements, etc. are spot announcements. Unsponsored time signals, weather announcements, etc., are program matter and not classified as announcements. Station identification announcements should *not* be classified as either sustaining public service or spot announcements, if limited to call letters, location, and identification of the licensee and network.

The Commission further proposes to amend Regulation 3.404 to provide in part that the program log shall contain:

An entry classifying each program as "network commercial" (NC); "network sustaining" (NS); "recorded commercial" (RC); "recorded sustaining" (RS); "wire commercial" (WC); "wire sustaining" (WS); "local live commercial" (LC); or "local live sustaining" (LS); and classifying each announcement as "spot announcement" (SA) or "sustaining public service announcement" (PSA).

The adoption of uniform definitions will make possible a fairer comparison of program representations and performance, and better statistical analyses.

2. Segments of the broadcast day

The Commission has always recognized, as has the industry, that different segments of the broadcast day have different characteristics and that different types of programming are therefore permissible. For example, the *NAB Code,* until recently, and many stations permit a greater proportion of advertising during the day than at night. The Commission's Chain Broadcasting Regulations recognize four segments: 8 a.m.–1 p.m., 1 p.m.–6 p.m., 6 p.m.–11 p.m., and all other hours. Most stations make distinctions of hours in their rate cards.

In general, sustaining and live programs have tended to be crowded out of the best listening hours from 6 to 11 p.m., and also in a degree out of the period from 8 a.m. to 6 p.m. At least some stations have improved the ratios shown in reports to the Commission, but not the service rendered the public, by crowding sustaining programs into the hours after 11 p.m. and before dawn when listeners are few and sponsors fewer still. Clearly the responsibility for public service cannot be met by broadcasting public service programs only during such hours. A well-balanced program structure requires balance during the best listening hours.

	8 a.m. 6 p.m.	6 p.m. 11 p.m.	All other hours	Total
Network commercial (NC)				
Network sustaining (NS)				
Recorded commercial (RC)				
Recorded sustaining (RS)				
Wire commercial (WC)				
Wire sustaining (WS)				
Live commercial (LC)				
Live sustaining (LS)				
Total[1]				
No. of Spot Announcements (SA)				
No. of Sustaining Public Service Announcements (PSA)				

[1] Totals should equal full operating time during each segment.

Statistical convenience requires that categories be kept to a minimum. In general, the segments of the broadcast day established in the Chain Broadcasting Regulations appear satisfactory, except that no good purpose appears to be served in connection with program analysis by calculating separately the segments from 8 a.m. to 1 p.m. and from 1 p.m. to 6 p.m. Accordingly, for present purposes it is proposed to merge these segments, so that the broadcast day will be composed of three segments only: 8 a.m.–6 p.m., 6 p.m.–11 p.m., and all other hours.

The categories set forth above, plus the segments herein defined, make possible a standard program log analysis as in the form shown on page 203.

The above schedule will be uniformly utilized in Commission application forms and annual report forms in lieu of the various types of schedules now prevailing. In using it, stations may calculate the length of programs to the nearest five minutes.

3. Annual reports and statistics

For some years, the Commission has called for a statement of the number of hours devoted to various classes of programs each year, in connection with the Annual Financial Reports of broadcast stations and networks. Requiring such figures for an entire year may constitute a considerable accounting burden on the stations, and may therefore impair the quality of the reports. Accordingly, the Commission proposes hereafter to require these data in the Annual Financial Reports only for one week.

To make the proposed week as representative as possible of the year as a whole, the Commission will utilize a procedure heretofore sometimes used by stations in presentations to the Commission. At the end of each year, it will select at random a Monday in January or February, a Tuesday in March, a Wednesday in April, a Thursday in May or June, a Friday in July or August, a Saturday in September or October, and a Sunday in November or December, and will ask for detailed program analyses for these seven days. The particular days chosen will vary from year to year, and will be drawn so as to avoid holidays and other atypical occasions.

The information requested will be in terms of the definitions and time periods set forth above. Statistical summaries and trends will be published annually.

The Commission will also call upon the networks for quarterly statements of the stations carrying and failing to carry network sustaining programs during a sample week in each quarter.

4. Revision of application forms

Since the establishment of the Federal Radio Commission, applicants for new stations have been required to set forth their program plans, and applications have been granted in part on the basis of representations concerning program plans. Applications for renewal of license, assignment of license, transfer of control of licensee corporation, and modification of license have similarly included, in various forms, representations concerning program service rendered or to be rendered. The program service questions now asked on the Commission's application forms are not uniform, and not closely integrated with current Commission policy respecting program service. It is proposed, accordingly, to revise the program service questions on all Commission forms to bring them into line with the policies set forth in this report.

Specifically, applicants for new stations will be required to fill out, as part of Form 301 or Form 319, a showing of their proposed program structure, utilizing the uniform schedule set forth on page 203. Applicants for renewal of license, consent to transfer of assignment, and modification of license will be required to fill out the same uniform schedule, both for a sample week under their previous licenses, and as an indication of their proposed operation if the application in question is granted.

The Commission, of course, recognizes that there is need for flexibility in broadcast operation. An application to the Commission should not be a straitjacket preventing a licensee from rendering an even better service than originally proposed. To provide the necessary flexibility, the information supplied in the uniform schedule will be treated as a responsible estimate rather than a binding pledge. However, attention should be called to the fact that the need for trustworthiness is at least as important with respect to representations concerning program service as with respect to statements concerning financial matters.

Stations will also be asked whether they propose to render a well-balanced program service, or to specialize in programs of a particular type or addressed to a particular audience. If their proposal is for a specialized rather than a balanced program service, a showing will be requested concerning the relative need for such service in the community as compared with the need for an additional station affording a balanced program service. On renewal, stations which have proposed a specialized service will be expected to show the extent to which they have in fact fulfilled their proposals during the period of their license.

Stations affiliated with a network will further be required to list network sustaining programs not carried during a representative week, and the programs carried in place of such programs.

If the Commission is able to determine from an examination of the application that a grant will serve the public interest, it will grant forthwith, as heretofore. If the Commission is unable to make such a determination on the basis of the application it will, as heretofore, designate the application for hearing.

5. Action on renewals

With the above changes in Commission forms and procedures, the Commission will have available in connection with renewal applications, specific data relevant to the finding of public interest required by the statute.

First, it will have available all the data concerning engineering, legal, accounting and other matters, as heretofore.

Second, it will have available a responsible estimate of the overall program structure appropriate for the station in question, as estimated by the licensee himself when making his previous application.

Third, it will have available affirmative representations of the licensee concerning the time to be devoted to sustaining programs, live programs, discussion programs, and advertising matter.

Fourth, it will have available from the annual reports to the Commission data concerning the actual program structure of the station during a sample week in each year under the existing license.

Fifth, it will have available a statement of the overall program structure of the station during a week immediately preceding the filing of the application being considered, and information concerning the carrying of network sustaining programs.

Sixth, it will have available the station's representations concerning program service under the license applied for.

If the Commission is able to determine on the basis of the data thus available that a grant will serve the public interest, it will continue as heretofore, to grant forthwith; otherwise, as heretofore, it will designate the renewal application for hearing.

THE 1960 PROGRAMMING
POLICY STATEMENT

4

Report and Statement of Policy re: Commission
en banc Programming Inquiry
FCC 60-970
July 29, 1960

Issued fourteen years after the "Blue Book," this programming policy statement was both milder in tone and more effectively enforced than its predecessor. This document is the one to which the Federal Communications Commission currently adheres.

On October 3, 1957, the Commission's Network Study Staff submitted its report on network broadcasting. While the scope and breadth of the network study as set forth in Order Number 1 issued November 21, 1955 encompassed a comprehensive study of programming, it soon became apparent that due to factors not within the control of the staff or the committee consideration of programming would be subject to substantial delay making it impracticable that the target dates for the overall report could be met in the program area. The principal reasons were: (a) the refusal of certain program distributors and producers to provide the committee's staff with certain information which necessitated protracted negotiations and ultimately legal action (FCC v. Ralph Cohn, et al., 154 F. Supp. 899); and (b) the fact that a coincidental and collateral investigation into certain practices was instituted by the Department of Justice. Accordingly the network study staff report recommended that the study of programming be continued and completed. The Director of the Network Study in his memorandum of transmittal of the Network Study Report stated:

The staff regrets that it was unable to include in the report its findings and conclusions in its study of programming. It is estimated that more than one-fourth of the time of the staff was expended in this area. However, the extended negotiations and litigation with some non-network program producers relative to supplying financial data necessary to this aspect of the study made it impossible to obtain this information from a sufficient number of these program producers to draw definitive conclusions on all the programming issues. Now that the Commission's right to obtain this information has been sustained, it is the hope of the staff that this aspect of the study will be completed and the results included in a supplement to the report. Unless the study of programming is completed, the benefit of much labor on this subject will have been substantially lost.

As a result on February 26, 1959, the Commission issued its "Order for Investigatory Proceeding," Docket No. 12782. That Order stated that during the course of the Network Study and otherwise, the Commission had obtained information and data regarding the acquisition, production, ownership, distribution, sale, licensing, and exhibition of programs for television broadcasting. Also, that that information and data had been augmented from other sources including hearings before Committees of Congress and from the Department of Justice, and that the Commission had determined that an overall inquiry should be made to determine the facts with respect to the television network program selection process. On November 9, 1959, the proceeding instituted by the Commission's Order of February 26, 1959 was amended and enlarged to include a general inquiry with respect to programming to determine, among other things, whether the general standards heretofore laid down by the Commission for the guidance of broadcast licensees in the selection of programs and other material intended for broadcast are currently adequate; whether the Commission should, by the exercise of its rule-making power, set out more detailed and precise standards for such broadcasters; whether the Commission's present review and consideration in the field of programming and advertising are adequate, under present conditions in the broadcast industry; and whether the Commission's authority under the Communications Act of 1934, as amended, is adequate, or whether legislation should be recommended to Congress.

This inquiry was heard by the Commission *en banc* between December 7, 1959, and February 1, 1960, and consumed 19 days in actual hearings. Over 90 witnesses testified relative to the problems involved, made suggestions and otherwise contributed from their background and experience to the solution of these problems. Several additional statements were submitted. The record in the *en banc* portion of the inquiry consisted of 3,775 pages of transcript plus 1,000 pages of exhibits. The Interim Report of the staff of the Office of Network Study was submitted to the Commission for consideration on June 15, 1960.

The Commission will make every effort to expedite its consideration of the entire docket proceeding and will take such definitive action as the Commission determines to be warranted. However, the Commission feels that a general statement of policy responsive to the issues in the *en banc* inquiry is warranted at this time.

Prior to the *en banc* hearing, the Commission had made its position clear that, in fulfilling its obligation to operate in the public interest, a broadcast station is expected to exercise reasonable care and prudence with respect to its broadcast material in order to assure that no matter is broadcast which will deceive or mislead the public. In view of the extent of the problem existing with respect to a number of licensees involving such practices as deceptive quiz shows and payola which had become apparent, the Commission concluded that certain proposed amendments to our Rules as well as proposed legislation would provide a basis for substantial improvements. Accordingly, on February 5, 1960, we adopted a Notice of Proposed Rule Making to deal with fixed quiz and other non-bona fide contest programs involving intellectual skill. These rules would prohibit the broadcasting of such programming unless accompanied by an announcement which would in all cases describe the nature of the program in a manner to sufficiently apprise the audience that the events in question are not in fact spontaneous or actual measures of knowledge or intellectual skill. Announcements would be made at the beginning and end of each program. Moreover, the proposed rules would require a station if it obtained such a program from networks, to be assured similarly that the network program has an accompanying announcement of this nature. This, we believe, would go a long way toward preventing any recurrence of problems such as those encountered in the recent quiz show programs.

We have also felt that this sort of conduct should be prohibited by statute. Accordingly, we suggested legislation designed to make it a crime for anyone to wilfully and knowingly participate or cause another to participate in or cause to be broadcast a program of intellectual skill or knowledge where the outcome thereof is prearranged or predetermined. Without the above-described amendment, the Commission's regulatory authority is limited to its licensing function. The Commission cannot reach networks directly or advertisers, producers, sponsors, and others who, in one capacity or another, are associated with the presentation of radio and television programs which may deceive the listening or viewing public. It is our view that this proposed legislation will help to assure that every contest of intellectual skill or knowledge that is broadcast will be in fact a bona fide contest. Under this proposal, all those persons responsible in any way for the broadcast of a deceptive program of this type would be penalized. Because of the far reaching effects of radio and television, we believe such sanctions to be desirable.

The Commission proposed on February 5, 1960 that a new section be added to the Commission's rules which would require the licensee of radio broadcast stations to adopt appropriate procedures to prevent the practice of payola amongst his employees. Here again the standard of due diligence would have to be met by the licensee. We have also approved on February 11 the language of proposed legislation which would impose criminal penalties for failure to announce sponsored programs, such as payola and others, involving hidden payments or other considerations. This proposal looks toward amending the United States Code to provide fines up to $5,000 or imprisonment up to one year, or both, for violators. It would prohibit the payment to any person or the receipt of payment by any person for the purpose of having as a part of the broadcast program any material on either a radio or television show unless an announcement is made as a part of the program that such material has been paid for or furnished. The Commission now has no direct jurisdiction over the employees of a broadcast station with respect to this type of activity. The imposition of a criminal penalty appears to us to be an effective manner for dealing with this practice. In addition, the Commission has made related legislative proposals with respect to fines, temporary suspension of licenses, and temporary restraining orders.

In view of our mutual interest with the Federal Trade Commission and in order to avoid duplication of effort, we have arrived at an arrangement whereby any information obtained by the FCC which might be of interest to FTC will be called to that Commission's attention by our staff. Similarly, FTC will advise our Commission of any information or data which it acquires in the course of its investigations which might be pertinent to matters under jurisdiction of the FCC. This is an understanding supplemental to earlier liaison arrangements between FCC and FTC.

Certain legislative proposals recently made by the Commission as related to the instant inquiry have been mentioned. It is appropriate now to consider whether the statutory authority of the Commission with respect to programming and program practices is, in other respects, adequate.

In considering the extent of the Commission's authority in the area of programming it is essential first to examine the limitations imposed upon it by the First Amendment to the Constitution and Section 326 of the Communications Act.

The First Amendment to the United States Constitution reads as follows:

Congress shall make no law respecting an establishment of religion or prohibiting the free exercise thereof; or abridging the freedom of speech, or of the press; or the right of the people peaceably to assemble, and to petition the Government for a redress of grievances.

Section 326 of the Communications Act of 1934, as amended, provides that:

Nothing in this chapter shall be understood or construed to give the Commission the power of censorship over the radio communications or signals transmitted by any radio station, and no regulation or condition shall be promulgated or fixed by the Commission which shall interfere with the right of free speech by means of radio communication.

The communication of ideas by means of radio and television is a form of expression entitled to protection against abridgement by the First Amendment to the Constitution. In *United States* v. *Paramount Pictures,* 334 U.S. 131, 166 (1948) the Supreme Court stated:

We have no doubt that moving pictures, like newspapers and radio are included in the press, whose freedom is guaranteed by the First Amendment.

As recently as 1954 in *Superior Films* v. *Department of Education,* 346 U.S. 587, Justice Douglas in a concurring opinion stated:

Motion pictures are, of course, a different medium of expression than the radio, the stage, the novel or the magazine. But the First Amendment draws no distinction between the various methods of communicating ideas.

Moreover, the free speech protection of the First Amendment is not confined solely to the exposition of ideas nor is it required that the subject matter of the communication be possessed of some value to society. In *Winters* v. *New York,* 333 U.S. 507, 510 (1948) the Supreme Court reversed a conviction based upon a violation of an ordinance of the City of New York which made it punishable to distribute printed matter devoted to the publication of accounts of criminal deeds and pictures of bloodshed, lust or crime. In this connection the Court said:

We do not accede to appellee's suggestion that the constitutional protection for a free press applies only to the exposition of ideas. The line between the informing and the entertaining is too elusive for the protection of that basic right. . . . Though we can see nothing of any possible value to society in these magazines, they are as much entitled to the protection of free speech as the best of literature.

Notwithstanding the foregoing authorities, the right to the use of the airwaves is conditioned upon the issuance of a license under a statutory scheme established by Congress in the Communications Act in the proper exercise of its power over commerce.[1] The question therefore arises as to whether because of the characteristics peculiar to broadcasting which justifies the government in regulating its operation through a licensing system, there exists the basis for a distinction as regards other media of mass communication with respect to application of the free speech provisions of the First Amendment? In other words, does it follow that because one may not engage in broadcasting without first obtaining a license, the terms thereof may be so framed as to unreasonably abridge the free speech protection of the First Amendment?

We recognize that the broadcasting medium presents problems peculiar to itself which are not necessarily subject to the same rules governing other media of communication. As we stated in our Petition in *Grove Press, Inc.* and *Readers Subscription, Inc.* v. *Robert K. Christenberry* (Case No. 25,861) filed in the U. S. Court of Appeals for the Second Circuit,

radio and TV programs enter the home and are readily available not only to the average normal adult but also to children and to the emotionally immature. . . . Thus, for example, while a nudist magazine may be within the protection

[1] *NBC* v. *United States,* 319 U. S. 190 (1943).

of the First Amendment . . . the televising of nudes might well raise a serious question of programming contrary to 18 U.S.C. 1464. . . . Similarly, regardless of whether the "four-letter words" and sexual description, set forth in "Lady Chatterley's Lover," (when considered in the context of the whole book) make the book obscene for mailability purposes, the utterance of such words or the depiction of such sexual activity on radio or TV would raise similar public interest and Section 1464 questions.

Nevertheless it is essential to keep in mind that "the basic principles of freedom of speech and the press like the First Amendment's command do not vary."[2]

Although the Commission must determine whether the total program service of broadcasters is reasonably responsive to the interests and needs of the public they serve, it may not condition the grant, denial or revocation of a broadcast license upon its own subjective determination of what is or is not a good program. To do so would "lay a forbidden burden upon the exercise of liberty protected by the Constitution."[3] The Chairman of the Commission during the course of his testimony recently given before the Senate Independent Offices Subcommittee of the Committee on Appropriations expressed the point as follows:

> Mr. Ford. When it comes to questions of taste, unles it is downright profanity or obscenity, I do not think that the Commission has any part in it.
> I don't see how we could possibly go out and say this program is good and that program is bad. That would be a direct violation of the law.[4]

In a similar vein Mr. Whitney North Seymour, President-elect of the American Bar Association, stated during the course of this proceeding that while the Commission may inquire of licensees what they have done to determine the needs of the community they propose to serve, the Commission may not impose upon them its private notions of what the public ought to hear.[5]

Nevertheless, several witnesses in this proceeding have advanced persuasive arguments urging us to require licensees to present specific types of programs on the theory that such action would enhance freedom of expression rather than tend to abridge it. With respect to this proposition we are constrained to point out that the First Amendment forbids governmental interference asserted in aid of free speech, as well as governmental action repressive of it. The protection against abridgement of freedom of speech and press flatly forbids governmental interference, benign or otherwise. The First Amendment "while regarding freedom in religion, in speech and printing and in assembling and petitioning the government for redress of griev-

---

[2] *Burstyn* v. *Wilson* 343 U.S. 495, 503 (1952).

[3] *Cantwell* v. *Connecticut,* 310 U. S. 926, 307 [*sic*].

[4] Hearings before the Subcommittee of the Committee on Appropriations, United States Senate, 86th Congress, 2nd Session on H.R. 11776 at page 775.

[5] Memorandum of Mr. Whitney North Seymour, Special Council to the National Association of Broadcasters at page 7.

ances as fundamental and precious to all, seeks only to forbid that Congress should meddle therein." (*Powe* v. *United States,* 109 F. 2nd 147)

As recently as 1959 in *Farmers Educational and Cooperative Union of America* v. *WDAY, Inc.* 360 U.S. 525, the Supreme Court succinctly stated:

. . . expressly applying this country's tradition of free expression to the field of radio broadcasting, Congress has from the first emphatically forbidden the Commission to exercise any power of censorship over radio communication.

An examination of the foregoing authorities serves to explain why the day-to-day operation of a broadcast station is primarily the responsibility of the individual station licensee. Indeed, Congress provided in Section 3(h) of the Communications Act that a person engaged in radio broadcasting shall not be deemed a common carrier. Hence, the Commission in administering the Act and the courts in interpreting it have consistently maintained that responsibility for the selection and presentation of broadcast material ultimately devolves upon the individual station licensee, and that the fulfillment of the public interest requires the free exercise of his independent judgment. Accordingly, the Communications Act "does not essay to regulate the business of the licensee. The Commission is given no supervisory control over programs, of business management or of policy . . . The Congress intended to leave competition in the business of broadcasting where it found it . . ."[6] The regulatory responsibility of the Commission in the broadcast field essentially involves the maintenance of a balance between the preservation of a free competitive broadcast system, on the one hand, and the reasonable restriction of that freedom inherent in the public interest standard provided in the Communications Act, on the other.

In addition, there appears a second problem quite unrelated to the question of censorship that would enter into the Commission's assumption of supervision over program content. The Commission's role as a practical matter, let alone a legal matter, cannot be one of program dictation or program supervision. In this connection we think the words of Justice Douglas are particularly appropriate.

The music selected by one bureaucrat may be as offensive to some as it is soothing to others. The news commentator chosen to report on the events of the day may give overtones to the news that pleases the bureaucrat but which rile the . . . audience. The political philosophy which one radio sponsor exudes may be thought by the official who makes up the programs as the best for the welfare of the people. But the man who listens to it . . . may think it marks the destruction of the Republic. . . . Today it is a business enterprise working out a radio program under the auspices of government. Tomorrow it may be a dominant, political or religious group. . . . Once a man is forced to submit to one type of program, he can be forced to submit to another. It may

[6] *FCC* v. *Sanders Brothers,* 309 U.S. 470 (1940).

be but a short step from a cultural program to a political program. . . . The strength of our system is in the dignity, resourcefulness and the intelligence of our people. Our confidence is in their ability to make the wisest choice. That system cannot flourish if regimentation takes hold.[7]

Having discussed the limitations upon the Commission in the consideration of programming, there remains for discussion the exceptions to those limitations and the area of affirmative responsibility which the Commission may appropriately exercise under its statutory obligation to find that the public interest, convenience and necessity will be served by the granting of a license to broadcast.

In view of the fact that a broadcaster is required to program his station in the public interest, convenience and necessity, it follows despite the limitations of the First Amendment and Section 326 of the Act, that his freedom to program is not absolute. The Commission does not conceive that it is barred by the Constitution or by statute from exercising any responsibility with respect to programming. It does conceive that the manner or extent of the exercise of such responsibility can introduce constitutional or statutory questions. It readily concedes that it is precluded from examining a program for taste or content, unless the recognized exceptions to censorship apply: for example, obscenity, profanity, indecency, programs inciting to riots, programs designed or inducing toward the commission of crime, lotteries, etc. These exceptions, in part, are written into the United States Code and, in part, are recognized in judicial decision. See Sections 1304, 1343, and 1464 of Title 18 of the United States Code (lotteries; fraud by radio; utterance of obscene, indecent or profane language by radio). It must be added that such traditional or legislative exceptions to a strict application of the freedom of speech requirements of the United States Constitution may very well also convey wider scope in judicial interpretation as applied to licensed radio than they have had or would have as applied to other communications media. The Commission's petition in the *Grove* case, *supra*, urged the court not unnecessarily to refer to broadcasting, in its opinion, as had the District Court. Such reference subsequently was not made though it must be pointed out there is no evidence that the motion made by the FCC was a contributing factor. It must nonetheless be observed that this Commission conscientiously believes that it should make no policy or take any action which would violate the letter or the spirit of the censorship prohibitions of Section 326 of the Communications Act.

As stated by the Supreme Court of the United States in *Joseph Burstyne, Inc.* v. *Wilson, supra:*

. . . Nor does it follow that motion pictures are necessarily subject to the precise rule governing any other particular method of expression. Each method tends to present its own peculiar problem. But the basic principles of freedom

---

7 *Public Utilities Commission* v. *Pollak*, 343 U. S. 451, 468, Dissenting Opinion.

of speech and the press, like the First Amendment's command, do not vary. Those principles, as they have frequently been enunciated by this Court, make freedom of expression the rule.

A review of the Communications Act as a whole clearly reveals that the foundation of the Commission's authority rests upon the public interest, convenience and necessity.[8] The Commission may not grant, modify or renew a broadcast station license without finding that the operation of such station is in the public interest. Thus, faithful discharge of its statutory responsibilities is absolutely necessary in connection with the implacable requirement that the Commission approve no such application for license unless it finds that "public interest, convenience, and necessity would be served." While the public interest standard does not provide a blueprint of all of the situations to which it may apply, it does contain a sufficiently precise definition of authority so as to enable the Commission to properly deal with the many and varied occasions which may give rise to its application. A significant element of the public interest is the broadcaster's service to the community. In the case of *NBC* v. *United States,* 319 U. S. 190, the Supreme Court described this aspect of the public interest as follows:

An important element of public interest and convenience affecting the issue of a license is the ability of the licensee to render the best practicable service to the community reached by broadcasts. . . . The Commission's licensing function cannot be discharged, therefore, merely by finding that there are no technological objections to the granting of a license. If the criterion of "public interest" were limited to such matters, how could the Commission choose between two applicants for the same facilities, each of whom is financially and technically qualified to operate a station? Since the very inception of federal regulation by radio, comparative considerations as to the services to be rendered have governed the application of the standard of "public interest, convenience, or necessity."

Moreover, apart from this broad standard which we will further discuss in a moment, there are certain other statutory indications.

It is generally recognized that programming is of the essence of radio service. Section 307(b) of the Communications Act requires the Commission to "make such distribution of licenses . . . among the several States and communities as to provide a fair, efficient, and equitable distribution of radio service to each of the same." Under this section the Commission has consistently licensed stations with the end objective of either providing new or additional programming service *to* a community, area or state, or of providing a new or additional "outlet" for broadcasting *from* a community, area, or state. Implicit in the former alternative is increased radio reception; implicit in the latter alternative is increased radio transmission and, in this connection, appropriate attention to local live programming is required.

[8] §307(d), 308, 309, *inter alia.*

Formerly by reason of administrative policy, and since September 14, 1959, by necessary implication from the amended language of Section 315 of the Communications Act, the Commission has had the responsibility for determining whether licensees "afford reasonable opportunity for the discussion of conflicting views on issues of public importance." This responsibility usually is of the generic kind and thus, in the absence of unusual circumstances, is not exercised with regard to particular situations but rather in terms of operating policies of stations as viewed over a reasonable period of time. This, in the past, has meant a review, usually in terms of filed complaints, in connection with the applications made each three year period for renewal of station licenses. However, that has been a practice largely traceable to workload necessities, and therefore not so limited by law. Indeed the Commission recently has expressed its views to the Congress that it would be desirable to exercise a greater discretion with respect to the length of licensing periods within the maximum three year license period provided by Section 307(d). It has also initiated rulemaking to this end.

The foundation of the American system of broadcasting was laid in the Radio Act of 1927 when Congress placed the basic responsibility for all matter broadcast to the public at the grass roots level in the hands of the station licensee. That obligation was carried forward into the Communications Act of 1934 and remains unaltered and undivided. The licensee, is, in effect, a "trustee" in the sense that his license to operate his station imposes upon him a non-delegable duty to serve the public interest in the community he had chosen to represent as a broadcaster.

Great confidence and trust are placed in the citizens who have qualified as broadcasters. The primary duty and privilege to select the material to be broadcast to his audience and the operation of his component of this powerful medium of communication is left in his hands. As was stated by the Chairman in behalf of this Commission in recent testimony before a Congressional Committee:[9]

Thus far Congress has not imposed by law an affirmative programming requirement on broadcast licenses. Rather, it has heretofore given licensees a broad discretion in the selection of programs. In recognition of this principle, Congress provided in section 3(h) of the Communications Act that a person engaged in radio broadcasting shall not be deemed a common carrier. To this end the Commission in administering the Act and the courts in interpreting it have consistently maintained that responsibility for the selection and presentation of broadcast material ultimately devolves upon the individual station licensee, and that the fulfillment of such responsibility requires the free exercise of his independent judgment.

[9] Testimony of Frederick W. Ford, May 16, 1960, before the Subcommittee on Communications of the Committee on Interstate & Foreign Commerce, United States Senate.

As indicated by former President Hoover, then Secretary of Commerce, in the Radio Conference of 1922–25:

The dominant element for consideration in the radio field is, and always will be, the great body of the listening public, millions in number, country wide in distribution. There is no proper line of conflict between the broadcaster and the listener, nor would I attempt to array one against the other. Their interests are mutual, for without the one the other could not exist.

There have been few developments in industrial history to equal the speed and efficiency with which genius and capital have joined to meet radio needs. The great majority of station owners today recognize the burden of service and gladly assume it. Whatever other motive may exist for broadcasting, the pleasing of the listener is always the primary purpose . . .

The greatest public interest must be the deciding factor. I presume that few will dissent as to the correctness of this principle, for all will agree that public good must ever balance private desire; but its acceptance leads to important and far-reaching practical effects, as to which there may not be the same unanimity, but from which, nevertheless, there is no logical escape.

The confines of the licensee's duty are set by the general standard "the public interest, convenience or necessity."[10] The initial and principal execution of that standard, in terms of the area he is licensed to serve, is the obligation of the licensee. The principal ingredient of such obligation consists of a diligent, positive and continuing effort by the licensee to discover and fulfill the tastes, needs and desires of his service area. If he has accomplished this, he has met his public responsibility. It is the duty of the Commission, in the first instance, to select persons as licensees who meet the qualifications laid down in the Act, and on a continuing basis to review the operations of such licensees from time to time to provide reasonable assurance to the public that the broadcast service it receives is such as its direct and justifiable interest requires.

Historically it is interesting to note that in its review of station performance the Federal Radio Commission sought to extract the general principles of broadcast service which should (1) guide the licensee in his determination of the public interest and (2) be employed by the Commission as an "index" or general frame of reference in evaluating the licensee's discharge of his public duty. The Commission attempted no precise definition of the components of the public interest but left the discernment of its limit to the practical operation of broadcast regulation. It required existing stations to report the types of service which had been provided and called on the public to express its views and preferences as to programs and other broadcast services. It sought information from as many sources as were available in its quest of a fair and equitable basis for the selection of those

[10] Cf. Communications Act of 1934, as amended, *inter alia,* Secs. 307, 309.

who might wish to become licensees and the supervision of those who already engaged in broadcasting.

The spirit in which the Radio Commission approached its unprecedented task was to seek to chart a course between the need of arriving at a workable concept of the public interest in station operation, on the one hand, and the prohibition laid on it by the First Amendment to the Constitution of the United States and by Congress in Section 29 of the Federal Radio Act against censorship and interference with free speech, on the other. The Standards or guidelines which evolved from that process, in their essentials, were adopted by the Federal Communications Commission and have remained as the basis for evaluation of broadcast service. They have in the main, been incorporated into various codes and manuals of network and station operation.

It is emphasized, that these standards or guidelines should in no sense constitute a rigid mold for station performance, nor should they be considered as a Commission formula for broadcast service in the public interest. Rather, they should be considered as indicia of the types and areas of service which, on the basis of experience, have usually been accepted by the broadcasters as more or less included in the practical definition of community needs and interests.

Broadcasting licensees must assume responsibility for all material which is broadcast through their facilities. This includes all programs and advertising material which they present to the public. With respect to advertising material the licensee has the additional responsibility to take all reasonable measures to eliminate any false, misleading, or deceptive matter and to avoid abuses with respect to the total amount of time devoted to advertising continuity as well as the frequency with which regular programs are interrupted for advertising messages. This duty is personal to the licensee and may not be delegated. He is obligated to bring his positive responsibility affirmatively to bear upon all who have a hand in providing broadcast matter for transmission through his facilities so as to assure the discharge of his duty to provide acceptable program schedule consonant with operating in the public interest in his community. The broadcaster is obligated to make a positive, diligent and continuing effort, in good faith, to determine the tastes, needs and desires of the public in his community and to provide programming to meet those needs and interests. This again, is a duty personal to the licensee and may not be avoided by delegation of the responsibility to others.

Although the individual station licensee continues to bear legal responsibility for all matter broadcast over his facilities, the structure of broadcasting, as developed in practical operation, is such—especially in television—that, in reality, the station licensee has little part in the creation, production, selection, and control of network program offerings. Licensees place "practical reliance" on networks for the selection and supervision of network programs which, of course, are the principal broadcast fare of the vast majority of television stations throughout the country.[11]

In the fulfillment of his obligation the broadcaster should consider the tastes, needs and desires of the public he is licensed to serve in developing his programming and should exercise conscientious efforts not only to ascertain them but also to carry them out as well as he reasonably can. He should reasonably attempt to meet all such needs and interests on an equitable basis. Particular areas of interest and types of appropriate service may, of course, differ from community to community, and from time to time. However, the Commission does expect its broadcast licensees to take the necessary steps to inform themselves of the real needs and interests of the areas they serve and to provide programming which in fact constitutes a diligent effort, in good faith, to provide for those needs and interests.

The major elements usually necessary to meet the public interest, needs and desires of the community in which the station is located as developed by the industry, and recognized by the Commission, have included: (1) Opportunity for Local Self-Expression, (2) The Development and Use of Local Talent, (3) Programs for Children, (4) Religious Programs, (5) Educational Programs, (6) Public Affairs Programs, (7) Editorialization by Licensees, (8) Political Broadcasts, (9) Agricultural Programs, (10) News Programs, (11) Weather and Market Reports, (12) Sports Programs, (13) Service to Minority Groups, (14) Entertainment Programming.

The elements set out above are neither all-embracing nor constant. We re-emphasize that they do not serve and have never been intended as a rigid mold or fixed formula for station operations. The ascertainment of the needed elements of the broadcast matter to be provided by a particular licensee for the audience he is obligated to serve remains primarily the function of the licensee. His honest and prudent judgments will be accorded great weight by the Commission. Indeed, any other course would tend to substitute the judgment of the Commission for that of the licensee.

The programs provided first by "chains" of stations and then by networks have always been recognized by this Commission as of great value to the station licensee in providing a well-rounded community service. The importance of network programs need not be re-emphasized as they have constituted an integral part of the well-rounded program service provided by the broadcast business in most communities.

Our own observations and the testimony in this inquiry have persuaded us that there is no public interest basis for distinguishing between sustaining and commercially sponsored programs in evaluating station performance. However, this does not relieve the station from responsibility for retaining the flexibility to accommodate public needs.

---

[11] The Commission, in recognition of this problem as it affects the licensees, has recently recommended to the Congress enactment of legislation providing for direct regulation of networks in certain respects.

Sponsorship of public affairs, and other similar programs may very well encourage broadcasters to greater efforts in these vital areas. This is borne out by statements made in this proceeding in which it was pointed out that under modern conditions sponsorship fosters rather than diminishes the availability of important public affairs and "cultural" broadcast programming. There is some convincing evidence, for instance, that at the network level there is a direct relation between commercial sponsorship and "clearance" of public affairs and other "cultural" programs. Agency executives have testified that there is unused advertising support for public affairs type programming. The networks and some stations have scheduled these types of programs during "prime time."

The Communication Act[12] provides that the Commission may grant construction permits and station licenses, or modifications or renewals thereof, "only upon written application" setting forth the information required by the Act and the Commission's Rules and Regulations. If, upon examination of any such application, the Commission shall find the public interest, convenience, and necessity would be served by the granting thereof, it shall grant said application. If it does not so find, it shall so advise the applicant and other known parties in interest of all objections to the application and the applicant shall then be given an opportunity to supply additional information. If the Commission cannot then make the necessary finding, the application is designated for hearing and the applicant bears the burden of providing proof of the public interest.

During our hearings there seemed to be some misunderstanding as to the nature and use of the "statistical" data regarding programming and advertising required by our application forms. We wish to stress that no one may be summarily judged as to the service he has performed on the basis of the information contained in his application. As we said long ago:

> It should be emphasized that the statistical data before the Commission constitute an index only of the manner of operation of the stations and are not considered by the Commission as conclusive of the over-all operation of the stations in question.
>
> Licensees will have an opportunity to show the nature of their program service and to introduce other relevant evidence which would demonstrate that in actual operation the program service of the station is, in fact, a well rounded program service and is in conformity with the promises and representations previously made in prior applications to the Commission.[13]

As we have said above, the principal ingredient of the licensee's obligation to operate his station in the public interest is the diligent, positive, and continuing effort by the licensee to discover and fulfill the tastes, needs, and desires of his community or service area, for broadcast service.

---

[12] Section 308(a).
[13] Public Notice (98501), Sept. 20, 1946, "Status of Standard Broadcast Applications."

To enable the Commission in its licensing functions to make the necessary public interest finding, we intend to revise PART IV of our application forms to require a statement by the applicant, whether for new facilities, renewal or modification, as to: (1) the measures he has taken and the effort he has made to determine the tastes, needs and desires of his community or service area, and (2) the manner in which he proposes to meet those needs and desires.

Thus we do not intend to guide the licensee along the path of programming; on the contrary the licensee must find his own path with the guidance of those whom his signal is to serve. We will thus steer clear of the bans of censorship without disregarding the public's vital interest. What we propose will not be served by pre-planned program format submissions accompanied by complimentary references from local citizens. What we propose is documented program submissions prepared as the result of assiduous planning and consultation covering two main areas: first, a canvass of the listening public who will receive the signal and who constitute a definite public interest figure; second, consultation with leaders in community life—public officials, educators, religious, the entertainment media, agriculture, business, labor—professional and eleemosynary organizations, and others who bespeak the interests which make up the community.

By the care spent in obtaining and reflecting the views thus obtained, which clearly cannot be accepted without attention to the business judgment of the licensee if his station is to be an operating success, will the standard of programming in the public interest be best fulfilled. This would not ordinarily be the case if program formats have been decided upon by the licensee before he undertakes his planning and consultation, for the result would show little stimulation on the part of the two local groups above referenced. And it is the composite of their contributive planning, led and sifted by the expert judgment of the licensee, which will assure to the station the appropriate attention to the public interest which will permit the Commission to find that a license may issue. By his narrative development, in his application, of the planning, consulting, shaping, revising, creating, discarding and evaluation of programming thus conceived or discussed, the licensee discharges the public interest facet of his business calling without Government dictation or supervision and permits the Commission to discharge its responsibility to the public without invasion of spheres of freedom properly denied to it. By the practicality and specificity of his narrative the licensee facilitates the application of expert judgment by the Commission. Thus, if a particular kind of educational program could not be feasibly assisted (by funds or service) by educators for more than a few time periods, it would be idle for program composition to place it in weekly focus. Private ingenuity and educational interest should look further, toward implemental suggestions of practical yet constructive value. The broadcaster's license is not intended to convert his business into "an instrumentality of the federal government";[14] neither, on the other hand, may he ignore the public interest which his application for a license should thus define and his operations thereafter reasonably observe.

Numbers of suggestions were made during the *en banc* hearings concerning possible uses by the Commission of codes of broadcast practices adopted by segments of the industry as part of a process of self-regulation. While the Commission has not endorsed any specific code of broadcast practices, we consider the efforts of the industry to maintain high standards of conduct to be highly commendable and urge that the industry persevere in these efforts.

The Commission recognizes that submissions, by applicants, concerning their past and future programming policies and performance provide one important basis for deciding whether—insofar as broadcast services are concerned—we may properly make the public interest finding requisite to the grant of an application for a standard FM or television broadcast station. The particular manner in which applicants are required to depict their proposed or past broadcast policies and services (including the broadcasting of commercial announcements) may therefore, have significant bearing upon the Commission's ability to discharge its statutory duties in the matter. Conscious of the importance of reporting requirements, the Commission on November 24, 1958 initiated proceedings (Docket No. 12673) to consider revisions to the rules prescribing the form and content of reports on broadcast programming.

Aided by numerous helpful suggestions offered by witnesses in the recent *en banc* hearings on broadcast programming, the Commission is at present engaged in a thorough study of this subject. Upon completion of that study we will announce, for comment by all interested parties, such further revisions to the present reporting requirements as we think will best conduce to an awareness, by broadcasters, of their responsibilities to the public and to effective, efficient processing, by the Commission, of applications for broadcast licenses and renewals.

To this end, we will initiate further rule making on the subject at the earliest practicable date.

Separate statement of Commissioner Hyde

I believe that the Commission's "Interim Report and Statement of Policy" in Docket No. 12782 misses the central point of the hearing conducted by the Commission en banc, December 7, 1959, to February 1, 1960.

It reiterates the legal position which was taken by the Federal Radio Commission in 1927, and which has been adhered to by the Federal Communications Commission since it was organized in 1934. This viewpoint was

---

14 "The defendant is not an instrumentality of the federal government but a privately owned corporation." *McIntire* v. *Wm. Penn Broadcasting Co.,* 151 F. 2d 597, 600.

accepted by the executives of the leading networks and by most other units of the broadcasting industry as well as the National Association of Broadcasters. The main concern requiring a fresh approach is what to do in the light of the law and the matters presented by many witnesses in the hearings. This, I understand, is to be the subject of a rule-making proceeding still to be initiated. I urged the preparation of an appropriate rule-making notice prior to the preparation of the instant statement.

I also disagree with the decision of the Commission to release the document captioned "Interim Report by the Office of Network Study, Responsibility for Broadcast Matter, Docket No. 12782." Since it deals in part with a hearing in which the Commission itself sat en banc, I feel that it does not have the character of a separate staff-study type of document, and that its release with the Commission policy statement will create confusion. Moreover, a substantial portion of the document is concerned with matter still under investigation process in Docket 12872. I think issuance of comment on these matters under the circumstances is premature and inappropriate.

5 THE SUBURBAN CASE

Patrick Henry et al., d/b as Suburban Broadcasters *v.*
Federal Communications Commission*
302 F.2d 191 (D.C. Cir.)
March 29, 1962

> *This Court of Appeals decision affirmed the FCC's right to apply
> the standards contained in its* 1960 Programming Policy Statement
> *when considering applications for permits to construct new stations.
> The Supreme Court declined review of the case (371 U.S. 821
> (1962)). The appellate court's ruling relies heavily on the Supreme
> Court's 1943* Network *decision, contained in Part IV.*

BAZELON, Circuit Judge.

Appellants, doing business as Suburban Broadcasters, filed the sole application for a permit to construct the first commercial F.M. station in Elizabeth, New Jersey.[1] Although the Federal Communications Commission found Suburban legally, technically and financially qualified, it designated the application for hearing on the issues raised by the claim of Metropolitan Broadcasting Company, the licensee of WNEW in New York, that a grant would result in objectionable interference. At Metropolitan's request, the Commission subsequently added another issue for hearing:

> To determine whether the program proposals of Suburban Broadcasters are designed to and would be expected to serve the needs of the proposed service area.

Upon hearing, the trial examiner found for Suburban on both issues. The Commission affirmed on the issue of objectionable interference but reversed on the issue relating to the program proposals and denied the application. Suburban appeals.

These are the pertinent facts disclosed by the record. None of Subur-

---

* Opinion taken with permission from Vol. 302, *Federal Reporter,* second series.
[1] The Communications Act of 1934 § 319, 48 Stat. 1089, 47 U.S.C.A. § 319 (1958), forbids the Commission to license a station unless its construction has previously been authorized by a permit issued pursuant to §§ 308 and 309, 48 Stat. 1084–1085 (1934), 47 U.S.C.A. §§ 308, 309 (1958).

ban's principals were residents of Elizabeth. They made no inquiry into the characteristics or programming needs of that community and offered no evidence thereon. Suburban's program proposals were identical with those submitted in its application for an F.M. facility in Berwyn, Illinois, and in the application of two of its principals for an F.M. facility in Alameda, California.[2]

Although the trial examiner resolved the program planning issue in favor of Suburban, he noted that its approach might be characterized as "cavalier" or little more than a "quick shrug." He also referred to the "Program Policy Statement," released by the Commission July 29, 1960, to the effect that the broadcaster's programming responsibility is measured by the statutory standard of "public interest, convenience or necessity," and that in meeting such standard the broadcaster is "obligated to make a positive, diligent and continuing effort, in good faith, to determine the tastes, needs and desires of the public in his community and to provide programming to meet those needs and interests." But the examiner stated that these standards were intended for existing licensees, rather than applicants for new stations, and were therefore inapplicable here.

In reversing the examiner, the Commission (with one Commissioner absent and two dissenting) stated:

> We agree [with the examiner] that Elizabeth has a presumptive need for a first local FM transmission service. We have generally presumed that an applicant for such a community would satisfy its programming needs, assuming that the applicant had at least a rudimentary knowledge of such needs. However, we cannot indulge in that presumption where the validity of the underlying assumption is questioned, a specific issue is added, and it is demonstrated that the applicant has taken no steps to familiarize himself with the community or its needs. It is not sufficient that the applicant will bring a first transmission service to the community—it must in fact provide a first local outlet for community self-expression. Communities may differ, and so may their needs; an applicant has the responsibility of ascertaining his community's needs and of programming to meet those needs. As found by the Examiner, Suburban's principals made no inquiry into the characteristics of Elizabeth or its particular programming needs. The instant program proposals were drawn up on the basis of the principals' apparent belief—unsubstantiated by inquiry, insofar as the record shows—that Elizabeth's needs duplicated those of Alameda, California, and Berwyn, Illinois, or, in the words of the Examiner, could "be served in the same manner that such 'needs' are served by FM broadcasters generally."

The Commission found that the "program proposals were not 'designed' to serve the needs of Elizabeth"; and that it could not determine whether the proposals "would be expected" to serve these needs, since no evidence of these needs was offered. "In essence," said the Commission, "we

[2] The application for the Berwyn facility was dismissed; the one for Alameda was granted.

are asked to grant an application prepared by individuals totally without knowledge of the area they seek to serve. We feel the public deserves something more in the way of preparation for the responsibilities sought by applicant than was demonstrated on this record." Accordingly, the Commission held that "it cannot be concluded that a grant . . . would serve the public interest, convenience and necessity."

Appellants contend that the statutory licensing scheme requires a grant where, as here, it is established that the sole applicants for a frequency are legally, financially and technically qualified. This view reflects an arbitrarily narrow understanding of the statutory words "public convenience, interest, or necessity."[3] It leaves no room for Commission consideration of matters relating to programming. Moreover, appellants urge that consideration of such matters is precluded by the statute's proscription of censorship[4] and the constitutional guarantee of free speech.

We think these broad contentions are beside the narrow point at issue upon this record. It may be that a licensee must have freedom to broadcast light opera even if the community likes rock and roll music, although that question is not uncomplicated. Even more complicated is the question whether he may feed a diet of rock and roll music to a community which hungers for opera. These are questions, however, that we need not here decide. As we see it, the question presented on the instant record is simply whether the Commission may require that an applicant demonstrate an earnest interest in serving a local community by evidencing a familiarity with its particular needs and an effort to meet them.

We think National Broadcasting Co. v. United States, 319 U.S. 190, 63 S.Ct. 997, 87 L.Ed. 1344 (1943), settles the narrow question before us in the affirmative. There, the Commission promulgated regulations which provided, *inter alia,* that no license would be granted to stations whose network contracts would prevent them from developing programs "to serve the needs of the local community." 319 U.S. at 203, 63 S.Ct. at 1003. National Broadcasting Company challenged the regulations on precisely the grounds appellants advance here: that since the regulations were calculated to affect program content, they exceeded statutory and constitutional limitations. In sustaining the regulations, the Supreme Court held that the Commission may impose reasonable restrictions upon the grant of licenses to assure programming designed to meet the needs of the local community. We

---

[3] Communications Act of 1934 § 307(a), 48 Stat. 1083, 47 U.S.C.A. § 307(a) (1958). The statute directs the Commission to grant a station license to any applicant "if public convenience, interest, or necessity will be served thereby."

[4] "Nothing in this Act shall be understood or construed to give the Commission the power of censorship over the radio communications or signals transmitted by any radio station, and no regulation or condition shall be promulgated or fixed by the Commission which shall interfere with the right of free speech by means of radio communication." Communications Act of 1934 § 326, 48 Stat. 1091, 47 U.S.C.A. § 326 (1958).

think it clear that the Commission's action in the instant case reflects no greater interference with a broadcaster's alleged right to choose its programs free from Commission control than the interference involved in National Broadcasting Co.[5]

Affirmed.

[5] Appellants also complain that they were surprised by the Commission's insistence that they be familiar with the needs of the community they sought to serve. But that requirement is not new. See Kentucky Broadcasting Corp. v. Federal Communications Comm., 84 U.S.App.D.C. 383, 174 F.2d 38 (1949); Sanders, 2 F.C.C. 365, 372 (1936); Egeland, 6 F.C.C. 278 (1938); Brownsville Broadcasting Co., 2 F.C.C. 336, 340 (1936) (alternative ground); Martin, 3 F.C.C. 461 (1936) (alternative ground); Goldwasser, 4 F.C.C. 223 (1937) (alternative ground); Kraft, 4 F.C.C. 354 (1937) (alternative ground). And the question whether appellants had demonstrated such familiarity was within the scope of the issues designated for hearing.

6 | THE CHARLIE WALKER CASE

In re Palmetto Broadcasting Company (WDKD)

Obscenity is not protected by the provisions of the First Amendment to the Constitution or by Section 326 of the Communications Act. Persons found guilty of uttering obscene language over the air are punishable under the provisions of Section 1464 of the Criminal Code.

In the "Charlie Walker" case, the FCC denied renewal of radio station WDKD's license because of certain "coarse, vulgar, and suggestive" material which the licensee permitted to be broadcast by an employee, among other reasons. The Commission's decision was upheld by the Court of Appeals because of the issue of licensee misrepresentation to the FCC. The programming issue and its freedom of speech overtones were thus largely unresolved (334 F.2d 534 (D.C. Cir. 1964)), and the Supreme Court refused to review the case (379 U.S. 843 (1964)). Walker, the WDKD disc jockey after whom the case is popularly named, was found guilty of violating Section 1464 of the Criminal Code in 1963.

All of the FCC Hearing Examiner's initial decision and that portion of the Commission's final decision relating to the programming issue appear below.

INITIAL DECISION OF HEARING EXAMINER THOMAS H. DONAHUE

33 FCC 265
December 8, 1961

PRELIMINARY STATEMENT

1. On March 15, 1961, the Commission adopted an order (FCC 61–344) which stated in essence that it had reviewed the above-captioned applications in the light of correspondence with applicant and a field investigation of applicant's station, and was unable to determine that grant of the applications would serve the public interest. The order specifically pointed out that in the Commission's possession was information to the effect that one Charlie Walker had broadcast over applicant's station material that was allegedly coarse, vulgar, suggestive, and susceptible of indecent double meaning. Hearing was directed to be held at the locale of applicant's station. Five issues were designated to be heard. By memorandum opinion and order released May 4, 1961 (FCC 61–588), the Commission amended one of the issues and designated another. The issues as finally designated read:

(1) To determine whether in its written or oral statements to the Commission with respect to the above matters, the licensee misrepresented facts to the Commission and/or was lacking in candor.

(2) To determine whether the licensee maintained adequate control or supervision of programing material broadcast over his station during the period of his most recent license renewal.

(3) To determine whether the licensee permitted program material to be broadcast over station WDKD on the Charlie Walker show, particularly during the period between January 1, 1960, and April 30, 1960, which program material was coarse, vulgar, suggestive, and susceptible of indecent, double meaning.

(4) To determine the manner in which the programing broadcast by the licensee during the period of his most recent license renewal has met the needs of the areas and populations served by the station.

(5) To determine whether, in light of the evidence adduced with respect to the foregoing issues, the licensee possesses the requisite qualifications to be a licensee of the Commission.

(6) To determine whether, in light of the evidence adduced with respect to the foregoing issues, a grant of the above-captioned applications would serve the public interest, convenience, or necessity.

Hearing was held in Kingstree on May 31, June 1, 2, and 5, 1961. Eighteen witnesses, including [licensee] Robinson, took the stand on behalf of the applicant. Ten witnesses testified on behalf of counsel for the Commission's Broadcast Bureau.

> *Did licensee misrepresent facts or lack candor in representing*
> *facts to the Commission?*

2. On May 11, 1960, the Commission sent a letter to the licensee, E. G. Robinson. In that letter reference was made to programs broadcast by Charlie Walker over WDKD, and the letter stated that in the Commission's possession were tape recordings of some of Walker's programs that were allegedly vulgar, suggestive, and susceptible of indecent double meaning. Pointing out that it was the practice of the Commission to associate complaints with station files and afford stations opportunity to submit comment, the applicant was directed to file a statement within 15 days. A copy of this letter was sent to the licensee's Washington counsel. (WDKD exhibit 3.)

3. On May 20, 1960, licensee's counsel wrote to the Commission. In that letter, counsel stated: WDKD had no knowledge of having broadcast vulgar or suggestive programs; counsel had requested the Commission's staff to be allowed to listen to tapes in the possession of the Commission but the request had been denied; counsel had been supplied with a tape of a typical Charlie Walker broadcast, but no instance of vulgarity or suggestiveness had been noted. Formal request was made that counsel be permitted to hear the tapes in the possession of the Commission and that full information concerning times and dates of the taped broadcasts, as well as the identity of the person making the charge, be provided. When such information was furnished, the letter continued, effort would be made to investigate the matter. In the meantime, concluded counsel's letter, Robinson, the licensee, had conferred with Walker who had denied knowledge of broadcasting anything vulgar or suggestive, but had nevertheless been admonished to be extremely circumspect in his broadcasts (WDKD exhibit 4).

4. On June 8, 1960, his counsel wrote Robinson. Tapes of the Charlie Walker programs in possession of the Commission had been heard. Eight excerpts from the tapes were set forth. The letter concluded with the following paragraph:

As you can see, these are indeed suggestive and in some respects, vulgar. With the temper of the Commission being as it presently is, with Congress looking into the programing of the industry as a whole, and with the South Carolina licenses coming up for renewal in December, I believe it is necessary for you to take direct affirmative action to stop all broadcasts of this type. Further, it is my suggestion that the services of Mr. Walker be dispensed with and that you submit to the Commission, under oath, a statement indicating the action you have taken and attach thereto a statement of policy, which you should prepare and circulate among all of your employees who work on the air. This statement should clearly spell out immediate dismissal should anything off-color be detected in any broadcast. Please supply us with copies of your proposed response to the Commission so that we may check it over and offer any suggestions before its filing (WDKD exhibit 5).

5. On June 10, 1960, Robinson wrote the Commission enclosing three affidavits. In that letter Robinson stated that he had just been informed in partial detail of the contents of the taped Charlie Walker programs. In significant part, the letter continued:

. . . These statements made by my employee, Charlie Walker, were not known to me, and I cannot help but agree that they are suggestive and, in some cases, of a vulgar nature. As a result of this information and in line with my avowed policy of maintaining a clean and decent radio station, I have unconditionally released Charlie Walker from my employ as of the date of this letter.

Repeating that he was unaware of the nature of the broadcasts, Robinson urged that the only accusation that could be leveled against him was that perhaps he "should have followed these matters more closely and should have known exactly what was going on." The letter concluded with a statement that immediately upon learning of the nature of the broadcasts, Walker had been discharged and that instructions had been issued and policy had been established insuring against such broadcasts being carried over WDKD in the future. Attached were affidavits formalizing the assertions made in the letter (WDKD exhibits 6, 7, 8, and 9).

> *Did applicant maintain adequate control and supervision over program material during the period of his most recent license renewal?*[1]

6. In this paragraph and the next six, Robinson's testimony on direct examination which appears to have bearing on the subject headnoted above is digested. He owns a small farm and a liquor store, besides his interest in the radio station.[2] The farm is operated on shares. The store is operated by a manager. Such work as he does at the farm is done from 5 to 8 a.m. From 80 to 90 percent of his time is spent on station affairs (Tr. 119–120).

---

[1] On the subject posed by the issue, Robinson's position appears to fall into four categories: (1) his lack of knowledge of the character of Walker's broadcasts; (2) the conventional nature of the station's organizational setup and his de facto management of all departments; (3) Walker's popularity and good works; and (4) his illness during which time the reins of management slipped from his fingers. After considerable thought, the examiner has chosen to present Robinson's testimony on the subject contemplated by the issue, in digest form, in the order in which it developed at the hearing. Only in this fashion can the full flavor of applicant's position on the matter be portrayed.

[2] In various applications filed with the Commission in the past, Robinson failed to report his ownership of the liquor store. This reporting failure, which is asserted to have been inadvertent, is the subject of a petition to amend filed during the course of hearing (Tr. 116-117).

7. For about a year following November 11, 1957, he was either hospitalized as a result of, or confined to his home recuperating from an automobile accident. During this period, his then assistant manager, Charles Green, looked after the radio station with some assistance from Mrs. Robinson on "inside" and "everyday" operations. Green had authority over station policy, but no major policy decisions that he could recall were made by Green (Tr. 121–124, WDKD exhibit 1).

8. The needs of WDKD's service area are identified by analyzing mail and contacting individuals and groups throughout the area. He is a member of a number of civic organizations (Tr. 127–128, 186).

9. Charlie Walker was with the station for 8 years as an announcer. Walker was on the air 4 hours a day handling the following programs: "Rise and Shine," "Grits and Gravy," "Mountain Jamboree," and "Sundown Hoedown." Walker's programs were very well received. A tremendous amount of mail was received by Walker. Sometimes a post office bag was required to carry it. He [Robinson] did not read Walker's mail (Tr. 136–138).

10. Over a period of years he talked to Walker some 8 or 10 times about "these different names that he called these different towns, what he said about me or some advertiser in a joking way," and about poking fun at his wife. In 1959 he called Walker in behind closed doors, "and went over with him this and told him that I was going to have to do something about it, it just couldn't continue, and from what I knew about it, he was going to have to go." Walker asked for another chance and promised to do better. With the public behind Walker the way they were and in his position of trying to serve the public, he "went along with this thing for 3 or 4 months." He called Walker in again on May 11 when he had a notice from the Commission. He handed Walker the letter and said, "Charlie, this is it. The Commission has notified me of complaints or proof of your programs. This is it." Walker remonstrated, wanting to know the particulars of what he had done. He told Walker that he thought he could very easily find out and he called Washington counsel. When he received the Commission's letter on June 10, he called Walker in and asked him "what about it." Walker responded, "Mr. Robinson, I don't remember saying those things; however, I imagine I did, if they've got it on tape." He asked Walker for his key and discharged him on the spot. He then called a staff meeting, went over with his employees what had happened and instructed them "to see that this didn't happen in the future, nothing pertaining to this sort of stuff." Following this, he typed up a notice, circulated it and put a copy on the bulletin board, and paid a visit to his local attorney (Tr. 138–139, 142, 146–148).

11. He had never received written or oral complaints concerning the Charlie Walker program. Rev. Donald Bailey of the Presbyterian church had asked him if he would change the type of music that was being played prior to the morning devotions program and he had agreed to make the change. Prior to his accident he picked up the mail in the mornings; since

then his traffic manager picks up the mail and he [Robinson] routes it. He is sure that if a written complaint had been received by the station about the Walker program he would have seen it. Mrs. Robinson did tell him of one occasion when Reverend Drennan, the Methodist minister, had "said something to her about Charlie Walker." Mrs. Robinson's reply had, of course, been that not everyone likes hillbilly music and that the minister should listen to the station at other times (Tr. 155–158).

12. Staff meetings at the station are scheduled for every 2 weeks. All aspects of station operations are discussed at the meetings. Suggestions are made by Robinson to his employees and by his employees to Robinson. When applications are made for employment at WDKD, applicants are carefully screened and if employed are provided with the rules of the Commission covering their duties. He personally has direct supervision over all departments of the station. To insure against repetition of "Walkerisms," he has held meetings, posted notices on the bulletin board, circulated rules and regulations with the understanding that if anything of the type happens again, the employee responsible will be released without notice. He has installed speakers in most of the offices at the station and he tries to monitor a portion of each program throughout the day (Tr. 159, 164, 166–167).

13. Charlie Walker did a great deal of public service work. Walker helped different people obtain money for operations, for a little boy's eyeglasses, for a burned-out family.[3] Walker obtained aid for those who needed food and clothing and people with braces. Walker was assistant county chairman of a Cancer Fund Drive and raised a record amount of money. On his own time Walker would go to merchants and solicit contributions of food and clothing for the needy. On his radio programs Walker very effectively carried on a campaign for March of Dimes contributions. WDKD at different times puts on contests to obtain audience reaction to programs. A considerable mail response is received. Charlie Walker's good works were much praised not only in contest mail but to him [Robinson] personally. In talking to people throughout the service area, he found no objection to Walker's programs. Such matters as the references Walker made to the various towns were included in these discussions, but he found no objection to this practice of Walker's and did nothing about it (Tr. 186–188, 208–211).

14. In this and the next six paragraphs Robinson's testimony on cross-examination is digested. He did have knowledge of the names Walker called the towns. Prior to filing his response to the Commission's letter of inquiry, the only knowledge he had of the unfavorable nature of Walker's broadcasts was the names Walker called the towns, what he said about him [Robinson] and what he said about different advertisers. Although he had no written policy against programs in bad taste, the subject was brought up every time a staff meeting was held and such meetings had been held, since

---

[3] A boy whom Walker aided in getting eyeglasses, Robert McDonald, was present, with his mother, and was identified at the hearing.

1956, regularly every 2 weeks and sometimes once a week. In an application filed with the Commission in May 1954 the following statement was made, "It has been the policy of this station and it will remain the policy of this station in its overall programing to offer programs that are in good taste and serve the educational, religious, and cultural background of people in and around Kingstree, South Carolina." That statement had been prepared by him on behalf of himself and his then partner, Marion Few. He did have occasion to warn and admonish Walker prior to May 1960. In 1959 as he had previously stated, he cautioned Walker several times about "those things." By "those things" he meant "Greeleyville; and Ann's Drawers for Andrews, Lake City—'City by the Lake' and all those sort of things." When asked what "those sort of things" meant, he continued, "Such as he called me 'money bags' and—I remember he said Mr. John Flagler was the only man he knew could stand up and milk a cow. . . ." He did not think the latter remark "too good" and called it to Walker's attention. Walker was employed in 1950. In 1952 Walker went into military service. Walker returned to the station in 1954. He could remember nothing prior to Walker's going into service. After Walker came out of service, particularly in 1956, "he certainly wasn't too bad about these things." Just now and then he would mention them. Walker actually got worse about them in 1959. That is when he noticed it. By "worse" he meant in calling towns by different names "and that sort of stuff" and by calling them by those names more frequently. Walker did not use any suggestive language. Walker did not use any language susceptible of indecent double meaning, that he heard. No one told him of any indecent thing Walker said. They always told about jokes Walker told and the jokes Walker told about him. They would not tell him the bad things Walker said. None of the jokes that were repeated to him had indecent double meaning. Walker's jokes were repeated to him hundreds of times. Beginning in 1959, he tried to monitor a portion of all of Walker's programs. Some of Walker's programs he monitored when he was in the hospital and at home recuperating. Other than the names of towns and that sort of thing, he never heard Walker broadcast anything objectionable. There is a speaker in the office next to his which he can hear very well. All of his employees have speakers in their offices. None of his employees ever told him that they had received complaints about Walker's programs being indecent. No advertiser ever told him that he wanted his advertising taken off the Walker program because it was indecent. As far as any minister telling him that he thought the Walker programs were coarse and suggestive, it had been brought to his attention by his wife, D. L. Taylor, and L. L. Law that Reverend Drennan had visited him at the hospital and said something about the Charlie Walker programs. He did not remember what Reverend Drennan had said and he did not remember what the people who reported the Drennan visit to him had told him Reverend Drennan had said. ("Well, sir, my condition, I'm sorry I didn't remember it.") No other minister, that he could remember, ever talked to him about the Walker programs in terms of their being indecent or susceptible of indecent double meaning. He never heard anyone comment on the indecency of the Walker programs. The names Walker called the towns were "Greasy Thrill" for Greeleyville and "Bloomersville" for Bloomville (Tr. 215, 220–233).

15. Besides the farm he had previously mentioned, he has another little farm of 52 acres that he does not cultivate. The market value of the two farms is $25,000 (Tr. 234, 236).

16. He goes to the station at 8 in the morning and stays until 12:30 p.m. He goes home for lunch and returns at 2 or 2:30 p.m. and stays there the rest of the day except when he goes into the field to service some 8 or 10 advertising accounts which he personally handles. WDKD is a daytime-only station. When he is away from the station and in his car, he makes it a practice to listen to the station although he does not keep the radio on all the time. From 1954 until he entered the hospital (in November 1957), he spent about 50 percent of his time at the station, the remainder he spent in the field selling advertising. He averaged about 6 hours a day at the station during that period (Tr. 240–242).

17. He has acted as station manager since 1953 or 1954. Prior to that time he and Few had hired a manager. This arrangement did not work out. Except for assistant managers from time to time, no one at the station (besides himself) exercises supervisory authority over programing. His first assistant manager was Charles Green who came in 1957. When Green left in 1960, Arnold Graham was made assistant manager. He has had program directors at the station. Program directors have supervision only over announcers and then not with respect to programing but with respect to quality of broadcast, being sure the announcer gives his best at all times, insuring that the announcer is checking his logs, pulling his "shows" beforehand, and filing records after completion of program. He could not remember whether Godwin had been a program director but Ashby Ward had held that position. At that time there were three announcers including Ward. Ward exercised supervision to the extent that he helped arrange the announcers' schedules. Employees were subject to his [Robinson's] control and supervision. Mrs. Robinson is bookkeeper at the station and bears the title of "operations manager." She works with the program director, the traffic department, the continuity writer, and assists them in correcting things that might come up and things to do other than policy—"that comes to me." Mrs. Robinson's authority on programing was solely "with the program director." Mrs. Robinson and the program director would discuss different programs and then come to him. As far as instructions were concerned, she worked through the program director. No one looked to Mrs. Robinson as running the station when he was absent. Personnel would go to her with problems and "she would translate those things to me." Mrs.

Robinson never brought him complaints to the effect that Charlie Walker's programs were susceptible of indecent double meaning (Tr. 243–249).

18. The second day of cross-examination continued in the following vein. In regard to his testimony that he had had discussions with Walker concerning his use of various nicknames for communities, he had learned of this practice of Walker's largely through listening to Walker over the air. The evening before his appearance that day he had jotted down everything that he could remember having heard Walker say. There were a few things that he had not previously mentioned. Walker called Olanta, S.C., "Chocolate Cake Cow Pasture"; Georgetown, "Stinkumville"; St. Stephens, "St. Step-Ins"; Lake City, "smooch me quick crossroads"; Monks Corners, "Monkey's Corners." On three separate occasions he called Walker's attention to using the phrase, "let it all hang out." He remembered hearing Walker on the air say something, he didn't catch it all, about carrying his girl to a cow pasture to relax and end up saying, "And that's right." He went to Walker immediately. Walker had no explanation. The only other terms not previously mentioned, that he could remember Walker using, was reference to himself [Walker] as "Banana Nose." When he heard Walker make such allusions he would go to him and talk to him. These discussions continued over a period of time. Walker would promise he would stop using such expressions. He thought he could recall that, as he had previously testified, he had to go back to Walker on these matters. This did not happen too often, once or twice. Walker did not use such expressions continuously, once or twice or perhaps three times, after he had talked to him. He had talked to Walker about his language over the air at least 10 times between 1954 and 1959. He could have had more or fewer discussions with Walker on the subject during that period. To his knowledge Walker used the phrase "let it all hang out," three times. He had never heard Walker use the phrase, "This is your Uncle Charlie letting it all hang out and drag in the sand." If he had heard Walker use that phrase, he thought he would have remembered it. No one, that he could recall, had ever complained to him about that language. He did not hear Walker tell the privy story. When he had confronted Walker with the digest of the privy story, Walker had said that he did not remember telling the story but wouldn't deny that he had. Walker did say that if it was on tape, he [Walker] had used the phrase. Walker's admission also applied to the Willie Tart story. He had not heard Walker broadcast the "Ain't you going to kiss me" item. No one had told him that they had heard it. People did not criticize Walker's programs to him. He could not say that he had had reports on the Willie Tart story. He could not recall that he had received such reports (Tr. 311–320, 322–327).

19. He could not recall Charlie Walker having ever been fired prior to 1960. Marion Few, his former partner, never discussed with him remarks made by Walker and did not state that they were suggestive and susceptible

of indecent double meaning. Few never complained that Walker's programs were vulgar and coarse (Tr. 331–332).

20. The station's staff is composed of a general manager [Robinson], an assistant manager and commercial manager, a part-time salesman, a program director and announcer, an announcer, a chief engineer and announcer, a continuity writer, a traffic director, and a bookkeeper [Mrs. Robinson] (Tr. 342).

21. Not all of Robinson's testimony noted above squares with the testimony of other witnesses. In the following 14 paragraphs, testimony on the subject here under scrutiny at odds with Robinson's is set forth.

22. Lloyd Ashby Ward, who worked at WDKD as an announcer from September 1958 to June 1960, testified that during his tenure Robinson spent 3 to 4 hours a day at the station. Carroll Godwin, who was an announcer at WDKD from June 1952 to October 1956, estimated that Robinson spent about 3 hours a day at the station (Tr. 523, 677).

23. S. Charles Green, who was employed at the station as salesman from June 1950 to October 1953 and from January of 1957 until February 1960, testified that when he was hired the second time, on the basis of his conversations with Robinson, he thought he was being hired as assistant manager, but when he went to work at the station no announcement was made to that effect and other station employees were never notified that he held that position. Moreover, Green was employed 5 days a week from 8 in the morning until 5 in the evening in the field selling advertising. Further, Robinson never told Green that he had authority at the station during his absence or that he had authority over programing. Aside from some correspondence and the handling of a minor personnel matter, Robinson had never given Green instructions on the conduct of station affairs outside the field of sales.[4] Ward testified that when he was at the station he had no knowledge that Green was assistant manager (Tr. 638, 639–640, 671).

24. Ward testified that only three or four staff meetings were held while he was at the station. Green estimated that only five or six staff meetings were held during his second period of employment there (Tr. 523, 639).

25. Ward was employed at WDKD through June 18, 1960. He testified that no notice was posted on the bulletin board while he was there which dealt with the broadcasting of indecent material or programs not in good taste[5] (Tr. 525).

26. Ward, who it will be recalled was identified by Robinson as pro-

---

[4] Although Green on occasion signed station correspondence over the title "Assistant Manager," it was merely an assumption of title on his part of the basis of his conversation with Robinson. Further, it might be here noted that Green did hold one staff meeting (Tr. 654, 655).

[5] Ward did testify that he understood that on June 13, 1960, a staff meeting was held at WDKD. He did not attend the meeting (Tr. 537).

gram director, testified that Mrs. Robinson did exercise supervisory authority over programing, did clear matters involving program content, and that he had no real authority to determine the scheduling of programs but that Mrs. Robinson almost always went along with his suggestions on such matters. While he was employed at WDKD, he was under the impression that Mrs. Robinson was second in command. Godwin also testified that the employees accepted Mrs. Robinson's authority the same as they did Mr. Robinson's (Tr. 530, 531, 542, 678).

27. In connection with Robinson's testimony concerning his knowledge of the character of Walker's broadcasts and the dearth of complaints he had received concerning those broadcasts, there is a good deal of evidence that speaks in another vein.

28. Marion L. Few testified that he was a partner and half owner with Robinson in WDKD from the time the station went on the air in 1949 until 1955 or early 1956. Walker was hired when the station went on the air and except for a period when he was in the Army, Walker was with the station during Few's entire association with the station. Walker's programs often contained suggestive and vulgar material. He often received complaints concerning the Walker programs. Nearly every time he received such a complaint, he passed it on to Robinson. Nothing was ever done in the way of improvement of the Walker programs. Although, for the most part, he had been an inactive partner in the day-to-day operation of the station, his concern over the Walker broadcasts led him, during the last 8 months of his association with the station, to increase the time he spent at the station. In 1955 or 1956 he fired Walker when he heard him broadcast the following story:

> Well, it seems that this couple had gotten married. After about three days the old boy got the first look at her feet, and he asked her why she had such big cracks between her toes. She said, "Well, you know, I got those big cracks between my big toes from walking in that Georgia mud barefooted." He said, "Are you sure that you didn't spend your time sitting in that Georgia mud?"

Walker, however, did not stay discharged. He was back at work the next day. Some 8 months later, he [Few] severed relations with Robinson and the station. The reason for this step was that Robinson was determined that Walker should be retained at the station and he [Few] was determined that he should go (Tr. 716–725, 729).

29. Bernard Smith Drennan testified that he was a minister in the South Carolina Conference of the Methodist Church and has lived in Kingstree 3½ years. He had heard Walker broadcast nicknames for the different towns and such jokes as those contained in FCC exhibit 2. (See par. 38.) Walker was a likable fellow; he did a lot of good and had a big following. He was very effective in raising money for charitable purposes. Walker got his following by the good that he did and then would inject into his programs

things that were in bad taste, that people could and did object to. His children did not listen to the Charlie Walker program because they had heard his objections and respected his judgment. He had on separate occasions discussed the Charlie Walker program with both Mr. and Mrs. Robinson. Sometime the latter part of 1957 he had met Mrs. Robinson at the home of a mutual friend. He had asked her if there wasn't something that could be done about the Walker program, that he heard many complaints concerning the suggestiveness of it, and wondered how Walker got by with it and why the FCC did not do something about it. He was informed by Mrs. Robinson that Walker received more mail at the station than anyone, that his program had been monitored and the only objection raised to it had been one reference to slop jars. In early 1958 when Robinson was in the hospital recuperating from an automobile accident, he called on him frequently. Toward the end of Robinson's recuperation he and Robinson were discussing devotional programs and he asked Robinson if it were not possible to do something about the Charlie Walker show, that many people complained and did not listen to the station because of the suggestive nature of the Walker programs. He told Robinson he thought the programs were giving the community a bad name. Robinson replied that the program did get pretty rough at times, that he had not had much opportunity to listen, and that he intended to talk to Walker and do something about it. After this discussion he noticed no improvement in the Walker program. The discussion took place 2 or 3 weeks before Robinson left the hospital. The Walker program was discussed at ministerial association meetings, but opinion there was to the effect that there was nothing much the association could do about it. One objection to the Walker program he raised before the association concerned the fact that after Saturday morning devotions on WDKD, Walker would come on with a smart-aleck statement or refer to things irrelevant to devotions. No formal complaint, however, was lodged (Tr. 546–562).

30. James Kirk Lawton testified that he is pastor of the Calvary Baptist Church, Florence, S. C., and was pastor at the First Baptist Church, Kingstree, from September 1953 to October 1957. The material contained in FCC exhibit 2 was typical of the type of material he had heard on the Walker program. He discussed the Walker program with Robinson on two separate occasions. Once when Robinson's daughter was ill, he called at Robinson's home. During the course of his conversation with Robinson, talk turned to spiritual matters and he suggested that one thing that would help a great deal would be improvement in the Charlie Walker situation, pointing out that the situation was not satisfactory, not proper, that Walker's material was suggestive and indecent. Robinson made no definite commitment. Another time he called upon Robinson at the latter's office. During a discussion of matters of general interest in the community, he again deplored the situation with respect to the Walker program and indicated hope of improvement. Following these conversations he noticed no improvement in the

Walker program. Members of his congregation frequently complained to him of the vulgar, suggestive, and sexy nature of the Walker programs. The Walker programs had been discussed at ministerial meetings. It was the consensus of opinion that the organization did not want to hurt Robinson and that individually the members would appeal to Robinson and see what he could do about it. Members of his present congregation at Florence had commented to him about the Walker program. The subject of these comments was the suggestive talk on the Walker program (Tr. 579–584, 586–588).

31. Green testified that when he was selling advertising for WDKD, an advertiser informed him that he did not care to use the station any longer because of the Charlie Walker programs (Tr. 642).

32. Godwin testified that when Walker was drafted he took over from Walker the handling of a program entitled, "Hymn Time." When Walker returned from the service he was again scheduled to announce the "Hymn Time" program. Godwin received some 50 letters objecting to Walker's return to the program. These objections were couched in terms of the filthy language used by Walker. Walker did handle the program for 2 or 3 days after he returned from the Army. Godwin then returned to the program. Walker frequently broadcast material that was suggestive or susceptible of indecent double meaning. An example of the type of material he had heard Walker broadcast was the following:

. . . he and his girl friend were out on a date the night before, and they ran out of gas far out into the country, away from town. So they proceeded to walk toward town, and they walked until they were completely exhausted, then they started crawling, and crawled until finally his girl collapsed, and he crawled on.

People frequently commented to him about the content of Walker's programs. On a few occasions he had accompanied Robinson on sales trips. There was a radio in Robinson's car. On those trips he had heard, over the car radio, Walker make such comments as "let it all hang out" (Tr. 674–675, 681–686, 689, 694, 696).

33. A. E. Creamer, general manager of Sears, Roebuck, Florence, S.C., testified that he directed cancellation of Sears' advertising on the Charlie Walker program over WDKD following reports by salesmen and friends that the program was off-color, had a certain amount of vulgarity attached to it, and was not in keeping with Sears' standards of advertising (Tr. 737, 739–740).

34. T. Doug Youngblood testified that he was general manager of WFIG, Sumter, S.C., and executive secretary of the South Carolina Broadcasters Association, and had heard material broadcast by Charlie Walker over WDKD that was susceptible of indecent double meaning or was coarse and vulgar. The Walker program was discussed among members of the as-

sociation in the context that it was not conducive to good broadcasting and at times downright indecent. He would not permit such programs as the Walker programs to be broadcast over his station. Programing that goes outside conventional concepts of decency does have a certain appeal. It is easy to sell smut. Pressure on competition is generated when other competitors lower standards of quality (Tr. 658, 661–662, 664–668).

35. Edward L. B. Osborne testified that he was president and general manager of WBCU, Union, S.C.; vice president of WAGS, Bishopville, S.C.; past president of the South Carolina Broadcasters Association; and had heard the Charlie Walker program on one occasion. En route to a convention he heard a program over WDKD, the contents of which he related to broadcasters at the convention and was informed, "Well, you heard the Charlie Walker show." The Walker programs have been a subject of discussion at biannual broadcasters conventions. Most broadcasters were concerned that the Walker program might hurt broadcasting. The concensus of opinion was that the program was degrading to radio in general (Tr. 749–753).

> *Did licensee, particularly during the period January 1–April 30, 1960, permit material to be broadcast that was coarse, vulgar, suggestive, and susceptible of indecent double meaning?*

36. James Roper, operations manager and chief engineer of station WJOT, Lake City, S.C., testified that between October 27, 1959, and April 25, 1960, he taped a total of 12 or 14 broadcasts over WDKD featuring Charlie Walker. Using an Eicor tape recorder and a Hallicrafters model S-85 communications receiver, the latter was tuned to WDKD and when by listening he ascertained that it was WDKD that was in fact being received and Charlie Walker broadcasting, the recorder was attached directly to the receiver and tapes were run. All tapes were monitored after they were made. Since the tapes were not cut as quality productions but for the purpose of calling to the attention of the Commission what was going on at WDKD, their quality was not high. Of the 12 or 14 broadcasts taped, only 6 were retained; the rest were discarded. The tapes retained were all intelligible to Roper. Stored in Roper's office under lock and key for some time, they were eventually turned over to the president of WJOT. The record does not disclose the story of their custody while in the latter's possession, but it may be safely assumed that during that period they were made available to the Commission and its staff. Returned to Roper and again kept under lock and key by him, they were again taken out and monitored by Roper in the presence of a Commission investigator and the two FCC counsel who tried this hearing. The tapes then monitored were the same as those Roper had made of the WDKD broadcasts. On this latter occasion the tapes were turned over to the FCC staff. Shortly before the hearing convened, Roper and the Commis-

sion's representatives again listened to the tapes, this time to identify the tapes with the days they were broadcast. This Roper did by listening for the announcer [Walker] to make reference to a particular day or event; e.g., reference to the Monday edition of the "Jamboree" program, reference to "Founder's Day Sale," and reference to the opening of "Black River Speedway." With such identification, the sequence of program material and spot announcements as disclosed by the tapes was compared with the station's program log for the day thus selected. As an additional check, other program logs were reviewed to insure against the possibility of duplication. At this same session a transcript of the broadcasts was checked against the tapes. Roper identified FCC exhibit 2 as an accurate transcript of the contents of the tapes which he had made of the Charlie Walker broadcasts (Tr. 595-623).

37. At the outset of Roper's testimony, counsel for the applicant conceded his qualifications to take tape recordings on the theory that "Anybody can take a tape recording." Thereafter, counsel for the applicant, when FCC exhibit 2 was offered into evidence, initiated a line of interrogation apparently designed to test the bona fides of the tapes from which FCC exhibit 2 was derived. At that point the examiner reminded applicant's counsel that the tapes had been made available to applicant's counsel prior to hearing, that already in evidence was Robinson's testimony that he had confronted Walker with excerpts from the tapes and had been told in effect that if the Commission had the tapes, he [Walker] had broadcast the material, that there was then in evidence testimony of witnesses corroborating various portions of the taped material, that the tapes were readily available for audition in the hearing room, and that there were a number of people then in the hearing room who knew Walker and were familiar with his program. Considering the state of the record, applicant's counsel was asked if he believed it profitable to further pursue the subject of the authenticity of the tapes. After brief interrogation of the witness concerning voice modulation and "tape level," counsel for the applicant stated he had no objection to the receipt into evidence of the subject exhibit (Tr. 623-631).

38. Indented below is a verbatim transcript of material broadcast by Charlie Walker on October 15 and 27, 1959, January 14 and 20, 1960, and on April 25, 1960.[6] All of the indented material comes from FCC exhibit 2. Selection was made from that exhibit to avoid redundancy and to eliminate matters not actually contained in quotes. In the latter connection, however, it should be noted that the Commission's exhibit makes clear that Walker on numerous occasions not included in the material below made reference to Greeleyville as "Greasy Thrill," Andrews as "Ann's Drawers," Bloomville as "Bloomersville," and St. Stephens as "St. Step-ins."

---

[6] Items contained on pp. 20 and 21 were presented during the period specifically mentioned in issue 3 (Jan. 1, 1960–Apr. 30, 1960). [The confusing page numbers probably refer to pages of FCC exhibit 2.—Ed.]

Next Saturday it is we gonna have the big grand opening over at the new W. P. Marshall store in Greasy Thrill and we gonna come over there and let it all hang out. Course if we let it all hang out in Greeleyville, there ain't gonna be enough room over there for nothin' else, is there?

He says: "I believe that old dog of mine is a Baptist." I asked him why he thought his old dog was a Baptist and he says, "you know, Uncle Charlie, it is that he's done baptized every hub cap around Ann's drawers." "You say it is all that all the hub caps in Spring Gully is going to Heaven?"

If you're goin' to see a gal over in Poston you got to go see her after it gets dark; I mean you can't go over there in the daylight. And the reason you can't go over there in the daylight is because it is that them gals around Poston are so wild, you know. They're so wild that you have to sneak up on 'em in the dark. . . . And the only thing about sneaking up on 'em in the dark it is that you is liable to make a mistake; well I mean like I did one night, I thought I was sneaking up on one of dem gals from Poston and I was sneaking up on a cow. And do you know it is that I didn't even know I had a cow until it is that it swatted a fly off the end of my nose with its tail. When it swatted a fly off the end of my nose with its tail. When it swatted a fly off the end of my nose with its tail I began to get suspicious. I knew them gals in Poston couldn't do that.

He was getting hard up. You ever been hard up? They tell, Uncle Charlie it is we hard up for a little bit of music right now but we ain't gonna get none. I say you take a flying bite out of my shirt tail, hear?[7]

Did you hear the one about the boy and the gal in the cow pasture? He was really lovin' that gal good. Boy he was lovin' that gal good. And it is that he was getting plenty whole-hearted cooperation. He was. He was lovin' that old gal good. She was givin' him something besides lovin'. She was giving him whole-hearted cooperation. She was. And he decided that this is the gal for me; says "this is the gal I want to marry, right here." So he came right out and asked her. He says: "Darling," he says, "will you marry me?" And she says, "well I don't know." She says, "tell me do you want a home?" And he says, "honey," he says, "I'm a regular home body." And she says, "And what about children?" And he says, "Oh," he says, "Honey, I just love children." And she says, "well," she says, "in that case," she says, "I'll marry you if you like children. We'll be in business in about six months!" [Laughter.] They gettin' a head start!

It is you give me barbecued iced water and a green-eyed gal and I can go hard.

Betsy says it is that not only will she flirt with dynamite, but it is that if it's single she'll propose to it. Fool, you couldn't marry no dynamite. Betsy says it is that she don't mind marrying a stick of dynamite if he's got a long fuse. A long fuse? Betsy, will you go make some French Market coffee and cut out your trash?

We's over in St. Step-ins yesterday. Had a glorious time.

I get so tired of people callin' me a jackass. Them people over in St. Stephens in Russelville. They wouldn't say, "Hello, Uncle Charlie," they's say,

---

[7] This comment followed a story concerning a husband whose wife beat him each morning; the husband bought a bulldog and the wife beat the bulldog.

"hello, jackass" . . . It is that so many people done called me a jackass that, I'll tell you the truth, it is that if I ain't got a saddle in the middle of my back I feel naked. All right, for everybody whose got ants in their pants, I'll tell you what you do. You make your self a big pot of French Market Coffee, and then, pour the French Market Coffee in the seat of your britches. If you got any ants in your pants that'll get rid of them. Of course, it didn't work with my red bugs, nothing ever does. I tried that to get rid of my red bugs. And my darn bugs were making mud pies out of that French Market Coffee, and throwing them at my black heads.

I don't wanta save everything I get my hands on. I had my hands on something last night and I guarantee you boy I didn't want to save it . . . It is that you better believe that.

You hear 'bout de gal dat had a brand new boy friend? And, well, it her brand new boy friend . . . and her brand new boy friend he had been coming over to see her a while, you know, and de gal's daddy decided that he'd better kinda lay down the law, you know, to his daughter's new boy friend, so he took the boy aside, you know, and he says, "Son," he says, "a man," he says, "a man should be the boss of his house" . . . and, he says, "I'm telling you, son, it won't take you long to find out that I'm the one who wears the pants in this family." And, the daughter's new boy friend says, "Oh, no, sir," he says, "I know that," he says, "I found it out last night, sir!" . . . And in October too, already.

Bill Hyman [or Heiman] you know that works for Willie Tar in Lake City he was telling me that, he used to have some ducks, you know, used to raise ducks, and says, "Uncle Charlie," he says, "them durn fool ducks," you know he used to have him a little patch of green peppers, you know, that hot green pepper, and he used to have it in the garden, and he said "them durn ducks would get in the garden and eat that green, and eat that hot green pepper," and he says, "then it is that the ducks had to fly backwards to keep from burning up" . . . [laughter] . . . "that's right," he said, "the durn, the old duck had to get up and fly backwards to keep from barbecuing himself" . . .

I'll tell you what that Snotty Cook at that Cook Shell station in the city by the Lake in Lake City says, and I believe this is the way that Lake City was born. You see, it is that Noah built his Ark, he took all the animals on board, see, I mean, he took all the animals on board, and of course, it rained for 40 days and 40 nights, but Noah had a problem, see? Because the Ark didn't have any bathroom on it. So the only thing Noah could do, of course, was to take all the animals up on deck. But then he had a problem of how to get rid of it all, so he took a shovel and they shoveled it all over the side of the Ark into the water. So, it is that all of it settled and that's where Lake City come from.[8]

Careful drivers can have accidents. Careful boy friends can have accidents too.

I seen something last night that I wanted. I wasn't too bashful to go get it, I was just too smart. She had her husband with her. My mama didn't raise no foolish young 'uns.

---

[8] At the end of this item Walker offered 10 printed copies of the lie he had just told for $1. This was followed by an offer of Bibles in exchange for coupons.

That's the scientific word for happy horse crud.[9]

Why don't you get off your ding dong friend, you'll never make a million lying up in the bed looking at the ceiling.

Betsy, you're not producing, you're not. Betsy says give her time, she's not married yet. Now you know what I'm talking about.

You always drink plenty of big value coffee and you'll have enough strength to tell your girl friend no when she wants to go to the cow pasture and you want to go to prayer meetin', you know, and it is you'll have enough strength to tell 'em no. That's right.

It is that I always tell them no, not because I'm such a good boy but because it is that I ain't got enough strength to do anything else.

It is that my girl still loves me when I let 'er. See I don't let her too often because I don't wanta spoil her, see. I mean if you give women everything they want you spoil them, see. It'll break you and spoil them.

Uncle Banana Nose lettin' it all hang out . . .

I used to go with this gal that worked in that five and dime over in Greeleyville and you know it is that I'd take the gal out you know and anytime it is I'd kiss the old gal or hug her or squeeze her or tease her she'd say "Will that be all, sir?" You see that's what they say all day long at the five and dime, will that be all, sir? I broke her of that habit though. It is that I broke her of that habit. It is that I got the ole gal to where she'd quit saying, "Will that be all sir?" She started saying, "That's enough, Charlie." You gotta break 'em.

You know that Betsy goes over to Lake City every night, she does, she goes over to Lake City and they beat the devil outta her but that don't make no difference. She go back right over there again tonight. Well, I ain't never seen nobody like you, Betsy, that likes to go 13 miles just to get your rear end cut. I'll tell you what, if you want to stay home tonight I'll be glad to do it for you and save you the trip. I don't know what makes them people so rough over there. Really I don't . . . People in Lake City don't love nobody. I know because I given them several opportunities to love me and they passed it up . . . I mean them girls over there have had several opportunities and they passed it up.

You farmers better get off of it and get out there and get in at them tobacco fields. We don't want no crop failures this year. It is that we don't want any farmers to have any crop failures. I know about eight farmers' daughters that I hope like the devil that have a crop failure. [Laughter.] All I got to say they better have one! If they don't have a crop failure I'm gonna have a heart failure.

I've always been a gentleman, I sure don't go around beating up my women before I love 'em . . . Tell me, would you go around bruising up your groceries before you eat 'em? Well, that's the way I feel about them gals.[10]

If Williamsburg County was a big old house, Lanes would be the privy.

You know they always told me if you had a problem the best thing to do

---

[9] This explanation followed reference to "noise distortion."
[10] This followed comment concerning Mickey Spillane beating up women before loving them since they then could not fight back.

was to go home and sleep on it. It is. Now I'll give you just three guesses what my problem is. I'll just give you three guesses as to what my problem is [Recorded girl's voice:] "Ain't you gonna kiss me" [Response in male voice:] "U'nh-u'nh." Well, that's my first problem right there. I get so tired of hearing that.

Old Willy Tart. You know Willy's getting kinda old now. Of course it is that he still likes to go out with the girls, but when he does it's only to refresh his memory because that's all he can do, refresh his memory. But we'll all be in the same boat one of these days, will we not?

I used to go out with a gal cause she had plenty of lovin' but now I go out with her cause she's got plenty of patience.

He was telling me, he says, "Uncle Charlie," he says, "we had 14 in the family. There was 14 of us not countin' the hogs too." He says, "There was 14 in the family," and he says "Uncle Charlie," he says, "we didn't have but one privy," he said, "one out-house, and that one out-house was sittin' on top the hill in back of the house." And he says, "do you know," he says, "in 3 years' time with all 14 in the family using it, in 3 years' time that privy was on flat ground. That family wore out that hill going back and forth. They did." He says "Uncle Charlie," he says, "they was always two of us going, two of us coming back, and one of us in there all the time, 24 hours a day." That's right, that's what he said, he says, "Uncle Charlie," he says, "that's the first time in my life I ever heard of a hole getting wore out." And you know, come to think of it, I never heard of no hole getting wore out.

You know they got a rooster down there at Frank Parsons Shell Station—a little ole bantam rooster and that bantam rooster's name is "Big Dick." And any time you go down to Frank Parsons and you wanta see that ole rooster all you gotta do is stand out there in the middle and holler "Hey Big Dick" and that old rooster will comma running.

I can remember back when I was single boy. It is that my britches used to be wrinkled all the time too, but the reason my britches was wrinkled when I was single is because gals was always sittin' on my lap and that's why it is that my britches was always wrinkled. Man, times do change. Now what I got in 'em's wrinkled.

I got some britches at home that it is that if the crease in those britches could talk . . . my wife woulda been done killed me a long time ago (FCC exhibit 2).

> *Has the programing of licensee's station met the needs of the population served during the station's most recent license renewal period?*

39. Kingstree, population 3,621, the county seat of Williamsburg County, population 43,807, is located in the southeastern part of South Carolina. It has a long and distinguished history dating back to 1732. The town has 3 hotels, a weekly newspaper, 2 hospitals, 2 banks, 2 high schools, 2 grade schools, 14 churches, a Carnegie library, 2 motion picture theaters, 2 parks, a considerable complement of both retail and manufacturing concerns, and

a number of civic organizations. The town operates under a mayor-council-type government and maintains independent fire and police departments. Williamsburg County is largely agricultural. Over 70 percent of its area is covered by timber. There are some 6,000 farms located in the county, averaging about 70 acres per farm. Tobacco, cotton, and corn are the leading crops. The colored population of Kingstree amounts to about 44 percent of its total population. In the county about 68 percent of the population is colored[11] (WDKD exhibit 2).

40. WDKD, a daytime-only station, is the only radio station in Kingstree. Roughly speaking, radii of its 0.5-mv/m contour extend about 35 miles. All of Williamsburg County and substantial areas beyond are served by the station. Twenty-six other stations furnish 0.5-mv/m contour. Only three of these stations, however, furnish 0.5-mv/m service to as much as half of that area. Of those three, WIS, Columbia, S.C., serves the largest portion, 63.4 percent (WDKD exhibit 23).

41. WDKD's programing for the composite week covering its last renewal period, exclusive of entertainment and commercial spot announcements, may be thus briefly described. Sunday (December 14, 1958): *Religion,* one 1-hour program; *News,* five programs, total duration 32 minutes and 4 seconds. Monday (February 2, 1959): *Religion,* 2 programs, total duration 29 minutes and 12 seconds; *Agriculture,* one 4-minute 20-second program; *Sports,* 2 programs total duration 13 minutes and 52 seconds; *News,* 12 programs, total duration 1 hour 1 minute and 32 seconds; *Speech,* one 14-minute and 20-second program. Tuesday (March 10, 1959): *Public service,* one 4-minute and 20-second program ("Fire Prevention"); *Religion,* one 14-minute and 50-second program; *Agriculture,* one 4-minute and 20-second program; *Sports,* 2 programs, total duration, 13 minutes and 52 seconds; *News,* 11 programs, total duration 57 minutes and 14 seconds; *Speech,* one 14-minute and 10-second program. Wednesday (April 29, 1959): *Public service,* 2 programs ("Fire Prevention" and "Army Bandstand") total duration 18 minutes and 50 seconds; *Religion,* one 14-minute and 20-second program; *Agriculture,* one 4-minute and 20-second program; *Sports,* 3 programs, total duration 18 minutes and 20 seconds; *News,* 13 programs, total duration 53 minutes and 30 seconds; *Speech,* one 14-minute and 20-second program. Thursday (May 21, 1959): *Public service,* one 14-minute and 30-second program (country music); *Religion,* one 14-minute and 20-second program; *Agriculture,* one 4-minute and 20-second program; *Sports,* 2 programs, total duration 13 minutes and 20 seconds; *News,* 11 programs, total duration 54 minutes and 42 seconds; *Speech,* one 14-minute and 20-second program. Friday (July 17, 1959): *Public service,* one 14-minute program ("Health Magazine"); *Religion,* one 14-minute and 30-second program; *Agriculture,* one 4-minute and 20-second program; *Sports,*

---

[11] Negligible portions of the foregoing findings relating to the history and composition of Kingstree are officially noted.

2 programs, total duration 15 minutes; *News,* 11 programs, total duration 54 minutes and 30 seconds; *Speech,* one 14-minute and 30-second program. Saturday (September 5, 1959): *Religion* 2 programs, total duration 28 minutes and 40 seconds; *Agriculture,* one 4-minute and 20-second program; *Sports,* 3 programs, total duration 1 hour 59 minutes and 40 seconds (ball game, 1 hour and 45 minutes); *News,* 11 programs, total duration 49 minutes and 40 seconds; *Speech,* one 14-minute and 20-second program[12] (FCC exhibit 3).

42. The presentation of spot announcements played a major role in WDKD's on-the-air operation during its last renewal period. Robinson in his renewal application stated that the station did not expect to present more than four spot announcements during any 14½-minute time period. This was a mistake, he testified; what he had intended to say was that not more than 4 minutes of spot announcement continuity would be included in any 14½-minute time segment (27 percent). Even this latter policy had been impossible of implementation due to the pressure from advertisers. Robinson admitted that on occasion the station presented as many as 10, 12, and 14 spot announcements during a 14½-minute time segment; that he would not be surprised if WDKD had not broadcast as many as 420 spot announcements in 1 day; that on occasion when announcers ran over the time scheduled for their programs, program material, including news, not spot announcements, were not carried to recapture time thus lost; and that announcers sometimes complained about the amount of commercial continuity they were required to present. Ward testified that it was not unusual when he was at WDKD for him to broadcast as many as 10 spot announcements in a 14½-minute time period, and that on one occasion he recalled presenting 15. Green testified that the station frequently carried more than six spot announcements during such time segments and that during sales trips he frequently heard complaints to the effect that the station was running too many spot announcements back to back and too close together (Tr. 177, 252, 254, 255, 258-262, 533, 536, 642, 644).

43. During WDKD's composite week the station carried 1,448 spot announcements.[13] This figure, while it may reflect an annual average, does not reflect the numerical peaks and concentration of spot announcements which the station frequently achieved. For example, on August 6 and 7, 1960, the station carried 448 and 475 spot announcements, respectively, on those 2 days. On October 16, 1959, the "Hymn Time" program which began at 10:10 a.m. contained spot announcements at the following intervals of time: 10:10, 10:12, 10:14, 10:18, 10:19, 10:21, 10:22, 10:23, 10:24,

---

[12] Time on the air for the station during the composite week was: Sunday, 10 hours and 44½ minutes; Monday, 12 hours and 27 minutes; Tuesday, 13 hours; Wednesday, 13 hours and 12 minutes; Thursday, 14 hours and 12 minutes; Friday, 14 hours and 29½ minutes; Saturday, 13 hours and 27 minutes.

[13] Robinson in his renewal application reported the number of spot announcements carried by WDKD during the composite week as 1,077 (FCC exhibit 4).

10:25, 10:27, 10:28. In the time segment between 10:45 and 10:59, spot announcements were carried at 10:48, 10:49, 10:50, 10:52, 10:53, 10:54, 10:55, 10:57, and 10:58. On October 9, 1959, the program "Three B's In Music" contained commercial spots carried at 2:03, 2:04, 2:05, 2:06, 2:07, 2:08, 2:09, 2:10, 2:11, and 2:12. On the program entitled, "Spiritual Crossroads" broadcast the same day between 2:30 and 2:44:30, spots were listed at 2:32, 2:34, 2:35, 2:36, 2:37, 2:38, 2:39, 2:40, 2:41, 2:42, and 2:43. On the program, "Memory Lane," beginning at 5:15 and ending 5:29:30 also broadcast on October 9, spots were carried at 5:18, 5:20, 5:21, 5:22, 5:23, 5:24, 5:25, 5:26, 5:27, 5:28, and 5:29. On October 22, 1959, on program "Records at Random," spot announcements were carried at 1:32, 1:34, 1:35, 1:36, 1:37, 1:38, 1:39, 1:40, 1:41, 1:42, 1:43, and 1:44. On October 10, 1959, the program "Hymn Time" included spot announcements at 10:30, 10:32:30, 10:33, 10:33:30, 10:34:30, 10:37:30, 10:38, 10:38:30, 10:39:30, 10:42, 10:42:30, 10:44. On Christmas Day 1959 on a program entitled "Christmas Music," WDKD carried commercials at the following times between 2:30 and 2:59:20: 2:31, 2:31:30, 2:32, 2:32:30, 2:33, 2:33:30, 2:34, 2:34:30, 2:35, 2:35:30, 2:36, 2:36:30, 2:38, 2:39, 2:40, 2:41, 2:42, 2:43, 2:46, 2:46:30, 2:47, 2:47:30, 2:48, 2:48:30, 2:49, 2:49:30, 2:50, 2:50:30, 2:51, 2:51:30, 2:52, 2:52:30, 2:53, 2:53:30, and 2:55; and during the time segment from 3:39:30 to 3:45 at the following times: 3:31:30, 3:32, 3:32:45, 3:33, 3:33:30, 3:34, 3:34:30, 3:36:30, 3:37, 3:37:45, 3:38, 3:38:30, 3:39, 3:39:30, 3:40:25, 3:41, 3:45 (Tr. 263, 265-267, 270, 271, 780-782, 787, and FCC exhibit 3).

44. Robinson testified that commercially, WDKD was a seasonal station, that the season ran from August to December. To offset the considerable evidence in the record reflecting the numerically high and heavily concentrated nature of WDKD's spot announcement performance, there was introduced into evidence on behalf of applicant a document entitled "Spot Announcements for a Week in February 1958, January 1959, and June 1960 (Off Season)." While the exhibit certainly demonstrates that not all of the 14½-minute time segments at WDKD during its "Off Season" were heavily saturated with spot announcements, the exhibit does show the following: For the week selected in February 1958 the station had twenty-eight 14½-minute time segments in which 5 spot announcements were carried, 9 such segments where 6 spots were carried, 8 where 7 were carried, 5 where 8 were carried, and a segment where 9 were carried. During the week in January 1959; the station had 27 segments where 5 spots were carried, 15 where 6 were carried, 7 where 7 were carried, 2 where 8 were carried, a segment where 9 were carried, and a segment where 10 were carried. During the June week in 1960, the station had 38 segments where 5 spots were carried, 27 where 6 were carried, 10 where 7 were carried, 8 where 8 were carried, 2 where 9 were carried, a segment where 10 were carried and

a segment where 11 were carried (Tr. 177, 771-774, and WDKD exhibit 22).

45. A picture of how WDKD operated during a broadcast day may be obtained from the description set forth in the paragraph below, which is taken from a WDKD program log chosen at random. The day described is *June 10, 1960,* a Friday, a good day for spot sales, looking as it does to Saturday merchandising, but a day that did not fall within WDKD's so-called "peak season," August-December. (See par. 44, above.)

46. The station signed on at 5 a.m. with recorded music. At 5:03 a musical record, participating program called "Rise and Shine" came on and ran until 6.[14] During the course of that program, 17 spot announcements were presented.[15] At 6 a 4-minute, sustaining "News" program came on, followed by a spot announcement.[16] At 6:05 a musical record, participating program was presented entitled "Grits and Gravy." This program lasted until 7, but was interrupted by 19 spot announcements and at 6:30 by a 4-minute musical record, commercial program called, "Dreher Jamboree." At 7 a sponsored "News" program came on for 4½ minutes, followed by a spot announcement. At 7:05 a sponsored "S.C. News and Weather" program came on for 4 minutes.[17] At 7:09 a sponsored "Weather Report" came on for 30 seconds. At 7:10 a sponsored "Sports" program came on for 9½ minutes, followed by a spot announcement. At 7:20 a musical record, participating show entitled "Musical Timetable" was presented. This program, which ran until 8:50, was interrupted by 20 spot announcements, for 4½ minutes at 8 for news and weather and for 4½ minutes at 8:25 for a transcribed commercial message on behalf of a political candidate. At 8:50 "Dreher Jamboree" returned for 4½ minutes, followed by a spot announcement. At 8:55 a sponsored "News" program came on for 4½ minutes, followed by a spot announcement. At 9 a participating musical record program entitled "Church by the Side of Road" came on for 15 minutes. The program contained nine spot announcements. At 9:15 "Morning Devotions" was presented live, sustaining, for 14½ minutes, followed by a spot announcement. At 9:30 "Melodies for M'Lady," a musical record, participating show was presented for 30 minutes. During this program

[14] A participating program is a program the time for which is not paid for by a sponsor but in which commercial spot announcements are intermittently broadcast throughout the program.

[15] In logging the "Rise and Shine" participating program, the station, as it did with all other participating shows, followed the practice of logging the last spot announcement separately from the program, thus disassociating the spot from the participating program. There seems to be no rational basis for this practice and the examiner in the interests of brevity has counted such announcements as one of the spot announcements carried during the participating program.

[16] A sustaining program is one not paid for by a sponsor.

[17] A sponsored program, or commercial program, is a program the time for which is paid for by a sponsor. Commercial messages on behalf of the sponsor are usually carried at the beginning of the program, at the end of the program, and not infrequently during the program.

16 spot announcements were broadcast. At 10 a 4½-minute, sponsored "News" program came on, followed by a spot announcement. At 10:05 "Hymn Time," a musical record, participating show, came on and continued until 10:55. This program was interrupted at 10:25 for 4½ minutes by a transcribed, commercial political message and 28 spot announcements. At 10:55 a sponsored "News and Weather" program came on for 4½ minutes, followed by a spot announcement. At 11 "Mountain Jamboree," a musical record, participating program, came on and continued until 12:20. This program was interrupted at 11:55 by a 4½-minute, sponsored program entitled "Weather and Streams," at 12 by a 4½-minute, sponsored "News" program and by 38 spot announcements. At 12:20 a 9½-minute, sponsored live, agricultural program entitled "Your Farm Agent Speaks" came on, followed by a spot announcement. At 12:30 a 4½-minute, sponsored "S.C. Market and Weather Report" came on, followed by a spot announcement. At 12:35 a 9½-minute musical record, participating program entitled "Western Startime" was presented. This program contained five spot announcements. At 12:45 a 14½-minute, sponsored "Exchange Bank News" program came on, followed by a spot announcement. At 1 a 14½-minute, sponsored program entitled "Old Trading Post," a kind of classified want ad program, was presented. This program was followed by a spot announcement. At 1:15 a 45-minute musical record, participating program, entitled "Records at Random," came on. This program included 18 spot announcements. At 2 a 30-minute musical record, participating program, entitled "Three B's in Music" was presented. Twelve spot announcements were included in this program. At 2:30 a 30-minute musical record, participating program entitled "Spiritual Crossroads" was presented. This program included 11 spot announcements. At 3 a 1-hour musical record, participating program entitled "Platter Party" came on. This program was interrupted at 3:25 by a 4½-minute transcribed presentation on behalf of a political candidate and by 21 spot announcements. At 4 an hour-and-a-half musical record, participating program entitled "Sundown Hoedown" was presented. This program was interrupted by 36 spot announcements and by a 4½-minute, sponsored "Dreher Jamboree" program at 4:30 and by a 4½-minute, sustaining "News" program at 5. At 5:30 a 30-minute musical record, participating program entitled "Pop Tunes" was presented. This program was interrupted by 14 spot announcements and, for 14½ minutes at 5:55 by a transcribed commercial message on behalf of a political candidate. At 6 a 4½-minute, sustaining "News" program came on, followed by a spot announcement. At 6:05 a 9½-minute, sustaining "Sports" program came on, followed by a spot announcement. At 6:15 a musical record, participating program entitled "Bandstand" came on for 45 minutes. This program included 20 spot announcements. At 7 a 4½-minute, sponsored "News" program came on, followed by a spot announcement. At 7:05 a musical record, participating program called "Sunset

Serenade" came on for 22 minutes. This program included six spot announcements. The station signed off at 7:27 (examiner's exhibit 1).

47. From the facts set forth in the previous paragraph, the following table may be obtained which will serve to give a bird's-eye view of how WDKD utilized the 14 hours and 27 minutes the station was on the air during the day under discussion:

News and weather	68 minutes.
Sports	19 minutes.
Transcribed political broadcasts	18 minutes.
Religion	14½ minutes.
Agriculture	9½ minutes.
Classified want ads	14½ minutes.
Musical records and commercial continuity, including 305 spot announcements.	12 hours 3½ minutes.
Total	14 hours 27 minutes.

Thus, some 17 percent of the station's broadcast day was devoted to material other than musical records and spot announcements. News and/or weather was presented 14 times during the day. On 10 occasions the program lasted 4½ minutes; twice, 4 minutes; once, 14½ minutes; and once, 30 seconds. Sports were presented twice, each program lasting 9½ minutes. There were four transcribed commercial political broadcasts, each lasting 4½ minutes. Religion, agriculture, and classified want ads were single programs.

48. The musical records played over WDKD fall into five general categories: (1) hillbilly, country and western; (2) popular music; (3) spirituals; (4) rock-'n-roll; and (5) popular music for teenagers. This record format is designed to reach the different type listners the station has determined the station serves, based on mail and personal interviews (Tr. 176).

49. In respect of other program categories, Robinson described WDKD's program activities at considerable length. The substance of his testimony may be thus digested: *Religion:* Years ago he adopted a policy of "religion No. 1, public service No. 2, the business will take care of itself." An hour each Sunday is set aside for church services. That hour is turned over to the local ministerial association. The association works out the scheduling of the services. The program rotates weekly from one church to another. Each morning the station also carries a 15-minute program entitled "Morning Devotions." This latter program also rotates among ministers respresenting various faiths. Some of the "Morning Devotions" programs are carried remote from churches, others originate in the station's studios. Further, the station also carries a tape-recorded program on Satur-

day morning called "Voice of Pentecost," which originates in Blaney, S.C.[18] It might be noted here that whatever the shortcomings of WDKD in other special program areas or in its overall program aspects, and notwithstanding the confusion in Robinson's testimony on the subject of religious programing, as noted below, the record does show that the station did in fact evince, during its last renewal period, a bona fide sensitivity and responsiveness to the religious needs of the community it served. *Education:* The station works closely with the schools. It cooperates in making announcements "and whatnot," with the training and industrial department of the high school, and when they have sales of light bulbs, boxes of candy, and things like that. The station supports and plugs football, basketball, and baseball games during the season and furnishes a sound truck if necessary. Robinson contacts the county superintendent and principals of the schools and offers them time for discussions "about the schools, and that sort of stuff." Announcements are made concerning preschool registration, kindergarten, and things like that.[19] *News:* The policy of the station is to have news headlines on the half hour and news on the hour. Headlines last 1 minute; news programs 5, 10, and 15 minutes. News originates from whatever information comes to the station during the day, plus information obtained from United Press wire service. Selection is made by announcers on the basis of what they believe the station's listeners would like to hear.[20] *Discussion:*

[18] Robinson at first testified that the station carried an hour-and-a-half religious program called "Hymn Time." Later he testified that this program was logged "commercial"—"entertainment." He also testified that the "Voice of Pentecost" was a 30-minute program. Introduced in applicant's behalf was an exhibit entitled "Public Service Type Programs and Announcements." This exhibit lists "Voice of Pentecost" as a 14½-minute program. Robinson testified that the station also carried on Sunday afternoons a live religious quartet originating in Lake City, S.C. Although the "Public Service Type Programs and Announcements" exhibit scrupulously lists WDKD's religious programs, it does not list any such program as the quartet. The exhibit does show, however, that the station did regularly carry, weekly, a 14½-minute program entitled "Catholic Hour" (Tr. 168-171, WDKD exhibit 10).

[19] On the whole record, it is doubtful if it can be found that WDKD carried any educational programs during its last renewal period. There is testimony in the record that educational programs may have been carried over the station in the past. (See par. 51, infra.) However, neither applicant's exhibit, "Public Service Type Programs and Announcements," nor Bureau counsel's analysis of WDKD's programing during the composite week shows any educational programs. The station did, however, from time to time carry announcements on behalf of schools within their service area (Tr. 172, WDKD exhibit 10, and FCC exhibit 3).

[20] Robinson appears to have given the station a little the best of it on regularity of news headlines and duration of news programs. Bureau counsel's analysis of applicant's composite week disclosed only three news headlines. These were carried at 1:59:30 on Wednesday, Thursday, and Friday. Moreover, reference to the time spent daily on news programs during the composite week shows little likelihood that 10- and 15-minute news programs were carried over WDKD with any such frequency as Robinson's testimony suggests. Bureau's analysis indicates that news and headlines were carried more on the order of their presentation as described in paragraph 46, above (FCC exhibit 3).

"Discussion programs . . . we don't have too many of them. We ask the people to come out, and we offer time for these discussion programs, but we've had very few of them." *Talk:* The station carried very few talk programs. Locally, it is hard to get people to put on this type program. *Public service* (programs on behalf of nonprofit organizations): The station schedules all public services and cooperates with churches, schools, civic organizations, or what have you. The station refuses nobody—"We take all that stuff, put it on the air, we solicit it, we do everything we possibly can to assist those people in these public services."[21] *Agriculture:* a farm program carried live from the county agent's office is presented 5 days a week from 12:20 to 12:30 p.m. A 5-minute market report is carried 6 days a week, giving market prices taken from the UP wire service. "The Old Trading Post" is carried from 1 to 1:15, 6 days a week. This program is sponsored and designed for both farm and city people to use as a vehicle for advertising lost-and-found items and trade items, including farm equipment, cows, dogs, houses to rent, and farms for sale. During the tobacco season (August-December) the station carries daily for 15 minutes, Monday through Friday, as a part of a small network, live market reports from the tobacco sales barn at Lake City. This program is carried annually for about a 6 weeks' period. A similar program originating in Kingstree is also carried by the station. Further, reports on the tobacco market in Hemingway are received by the station by telephone and presented over WDKD in the form of spot announcements (Tr. 129-136, 167-168, 171-172, 173-175, 176, 179-184).

Evidence of community support for Robinson and his stewardship of WDKD

50. As before mentioned, 17 witnesses besides Robinson took the stand on his behalf. Who they were and the essence of what they testified to is digested in the following paragraphs.

---

[21] In support of Robinson's testimony here, it should be noted that applicant's exhibit "Public Service Type Programs and Announcements," which lists the programs and announcements carried by WDKD on behalf of nonprofit organizations for the year 1958, all but June, October, and November of 1959 and all but November and December of 1960 is slightly over 150 pages long, with programs and announcements listed on each page single space to an item. The examiner counted 1,880 programs of this type carried by the station during the period covered. The average in round figures is 60 per month, or roughly 2 a day. From the examiner's inspection, it would appear that virtually all of these programs were recorded and furnished by the sponsoring agency. Another exhibit of applicant's which speaks on behalf of its programing in the category under discussion is entitled "Awards Received by WDKD During Last Renewal Period." This exhibit shows that expressions of commendation were received by the station from the Army, the Thor Research Center for Better Farm Living, Navy-Marine Corps, National Guard, Crippled Children's Society, Methodist Men's Hour, U.S. Olympic Association, and U.S. Department of Agriculture (WDKD exhibits 10 and 11).

51. *Lawrence Harry Fry* is a teacher of vocational subjects at Kingstree High School. WDKD participates in the on-the-job training aspects of the high schools' diversified occupations program. Three students have been trained at WDKD in connection with that program. WDKD for years carried a weekly program entitled "Your School Speaks," which covered various substantive areas of the schools' academic program; e.g., music, English, and history. On one or two occasions he appeared on that program. The station also carried a music program for teenagers called "Teen-Age Beat." The station taped home football games for rebroadcast and, when possible, similarly taped games away from home. Any time the school requests that an announcement be broadcast, the station is always cooperative. Charlie Walker was continually doing public service work. He recalled that Walker on one occasion came to the school and auctioned off cakes on behalf on the March of Dimes. That year Walker worked with the March of Dimes drive, and the drive raised as much, or more, money than had ever been similarly raised for that cause. Walker also aided underprivileged children. He had not listened to Walker broadcast over WDKD to any great extent. When he had listened, he had not heard anything offensive—"a joke about some individual, something like that; I mean no more than you hear on television today." In response to a question as to whether WDKD had served the needs of the community, Fry responded:

> I feel this, in my own mind, because, as I say, I've worked with it closely for the last 3 to 4 years, and I have asked them on numbers of occasions to help with some particular function that was going on at the school and also some of my students were putting on, and anything else—I've heard the statements made throughout the town: If you want something, help, call the radio station and they'll help you. I've heard that statement made all the time. And they have always cooperated a hundred percent in anything you ever asked them to do. I don't know of any time a worthwhile project they haven't helped in any way they could (Tr. 361, 362, 366–369, 370, 372, 377).

52. *Ralph Cleo Fennell* is county superintendent of education and member of the board of the Greeleyville Methodist Church. In connection with a fundraising drive for his church he, as advertising chairman, requested WDKD to carry publicity for the drive. The station carried those announcements. Charlie Walker in connection with the March of Dimes drive visited each of the classes in the Greeleyville area schools. He generated a great deal of enthusiasm among the students. They participated in the drive. The drive was a success and Walker gave the winning class a party. When because of bad weather county schools were forced to close, WDKD worked in close cooperation with the county board of education in issuing over the station early morning notices of school status. He had heard comments about the Walker programs. He was not interested in what was said. He recalled having heard Walker make references to towns by nick-

names; he did not pay much attention; he was trying to listen to the announcements. He did not remember having heard Walker tell any stories. He did recall hearing him make about the best plea for a family that had been burned out that he had ever heard. The response to that plea was, he believed, great. While Walker had made some mistakes, that is past and gone. While he is condemned, he had his good side too. WDKD, in his opinion, has met the needs of the community in which it serves. In connection with the work for which he is responsible, it has certainly met those needs (Tr. 381-384, 385, 387, 388, 390, 391).

53. *Louis L. Law* is president and cashier of the Williamsburg State Bank in Kingstree, a director of the local and State tuberculosis association, on the executive council of the South Carolina Banking Association, and on the board of stewards of the Kingstree Methodist Church. He has heard the station carry material on behalf of a large number of nonprofit organizations—State, National, and local. Material on behalf of churches and the highway department he knew to be programs; the remainder could have been spot announcements. His son works at WDKD. His son went to the station through the schools' diversified occupations program. The boy, 16 years old, had difficulty in adjustment, but since employment with WDKD has been thoroughly happy. He has improved in many ways, particularly in voice, poise, and diction. Credit for the improvement goes to the Robinsons. On his own volition he went to Robinson and asked if there was anything he could do for him in connection with the instant hearing. He was present at a discussion of the hearing (then forthcoming) in Charlestown, S.C., a discussion which included Mr. Lane, Mr. Taylor, and E. D. Rivers, manager of WCSC at Charleston. Mr. Rivers reported that Carroll Godwin would testify and would tell the truth. This was all that he, Law, asked; it was all that he wanted. It would be inaccurate to suggest that his call with others upon Rivers was to suggest that Godwin not testify at the hearing as an employee of Rivers. Through Law, a document entitled "Resolution of Kingstree Business Men" was introduced. The resolution states that Robinson is a fit and proper person to operate WDKD; that he would not knowingly allow anything of an immoral nature to be broadcast over his station; that WDKD has served the county of Williamsburg and surrounding areas in a good and proper manner; that Robinson's policy is, when opportunity presents itself, to perform proper service; that Robinson should be allowed to continue management of WDKD and perform the same service as the station has performed in the past. The document is signed by two bank presidents, the county superintendent of education, chairman of the board of the local hospital, the county farm agent, the county sheriff, the county health officer, the president of the chamber of commerce, and the president of the junior chamber of commerce (Tr. 393-401, 406-409, and WDKD exhibit 12).

54. *Cornelius Graham Bass* is secretary-treasurer of the Santee Oil

Co., secretary-treasurer and general manager of Services, Inc., partner and general manager of the S & P Tire Co., president of Warsaw Manufacturing Co., president of Kingstree Industrial Development Corp., chairman of the county board of education. He listens to WDKD. He advertises over WDKD. At times he requested that his advertising over the station be handled by Charlie Walker because Walker's listening audience was the largest that could be reached by any media in the area. He confirmed previous testimony relating to WDKD's cooperation with local schools. WDKD had been helpful through the use of spot announcements in obtaining for the chamber of commerce a register of potential employees for an industry which at the time was considering moving to Kingstree and subsequently did move there. Any request for time over WDKD by any Boy Scout or chamber of commerce drive he had been connected with had always met with generous response. The Lions Club used the station to promote a sale to aid underprivileged children. He listened to Charlie Walker over WDKD; whether what he heard was suggestive depended on whether you used preacher standards or the standards prevalent on radio and TV. Under his personal standards he didn't regard the Walker material as suggestive, vulgar, obscene, or indecent. He had heard material that could be considered subject to double meaning. He had heard such remarks as "that guy Charlie Walker. I just don't know how he gets away with it," made in the community during discussions of the Charlie Walker show. His testimony concerning the Walker broadcasts was based on what he had heard Walker broadcast. He had heard Walker refer to "Brown, the Clown," "Candy Man," and "Ann Drawers." He had not heard Walker make reference to taking his girl to a cow pasture. He had heard Walker make reference to "letting it all hang out" in service stations, but didn't know whether he had heard him use that phrase over the air. In his opinion WDKD has "very definitely" met the needs of the public which it serves. It would be a great loss to the area if the station were to be lost. (Tr. 413–416, 419–423).

55. *Donald L. Taylor* is president of the Exchange Bank of Kingstree. The bank has advertised over WDKD for from 6 to 10 years. The board of directors conditioned their sponsorship of a 15-minute program over WDKD on Charlie Walker handling it. The program ran several years for 6 or 8 weeks during the Kingstree Tobacco Market. The bank has since then, and for several years, also sponsored another 15-minute program over WDKD. He seldom listens to radio. He does not have the time. He is a personal friend of Robinson's. Robinson is a stockholder in the bank. He went with Law and Lane to Charleston to talk to E. D. Rivers. He and Law contacted Lane to set up an appointment with Rivers. Lane introduced both him and Law to Rivers and said they were interested as to whether Godwin was antagonistic toward WDKD. Rivers took over and assured them Godwin was telling the truth. The only reason they talked to

Rivers rather than Godwin was a matter of choice. There was no idea of putting pressure on anybody. In his opinion, based on his knowledge of the community and the things WDKD had done, he believes the station has served the community (Tr. 424–426, 428–431, 433, 434).

56. *James N. Hinnant* is owner of the Southern Discount Co., the principal business of which is financing and sale of automobiles. He is past chairman of the Polk National Foundation Fund for Infantile Paralysis and past chairman of the county Red Cross chapter. He has served as president of Little League Baseball; State director of the recreational association; alderman of Kingstree (two terms); on board of directors of Rotary Club; president of Royal Motors, Inc.; board member, trustee, and president of Bible Class of Methodist Church. At present he is chairman of the citizens councils of the county, on the State board from the county, and on the State executive committee. He listens to WDKD. He advertises over WDKD. Conservatively speaking, 90 percent of his advertising was placed on the Charlie Walker program at his request. This was because of Walker's extensive coverage. Through Charlie Walker the station promoted the Little League Baseball's fund drives for charities, a family that was burned out, financing the hospitalization of a boy who was a victim of that fire (in 2 or 3 days necessary funds were oversubscribed). Cancer drives and a very successful March of Dimes drive were handled by the station. In expressing his opinion of the station, the witness testified:

> I think that the greatest thing that Kingstree has and Williamsburg County has to date as a civic thing and promotional of Williamsburg County is radio station WDKD. I think they have done more than any other two or three organizations due to the facilities that they have in the promotion and progress of Williamsburg County.

> If there is such a thing as an organization exceeding its public debt . . . to a community, they have done that . . . (Tr. 437–443).

57. *John C. Flagler* is owner and operator of 10 general merchandise stores in Williamsburg, Georgetown, and Clarendon Counties. He advertises over WDKD. He requested that his advertising be presented by Charlie Walker. He did this because Walker brought customers into his store, and he is interested in making money. He was not offended when Walker referred to him over the air as the only man in the county who could stand up and milk a cow. Whenever there was a need for fundraising or for blood donors, Walker always carried the ball. Walker was serious about such promotions and spoke from the heart. His business fell off about 20 percent after Walker left. Business is improving, but recovery is slow. He has to work hard. When Walker was on WDKD he did not have to work so hard. In his opinion, WDKD has definitely met the needs of the populations it serves, and more (Tr. 445–448).

58. *Lucius Kennedy Montgomery* is an architectural designer, a mem-

ber of the Kingstree City Council, and secretary of the board of trustees of the Kingstree Methodist Church. He has been president of the Kingstree Chamber of Commerce for 7 years. WDKD has carried spot announcements on behalf of the chamber. He corroborated previous testimony concerning WDKD's role in securing an employment pool for an industry moving into Kingstree. He did not know of WDKD ever having aired a program for the chamber of commerce, but neither did he know that the chamber had ever made request for a program. In his opinion WDKD very definitely has met the needs of the areas and populations which it serves. Through this witness two exhibits were introduced; both are resolutions. Both are to the same purport as the resolution of the Kingstree businessmen. The first is entitled, "Resolution of Mayor and Council of Kingstree," and is signed by the mayor and six councilmen, one of whom is Montgomery. The second, signed by Montgomery as president and eight other members of the board of directors, is entitled "Resolution of the Chamber of Commerce" (Tr. 459–465 and WDKD exhibits 13 and 14).

59. *Weldon B. Bower* is plant manager of a branch of the Drexel Furniture Co. and is mayor of Kingstree. He has occasionally listened to WDKD. He agreed wholeheartedly with statements on behalf of the station made by previous witnesses. The station has performed excellent service in Kingstree. He has made a decision not to listen to the Charlie Walker program because of its content. He only listens to radio when he is in his car. He does not subscribe to the type of program or music that is usually heard on local radio. Unless it is something he enjoys, he turns it off. He did not listen to the radio for the Charlie Walker program. On occasion he had heard that program. He had heard material that could be interpreted as being of a suggestive nature. He could not answer as to whether the Walker program grew progressively worse. Everybody at first listened to Walker; it was an innovation, a novelty. He did not care for that type of broadcasting —its flippancy. He could not say there were obscenities; he just didn't like that kind of broadcasting. The only reference he could recall made by Walker was to "Smooch Me Quick Crossroads." He thought Walker called Andrews "Ann drawers." He had no recollection of Robinson ever approaching him for the broadcast of material of interest to him or to the city council (Tr. 466–472).

60. *James Hugh McCutchen* is manager of the Williamsburg Livestock Co., dealing in farm machinery, and ruling elder of the Williamsburg Presbyterian Church. He has listened to WDKD and the Charlie Walker show. He had no objection to his wife or children listening to that program. He believed that he could affirm all of the testimony previously given by WDKD witnesses concerning the public-service work of WDKD. Along with supporting Red Cross and Boy and Girl Scout activities, the station had always carried church services. He did not believe that a fundraising activity could be named in which WDKD had not taken part. The station has

very definitely met the needs of the area. Those it serves would be in bad shape if they did not have the station (Tr. 449–450).

61. *J. Lindwood Tyler* farms and also manages Belk's Department Store. He listens to WDKD. His store advertises over WDKD. He requested that to the extent possible the store's spots be handled by Charlie Walker. Walker had a good following and he was well accepted by many customers who would remark that they had heard Walker advertising for Belk's. He had listened to Walker's broadcasts but did not think he had heard a complete program. The civic activities of WDKD previously testified to cover his knowledge of that field and are correct. The store places so many spot announcements with WDKD it would be impossible for one announcer to handle them all. The store places as many as 60 spots over a 3-day period. He did not know whether the store carried 30-second spots or 1-minute spots. He has never been dissatisfied with the duration of the Belk's announcements. In his opinion, he believes the station has met the needs of the population and areas it serves (Tr. 452–459).

62. *Clarence P. Snowden, Jr.,* is a member of the town council of Hemingway, S.C. Through the witness an exhibit entitled "Hemingway Resolution" was introduced. This exhibit, which, except for the words "town of Hemingway" in place of "town of Kingstree" is, in its body, identical with the resolution of the Kingstree businessmen. It is signed by the mayor of Hemingway and four councilmen (Tr. 473–474, 476, and WDKD exhibit 16).

63. *T. E. Ruffin* operates department stores in Hemingway and Andrews, S.C. He advertises over WDKD 3, 4, and perhaps 5 days a week, utilizing 8 to 15 spots per day. Through this witness an exhibit entitled "Hemingway Businessmen" was introduced. The exhibit is a resolution framed to the same general purport as the other resolutions introduced into evidence by WDKD and is signed by the president of the Hemingway Merchants Association, secretary of Hemingway Merchants Association, president of Ruffin's Department Store, Inc., president of Ratcliff's Department Store, Inc., vice president of Hyman Motors, Inc., a representative of Red and White Supermarket, president of Stuckey Bros. Furniture Co., pastor of Old Johnsonville Methodist Church, vice president of Anderson State Bank, Inc., a representative of the Hemingway Home Development Co., and the principal of the Hemingway schools (Tr. 477–478, 481, 482, and WDKD exhibit 17).

64. *Leonard Grossman* is manager of the General Drygoods Store and alderman [councilman] of the town of Greeleyville, S.C. Through this witness a resolution was introduced similar in content to those previously introduced and entitled "Greeleyville Resolution." It is signed by the mayor and four councilmen of that town (Tr. 488–489 and WDKD exhibit 19).

65. *W. Frank Mishoe* is a member of the South Carolina House of Representatives. He farms and has a retail feed and seed business. He ad-

vertises over WDKD. The station carried about 20 to 25 of his spots a month. He occasionally listens to WDKD. Years ago he listened to Charlie Walker. He was not sure that he had or had not heard Walker during the last 3 years. He could not recall anything suggestive that Walker had broadcast. He did not pay that much attention to it. Through this witness an exhibit entitled "Resolution of Legislative Delegation" was introduced. In its entirety, as received, it reads:

This is to certify that we the undersigned members of the Williamsburg County legislative delegation are of the opinion that radio station WDKD has met the commercial and civic needs of the people of Williamsburg County in the field of communications, information, and entertainment (Tr. 492–497 and WDKD exhibit 20).

66. *Woody Brooks* is president and general manager of the Brooks Veneer Co. in Andrews, S.C., and mayor of Andrews. He has listened to the Charlie Walker program perhaps a half-dozen times. His testimony on the Walker program was based on knowledge of the program thus gained. Whether what Walker broadcast was suggestive depended on the listener's frame of mind. He had heard Walker use the term "Ann drawers" and if one had the mind, that reference could be considered a little off color. He thought Walker was "sort of a nut." He seldom listened to him. He had never heard Walker talk of taking his girl to a cow pasture. He made a point to turn Walker off most of the time when he heard him. He did this not because Walker's programs were objectionable but because they were of a type he did not appreciate. He does not like country music. He had no particular objection to Walker's language. It was not only the music in the Walker programs that he objected to, but it was the entire format of the program. He did not like the " 'Uncle Willie this and that,' 'you know, boys,' that kind of jazz." He did not purport to be an expert on Walker's type of entertainment. Through this witness a document entitled "Resolution of Citizens of Andrews" was introduced. It, too, commends the general operation of WDKD and Robinson and recommends renewal of the station's license. It is signed by the mayor and the chief of police of Andrews; Reynolds, of the Reynolds Drug Co.; the president of Blakeley Bros.; the president of Hemingway Motor Co.; superintendent of schools of Andrews; and an agriculture teacher (Tr. 483–487 and WDKD exhibit 18).

67. *Roger R. Nettles* is president of Moore-Nettles Co., Inc. (wholesale sand and gravel), and member of the City Council of Lake City, S.C. Robinson had never approached him to put on programs of civic importance. Lake City recently had a bond issue of major local concern. He did request that WDKD run a local civic notice and the station carried the item. Through this witness an exhibit entitled "Resolution of Mayor of Lake City and Others" was introduced. Similar in content to the other resolutions, it was signed, besides Nettles, by the mayor of Lake City,

president of the Lake City Rotary Club, worshipful master of Lake City No. 193 AFM, the president of W. Lee Flowers Co., the president of Lake City Chamber of Commerce, the president of the Council of Women's Federated Clubs of South Carolina, and the president of Lake City State Bank (Tr. 498–502 and WDKD exhibit 15).

CONCLUSIONS

1. The pivotal issue in this case is issue 3—did Robinson permit Walker to broadcast over his station material that was coarse, vulgar, suggestive, and susceptible of indecent, double meaning? Putting aside for the moment Robinson's role in the Walker broadcasts, a subject which will be treated below in connection with the second issue, the character of those broadcasts is now considered. In dealing with this matter one is faced at the outset with the free-speech implications surrounding the subject. This is so, not only because of Robinson's claims of first-amendment protection for the Walker broadcasts, but because words spoken by an individual are here involved and due regard for a precious heritage of the American people requires anyone, cast in the role of assaying the import of words spoken with a corollary responsibility to do something about them, to approach the task with an awareness that he is operating on near-sacred ground. The agency on whose behalf the examiner initially speaks, charged with the responsibility for determining the composition of traffic over the air, *NBC* v. *U.S.,* 319 U.S. 190, 216, has traditionally been most assiduous in leaning over backward to avoid exercising its authority in such fashion as to make even the slightest incursion into those liberties protected by the first amendment.

2. Robinson in his proposed findings attempts to place the Commission on the horns of a dilemma. He contends that if the Commission should find the Walker broadcasts to be obscene or indecent it would be acting ultra vires since the United States Code, 18 U.S.C. 1464, makes the broadcast of obscene and indecent material a crime, and determination of crime is for courts alone, not for administrative agencies.[22] If the Commission were to find the Walker broadcasts to be something less than obscene or indecent, claims Robinson, it would be violating the free-speech protection afforded by the first amendment.

3. The first thrust of Robinson's argument may be disposed of briefly. In doing so, it is unnecessary to attempt to draw hairline distinctions between the meaning of "coarse, vulgar, suggestive, and susceptible of indecent, double meaning" as used in the issue, and "obscene and indecent" as used in the statute. Webster's New Collegiate Dictionary (2d ed., 1951)

---

[22] Title 18 U.S.C. 1464: "Whoever utters any obscene, indecent, or profane language by means of radio communication shall be fined not more than $10,000 or imprisoned not more than two years, or both." June 25, 1948, ch. 645, 62 Stat. 769.

defines "coarse" as ". . . common, of inferior quality or appearance; mean; . . . harsh, rough, or rude as opposed to delicate or dainty. . . . unrefined; vulgar; gross." "Vulgar" is defined as ". . . boorish; also offensive to good taste or refined feelings; low, coarse . . . obscene; . . . low; as a vulgar joke." "Suggestive" is defined ". . . tending to suggest what is improper, indecent, or the like." "Indecent" is defined as "not decent; specif. . . . unbecoming or unseemly; indecorous . . . morally offensive; unfit to be seen or heard." "Obscene" is defined as ". . . foul; disgusting . . . offensive to chastity or to modesty; lewd." While it might be possible to eke out from those definitions a theory that the words used in the issue are of different import than those used in the statute, such an exercise in semantics would, in the view of the examiner, smack more of logomachy than law or logic, and would be cynical treatment, indeed, of a defense seriously advanced. The examiner is as willing to brand the Walker broadcasts "obscene" and "indecent" as he is to dub them with the adjectives used in the issue. Having conceded that the broadcasts do fall within the proscriptive language of 18 U.S.C. 1464, and at the same time noting that a hearing on a radio station license renewal is in no sense a judicial proceeding looking toward the existence or nonexistence of a crime, the examiner hastens to dispose of the first thrust of Robinson's argument by pointing out that from time to time over the years the theory has been advanced before both the Commission and the courts that when a licensee's conduct has been so bad as to fall afoul of criminal sanctions, that conduct is for "eyes only" of the courts. That view has consistently been rejected by both the courts and the Commission. See *Report on Uniform Policy as to Violation by Applicants of the Laws of the United States,* 1 R.R., part 3, 495, and cases cited therein. Further, by amendment to the Communications Act, effective September 1960, Congress specifically conferred authority on the Commission to act on matters involving violation of 18 U.S.C. 1464. See pages 275–276, infra.

4. In advancing the second front of his argument, Robinson urges that the test for obscenity set forth by the Supreme Court in *Roth* v. *U.S.,* 354 U.S. 476, must be adopted here. That test is: "Whether to the average person, applying contemporary community standards, the dominant theme of the material taken as a whole appeals to prurient interests," id. at 489.[23] Under that test, Robinson contends, the Walker material cannot be found to be obscene because: (1) Walker broadcast a great deal of material that was not of the same nature as the material quoted above and (2) the Walker broadcasts, on the whole, achieved a good deal of acceptability in the community. As will be pointed out in more detail later, contrary to

[23] Webster's New International Dictionary (unabridged, 2d ed., 1934) defines "prurient" in pertinent part as follows: " . . . Itching; longing; uneasy with desire or longing; or persons, having itching, morbid, or lascivious longings; of desire, curiosity, or propensity, lewd. . . .

Robinson's contention, the examiner is of the view that the Walker material at issue here can be found to be obscene under the test approved in *Roth*. However, the instant matter is a case of first impression and, because it is, it is important, if possible, to avoid adopting measures which ripening into precedent might unduly hamper effective radio regulation.[24] It must be conceded that the Court in the *Roth* case did apparently prescribe the test quoted above for use by the Postmaster General in determining the mailability of publications by courts in reviewing his orders, and by State officials in enforcing State laws designed to prevent the origination, sale, advertising, and distribution of obscene writings and photographs. In the view of the examiner, however, the *Roth* case did not purport to establish the test as one that must be applied wherever or whenever a question of obscenity is to be determined.

5. In this and the following two paragraphs the examiner will attempt to explain why he does not believe the *Roth* test was intended for uniform application in all cases where a question of obscenity is involved. The *Roth* decision involved two cases, *Roth* v. *U.S.* and *Alberts* v. *California*. The one involving Roth came up following conviction for violation of a Federal statute prohibiting utilization of the U.S. mails for the dissemination of obscene matter (18 U.S.C. 1461). The other, involving Alberts, came up following conviction for violation of provisions of the California Penal Code prohibiting the authorship, publication, advertising, sale or distribution of obscene matter (West's Cal. Penal Code Ann. 1955, sec. 311). In its decision, the court did the following: It affirmed both convictions below. It unequivocally held that obscenity is not within the area of constitutionally protected speech or press. It rejected a contention that constitutional guarantees had been violated because of failure of proof below to show that the material at issue would have perceptibly created a clear and present danger of antisocial conduct or would probably have induced such conduct. It warned that sex and obscenity are not synonymous and that portrayal of sex in art, literature, and scientific works is not in itself reason to deny first-amendment protection. It warned that ceaseless vigilance is the price of retention of a fundamental liberty; that freedom of speech and press has contributed much to our free society; that the door to Federal and State intrusion into the area of free speech and press must be kept tightly closed, and opened only to the extent necessary to prevent encroachment upon more important interests; that it is vital that the standards for judging ob-

---

[24] As far as the examiner has been able to ascertain, this is the first case the Federal Communications Commission has had where questionable language over the air has been at issue in a renewal proceeding. The Federal Radio Commission did have such a case, *Trinity Methodist Church South* v. *Federal Radio Commission*, 61 App. D.C. 311 (cert. den., 284 U.S. 685). Based upon his review of more recent "free speech" decisions, it is this examiner's considered opinion that there is room for doubt that the courts would now adopt the somewhat sweeping rationale of that decision.

scenity safeguard freedom of speech and press with respect to material which does not treat sex in a manner appealing to prurient interest. It rejected as unconstitutional the *Hicklin* test[25] which allowed judgment of obscenity to turn on the effect excerpts of the material at issue would have upon particularly susceptible persons. It noted with approval the test quoted in the above paragraph as employed in cases subsequent to those which employed the *Hicklin* test. It held that the courts below in their instructions to the jury had sufficiently followed the proper test. It brushed aside objections that the statutes involved were so vague as to deny due process. It concluded that, in light of its holding that obscenity is not protected by the first amendment, the contention that the Federal censorship statute unconstitutionally encroached upon powers reserved to the States and to the people was without merit. It rejected a plea by Alberts that the California statute was void as against him on the ground that his was a mail-order business and Congress had preempted the field in regulation of the mail. As the examiner reads the decision, the foregoing is what the Court held in the *Roth* case and all that it held. The Court did not say that the test therein approved for obscenity was for universal application and, significantly, in coining a short term for the Federal statute involved, it did not refer to "Federal obscenity statutes" but instead to the "Federal obscenity statute"; i.e., the one contained in the U.S. postal laws. Moreover, as the examiner will attempt to point out below, the circumstances surrounding other areas where obscenity is a problem, in and of themselves, speak firmly to the effect that the Court in *Roth* did not intend the test therein approved to be one required for application in all obscenity cases.

6. It hardly seems reasonable that the sideshow barker could publicly describe the physical attributes of his dancing girls in the same terms he might describe them in private and successfully defend against prosecution for public utterance of obscenity with proof that the *average* person was repelled, not moved by the coarseness of his "pitch." It hardly seems reasonable that a motion-picture exhibitor could or should be able to defend against an obscenity charge after intermittently interspersing in an otherwise artistic feature unrelated clips of pure erotica on the ground that the *dominant theme* of the picture viewed in its entirety did not appeal to prurient interests. It hardly seems reasonable that the huckster operating in "skid row" could seek to draw attention to his produce by raucously bawling vulgarities and defend against an obscenity charge on the ground that, considering the complex of the community and its contemporary standards, his language had no appeal to *prurient interest*. While the foregoing examples are, of course, purely hypothetical, it is certainly conceivable that such situations, or some variant of them, could occur.

7. The field of broadcast regulation is perhaps an area as ill adapted as any for employment of the *Roth* test. First, it must be remembered that,

---

[25] *Regina* v. *Hicklin* (1868) L.R. 3 Q.B. 360.

unlike the acquisition of books and pictures, broadcast material is available at the flick of a switch to young and old alike, to the sensitive and the indifferent, to the sophisticated and the credulous. Further, broadcast material is delivered on a route commonly owned by the public on a vehicle especially licensed to serve them and is received on property owned by the consignee. In short, there is a universality of utility and a public stake present in broadcasting wholly lacking in the kind of thing that was involved in *Roth.* Two hypothetical situations may serve to illustrate the disparity between the free-speech problems that were involved there and the kind that can be present in broadcasting. All hands would agree, it is supposed, that the Postmaster General would be hard put to ban the Bible from the mails. Would they not also agree that the Commission might be justified in holding that a licensee who telecast a documentary, live, in depth, of the "Song of Solomon" had not met the public-interest standard? Joyce's "Ulysses" and Lawrence's "Lady Chatterley's Lover" have both been found by the courts not to be obscene within the meaning of the postal laws, *U.S.* v *One Book Called Ulysses,* D.C., S.D.N.Y., 5 F. Supp. 182, affirmed 2 Cir., 72 F. 2d. 705; *Grove Press, Inc.* v. *Christenberry,* 175 F. Supp. 488. However, were dramatizations of those works to be telecast with coverage, in depth, of their more lurid details (e.g., the Mollie Bloom flashbacks in pt. 3 of "Ulysses"), should not the Commission be able to seriously question the qualifications of the licensee over whose station the programs were presented? Those who believe that any prior restraint constitutes censorship and per se violation of the first amendment might wish to consider whether or not, in this latter situation, despite their views, Federal or State authority, armed with notice and in full possession of the facts concerning proposal to present such telecasts, ought not to be able successfully to seek injunction.[26] Similar hypothetical situations where it would appear free-speech problems differ profoundly in broadcasting and in the fields of letters and art might be propounded at length. The examiner is hopeful, however, that the foregoing will suffice to justify moving on to the following observations, all of which are at odds with doctrine enunciated in *Grove Press,* id., at 496–497, 499, a case in which the *Roth* rule was applied and one on which Robinson also relies. In determining obscenity in broadcasting, questionable material should not always have to be weighed within the context of everything else that is presented with it. Brief injections of erotica, pornography, or smut are enough to seriously prejudice, if not destroy, the general utility of radio and television. "The effect on the average man of normal sensual impulses" test hardly serves to protect tots from getting an eye or earful of smut which their parents, quite legitimately, may desire they be shielded from, nor does it protect the adult of tender sensibilities from being exposed

[26] To those who may regard the examiner's "strawmen" as falling outside the realm of possibility, let them again review the Walker anecdotes set out in pars. 28, 32, and 38, above.

to that which to him or her is truly revolting. Both types of listeners and viewers have a considerable stake in broadcasting. Considering the "universality of utility" aspect of broadcasting, it would seem that whether broadcast material is in bad taste and shocks and offends substantial segments of a community might well be a perfectly proper consideration for determining whether such material is obscene. The "shamful and morbid interest in sex so pervasive as to submerge any ideas of redeeming social importance" test and the requirement that the material in question to be obscene must exceed limits of tolerance imposed by current standards of a community certainly would appear to permit a lot of broadcast material to find first-amendment protection that nevertheless would be highly offensive to large segments of a listening or viewing audience. The reaction of even minority blocs of the public are entitled to consideration when public-interest judgment is made. A high degree of acceptability among literary cognoscenti as a test for obscenity seems woefully inadequate when used in connection with a medium the very nature of which is general public acceptability. Although the converse of all the foregoing propositions was found by the Court to be appropriate for application under the facts present in *Grove Press,* it appears manifest that such application in broadcast cases would be unduly restrictive to regulation in the public interest. All hands would agree, it is supposed, that the radio or television set should never require that sequestered treatment accorded the family revolver, the rat poison, or the book on love and marriage. Similar agreement may be assumed for the proposition that the dials of those sets should not have to be approached timidly and in fear of receiving offense by those of highly developed sensibilities.

8. The foregoing views are in no sense intended to suggest that under appropriate circumstances bona fide works of art, literature, or science dealing in candid fashion with subjects that may have been socially and legally taboo in some bygone period may not be aired. Nor are those views intended to suggest that the *Roth* test is not appropriate for determination of obscenity where obscenity laws are directed at books, art, or the theater. The sole purpose of the foregoing discussion is to point up the reasons behind the examiner's view that the *Roth* test was not advanced by the Supreme Court as a universal standard for determining obscenity and, of course, as a correlative to point up the lack of merit in Robinson's contention that the test must be applied here.

9. As earlier indicated, the *Roth* test can be applied to the Walker material here at issue and a conclusion reached that it is obscene. The material on its face is of such nature that only the very young or the very naive can fail to recognize in it a common vein of thinly veiled reference to the procreatory or excretory functions of man or beast or some ramification of, or appurtenance to, those functions. With the extremities of youth and credulity lopped off, the average man is left to make the test. If the

testimony of those few witnesses who were interrogated about the Walker material and who indicated they knew anything about it and nevertheless found it inoffensive is discounted (see, e.g., pars. 52, 54, and 60 above) on the ground that their zeal in coming to the aid of a medium that had served them well overpowered their judgment (a conclusion the examiner is willing to reach), there is clear evidence that the average man in Kingstree and its environs found the Walker material highly objectionable. Clergymen received complaints about the Walker broadcasts (see pars. 29 and 30, above); other broadcasters feared the broadcasts would be detrimental to broadcasting (see pars. 34 and 35, above); at least one advertiser canceled his advertising over the station because of the Walker broadcasts (see par. 33, above); and a former partner of the respondent not only fired Walker because of the character of his broadcasts but left the partnership for the same reason (see par. 28, above). Of course, the average man's complaint was not couched in terms of "appealing to prurient interests," but for laymen the witnesses did pretty well in meeting the meaning of that phrase with such characterizations as "vulgar, suggestive, and sexy" (see par. 30, above); "bad taste that people could and did object to"; "the suggestiveness of it" (see par. 29, above); "filthy" (see par. 32, above); "off color"; "a certain amount of vulgarity" (see par. 33, above); "downright indecent" (see par. 34, above); and "degrading to radio" (see par. 35). Insofar as the "dominant theme" requirement of the *Roth* test is concerned, when Walker's remarkable popularity with the local advertisers is taken into account (see, e.g., pars. 54, 56, 61, and 63, above) and it is recalled that his primary function over the air, along with musical records, was to serve as filler between spot announcements, it becomes pretty apparent that his principal appeal lay in his smut and that his smut signalized, characterized, and was in fact the dominant note in his broadcasts.[27]

10. On the basis of the foregoing considerations, the examiner concludes that even under the *Roth* test the Walker broadcasts here at issue are obscene and indecent and, a fortiori, coarse, vulgar, suggestive, and susceptible of indecent double meaning. Without employing the *Roth* test, he holds the material in question obscene and indecent on its face.

11. In respect of the question posed by the second issue—whether Robinson maintained adequate control or supervision of the programs broadcast over his station—it has now become apparent that the question is rhetorical. Robinson clearly did not exercise adequate control over that aspect of his station's operation. Had he done so, the Walker material here at issue would not have been broadcast. Broadcasting licensees must assume responsibility for all material which is broadcast through their facilities, *Commission Policy on Programing.* 20 R.R. 1901. Absent intervening fac-

[27] Webster's New International Dictionary (unabridged, 2d ed., 1934) defines "smut" in pertinent part as follows: ". . . 3. Indecent or ribald language, jests, etc.; obscenity."

tors of such nature as would make licensee accountability wholly unreasonable, that principle must, by the very nature of our system of radio regulation, be maintained inviolate. Suggestions, such as Robinson advanced during the trial of this proceeding, that ill health, inadequate subordinates, extreme popularity of talent, or ignorance of the true character of the broadcast material in question, cannot be accepted as in any way relieving him of full responsibility for his station's operation.

12. When the facts set forth in paragraphs 9 to 14, 18, 19, and 28 to 35 of the above findings are carefully evaluated, it is apparent that Walker had for years been broadcasting over his station the kind of bucolic double entendre that is set out in paragraphs 28, 32, and 38 of the findings. Further, it is apparent that Robinson well knew the true character of those broadcasts. It is, therefore, clear from the correspondence between Robinson, his counsel, and the Commission (see pars. 2 to 5, above) that Robinson was attempting to palm off on the Commission representation that the Walker broadcasts were but a slight station contretemps which had been promptly corrected when its origin was called to his attention. Such a representation hardly squares with the fact, as this record amply demonstrates, that for years he had been featuring over his station a smut artist as disk-jockey. Thus, it only can be held that his representations to the Commission here under consideration were not only lacking in candor but were, under the circumstances, studied misrepresentation of fact. The question propounded by the first issue must be concluded adversely to Robinson.

13. Issue 4 inquires as to the manner in which WDKD served the needs of its community. In the *Commission's Policy on Programing* (id. at 1912–1913), the Commission after pointing out at considerable length that it was not its function to provide rigid formula for broadcast service in the public interest went on to say:

> Broadcast licensees must assume responsibility for all material which is broadcast through their facilities. This includes all programs and advertising material which they present to the public. With respect to advertising material the licensee has the additional responsibility to take all reasonable measures to eliminate any false, misleading, or deceptive matter and to avoid abuses with respect to the total amount of time devoted to advertising continuity as well as the frequency with which regular programs are interrupted for advertising messages. This duty is personal to the licensee and may not be delegated. He is obligated to bring his positive responsibility affirmatively to bear upon all who have a hand in providing broadcast matter for transmission through his facilities so as to assure the discharge of his duty to provide acceptable program schedule consonant with operating in the public interest in his community. The broadcaster is obligated to make a positive, diligent, and continuing effort, in good faith, to determine the tastes, needs, and desires of the public in his community and to provide programing to meet those needs and interests. This again, is a duty personal to the licensee and may not be avoided by delegation of the responsibility to others.

In the fulfillment of his obligation the broadcaster should consider the tastes, needs, and desires of the public he is licensed to serve in developing his programing and should exercise conscientious efforts not only to ascertain them but also to carry them out as well as he reasonably can. He should reasonably attempt to meet all such needs and interests on an equitable basis. Particular areas of interest and types of appropriate service may, of course, differ from community to community, and from time to time. However, the Commission does expect its broadcast licensees to take the necessary steps to inform themselves of the real needs and interests of the areas they serve, and to provide programing which in fact constitutes a diligent effort, in good faith, to provide for those needs and interests.

The major element usually necessary to meet the public interest, needs, and desires of the community in which the station is located as developed by the industry, and recognized by the Commission, have included: (1) Opportunity for local self-expression, (2) the development and use of local talent, (3) programs for children, (4) religious programs, (5) educational programs, (6) public affairs programs, (7) editorialization by licensees, (8) political broadcasts, (9) agricultural programs, (10) news programs, (11) weather and market reports, (12) spot programs, (13) service to minority groups, (14) entertainment programing.

14. It has already been concluded that in one important area, insuring decency of programs, Robinson has been woefully inadequate in discharging his broadcast licensee responsibilities. Review of paragraphs 42 through 46 discloses that he has been similarly deficient in "avoid[ing] abuses with respect to the total amount of time devoted to advertising continuity as well as the frequency with which regular programs are interrupted for advertising messages."[28] As far as making a diligent and continuing effort to determine the tastes and needs of the community, the program performance of his station certainly does not reflect that the efforts Robinson put out in that regard (and he did put out some), were very fruitful. As to the 14 elements necessary to meet the interests, desires, and needs of a community, based on the record facts (see pars. 39 to 49, above), the examiner would grade WDKD's performance thus: *opportunity for local self-expression—* virtually nil as far as performance was concerned; *development of local talent—*feeble, some attention to this subject as evidenced by the station's co-operation with the schools' vocational training program; *programs for children—*nil, except for musical record programs directed at teenage audiences; *religious programs—*fully met obligation as broadcast licensee; *educational programs—*nil; *public affairs programs—*nil; *editorializing by licensee—* nil; *political broadcasts—*met obligation as broadcast licensee; *agricultural programs—*adequate discharge of licensee responsibility; *news programs—* performance variable and skimpy, little attention to news in depth, standard

---

[28] In this connection, it may be of interest to recall that at WDKD not only were programs interrupted by spot announcements but programs were interrupted by programs. See par. 46, above.

for judgment in news selection, poor (see par. 49, above); *weather and market reports*—fully met responsibility as broadcast licensee; *sports*—met responsibility as broadcast licensee; *service to minority groups*—nil, except for musical records directed at colored audience; *entertainment program-ing*—adequate time devoted but scope too narrow due to reliance on re-corded music. On the basis of the foregoing "report card," it follows that in the 14 categories, WDKD has "failed" in 6, "passed" in 5 (with a high mark in one—religion), and has "conditions" in 3.

15. If the foregoing marks were to be evaluated for honors in making contribution to enlargement of the American mind, Robinson would surely fail. If those marks were to be evaluated to determine whether Robinson's performance as licensee enabled his station to show adequate performance in even a majority of the above program categories, conclusion adverse to him would follow. But considerations such as the foregoing are not appro-priate criteria against which WDKD's performance should be measured to obtain final response to the issue. Since at final issue here is the question of whether a man should retain a license that is the foundation of his business and since his is a regulated business, fairness dictates that the performance must be finally evaluated in terms of the performance of other licensed operations of like scope, size, and situation. This, of course, involves a purely subjective determination. It is the examiner's judgment that, exclud-ing the fact that obscenities were broadcast over the station, WDKD's record of past performance has met the needs of the community it serves little better or little worse than most other standard broadcast stations op-erating under like conditions. The foregoing conclusion is about as far as the examiner can appropriately go in responding to issue 4.

16. Issues 5 and 6 are conclusionary issues and, read together, call for the examiner to make initial determination as to whether the public in-terest would be served by renewal of WDKD's license in the light of facts developed on the record. Before entering this final stage, the examiner should, perhaps, make perfectly clear where in his judgment the weight of the evidence lies in matters involving conflict of testimony. The only area where such conflict is significant is to be found in the clash between Robin-son's testimony and the testimony of others. In all such instances the ex-aminer holds against Robinson. The examiner has no reasonable basis to doubt the veracity of those whose testimony was at odds with that given by Robinson. He does have cause to doubt that on the stand Robinson at all times testified to the whole truth. A careful reading of Robinson's testimony as digested above will show that it is often marked by vagueness and ambiv-alence; a poor earnest of probity. Further, there is an immense amount of proof in this record tending to show that over a considerable period of time Walker had been broadcasting obscenities over WDKD. There is ample proof that those broadcasts had been a source of concern to many mem-bers of the community. That this concern had been made clear to Robinson

on a number of occasions has been attested by several witnesses. There is no dispute that for years Robinson has been owner-manager of WDKD. Weighed against Robinson's efforts on the stand and in his correspondence with the Commission to create the impression that he was not fully aware of the character of Walker's broadcasts, such massive refutation not only destroys the point Robinson sought to make but effectively serves to impeach his credibility generally. Returning to the final issues, the pros and cons of Robinson's position will now be considered.

17. On the debit side of Robinson's ledger we find that in correspondence and at hearing, his record for candor is bad. He has lent his facilities to the broadcast of obscene material. His station, aside from the obscene matter broadcast, while it may not have differed in marked degree from the performance of other stations having similar characteristics, has carried a horrendous number of commercial spot announcements and has not approached programing to meet that complex of program needs and interests to be found in a community. Thus, there is ample basis for denying Robinson's application for renewal of station license—character deficiency and bad past operation.

18. There are, however, some considerations that militate against taking the action suggested above. The WDKD license is the foundation upon which Robinson's business and, it is presumed, his principal source of livelihood is based. To take it away would be punishment more severe in many respects than many penalties that might be assessed by a court following conviction for a crime. Such a harsh measure is to be avoided if alternative can be found.

19. The Government is not wholly without fault in this matter. Had a representative of the Department of Justice or of the Commission called upon Robinson in the early days of the Walker broadcasts and showed Walker and Robinson the provisions of 18 U.S.C. 1464 with a warning that rustic jokes with hidden meaning might well come within the purview of that law, it is inconceivable to the examiner that Robinson would have permitted those broadcasts to continue or that Walker would have wished to continue presenting them. While inaction by the Government does not form an excuse for Robinson's permitting the broadcasts to be aired, it does place one in the position of the examiner, who is also a "clerk in the same store" as those who might have taken such prophylactic action, to wonder if, under the circumstances, a little leniency toward Robinson might not be amiss to compensate for the bobble of his brethren.

20. It is apparent from the description of the town and the employment of the witnesses that Kingstree and the surrounding areas, like many other parts of the South, are engaged in the process of converting from what was once almost entirely an agricultural economy to one more balanced by business and industry. It is also apparent from the testimony of the witnesses

and the record of the station operation that Robinson and WDKD are an integral part of that movement. While it is clear that in playing his role Robinson overacted his part (the Walker broadcasts and the station's "over-commercialization"), it cannot be said that Robinson's activity in this behalf was wholly without public-interest connotations.

21. Without going into a dissertation on why the gap exists and whether or not it is narrowing, the examiner feels justified in pointing out that one has only to look at standard broadcast operation in general today to appreciate that there is a considerable gap between what the Commission regards as good programing practice as stated in its *Commission Policy on Programing* and what broadcasters in general apparently believe that standard to be. As will be pointed out more fully later, the examiner does not believe that Robinson would again permit obscene matter to be aired over WDKD. Considering the hiatus between policy and performance just mentioned, it appears fair to say that at least it is highly doubtful that were the stewardship of WDKD to be altered a change for the better would result. Particularly does this observation seem warranted, when it is remembered that in one program category, religion, Robinson opened up the "spot and platter" format of his operation (sometimes euphemistically referred to in the trade as "news and music") to admit local live programing in real depth and that in four other program categories the performance of his station has been found to be adequate.

22. While Robinson did lack candor in his representations to the Commission, vis-a-vis the Walker matter, while he did exercise execrable judgment in permitting such broadcasts, and while his performance on the stand was a good deal below par, it is not the examiner's judgment that he is a venal man of evil purpose or that he is a congenital liar. Rather, Robinson is, in the examiner's judgment, typical of a type of modern American businessman. With financial success as the goal, he is in a hurry to get on with the job and more interested in results than means or methods. As far as candor is concerned in most matters, he is no different than others. However, the rules under which he plays regrettably appear to countenance misrepresentation to the Government as a kind of "white lie." It can, of course, be cogently urged that such people are precisely the kind that should not be the holders of Government franchises. On the other hand, the Commission is not in the business of reforming the morals of the American businessman. Its principal concern in the field of license qualification is selection of reliable persons who can be counted on to carry out their public-service responsibilities. A chastened malefactor is sometimes a better bet to carry out responsibilities under law than one who has not been subjected to discipline for wrongdoing. It is the examiner's belief that Robinson is now truly contrite. In this connection, it should be noted that on the stand he testified:

. . . I have made a mistake in this thing. I'm very sorry. It hasn't happened at the station since. And I promise that it won't happen in the future (Tr. 167).

It is the examiner's opinion those words were spoken with real conviction.

23. The examiner cannot view the testimony of the 17 witnesses who testified on behalf of Robinson as being persuasive insofar as that testimony is directed to the overall merit of WDKD's performance from the public-interest standpoint. Those who have nothing to eat but rice like rice. WDKD is the only radio station for miles around. Moreover, there can be no doubt that the station is, and has been, an effective advertising medium for local merchants and in all probability an inexpensive one. Most of the witnesses who testified for Robinson had good reason to admire the station for reasons other than the quality of its programing. To the merchant, loss of inexpensive and effective aural billboard space is no less regrettable than loss of such space from a highway sign. There is, however, no blinking the fact that Robinson did marshal a formidable expression of community support for retention of his station's license. This is no matter to be lightly brushed aside. It is not now and never has been the policy of this Commission to approach its regulatory responsibility in paternalistic fashion. The wishes of local communities, as far as this examiner is aware, have always been given great weight by the FCC in the performance of its duties. In a Government such as ours, politics, in the highest sense of the term, requires such an approach to regulation. This is not to say that local desires invariably counterbalance national interest or that regulatory action may not be required in the national interest which is at odds with local desires. It does mean, in the latter case, that local sentiment has been placed in the scales with national interest and found wanting. In his final evaluation here, the examiner gives great weight to the expressions of local support collected by Robinson in defense of his license. By the same token, however, he is not unmindful that the disposition that will eventually be made of this case may have large-scale national implications in the field of broadcasting since it will reflect the policy of the Commission not only in respect of obscenity over the air but in regard to programing that misses by far measuring up to what the Commission has suggested is required to meet the public-interest standard.[29]

[29] The examiner should not depart from consideration of the testimony of Robinson's witnesses without comment on an aspect of the case upon which the Bureau lays much stress in its proposed findings. It will be noted that Louie L. Law and Donald L. Taylor both testified that they had visited the employer of one of the Bureau's witnesses, Carroll Godwin. Law testified that the purpose of the visit was to insure that Godwin was going to testify to the truth in the instant proceeding. Taylor testified that the purpose of the visit was to determine whether Godwin was antagonistic toward WDKD. (See pars. 53 and 55, above.) Moreover, it should be found here and noted, that Reverend Drennan testified that Law and Taylor, both of whom were members of his church, had called upon him and told him that if he testified in the instant matter he would hurt himself in the community and would also hurt his church (Tr. 563). The examiner does not

24. As a final consideration running in Robinson's favor, the following might be noted. The determination that will be ultimately made of this matter may also be interpreted by the industry and the public as one of a series of events signalizing abandonment by the Commission of a laissez faire policy of regulation in the field of programing and indicative of a rebirth of interest and concern by the Commission in that area of station operation. (See counsel's letter to Robinson, par. 4 of the findings.) In the complex of broadcasting in the United States, WDKD is not a large operation. If such an interpretation as that suggested is correct, it would be regrettable that the significance of the pronouncement be watered down by any conflicting interpretation to the effect that a small station is being harshly used merely as a whipping boy in a regulatory gesture.

25. The question of what to do with the applications at issue is a close one. The examiner has spent no little time and thought in considering the possibility of conditional renewal with forfeiture. Section 503(b) of the Communications Act of 1934 provides:

> (b) (1) Any licensee or permittee of a broadcast station who—
> (A) willfully or repeatedly fails to operate such station substantially as set forth in his license or permit,
> (B) willfully or repeatedly fails to observe any of the provisions of this Act or of any rule or regulation of the Commission pre-

---

believe that the interrogation of Law and Taylor in connection with the Godwin matter by any means developed the full story behind the visit to Godwin's employer. Further, he fully accepts the testimony of Reverend Drennan on the visit of Law and Taylor to him. He has no doubt that the fact that two of the town's leading bankers were busying themselves interviewing prospective witnesses and their employers did not make Bureau counsel's task any easier in assembling evidence with which to respond to the issues. The examiner does not believe, however, that the record will support findings that these interviews can be found to reflect unfavorably upon Robinson or that they were instituted or conducted by Law and Taylor with bad intent. Rather, they appear to be overzealous efforts inaugurated solely by Law and Taylor to help a friend and business associate who was in trouble, a course of action passively viewed by Robinson with gratitude. Proof that Robinson triggered the visits is missing. Proof, other than that which can be drawn from the circumstances themselves, that the intent of Law and Taylor in making the visits was bad is also missing. In this connection, it is important to note that neither the testimony of Godwin or Reverend Drennan appears to have in any way been inhibited by the visits. The examiner closes the door on these incidents with the observation that in his view it is poor judgment on the part of anyone not officially connected with a matter in hearing to discuss with witnesses or the employer of witnesses anything having to do with their prospective testimony. Friendship and misplaced zeal in this area could result in conduct falling within the purview of title 18, section 1505, of the United States Code, which provides in pertinent part:

"Whoever corruptly or by threats of force, or by any threatening letter or communication, endeavors to influence, intimidate, or impede any witness in any proceeding pending before any department or agency of the United States . . .

Shall be fined not more than $5,000 or imprisoned not more than five years or both" (June 25, 1948, ch. 645, 62 Stat. 770).

scribed under authority of this Act or under authority of any
treaty ratified by the United States,

(C) fails to observe any final cease and desist order issued by
the Commission,

(D) violates section 317(c) or section 509(a)(4) of this act, or

(E) violates section 1304, 1343, or 1464 of title 18 of the
United States Code,

shall forfeit to the United States a sum not to exceed $1,000. Each day during
which such violation occurs shall constitute a separate offense. Such forfeiture
shall be in addition to any other penalty provided by this act.

(2) No forfeiture liability under paragraph (1) of this subsection
(b) shall attach unless a written notice of apparent liability shall have been issued by the Commission and such notice has been received by the licensee or
permittee or the Commission shall have sent such notice by registered or certified mail to the last known address of the licensee or permittee. A licensee or
permittee so notified shall be granted an opportunity to show in writing, within
such reasonable period as the Commission shall by regulations prescribe, why
he should not be held liable. A notice issued under this paragraph shall not be
valid unless it sets forth the date, facts, and nature of the act or omission with
which the licensee or permittee is charged and specifically identifies the particular provision or provisions of the law, rule, or regulation or the license,
permit, or cease and desist order involved.

(3) No forfeiture liability under paragraph (1) of this subsection
(b) shall attach for any violation occurring more than one year prior to the
date of issuance of the notice of apparent liability and in no event shall the
forfeiture imposed for the acts or omissions set forth in any notice of apparent
liability exceed $10,000.[30]

The foregoing provision of the act appears to provide a good auxiliary tool
for use in proceedings such as this. It might well be that the public interest
would best be served here, all things considered, with ultimate disposition
being made in some such fashion as the following: Payment by Robinson
into the Treasury of the United States of $1,000 for each day the record
shows obscenity was broadcast over his station; continuation of license on
temporary basis pending Robinson filing with the Commission (1) a statement to the effect that he has read and studied the *"Commission's Policy
Report on Programing,"* 20 R.R. 1901, particularly those parts dealing with
licensee responsibility, programing to meet a diversity of community needs
and the undesirability of a station carrying an excess of commercial continuity; "section 312(a) of the Communications Act," with particular attention to subparagraph 1 of that section which, among other things, authorizes the Commission to revoke licenses for false statements knowingly
made and for violations of 18 U.S.C. 1464; and *"FCC v. WOKO, Inc."* 329
U.S. 223 (1946), a case involving refusal to renew a license for false information having been filed; and (2) an amended renewal application re-

[30] Sec. 503 was amended to read as above by Public Law 86-752, approved Sept. 13,
1960, 74 Stat. 889.

flecting that he has, in fact, read the foregoing material in the particulars mentioned. Upon receipt of such statement and amended application, license would be renewed for a 1-year period with the understanding that at the end of that period, if the performance of the station measured up to the representations made in the amended application, license would issue for a regular term.

26. Imposition of such forfeiture sanction as that suggested above appears to be out of the question. This is so not because this proceeding fails to provide precisely the kind of situation with which Congress apparently intended section 503(b) to cope. Nor is it because of any lack of opportunity to be heard afforded Robinson. The sanction cannot be imposed because the notice provisions of sections 503(b) (2) and (3) have not been met in this proceeding. Since forfeiture law is involved, provisions must be strictly construed and procedures provided by such law scrupulously observed.

27. The examiner appears to have no alternative but to recommend grant or denial of the applications at issue. In his opinion, it would be unconscionable to permit Robinson to come off here with only token punishment for the grievous deviation he has permitted his station to make from the public-interest norm. It is also important that disposition here should stand as a warning to others that such licensee misconduct is not to be condoned. In the end, to the examiner, these considerations override those running in favor of granting the applications.

Accordingly, *It is ordered,* This 8th day of December 1961, that unless an appeal from this initial decision is taken to the Commission by any of the parties, or unless the Commission reviews the initial decision on its own motion in accordance with the provisions of section 1.153 of the rules, the applications of E. G. Robinson, Jr., tr/as Palmetto Broadcasting Co. (WDKD), Kingstree, S.C., for renewal of license and for license to cover construction permit, *Are denied.*

B | DECISION BY THE COMMISSION

33 FCC 250, 255
July 25, 1962

(COMMISSIONER CROSS NOT PARTICIPATING)

17. We turn now to issue 3. WDKD argues regarding issue 3 that since 18 U.S.C. 1464 makes the broadcast of obscene and indecent material a crime[4] and since only the courts may adjudicate criminal conduct, the Commission would exceed its authority were it to find the material in issue "obscene" or "indecent." On the other hand, were we to avoid determinations thereon but still deny the applications on the basis of impropriety of the material in terms other than "obscene" or "indecent," we would be, according to WDKD, ". . . straying into the area which the courts have held to be clearly marked off-limits by the First Amendment."

18. The examiner rejected WDKD's arguments and concluded that the material was "obscene and indecent and [certainly] coarse, vulgar, suggestive and susceptible of indecent double meaning." He did not make any distinction for the purposes of this proceeding between the adjectives used in issue 3 and those used in 18 U.S.C. 1464.

19. WDKD is wrong in its assertion that the Commission cannot find the material in issue to violate section 1464 of title 18 and to take that into account in its determination as to whether or not to renew. *FCC* v. *American Broadcasting Co.,* 347 U.S. 284, 289, note 7, clearly establishes the authority to do so.[5] The Communications Act itself imposes upon the Commission several obligations with respect to this specific section of the Criminal Code. See sections 312 (a), (b); section 503 (b) (1) (E). But while we have the authority to base our decision on section 1464, the short an-

---

[4] That section provides that "Whoever utters any obscene, indecent, or profane language by means of radio communication shall be fined not more than $10,000 or imprisoned not more than 2 years, or both."

[5] The Commission's rule in that case was based on 18 U.S.C. 1304 (the radio lottery statute). The court there stated (note 7): "The 'public interest, convenience, or necessity' standard for the issuance of licenses would seem to imply a requirement that the applicant be law-abiding. In any event, the standard is sufficiently broad to permit the Commission to consider the applicant's past or proposed violation of a Federal criminal statute especially designed to bar certain conduct by operators of radio and television stations." Cf., also, *Southern S.S. Co.* v. *NLRB,* 316 U.S. 31, 47.

swer to this entire question is that the question of violation of this section is not encompassed within issue 3. The issue has been drawn not in terms of violation of section 1464 or of the statutory language ("obscene, indecent, or profane"), but rather in different terms—"coarse, vulgar, suggestive, and susceptible of indecent, double meaning." We do not think these terms can be equated with the statutory "obscene" or "indecent." See note 7, infra.

20. We turn now to WDKD's second argument (see par. 17). Before dealing with the essence of that argument, we shall discuss several pertinent principles which we believe are now well established. First, there is no question but that the Commission, in discharging its licensing functions, may take into account under the public-interest standard activities which may also be violations of Federal laws. See *National Broadcasting Co.* v. *U.S.*, 319 U.S. 190, 223; *Mansfield Journal Co.* v. *FCC*, 180 F. 2d 28 (C.A.D.C.). Second, there is no question but that the Commission is charged with the responsibility of insuring that a broadcast licensee's operation is in the public interest. It can grant permits and renewals only upon a finding that the public interest would be served by the grant. Sections 309(a), 307(d). Accordingly, both the Commission and its predecessor have, at the time of renewal, reviewed the station's overall operation, including its programing record, in order to determine whether a renewal is in the public interest. See *Report and Statement of Policy Re: Commission en Banc Programing Inquiry.* Such review is called for by the statute and its legislative history and is supported by all the judicial pronouncements.[6] A denial of renewal of license upon the grounds that the applicant's overall past programing has not been in the public interest, if supported by the record of the case, is not censorship in violation of section 326 or of the first amendment. See *KFKB Broadcasting Assn. Inc.* v. *FRC*, 60 App. D.C. 79, 47 F. 2d 670; *Trinity Methodist Church, South* v. *FRC*, 61 App. D.C. 311, 62 F. 2d 850, cert. den., 284 U.S. 685, 288 U.S. 599.

21. With this as background, we consider WDKD's argument that at the time of renewal, the Commission may not constitutionally consider whether the station has carried extensive amounts of coarse, vulgar, suggestive, double-meaning programing. If this argument is correct, a station could present, for 75 precent or 80 percent of its broadcast day, entertainment which consisted of records interspersed with the type of smut set out in the examiner's initial decision (par. 38); and it would nevertheless be no concern of the Commission at the time of renewal. Inasmuch as record-

---

[6] See, e.g., *National Bctg. Co.* v. *U.S.*, 319 U.S. 190; *Regents of the University System of Georgia* v. *Carroll*, 338 U.S. 586, 598; *Farmers Educational & Coop. Union* v. *WDAY, Inc.*, 360 U.S. 525, 534-535; *Bay State Beacon, Inc.* v. *FCC*, 84 U.S. App. D.C. 216, 217, 171 F.2d 826, 827; *Johnston Bctg. Co.* v. *FCC*, 85 U.S. App. D.C. 40, 48, 175 F.2d 351, 359; *Independent Bctg. Co.* v. *FCC*, 89 U.S. App. D.C.. 396, 193 F.2d 900, cert. den. 344 U.S. 837; *Wrather-Alvarez Bctg., Inc.* v. *FCC*, 101 U.S. App. D.C. 324, 329, 248 F.2d 646, 651.

discjockey type of entertainment is so popular and widespread on radio, the argument comes down to this: Radio could become predominantly a purveyor of smut and patent vulgarity—yet unless the matter broadcast reached the level of obscenity under 18 U.S.C. 1464,[7] the Commission, even though charged to issue licenses only when it is in the public interest, would be powerless to prevent this perversion or misuse of a valuable national resource. The housewife, the teenager, the young child—all—would simply be subjected to the great possibility of hearing such patently offensive programing whenever they turn the dial. It would truly be an oddity that this Commission could deny a permit to an applicant who chose to "plug into" the network (and thus not to serve the local needs of his area)[8] and yet would have to grant a permit to one who proposed to broadcast, for a large part of the day, programing of the type described in paragraph 38.

22. We do not slough aside the argument advanced here by WDKD. On the contrary, we recognize the great importance of the first amendment and censorship (sec. 326) considerations here. Programing statement of July 29, 1960, supra; *U.S.* v. *Paramount Pictures,* 334 U.S. 131, 166; *Superior Films, Inc.* v. *Department of Education of State of Ohio,* 346 U.S. 587, 589. But this does not mean that the Commission has no authority to act under the public-interest standard. Rather, it means that the Commission cannot substitute its taste for that of the broadcaster or his public— that it cannot set itself up as a national arbiter of taste. Such wholly improper action by the Commission would be disastrous to our system of broadcasting and would not be tolerated by the courts or by the Congress. Turning to the specific issue before us, this means that we cannot decide that some pattern of broadcasts is "vulgar," "suggestive," "coarse," and "susceptible of indecent, double meaning" on the basis of our own taste or preference for what we believe should be broadcast. What we must find is that the broadcasts in question are flagrantly offensive—that by any standard, however reasonably weighted for the licensee, taking into account the record evidence, the broadcasts are obviously offensive or patently vulgar. In short, the licensee necessarily and properly has wide discretion in choosing *every* type of programing to be broadcast to meet the needs and interests of the public in his area. Programing statement of July 29, 1960. It follows that in dealing with the issue before us, we cannot act to deny renewal where the matter is a close one, susceptible to reasonable interpretation either way. We can only act where the record evidence establishes a patently offensive course of broadcasts. It is, we think, incorrect to say

[7] The legal considerations applicable to 18 U.S.C. 1464 are not clear, because of the dearth of court decisions dealing with this section. See *Report and Statement re: Commission en Banc Programing Inquiry,* 25 F.R. 7291, 20 Pike & Fischer, R.R. 1901, 1905–1906; cf. *Burstyn* v. *Wilson,* 343 U.S. 495, 502, 503 ("Each method [of communication] tends to present its own peculiar problems"); *Manual Enterprises, Inc.* v. *Day,* 370 U.S. 478, decided June 25, 1962.

[8] *Simmons* v. *FCC,* 83 U.S. App. D.C. 262, 169 F.2d 670, cert. den. 354 U.S. 846.

that in so acting under the public-interest standard, the Commission poses any danger to free expression in the broadcasting field. Our whole history establishes that this is not so—that we have acted with great circumspection in this sensitive area, and that where the drastic action of denial of renewal has been used, it has been because the situation itself was a drastic or flagrant one. In the circumstances, we think that the greater danger to broadcasting would be in our failure to protect the public interest; and we note that there is evidence in the record by local broadcasters which would support that conclusion (pars. 34–35, initial decision).

23. Clearly, this case presents that flagrant situation calling for drastic administrative action. The material broadcast, examples of which are set out in paragraph 38 of the initial decision (and see also pars. 28, 32; FCC exhibit 2), is not "buffoonery and attempted bucolic badinage," as WDKD claims. We find that such material, on its face, is coarse, vulgar, suggestive, and of indecent double meaning. By any standards, it is flagrantly and patently offensive in the context of the broadcast field (see par. 21), and thus contrary to the public interest. In this connection, we have also taken into account the testimony of the witnesses who heard the broadcasts.[9] We further note the evidence showing that the Charlie Walker program was on the air for a substantial portion of the broadcast day (25 percent) over a lengthy period of time (1949–52; 1954 to June 1960), and that this type of flagrant vulgarity was heard outside the period between January 1, 1960, and April 30, 1960; in short, the record reasonably establishes, and we so find, that this was the manner in which the station was operated for a substantial period of its broadcast day over many years. Thus, we are not saying that a single off-color joke or program suffices to taint an entire operation. That question is clearly not presented by the record before us. We are saying that this licensee's devotion of so substantial a portion of broadcast time to the type of programing set forth in the examiner's initial decision is inconsistent with the public interest and, indeed, represents an intolerable waste of the only operating broadcast facilities in the community—facilities which were granted to this licensee to meet the needs and interests of the Kingstree area. In the circumstances, on this issue alone (No. 3), we find that a denial of the application for renewal of license is called for.

[9] WDKD's contention that contemporary community standards of Kingstree were not offended as evidenced by the general acceptance of the Walker programs throughout the area is inaccurate. The record herein indicates no general acceptance of the Walker fare. On the contrary, the preponderance of testimony shows the programs were unacceptable.

7 THE PACIFICA CASE

In re Pacifica Foundation
36 FCC 147
January 22, 1964

This decision resulted in grants to the Pacifica Foundation for an initial license for KPFK, Los Angeles, renewals of the licenses of KPFA-FM and KPFB, Berkeley, and WBAI-FM, New York, and permission to transfer control of the stations. The authorizations were made by the Commission despite the fact that complaints had been received regarding the stations' programming, which some persons found offensive. The Pacifica *decision can be considered the FCC's affirmation of principles of free speech as applied to broadcasting.*

BY THE COMMISSION: COMMISSIONER LEE CONCURRING AND ISSUING A STATEMENT.

1. The Commission has before it for consideration the above-pending applications of the listed broadcast stations licensed to Pacifica Foundation. There are three aspects to our consideration: (*a*) Certain programing issues raised by complaints; (*b*) issues of possible Communist Party affiliation of principals of Pacifica; and (*c*) a question of possible unauthorized transfer of control. We shall consider each in turn.

2. *The programing issues.*—The principal complaints are concerned with five programs: (i) a December 12, 1959, broadcast over KPFA, at 10 p.m., of certain poems by Lawrence Ferlinghetti (read by the poet himself); (ii) "The Zoo Story," a recording of the Edward Albee play broadcast over KPFK at 11 p.m., January 13, 1963; (iii) "Live and Let Live," a program broadcast over KPFK at 10:15 p.m. on January 15, 1963, in which eight homosexuals discussed their attitudes and problems; (iv) a program broadcast over KPFA at 7:15 p.m. on January 28, 1963, in which the poem, "Ballad of the Despairing Husband," was read by the author Robert Creeley; and (v) "The Kid," a program broadcast at 11 p.m. on January 8, 1963, over KPFA, which consisted of readings by Edward Pomerantz from his unfinished novel of the same name. The complaints

charge that these programs were offensive or "filthy" in nature, thus raising the type of issue we recently considered in *Palmetto Bctg. Co.*, 33 FCC 483; 34 FCC 101. We shall consider the above five matters in determining whether, on an overall basis, the licensee's programing met the public-interest standard laid down in the Communications Act.[1] *Report and Statement of Policy re: Commission En Banc Programing Inquiry*, 20 Pike & Fischer R.R. 1901.

3. When the Commission receives complaints of the general nature here involved, its usual practice is to refer them to the licensee so as to afford the latter an opportunity to comment. When the Commission reviews, on an overall basis, the station's operation at the time of renewal, it thus has before it a complete file, containing all the sides of any matter which may have arisen during the license period. Specifically, with respect to the programing issue in this case, the Commission, barring the exceptions noted in the *Programing Statement (supra,* at p. 1909), is not concerned with individual programs—nor is it at any time concerned with matters essentially of licensee taste or judgment. Cf. *Palmetto Bctg. Co., supra,* paragraph 22. As shown by the cited case, its very limited concern in this type of case is whether, upon the overall examination, some substantial pattern of operation inconsistent with the public-interest standard clearly and patently emerges. Unlike *Palmetto* where there was such a substantial pattern (id. at par. 23; see par. 7, infra), here we are dealing with a few isolated programs, presented over a 4-year period. It would thus appear that there is no substantial problem, on an overall basis, warranting further inquiry.[2] While this would normally conclude the matter, we have determined to treat the issues raised by Pacifica's response to the complaints, because we think it would serve a useful purpose, both to the industry and the public. We shall therefore turn to a more detailed consideration of the issues raised by the complaints as to these five programs. Because of Pacifica's different response to the complaints as to (i) and (iv), paragraph 2 above, we shall treat these two broadcasts separately. (See pars. 6-7, infra.)

4. There is, we think, no question but that the broadcasts of the programs, "The Zoo Story," "Live and Let Live," and "The Kid," lay well within the licensee's judgment under the public-interest standard. The situation here stands on an entirely different footing than *Palmetto, supra,* where the licensee had devoted a substantial period of his broadcast day to mate-

---

[1] The Commission may also enforce the standard of sec. 1464 of title 18 (dealing with "obscene, indecent, or profane language"). See secs. 312 (a), (b); sec. 503(b)(1)(E). In our view, enforcement proceedings under sec. 1464 are not warranted, and therefore, no further consideration need be given this section.

[2] While, for reasons developed in this opinion, it is unnecessary to detail the showings here, we have examined the licensee's overall showings as to its stations' operations and find that those operations did serve the needs and interests of the licensee's areas. *Programing Statement, supra,* at pp. 1913-1916. In this connection, we have also taken into account the showing made in the letter of Apr. 16, 1963.

rial which we found to be patently offensive—however much we weighted that standard in the licensee's favor—and as to which programing the licensee himself never asserted that it was not offensive or vulgar, *or that it served the needs of his area or had any redeeming features.* In this case, Pacifica has stated its judgment that the three above-cited programs served the public interests and specifically, the needs and interests of its listening public. Thus, it has pointed out that in its judgment, "The Zoo Story" is a "serious work of drama" by an eminent and "provocative playwright"—that it is "an honest and courageous play" which Americans "who do not live, near Broadway ought to have the opportunity to hear and experience. . . ." Similarly, as to "The Kid," Pacifica states, with supporting authority, that Mr. Pomerantz is an author who has obtained notable recognition for his writings and whose readings from his unfinished novel were fully in the public interest as a serious work meriting the attention of its listeners; Pacifica further states that prior to broadcast, the tape was auditioned by one of its employees who edited out two phrases because they did not meet Pacifica's broadcast standards of good taste; and that while "certain minor swear words are used, . . . these fit well within the context of the material being read and conform to the standards of acceptability of reasonably intelligent listeners." Finally, as to the program, "Live and Let Live," Pacifica states that "so long as the program is handled in good taste, there is no reason why subjects like homosexuality should not be discussed on the air"; and that it "conscientiously believes that the American people will be better off as a result of hearing a constructive discussion of the problem rather than leaving the subject to ignorance and silence."

5. We recognize that as shown by the complaints here, such provocative programing as here involved may offend some listeners. But this does not mean that those offended have the right, through the Commission's licensing power, to rule such programing off the airwaves. Were this the case, only the wholly inoffensive, the bland, could gain access to the radio microphone or TV camera. No such drastic curtailment can be countenanced under the Constitution, the Communications Act, or the Commission's policy, which has consistently sought to insure "the maintenance of radio and television as a medium of freedom of speech and freedom of expression for the people of the Nation as a whole" (*Editorializing Report,* 13 FCC 1246, 1248). In saying this, we do not mean to indicate that those who have complained about the foregoing programs are in the wrong as to the worth of these programs and should listen to them. This is a matter solely for determination by the individual listeners. Our function, we stress, is not to pass on the merits of the program—to commend or to frown. Rather, as we stated (par. 3), it is the very limited one of assaying, at the time of renewal, whether the licensee's programing, on an overall basis, has been in the public interest and, in the context of this issue, whether he has made pro-

graming judgments reasonably related to the public interest. This does not pose a close question in the case: Pacifica's judgments as to the above programs clearly fall within the very great discretion which the act wisely vests in the licensee. In this connection, we also note that Pacifica took into account the nature of the broadcast medium when it scheduled such programing for the late evening hours (after 10 p.m., when the number of children in the listening audience is at a minimum).[3]

6. As to the Ferlinghetti and Creeley programs, the licensee asserts that in both instances, some passages did not measure up to "Pacifica's own standards of good taste." Thus, it states that it did not carefully screen the Ferlinghetti tape to see if it met its standards, "because it relied upon Mr. Ferlinghetti's national reputation and also upon the fact that the tape came to it from a reputable FM station." It acknowledges that this was a mistake in its procedures and states that "in the future, Pacifica will make its own review of all broadcasts. . . ." With respect to the Creeley passage (i.e., the poem, "Ballad of a Despairing Husband"),[4] Pacifica again states that in its judgment it should not have been broadcast. It "does not excuse the broadcast of the poem in question," but it does explain how the poem "slipped by" KPFA's drama and literature editor who auditioned the tape. It points out that prior to the offending poem, Mr. Creeley, who "has a rather flat, monotonous voice," read 18 other perfectly acceptable poems—and that the station's editor was so lulled thereby that he did not catch the few offensive words on the 19th poem. It also points out that each of the nine poems which followed was again perfectly acceptable, and that before rebroadcasting the poem on its Los Angeles station, it deleted the objectionable verse.

7. In view of the foregoing, we find no impediment to renewal on this score. We are dealing with two isolated errors in the licensee's application of its own standards—one in 1959 and the other in 1963. The explanations given for these two errors are credible. Therefore, even assuming, arguendo, that the broadcasts were inconsistent with the public-interest standard, it is clear that no unfavorable action upon the renewal applications is called for. The standard of public interest is not so rigid that an honest mistake or error on the part of a licensee results in drastic action against him where his overall record demonstrates a reasonable effort to serve the needs and interests of his community. (See note 2, supra.) Here again, this case contrasts sharply with *Palmetto,* where instead of two isolated instances, years

---

[3] Pacifica states that it "is sensitive to its responsibilities to its listening audience and carefully schedules for late night broadcasts those programs which may be misunderstood by children although thoroughly acceptable to an adult audience."

[4] The program containing this passage was a taped recording of Mr. Creeley's readings of selections from his poetry to students at the University of California. KPFA broadcasts many such poetry readings at the university, which are recorded by a university employee for the school's archives (and made available to the station).

apart, we found that the patently offensive material was broadcast for a substantial period of the station's broadcast day for many years. (See par. 3, supra.)

8. We find, therefore, that the programing matters raised with respect to the Pacifica renewals pose no bar to a grant of renewal.[5] Our holding, as is true of all such holdings in this sensitive area, is necessarily based on, and limited to, the facts of the particular case. But we have tried to stress here, as in *Palmetto,* an underlying policy—that the licensee's judgment in this freedom-of-speech area is entitled to very great weight and that the Commission, under the public-interest standard, will take action against the licensee at the time of renewal only where the facts of the particular case, established in a hearing record, flagrantly call for such action. We have done so because we are charged under the act with "promoting the larger and more effective use of radio in the public interest" (sec. 303(g)), and obviously, in the discharge of that responsibility, must take every precaution to avoid inhibiting broadcast licensees' efforts at experimenting or diversifying their programing. Such diversity of programing has been the goal of many Commission policies (e.g., multiple ownership, development of UHF, the fairness doctrine). Clearly, the Commission must remain faithful to that goal in discharging its functions in the actual area of programing itself.

9. *Communist Party affiliation issue.*—Under the public-interest standard, it is relevant and important for the Commission to determine in certain cases whether its applicants, or the principals of its applicants, for broadcast licenses or radio operator licenses are members of the Communist Party or of organizations which advocate or teach the overthrow of the Government by force or violence. Sections 307(a), 307(d), 308(b), 309, 47 U.S.C. 307(a), 307(d), 308(b), 309; *Borrow* v. *F.C.C.,* 285 F. 2d 666, 669 *cert. den.,* 366 U.S. 904; *Cronan* v. *F.C.C.,* 285 F. 2d 288 (C.A.D.C.), *cert den.,* 366 U.S. 904; *Blumenthal* v. *F.C.C.,* 318 F. 2d 276 (C.A.D.C.), *cert. den.,* Case No. 1026, June 3, 1963; cf. *Beilan* v. *Board of Education,* 357 U.S. 399, 405; *Adler* v. *Board of Education,* 342 U.S. 485, 493; *Garner* v. *Los Angeles Board,* 341 U.S. 716, 720; *Speiser* v. *Randall,* 357 U.S. 513, 527. The Commission therefore has followed a policy of inquiring as to Communist Party membership in those radio-licensing situations where it has information making such inquiry appropriate. Because of information coming to the Commission's attention from several sources, the Commission requested

[5] One other programing aspect deserves emphasis. Complaint has also been made concerning Pacifica's presentation of "far-left" programing. Pacifica has stated that it follows a policy of presenting programs covering the widest range of the political or controversial issue spectrum—from the members of the Communist Party on the left to members of the John Birch Society on the right. Again, we point out that such a policy (which must, of course, be carried out consistently with the requirements of the fairness doctrine) is within the licensee's area of programing judgment.

information from Pacifica Foundation on this score. On the basis of information obtained from Government sources, the foundation, and our own inquiry, we do not find any evidence warranting further inquiry into the qualifications in this respect of Pacifica Foundation.

10. *The unauthorized transfer of control.*—Until September 30, 1961, control of Pacifica was vested in executive members, who elected a committee of directors, who in turn elected officers and controlled the foundation's activities. On September 30, 1961, the executive membership and the committee of directors were abolished. In their place, Pacifica is controlled—pursuant to its bylaws—by a board of directors, which elects officers and controls the foundation's activities. The new bylaws which accomplished this result were appropriately reported to the Commission at the time they were adopted. However, no application for consent to a transfer of control was then filed.

11. This matter was brought to Pacifica's attention by a letter of February 7, 1963. The licensee's response of April 26, 1963, takes the position that no transfer of actual control had in fact taken place. However, in the event that the Commission deemed an application for consent to transfer of control to be necessary, Pacifica simultaneously filed such an application (BTC-4284). Pacifica argues that in actual practice, control had been in the so-called committee of directors, and that this practice had been formalized in an amendment to the bylaws of October 20, 1960, which read, in relevant part:

Except as hereinafter provided, the powers of this corporation shall be exercised, its property controlled, and its affairs conducted by a Committee of Directors which shall consist of 21 Executive Members of this corporation.

The new board of directors, elected on September 30, 1961, was identical with the then existing committee of directors, and the officers of the foundation likewise remained the same.

12. Although the September 30, 1961, revision in the bylaws does appear to have been only the formal recognition of a development in the actual control of Pacifica which had occurred over a period of years, and although there may well be merit in Pacifica's contention that changes in the composition of its executive membership (or, for that matter, of its present board of directors) should not be regarded as transfers of control, the September 30, 1961, revision in the bylaws did transfer legal control. Prior to that date, the executive membership elected directors, who elected officers. After that date, the directors themselves have elected new directors, as well as officers. The fact that the legal control vested in the executive members did not, in practice, amount to actual control does not mean that its existence can be ignored—any more than the legal control of a 51-percent stockholder in a commercial corporation can be ignored because he fails to exer-

cise it. See *ABC-Paramount Merger Case,* 8 Pike & Fischer R.R. 541, 619; *Press-Union Publishing Co., Inc.,* 7 Pike & Fischer R.R. 83, 96; *Universal Carloading Co.* v. *Railroad Retirement Board,* 71 F. Supp. 369.

13. On the other hand, it is clear that Pacifica did not seek to conceal or misrepresent any facts concerning those who control its affairs, and that the failure to file involved was an excusable one. We therefore grant the pending application for transfer of control.

Conclusion

14. In view of the foregoing, *It is ordered,* This 22d day of January 1964, that the above-entitled applications of Pacifica Foundation *Are granted* as serving the public interest, convenience, and necessity.

Concurring statement of Commissioner Robert E. Lee

I concur in the action of the Commission in granting the several applications of Pacifica Foundation. However, I feel constrained to comment on at least one program coming to our attention insofar as it may or may not reflect these stations' program policies.

Having listened carefully and painfully to a 1½-hour tape recording of a program involving self-professed homosexuals, I am convinced that the program was designed to be, and succeeded in being, contributory to nothing but sensationalism. The airing of a program dealing with sexual aberrations is not to my mind, per se, a violation of good taste nor contrary to the public interest. When these subjects are discussed by physicians and sociologists, it is conceivable that the public could benefit. But a panel of eight homosexuals discussing their experiences and past history does not approach the treatment of a delicate subject one could except by a responsible broadcaster. A microphone in a bordello, during slack hours, could give us similar information on a related subject. Such programs, obviously designed to be lurid and to stir the public curiosity, have little place on the air.

I do not hold myself to be either a moralist or a judge of taste. Least of all do I have a clear understanding of what may constitute obscenity in broadcasting.

8 FCC PROGRAM PROPOSAL QUESTIONNAIRE

FCC Form 301, Section IV-A
December, 1966

FCC Form 301 must be filled out by any applicant wishing to construct a new commercial broadcast station. Section IV-A of the form pertains to the programming plans of radio station applicants; it is similar to Section IV-B, which must be completed by applicants for television stations. Other sections of the application form deal with the legal, financial, and technical qualifications of the prospective broadcaster.

Section IV becomes particularly crucial when there are competing applications for the same broadcast facilities. If the several applicants are equal in all other respects, then the Federal Communications Commission will award a grant to the applicant whose programming proposal best serves the public interest.

Although licensees are not expected to "adhere inflexibly in day-to-day operation to the representations" made in Section IV, the proposal is again taken into account when it is compared with the station's performance at license renewal time. Renewal applicants must list information regarding their past programming during a "composite week" and must also indicate the nature of the program service they intend to render in the future on the application for renewal, FCC Form 303.

STATEMENT OF AM OR FM
PROGRAM SERVICE
(See instructions, Sec. IV-A, pages 7 and 8.)

Name of Applicant

City and state which station is licensed to serve

Call letters of station

PART I

Ascertainment of Program Needs

1. A. State in Exhibit No._____ the methods used by the applicant to ascertain the needs and interests of the public served by the station. Such information shall include (1) identification of representative groups, interests and organizations which were consulted and (2) the major communities or areas which applicant principally undertakes to serve.

B. Describe in Exhibit No._____ the significant needs and interests of the public which the applicant believes his station will serve during the coming license period, including those with respect to national and international matters.

C. List in Exhibit No._____ typical and illustrative programs or program series (excluding Entertainment and News) that applicant plans to broadcast during the coming license period to meet those needs and interests.

NOTE: Sufficient records shall be kept on file at the station, open for inspection by the Commission, for a period of 3 years from the date of filing of this statement (unless requested to be kept longer by the Commission) to support the representations required in answer to Question 1. These records should **not** be submitted with this application and need not be available for public inspection.

PART II

Past Programming

2. A. State the total hours of operation during the composite week: _____

B. Attach as Exhibit No._____ one exact copy of the program logs for the composite week used as a basis for responding to questions herein. Applicants utilizing automatic program logging devices must comply with the provisions of Sections 73.112(c) and 73.282(c). Automatic recordings will be returned to the applicant. Exact copies will not be returned.

If applicant has not operated during all of the days of the composite week which would be applicable to the use of this form, applicant should so notify the Commission and request the designation of substitute day or days as required.

3. A. State the amount of time (rounded to the nearest minute) the applicant devoted in the composite week to the program types (see Definitions) listed below. Commercial matter within a program segment shall be excluded in computing time devoted to that particular program segment (e.g., a 15-minute news program containing 3 minutes' commercial matter shall be counted as a 12-minute news program).

	Hours	Minutes	% of Total Time on Air
(1) News	....	....	.... %
(2) Public Affairs	....	....	.... %
(3) All other programs, exclusive of Entertainment and Sports	....	....	.... %

B. If in the applicant's judgment the composite week does not adequately represent the station's past programming, applicant may in addition provide in Exhibit No. ____ the same information as required in 3-A above (using the same format) for a calendar month or longer during the year preceding the filing of this application. Applicant shall identify the time period used. Applicant need not file the program logs used in responding to this question unless requested by the Commission.

4. List in Exhibit No. ____ typical and illustrative programs or program series (excluding Entertainment and News) broadcast during the year preceding the filing of this application which have served public needs and interests in applicant's judgment. Denote, by underlining the Title, those programs, if any, designed to inform the public on local, national or international problems of greatest public importance in the community served by the applicant. Use the format below.

Title	Source*	Type*	Brief Description	Time Broadcast & Duration	How Often Broadcast

5. Submit in Exhibit No. ____ the following information concerning the applicant's news programs:

A. The staff, news gathering facilities, news services and other sources utilized; and

B. An estimate of the percentage of news program time devoted to local and regional news during the composite week.

6. In connection with the applicant's public affairs programming, describe its policy during the past renewal period with respect to making time available for the discussion of public issues and the method of selecting subjects and participants.

*See Definitions Section IV-A, Page 7

291

7. Describe briefly the applicant's program format(s) during the past 12 months (e.g., country and western music, talk, folk music, classical music, foreign language, jazz, standard pops, etc.) and the approximate percentage of time per week devoted to such format(s).

8. State how and to what extent (if any) applicant's station contributed during the past license period to the over-all diversity of program services available in the area or communities served.

9. Was the applicant affiliated with one or more national, regional or special radio networks during the past license period? Yes_____ No_____. If "yes," give name(s) of network(s): _____

10. State the number of public service announcements broadcast by the applicant during the composite week: _____

11. A. If this application is for an FM station, did the programming duplicate that of any AM station? Yes_____ No_____.("Duplicate" means simultaneous broadcasting of a particular program over both the AM and FM stations or the broadcast of a particular FM program within 24 hours before or after the identical program is broadcast over the AM station—Section 73.242(a) of the Rules and Regulations.)

   B. If the answer is "yes," identify the AM station by call letters; describe its relation to the FM station; and state the number of hours each day in the composite week that were duplicated.

12. A. In applicant's judgment, does the information supplied in this Part II adequately reflect its past programming?

Yes _____ No _____ .

B. If "no," applicant may attach as Exhibit No. _____ such additional information as may be necessary to describe accurately and present fairly its program service.

C. If applicant's programming practices for the period covered by this statement varied substantially from the programming representations made in applicant's last renewal application, the applicant shall submit as Exhibit No. _____ a statement explaining the variations and the reasons therefor.

PART III

Proposed Programming

13. State the proposed total hours of operation during a typical week: _____

14. State the minimum amount of time the applicant proposes to devote normally each week to the program types (see Definitions) listed below. Commercial matter within a program segment shall be excluded in computing time devoted to that particular program segment (e.g., a fifteen-minute news program containing 3 minutes' commercial matter shall be computed as a 12-minute news program.)

	Hours	Minutes	% of Total Time on Air
(1) News	....	....	.... %
(2) Public Affairs	....	....	.... %
(3) All other programs, exclusive of Entertainment and Sports	....	....	.... % .... %

15. Submit in Exhibit No. _____ the following information concerning the applicant's proposed news programs:

A. The staff, news gathering facilities, news services and other sources to be utilized; and

B. An estimate of the percentage of news program time to be devoted to local and regional news during a typical week.

293

16. In connection with the applicant's proposed public affairs programming describe its policy with respect to making time available for the discussion of public issues and the method of selecting subjects and participants.

17. Describe the applicant's proposed programming format(s), e.g., country and western music, talk, folk music, classical music, foreign language, jazz, standard pops, etc., and the approximate percentage of time per week to be devoted to such format(s).

18. State how and to what extent (if any) applicant proposes to contribute to the over-all diversity of program services available in the area or communities to be served.

19. State the minimum number of public service announcements applicant proposes to present during a typical week: _____

20. Will the applicant be affiliated with one or more national, regional, or special radio networks? Yes _____ No _____ .

   If "yes," give name(s) of network(s): _____

21. A. If this application is for an FM station will the programming duplicate that of any AM station? Yes _____ No _____ . ("Duplicate" means simultaneous broadcasting of a particular program over both AM and FM stations or the broadcast of a particular FM program within 24 hours before or after the identical program is broadcast over the AM station—Section 73.242(a) of the Rules and Regulations.)

   B. If the answer is "yes," identify the AM station by call letters; describe its relation to the FM station; and state the number of hours each day proposed to be duplicated.

PART IV

Past Commercial Practices

22. Give the following information with respect to the composite week:

	All Hours	6 A.M. – 6 P.M.
A. Total broadcast time	....	....
B. Time devoted to commercial matter:		
(1) Amount in hours and minutes	.... %	....
(2) Percentage	.... %	.... %

295

23. State the number of 60-minute segments of the composite week (beginning with the first full clock hour and ending with the last clock hour of each broadcast day) containing the following amounts of commercial matter:

A. Up to and including 10 minutes ....

B. Over 10 and up to and including 14 minutes ....

C. Over 14 and up to and including 18 minutes ....

D. Over 18 minutes ....

List each segment in category (D) above, specifying the amount of commercial time in the segment, and the day and time broadcast.

24. A. In the applicant's judgment, does the information supplied in this Part IV for the composite week adequately reflect its commercial practices?   Yes_____ No_____.

B. If "no," applicant may attach as Exhibit No._____ such additional material as may be necessary to describe adequately and present fairly its commercial practices.

C. If applicant's commercial practices for the period covered by this statement varied substantially from the commercial representations made in applicant's last renewal application, the applicant shall submit as Exhibit No._____ a statement explaining the variations and the reasons therefor.

PART V

Proposed Commercial Practices

25. State the maximum percentage of commercial matter which the applicant proposes normally to allow during the following segments of a typical week:

6 a.m. - 6 p.m. .... _____ %

All hours .... _____ %

If applicant proposes to permit this level to be exceeded at times, state under what circumstances and how often this is expected to occur, and the limits that would then apply.

26. What is the maximum amount of commercial matter in any 60-minute segment which the applicant proposes normally to allow?

If applicant proposes to permit this amount to be exceeded at times, state under what circumstances and how often this is expected to occur, and the limits that would then apply.

PART VI

General Station Policies and Procedures

27. State the name(s) and position of the person(s) who determines the day-to-day programming, makes decisions, and directs the operation of the station covered by this application and whether he is employed full-time in the operation of the station.

28. A. Does the applicant have established policies with respect to programming and advertising standards (whether developed by the station or contained in a code of broadcasting standards and practices) to guide the operation of the station?

    Yes _____ No _____.

    B. If "yes," attach as Exhibit No. _____ a brief summary of such policies. (If the station relies exclusively upon the published code of any national organization or trade association, a statement to that effect will suffice)

29. State the methods by which applicant undertakes to keep informed of the requirements of the Communications Act and the Commission's Rules and Regulations, and a description of the procedures established to acquaint applicant's employees and agents with such requirements and to ensure their compliance.

30. If, as an integral part of its station identification announcements, applicant makes or proposes to make reference to any business, profession or activity other than broadcasting in which applicant or any affiliate or stockholder is engaged or financially interested, directly or indirectly, set forth typical examples and approximate frequency of their use.

31. State the number of station employees: _____ . If the station has or proposes to have ten or more employees, state in Exhibit No. _____ the number of full-time and part-time employees in the programming, sales, technical, and general and administrative departments. Do not list the same employee in more than one category. However, if an employee performs multiple services, this may be so shown by identifying him with his various duties e.g., if two employees are combination announcers and salesmen, the list would include an entry of "two programming-sales".

PART VII

Other Matters and Certification

32. Applicant may submit as Exhibit No. _____ any additional information which, in its judgment, is necessary adequately to describe or to present fairly its services and operations in relation to the public interest.

33. The undersigned has familiarized himself with paragraph 7 of the instructions on page 7 of Section IV-A concerning signature requirements and in light of its provisions does hereby:

A. Acknowledge that all the statements made in this Section IV-A and the attached exhibits are considered material representations and that all the exhibits are a material part hereof and are incorporated herein as if set out in full in the application form; and

B. Certify that the statements herein are true, complete, and correct to the best of his knowledge and belief and are made in good faith.

SIGNED AND DATED this .... day of .... , 19 ....

....
(NAME OF APPLICANT)

By: ....
(SIGNATURE)

....
(PLEASE PRINT NAME OF PERSON SIGNING)

(TITLE)

WILLFUL FALSE STATEMENTS MADE IN THIS FORM ARE PUNISHABLE BY FINE AND IMPRISONMENT. U. S. CODE, TITLE 18, SECTION 1001.

Instructions, General Information and Definitions

1. *Applicants for new AM or FM stations, and major changes when required* (see paragraph 2), shall file this Section IV-A with respect to Ascertainment of Program Needs (Part I), Proposed Programming (Part III), Proposed Commercial Practices (Part V), General Station Policies and Practices (Part VI) and Other Matters and Certification (Part VII).

2. *Applicants for major changes in facilities* (as defined in Sections 1.571(a)(1) and 1.573(a)(1) of the Commission's Rules) need not file this Section IV-A unless a substantial change in programming is proposed or unless the information is requested by the Commission.

3. A. The replies to the following questions constitute representations on which the Commission will rely in considering this application. Thus time and care should be devoted to the replies so that they will reflect accurately applicant's responsible consideration of the questions asked. It is not, however, expected that the licensee will or can adhere inflexibly in day-to-day operation to the representations made herein.

   B. Replies relating to future operation constitute representations against which the subsequent operation of the station will be measured. Accordingly, if during the license period the station substantially alters its programming format or commercial practices, the licensee should notify the Commission of such changes; otherwise it is presumed the station is being operated substantially as last proposed.

4. The applicant's attention is called to the Commission's "Report and Statement of Policy re: Commission En Banc Programming Inquiry," (FCC 60-970; 25 Federal Register 7291; 20 Pike and Fischer Radio Regulation 1902), copies of which are available upon request to the Commission; and also to the material contained in Attachment A to this Section.

5. A legible copy of this Section IV-A and the exhibits submitted therewith shall be kept on file available for public inspection at any time during regular business hours. It shall be maintained at the main studio of the station or any other accessible place (such as a public registry for documents or an attorney's office) in the community to which the station is or is proposed to be licensed.

6. *Network Programs.* Where information for the composite week is called for herein with respect to commercial matter or program type classification in connection with national network programs, the applicant may rely on information furnished by the network.

7. *Signature.*

   This Section IV-A shall be signed in the space provided at the end hereof. It shall be personally signed by the applicant, if the applicant is an individual; by one of the partners, if the applicant is a partnership; by an officer of applicant, if a corporation or association. *SIGNING OF THIS SECTION IS A REPRESENTATION THAT THE PERSON WHO SIGNS IS FAMILIAR WITH THE CONTENTS OF THIS SECTION AND ASSOCIATED EXHIBITS, AND SUPPORTS AND APPROVES THE REPRESENTATIONS THEREIN ON BEHALF OF THE APPLICANT.*

Definitions

The definitions set out below are to be followed in furnishing the information called for by the questions of this Section IV-A. The inclusion of various types and sources of programs in the paragraphs which follow is not intended to establish a formula for station operation, but is a method for analyzing and reporting station operation.

8. **Sources** of programs are defined as follows:

   (a) **A local program** (L) is any program originated or produced by the station, or for the production of which the station is primarily responsible, and employing live talent more than 50% of the time. Such a program, taped or recorded for later broadcast, shall be classified as local. A local program fed to a network shall be classified by the originating station as local. All non-network news programs may be classified as local. Programs primarily featuring records or transcriptions shall be classified as recorded even though a station announcer appears in connection with such material. However, identifiable units of such programs which are live and separately logged as such may be classified as local (e.g., if during the course of a program featuring records or transcriptions a non-network 2-minute news report is given and logged as a news program, the report may be classified as local).

   (b) **A network program** (NET) is any program furnished to the station by a network (national, regional or special). Delayed broadcasts of programs originated by networks are classified as network.

   (c) **A recorded program** (REC) is any program not defined above, including, without limitation, those using recordings, transcriptions, or tapes.

9. **Types** of programs are defined as follows:

   If a program contains two or more identifiable units of program material which constitute different program types as herein defined, each such unit may be separately logged and classified.

   The definitions of the first eight types of programs, (a) through (h) are not intended to overlap each other, and these types will normally include all the programs broadcast. The programs classified under (i) through (k) will have been classified under the first eight and there may be further duplication among types (i) through (k).

   (a) **Agricultural programs** (A) include market reports, farming or other information specifically addressed, or primarily of interest, to the agricultural population.

303

Definitions - Cont.

(b) *Entertainment programs* (E) include all programs intended primarily as entertainment, such as music, drama, variety, comedy, quiz, etc.

(c) *News programs* (N) include reports dealing with current local, national, and international events, including weather and stock market reports; and when an integral part of a news program, commentary, analysis and sports news.

(d) *Public Affairs programs* (PA) include talks, commentaries, discussions, speeches, editorials, political programs, documentaries, forums, panels, round tables, and similar programs primarily concerning local, national, and international public affairs.

(e) *Religious programs* (R) include sermons or devotionals; religious news; and music, drama, and other types of programs designed primarily for religious purposes.

(f) *Instructional programs* (I) include programs, other than those classified under Agricultural, News, Public Affairs, Religious or Sports, involving the discussion of, or primarily designed to further an appreciation or understanding of, literature, music, fine arts, history, geography, and the natural and social sciences; and programs devoted to occupational and vocational instruction, instruction with respect to hobbies, and similar programs intended primarily to instruct.

(g) *Sports programs* (S) include play-by-play and pre- or post-game related activities and separate programs of sports instruction, news, or information (e.g., fishing opportunities, golfing instruction, etc.).

(h) *Other programs* (O) include all programs not falling within definitions (a) through (g).

                        *   *   *   *   *

(i) *Editorials* (EDIT) include programs presented for the purpose of stating opinions of the licensee.

(j) *Political programs* (POL) include those which present candidates for public office or which give expression (other than in station editorials) to views on such candidates or on issues subject to public ballot.

(k) *Educational Institution programs* (ED) include any program prepared by, in behalf of, or in cooperation with, educational institutions, educational organizations, libraries, museums, PTA's or similar organizations. Sports programs shall not be included.

10. *Commercial matter* (CM) includes commercial continuity (network and non-network) and commercial announcements (network and non-network) as follows:

(a) *Commercial continuity* (CC) is the advertising message of a program sponsor.

(b) *A commercial announcement* (CA) is any other advertising message for which a charge is made, or other consideration is received.

(1) Included are (i) "bonus" spots, (ii) trade-out spots, and (iii) promotional announcements of a future program where consideration is received for such an announcement or where such announcement identifies the sponsor of the future program beyond mention of the sponsor's name as an integral part of the title of the program (e.g., when the agreement for the sale of time provides that the sponsor will receive promotional announcements, or when the promotional announcement contains a statement such as "LISTEN TOMORROW FOR THE ⎣NAME OF PROGRAM⎤ BROUGHT TO YOU BY ⎣SPONSOR'S NAME⎤").

(2) Other announcements including but not limited to the following are *not* commercial announcements:

    (i) Promotional announcements, except as defined above;

    (ii) Station identification announcements for which no charge is made;

    (iii) Mechanical reproduction announcements;

    (iv) Public service announcements;

    (v) Announcements made pursuant to Sections 73.119(d) or 73.289(d) of the Rules that materials or services have been furnished as an inducement to broadcast a political program or a program involving the discussion of controversial public issues;

    (vi) Announcements made pursuant to the local notice requirements of Sections 1.580 (pre-grant) and 1.594 (designation for hearing) of the Rules.

11. **A *public service announcement* (PSA)** is any announcement (including network) for which no charge is made and which promotes programs, activities, or services of federal, state or local governments (e.g., recruiting, sales of bonds, etc.) or the programs, activities or services of non-profit organizations (e.g., UGF, Red Cross blood donations, etc.), and other announcements regarded as serving community interests, excluding time signals, routine weather announcements and promotional announcements.

12. **A *program*** is an identifiable unit of program material, logged as such, which is not an announcement as defined above (e.g., if, within a 30-minute entertainment program, a station broadcasts a one-minute news and weather report, this news and weather report may be separately logged and classified as a one-minute news program and the entertainment portion as a 29-minute program).

13. **Composite Week** - Seven days designated annually by the Commission in a Public Notice and consisting of seven different days of the week.

14. **Typical Week** - A week which an applicant projects as typical of his proposed weekly operation.

STATEMENT OF AM OR FM PROGRAM SERVICE

ATTACHMENT A

Attention is invited to the Commission's "Report and Statement of Policy Re: Commission En Banc Programming Inquiry" released July 29, 1960 - FCC 60-970 (25 Federal Register 7291; 20 Pike and Fischer Radio Regulation 1902).

Pursuant to the Communications Act of 1934, as amended, the Commission cannot grant, renew or modify a broadcast authorization unless it makes an affirmative finding that the operation of the station, as proposed, will serve the public interest, convenience and necessity. Programming is of the essence of broadcasting.

A broadcast station's use of a channel for the period authorized is premised on its serving the public. Thus, the public has a legitimate and continuing interest in the program service offered by the station, and it is the duty of all broadcast permittees and licensees to serve as trustees for the public in the operation of their stations. Broadcast permittees and licensees must make positive, diligent and continuing efforts to provide a program schedule designed to serve the needs and interests of the public in the areas to which they transmit an acceptable signal.

In its above-referenced "Policy Statement," the Commission has indicated the general nature of the inquiry which should be made in the planning and devising of a program schedule:

"Thus we do not intend to guide the licensee along the path of programming; on the contrary, the licensee must find his own path with the guidance of those whom his signal is to serve. We will thus steer clear of the bans of censorship without disregarding the public's vital interest. What we propose will not be served by pre-planned program format submissions accompanied by complimentary references from local citizens. What we propose is documented program submissions prepared as the result of assiduous planning and consultation covering two main areas: first, a canvass of the listening public who will receive the signal and who constitute a definite public interest figure; second, consultation with leaders in community life -- public officials, educators, religious (groups), the entertainment media - agriculture, business, labor, professional and eleemosynary organizations, and others who bespeak the interests which make up the community."

Over the years, experience has shown both broadcasters and the Commission that certain recognized elements of broadcast service have frequently been found necessary or desirable to serve the broadcast needs and interests of many communities. In the Policy Statement, referred to above, the Commission set out fourteen such elements. The Commission stated:

"The major elements usually necessary to meet the public interest, needs and desires of the community in which the station is located as developed by the industry, and recognized by the Commission, have included: (1) Opportunity for Local Self-Expression, (2) The Development and Use of Local Talent (3) Programs for Children, (4) Religious Programs, (5) Educational Programs, (6) Public Affairs Programs, (7) Editorialization by licensees, (8) Political Broadcasts, (9) Agricultural Programs, (10) News Programs, (11) Weather and Market Reports, (12) Sports Programs, (13) Service to Minority Groups, (14) Entertainment Programming."

It is emphasized that broadcasters, mindful of the public interest, must assume and discharge responsibility for planning, selecting and supervising all matter broadcast by their stations, whether such matter is produced by them or provided by networks or others. This duty was made clear in the Commission's Policy Statement, page 14, paragraph 3:

"Broadcasting licensees must assume responsibility for all material which is broadcast through their facilities. This includes all programs and advertising material which they present to the public. With respect to advertising material the licensee has the additional responsibility to take all reasonable measures to eliminate any false, misleading, or deceptive matter and to avoid abuses with respect to the total amount of time devoted to advertising continuity as well as the frequency with which regular programs are interrupted for advertising messages. This duty is personal to the licensee and may not be delegated. He is obligated to bring his positive responsibility affirmatively to bear upon all who have a hand in providing broadcast matter for transmission through his facilities so as to assure the discharge of his duty to provide (an) acceptable program schedule consonant with operating in the public interest in his community. The broadcaster is obligated to make a positive, diligent and continuing effort, in good faith, to determine the tastes, needs and desires of the public in his community and to provide programming to meet those needs and interests. This, again, is a duty personal to the licensee and may not be avoided by delegation of the responsibility to others."

307

9 SELF-REGULATION

*Broadcasters first voluntarily imposed regulation on themselves
through their trade association, the National Association of Broadcasters (NAB), in 1929. The remarkable growth and increased
complexity of self-regulation are made evident by comparing the
original codes with their contemporary counterparts.*

*About half of all commercial radio and television stations sub-
scribe to the current codes. Additionally, many networks and stations have their own formulations of programming standards to
which they adhere, although the NAB codes have gained wider acceptance than any others.*

*The documents below appear here through the courtesy of The
Code Authority, National Association of Broadcasters.*

A NAB CODE OF ETHICS *
MARCH 25, 1929

First.   Recognizing that the Radio audience includes persons
of all ages and all types of political, social and religious belief, every broadcaster will endeavor to prevent the broadcasting of any matter which would
commonly be regarded as offensive.

Second.   When the facilities of a broadcaster are used by others than
the owner, the broadcaster shall ascertain the financial responsibility and
character of such client, that no dishonest fradulent or dangerous person,
firm or organization may gain access to the Radio audience.

Third.   Matter which is barred from the mails as fraudulent, deceptive
or obscene shall not be broadcast.

Fourth.   Every broadcaster shall exercise great caution in accepting
any advertising matter regarding products or services which may be in-
jurious to health.

* Reprinted by permission of The Code Authority, National Association of Broadcasters.

Fifth. No broadcaster shall permit the broadcasting of advertising statements or claims which he knows or believes to be false, deceptive or grossly exaggerated.

Sixth. Every broadcaster shall strictly follow the provisions of the Radio Act of 1927 regarding the clear identification of sponsored or paid-for material.

Seventh. Care shall be taken to prevent the broadcasting of statements derogatory to other stations, to individuals, or to competing products or services, except where the law specifically provides that the station has no right of censorship.

Eighth. Where charges of violation of any article of the Code of Ethics of The National Association of Broadcasters are filed in writing with the Managing Director, the Board of Directors shall investigate such charges and notify the station of its findings.

 ## NAB STANDARDS OF COMMERCIAL PRACTICE*, MARCH 25, 1929

I. *Program Content and Presentation*

    (A) There is a decided difference between what may be broadcast before and after 6:00 p.m. Time before 6:00 p.m. is included in the business day and, therefore, may be devoted in part, at least, to broadcasting programs of a business nature; while time after 6:00 p.m. is for recreation and relaxation, and commercial programs should be of the good-will type.

    (B) Commercial announcements, as the term is generally understood, should not be broadcast between 7:00 and 11:00 p.m.

    (C) A client's business and his product should be mentioned sufficiently to insure him an adequate return on his investment—but never to the extent that it loses listeners to the station.

    (D) The use of records should be governed by the following:

        1. The order of the Commission with reference to identifying "Phonograph Records" and other means of mechanical reproduction should be completely carried out.

        2. Phonograph records (those for sale to the public) should not be broadcast between 6:00 and 11:00 p.m. except in the case

* Reprinted by permission of The Code Authority, National Association of Broadcasters.

of pre-release records used in programs sponsored either by the manufacturer or the local distributor.

3. When mechanical reproductions prepared for radio use only are not for public sale, and are of such quality to recommend their being broadcast, no limitation should be placed on their use, except as individual station policy may determine.

II. *Salesmen and Representatives*

(A) Salesmen on commission or salary should have:
1. Definite responsibility to the station for which they solicit;
2. Some means of identification.

Furthermore, contracts should state specifically that they will not be considered as acceptable until signed by an officer of the station; that no agreements, verbal or understood, can be considered as part of the contract. The salesmen's conference with the client should always be confirmed by an officer of the station.

(B) The standard commission allowed by all advertising media to recognized agencies should be allowed by broadcasting stations. If selling representatives are maintained by stations in cities where they otherwise have no representation, the station itself should make its own arrangements as to payment for such representation.

(C) Blanket time should not be sold to clients to be resold by them as they see fit.

III. *Agencies*

(A) Agencies have three functions in broadcasting:
1. Credit responsibility.
2. Account service and contact.
3. Program supervision in the interest of the client.

(B) Commission should be allowed only to agencies of recognized standing.

IV. *Sales Data.*—The best sales data is result data.

V. *Rate Cards*

(A) There should be no deviation whatsoever from rates quoted on a rate card or cards.

(B) Wherever practicable, the standard rate card form recommended by this Association should be used.

VI. *Clients*

(A) Client standards of credit should be maintained similar to those established in other fields of advertising.

(B) In deciding what accounts or classes of business are acceptable for broadcast advertising, member stations should be governed by the Code of Ethics adopted by this Association.

 NAB RADIO CODE *

13th Edition, September, 1967
(Amended to June 19, 1968)

THE RADIO BROADCASTER'S CREED

We Believe:

That Radio Broadcasting in the United States of America is a living symbol of democracy; a significant and necessary instrument for maintaining freedom of expression, as established by the First Amendment to the Constitution of the United States;

That its influence in the arts, in science, in education, in commerce, and upon the public welfare is of such magnitude that the only proper measure of its responsibility is the common good of the whole people;

That it is our obligation to serve the people in such manner as to reflect credit upon our profession and to encourage aspiration toward a better estate for all mankind; by making available to every person in America such programs as will perpetuate the traditional leadership of the United States in all phases of the broadcasting art;

That we should make full and ingenious use of man's store of knowledge, his talents, and his skills and exercise critical and discerning judgment concerning all broadcasting operations to the end that we may, intelligently and sympathetically:

Observe the properties and customs of civilized society;

Respect the rights and sensitivities of all people;

Honor the sanctity of marriage and the home;

Protect and uphold the dignity and brotherhood of all mankind;

* Reprinted by permission of The Code Authority, National Association of Broadcasters.

Enrich the daily life of the people through the factual reporting and analysis of news, and through programs of education, entertainment, and information;

Provide for the fair discussion of matters of general public concern; engage in works directed toward the common good; and volunteer our aid and comfort in times of stress and emergency;

Contribute to the economic welfare of all by expanding the channels of trade, by encouraging the development and conservation of natural resources, and by bringing together the buyer and seller through the broadcasting of information pertaining to goods and services.

Toward the achievement of these purposes we agree to observe the following:

I. PROGRAM STANDARDS

A. News

Radio is unique in its capacity to reach the largest numbers of people first with reports on current events. This competitive advantage bespeaks caution—being first is not as important as being right. The following Standards are predicated upon that viewpoint.

1. NEWS SOURCES.   Those responsible for news on radio should exercise constant professional care in the selection of sources—for the integrity of the news and the consequent good reputation of radio as a dominant news medium depend largely upon the reliability of such sources.

2. NEWS REPORTING.   News reporting shall be factual and objective. Good taste shall prevail in the selection and handling of news. Morbid, sensational, or alarming details not essential to factual reporting should be avoided. News should be broadcast in such a manner as to avoid creation of panic and unnecessary alarm. Broadcasters shall be diligent in their supervision of content, format, and presentation of news broadcasts. Equal diligence should be exercised in selection of editors and reporters who direct news gathering and dissemination, since the station's performance in this vital informational field depends largely upon them.

3. COMMENTARIES AND ANALYSES.   Special obligations devolve upon those who analyze and/or comment upon news developments, and management should be satisfied completely that the task is to be performed in the best interest of the listening public. Programs of news analysis and commentary shall be clearly identified as such, distinguishing them from straight news reporting.

4. EDITORIALIZING.   Broadcasts in which stations express their own opinions about issues of general public interest should be clearly identified as

editorials and should be clearly distinguished from news and other program material.

5. COVERAGE OF NEWS AND PUBLIC EVENTS.   In the coverage of news and public events the broadcaster has the right to exercise his judgment consonant with the accepted standards of ethical journalism and especially the requirements for decency and decorum in the broadcast of public and court proceedings.

6. PLACEMENT OF ADVERTISING.   A broadcaster should exercise particular discrimination in the acceptance, placement and presentation of advertising in news programs so that such advertising should be clearly distinguishable from the news content.

B. Controversial public issues

1.   Radio provides a valuable forum for the expression of responsible views on public issues of a controversial nature. The broadcaster should develop programs relating to controversial public issues of importance to his fellow citizens; and give fair representation to opposing sides of issues which materially affect the life or welfare of a substantial segment of the public.

2.   Requests by individuals, groups or organizations for time to discuss their views on controversial public issues should be considered on the basis of their individual merits, and in the light of the contributions which the use requested would make to the public interest.

3.   Programs devoted to the discussion of controversial public issues should be identified as such. They should not be presented in a manner which would create the impression that the program is other than one dealing with a public issue.

C. Community responsibility

1.   A broadcaster and his staff occupy a position of responsibility in the community and should conscientiously endeavor to be acquainted with its needs and characteristics in order to serve the welfare of its citizens.

2.   Requests for time for the placement of public service announcements or programs should be carefully reviewed with respect to the character and reputation of the group, campaign or organization involved, the public interest content of the message, and the manner of its presentation.

D. Political broadcasts

1.   Political broadcasts, or the dramatization of political issues designed to influence an election, shall be properly identified as such.

2.   They should be presented in a manner which would properly identify the nature and character of the broadcast.

3.   Because of the unique character of political broadcasts and the necessity to retain broad freedoms of policy void of restrictive interference, it is incumbent upon all political candidates and all political parties to observe the canons of good taste and political ethics, keeping in mind the intimacy of broadcasting in the American home.

E. *Advancement of education and culture*

1.   Because radio is an integral part of American life, there is inherent in radio broadcasting a continuing opportunity to enrich the experience of living through the advancement of education and culture.

2.   The radio broadcaster, in augmenting the educational and cultural influences of the home, the church, schools, institutions of higher learning, and other entities devoted to education and culture:

(a) Should be thoroughly conversant with the educational and cultural needs and aspirations of the community served;

(b) Should cooperate with the responsible and accountable educational and cultural entities of the community to provide enlightenment of listeners;

(c) Should engage in experimental efforts designed to advance the community's cultural and educational interests.

F. *Religion and religious programs*

1.   Religious programs shall be presented by responsible individuals, groups or organizations.

2.   Radio broadcasting, which reaches men of all creeds simultaneously, shall avoid attacks upon religious faiths.

3.   Religious programs shall be presented respectfully and without prejudice or ridicule.

4.   Religious programs shall place emphasis on religious doctrines of faith and worship.

G. *Dramatic Programs*

1.   In determining the acceptability of any dramatic program containing any element of crime, mystery, or horror, proper consideration should be given to the possible effect on all members of the family.

2.   Radio should reflect realistically the experience of living, in both its pleasant and tragic aspects, if it is to serve the listener honestly. Nevertheless, it holds a concurrent obligation to provide programs which will encourage better adjustments to life.

3.   This obligation is apparent in the area of dramatic programs par-

ticularly. Without sacrificing integrity of presentation, dramatic programs on radio shall avoid:

(a) Techniques and methods of crime presented in such manner as to encourage imitation, or to make the commission of crime attractive, or to suggest that criminals can escape punishment;

(b) Detailed presentation of brutal killings, torture, or physical agony, horror, the use of supernatural or climactic incidents likely to terrify or excite unduly;

(c) Sound effects calculated to mislead, shock, or unduly alarm the listener;

(d) Disrespectful portrayal of law enforcement;

(e) The portrayal of suicide as a satisfactory solution to any problem.

H. Responsibility toward children

The education of children involves giving them a sense of the world at large. It is not enough that programs broadcast for children shall be suitable for the young and immature. In addition, programs which might reasonably be expected to hold the attention of children and which are broadcast during times when children may be normally expected to constitute a substantial part of the audience should be presented with due regard for their effect on children.

1.   Programs specifically designed for listening by children shall be based upon sound social concepts and shall reflect respect for parents, law and order, clean living, high morals, fair play, and honorable behavior.

2.   They shall convey the commonly accepted moral, social and ethical ideals characteristic of American life.

3.   They should contribute to the healthy development of personality and character.

4.   They should afford opportunities for cultural growth as well as for wholesome entertainment.

5.   They should be consistent with integrity of realistic production, but they should avoid material of extreme nature which might create undesirable emotional reaction in children.

6.   They shall avoid appeals urging children to purchase the product specifically for the purpose of keeping the program on the air or which, for any reason, encourage the children to enter inappropriate places.

7.   They should present such subjects as violence and sex without undue emphasis and only as required by plot development or character delineation. Crime should not be presented as attractive or as a solution to human problems, and the inevitable retribution should be made clear.

8.   They should avoid reference to kidnapping or threats of kidnapping of children.

I. General

1.   The intimacy and confidence placed in Radio demand of the broadcaster, the networks and other program sources that they be vigilant in protecting the audience from deceptive program practices.

2.   Sound effects and expressions characteristically associated with news broadcasts (such as "bulletin," "flash," "we interrupt this program to bring you," etc.) shall be reserved for announcement of news, and the use of any deceptive techniques in connection with fictional events and non-news programs shall not be employed.

3.   The acceptance of cash payments or other considerations for including identification of commercial products or services, trade names or advertising slogans, including the identification of prizes, etc., must be disclosed in accordance with provisions of the Communications Act.

4.   When plot development requires the use of material which depends upon physical or mental handicaps, care should be taken to spare the sensibilities of sufferers from similar defects.

5.   Stations should avoid broadcasting program material which would tend to encourage illegal gambling or other violations of Federal, State and local laws, ordinances, and regulations.

6.   Simulation of court atmosphere or use of the term "court" in a program title should be done only in such manner as to eliminate the possibility of creating the false impression that the proceedings broadcast are vested with judicial or official authority.

7.   Quiz and similar programs that are presented as contests of knowledge, information, skill or luck must in fact, be genuine contests and the results must not be controlled by collusion with or between contestants, or any other action which will favor one contestant against any other.

8.   No program shall be presented in a manner which through artifice or simulation would mislead the audience as to any material fact. Each broadcaster must exercise reasonable judgment to determine whether a particular method of presentation would constitute a material deception, or would be accepted by the audience as normal theatrical illusion.

9.   Legal, medical and other professional advice will be permitted only in conformity with law and recognized ethical and professional standards.

10.   Narcotic addiction shall not be presented except as a vicious habit. The misuse of hallucinogenic drugs shall not be presented or encouraged as desirable or socially acceptable.

11.   Program material pertaining to fortune-telling, occultism, astrology, phrenology, palm-reading, numerology, mind-reading, character-

reading, or subjects of a like nature, is unacceptable when presented for the purpose of fostering belief in these subjects.

12. The use of cigarettes shall not be presented in a manner to impress the youth of our country that it is a desirable habit worthy of imitation in that it contributes to health, individual achievement or social acceptance.

13. Profanity, obscenity, smut and vulgarity are forbidden. From time to time, words which have been acceptable, acquire undesirable meanings, and broadcasters should be alert to eliminate such words.

14. Words (especially slang) derisive of any race, color, creed, nationality or national derivation, except wherein such usage would be for the specific purpose of effective dramatization, such as combating prejudice, are forbidden.

15. Respect is maintained for the sanctity of marriage and the value of the home. Divorce is not treated casually as a solution for marital problems.

16. Broadcasts of actual sporting events at which on-the-scene betting is permitted should concentrate on the subject as a public sporting event and not on the aspects of gambling.

II. ADVERTISING STANDARDS

Advertising is the principal source of revenue of the free, competitive American system of radio broadcasting. It makes possible the presentation to all American people of the finest programs of entertainment, education, and information.

Since the great strength of American radio broadcasting derives from the public respect for and the public approval of its programs, it must be the purpose of each broadcaster to establish and maintain high standards of performance, not only in the selection and production of all programs, but also in the presentation of advertising.

This Code establishes basic standards for all radio broadcasting. The principles of acceptability and good taste within the Program Standards section govern the presentation of advertising where applicable. In addition, the Code establishes in this section special standards which apply to radio advertising.

A. General advertising standards

1. A commercial radio broadcaster makes his facilities available for the advertising of products and services and accepts commercial presentations for such advertising. However, he shall, in recognition of his responsibility to the public, refuse the facilities of his station to an advertiser where he has good reason to doubt the integrity of the advertiser, the truth of the

advertising representations, or the compliance of the advertiser with the spirit and purpose of all applicable legal requirements.

2.   In consideration of the customs and attitudes of the communities served, each radio broadcaster should refuse his facilities to the advertisement of products and services, or the use of advertising scripts, which the station has good reason to believe would be objectionable to a substantial and responsible segment of the community. These standards should be applied with judgment and flexibility, taking into consideration the characteristics of the medium, its home and family audience, and the form and content of the particular presentation.

B. Presentation of advertising

1.   The advancing techniques of the broadcast art have shown that the quality and proper integration of advertising copy are just as important as measurement in time. The measure of a station's service to its audience is determined by its overall performance.

2.   The final measurement of any commercial broadcast service is quality. To this, every broadcaster shall dedicate his best effort.

3.   Great care shall be exercised by the broadcaster to prevent the presentation of false, misleading or deceptive advertising. While it is entirely appropriate to present a product in a favorable light and atmosphere, the presentation must not, by copy or demonstration, involve a material deception as to the characteristics or performance of a product.

4.   The broadcaster and the advertiser should exercise special caution with the content and presentation of commercials placed in or near programs designed for children. Exploitation of children should be avoided. Commercials directed to children should in no way mislead as to the product's performance and usefulness.

5.   Appeals involving matters of health which should be determined by physicians should be avoided.

6.   Reference to the results of research, surveys or tests relating to the product to be advertised shall not be presented in a manner so as to create an impression of fact beyond that established by the study. Surveys, tests or other research results upon which claims are based must be conducted under recognized research techniques and standards.

C. Acceptibility of advertisers and products

In general, because radio broadcasting is designed for the home and the entire family, the following principles shall govern the business classifications:

1.   The advertising of hard liquor shall not be accepted.

2.   The advertising of beer and wines is acceptable when presented in the best of good taste and discretion.

3.   The advertising of fortune-telling, occultism, astrology, phrenology, palm-reading, numerology, mind-reading, character-reading, or subjects of a like nature, is not acceptable.

4.   Because the advertising of all products of a personal nature raises special problems, such advertising, when accepted, should be treated with emphasis on ethics and the canons of good taste, and presented in a restrained and inoffensive manner.

5.   The advertising of tip sheets, publications, or organizations seeking to advertise for the purpose of giving odds or promoting betting or lotteries is unacceptable.

6.   The advertising of cigarettes shall not state or imply claims regarding health and shall not be presented in such a manner as to indicate to the youth of our country that the use of cigarettes contributes to individual achievement, personal acceptance, or is a habit worthy of imitation.

7.   An advertiser who markets more than one product shall not be permitted to use advertising copy devoted to an acceptable product for purposes of publicizing the brand name or other identification of a product which is not acceptable.

8.   Care should be taken to avoid presentation of "bait-switch" advertising whereby goods or services which the advertiser has no intention of selling are offered merely to lure the customer into purchasing higher-priced substitutes.

9.   Advertising should offer a product or service on its positive merits and refrain from discrediting, disparaging or unfairly attacking competitors, competing products, other industries, professions or institutions.

Any identification or comparison of a competitive product or service, by name, or other means, should be confined to specific facts rather than generalized statements or conclusions, unless such statements or conclusions are not derogatory in nature.

10.   Advertising testimonials should be genuine and reflect an honest appraisal of personal experience.

11.   Advertising by institutions or enterprises offering instruction with exaggerated claims for opportunities awaiting those who enroll, is unacceptable.

12.   The advertising of firearms/ammunition is acceptable provided it promotes the product only as sporting equipment and conforms to recognized standards of safety as well as all applicable laws. Advertisements of firearms/ammunition by mail order are unacceptable.

D. *Advertising of medical products*

Because advertising for over-the-counter products involving health considerations are of intimate and far-reaching importance to the consumer, the following principles should apply to such advertising:

1.   When dramatized advertising material involves statements by doctors, dentists, nurses or other professional people, the material should be presented by members of such profession reciting actual experience, or it should be made apparent from the presentation itself that the portrayal is dramatized.

2.   Because of the personal nature of the advertising of medical products, the indiscriminate use of such words as "Safe," "Without Risk," "Harmless," or other terms of similar meaning, either direct or implied, should not be expressed in the advertising of medical products.

3.   Advertising material which offensively describes or dramatizes distress or morbid situations involving ailments is not acceptable.

E. Time standards for advertising copy

1.   The amount of time to be used for advertising should not exceed 18 minutes within any clock hour. The Code Authority, however, for good cause may approve advertising exceeding the above standard for special circumstances.

2.   The maximum time to be used for advertising allowable to any single sponsor beyond mention of sponsor's name and address at the opening and close of the program shall be:

5-minute program	1:30
10-minute program	2:30
15-minute program	3:00

3.   Any reference to another's products or services under any trade name, or language sufficiently descriptive to identify it, shall, except for normal guest identifications, be considered as advertising copy.

4.   For the purpose of determining advertising limitations, such program types as "classified," "swap shop," "shopping guides," and "farm auction" programs, etc., shall be regarded as containing one and one-half minutes of advertising for each five-minute segment.

F. Contests

1.   Contests shall be conducted with fairness to all entrants, and shall comply with all pertinent laws and regulations.

2.   All contest details, including rules, eligibility requirements, opening and termination dates, should be clearly and completely announced or easily accessible to the listening public; and the winners' names should be released as soon as possible after the close of the contest.

3.   When advertising is accepted which requests contestants to submit items of product identification or other evidence of purchase of products, reasonable facsimiles thereof should be made acceptable. However,

when the award is based upon skill and not upon chance, evidence of purchase may be required.

4.   All copy pertaining to any contest (except that which is required by law) associated with the exploitation or sale of the sponsor's product or service, and all references to prizes or gifts offered in such connection should be considered a part of and included in the total time limitations heretofore provided. (See Time Standards For Advertising Copy.)

G. *Premiums and offers*

1.   The broadcaster should require that full details of proposed offers be submitted for investigation and approval before the first announcement of the offer is made to the public.

2.   A final date for the termination of an offer should be announced as far in advance as possible.

3.   If a consideration is required, the advertiser should agree to honor complaints indicating dissatisfaction with the premium by returning the consideration.

4.   There should be no misleading descriptions or comparisons of any premiums or gifts which will distort or enlarge their value in the minds of the listeners.

 NAB TELEVISION CODE*

12th Edition, October, 1967
(Amended to June 20, 1968)

PREAMBLE

Television is seen and heard in every type of American home. These homes include children and adults of all ages, embrace all races and all varieties of religious faith, and reach those of every educational background. It is the responsibility of television to bear constantly in mind that the audience is primarily a home audience, and consequently that television's relationship to the viewers is that between guest and host.

* Reprinted by permission of The Code Authority, National Association of Broadcasters.

The revenues from advertising support the free, competitive American system of telecasting, and make available to the eyes and ears of the American people the finest programs of information, education, culture and entertainment. By law the television broadcaster is responsible for the programming of his station. He, however, is obligated to bring his positive responsibility for excellence and good taste in programming to bear upon all who have a hand in the production of programs, including networks, sponsors, producers of film and of live programs, advertising agencies, and talent agencies.

The American businesses which utilize television for conveying their advertising messages to the home by pictures with sound, seen free-of-charge on the home screen, are reminded that their responsibilities are not limited to the sale of goods and the creation of a favorable attitude toward the sponsor by the presentation of entertainment. They include, as well, responsibility for utilizing television to bring the best programs, regardless of kind, into American homes.

Television and all who participate in it are jointly accountable to the American public for respect for the special needs of children, for community responsibility, for the advancement of education and culture, for the acceptibility of the program materials chosen, for decency and decorum in production, and for propriety in advertising. This responsibility cannot be discharged by any given group of programs, but can be discharged only through the highest standards of respect for the American home, applied to every moment of every program presented by television.

In order that television programming may best serve the public interest, viewers should be encouraged to make their criticisms and positive suggestions known to the television broadcasters. Parents in particular should be urged to see to it that out of the richness of television fare, the best programs are brought to the attention of their children.

I. Advancement of education and culture

1.   Commercial television provides a valuable means of augmenting the educational and cultural influence of schools, institutions of higher learning, the home, the church, museums, foundations, and other institutions devoted to education and culture.

2.   It is the responsibility of a television broadcaster to call upon such institutions for counsel and cooperation and to work with them on the best methods of presenting educational and cultural materials by television. It is further the responsibility of stations, networks, advertising agencies and sponsors consciously to seek opportunities for introducing into telecasts factual materials which will aid in the enlightenment of the American public.

3.   Education via television may be taken to mean that process by

which the individual is brought toward informed adjustment to his society. Television is also responsible for the presentation of overtly instructional and cultural programs, scheduled so as to reach the viewers who are naturally drawn to such programs, and produced so as to attract the largest possible audience.

4. The television broadcaster should be thoroughly conversant with the educational and cultural needs and desires of the community served.

5. He should affirmatively seek out responsible and accountable educational and cultural institutions of the community with a view toward providing opportunities for the instruction and enlightenment of the viewers.

6. He should provide for reasonable experimentation in the development of programs specifically directed to the advancement of the community's culture and education.

7. It is in the interest of television as a vital medium to encourage and promote the broadcast of programs presenting genuine artistic or literary material, valid moral and social issues, significant controversial and challenging concepts and other subject matter involving adult themes. Accordingly, none of the provisions of this code, including those relating to the responsibility toward children, should be construed to prevent or impede their broadcast. All such programs, however, should be broadcast with due regard to the composition of the audience. The highest degree of care should be exercised to preserve the integrity of such programs and to ensure that the selection of themes, their treatment and presentation are made in good faith upon the basis of true instructional and entertainment values, and not for the purposes of sensationalism, to shock or exploit the audience or to appeal to prurient interests or morbid curiosity.

II. Responsibility toward children

1. The education of children involves giving them a sense of the world at large. It is not enough that only those programs which are intended for viewing by children shall be suitable to the young and immature. In addition, those programs which might be reasonably expected to hold the attention of children and which are broadcast during times of the day when children may be normally expected to constitute a substantial part of the audience should be presented with due regard for their effect on children. *(Afterschool Special)*

2. Such subjects as violence and sex shall be presented without undue emphasis and only as required by plot development or character delineation. Crime should not be presented as attractive or as a solution to human problems, and the inevitable retribution should be made clear.

3. The broadcaster should afford opportunities for cultural growth as well as for wholesome entertainment.

4. He should develop programs to foster and promote the com-

monly accepted moral, social and ethical ideals characteristic of American life.

5.   Programs should reflect respect for parents, for honorable behavior, and for the constituted authorities of the American community.

6.   Exceptional care should be exercised with reference to kidnapping or threats of kidnapping of children in order to avoid terrorizing them.

7.   Material which is excessively violent or would create morbid suspense, or other undesirable reactions in children, should be avoided.

8.   Particular restraint and care in crime or mystery episodes involving children or minors, should be exercised.

up to parents to restrict some show from

III. Community responsibility

1.   A television broadcaster and his staff occupy a position of responsibility in the community and should conscientiously endeavor to be acquainted fully with its needs and characteristics in order better to serve the welfare of its citizens.

2.   Requests for time for the placement of public service announcements or programs should be carefully reviewed with respect to the character and reputation of the group, campaign or organization involved, the public interest content of the message, and the manner of its presentation.

IV. General program standards

1.   Program materials should enlarge the horizons of the viewer, provide him with wholesome entertainment, afford helpful stimulation, and remind him of the responsibilities which the citizen has towards his society. The intimacy and confidence placed in television demand of the broadcaster, the network and other program sources that they be vigilant in protecting the audience from deceptive program practices.

2.   Profanity, obscenity, smut and vulgarity are forbidden, even when likely to be understood only by part of the audience. From time to time, words which have been acceptable, acquire undesirable meanings, and telecasters should be alert to eliminate such words.

3.   Words (especially slang) derisive of any race, color, creed, nationality or national derivation, except wherein such usage would be for the specific purpose of effective dramatization such as combating prejudice, are forbidden, even when likely to be understood only by part of the audience. From time to time, words which have been acceptable, acquire undesirable meanings, and telecasters should be alert to eliminate such words.

4.   Racial or nationality types shall not be shown on television in such a manner as to ridicule the race or nationality.

5.   Attacks on religion and religious faiths are not allowed. Rev-

erence is to mark any mention of the name of God, His attributes and powers. When religious rites are included in other than religious programs the rites shall be accurately presented. The office of minister, priest or rabbi shall not be presented in such a manner as to ridicule or impair its dignity.

6. Respect is maintained for the sanctity of marriage and the value of the home. Divorce is not treated casually as a solution for marital problems.

7. In reference to physical or mental afflictions and deformities, special precautions must be taken to avoid ridiculing sufferers from similar ailments and offending them or members of their families.

8. Excessive or unfair exploitation of others or of their physical or mental afflictions shall not be presented as praiseworthy.

The presentation of cruelty, greed and selfishness as worthy motivations is to be avoided.

9. Law enforcement shall be upheld and, except where essential to the program plot, officers of the law portrayed with respect and dignity.

10. Legal, medical and other professional advice, diagnosis and treatment will be permitted only in conformity with law and recognized ethical and professional standards.

11. The use of animals both in the production of television programs and as part of television program content, shall at all times, be in conformity with accepted standards of humane treatment.

12. Care should be exercised so that cigarette smoking will not be depicted in a manner to impress the youth of our country as a desirable habit worthy of imitation.

13. Criminality shall be presented as undesirable and unsympathetic. The condoning of crime and the treatment of the commission of crime in a frivolous, cynical or callous manner is unacceptable.

The presentation of techniques of crime in such detail as to invite imitation shall be avoided.

14. The presentation of murder or revenge as a motive for murder shall not be presented as justifiable.

15. Suicide as an acceptable solution for human problems is prohibited.

16. Illicit sex relations are not treated as commendable.

Sex crimes and abnormalities are generally unacceptable as program material.

The use of locations closely associated with sexual life or with sexual sin must be governed by good taste and delicacy.

17. Drunkenness should never be presented as desirable or prevalent.

The use of liquor in program content shall be de-emphasized.

The consumption of liquor in American life, when not required by the plot or for proper characterization, shall not be shown.

18.   Narcotic addiction shall not be presented except as a vicious habit. The administration of illegal drugs will not be displayed. The use of hallucinogenic drugs shall not be shown or encouraged as desirable or socially acceptable.

19.   The use of gambling devices or scenes necessary to the development of plot or as appropriate background is acceptable only when presented with discretion and in moderation, and in a manner which would not excite interest in or foster betting nor be instructional in nature.

20.   Telecasts of actual sport programs at which on-the-scene betting is permitted by law should be presented in a manner in keeping with Federal, state and local laws, and should concentrate on the subject as a public sporting event.

21.   Program material pertaining to fortune-telling, occultism, astrology, phrenology, palm-reading, numerology, mind-reading, or character-reading, is unacceptable when presented for the purpose of fostering belief in these subjects.

22.   Quiz and similar programs that are presented as contests of knowledge, information, skill or luck must, in fact, be genuine contests and the results must not be controlled by collusion with or between contestants, or any other action which will favor one contestant against any other.

23.   No program shall be presented in a manner which through artifice or simulation would mislead the audience as to any material fact. Each broadcaster must exercise reasonable judgment to determine whether a particular method of presentation would constitute a material deception, or would be accepted by the audience as normal theatrical illusion.

24.   The appearances or dramatization of persons featured in actual crime news will be permitted only in such light as to aid law enforcement or to report the news event.

25.   The use of horror for its own sake will be eliminated; the use of visual or aural effects which would shock or alarm the viewer, and the detailed presentation of brutality or physical agony by sight or by sound are not permissible.

26.   Contests may not constitute a lottery.

27.   The costuming of all performers shall be within the bounds of propriety and shall avoid such exposure or such emphasis on anatomical detail as would embarrass or offend home viewers.

28.   The movements of dancers, actors, or other performers shall be kept within the bounds of decency, and lewdness and impropriety shall not be suggested in the positions assumed by performers.

29.   Camera angles shall avoid such views of performers as to emphasize anatomical details indecently.

30.   The use of the television medium to transmit information of any

kind by the use of the process called "subliminal perception," or by the use of any similar technique whereby an attempt is made to convey information to the viewer by transmitting messages below the threshold of normal awareness, is not permitted.

31.   The broadcaster shall be constantly alert to prevent activities that may lead to such practices as the use of scenic properties, the choice and identification of prizes, the selection of music and other creative program elements and inclusion of any identification of commercial products or services, their trade names or advertising slogans, within a program dictated by factors other than the requirements of the program itself. The acceptance of cash payments or other considerations in return for including any of the above within the program is prohibited except in accordance with Sections 317 and 508 of the Communications Act.

32.   A television broadcaster should not present fictional events or other non-news material as authentic news telecasts or announcements, nor should he permit dramatizations in any program which would give the false impression that the dramatized material constitutes news. Expletives (presented aurally or pictorially) such as "flash" or "bulletin" and statements such as "we interrupt this program to bring you . . ." should be reserved specifically for news room use. However, a television broadcaster may properly exercise discretion in the use in non-news programs of words or phrases which do not necessarily imply that the material following is a news release.

33.   Program content should be confined to those elements which entertain or inform the viewer and to the extent that titles, teasers and credits do not meet these criteria, they should be restricted or eliminated.

34.   The creation of a state of hypnosis by act or demonstration on the air is prohibited and hypnosis as an aspect of "parlor game" antics to create humorous situations within a comedy setting cannot be used.

V. Treatment of news and public events

News

1.   A television station's news schedule should be adequate and well-balanced.

2.   News reporting should be factual, fair and without bias.

3.   A television broadcaster should exercise particular discrimination in the acceptance, placement and presentation of advertising in news programs so that such advertising should be clearly distinguishable from the news content.

4.   At all times, pictorial and verbal material for both news and comment should conform to other sections of these standards, wherever such sections are reasonably applicable.

5. Good taste should prevail in the selection and handling of news:

Morbid, sensational or alarming details not essential to the factual report, especially in connection with stories of crime or sex, should be avoided. News should be telecast in such a manner as to avoid panic and unnecessary alarm.

6. Commentary and analysis should be clearly identified as such.

7. Pictorial material should be chosen with care and not presented in a misleading manner.

8. All news interview programs should be governed by accepted standards of ethical journalism, under which the interviewer selects the questions to be asked. Where there is advance agreement materially restricting an important or newsworthy area of questioning, the interviewer will state on the program that such limitation has been agreed upon. Such disclosure should be made if the person being interviewed requires that questions be submitted in advance or if he participates in editing a recording of the interview prior to its use on the air.

9. A television broadcaster should exercise due care in his supervision of content, format, and presentation of newscasts originated by his station, and in his selection of newscasters, commentators, and analysts.

Public events

1. A television broadcaster has an affirmative responsibility at all times to be informed of public events, and to provide coverage consonant with the ends of an informed and enlightened citizenry.

2. The treatment of such events by a television broadcaster should provide adequate and informed coverage.

VI. Controversial public issues

1. Television provides a valuable forum for the expression of responsible views on public issues of a controversial nature. The television broadcaster should seek out and develop with accountable individuals, groups and organizations, programs relating to controversial public issues of import to his fellow citizens; and to give fair representation to opposing sides of issues which materially affect the life or welfare of a substantial segment of the public.

2. Requests by individuals, groups or organizations for time to discuss their views on controversial public issues, should be considered on the basis of their individual merits, and in the light of the contribution which the use requested would make to the public interest, and to a well-balanced program structure.

3. Programs devoted to the discussion of controversial public issues should be identified as such. They should not be presented in a manner which would mislead listeners or viewers to believe that the program is purely of an entertainment, news, or other character.

4.   Broadcasts in which stations express their own opinions about issues of general public interest should be clearly identified as editorials. They should be unmistakably identified as statements of station opinion and should be appropriately distinguished from news and other program material.

VII. Political telecasts

1.   Political telecasts should be clearly identified as such. They should not be presented by a television broadcaster in a manner which would mislead listeners or viewers to believe that the program is of any other character.

(Ref.: Communications Act of 1934, as amended, Secs. 315 and 317, and FCC Rules and Regulations, Secs. 3.654, 3.657, 3.663, as discussed in NAB's "A Political Catechism.")

VIII. Religious programs

1.   It is the responsibility of a television broadcaster to make available to the community appropriate opportunity for religious presentations.

2.   Telecasting which reaches men of all creeds simultaneously should avoid attacks upon religion.

3.   Religious programs should be presented respectfully and accurately and without prejudice or ridicule.

4.   Religious programs should be presented by responsible individuals, groups and organizations.

5.   Religious programs should place emphasis on broad religious truths, excluding the presentation of controversial or partisan views not directly or necessarily related to religion or morality.

6.   In the allocation of time for telecasts of religious programs the television station should use its best efforts to apportion such time fairly among the representative faith groups of its community.

IX. General advertising standards

1.   This Code establishes basic standards for all television broadcasting. The principles of acceptability and good taste within the Program Standards section govern the presentation of advertising where applicable. In addition, the Code establishes in this section special standards which apply to television advertising.

2. A commercial television broadcaster makes his facilities available for the advertising of products and services and accepts commercial presentations for such advertising. However, a television broadcaster should, in recognition of his responsibility to the public, refuse the facilities of his station to an advertiser where he has good reason to doubt the integrity of the advertiser, the truth of the advertising representations, or the com-

pliance of the advertiser with the spirit and purpose of all applicable legal requirements.

3.   Identification of sponsorship must be made in all sponsored programs in accordance with the requirements of the Communications Act of 1934, as amended, and the Rules and Regulations of the Federal Communications Commission.

4.   Representations which disregard normal safety precautions shall be avoided.

Children shall not be represented, except under adult supervision, as being in contact with, or demonstrating a product recognized as potentially dangerous to them.

5.   In consideration of the customs and attitudes of the communities served, each television broadcaster should refuse his facilities to the advertisement of products and services, or the use of advertising scripts, which the station has good reason to believe would be objectionable to a substantial and responsible segment of the community. These standards should be applied with judgment and flexibility, taking into consideration the characteristics of the medium, its home and family audience, and the form and content of the particular presentation.

6.   The advertising of hard liquor (distilled spirits) is not acceptable.

7.   The advertising of beer and wines is acceptable only when presented in the best of good taste and discretion, and is acceptable only subject to Federal and local laws.

8.   The advertising of cigarettes shall not state or imply claims regarding health and shall not be presented in such a manner as to indicate to youth that the use of cigarettes contributes to individual achievement, personal acceptance or is a habit worthy of imitation.

9.   Advertising by institutions or enterprises which in their offers of instruction imply promises of employment or make exaggerated claims for the opportunities awaiting those who enroll for courses is generally unacceptable.

10.   The advertising of firearms/ammunition is acceptable provided it promotes the product only as sporting equipment and conforms to recognized standards of safety as well as all applicable laws and regulations. Advertisements of firearms/ammunition by mail order are unacceptable. The advertising of fireworks is acceptable subject to all applicable laws.

11.   The advertising of fortune-telling, occultism, astrology, phrenology, palm-reading, numerology, mind-reading, character reading or subjects of a like nature is not permitted.

12.   Because all products of a personal nature create special problems, such products, when accepted, should be treated with especial emphasis on ethics and the canons of good taste. Such advertising of personal products as is accepted must be presented in a restrained and obviously inoffensive manner.

The advertising of particularly intimate products which ordinarily are not freely mentioned or discussed is not acceptable.

13. The advertising of tip sheets, race track publications, or organizations seeking to advertise for the purpose of giving odds or promoting betting or lotteries is unacceptable.

14. An advertiser who markets more than one product should not be permitted to use advertising copy devoted to an acceptable product for purposes of publicizing the brand name or other identification of a product which is not acceptable.

15. "Bait-switch" advertising, whereby goods or services which the advertiser has no intention of selling are offered merely to lure the customer into purchasing higher-priced substitutes, is not acceptable.

16. Personal endorsements (testimonials) shall be genuine and reflect personal experience. They shall contain no statement that cannot be supported if presented in the advertiser's own words.

X. Presentation of advertising

1. Advertising messages should be presented with courtesy and good taste; disturbing or annoying material should be avoided; every effort should be made to keep the advertising message in harmony with the content and general tone of the program in which it appears.

2. The role and capability of television to market sponsors' products are well recognized. In turn, this fact dictates that great care be exercised by the broadcaster to prevent the presentation of false, misleading or deceptive advertising. While it is entirely appropriate to present a product in a favorable light and atmosphere, the presentation must not, by copy or demonstration, involve a material deception as to the characteristics, performance or appearance of the product.

3. The broadcaster and the advertiser should exercise special caution with the content and presentation of television commercials placed in or near programs designed for children. Exploitation of children should be avoided. Commercials directed to children should in no way mislead as to the product's performance and usefulness.

Appeals involving matters of health which should be determined by physicians should not be directed primarily to children.

4. Appeals to help fictitious characters in television programs by purchasing the advertiser's product or service or sending for a premium should not be permitted, and such fictitious characters should not be introduced into the advertising message for such purposes.

5. Commercials for services or over-the-counter products involving health considerations are of intimate and far-reaching importance to the consumer. The following principles should apply to such advertising:

a. Physicians, dentists or nurses, or actors representing physicians, dentists or nurses shall not be employed directly or by implication. These restrictions also apply to persons professionally engaged in medical services (e.g., physical therapists, pharmacists, dental assistants, nurses' aides).

　　b. Visual representations of laboratory settings may be employed, provided they bear a direct relationship to bona fide research which has been conducted for the product or service. (*See Television Code, X, 10*) In such cases, laboratory technicians shall be identified as such and shall not be employed as spokesmen or in any other way speak on behalf of the product.

　　c. Institutional announcements not intended to sell a specific product or service to the consumer and public service announcements by non-profit organizations may be presented by accredited physicians, dentists or nurses, subject to approval by the broadcaster. An accredited professional is one who has met required qualifications and has been licensed in his resident state.

　　6.　　Advertising should offer a product or service on its positive merits and refrain by identification or other means from discrediting, disparaging or unfairly attacking competitors, competing products, other industries, professions or institutions.

　　7.　　A sponsor's advertising messages should be confined within the framework of the sponsor's program structure. A television broadcaster should avoid the use of commercial announcements which are divorced from the program either by preceding the introduction of the program (as in the case of so-called "cow-catcher" announcements) or by following the apparent sign-off of the program (as in the case of so-called trailer or "hitch-hike" announcements). To this end, the program itself should be announced and clearly identified, both audio and video, before the sponsor's advertising material is first used, and should be signed off, both audio and video, after the sponsor's advertising material is last used.

　　8.　　Since advertising by television is a dynamic technique, a television broadcaster should keep under surveillance new advertising devices so that the spirit and purpose of these standards are fulfilled.

　　9.　　A charge for television time to churches and religious bodies is not recommended.

　　10.　　Reference to the results of bona fide research, surveys or test relating to the product to be advertised shall not be presented in a manner so as to create an impression of fact beyond that established by the work that has been conducted.

XI. *Advertising of medical products*

　　1.　　The advertising of medical products presents considerations of intimate and far-reaching importance to the consumer because of the direct bearing on his health.

2. Because of the personal nature of the advertising of medical products, claims that a product will effect a cure and the indiscriminate use of such words as "safe," "without risk," "harmless," or terms of similar meaning should not be accepted in the advertising of medical products on television stations.

3. A television broadcaster should not accept advertising material which in his opinion offensively describes or dramatizes distress or morbid situations involving ailments, by spoken word, sound or visual effects.

XII. Contests

1. Contests shall be conducted with fairness to all entrants, and shall comply with all pertinent laws and regulations. Care should be taken to avoid the concurrent use of the three elements which together constitute a lottery—prize, chance and consideration.

2. All contest details, including rules, eligibility requirements, opening and termination dates should be clearly and completely announced and/or shown, or easily accessible to the viewing public, and the winners' names should be released and prizes awarded as soon as possible after the close of the contest.

3. When advertising is accepted which requests contestants to submit items of product identification or other evidence of purchase of products, reasonable facsimiles thereof should be made acceptable unless the award is based upon skill and not upon chance.

4. All copy pertaining to any contest (except that which is required by law) associated with the exploitation or sale of the sponsor's product or service, and all references to prizes or gifts offered in such connection should be considered a part of and included in the total time allowances as herein provided. (*See Television Code, XIV*)

XIII. Premiums and offers

1. Full details of proposed offers should be required by the television broadcaster for investigation and approved before the first announcement of the offer is made to the public.

2. A final date for the termination of an offer should be announced as far in advance as possible.

3. Before accepting for telecast offers involving a monetary consideration, a television broadcaster should satisfy himself as to the integrity of the advertiser and the advertiser's willingness to honor complaints indicating dissatisfaction with the premium by returning the monetary consideration.

4. There should be no misleading descriptions or visual representations of any premiums or gifts which would distort or enlarge their value in the minds of the viewers.

5.   Assurances should be obtained from the advertiser that premiums offered are not harmful to person or property.

6.   Premiums should not be approved which appeal to superstition on the basis of "luck-bearing" powers or otherwise.

XIV. Time standards for non-program material*

In order that the time for non-program material and its placement shall best serve the viewer, the following standards are set forth in accordance with sound television practice:

1.   *Non-Program Material Definition:* Non-program material, in both prime time and all other time, includes billboards, commercials, all credits in excess of 30 seconds and promotional announcements. Public service announcements and promotional announcements for the same program are excluded from this definition.

2.   *Allowable Time for Non-Program Material.*

A. In prime time, non-program material shall not exceed 10 minutes in any 60-minute period.

Prime time is a continuous period of not less than three consecutive evening hours per broadcast day as designated by the station between the hours of 6:00 PM and Midnight.

B. In all other time, non-program material shall not exceed 16 minutes in any 60-minute period.

3.   *Program Interruptions.*

A. *Definition:* A program interruption is any occurrence of non-program material within the main body of the program.

B. In prime time, the number of program interruptions shall not exceed two within any 30-minute program, or four within any 60-minute program.

Programs longer than 60 minutes shall be pro-rated at two interruptions per half-hour.

The number of interruptions in 60-minute variety shows shall not exceed five.

C. In all other time, the number of interruptions shall not exceed four within any 30-minute program period.

D. In both prime time and all other time, the following interruption standard shall apply within programs of 15 minutes or less in length:

> 5-minute program—1 interruption;
> 10-minute program—2 interruptions;
> 15-minute program—2 interruptions.

E. News, weather, sports and special events programs are ex-

* This section is effective September 15, 1968. [Ed.]

empt from the interruption standard because of the nature of such programs.

4. No more than four commercial announcements shall be scheduled consecutively within programs, and no more than three commercial announcements shall be scheduled consecutively during station breaks. The consecutive commercial message limitation shall not apply to a single sponsor who wishes to further reduce the number of interruptions in the program.

5. A multiple product announcement is one in which two or more products or services are presented within the framework of a single announcement.

A multiple product announcement shall be counted as a single announcement provided the products or services are so treated in audio and video throughout the announcement as to appear to the viewer as a single unit. Multiple product announcements not meeting this definition shall be counted as two or more announcements under this section of the Code. This provision shall not apply to retail or service establishments.

6. The use of billboards, in prime time and all other time, shall be confined to programs sponsored by a single or alternate week advertiser and shall be limited to the products advertised in the program.

7. Reasonable and limited identification of prizes and donors' names where the presentation of contest awards or prizes is a necessary part of program content shall not be included as non-program material as defined above.

8. Programs presenting women's service features, shopping guides, fashion shows, demonstrations and similar material provide a special service to the public in which certain material normally classified as non-program is an informative and necessary part of the program content. Because of this, the time standards may be waived by the Code Authority to a reasonable extent on a case-by-case basis.

9. Gratuitous references in a program to a non-sponsor's product or service should be avoided except for normal guest identification.

10. Stationary backdrops or properties in television presentations showing the sponsor's name or product, the name of his product, his trademark or slogan should be used only incidentally and should not obtrude on program interest or entertainment.

RELATED READING

ADVERTISING ADVISORY COMMITTEE TO THE SECRETARY OF COMMERCE. *Self-Regulation in Advertising.* Washington: Government Printing Office, 1964.

ANELLO, Douglas A., and Robert V. CAHILL. "Legal Authority of the FCC to Place Limits on Broadcast Advertising Time," *Journal of Broadcasting,* VII (Fall, 1963), 285-303.

ATKIN, Kenward L. "Federal Regulation of Broadcast Advertising," *Journal of Broadcasting,* III (Fall, 1959), 326-340.

BAIRD, Frank L. "Program Regulation on the New Frontier," *Journal of Broadcasting,* XI (Summer, 1967), 231-243.

BRINDZE, Ruth. *Not to Be Broadcast.* New York: Vanguard Press, 1937.

Broadcasting and Government Regulation in a Free Society. Santa Barbara, Cal.: Center for the Study of Democratic Institutions, 1959.

Broadcasting and the Bill of Rights. Washington: National Association of Broadcasters, 1947.

BRONSON, Edward H. "Self-Regulation by Stations," *Journal of Broadcasting,* I (Spring, 1957), 119-123.

BRYANT, Ashbrook. "Responsibility for Broadcast Matter," *Journal of Broadcasting,* V (Winter, 1960-61), 3-16.

CARSON, Gerald. *The Roguish World of Doctor Brinkley.* New York: Holt, Rinehart and Winston, 1960.

COGLEY, John. *Report on Blacklisting: Radio-Television.* Vol. II. New York: Fund for the Republic, 1956.

CONE, Fairfax M. "Wasteland Revisited," *Television Quarterly,* II (Summer, 1963), 27-39.

COONS, John E., ed. *Freedom and Responsibility in Broadcasting.* Evanston: Northwestern University Press, 1961.

COX, Kenneth A. "Broadcasters as Revolutionaries," *Television Quarterly,* VI (Winter, 1967), 13-19.

CROSBY, John. *Out of the Blue.* New York: Simon and Schuster, 1952.

EMERY, Walter B. "Broadcasting Rights and Responsibilities in Democratic Society," *NAEB Journal,* XXIV (March-April, 1965), 72-84.

————. "Government's Role in the American System of Broadcasting," *Television Quarterly,* I (February, 1962), 7-13.

————. "Legal Restrictions on Use of Program Materials," *Journal of Broadcasting,* IV (Summer, 1960), 241-252.

ERNST, Morris L. *The First Freedom.* New York: Macmillan, 1946.

FEDERAL COUNCIL OF CHURCHES OF CHRIST IN AMERICA. *Broadcasting and the Public.* New York: Abingdon Press, 1938.

FOWLER, Paul C. "The Policy of the FCC with Respect to Programming," *Journal of Broadcasting,* II (Spring, 1958), 99-109.

FROST, S. E., Jr. *Is American Radio Democratic?* Chicago: University of Chicago Press, 1937.

GERBNER, George. "Mental Illness on Television: A Study of Censorship," *Journal of Broadcasting,* III (Fall, 1959), 293-303.

HAWES, William. "Television Censorship: Myth or Menace?," *Television Quarterly,* IV (Summer, 1965), 63-73.

HELFFRICH, Stockton. "Broadcast Censorship: Past, Present, Future," *Television Quarterly,* I (November, 1962), 62-68.

————. "Self-Regulation by Networks," *Journal of Broadcasting,* I (Spring, 1957), 124-128.

————. "Self-Regulation in TV Advertising," *Television Quarterly,* III (Summer, 1964), 74-77.

HENRY, E. William. "The '50-50' Rule," *Television Quarterly,* IV (Fall, 1965), 7-12.

HOGGART, Richard. "Not So Popular as 'Gunsmoke,' But—," *New York Times Magazine,* November 4, 1962, 22, 112-115.

HUGGINS, Roy B. "The Bloodshot Eye: A Comment on the Crisis in American Television," *Television Quarterly,* I (August, 1962), 6-22.

"Interpreting the FCC Rules and Regulations: 'Overcommercialization' Reviewed," *Broadcast Management/Engineering,* III (March, 1967), 18-25, 75.

"Interpreting the FCC Rules and Regulations: The Commission vs. Programming Responsibility," *Broadcast Management/Engineering,* I (January, 1965), 12-14.

JOHNSON, Nicholas. "Crisis in Communications," *Television Quarterly,* VI (Winter, 1967), 21-28.

KELLY, Frank. *Who Owns the Air?* Santa Barbara, Cal.: Center for the Study of Democratic Institutions, 1960.

KROEGER, Albert R. "A Long, Hard Look at the Genealogy of Network TV," *Television,* XXIII (April, 1966), 33-39.

LACY, Dan. *Freedom and Communications,* 2nd ed. Urbana: University of Illinois Press, 1965.

LAMB, Edward. *"Trial by Battle."* Santa Barbara, Cal.: Center for the Study of Democratic Institutions, 1964.

LOEVINGER, Lee. "The Limits of Technology in Broadcasting," *Journal of Broadcasting,* X (Fall, 1966), 285-298.

————. "The Role of Law in Broadcasting," *Journal of Broadcasting,* VIII (Spring, 1964), 113-126.

LONGLEY, Lawrence D. "The FCC's Attempt to Regulate Commercial Time," *Journal of Broadcasting,* XI (Winter, 1966-67), 83-89.

MEYER, Richard J. "Charles A. Siepmann," *NAEB Journal,* XXII (May-June, 1963), 64-68.

————. "Reaction to the 'Blue Book,'" *Journal of Broadcasting,* VI (Fall, 1962), 295-312.

————. "'The Blue Book,'" *Journal of Broadcasting,* VI (Summer, 1962), 197-207.

MILL, John Stuart. *On Liberty,* ed. by Alburey Castell. New York: Appleton-Century-Crofts, 1947.

MILLER, Merle, and Evan RHODES. *Only You, Dick Daring!* New York: William Sloane Associates, 1964.

MILTON, John. *Areopagitica and Of Education,* ed. by George H. Sabine. New York: Appleton-Century-Crofts, 1951.

MINOW, Newton N. *Equal Time: The Private Broadcaster and the Public Interest,* ed. by Lawrence Laurent. New York: Atheneum, 1964.

PIERSON, W. Theodore. "The Active Eyebrow—A Changing Style for Censorship," *Television Quarterly,* I (February, 1962), 14-21.

———. "What Is the American System of Broadcasting?," *Journal of Broadcasting,* X (Summer, 1966), 191-198.

RATNER, Victor M. "The Freedom of Taste," *Television,* XIX (November, 1962), 61-64.

The Relation of the Writer to Television. Santa Barbara, Cal.: Center for the Study of Democratic Institutions, 1960.

SCHWARTZ, Bernard. *The Professor and the Commissions.* New York: Knopf, 1959.

SEYMOUR, Whitney N. "Authority of the FCC over Broadcast Content," *Journal of Broadcasting,* IV (Winter, 1959-60), 18-26.

SELDES, Gilbert. *The Public Arts.* New York: Simon and Schuster, 1956.

SERLING, Rod. "About Writing for Television," *Patterns.* New York: Bantam, 1958.

———. "Controversy in Broadcasting,'" *NAEB Journal,* XX (January-February, 1961), 1-3.

SIEPMANN, Charles A. *Radio's Second Chance.* Boston: Little, Brown, 1946.

———. "What Is Wrong With TV—and With Us," *New York Times Magazine,* April 19, 1964, 13, 112-114.

SMEAD, Elmer E. *Freedom of Speech by Radio and Television.* Washington: Public Affairs Press, 1959.

STANLEY, Earl R. "Revocation, Renewal of License, and Fines and Forfeiture Cases before the Federal Communications Commission," *Journal of Broadcasting,* VIII (Fall, 1964), 371-382.

STEINER, Gary A. *The People Look at Television: A Study of Audience Attitudes.* New York: Knopf, 1963.

SUMMERS, H. B., ed. *Radio Censorship.* New York: H. W. Wilson Company, 1939.

SUMMERS, Robert E., and SUMMERS, Harrison B. *Broadcasting and the Public.* Belmont, Cal.: Wadsworth, 1966.

WEINBERG, Meyer. *TV in America: The Morality of Hard Cash.* New York: Ballantine, 1962.

WINICK, Charles. *Taste and the Censor in Television.* New York: Fund for the Republic, 1959.

———. "Censor and Sensibility: A Content Analysis of the TV Censor's Comments," *Journal of Broadcasting,* V (Spring, 1961), 117-135.

PART THREE

FREEDOM OF EXPRESSION: BROADCAST JOURNALISM

NEWS HAS BEEN a staple of broadcasting since radio's beginnings. As newspapers felt the pinch of journalistic competition from the electronic medium, publishers and the press associations they controlled attempted to minimize the amount of news radio stations could broadcast. The infamous "Biltmore Agreement" of 1933 marked a low point for broadcast journalism.

But stations and networks developed their own sources of news, built their own news staffs, and nurtured such journalistic forms as the radio (later television) documentary and news commentary. The newspapers' strategy backfired, and the resultant "if you can't fight 'em, join 'em" philosophy motivated many a publisher to secure a financial interest in broadcasting.

Broadcasting gained its greatest journalistic impetus during World War II. Its ability to be "on the spot" to describe events as they were happening surpassed the best efforts of the newspapers, which could only put out "extra" editions hours after an event was reported by radio. In addition, broadcasting benefited financially from newsprint shortages during the war, as advertisers, unable to secure print space, turned increasingly to radio.

While newspapers still occupy a prominent position, broadcasting, especially television, appears to be the primary source of news for most people.[1] The increase in the number of broadcast stations and the concurrent decrease in the number of daily newspapers indicate further the journalistic shift from print to electronic media.

Broadcasters fulfill their journalistic responsibilities under greater restraints than their newspaper colleagues, who have no equivalent of Sec-

---

[1] Burns W. Roper. *Emerging Profiles of Television and Other Mass Media: Public Attitudes, 1959-1967* (New York: Television Information Office, 1967).

tion 315 or the "Fairness Doctrine." Canon 35 permits the pencil-and-pad reporter to ply his trade in the courtroom, but denies broadcasters the use of their tools—microphones and cameras. Whether such restrictions might properly be applied to the print media, or whether the removal of such restrictions on electronic media would tend to better serve the information needs of the public, dependent as it is on broadcast news, are questions every person must decide for himself. In doing so, it may help to recall the paradox in two of Thomas Jefferson's remarks:

Ignorance is preferable to error; and he is less remote from the truth who believes nothing, than he who believes what is wrong. (From *Notes on the State of Virginia.*)

The basis of our government being the opinion of the people, the very first object should be to keep that right; and were it left to me to decide whether we should have a government without newspapers, or newspapers without a government, I should not hesitate a moment to prefer the latter. But I should mean that every man should receive those papers, and be capable of reading them. (From a letter to Colonel Edward Carrington.)

1 | A BENCHMARK

The Requirements for *A Free and Responsible Press** (1947)

A Free and Responsible Press *was a report by the Commission on Freedom of the Press, a group whose independent inquiry was supported by grants from Time, Inc., and Encyclopaedia Britannica, Inc. Among the notable individuals who served on this distinguished Commission were Harold Lasswell, Archibald MacLeish, Reinhold Niebuhr, Beardsley Ruml, and Arthur M. Schlesinger. The Commission was chaired by Robert M. Hutchins, then Chancellor of The University of Chicago.*

The selection that follows comprises the chapter entitled "The Requirements" in the Commission's report. It is as clear and consise a description of what the press (including broadcasting) should be as has yet been issued.

If the freedom of the press is freighted with the responsibility of providing the current intelligence needed by a free society, we have to discover what a free society requires. Its requirements in America today are greater in variety, quantity, and quality than those of any previous society in any age. They are the requirements of a self-governing republic of continental size, whose doings have become, within a generation, matters of common concern in new and important ways. Its internal arrangements, from being thought of mainly as matters of private interest and automatic market adjustments, have become affairs of conflict and conscious compromise among organized groups, whose powers appear not to be bounded by "natural law," economic or other. Externally, it has suddenly assumed a leading role in the attempt to establish peaceful relationships among all the states on the globe.

Today our society needs, first, a truthful, comprehensive, and intelligent account of the day's events in a context which gives them meaning;

* Reprinted from *A Free and Responsible Press* by The Commission on Freedom of the Press, by permission of the University of Chicago Press. Copyright 1947 by The University of Chicago.

second, a forum for the exchange of comment and criticism; third, a means of projecting the opinions and attitudes of the groups in the society to one another; fourth, a method of presenting and clarifying the goals and values of the society; and, fifth, a way of reaching every member of the society by the currents of information, thought, and feeling which the press supplies.

The Commission has no idea that these five ideal demands can ever be completely met. All of them cannot be met by any one medium; some do not apply at all to a particular unit; nor do all apply with equal relevance to all parts of the communications industry. The Commission does not suppose that these standards will be new to the managers of the press; they are drawn largely from their professions and practices.

A truthful, comprehensive, and intelligent account of the day's events in a context which gives them meaning

The first requirement is that the media should be accurate. They should not lie.

Here the first link in the chain of responsibility is the reporter at the source of the news. He must be careful and competent. He must estimate correctly which sources are most authoritative. He must prefer firsthand observation to hearsay. He must know what questions to ask, what things to observe, and which items to report. His employer has the duty of training him to do his work as it ought to be done.

Of equal importance with reportorial accuracy are the identification of fact as fact and opinion as opinion, and their separation, so far as possible. This is necessary all the way from the reporter's file, up through the copy and makeup desks and editorial offices, to the final, published product. The distinction cannot, of course, be made absolute. There is no fact without a context and no factual report which is uncolored by the opinions of the reporter. But modern conditions require greater effort than ever to make the distinction between fact and opinion. In a simpler order of society published accounts of events within the experience of the community could be compared with other sources of information. Today this is usually impossible. The account of an isolated fact, however accurate in itself, may be misleading and, in effect, untrue.

The greatest danger here is in the communication of information internationally. The press now bears a responsibility in all countries, and particularly in democratic countries, where foreign policies are responsive to popular majorities, to report international events in such a way that they can be understood. It is no longer enough to report *the fact* truthfully. It is now necessary to report *the truth about the fact*.

In this country a similar obligation rests upon the press in reporting domestic news. The country has many groups which are partially insulated from one another and which need to be interpreted to one another. Factually correct but substantially untrue accounts of the behavior of members of one of these social islands can intensify the antagonisms of others toward them. A single incident will be accepted as a sample of group action unless the press has given a flow of information and interpretation concerning the relations between two racial groups such as to enable the reader to set a single event in its proper perspective. If it is allowed to pass as a sample of such action, the requirement that the press present an accurate account of the day's events in a context which gives them meaning has not been met.

A forum for the exchange of comment and criticism

The second requirement means that the great agencies of mass communication should regard themselves as common carriers of public discussion.[1] The units of the press have in varying degrees assumed this function and should assume the responsibilities which go with it, more generally and more explicitly.

It is vital to a free society that an idea should not be stifled by the circumstances of its birth. The press cannot and should not be expected to print everybody's ideas. But the giant units can and should assume the duty of publishing significant ideas contrary to their own, as a matter of objective reporting, distinct from their proper function of advocacy. Their control over the various ways of reaching the ear of America is such that, if they do not publish ideas which differ from their own, those ideas will never reach the ear of America. If that happens, one of the chief reasons for the freedom which these giants claim disappears.

Access to a unit of the press acting as a common carrier is possible in a number of ways, all of which, however, involve selection on the part of the managers of the unit. The individual whose views are not represented on an editorial page may reach an audience through a public statement reported as news, through a letter to the editor, through a statement printed in advertising space, or through a magazine article. But some seekers for space are bound to be disappointed and must resort to pamphlets or such duplicating devices as will spread their ideas to such public as will attend to them.

But all the important viewpoints and interests in the society should be represented in its agencies of mass communication. Those who have these viewpoints and interests cannot count on explaining them to their fellow-citizens through newspapers or radio stations of their own. Even if they could make the necessary investment, they could have no assurance that

---

[1] By the use of this analogy the Commission does not intend to suggest that the agencies of communication should be subject to the legal obligations of common carriers, such as compulsory reception of all applicants for space, the regulation of rates, etc.

their publications would be read or their programs heard by the public outside their own adherents. An ideal combination would include general media, inevitably solicitous to present their own views, but setting forth other views fairly. As checks on their fairness, and partial safeguards against ignoring important matters, more specialized media of advocacy have a vital place. In the absence of such a combination the partially insulated groups in society will continue to be insulated. The unchallenged assumptions of each group will continue to harden into prejudice. The mass medium reaches across all groups; through the mass medium they can come to understand one another.

Whether a unit of the press is an advocate or a common carrier, it ought to identify the sources of its facts, opinions, and arguments so that the reader or listener can judge them. Persons who are presented with facts, opinions, and arguments are properly influenced by the general reliability of those who offer them. If the veracity of statements is to be appraised, those who offer them must be known.

Identification of source is necessary to a free society. Democracy, in time of peace, at least, has a justifiable confidence that full and free discussion will strengthen rather than weaken it. But, if the discussion is to have the effect for which democracy hopes, if it is to be really full and free, the names and the characters of the participants must not be hidden from view.

The projection of a representative picture of the constituent groups in the society

This requirement is closely related to the two preceding. People make decisions in large part in terms of favorable or unfavorable images. They relate fact and opinion to stereotypes. Today the motion picture, the radio, the book, the magazine, the newspaper, and the comic strip are principal agents in creating and perpetuating these conventional conceptions. When the images they portray fail to present the social group truly, they tend to pervert judgment.

Such failure may occur indirectly and incidentally. Even if nothing is said about the Chinese in the dialogue of a film, yet if the Chinese appear in a succession of pictures as sinister drug addicts and militarists, an image of China is built which needs to be balanced by another. If the Negro appears in the stories published in magazines of national circulation only as a servant, if children figure constantly in radio dramas as impertinent and ungovernable brats—the image of the Negro and the American child is distorted. The plugging of special color and "hate" words in radio and press dispatches, in advertising copy, in news stories—such words as "ruthless," "confused," "bureaucratic"—performs inevitably the same image-making function.

Responsible performance here simply means that the images repeated and emphasized be such as are in total representative of the social group as it is. The truth about any social group, though it should not exclude its weaknesses and vices, includes also recognition of its values, its aspirations, and its common humanity. The Commission holds to the faith that if people are exposed to the inner truth of the life of a particular group, they will gradually build up respect for and understanding of it.

> *The presentation and clarification of the goals and values of the society*

The press has a similar responsibility with regard to the values and goals of our society as a whole. The mass media, whether or not they wish to do so, blur or clarify these ideals as they report the failings and achievements of every day.[2] The Commission does not call upon the press to sentimentalize, to manipulate the facts for the purpose of painting a rosy picture. The Commission believes in realistic reporting of the events and forces that militate against the attainment of social goals as well as those which work for them. We must recognize, however, that the agencies of mass communication are an educational instrument, perhaps the most powerful there is; and they must assume a responsibility like that of educators in stating and clarifying the ideals toward which the community should strive.

> *Full access to the day's intelligence*

It is obvious that the amount of current information required by the citizens in a modern industrial society is far greater than that required in any earlier day. We do not assume that all citizens at all times will actually use all the material they receive. By necessity or choice large numbers of people voluntarily delegate analysis and decision to leaders whom they trust. Such leadership in our society is freely chosen and constantly changing; it is informal, unofficial, and flexible. Any citizen may at any time assume the power of decision. In this way government is carried on by consent.

But such leadership does not alter the need for the wide distribution of news and opinion. The leaders are not identified; we can inform them only by making information available to everybody.

[2] A striking indication of the continuous need to renew the basic values of our society is given in the recent poll of public opinion by the National Opinion Research Center at Denver, in which one out of every three persons polled did not think the newspapers should be allowed to criticize the American form of government, even in peacetime. Only 57 per cent thought that the Socialist party should be allowed, in peacetime, to publish newspapers in the United States. Another poll revealed that less than a fourth of those questioned had a "reasonably accurate idea" of what the Bill of Rights is. Here is widespread ignorance with regard to the value most cherished by the press—its own freedom—which seems only dimly understood by many of its consumers.

The five requirements listed in this chapter suggest what our society is entitled to demand of its press. We can now proceed to examine the tools, the structure, and the performance of the press to see how it is meeting these demands.

Let us summarize these demands in another way.

The character of the service required of the American press by the American people differs from the service previously demanded, first, in this—that it is essential to the operation of the economy and to the government of the Republic. Second, it is a service of greatly increased responsibilities both as to the quantity and as to the quality of the information required. In terms of quantity, the information about themselves and about their world made available to the American people must be as extensive as the range of their interests and concerns as citizens of a self-governing, industrialized community in the closely integrated modern world. In terms of quality, the information provided must be provided in such a form, and with so scrupulous a regard for the wholeness of the truth and the fairness of its presentation, that the American people may make for themselves, by the exercise of reason and of conscience, the fundamental decisions necessary to the direction of their government and of their lives.

2 | THE MAYFLOWER DECISION

In the Matter of The Mayflower Broadcasting Corporation
and The Yankee Network, Inc. (WAAB)
8 FCC 333, 338
January 16, 1941

*This case began when the Mayflower Broadcasting Corporation
filed an application for a construction permit, requesting the facilities of station WAAB in Boston, whose license was being considered for renewal by the FCC. Although Mayflower's application
was denied because of misrepresentations made to the Commission
and lack of financial qualifications, the proceedings revealed that
WAAB had editorialized for some period of time. The Commission's ruling on this matter effectively discouraged broadcast editorials until the FCC issued its "Fairness Doctrine" in 1949.*

DECISION AND ORDER

These proceedings were instituted upon the filing by The Mayflower Broadcasting Corporation of an application for a construction permit to authorize a new radiobroadcast station at Boston, Mass., to operate
on the frequency 1410 kilocycles with power of 500 watts night and 1
kilowatt day, unlimited time. These are the facilities now assigned to Station
WAAB, Boston, Mass. The Commission designated this application for
hearing along with the applications of The Yankee Network, Inc. (licensee
of Station WAAB) for renewal of licenses for this station's main and auxiliary transmitters. The hearing was held in Boston, Mass., during November 1939. On May 31, 1940, the Commission issued proposed findings of
fact and conclusions proposing to deny the application of The Mayflower
Broadcasting Corporation and to grant the applications of The Yankee
Network, Inc., for renewal of licenses. Exceptions to the proposed findings
and conclusions were filed by Mayflower Broadcasting Corporation and at
its request oral argument was held on July 25, 1940, with The Yankee
Network, Inc., participating. Due to the absence of a quorum of the Com-

mission at that time, the case was reargued before the full Commission by counsel for both parties on September 26, 1940.

In its proposed findings the Commission concluded that The Mayflower Broadcasting Corporation was not shown to be financially qualified to construct and operate the proposed station and, moreover, that misrepresentations of fact were made to the Commission in the application. After careful consideration of the applicant's exceptions and of the oral arguments presented, the Commission is unable to change these conclusions. The proposed findings and conclusions as to the application of The Mayflower Broadcasting Corporation will therefore, be adopted and made final.

More difficult and less easily resolvable questions are, however, presented by the applications for renewal of The Yankee Network, Inc. The record shows without contradiction that beginning early in 1937 and continuing through September 1938, it was the policy of Station WAAB to broadcast so-called editorials from time to time urging the election of various candidates for political office or supporting one side or another of various questions in public controversy. In these editorials, which were delivered by the editor-in-chief of the station's news service, no pretense was made at objective, impartial reporting. It is clear—indeed the station seems to have taken pride in the fact—that the purpose of these editorials was to win public support for some person or view favored by those in control of the station.

No attempt will be made here to analyze in detail the large number of broadcasts devoted to editorials. The material in the record has been carefully considered and compels the conclusion that this licensee during the period in question, has revealed a serious misconception of its duties and functions under the law. Under the American system of broadcasting it is clear that responsibility for the conduct of a broadcast station must rest initially with the broadcaster. It is equally clear that with the limitations in frequencies inherent in the nature of radio, the public interest can never be served by a dedication of any broadcast facility to the support of his own partisan ends. [Radio can serve as an instrument of democracy only when devoted to the communication of information and the exchange of ideas fairly and objectively presented. A truly free radio cannot be used to advocate the causes of the licensee. It cannot be used to support the candidacies of his friends. It cannot be devoted to the support of principles he happens to regard most favorably. In brief, the broadcaster cannot be an advocate]

Freedom of speech on the radio must be broad enough to provide full and equal opportunity for the presentation to the public of all sides of public issues. Indeed, as one licensed to operate in a public domain the licensee has assumed the obligation of presenting all sides of important public questions, fairly, objectively and without bias. The public interest—not the private—is paramount. These requirements are inherent in the conception of public interest set up by the Communications Act as the criterion of regulation. And while the day to day decisions applying these requirements are the licensee's responsibility, the ultimate duty to review generally the course of conduct of the station over a period of time and to take appropriate action thereon is vested in the Commission.

Upon such a review here, there can be no question that The Yankee Network, Inc., in 1937 and 1938 continued to operate in contravention of these principles. The record does show, however, that, in response to a request of the Commission for details as to the conduct of the station since September 1938, two affidavits were filed with the Commission by John Shepard 3d, president of The Yankee Network, Inc. Apparently conceding the departures from the requirements of public interest by the earlier conduct of the station, these affidavits state, and they are uncontradicted, that no editorials have been broadcast over Station WAAB since September 1938 and that it is not intended to depart from this uninterrupted policy. The station has no editorial policies. In the affidavits there is further a description of the station's procedure for handling news items and the statement is made that since September 1938 "no attempt has ever been or will ever be made to color or editorialize the news received" through usual sources. In response to a question from the bench inquiring whether the Commission should rely on these affidavits in determining whether to renew the licenses, counsel for The Yankee Network, Inc., stated at the second argument, "There are absolutely no reservations whatsoever, or mental reservations of any sort, character, or kind with reference to those affidavits. They mean exactly what they say in the fullest possible amplification that the Commission wants to give to them."

Relying upon these comprehensive and unequivocal representations as to the future conduct of the station and in view of the loss of service to the public involved in the deletion of this station, it has been concluded to grant the applications for renewal. Should any future occasion arise to examine into the conduct of this licensee, however, the Commission will consider the facts developed in this record in its review of the activities as a whole. . . .

3 GLIMMERINGS OF "FAIRNESS"

The WHKC *and* Scott *decisions both deal with the programming of controversial issues and with requests for license non-renewal or revocation by those who alleged that their right of free speech was denied by the stations in question. The FCC's disposition of the two cases can be regarded as a portent of the "Fairness Doctrine" that was issued a few years later. The* Scott *case is particularly interesting because of the Commission's treatment of religious liberty as related to freedom of expression in broadcasting.*

A THE WHKC CASE

In re United Broadcasting Co. (WHKC)
10 FCC 515
June 26, 1945

DECISION AND ORDER

BY THE COMMISSION:

1. The Commission has before it a joint motion filed by the International Union, United Automobile, Aircraft, and Agricultural Implement Workers of America, affiliated with the Congress of Industrial Organizations and Local 927, UAW-CIO, Columbus, Ohio (herein called the "UAW-CIO" or the petitioner), and the United Broadcasting Co., licensee of Station WHKC (herein called the licensee), requesting the Commission to adopt a statement of policy which has been agreed upon by the parties, and to enter an order dismissing the proceedings.

2. The background of this matter may be set forth as follows: On June 2, 1944, the UAW-CIO filed a petition directed against the Commission's action granting the application of the licensee for renewal of license for operation of Station WHKC. The petition alleged that the li-

censee was throttling free speech and was therefore not operating in the public interest for the following reasons.

(a) The station had a policy not to permit the sale of time for programs which solicit memberships, discuss controversial subjects, race, religion, and politics.

(b) The station did not apply this practice uniformly, but on the contrary applied that policy "strictly to those with whom the management of Station WHKC disagrees, including petitioners, and loosely or not at all with respect to others."

(c) The station unfairly censored scripts submitted by petitioners.

Upon consideration of this petition and an opposition thereto filed by the licensee, the Commission designated the petition for hearing, and pursuant to the provisions of section 308 (b) and 312 (a) of the Communications Act of 1934, as amended, directed the station licensee to file with the Commission on or before the 5th day of August 1944, a statement of fact concerning the operation of WHKC with particular reference to the allegations of the petition and as to whether the station had been operated in the public interest. The Commission further directed the licensee to be prepared at said hearing to offer evidence in support of its statement of fact. Pursuant to the Commission's action, the licensee filed its statement of fact and a hearing was held before a member of the Commission from August 16 through August 24, 1944.

3. The evidence adduced at the hearing showed that the station's policy upon which the petition was predicated was governed by the provisions of the Code of the National Association of Broadcasters. The code is a voluntary one without legal effect upon the members of the National Association of Broadcasters. The purpose of the Code as stated in its foreword is "to formulate basic standards" for the guidance of broadcasters. At pages 3 and 4 it provides that no time shall be sold for the presentation of public controversial issues, with the exception of political broadcasts and the public forum type of programs; and that solicitation of memberships in organizations, whether on paid or free time, should not be permitted except for charitable organizations, such as the American Red Cross and "except where such memberships are incidental to the rendering of commercial services, such as an insurance plan either in respect to casualty, to life, or to property."

4. On October 20, 1944, the petitioner and the licensee filed the instant joint motion which contained the following agreed statement:

The record of the hearing discloses that Station WHKC in the past had pursued a policy which it believed to be in the best interests of the public and at no time did the station believe that the application of this policy was contrary to the interests of labor. The record testimony further discloses that at the time of the hearing the station enunciated a revised policy which it had adopted prior to the hearing and which it intends to follow in the future. This policy is as follows:

(a) It will be the future policy of Station WHKC to consider each request for time solely on its individual merits without discriminations and without prejudice because of the identity of the personality of the individual, corporation, or organization desiring such time.

(b) With respect to public issues of a controversial nature, the station's policy will be one of open-mindedness and impartiality. Requests of all individuals, groups, or organizations will of necessity have to be considered in the light of the contribution which their use of time would make toward a well-balanced program schedule, which the station will try at all times to maintain in the interest of the people it serves.

(c) Station WHKC will make time available, primarily on a sustaining basis, but also on a commercial basis, for the full and free discussion of issues of public importance, including controversial issues, and dramatizations thereof, in order that broadcasting may achieve its full possibilities as a significant medium for the dissemination of news, ideas, and opinions. And, in doing so, there will be no discrimination between business concerns and nonprofit organizations either in making time available or restricting the use of such time. Nonprofit organizations will have the right to purchase time for solicitation of memberships.

(d) Station WHKC will, if it refuses time for public discussion, do so in writing showing reasons for such denial to the extent that requests for time are made in writing.

(e) The censorship of scripts is an evil repugnant to the American tradition of free speech and a free press, whether enforced by a Government agency or by a private radio station licensee. Broadcasts by candidates for public office may not be censored under the law. But as to all other broadcasts, Station WHKC will not censor scripts, or delete any matter contained in them, except for reasons which it believes to be in accordance with the law and existing regulations as set forth in its statement of policy and as explained and interpreted in the record testimony. In the light of future experience this policy may be changed through action by the courts, the legislature, or by rules of Government bodies having jurisdiction over particular subject matter. It will be the policy of the station to adjust its practices to such changes, reflecting at all times the tolerance which the interest of the public renders essential.

(f) The station will see that its broadcasts on controversial issues, considered on an over-all basis, maintain a fair balance among the various points of view, i. e., over the weeks and months it will maintain such a balance with respect to local and network programs, both sustaining and commercial alike.

The parties believe that the above statement of policy properly sets forth the duties of a licensee under the Communications Act of 1934 with respect to the availability of time for discussion of issues of public importance, the censoring of scripts by licensees, and the maintenance of an over-all program balance.

5.   As indicated in paragraph 2 hereof, the present proceeding puts in issue the duties of a licensee, under the statutory mandate, to operate in

the public interest, convenience, and necessity, to maintain an over-all program balance by providing time on a nondiscriminatory basis for discussion of public controversial issues and for the solicitation of memberships for nonprofit organizations. It is recognized, of course, that the physical limitations on the amount of spectrum space available for radio broadcasting and the large demands upon radio stations for use of time make it impossible for every person desiring to use the facilities of a station to be granted this privilege. Under section 3 (h) of the act, broadcast stations are expressly declared not to be common carriers. These facts, however, in no way impinge upon the duty of each station licensee to be sensitive to the problems of public concern in the community and to make sufficient time available, on a nondiscriminatory basis, for full discussion thereof, without any type of censorship which would undertake to impose the views of the licensee upon the material to be broadcast. The spirit of the Communications Act of 1934 requires radio to be an instrument of free speech, subject only to the general statutory provisions imposing upon the licensee the responsibility of operating its station in the public interest.

6. No single or exact rule of thumb for providing time, on a nondiscriminatory basis, can be stated for application to all situations which may arise in the operation of all stations. The Commission, however, is of the opinion that the operation of any station under the extreme principles that no time shall be sold for the discussion of controversial public issues and that only charitable organizations and certain commercial interests may solicit memberships is inconsistent with the concept of public interest established by the Communications Act as the criterion of radio regulations (cf. in re the Mayflower Broadcasting Co., 8 FCC 338). The Commission recognizes that good program balance may not permit the sale or donation of time to all who may seek it for such purposes and that difficult problems calling for careful judgment on the part of station management may be involved in deciding among applicants for time when all cannot be accommodated. However, competent management should be able to meet such problems in the public interest and with fairness to all concerned. The fact that it places an arduous task on management should not be made a reason for evading the issue by a strict rule against the sale of time for any programs of the type mentioned.

7. The agreed statement of policy submitted by the parties herein appears to set forth generally a fair and nondiscriminatory policy which WHKC, the licensee, has undertaken to apply to the presentation of controversial public issues and to the solicitation of memberships by nonprofit organizations in the maintenance of over-all program balance. On the basis of this undertaking, we are of the opinion that the joint motion should be granted and the proceeding dismissed, and it is so ordered this 26th day of June 1945.

THE SCOTT CASE

In re Petition of Robert Harold Scott for Revocation of
Licenses of Radio Stations KQW, KPO and KFRC
11 FCC 372
July 19, 1946

MEMORANDUM OPINION AND ORDER

On March 27, 1945, Robert Harold Scott, of Palo Alto, Calif., filed a petition requesting that the Commission revoke the licenses of radio stations KQW, San Jose, Calif., and KPO and KFRC, both of San Francisco, Calif. The ground on which the petitioner seeks to have the Commission take this action is that these stations have refused to make any time available to him, by sale or otherwise, for the broadcasting of talks on the subject of atheism, while they have permitted the use of their facilities for direct statements and arguments against atheism as well as for indirect arguments, such as church services, prayers, Bible reading, and other kinds of religious programs. It is petitioner's contention that the question of the existence or nonexistence of a Divine Being is, in itself a controversial issue, and that in refusing to make time available for arguments in support of the atheistic point of view, the stations complained of are not presenting all sides of the issue and, therefore, are not operating in the public interest.

After having secured further information from the petitioner, the Commission notified the stations of the petition and invited their comments on the matter. Don Lee Broadcasting System, licensee of Station KFRC, expressed its "firm belief that it would not be in the public interest to lend our facilities to Mr. Scott for the dissemination and propagation of atheism." National Broadcasting Co., Inc., licensee of KPO, asserted that "it is difficult to imagine that a controversial public issue exists in the usual sense of that phrase, on the subject of the existence of a God merely because of the nonbelief of a relatively few." Station KQW, in its reply, stated that it refused time to petitioner for the "broadcasting of atheistic talks," and contended that such talks would not be in the public interest. The answer stated that the management of KQW did not consider the "proposed atheistic broadcasts" as presenting a "controversial" public question and that, in any event, "if a public controversial question was tendered, it was not of sufficient public moment and did not present a question so uppermost or important in the minds of the public to justify its broadcast in the public interest with consequent displacement of an existing program service." The answer alleged further that "KQW acted within its legal rights and the Commission is not by statute authorized to substitute its judgment for that of the licensee under the circumstances here presented."

In his petition, Mr. Scott says: "I do not throw stones at church windows. I do not mock a people kneeling in prayer. I respect every man's right to have and to express any religious belief whatsoever. But I abhor and denounce those who, while asserting this right, seek, in one way or another, to prevent others from expressing contrary views."

It therefore appears, both from licensees' responses to Mr. Scott's requests for time and from his statement of his own position, that the question here presented does not involve blasphemous attacks upon the Deity, or abusive or intemperate attacks upon any religious belief or organization, but only such criticisms as would necessarily be implied in the logical development of arguments supporting atheism. The licensees of the stations involved appear to have treated atheism as a special type of controversy and to have interpreted their obligation to operate in the public interest as requiring or permitting them to bar access to their facilities for the presentation of the atheistic point of view, not because of the manner in which the point of view is to be presented, but because they believe its substance to be distasteful or objectionable to a large majority of the listening audience.

As in the case of the petition of the Reverend Sam Morris for a denial of the application of renewal of license of Station KRLD, Dallas, Tex. (file No. B3–R–397), the issue here involved is one of broad scope and it is not restricted to the three stations which are the subject of Mr. Scott's complaint. We therefore do not feel that we would be warranted on the basis of this single complaint in selecting these three stations as the subject of a hearing looking toward terminations of their licenses, when there is no urgent ground for selecting them rather than many other stations. But, lest our dismissal of Mr. Scott's petition be misconstrued, we feel that we should make our position entirely clear, as we did in dismissing the petition of the Reverend Sam Morris.

The first amendment to our Constitution guarantees both religious freedom[1] and freedom of speech. While these guarantees are expressed in terms of limitation on governmental action, they are far more than narrow legalistic concepts. They are essential parts of the fundamental philosophy underlying the form of government and the way of life which we call "American."

---

[1] No principle is more firmly imbedded in our Constitution than that of religious freedom. In addition to the first amendment, art. VI repudiates any religious tests as to qualification to any office of political trust under the United States. The same section, in the interests of freedom of conscience, permits affirmation rather than oath in the pledge to support the Constitution required of State and Federal officials. Likewise, sec. 1 of art. II permits the substitution of an affirmation for the oath of office required of the President of the United States.

Freedom of religious belief necessarily carries with it freedom to disbelieve, and freedom of speech means freedom to express disbeliefs as well as beliefs. If freedom of speech is to have meaning, it cannot be predicated on the mere popularity or public acceptance of the ideas sought to be advanced. It must be extended as readily to ideas which we disapprove or abhor as to ideas which we approve. Moreover, freedom of speech can be as effectively denied by denying access to the public means of making expression effective—whether public streets, parks, meeting halls, or the radio —as by legal restraints or punishment of the speaker.

It is true that in this country an overwhelming majority of the people profess a belief in the existence of a Divine Being. But the conception of the nature of the Divine Being is as varied as religious denominations and sects and even differs with the individuals belonging to the same denominations or sects.

God is variously thought of as a "Spirit, infinite, eternal, and unchangeable," and as having a tangible form resembling man who, in turn, was created in His image; as consisting of a Trinity and a single Godhead; as a Divine Lawgiver, laying down infallible natural and moral laws by which man is governed, and as a God who concerns himself with the personal affairs of individuals, however petty; as a God to whom each person is individually accountable and as a God to be approached only through ordained intermediaries; a God of the powerful who divinely appoints kings and other rulers of men, and as a God of the meek and lowly; as a God of stern justice and a God of mercy; as a God to be worshipped or appeased primarily through ritual and as a God to be served primarily through service to one's fellow man; as a God whose rewards and punishments are mainly reserved for a future life and as a God who also rewards or punishes through spiritual enrichment or impoverishment of man's present existence. These are only a few of the many differing conceptions which might be cited by way of illustration.

So diverse are these conceptions that it may be fairly said, even as to professed believers, that the God of one man does not exist for another. And so strongly may one believe in his own particular conception of God that he may easily be led to say, "Only my God exists, and therefore he who denies my God is an atheist, irrespective of his professed belief in *a* God." For example, the early Christians were to the Romans atheists because they denied the existence of the pagan gods in which the Romans believed.[2]

---

[2] "Atheism is a term of varying application and significance. . . . Its meaning is dependent upon the particular type of 'theism' with which at the moment it is being contrasted. . . . The atheist is conceived as the man who denies or despises what he ought not only to fear but to respect. It is intelligible, then, that the early Christians should be called 'atheists' by their persecutors. The Christians denied, after all, many more gods than they acknowledged. The pagan was morally offended at this wholesale rejection of familiar loyalties." [Encyclopedia Britannica, 14th Ed., vol. 2 (article on "Atheism" by the Reverend Charles John Shebbeare, M.A., rector of Stanhope, County Durham, and chaplain to His Majesty the King).]

A rule which denies freedom of expression to the professed atheist should certainly be applied with equal, if not greater, strictness to one whose views are, in fact, atheistic, but who seeks to deny or conceal his atheism. Thus, the necessity arises of making determinations on the basis of personal judgment as to whether views sought to be expressed are, in fact, atheistic. The power then is vested in those making such determination to attach the label of atheism to the believer whose particular belief they may happen to disapprove, and thus of effectively denying the believer the right to express his views. Under such a course, Jefferson, Jackson, Lincoln, and others whose names we revere could, today, be barred from access to the air to express their own particular religious philosophies. The first two were denounced with particular vigor from the pulpits of some of the wealthier and better established churches, and the label of "atheist" was freely attached to Jefferson by those who had come to feel that their favored positions, which were threatened by his social, economic, and political philosophies, were rewards which the Deity had bestowed upon them because of their special virtues and accomplishments.

Underlying the conception of freedom of speech is not only the recognition of the importance of the free flow of ideas and information to the effective functioning of democratic forms of government and ways of life, but also belief that immunity from criticism is dangerous—dangerous to the institution or belief to which the immunity is granted as well as to the freedom of the people generally. Sound and vital ideas and institutions become strong and develop with criticism so long as they themselves have full opportunity for expression; it is dangerous that the unsound be permitted to flourish for want of criticism.

Moreover, however strongly we may feel about the sacredness of religious beliefs, we should be mindful of the fact that immunity from criticism cannot be granted to religion without, at the same time, granting it to those who use the guise of religion to further their ends of personal profit or power, to promote their own particular political or economic philosophies, or to give vent to their personal frustrations and hatreds. "False prophets" are not phenomena peculiar to Biblical days. Their danger now, as then, lies essentially in the difficulty of recognizing them as such. This difficulty is increased to the extent that their doctrines and motives are shielded from critical examination.

We recognize that in passing upon requests for time, a station licensee is constantly confronted with most difficult problems. Since the demands for time may far exceed the amount available for broadcasting a licensee must inevitably make a selection among those seeking it for the expression of their views. He may not even be able to grant time to all religious groups who might desire the use of his facilities, much less to all who might want to oppose religion. Admittedly, a very real opportunity exists for him to be arbitrary and unreasonable, to indulge his own preferences, prejudices, or whims; to pursue his own private interest or to favor those who espouse his views, and discriminate against those of opposing views. The indulgence of that opportunity could not conceivably be characterized as an exercise of the broadcaster's right of freedom of speech. Nor could it fairly be said to afford the listening audience that opportunity to hear a diversity and balance of views, which is an inseparable corollary of freedom of expression. In making a selection with fairness, the licensee must, of course, consider the extent of the interest of the people in his service area in a particular subject to be discussed as well as the qualifications of the person selected to discuss it. Every idea does not rise to the dignity of a "public controversy," and every organization, regardless of membership or the seriousness of its purposes, is not per se entitled to time on the air. But an organization or idea may be projected into the realm of controversy by virtue of being attacked. The holders of a belief should not be denied the right to answer attacks upon them or their belief solely because they are few in number.

The fact that a licensee's duty to make time available for the presentation of opposing views on current controversial issues of public importance may not extend to all possible differences of opinion within the ambit of human contemplation cannot serve as the basis for any rigid policy that time shall be denied for the presentation of views which may have a high degree of unpopularity. The criterion of the public interest in the field of broadcasting clearly precludes a policy of making radio wholly unavailable as a medium for the expression of any view which falls within the scope of the constitutional guarantee of freedom of speech.

Because, as we have stated above, the problem here presented is far broader in scope than the complaint against the particular stations here involved, we feel that the petition should be denied, notwithstanding the views which we have expressed.

It is therefore ordered, this 19th day of July 1946, that the petition be and it is hereby denied.

THE FAIRNESS DOCTRINE

In the Matter of Editorializing by Broadcast Licensees
13 FCC 1246
June 1, 1949

> *This document served to reverse the Commission's previous policy
> regarding broadcast editorials enunciated in the* Mayflower *decision.
> FCC adherence to the "Fairness Doctrine" from 1949 to date has
> encouraged increasing numbers of stations to express their editorial
> views on the air. The edited version below omits the "additional
> views" of Commissioner Webster and the separate opinion of Com-
> missioner Jones.*

REPORT OF THE COMMISSION

1. This report is issued by the Commission in connection with its
hearings on the above entitled matter held at Washington, D. C., on March
1, 2, 3, 4, and 5, and April 19, 20, and 21, 1948. The hearing had been
ordered on the Commission's own motion on September 5, 1947, because
of our belief that further clarification of the Commissioner's position with
respect to the obligations of broadcast licensees in the field of broadcasts of
news, commentary and opinion was advisable. It was believed that in view of
the apparent confusion concerning certain of the Commission's previous
statements on these vital matters by broadcast licensees and members of the
general public, as well as the professed disagreement on the part of some
of these persons with earlier Commission pronouncements, a reexamina-
tion and restatement of its views by the Commission would be desirable.
And in order to provide an opportunity to interested persons and organizations to acquaint the Commission with their views, prior to any Commission determination, as to the proper resolution of the difficult and complex
problems involved in the presentation of radio news and comment in a
democracy, it was designated for public hearing before the Commission *en
banc* on the following issues:

> 1. To determine whether the expression of editorial opinions by broadcast
> station licensees on matters of public interest and controversy is con-

sistent with their obligations to operate their stations in the public interest.

2. To determine the relationship between any such editorial expression and the affirmative obligation of the licensees to insure that a fair and equal presentation of all sides of controversial issues is made over their facilities.

2.   At the hearings testimony was received from some 49 witnesses representing the broadcasting industry and various interested organizations and members of the public. In addition, written statements of their position on the matter were placed into the record by 21 persons and organizations who were unable to appear and testify in person. The various witnesses and statements brought forth for the Commission's consideration, arguments on every side of both of the questions involved in the hearing. Because of the importance of the issues considered in the hearing, and because of the possible confusion which may have existed in the past concerning the policies applicable to the matters which were the subject of the hearing, we have deemed it advisable to set forth in detail and at some length our conclusions as to the basic considerations relevant to the expression of editorial opinion by broadcast licensees and the relationship of any such expression to the general obligations of broadcast licensees with respect to the presentation of programs involving controversial issues.

3.   In approaching the issues upon which this proceeding has been held, we believe that the paramount and controlling consideration is the relationship between the American system of broadcasting carried on through a large number of private licensees upon whom devolves the responsibility for the selection and presentation of program material, and the congressional mandate that this licensee responsibility is to be exercised in the interests of, and as a trustee for the public at large which retains ultimate control over the channels of radio and television communications. One important aspect of this relationship, we believe, results from the fact that the needs and interests of the general public with respect to programs devoted to news commentary and opinion can only be satisfied by making available to them for their consideration and acceptance or rejection, of varying and conflicting views held by responsible elements of the community. And it is in the light of these basic concepts that the problems of insuring fairness in the presentation of news and opinion and the place in such a picture of any expression of the views of the station licensee as such must be considered.

4.   It is apparent that our system of broadcasting, under which private persons and organizations are licensed to provide broadcasting service to the various communities and regions, imposes responsibility in the selection and presentation of radio program material upon such licensees. Congress has recognized that the requests for radio time may far exceed the amount of time reasonably available for distribution by broadcasters. It pro-

vided, therefore, in Section 3 (h) of the Communications Act that a person engaged in radio broadcasting shall not be deemed a common carrier. It is the licensee, therefore, who must determine what percentage of the limited broadcast day should appropriately be devoted to news and discussion or consideration of public issues, rather than to the other legitimate services of radio broadcasting, and who must select or be responsible for the selection of the particular news items to be reported or the particular local, State, national or international issues or questions of public interest to be considered, as well as the person or persons to comment or analyze the news or to discuss or debate the issues chosen as topics for radio consideration: "The life of each community involves a multitude of interests some dominant and all pervasive such as interest in public affairs, education and similar matters and some highly specialized and limited to few. The practical day-to-day problem with which every licensee is faced is one of striking a balance between these various interests to reflect them in a program service which is useful to the community, and which will in some way fulfill the needs and interests of the many." *Capital Broadcasting Company,* 4 Pike & Fischer, R.R. 21; *The Northern Corporation (WMEX)* 4 Pike & Fischer, R.R. 333, 338. And both the Commission and the courts have stressed that this responsibility devolves upon the individual licensees, and can neither be delegated by the licensee to any network or other person or group, or be unduly fettered by contractual arrangements restricting the licensee in his free exercise of his independent judgments. *National Broadcasting Company* v. *United States,* 319 U.S. 190 (upholding the Commission's chain broadcasting regulations, Section 3.101–3.108, 3.231–3.238, 3.631–3.638), *Churchhill Tabernacle* v. *Federal Communications Commission,* 160 F. 2d 244 (See, rules and regulations, Sections 3.109, 3.239, 3.639); *Allen T. Simmons* v. *Federal Communications Commission,* 169 F. 2d 670, *certiorari denied* 335 U.S. 846.

5.   But the inevitability that there must be some choosing between various claimants for access to a licensee's microphone, does not mean that the licensee is free to utilize his facilities as he sees fit or in his own particular interests as contrasted with the interests of the general public. The Communications Act of 1934, as amended, makes clear that licenses are to be issued only where the public interest, convenience or necessity would be served thereby. And we think it is equally clear that one of the basic elements of any such operation is the maintenance of radio and television as a medium of freedom of speech and freedom of expression for the people of the Nation as a whole. Section 301 of the Communications Act provides that it is the purpose of the act to maintain the control of the United States over all channels of interstate and foreign commerce. Section 326 of the act provides that this control of the United States shall not result in any impairment of the right of free speech by means of such radio communications. It would be inconsistent with these express provisions to assert that,

while it is the purpose of the act to maintain the control of the United States over radio channels, but free from any regulation or condition which interferes with the right of free speech, nevertheless persons who are granted limited rights to be licensees of radio stations, upon a finding under Sections 307 (a) and 309 of the act that the public interest, convenience, or necessity would be served thereby, may themselves make radio unavailable as a medium of free speech. The legislative history of the Communications Act and its predecessor, the Radio Act of 1927 shows, on the contrary, that Congress intended that radio stations should not be used for the private interest, whims, or caprices of the particular persons who have been granted licenses, but in manner which will serve the community generally and the various groups which make up the community.[1] And the courts have consistently upheld Commission action giving recognition to and fulfilling that intent of Congress. *KFKB Broadcasting Association* v. *Federal Radio Commission*, 47 F. 2d 670; *Trinity Methodist Church, South* v. *Federal Radio Commission*, 62 F. 2d 850, *certiorari denied*, 288 U.S. 599.

6.   It is axiomatic that one of the most vital questions of mass communication in a democracy is the development of an informed public opinion through the public dissemination of news and ideas concerning the vital public issues of the day. Basically, it is in recognition of the great contribution which radio can make in the advancement of this purpose that portions of the radio spectrum are allocated to that form of radio communications known as radiobroadcasting. Unquestionably, then, the standard of public interest, convenience and necessity as applied to radiobroadcasting must be interpreted in the light of this basic purpose. The Commission has consequently recognized the necessity for licensees to devote a reasonable percentage of their broadcast time to the presentation of news and programs devoted to the consideration and discussion of public issues

---

[1] Thus in the Congressional debates leading to the enactment of the Radio Act of 1927 Congressman (later Senator) White stated (67 Cong. Rec. 5479, March 12, 1926):

"We have reached the definite conclusion that the right of all our people to enjoy this means of communication can be preserved only by the repudiation of the idea underlying the 1912 law that anyone who will, may transmit and by the assertion in its stead of the doctrine that the right of the public to service is superior to the right of any individual to use the ether . . . the recent radio conference met this issue squarely. It recognized that in the present state of scientific development there must be a limitation upon the number of broadcasting stations and it recommended that licenses should be issued only to those stations whose operation would render a benefit to the public, are necessary in the public interest or would contribute to the development of the art. This principle was approved by every witness before your committee. We have written it into the bill. *If enacted into law, the broadcasting privilege will not be a right of selfishness. It will rest upon an assurance of public interest to be served.*" (Italics added.)

And this view that the interest of the listening public rather than the private interests of particular licensees was reemphasized as recently as June 9, 1948, in a unanimous report of the Senate Committee on Interstate and Foreign Commerce on S. 1333 (80th Cong.) which would have amended the present Communications Act in certain respects. See S. Rept. No. 1567, 80th Cong. 2nd Sess., pp. 14–15.

of interest in the community served by the particular station. And we have recognized, with respect to such programs, the paramount right of the public in a free society to be informed and to have presented to it for acceptance or rejection the different attitudes and viewpoints concerning these vital and often controversial issues which are held by the various groups which make up the community.[2] It is this right of the public to be informed, rather than any right on the part of the Government, any broadcast licensee or any individual member of the public to broadcast his own particular views on any matter, which is the foundation stone of the American system of broadcasting.

7.   This affirmative responsibility on the part of broadcast licensees to provide a reasonable amount of time for the presentation over their facilities of programs devoted to the discussion and consideration of public issues has been reaffirmed by this Commission in a long series of decisions. The *United Broadcasting Co. (WHKC)* case, 10 FCC 675, emphasized that this duty includes the making of reasonable provision for the discussion of controversial issues of public importance in the community served, and to make sufficient time available for full discussion thereof. The *Scott* case, 3 Pike & Fischer, Radio Regulation 259, stated our conclusions that this duty extends to all subjects of substantial importance to the community coming within the scope of free discussion under the first amendment without regard to personal views and opinions of the licensees on the matter, or any determination by the licensee as to the possible unpopularity of the views to be expressed on the subject matter to be discussed among particular elements of the station's listening audience. Cf., *National Broadcasting Company* v. *United States,* 319 U.S. 190; *Allen T. Simmons,* 3 Pike & Fischer, R.R. 1029, *affirmed; Simmons* v. *Federal Communications Commission,* 169 F. 2d 670, *certiorari denied,* 335 U.S. 846; *Bay State Beacon,* 3 Pike & Fischer, R.R. 1455, *affirmed; Bay State Beacon* v. *Federal Communications Commission,* U.S. App. D.C., decided December 20, 1948; *Petition of Sam Morris,* 3 Pike & Fischer, R.R. 154; *Thomas N. Beach,* 3 Pike & Fischer R.R. 1784. And the Commission has made clear that in such presentation of news and comment the public interest requires that the licensee must operate on a basis of overall fairness, making his facilities available for the expression of the contrasting views of all responsible elements in the community on the various issues which arise. *Mayflower Broadcasting Co.,* 8 F. C. C. 333; *United Broadcasting Co. (WHKC)* 10 F. C. C. 515; Cf. *WBNX Broadcasting Co., Inc.,* 4 Pike & Fischer, R.R. 244 (memorandum opinion). Only where the licensee's discretion in the choice of the particular programs to be broadcast over his facilities is exercised so as to afford a reasonable opportunity for the presentation of all responsible positions on matters of sufficient importance to be

[2] Cf., *Thornhill* v. *Alabama,* 310 U.S. 88, 95, 102; *Associated Press* v. *United States* 326 U.S. 1, 20.

afforded radio time can radio be maintained as a medium of freedom of speech for the people as a whole. These concepts, of course, do restrict the licensee's freedom to utilize his station in whatever manner he chooses but they do so in order to make possible the maintenance of radio as a medium of freedom of speech for the general public.

8.   It has been suggested in the course of the hearings that licensees have an affirmative obligation to insure fair presentation of all sides of any controversial issue before any time may be allocated to the discussion or consideration of the matter. On the other hand, arguments have been advanced in support of the proposition that the licensee's sole obligation to the public is to refrain from suppressing or excluding any responsible point of view from access to the radio. We are of the opinion, however, that any rigid requirement that licensees adhere to either of these extreme prescriptions for proper station programing techniques would seriously limit the ability of licensees to serve the public interest. Forums and roundtable discussions, while often excellent techniques of presenting a fair cross section of differing viewpoints on a given issue, are not the only appropriate devices for radio discussion, and in some circumstances may not be particularly appropriate or advantageous. Moreover, in many instances the primary "controversy" will be whether or not the particular problem should be discussed at all; in such circumstances, where the licensee has determined that the subject is of sufficient import to receive broadcast attention, it would obviously not be in the public interest for spokesmen for one of the opposing points of view to be able to exercise a veto power over the entire presentation by refusing to broadcast its position. Fairness in such circumstances might require no more than that the licensee make a reasonable effort to secure responsible representation of the particular position and, if it fails in this effort, to continue to make available its facilities to the spokesmen for such position in the event that, after the original programs are broadcast, they then decide to avail themselves of a right to reply to present their contrary opinion. It should be remembered, moreover, that discussion of public issues will not necessarily be confined to questions which are obviously controversial in nature, and, in many cases, programs initiated with no thought on the part of the licensee of their possibly controversial nature will subsequently arouse controversy and opposition of a substantial nature which will merit presentation of opposing views. In such cases, however, fairness can be preserved without undue difficulty since the facilities of the station can be made available to the spokesmen for the groups wishing to state views in opposition to those expressed in the original presentation when such opposition becomes manifest.

9.   We do not believe, however, that the licensee's obligations to serve the public interest can be met merely through the adoption of a general policy of not refusing to broadcast opposing views where a demand is made of the station for broadcast time. If, as we believe to be the case, the public interest

is best served in a democracy through the ability of the people to hear expositions of the various positions taken by responsible groups and individuals on
particular topics and to choose between them, it is evident that broadcast
licensees have an affirmative duty generally to encourage and implement the
broadcast of all sides of controversial public issues over their facilities, over
and beyond their obligation to make available on demand opportunities for
the expression of opposing views. It is clear that any approximation of
fairness in the presentation of any controversy will be difficult if not impossible of achievement unless the licensee plays a conscious and positive
role in bringing about balanced presentation of the opposing viewpoints.

10. It should be recognized that there can be no one all embracing
formula which licensees can hope to apply to insure the fair and balanced
presentation of all public issues. Different issues will inevitably require different techniques of presentation and production. The licensee will in each
instance be called upon to exercise his best judgment and good sense in determining what subjects should be considered, the particular format of the
programs to be devoted to each subject, the different shades of opinion to
be presented, and the spokesmen for each point of view. In determining
whether to honor specific requests for time, the station will inevitably be
confronted with such questions as whether the subject is worth considering,
whether the viewpoint of the requesting party has already received a sufficient amount of broadcast time, or whether there may not be other available groups or individuals who might be more appropriate spokesmen for
the particular point of view than the person making the request. The latter's personal involvement in the controversy may also be a factor which
must be considered, for elementary considerations of fairness may dictate
that time be allocated to a person or group which has been specifically attacked over the station, where otherwise no such obligation would exist.
Undoubtedly, over a period of time some licensees may make honest errors
of judgment. But there can be no doubt that any licensee honestly desiring
to live up to its obligation to serve the public interest and making a reasonable effort to do so, will be able to achieve a fair and satisfactory resolution
of these problems in the light of the specific facts.

11. It is against this background that we must approach the question
of "editorializing"—the use of radio facilities by the licensees thereof for
the expression of the opinions and ideas of the licensee on the various controversial and significant issues of interest to the members of the general
public afforded radio (or television) service by the particular station: In
considering this problem it must be kept in mind that such editorial expression may take many forms ranging from the overt statement of position by
the licensee in person or by his acknowledged spokesmen to the selection
and presentation of news editors and commentators sharing the licensee's
general opinions or the making available of the licensee's facilities, either
free of charge or for a fee to persons or organizations reflecting the licen-

see's viewpoint either generally or with respect to specific issues. It should also be clearly indicated that the question of the relationship of broadcast editorialization, as defined above, to operation in the public interest, is not identical with the broader problem of assuring "fairness" in the presentation of news, comment or opinion, but is rather one specific facet of this larger problem.

12. It is clear that the licensee's authority to determine the specific programs to be broadcast over his station gives him an opportunity, not available to other persons, to insure that his personal viewpoint on any particular issue is presented in his station's broadcasts, whether or not these views are expressly identified with the licensee. And, in the absence of governmental restraint, he would, if he so choose, be able to utilize his position as a broadcast licensee to weight the scales in line with his personal views, or even directly or indirectly to propagandize in behalf of his particular philosophy or views on the various public issues to the exclusion of any contrary opinions. Such action can be effective and persuasive whether or not it is accompanied by any editorialization in the narrow sense of overt statement of particular opinions and views identified as those of licensee.

13. The narrower question of whether any overt editorialization or advocacy by broadcast licensees, identified as such is consonant with the operation of their stations in the public interest, resolves itself, primarily into the issue of whether such identification of comment or opinion broadcast over a radio or television station with the licensee, as such, would inevitably or even probably result in such overemphasis on the side of any particular controversy which the licensee chooses to espouse as to make impossible any reasonably balanced presentation of all sides of such issues or to render ineffective the available safeguards of that overall fairness which is the essential element of operation in the public interest. We do not believe that any such consequence is either inevitable or probable, and we have therefore come to the conclusion that overt licensee editorialization, within reasonable limits and subject to the general requirements of fairness detailed above, is not contrary to the public interest.

14. The Commission has given careful consideration to contentions of those witnesses at the hearing who stated their belief that any overt editorialization or advocacy by broadcast licensee is *per se* contrary to the public interest. The main arguments advanced by these witnesses were that overt editorialization by broadcast licensees would not be consistent with the attainment of balanced presentations since there was a danger that the institutional good will and the production resources at the disposal of broadcast licensees would inevitably influence public opinion in favor of the positions advocated in the name of the licensee and that, having taken an open stand on behalf of one position in a given controversy, a license is not likely to give a fair break to the opposition. We believe, however, that these fears are largely misdirected, and that they stem from a confusion of

the question of overt advocacy in the name of the licensee, with the broader issue of insuring that the station's broadcasts devoted to the consideration of public issues will provide the listening public with a fair and balanced presentation of differing viewpoints on such issues, without regard to the particular views which may be held or expressed by the licensee. Considered, as we believe they must be, as just one of several types of presentation of public issues, to be afforded their appropriate and nonexclusive place in the station's total schedule of programs devoted to balanced discussion and consideration of public issues, we do not believe that programs in which the licensee's personal opinions are expressed are intrinsically more or less subject to abuse than any other program devoted to public issues. If it be true that station good will and licensee prestige, where it exists, may give added weight to opinion expressed by the licensee, it does not follow that such opinion should be excluded from the air any more than it should in the case of any individual or institution which over a period of time has built up a reservoir of good will or prestige in the community. In any competition for public acceptance of ideas, the skills and resources of the proponents and opponents will always have some measure of effect in producing the results sought. But it would not be suggested that they should be denied expression of their opinions over the air by reason of their particular assets. What is against the public interest is for the licensee "to stack the cards" by a deliberate selection of spokesmen for opposing points of view to favor one viewpoint at the expense of the other, whether or not the views of those spokesmen are identified as the views of the licensee or of others. Assurance of fairness must in the final analysis be achieved, not by the exclusion of particular views because of the source of the views, or the forcefulness with which the view is expressed, but by making the microphone available for the presentation of contrary views without deliberate restrictions designed to impede equally forceful presentation.

15. Similarly, while licensees will in most instances have at their disposal production resources making possible graphic and persuasive techniques for forceful presentation of ideas, their utilization for the promulgation of the licensee's personal viewpoints will not necessarily or automatically lead to unfairness or lack of balance. While uncontrolled utilization of such resources for the partisan ends of the licensee might conceivably lead to serious abuses, such abuses could as well exist where the station's resources are used for the sole use of his personal spokesmen. The prejudicial or unfair use of broadcast production resources would, in either case, be contrary to the public interest.

16. The Commission is not persuaded that a station's willingness to stand up and be counted on these particular issues upon which the licensee has a definite position may not be actually helpful in providing and maintaining a climate of fairness and equal opportunity for the expression of contrary views. Certainly the public has less to fear from the open partisan

than from the covert propagandist. On many issues, of sufficient importance to be allocated broadcast time, the station licensee may have no fixed opinion or viewpoint which he wishes to state or advocate. But where the licensee, himself, believes strongly that one side of a controversial issue is correct and should prevail, prohibition of his expression of such position will not of itself insure fair presentation of that issue over his station's facilities, nor would open advocacy necessarily prevent an overall fair presentation of the subject. It is not a sufficient answer to state that a licensee *should* occupy the position of an impartial umpire, where the licensee is *in fact* partial. In the absence of a duty to present all sides of controversial issues, overt editorialization by station licensees could conceivably result in serious abuse. But where, as we believe to be the case under the Communications Act, such a responsibility for a fair and balanced presentation of controversial public issues exists, we cannot see how the open espousal of one point of view by the licensee should necessarily prevent him from affording a fair opportunity for the presentation of contrary positions or make more difficult the enforcement of the statutory standard of fairness upon any licensee.

17. It must be recognized, however, that the licensee's opportunity to express his own views as part of a general presentation of varying opinions on particular controversial issues, does not justify or empower any licensee to exercise his authority over the selection of program material to distort or suppress the basic factual information upon which any truly fair and free discussion of public issues must necessarily depend. The basis for any fair consideration of public issues, and particularly those of a controversial nature, is the presentation of news and information concerning the basic facts of the controversy in as complete and impartial a manner as possible. A licensee would be abusing his position as public trustee of these important means of mass communication were he to withhold from expression over his facilities relevant news or facts concerning a controversy or to slant or distort the presentation of such news. No discussion of the issues involved in any controversy can be fair or in the public interest where such discussion must take place in a climate of false or misleading information concerning the basic facts of the controversy.

18. During the course of the hearing, fears have been expressed that any effort on the part of the Commission to enforce a reasonable standard of fairness and impartiality would inevitably require the Commission to take a stand on the merits of the particular issues considered in the programs broadcast by the several licensees, as well as exposing the licensees to the risk of loss of license because of "honest mistakes" which they may make in the exercise of their judgment with respect to the broadcasts of programs of a controversial nature. We believe that these fears are wholly without justification, and are based on either an assumption of abuse of power by the Commission or a lack of proper understanding of the role

of the Commission, under the Communications Act, in considering the program service of broadcast licensees in passing upon applications for renewal of license. While this Commission and its predecessor, the Federal Radio Commission, have, from the beginning of effective radio regulation in 1927, properly considered that a licensee's overall program service is one of the primary indicia of his ability to serve the public interest, actual consideration of such service has always been limited to a determination as to whether the licensee's programing, taken as a whole, demonstrates that the licensee is aware of his listening public and is willing and able to make an honest and reasonable effort to live up to such obligations. The action of the station in carrying or refusing to carry any particular program is of relevance only as the station's actions with respect to such programs fits into its overall pattern of broadcast service, and must be considered in the light of its other program activities. This does not mean, of course, that stations may, with impunity, engage in a partisan editorial campaign on a particular issue or series of issues provided only that the remainder of its program schedule conforms to the statutory norm of fairness; a licensee may not utilize the portion of its broadcast service which conforms to the statutory requirements as a cover or shield for other programing which fails to meet the minimum standards of operation in the public interest. But it is clear that the standard of public interest is not so rigid that an honest mistake or error in judgment on the part of a licensee will be or should be condemned where his overall record demonstrates a reasonable effort to provide a balanced presentation of comment and opinion on such issues. The question is necessarily one of the reasonableness of the station's actions, not whether any absolute standard of fairness has been achieved. It does not require any appraisal of the merits of the particular issue to determine whether reasonable efforts have been made to present both sides of the question. Thus, in appraising the record of a station in presenting programs concerning a controversial bill pending before the Congress of the United States, if the record disclosed that the licensee had permitted only advocates of the bill's enactment to utilize its facilities to the exclusion of its opponents, it is clear that no independent appraisal of the bill's merits by the Commission would be required to reach a determination that the licensee has misconstrued its duties and obligations as a person licensed to serve the public interest. The Commission has observed, in considering this general problem that "the duty to operate in the public interest is no esoteric mystery, but is essentially a duty to operate a radio station with good judgment and good faith guided by a reasonable regard for the interests of the community to be served." *Northern Corporation (WMEX),* 4 Pike & Fischer, R.R. 333, 339. Of course, some cases will be clearer than others, and the Commission in the exercise of its functions may be called upon to weigh conflicting evidence to determine whether the licensee has or has not made reasonable efforts to present a fair and well-rounded presentation of particular public issues. But the standard of reasonableness and the reasonable approximation of a statutory norm is not an arbitrary standard incapable of administrative or judicial determination, but, on the contrary, one of the basic standards of conduct in numerous fields of Anglo-American law. Like all other flexible standards of conduct, it is subject to abuse and arbitrary interpretation and application by the duly authorized reviewing authorities. But the possibility that a legitimate standard of legal conduct might be abused or arbitrarily applied by capricious governmental authority is not and cannot be a reason for abandoning the standard itself. And broadcast licensees are protected against any conceivable abuse of power by the Commission in the exercising of its licensing authority by the procedural safeguards of the Communications Act and the Administrative Procedure Act, and by the right of appeal to the courts from final action claimed to be arbitrary or capricious.

19. There remains for consideration the allegation made by a few of the witnesses in the hearing that any action by the Commission in this field enforcing a basic standard of fairness upon broadcast licensees necessarily constitutes an "abridgment of the right of free speech" in violation of the first amendment of the United States Constitution. We can see no sound basis for any such conclusion. The freedom of speech protected against governmental abridgment by the first amendment does not extend any privilege to government licensees of means of public communications to exclude the expression of opinions and ideas with which they are in disagreement. We believe, on the contrary, that a requirement that broadcast licensees utilize their franchises in a manner in which the listening public may be assured of hearing varying opinions on the paramount issues facing the American people is within both the spirit and letter of the first amendment. As the Supreme Court of the United States has pointed out in the *Associated Press* monopoly case:

> It would be strange indeed, however, if the grave concern for freedom of the press which prompted adoption of the first amendment should be read as a command that the Government was without power to protect that freedom. . . . *That amendment rests on the assumption that the widest possible dissemination of information from diverse and antagonistic sources is essential to the welfare of the public, that a free press is a condition of free society. Surely a command that the Government itself shall not impede the free flow of ideas does not afford nongovernmental combinations a refuge if they impose restraints upon that constitutionally guaranteed freedom.* Freedom to publish means freedom for all and not for some. Freedom to publish is guaranteed by the Constitution but freedom to combine to keep others from publishing is not. (*Associated Press* v. *United States*, 326 U.S. 1 at p. 20.)

20. We fully recognize that freedom of the radio is included among the freedoms protected against governmental abridgment by the first amendment. *United States* v. *Paramount Pictures, Inc., et al.,* 334 U.S. 131,

166. But this does not mean that the freedom of the people as a whole to enjoy the maximum possible utilization of this medium of mass communication may be subordinated to the freedom of any single person to exploit the medium for his own private interest. Indeed, it seems indisputable that full effect can only be given to the concept of freedom of speech on the radio by giving precedence to the right of the American public to be informed on all sides of public questions over any such individual exploitation for private purposes. Any regulation of radio, especially a system of limited licensees, is in a real sense an abridgment of the inherent freedom of persons to express themselves by means of radio communications. It is however, a necessary and constitutional abridgment in order to prevent chaotic interference from destroying the great potential of this medium for public enlightment and entertainment. *National Broadcasting Company* v. *United States,* 319 U. S. 190, . . . ;   cf. *Federal Radio Commission* v. *Nelson Brothers Bond & Mortgage Co.,* 289 U. S. 266; *Fisher's Blend Station, Inc.* v. *State Tax Commission,* 277 U. S. 650. Nothing in the Communications Act or its history supports any conclusion that the people of the Nation, acting through Congress, have intended to surrender or diminish their paramount rights in the air waves, including access to radio broadcasting facilities to a limited number of private licensees to be used as such licensees see fit, without regard ⅾ the paramount interests of the people. The most significant meaning of freedom of the radio is the right of the American people to listen to this great medium of communications free from any governmental dictation as to what they can or cannot hear and free alike from similar restraints by private licensees.

21. To recapitulate, the Commission believes that under the American system of broadcasting the individual licensees of radio stations have the responsibility for determining the specific program material to be broadcast over their stations. This choice, however, must be exercised in a manner consistent with the basic policy of the Congress that radio be maintained as a medium of free speech for the general public as a whole rather than as an outlet for the purely personal or private interests of the licensee. This requires that licensees devote a reasonable percentage of their broadcasting time to the discussion of public issues of interest in the community served by their stations and that such programs be designed so that the public has a reasonable opportunity to hear different opposing positions on the public issues of interest and importance in the community. The particular format best suited for the presentation of such programs in a manner consistent with the public interest must be determined by the licensee in the light of the facts of each individual situation. Such presentation may include the identified expression of the licensee's personal viewpoint as part of the more general presentation of views or comments on the various issues, but the opportunity of licensees to present such views as they may have on matters of controversy may not be utilized to achieve a partisan

or one-sided presentation of issues. Licensee editorialization is but one aspect of freedom of expression by means of radio. Only insofar as it is exercised in conformity with the paramount right of the public to hear a reasonably balanced presentation of all responsible viewpoints on particular issues can such editorialization be considered to be consistent with the licensee's duty to operate in the public interest. For the licensee is a trustee impressed with the duty of preserving for the public generally radio as a medium of free expression and fair presentation.

DISSENTING VIEWS OF COMMISSIONER HENNOCK

I agree with the majority that it is imperative that a high standard of impartiality in the presentation of issues of public controversy be maintained by broadcast licensees. I do not believe that the Commission's decision, however, will bring about the desired end. The standard of fairness as delineated in the report is virtually impossible of enforcement by the Commission with our present lack of policing methods and with the sanctions given us by law. We should not underestimate the difficulties inherent in the discovery of unfair presentation in any particular situation, or the problem presented by the fact that the sole sanction the Commission possesses is total deprivation of broadcast privileges in a renewal or revocation proceeding which may occur long after the violation.

In the absence of some method of policing and enforcing the requirement that the public trust granted a licensee be exercised in an impartial manner, it seems foolhardy to permit editorialization by licensees themselves. I believe that we should have such a prohibition, unless we can substitute for it some more effective method of insuring fairness. There would be no inherent evil in the presentation of a licensee's viewpoint if fairness could be guaranteed. In the present circumstances, prohibiting it is our only instrument for insuring the proper use of radio in the public interest.

FAIRNESS DOCTRINE INTERPRETATIONS

The three documents below clarify the intent of the "Fairness Doctrine." FCC 63-734 deals with methods of ensuring fair opportunity to respond to personal attacks, political partisanship, and racial viewpoints. The Commission codified its policy in the first two areas on July 5, 1967 (FCC 67-795, adding Sections 73.123, 73.300, 73.598, and 73.679 to the Commission's Rules), but softened its approach during the pendency of court appeals in 1968.

The question-answer format of the 1964 "Fairness Primer" provides policy determinations made by the Commission on a case-by-case basis.

FCC 67-641, linking the "Fairness Doctrine" to cigarette advertising, is the first application of the doctrine to broadcast commercials. Broadcasters were so disturbed by this ruling that they prepared to seek relief from the Supreme Court.

A   BROADCAST LICENSEES ADVISED . . .

Broadcast Licensees Advised Concerning Stations' Responsibilities Under the Fairness Doctrine as to Controversial Issue Programming
FCC 63-734, July 25, 1963

Several recent incidents suggest the desirability of calling the attention of broadcast licensees to the necessity for observance of the fairness doctrine stated by the Commission in its opinion of June 1, 1949 in Docket No. 8516. The Commission adheres to the views expressed in that opinion and continues to apply that policy, namely, that the licensee has an affirmative obligation to afford reasonable opportunity for the presentation of contrasting viewpoints on any controversial issue which he chooses to cover.

The Commission has undertaken a study to consider what actions, perhaps in the form of a primer or rules, might be appropriate better to define certain of the licensee's responsibilities in this area. Without undertaking at the present time to specify all, or the most important, applications of the policy, it is appropriate to call attention to the Commission's view of its application in three currently important situations:

(a) When a controversial program involves a personal attack upon an individual or organization, the licensee must transmit the text of the broadcast to the person or group attacked, wherever located, either prior to or at the time of the broadcast, with a specific offer of his station's facilities for an adequate response (*Clayton W. Mapoles,* 23 Pike & Fischer, R.R. 586, 591; *Billings Broadcasting Company,* 23 Pike & Fischer, R.R. 951, 953).

(b) When a licensee permits the use of his facilities by a commentator or any person other than a candidate to take a partisan position on the issues involved in a contest for political office or to attack one candidate or support another by direct or indirect identification, he must immediately send a transcript of the pertinent continuity in each such program to each candidate concerned and offer a comparable opportunity for an appropriate spokesman to answer the broadcast (*Times-Mirror Broadcasting Co.,* 24 Pike & Fischer, R.R. 404, 405).

(c) When a licensee permits the use of his facilities for the presentation of views regarding an issue of current importance such as racial segregation, integration, or discrimination, or any other issue of public importance, he must offer spokesmen for other responsible groups within the community similar opportunities for the expression of the contrasting viewpoints of their respective groups. In particular, the views of the leaders of the Negro and other community groups as to the issue of racial segregation, integration, or discrimination, and of the leaders of appropriate groups in the community as to other issues of public importance, must obviously be considered and reflected, in order to insure that fairness is achieved with respect to programming dealing with such controversial issues (*Editorializing Report,* 1 (Part three) Pike & Fischer, R.R. 201, 204-206; cf. *WBNX Bctg. Co., Inc.,* 4 Pike & Fischer, R.R. 242, 248).

In determining compliance with the fairness doctrine the Commission looks to substance rather than to label or form. It is immaterial whether a particular program or viewpoint is presented under the label of "Americanism," "anti-communism" or "states' rights," or whether it is a paid announcement, official speech, editorial or religious broadcast. Regardless of label or form, if one viewpoint of a controversial issue of public importance is presented, the licensee is obligated to make a reasonable effort to present the other opposing viewpoint or viewpoints.

The Commission does not seek to prevent the expression of any viewpoint by any licensee on any issue. It does seek to prevent the suppression of other contrasting viewpoints by any licensee on any issue when licensed broadcast facilities have been used for the presentation of one view of the issue. This is required by the public interest standard of the law.

THE FAIRNESS PRIMER

Applicability of the Fairness Doctrine in the Handling of
Controversial Issues of Public Importance
29 Fed. Reg. 10416
Adopted July 1, 1964; Printed July 25, 1964

PART I—INTRODUCTION

It is the purpose of this Public Notice to advise broadcast licensees and members of the public of the rights, obligations, and responsibilities of such licensees under the Commission's "fairness doctrine," which is applicable in any case in which broadcast facilities are used for the discussion of a controversial issue of public importance. For this purpose, we have set out a digest of the Commission's interpretative rulings on the fairness doctrine. This Notice will be revised at appropriate intervals to reflect new rulings in this area. In this way, we hope to keep the broadcaster and the public informed of pertinent Commission determinations on the fairness doctrine, and thus reduce the number of these cases required to be referred to the Commission for resolution. Before turning to the digest of the rulings, we believe some brief introductory discussion of the fairness doctrine is desirable.

The basic administrative action with respect to the fairness doctrine was taken in the Commission's 1949 Report, Editorializing by Broadcast Licensees, 13 FCC 1246; Vol. 1, Part 3, R.R. 91–201.[1] This report is attached hereto because it still constitutes the Commission's basic policy in this field.[2]

Congress recognized this policy in 1959. In amending Section 315 so as to exempt appearances by legally qualified candidates on certain news-type programs from the "equal opportunities" provision, it was stated in the statute that such action should not be construed as relieving broadcasters " . . . from the obligation imposed upon them under this Act to operate in the public interest and to afford reasonable opportunity for the discussion of conflicting views on issues of public importance" (Public

[1] Citations in "R.R." refer to Pike & Fischer, Radio Regulations. The above report thus deals not only with the question of editorializing but also the requirements of the fairness doctrine.
[2] The report (par. 6) also points up the responsibility of broadcast licensees to devote a reasonable amount of their broadcast time to the presentation of programs dealing with the discussion of controversial issues of public importance. See Appendix A. [Appendix A, the Commission's 1949 Report, is omitted here; it appears, however, on pp. 361–374 of this volume.—Ed.]

Law 86–274, approved September 14, 1959, 73 Stat. 557).[3] The legislative history[4] establishes that this provision "is a restatement of the basic policy of the 'standard of fairness' which is imposed on broadcasters under the Communications Act of 1934" (H. Rept. No. 1069, 86th Cong., 1st Sess., p. 5).

While Section 315 thus embodies both the "equal opportunities" requirement and the fairness doctrine, they apply to different situations and in different ways. The "equal opportunities" requirement relates solely to use of broadcast facilities by candidates for public office. With certain exceptions involving specified news-type programs, the law provides that if a licensee permits a person who is a legally qualified candidate for public office to use a broadcast station, he shall afford equal opportunities to all other such candidates for that office in the use of the station. The Commission's Public Notice on Use of Broadcast Facilities by Candidates for Public Office, 27 Fed. Reg. 10063 (October 12, 1962), should be consulted with respect to "equal opportunities" questions involving political candidates.

The fairness doctrine deals with the broader question of affording reasonable opportunity for the presentation of contrasting viewpoints on controversial issues of public importance. Generally speaking, it does not apply with the precision of the "equal opportunities" requirement. Rather, the licensee, in applying the fairness doctrine, is called upon to make reasonable judgments in good faith on the facts of each situation—as to whether a controversial issue of public importance is involved, as to what viewpoints have been or should be presented, as to the format and spokesmen to present the viewpoints, and all the other facets of such programming. See par. 9, Editorializing Report. In passing on any complaint in this area, the Commission's role is not to substitute its judgment for that of the licensee as to any of the above programming decisions, but rather to determine whether the licensee can be said to have acted reasonably and in good faith. There is thus room for considerably more discretion on the part of the licensee under the fairness doctrine than under the "equal opportunities" requirement.

Interpretative rulings—Commission procedure

We set forth below a digest of the Commission's rulings on the fairness doctrine. References, with citations, to the Commission's decisions or rul-

---

[3] The full statement in Section 315(a) reads as follows: "Nothing in the foregoing sentence [i.e., exemption from equal time requirements for news-type programs] shall be construed as relieving broadcasters, in connection with the presentation of newscasts, news interviews, news documentaries, and on-the-spot coverage of news events, from the obligation imposed upon them under this chapter to operate in the public interest and to afford reasonable opportunity for the discussion of conflicting views on issues of public importance."

[4] See Appendix B. [Appendix B, "The History of the Fairness Doctrine," is omitted. —Ed.]

ings are made so that the researcher may, if he desires, review the complete text of the Commission's ruling. Copies of rulings may be found in a "Fairness Doctrine" folder kept in the Commission's Reference Room.

In an area such as the fairness doctrine, the Commission's rulings are necessarily based upon the facts of the particular case presented, and thus a variation in facts might call for a different or revised ruling. We therefore urge that interested persons, in studying the rulings for guidance, look not only to the language of the ruling but the specific factual context in which it was made.

It is our hope, as stated, that this Notice will reduce significantly the number of fairness complaints made to the Commission. Where complaint is made to the Commission, the Commission expects a complainant to submit specific information indicating (1) the particular station involved; (2) the particular issue of a controversial nature discussed over the air; (3) the date and time when the program was carried; (4) the basis for the claim that the station has presented only one side of the question; and (5) whether the station had afforded, or has plans to afford, an opportunity for the presentation of contrasting viewpoints.[5] (Lar Daly, 19 R.R. 1104, March 24, 1960; cf. Cullman Bctg. Co., FCC 63–849, Sept. 18, 1963.)

If the Commission determines that the complaint sets forth sufficient facts to warrant further consideration, it will promptly advise the licensee of the complaint and request the licensee's comments on the matter. Full opportunity is given to the licensee to set out all programs which he has presented, or plans to present, with respect to the issue in question during an appropriate time period. Unless additional information is sought from either the complainant or the licensee, the matter is then usually disposed of by Commission action. (Letter of September 18, 1963 to Honorable Oren Harris, FCC 63–851.)

Finally, we repeat what we stated in our 1949 Report:

. . . It is this right of the public to be informed, rather than any right on the part of the Government, any broadcast licensee or any individual member of the public to broadcast his own particular views on any matter, which is the foundation stone of the American system of broadcasting.

PART II—COMMISSION RULINGS

A. Controversial issue of public importance

1. *Civil rights as controversial issue.* In response to a Commission inquiry, a station advised the Commission, in a letter dated March 6, 1950, that it had broadcast editorial programs in support of a National Fair Employment Practices Commission on January 15–17, 1950, and that it had

[5] The complainant can usually obtain this information by communicating with the station

taken no affirmative steps to encourage and implement the presentation of points of view with respect to these matters which differed from the point of view expressed by the station.

Ruling. The establishment of a National Fair Employment Practices Commission constitutes a controversial question of public importance so as to impose upon the licensee the affirmative duty to aid and encourage the broadcast of opposing views. It is a matter of common knowledge that the establishment of a National Fair Employment Practices Commission is a subject that has been actively controverted by members of the public and by members of the Congress of the United States and that in the course of that controversy numerous differing views have been espoused. The broadcast by the station of a relatively large number of programs relating to this matter over a period of three days indicates an awareness of its importance and raises the assumption that at least one of the purposes of the broadcasts was to influence public opinion. In our report In the Matter of Editorializing by Broadcast Licensees, we stated that:

. . . In appraising the record of a station in presenting programs concerning a controversial bill pending before the Congress of the United States, if the record disclosed that the licensee had permitted only advocates of the bill's enactment to utilize its facilities to the exclusion of its opponents, it is clear that no independent appraisal of the bill's merits by the Commission would be required to reach a determination that the licensee had misconstrued its duties and obligations as a person licensed to serve the public interest.

In light of the foregoing the conduct of the licensee was not in accord with the principles set forth in the report. (New Broadcasting Co. (WLIB), 6 R.R. 258, April 12, 1950.)

2. *Political spot announcements.* In an election an attempt was made to promote campaign contributions to the candidates of the two major parties through the use of spot announcements on broadcast stations. Certain broadcast stations raised the question whether the airing of such announcements imposed an obligation under Section 315 of the Act and/or the fairness doctrine to broadcast such special announcements for all candidates running for a particular office in a given election.

Ruling. The "equal opportunities" provision of Section 315 applies only to uses by candidates and not to those speaking in behalf of or against candidates. Since the above announcements did not contemplate the appearance of a candidate, the "equal opportunities" provision of Section 315 would not be applicable. The fairness doctrine is, however, applicable. (Letter to Lawrence M. C. Smith, FCC 63–358, 25 R.R. 291, April 17, 1963.) See Ruling No. 13.

3. *"Reports to the People."* The complaint of the Chairman of the Democratic State Committee of New York alleged that an address by Governor Dewey over the facilities of the stations affiliated with the CBS net-

work on May 2, 1949, entitled "A Report to the People of New York State," was political in nature and contained statements of a controversial nature. The CBS reply stated, in substance, that it was necessary to distinguish between the reports made by holders of office to the people whom they represented and the partisan political activities of the individuals holding office.

Ruling. The Commission recognizes that public officials may be permitted to utilize radio facilities to report on their stewardship to the people and that "the mere claim that the subject is political does not automatically require that the opposite political party be given equal facilities for a reply." On the other hand, it is apparent that so-called reports to the people may constitute attacks on the opposite political party or may be a discussion of a public controversial issue. Consistent with the views expressed by the Commission in the Editorializing Report, it is clear that the characterization of a particular program as a report to the people does not necessarily establish such a program as noncontroversial in nature so as to avoid the requirement of affording time for the expression of opposing views. In that Report, we stated ". . . that there can be no one all embracing formula which licensees can hope to apply to insure the fair and balanced presentation of all public issues . . . . The licensee will in each instance be called upon to exercise his best judgment and good sense in determining what subjects should be considered the particular format of the programs to be devoted to each subject, the different shades of opinion to be presented, and the spokesmen for each point of view." The duty of the licensee to make time available for the expression of differing views is invoked where the facts and circumstances in each case indicate an area of controversy and differences of opinion where the subject matter is of public importance. In the light of the foregoing, the Commission concludes that "it does not appear that there has been the abuse of judgment on the part of [CBS] such as to warrant holding a hearing on its applications for renewal of license." (Paul E. Fitzpatrick, 6 R.R. 543, July 21, 1949; (see also, California Democratic State Central Committee, Public Notice 95873, 20 R.R. 867.869, October 31, 1960.))

4. *Controversial issue within service area.* A station broadcast a statement by the President of CBS opposing pay TV; two newscasts containing the views of a Senator opposed to pay TV; one newscast reporting the introduction by a Congressman of an anti-pay TV bill; a half-hour network program on pay TV in which both sides were represented, followed by a ten-minute film clip of a Senator opposing pay TV; a half-hour program in which a known opponent of pay TV was interviewed by interrogators whose questions in some instances indicated an opinion by the questioner favorable to pay TV. In a hearing upon the station's application for modification of its construction permit, an issue was raised whether the station had complied with the requirements of the fairness doctrine. The licensee stated

that while nationally pay TV was "certainly" a controversial issue, it regarded pay TV as a local controversial issue only to a very limited extent in its service area, and therefore it was under no obligation to take the initiative to present the views of advocates of pay TV.

Ruling. The station's handling of the pay TV question was improper. It could be inferred that the station's sympathies with the opposition to pay TV made it less than a vigorous searcher for advocates of subscription television. The station evidently thought the subject of sufficient general interest (beyond its own concern in the matter) to devote broadcast time to it, and even to preempt part of a local program to present the views of the Senator in opposition to pay TV immediately after the balanced network discussion program, with the apparent design of neutralizing any possible public sympathy for pay TV which might have arisen from the preceding network forum. The anti-pay TV side was represented to a greater extent on the station than the other, though it cannot be said that the station choked off the expression of all views inimical to its interest. A licensee cannot excuse a one-sided presentation on the basis that the subject matter was not controversial in its service area, for it is only through a fair presentation of all facts and arguments on a particular question that public opinion can properly develop. (In re The Spartan Radiocasting Co., 33 F.C.C., 765, 771, 794–795, 802–803, November 21, 1962.)

5. *Substance of broadcast.* A number of stations broadcast a program entitled "Living Should Be Fun," featuring a nutritionist giving comment and advice on diet and health. Complaint was made that the program presented only one side of controversial issues of public importance. Several licensees contended that a program dealing with the desirability of good health and nutritious diet should not be placed in the category of discussion of controversial issues.

Ruling. The Commission cannot agree that the program consisted merely of the discussion of the desirability of good health and nutritious diet. Anyone who listened to the program regularly—and station licensees have the obligation to know what is being broadcast over their facilities— should have been aware that at times controversial issues of public importance were discussed. In discussing such subjects as the fluoridation of water, the value of krebiozen in the treatment of cancer, the nutritive qualities of white bread, and the use of high potency vitamins without medical advice, the nutritionist emphasized the fact that his views were opposed to many authorities in these fields, and on occasions on the air, he invited those with opposing viewpoints to present such viewpoints on his program. A licensee who did not recognize the applicability of the fairness doctrine failed in the performance of his obligations to the public. (Report on "Living Should be Fun" Inquiry, 33 F.C.C. 101, 107, 23 R.R. 1599, 1606, July 18, 1962.)

6. *Substance of broadcast.* A station broadcast a program entitled

"Communist Encirclement" in which the following matters, among others, were discussed: socialist forms of government were viewed as a transitory form of government leading eventually to communism; it was asserted that this country's continuing foreign policy in the Far East and Latin America, the alleged infiltration of our government by communists, and the alleged moral weakening in our homes, schools and churches have all contributed to the advance of international communism. In response to complaints alleging one-sided presentation of these issues, the licensee stated that since it did not know of the existence of any communist organizations or communists in its community, it was unable to afford opportunity to those who might wish to present opposing views.

Ruling. In situations of this kind, it was not and is not the Commission's intention to require licensees to make time available to communists or the communist viewpoints. But the matters listed above raise controversial issues of public importance on which persons other than communists hold contrasting views. These are responsible contrasting viewpoints on the most effective methods of combatting communism and communist infiltration. Broadcast of proposals supporting only one method raises the question whether reasonable opportunity has been afforded for the expression of contrasting viewpoints. (Letter to Tri-State Broadcasting Company, Inc., April 26, 1962 (staff letter).)

7. *Substance of broadcast.* In 1957, a station broadcast a panel discussion entitled "The Little Rock Crisis" in which several public officials appeared, and whose purpose, a complainant stated, was to stress the maintenance of segregation and to express an opinion as to what the Negro wants or does not want. A request for time to present contrasting viewpoints was refused by the licensee who stated that the program was most helpful in preventing trouble by urging people to keep calm and look to their elected representatives for leadership, that it was a report by elected officials to the people, and that therefore no reply was necessary or advisable.

Ruling. If the matters discussed involved no more than urging people to remain calm, it can be urged that no question exists as to fair presentation. However, if the station permitted the use of its facilities for the presentation of one side of the controversial issue of racial integration, the station incurred an obligation to afford a reasonable opportunity for the expression of contrasting views. The fact that the proponents of one particular position were elected officials did not in any way alter the nature of the program or remove the applicability of the fairness doctrine. See Ruling No. 3. (Lamar Life Insurance Co., FCC 59–651, 18 R.R. 683, July 1, 1959.)

8. *National controversial issues.* Stations broadcast a daily commentary program six days a week, in three of which views were expressed critical of the proposed nuclear weapons test ban treaty. On one of the stations the program was sponsored six days a week and on the other one day a

week. A national committee in favor of the proposed treaty requested that the stations afford free time to present a tape of a program containing viewpoints opposed to those in the sponsored commentary program. The stations indicated, among other things, that it was their opinion that the fairness doctrine is applicable only to local issues.

Ruling. The keystone of the fairness doctrine and of the public interest is the right of the public to be informed—to have presented to it the "conflicting views of issues of public importance." Where a licensee permits the use of its facilities for the expression of views on controversial local or national issues of public importance such as the nuclear weapons test ban treaty, he must afford reasonable opportunities for the presentation of contrasting views by spokesmen for other responsible groups. (Letter to Cullman Broadcasting Co., Inc., FCC 63–849, September 18, 1963.) See Rulings No. 16 and 17 for other aspects of the Cullman decision.

B. Licensee's obligation to afford reasonable opportunity for the presentation of contrasting viewpoints

9. *Affirmative duty to encourage.* In response to various complaints alleging that a station had been "one-sided" in its presentations on controversial issues of public importance, the licensee concerned rested upon its policy of making time available, upon request, for "the other side."

Ruling. The licensee's obligations to serve the public interest cannot be met merely through the adoption of a general policy of not refusing to broadcast opposing views where a demand is made of the station for broadcast time. As the Commission pointed out in the Editorializing Report (par. 9):

. . . If, as we believe to be the case, the public interest is best served in a democracy through the ability of the people to hear expositions of the various positions taken by responsible groups and individuals on particular topics and to choose between them, it is evident that broadcast licensees have an affirmative duty generally to encourage and implement the broadcast of all sides of controversial public issues over their facilities, over and beyond their obligation to make available on demand opportunities for the expression of opposing views. It is clear that any approximation of fairness in the presentation of any controversy will be difficult if not impossible of achievement unless the licensee pays a conscious and positive role in bringing about balanced presentations of the opposing viewpoints. (John J. Dempsey, 6 R.R. 615, August 16, 1950; Editorializing Report, par. 9.) (See also Metropolitan Bctg. Corp., Public Notice 82386, 19 R.R. 602, 604, December 29, 1959.)

10. *Non-delegable duty.* Approximately 50 radio stations broadcast a program entitled "Living Should Be Fun," featuring a nutritionist giving comment and advice on diet and health. The program was syndicated and taped for presentation, twenty-five minutes a day, five days a week. Many

of the programs discussed controversial issues of public importance. In response to complaints that the stations failed to observe the requirements of the fairness doctrine, some of the licensees relied upon (i) the nutritionist's own invitation to those with opposing viewpoints to appear on his program or (ii) upon the assurances of the nutritionist or the sponsor that the program fairly represented all responsible contrasting viewpoints on the issues with which it dealt, as an adequate discharge of their obligations under the fairness doctrine.

Ruling. Those licensees who relied solely upon the assumed built-in fairness of the program itself, or upon the nutritionist's invitation to those with opposing viewpoints, cannot be said to have properly discharged their responsibilities. Neither alternative is likely to produce the fairness which the public interest demands. There could be many valid reasons why the advocate of an opposing viewpoint would be unwilling to appear upon such a program. In short, the licensee may not delegate his responsibilities to others, and particularly to an advocate of one particular viewpoint. As the Commission said in our Report in the Matter of Editorializing by Broadcast Licensees, "It is clear that any approximation of fairness in the presentation of any controversy will be difficult if not impossible of achievement unless the licensee plays a conscious and positive role in bringing about balanced presentation of the opposing viewpoints." (Report on "Living Should Be Fun" Inquiry, 33 FCC 101, 107, 23 R.R. 1599, 1606, July 18, 1962.)

11. *Reliance upon other media.* In January 1958, the issue of subscription television was a matter of public controversy, and it was generally known that the matter was the subject of Congressional hearings being conducted by the House and Senate Interstate and Foreign Commerce Committees. On Monday, January 27, 1958, between 9:30 and 10:00 p.m., WSOC-TV broadcast the program "Now It Can Be Told" (simultaneously with the other Charlotte television station, WBTV), a program consisting of a skit followed by a discussion in which the president of WSOC-TV and the vice president and general manager of Station WBTV were interviewed by employees of the two stations. The skit and interview were clearly weighted against subscription TV, and in the program the station made clear its preference for the present TV system. On Saturday, February 1, 1958, WSOC-TV presented for 15 minutes, beginning at 3:35 p.m., a film clip in which a United States Representative discussed subscription television and expressed his opposition thereto. From January 24 to January 30, 1958, inclusive, WSOC-TV presented a total of 43 spot announcements, all of them against subscription television, and urged viewers, if they opposed it, to write their Congressmen without delay to express their opposition. WSOC-TV did not broadcast any programs or announcements presenting a viewpoint favorable to subscription television although on February 28, 1958, the station did (together with the management of Station WBTV)

send a telegram to the three chief subscription television groups, offering them joint use of the two Charlotte stations, without charge, at a time mutually agreeable to all parties concerned, for the purpose of putting on a program by the proponents of pay TV. This offer was refused by Skiatron, one of the three groups. In its reply to the Commission's inquiry, the station referred to "the large amount of publicity already given by the Pay-TV proponents in newspapers, magazines and by direct mail," and asserted that its decision in this matter was taken "in an effort to furnish the public with the opposing viewpoints on the subject . . . "

Ruling. The station's broadcast presentation of the subscription TV issue was essentially one-sided, and, taking into account the circumstances of the situation existing at the time, the station did not make any timely effort to secure the presentation of the other side of the issue by responsible representatives. It is the Commission's view that the requirement of fairness, as set forth in the Editorializing Report, applies to a broadcast licensee irrespective of the position which may be taken by other media on the issue involved; and that the licensee's own performance in this respect, in and of itself, must demonstrate compliance with the fairness doctrine. (Letter to WSOC Broadcasting Co., FCC 58–686, 17 R.R. 548, 550, July 16, 1958.)

C. Reasonable opportunity for the presentation of contrasting viewpoints

12. *"Equal time" not required.* Licensee broadcast over its several facilities on October 28, 1960, a 30-minute documentary concerning a North Dakota hospital. The last five minutes of the program consisted of an interview of the Superintendent of the hospital and the Chairman of the Board of Administration for State Institutions who responded to charges that the complainant, a candidate for the office of Attorney General of North Dakota, had publicly leveled against the Superintendent and Chairman concerning the administration of the hospital. On November 4, 1960 and at about the same viewing time as the preceding documentary, complainant's 30-minute broadcast was aired over the Stations in which complainant presented his allegations about the professional, administrative, and disciplinary conditions at the hospital and a state training school. The following day (November 5) licensee presented a 30-minute documentary on the state training school, the last five minutes of which consisted of a discussion of the charges made by complainant on his November 4 program by a spokesman for the opposing political party, and by the interviewees of the October 28 program. Licensee refused complainant's request for "equal time" to reply to the November 5 broadcast.

Ruling. In view of the fact that the "equal opportunities" requirement of Section 315 becomes applicable only when an opposing candidate for the same office has been afforded broadcast time, and that the complainant's political opponent did not appear on any of the programs in question (and, in fact, was never mentioned during the broadcast of these programs), the Commission reviewed the matter in light of the fairness doctrine. Unlike the "equal opportunities" requirement of Section 315, the fairness doctrine requires that where a licensee affords time over his facilities for an expression of one opinion on a controversial issue of public importance, he is under obligation to insure that proponents of opposing viewpoints are afforded a reasonable opportunity for the presentation of such views. The Commission concludes that on the facts before it, the licensee's actions were not inconsistent with the principles enunciated in the Editorializing Report. (Hon. Charles L. Murphy, FCC 62–737, 23 R.R. 953, July 13, 1962.)

13. *"Equal time" not required.* During a state-wide election an attempt was made to promote bipartisan campaign contributions, particularly for the candidates of the two major parties running for Governor and Senator, through the use of spot announcements on broadcast stations. Several stations raised the question whether the broadcast of these announcements would impose upon them the obligation, under the fairness doctrine, to broadcast such special announcements for all candidates running for a particular office in a given election.

Ruling. If there were only the two candidates of the major parties for the office in question, fairness would obviously require that these two be treated roughly the same with respect to the announcements. But it does not follow that if there were, in addition, so-called minority party candidates for the office of Senator, these candidates also would have to be afforded a roughly equivalent number of similar announcements. In such an event, the licensee would be called upon to make a good faith judgment as to whether there can reasonably be said to be a need or interest in the community calling for some provision of announcement time to these other parties or candidates and, if so, to determine the extent of that interest or need and the appropriate way to meet it. In short, the licensee's obligation under the fairness doctrine is to afford a reasonable opportunity for the presentation of opposing views in the light of circumstances—an obligation calling for the same kind of judgment as in the case where party spokesmen (rather than candidates) appear. (Letter to Mr. Lawrence M. C. Smith, FCC 63–658, April 18, 1963.)

14. *No necessity for presentation on same program.* In the proceedings leading to the Editorializing Report, it was urged, in effect, that contrasting viewpoints with respect to a controversial issue of public importance should be presented on the same program.

Ruling. The Commission concluded that any rigid requirement in this respect would seriously limit the ability of the licensees to serve the public interest, "Forums and roundtable discussions, while often excellent techniques of presenting a fair cross section of differing viewpoints on a given issue, are not the only appropriate devices for radio discussion, and in some circumstances may not be particularly appropriate or advantageous." (Par. 8, Editorializing Report.)

15. *Overall performance on the issue.* A licensee presented a program in which views were expressed critical of the proposed nuclear weapons test ban treaty. The licensee rejected a request of an organization seeking to present views favorable to the treaty, on the ground, among others, that the contrasting viewpoint on this issue had already been presented over the station's facilities in other programming.

Ruling. The licensee's overall performance is considered in determining whether fairness has been achieved on a specific issue. Thus, where complaint is made, the licensee is afforded the opportunity to set out all the programs, irrespective of the programming format, which he has devoted to the particular controversial issue during the appropriate time period. In this case, the Commission files contained no complaints to the contrary, and therefore, if it was the licensee's good faith judgment that the public had had the opportunity fairly to hear contrasting views on the issue involved in his other programming, it appeared that the licensee's obligation pursuant to the fairness doctrine had been met. (Letter to Cullman Bctg. Co., FCC 63–849, September 18, 1963; Letter of September 20, 1963, FCC 63–851, to Honorable Oren Harris.)

D. *Limitations which may reasonably be imposed by the licensee*

16. *Licensee discretion to choose spokesman.* See Ruling 8 for facts.

Ruling. Where a licensee permits the use of its facilities for the expression of views on controversial local or national issues of public importance such as the nuclear weapons test ban treaty, he must afford reasonable opportunities for the presentation of contrasting views by spokesmen for other responsible groups. There is, of course, no single method by which this obligation is to be met. As the Editorializing Report makes clear, the licensee has considerable discretion as to the techniques or formats to be employed and the spokesmen for each point of view. In the good faith exercise of his best judgment, he may, in a particular case, decide upon a local rather than regional or national spokesmen—or upon a spokesman for a group which also is willing to pay for the broadcast time. Thus, with the exception of the broadcast of personal attacks (see Part E), there is no single group or person entitled as a matter of right to present a viewpoint differing from that previously expressed on the station. (Letter to Cullman Broadcasting Co., Inc., FCC 63–849, September 18, 1963.)

17. *Non-local spokesman; paid sponsorship.* See Ruling 8 for facts. The stations contended that their obligation under the fairness doctrine extended only to a local group or its spokesman, and also inquired whether

they were required to give free time to a group wishing to present viewpoints opposed to those aired on a sponsored program.

Ruling. Where the licensee has achieved a balanced presentation of contrasting views, either by affording time to a particular group or person of its own choice or through its own programming, the licensee's obligations under the fairness doctrine—to inform the public—will have been met. But, it is clear that the public's paramount right to hear opposing views on controversial issues of public importance cannot be nullified by either the inability of the licensee to obtain paid sponsorship of the broadcast time or the licensee's refusal to consider requests for time to present a conflicting viewpoint from an organization on the sole ground that the organization has no local chapter. In short, where the licensee has chosen to broadcast a sponsored program which for the first time presents one side of a controversial issue, has not presented (or does not plan to present) contrasting viewpoints in other programming, and has been unable to obtain paid sponsorship for the appropriate presentation of the opposing viewpoint or viewpoints, he cannot reject a presentation otherwise suitable to the licensee—and thus leave the public uninformed—on the ground that he cannot obtain paid sponsorship for that presentation. (Letter to Cullman Broadcasting, Co., Inc., FCC 63–849, September 18, 1963.)

18. *Unreasonable limitation; refusal to permit appeal not to vote.* A station refused to sell broadcast time to the complainant who, as a spokesman for a community group, was seeking to present his point of view concerning a bond election to be held in the community; the station had sold time to an organization in favor of the bond issue. The complainant alleged that the station had broadcast editorials urging people to vote in the election and that his group's position was that because of the peculiarities in the bond election law (more than 50 percent of the electorate had to vote in the election for it to be valid), the best way to defeat the proposed measure was for people not to vote in the election. The complainant alleged, and the station admitted, that the station refused to sell him broadcast time because the licensee felt that to urge people not to vote was improper.

Ruling. Because of the peculiarities of the state election law, the sale of broadcast time to an organization favoring the bond issue, and the urging of listeners to vote, the question of whether to vote became an issue. Accordingly, by failing to broadcast views urging listeners not to vote, the licensee failed to discharge the obligations imposed upon him by the Commission's Report on Editorializing. (Letter to Radio Station WMOP, January 21, 1962 (staff ruling).)

19. *Unreasonable limitation; insistence upon request from both parties to dispute.* During the period of a labor strike which involved a matter of paramount importance to the community and to the nation at large, a union requested broadcast time to discuss the issues involved. The request was denied by the station solely because of its policy to refuse time for such

discussion unless both the union and the management agreed, in advance, that they would jointly request and use the station, and the management of the company involved in the strike had refused to do so.

Ruling. In view of the licensee's statement that the issue was "of paramount importance to the community . . ." the licensee's actions were not in accordance with the principles enunciated in the Editorializing Report, specifically that portion of par. 8, which states that:

. . . where the licensee has determined that the subject is of sufficient import to receive broadcast attention, it would obviously not be in the public interest for spokesmen for one of the opposing points of view to be able to exercise a veto power over the entire presentation by refusing to broadcast its position. Fairness in such circumstances might require no more than that the licensee make a reasonable representation of the particular position and if it fails in this effort, to continue to make available its facilities to the spokesmen for such position in the event that, after the original programs are broadcast, they then decide to avail themselves of a right to present their contrary opinion. (Par. 8, Report on Editorializing by Broadcast Licensees; The Evening News Ass'n (WWJ), 6 R.R. 283, April 21, 1950.)

E. Personal attack principle

20. *Personal attack.* A newscaster on a station, in a series of broadcasts, attacked certain county and state officials, charging them with nefarious schemes and the use of their offices for personal gain, attaching derisive epithets to their names, and analogizing their local administration with the political methods of foreign dictators. At the time of renewal of the station's license, the persons attacked urged that the station had been used for the licensee's selfish purposes and to vent his personal spite. The licensee denied the charge, and asserted that the broadcasts had a factual basis. On several occasions, the persons attacked were invited to use the station to discuss the matters in the broadcasts.

Ruling. Where a licensee expresses an opinion concerning controversial issues of public importance, he is under obligation to see that those holding opposing viewpoints are afforded a reasonable opportunity for the presentation of their views. He is under a further obligation not to present biased or one-sided news programming (viewing such programming on an overall basis) and not to use his station for his purely personal and private interests. Investigation established that the licensee did not subordinate his public interest obligations to his private interests, and that there was "a body of opinion" in the community "that such broadcasts had a factual basis."

As to the attacks, the *Editorializing Report* states that ". . . elementary considerations of fairness may dictate that time be allocated to a person or group which has been specifically attacked over the station, where otherwise no such obligation would exist . . ." In this case, the attacks were of a highly personal nature, impugning the character and honesty of named individuals. In such circumstances, the licensee has an affirmative duty to take all appropriate steps to see to it that the persons attacked are afforded the fullest opportunity to respond. Here, the persons attacked knew of the attacks, were generally apprised of their nature, and were aware of the opportunities afforded them to respond. Accordingly, the license was renewed. (Clayton W. Mapoles, FCC 62–501, 23 R.R. 586, May 9, 1962.)

21. *Personal attack.* For a period of five days, September 18–22, a station broadcast a series of daily editorials attacking the general manager of a national rural electric cooperative association in connection with a pending controversial issue of public importance. The manager arrived in town on September 21 for a two-day stay and, upon being informed of the editorials, on the morning of September 22d sought to obtain copies of them. About noon of the same day, the station approached the manager with an offer of an interview to respond to the statements made in the editorials. The manager stated, however, that he would not have had time to prepare adequately a reply which would require a series of broadcasts. He complained to the Commission that the station had acted unfairly.

Ruling. Where, as here, a station's editorials contain a personal attack upon an individual by name, the fairness doctrine requires that a copy of the specific editorial or editorials shall be communicated to the person attacked either prior to or at the time of the broadcast of such editorials so that a reasonable opportunity is afforded that person to reply. This duty on the part of the station is greater where, as here, interest in the editorials was consciously built up by the station over a period of days and the time within which the person attacked would have an opportunity to reply was known to be so limited. The Commission concludes that in failing to supply copies of the editorials promptly to the manager and delaying in affording him the opportunity to reply to them, the station had not fully met the requirements of the Commission's fairness doctrine. (Billings Bctg. Co., FCC 62–736. 23 R.R. 951, July 13, 1962.)

22. *No personal attack merely because individual is named.* A network program discussed the applicability of Section 315 to appearances by candidates for public office on TV newscasts and the Commission's decision holding that the mayoralty candidate, Lar Daly, was entitled to equal time when the Mayor of Chicago appeared on a newscast. The program contained the editorial views of the President of CBS opposing the interpretation of the Commission and urging that Section 315 not apply to newscasts. Three other persons on the program expressed contrasting points of view. Lar Daly's request that he be afforded time to reply to the President of CBS, because he was "directly involved" in the Commission's decision which was discussed over the air and because he was the most qualified

spokesman to present opposing views, was denied by the station. Did the fairness doctrine require that his request be granted?

Ruling. It was the newscast question involved in the Commission's decision, rather than Lar Daly, which was the controversial issue which was presented. Since the network presented several spokesmen, all of whom appeared qualified to state views contrasting with those expressed by the network President, the network fulfilled its obligation to provide a "fair and balanced presentation of an important public issue of a controversial nature." (Lar Daly, 19 R.R. 1103, at 1104, Mar. 24, 1960.)[6]

23. *Licensee involvement in personal attack.* It was urged that in Mapoles, Billings, and Times-Mirror (see Rulings 20, 21, 25), the station was, in effect, "personally involved"; that the personal attack principle should be applied only when the licensee is personally involved in the attack upon a person or group (i.e., through editorials or through station commentator programming), and not where the attack is made by a party unconnected with the station.

Ruling. Under fundamental communications policy, the licensee, with the exception of appearances of political candidates subject to the equal opportunity requirements of Section 315 is fully responsible for all matter which is broadcast over his station. It follows that when a program contains a personal attack, the licensee must be fully aware of the contents of the program, whatever its source or his actual involvement in the broadcast. The crucial consideration, as the Commission stated in Mapoles, is that "his broadcast facilities [have been] used to attack a person or group." (Letter of September 18, 1963 to Douglas A. Anello, FCC 63–850.)

24. *Personal attack—no tape or transcript.* In the same inquiry as above (Ruling 23), the question was also raised as to the responsibility of the licensee when his facilities are used for a personal attack in a program dealing with a controversial issue of public importance and the licensee has no transcript or tape of the program.

Ruling. Where a personal attack is made and no script or tape is available, good sense and fairness dictate that the licensee send as accurate a summary as possible of the substance of the attack to the person or group involved. (Letter of September 18, 1963 to Douglas A. Anello, FCC 63–850.)

---

[6] As seen from the above rulings, the personal attack principle is applicable where there are statements, in connection with a controversial issue of public importance, attacking an individual's or group's integrity, character, or honesty or like personal qualities, and not when an individual or group is simply named or referred to. Thus, while a definitive Commission ruling must await a complaint involving specific facts—see introduction, p. 379, the personal attack principle has not been applied where there is simply stated disagreement with the views of an individual or group concerning a controversial issue of public importance. Nor is it necessary to send a transcript or summary of the attack, with an offer of time for response, in the case of a personal attack upon a foreign leader, even assuming such an attack occurred in connection with a controversial issue of public importance.

25. *Personal attacks on, and criticism of, candidate; partisan position on campaign issues.* In more than 20 broadcasts, two station commentators presented their views on the issues in the 1962 California gubernatorial campaign between Governor Brown and Mr. Nixon. The views expressed on the issues were critical of the Governor and favored Mr. Nixon, and at times involved personal attacks on individuals and groups in the gubernatorial campaign, and specifically on Governor Brown. The licensee responded that it had presented opposing viewpoints but upon examination there were two instances of broadcasts featuring Governor Brown (both of which were counterbalanced by appearances of Mr. Nixon) and two instances of broadcasts presenting viewpoints opposed to two of the issues raised by the above-noted broadcasts by the commentators. It did not appear that any of the other broadcasts cited by the station dealt with the issues raised as to the gubernatorial campaign.

Ruling. Since there were only two instances which involved the presentation of viewpoints concerning the gubernatorial campaign, opposed to the more than twenty programs of the commentators presenting their views on many different issues of the campaign for which no opportunity was afforded for the presentation of opposing viewpoints, there was not a fair opportunity for presentation of opposing viewpoints with respect to many of the issues discussed in the commentators' programs. The continuous, repetitive opportunity afforded for the expression of the commentators' viewpoints on the gubernatorial campaign, in contrast to the minimal opportunity afforded to opposing viewpoints, violated the right of the public to a fair presentation of views. Further, with respect to the personal attacks by the one commentator on individuals and groups involved in the gubernatorial campaign, the principle in Mapoles and Billings should have been followed. In the circumstances, the station should have sent a transcript of the pertinent continuity on the above programs to Governor Brown and should have offered a comparable opportunity for an appropriate spokesman to answer the broadcasts. (Times-Mirror, FCC 62–1130, 24 R.R. 404, Oct. 26, 1962; FCC 62–1109, 24 R.R. 407, Oct. 19, 1962.)

26. *Personal attacks on, and criticism of, candidates; partisan position on campaign issues—appropriate spokesman.* See facts above. The question was raised whether the candidate has the right to insist upon his own appearance, to respond to the broadcasts in question.

Ruling. Since a response by a candidate would, in turn, require that equal opportunities under Section 315 be afforded to the other legally-qualified candidates for the same office, the fairness doctrine requires only that the licensee afford the attacked candidate an opportunity to respond through an appropriate spokesman. The candidate should, of course, be given a substantial voice in the selection of the spokesman to respond to the attack or to the statement of support. (Times-Mirror Bctg. Co., FCC 62–1130, 24 R.R. 404, 406, Oct. 19, 1962, Oct. 26, 1962.)

27. *Personal attacks on, and criticism of, candidate; partisan position on campaign issues.* During the fall of an election year, a news commentator on a local affairs program made several critical and uncomplimentary references to the actions and public positions of various political and nonpartisan candidates for public office and of the California Democratic Clubs and demanded the resignation of an employee of the staff of the County Superintendent of Schools. In response to a request for time to respond by the local Democratic Central Committee, and after negotiations between the licensee and the complaining party, the licensee offered two five-minute segments of time on November 1 and 2, 1962, and instructed its commentator to refrain from expressing any point of view on partisan issues on November 5, or November 6, election eve and election day, respectively.

Ruling. On the facts of this case, the comments of the news commentator constituted personal attacks on candidates and others and involved the taking of a partisan position on issues involved in a race for political office. Therefore, under the ruling of the Times-Mirror case, the licensee was under an obligation to "send a transcript of the pertinent continuity in each such program to the appropriate candidates immediately and [to] offer a comparable opportunity for an appropriate spokesman to answer the broadcast." However, upon the basis of the showing, the licensee's offer of time, in response to the request, was not unreasonable under the fairness doctrine. (Letter to The McBride Industries, Inc., FCC 63–756, July 31, 1963.)

F. *Licensee editorializing*

28. *Freedom to editorialize.* The Editorializing Report and the 1960 Programming Statement, while stating that the licensee is not required to editorialize, make clear that he is free to do so, but that if he does, he must meet the requirements of the fairness doctrine.

The Fairness Doctrine

Jeffrey Murphy

Communication . 210.

THE "FAIRNESS DOCTRINE" APPLIED TO CIGARETTE ADVERTISING

FCC 67-641
June 2, 1967

FEDERAL COMMUNICATIONS COMMISSION
Washington 25, D.C.
June 2, 1967

Television Station WCBS-TV
51 West 52 Street
New York, New York

Gentlemen:

This letter constitutes the Commission's ruling upon the complaint of Mr. John F. Banzhaf, III, against Station WCBS-TV, New York, N.Y. Mr. Banzhaf, by letter dated January 5, 1967, filed a fairness doctrine complaint, asserting that WCBS-TV, after having aired numerous commercial advertisements for cigarette manufacturers, has not afforded him or some other responsible spokesman an opportunity "to present contrasting views on the issue of the benefits and advisability of smoking."

Mr. Banzhaf's letter cites as examples three particular commercials over WCBS-TV which present the point of view that smoking is "socially acceptable and desirable, manly, and a necessary part of a rich full life." Mr. Banzhaf, in his letter to you of December 1, 1966, requested free time be made available to "responsible groups" roughly approximate to that spent on the promotion of "the virtues and values of smoking."

Your responsive letter of December 30, 1966, cites programs which WCBS-TV has broadcast dealing with the effect of smoking on health, beginning in September 1962 and continuing to date. It cites six reports on this issue in its evening news programs since May 1966, five major reports by its Science Editor since September 1966 and five one minute messages, which advance the view that smoking is undesirable, broadcast without charge within the last few months for the American Cancer Society. The letter also refers to half hour and hour programs on smoking and health broadcast in 1962 and 1964. You take the position that the above programs have provided contrasting viewpoints on this issue by responsible authorities, and therefore, that it is unnecessary to consider whether the "fairness doctrine" may be applied to commercial announcements solely aimed at selling products. You state your view that it may not.

In Mr. Banzhaf's complaint to the Commission, he asserts that the programs cited by you as showing compliance with the "fairness doctrine" are insufficient to offset the effects of paid advertisements broadcast daily for a total of five to ten minutes each broadcast day. He also states that the very point of his letters is to establish the applicability of the doctrine to cigarette advertisements.

We hold that the fairness doctrine is applicable to such advertisements. We stress that our holding is limited to this product—cigarettes. Governmental and private reports (e.g., the 1964 Report of the Surgeon General's Committee) and Congressional action (e.g., the Federal Cigarette Labeling and Advertising Act of 1965) assert that normal use of this product can be a hazard to the health of millions of persons. The advertisements in question clearly promote the use of a particular cigarette as attractive and enjoyable. Indeed, they understandably have no other purpose. We believe that a station which presents such advertisements has the duty of informing its audience of the other side of this controversial issue of public importance—that however enjoyable, such smoking may be a hazard to the smoker's health.

We reject, however, Mr. Banzhaf's claim that the time to be afforded "roughly approximate" that devoted to the cigarette commercials. The fairness doctrine does not require "equal time" (see Ruling No. II C. 12, 29 F.R. 10416) and, equally important, a requirement of such "rough approximation" would, we think, be inconsistent with the Congressional direction in this field—the 1965 Cigarette Labeling and Advertising Act. The practical result of any roughly one-to-one correlation would probably be either the elimination or substantial curtailment of broadcast cigarette advertising. But in the 1965 Act Congress made clear that it did not favor such a "drastic" step, but rather wished to afford an opportunity to consider "the combined impact of voluntary limitations on advertising under the Cigarette Advertising Code, the extensive smoking education campaigns now underway, and the compulsory warning on the package . . . [on the problem of] adequately alert[ing] the public to the potential hazard from smoking" (Sen. Rept. No. 195, 89th Cong., 1st Sess., p. 5). At the conclusion of a three year period (to end July 1, 1969), and upon the basis of reports from the Federal Trade Commission and the Department of Health, Education, and Welfare (HEW) and other pertinent sources, the Congress would then decide what further remedial action, if any, is appropriate. In the meantime, Congress has promoted extensive smoking education campaigns by appropriating substantial sums for HEW in this area. See P.L. 89–156, Title II, Public Health Service, Chronic Diseases and Health of the Aged.

Our action here, therefore, must be tailored so as to carry out the above Congressional purpose. We believe that it does. It requires a station which carries cigarette commercials to provide a significant amount of time for the other viewpoint, thus implementing the "smoking education campaigns" referred to as a basis for Congressional action in the 1965 Act. See Cigarette Labeling and Advertising Act; remarks of Senator Warren Magnuson, floor manager in the Senate of the bill which became that Act, Cong. Rec. (Daily Edition) Jan. 16, 1967, p. S. 317, 319. But this requirement will not preclude or curtail presentation by stations of cigarette advertising which they choose to carry.

A station might, for example, reasonably determine that the above noted responsibility would be discharged by presenting each week, in addition to appropriate news reports or other programming dealing with the subject, a number of the public service announcements of the American Cancer Society or HEW in this field. We stress, however, that in this, as in other areas under the fairness doctrine, the type of programming and the amount and nature of time to be afforded is a matter for the good faith, reasonable judgment of the licensee, upon the particular facts of his situation. See Cullman Broadcasting Co., F.C.C. 63–849 (Sept. 18, 1963).

In this case, we note that WCBS-TV is aware of its responsibilities in this area, in light of the programming described in the third paragraph. While we have rejected Mr. Banzhaf's claim of "rough approximation of time," the question remains whether in the circumstances a sufficient amount of time is being allocated each week to cover the viewpoint of the health hazard posed by smoking. We note in this respect that, particularly in light of the recent American Cancer Society announcements, you appear to have a continuing program in this respect. The guidelines in the foregoing discussion are brought to your attention so that in connection with the above continuing program you may make the judgment whether sufficient time is being allocated each week in this area.

BY DIRECTION OF THE COMMISSION

Ben F. Waple
Secretary

6 EDITORIAL POLICY

Corinthian Broadcasting Corporation*
August 1, 1963

Many broadcasters have found it desirable to establish written guidelines to clarify for both their staffs and the public necessary procedures to be followed in editorializing. The policy statement of the Corinthian Broadcasting Corporation, licensee of stations KHOU-TV in Houston, KOTV in Tulsa, KXTV in Sacramento, WISH-TV in Indianapolis, and WANE-AM-TV in Fort Wayne is typical. It is made available through the courtesy of the Corinthian Broadcasting Corporation.

A free society is an informed society. The responsible expression of opinion as well as the accurate presentation of facts contributes to public understanding of vital issues.

It shall be the policy of Corinthian Stations to present editorial opinion on a regular basis. Such opinion shall be developed and presented in accordance with the following principles, which are discussed under the headings of:

    I.   Responsibility and organization
    II. Subject matter
    III. Method of presentation
    IV. Treatment of opposing views

I. Responsibility and organization

A. The responsibility for editorializing at a Corinthian station shall ultimately rest with the Vice President and General Manager of that station. He may delegate such elements of the editorial function as he deems necessary and appropriate.

B. To assist the manager in carrying out his editorial function, each Corinthian station will establish an editorial board of about five persons.

* Reprinted by permission of the Corinthian Broadcasting Corporation.

Normally, the editorial board will consist of the manager, program manager, the news director, the editorial writer and such other personnel as may be designated by the manager. The editorial board will meet regularly, normally at least once each week. A brief memorandum of the topics discussed at each meeting, as well as a copy of each editorial presented on the air, shall be kept in the station files for at least three years.

C. The editorial board shall assist the manager in carrying out the station's editorial responsibility in:

1. selecting topics;
2. determining the station's position on particular issues;
3. evaluating editorial performance and results.

D. No editorial shall be presented on the air unless it has been read in advance by at least one member of the editorial board who has not been substantially involved in its detailed preparation. Wherever possible, the General Manager shall read each editorial before it is presented on the air.

E. Care will be exercised in the preparation of all editorial copy. All necessary facts will be assembled, and they will be checked for accuracy before presentation. Where feasible, research will include talks with persons vitally involved in the issue which is the subject of an editorial. Where the issue is controversial, responsible persons with differing viewpoints should be contacted unless the various viewpoints are already available.

F. A clear distinction shall be made in editorials between facts and opinion. Reference to the opinions of others, whether quoted or paraphrased, shall be verified in advance of broadcast.

G. Everyone involved in the preparation, review, and presentation of an editorial shall be responsible for the maintenance of editorial standards.

II. Subject Matter

A. Editorials may be presented on any subject which, in the judgment of the station, is of significance or interest to the people served by the station. The only exception is that, for the present, editorials shall not endorse or oppose particular candidates for political office.

B. The choice of topics rests with local station management. Editorial attention may be focused on international, national, regional or local topics. Normally, only one subject shall be treated in each editorial.

C. An editorial may state a point of view on an issue, catalog relevant facts, or simply raise pertinent questions. Each contributes to public understanding. Where expression of a point of view is desirable, each particular station management has the authority to decide what that view shall be. The only limitation is that, where the proposed position on a matter of basic principle is known to be contrary to that of Corinthian ownership, the position will be discussed in advance by the General Manager with a higher Corporate official. In such cases, the station is always free not to editorialize on the matter or to editorialize without taking any position.

D. Highly controversial and sensitive subjects should be selected with mature judgment and presented with balance and good taste. Such subjects should not be avoided. Neither persons nor organizations shall be ridiculed, but critical comment based on fact is permissible. The activities of individuals will be discussed only when they relate to matters of public importance. Editorials shall focus on issues rather than on personalities.

E. In selecting subjects, the practical requirements of Section IV following (dealing with the presentation of opposing views) shall be taken into account. Thus, editorials on particular controversial subjects must be so timed as to leave an opportunity for a request to reply to be made and honored, except in the most extraordinary circumstances where this is impossible and the editorial is of such vital and overriding importance as to justify an exceptional departure from this rule.

III. Method of Presentation

A. Editorials are opinion, not hard news. They reflect the views of the station, not of a particular writer or presenter. Both of these facts should be made clear both aurally and visually when editorials are being presented on the air. Introductory and closing copy must state that the material presented is "editorial opinion and represents the views of the station." Visual and aural reference such as "KOTV Editorial Opinion" or "An Editorial Viewpoint by WISH-TV" should be used at least at the opening of the editorial and at its close. The visual identification may most easily be done by means of a placard on the flat behind the presenter of the editorial that is seen in both the opening and closing shots. It is not necessary that this identification be in constant view during the course of the editorial.

B. Editorials will be presented on the air by a person, designated by the station manager, who has the authority, sincerity and technical skill to present the station's editorial position appropriately to the public.

1. The presenter will not be identified by name on the air, except when the general manager is giving the editorial.
2. On-the-air newscasters or other on-the-air personalities shall not be used to present editorials.
3. Station managers occasionally may present editorials where the subject matter is of particular importance.
4. From time to time presenters may be changed so as to indicate to the viewing public that the editorials reflect station position rather than the views of any particular man.
5. No person shall be required to present an editorial on the air ex-

pressing a position with which he personally disagrees, but every effort should be made to use presenters who understand that a station opinion is not necessarily that of the presenter.

C. Normal editorial length shall not exceed two minutes, although different lengths are acceptable in accordance with the requirements of the subject matter.

D. Since the purpose of editorializing is to contribute to public understanding rather than to sell a specific point of view, a particular editorial will *not* normally be run more than three times or be broadcast over a period longer than 24 hours.

IV. Treatment of Opposing Views

A. A copy of each editorial shall be mailed on the day of broadcast to each person or group specifically named in the editorial, to representative persons or groups who are directly involved in matters discussed in an editorial, and to those who, according to information available, are thought to hold views opposite from those expressed by the station in the editorial.

B. The covering letter sending copies of editorials pursuant to "A," preceding, shall contain an offer of a reasonable opportunity for the presentation of contrasting views, if the request is made within five days after the date of broadcast of the editorial. Where more than one such request is received, the station reserves the right to designate the spokesman to present such views. The copy stating the opposing view shall be submitted to the station 24 hours in advance of presentation. It shall be edited only to the extent necessary to eliminate libelous, indecent or profane material. The presentation by spokesmen of an opposing view shall be made at times comparable to, although not necessarily the same as, the editorials and shall be clearly labeled at the beginning and end of the broadcast. An appropriate introduction might be as follows:

In accordance with its policy of encouraging broad discussion of public issues, KOTV is making (has made) its facilities available to (   ) who will speak (spoke) on behalf of some of those who disagree with the position on (   ) recently taken by this station.

7 | FARMERS UNION v. WDAY

Farmers Educational & Cooperative Union of America,
North Dakota Division, *v.* WDAY, Inc.
360 U.S. 525
June 29, 1959

> *Political broadcasting is an important aspect of broadcasting's jour-*
> *nalistic function. This 5-4 Supreme Court decision granted broad-*
> *cast stations immunity from defamation suits based on remarks*
> *made by political candidates over the air. The grant of immunity*
> *derives from the Congressional prohibition regarding licensee cen-*
> *sorship of political talks under Section 315 of the Communications*
> *Act.*
>
> > *Justice Frankfurter's dissent, omitted here, relies heavily on the*
> > *contention of a lack of sufficient reason to conclude that Congress*
> > *intended such immunity. Hence the States retain "the power to de-*
> > *termine the nature and extent of the liability, if any, of broad-*
> > *casters to third persons." (360 U.S. 525, 547)*

MR. JUSTICE BLACK delivered the opinion of the Court.

We must decide whether § 315 of the Federal Communications
Act of 1934 bars a broadcasting station from removing defamatory statements contained in speeches broadcast by legally qualified candidates for
public office, and if so, whether that section grants the station a federal immunity from liability for libelous statements so broadcast. Section 315
reads:

(a) If any licensee shall permit any person who is a legally qualified
candidate for any public office to use a broadcasting station, he shall afford
equal opportunities to all other such candidates for that office in the use of such
broadcasting station: *Provided,* That such licensee shall have no power of censorship over the material broadcast under the provisions of this section. No obligation is imposed upon any licensee to allow the use of its station by any such
candidate.[1]

[1] 48 Stat. 1088, as amended, 47 U. S. C. § 315 (a). See also, § 18 of the Radio Act
of 1927, 44 Stat. 1170.

This suit for libel arose as a result of a speech made over the radio and television facilities of respondent, WDAY, Inc., by A. C. Townley—a legally qualified candidate in the 1956 United States senatorial race in North Dakota. Because it felt compelled to do so by the requirements of § 315, WDAY permitted Townley to broadcast his speech, uncensored in any respect, as a reply to previous speeches made over WDAY by two other senatorial candidates. Townley's speech, in substance, accused his opponents, together with petitioner, Farmers Educational and Cooperative Union of America, of conspiring to "establish a Communist Farmers Union Soviet right here in North Dakota." Farmers Union then sued Townley and WDAY for libel in a North Dakota State District Court. That court dismissed the complaint against WDAY on the ground that § 315 rendered the station immune from liability for the defamation alleged. The Supreme Court of North Dakota affirmed, stating: "Section 315 imposes a mandatory duty upon broadcasting stations to permit all candidates for the same office to use their facilities if they have permitted one candidate to use them. Since power of censorship of political broadcasts is prohibited it must follow as a corollary that the mandate prohibiting censorship includes the privilege of immunity from liability for defamatory statements made by the speakers." For this reason it held that the state libel laws could not apply to WDAY. 89 N. W. 2d 102, 110. We granted certiorari because the questions decided are important to the administration of the Federal Communications Act. 358 U. S. 810.

I

Petitioner argues that § 315's prohibition against censorship leaves broadcasters free to delete libelous material from candidates' speeches, and that therefore no federal immunity is granted a broadcasting station by that section. The term censorship, however, as commonly understood, connotes *any* examination of thought or expression in order to prevent publication of "objectionable" material. We find no clear expression of legislative intent, nor any other convincing reason to indicate Congress meant to give "censorship" a narrower meaning in § 315. In arriving at this view, we note that petitioner's interpretation has not generally been favored in previous considerations of the section. Although the first, and for years the only judicial decision dealing with the censorship provision did hold that a station may remove defamatory statements from political broadcasts,[2] subsequent judicial interpretations of § 315 have with considerable

---

[2] *Sorensen* v. *Wood,* 123 Neb. 348, 243 N. W. 82. Following this decision the case was remanded for a new trial. Appeal from a judgment for plaintiff was dismissed by the Supreme Court of Nebraska. Appeal to this Court was dismissed *sub nom. KFAB Broadcasting Co.* v. *Sorensen,* 290 U. S. 599, because, as the records of this Court disclose, the Supreme Court of Nebraska's holding had been based on adequate state grounds, namely, that the case had become moot through settlement.

uniformity recognized that an individual licensee has no such power.[3] And while for some years the Federal Communications Commission's views on this matter were not clearly articulated,[4] since 1948 it has continuously held that licensees cannot remove allegedly libelous matter from speeches by candidates.[5] Similarly, the legislative history of the measure both prior to its first enactment in 1927, and subsequently, shows a deep hostility to censorship either by the Commission or by a licensee.[6]

More important, it is obvious that permitting a broadcasting station to censor allegedly libelous remarks would undermine the basic purpose for which § 315 was passed—full and unrestricted discussion of political issues by legally qualified candidates. That section dates back to, and was adopted verbatim from, the Radio Act of 1927. In that Act, Congress provided for the first time a comprehensive federal plan for regulating the new and expanding art of radio broadcasting. Recognizing radio's potential importance as a medium of communication of political ideas, Congress sought to foster its broadest possible utilization by encouraging broadcasting stations to make their facilities available to candidates for office with-

---

[3] See *Lamb* v. *Sutton,* 164 F. Supp. 928; *Yates* v. *Associated Broadcasters, Inc.,* 7 Pike and Fischer Radio Reg. 2088; *Felix* v. *Westinghouse Radio Stations, Inc.,* 89 F. Supp. 740, rev'd on other grounds, 186 F. 2d 1; *Charles Parker Co.* v. *Silver City Crystal Co.,* 142 Conn. 605, 116 A. 2d 440; *Josephson* v. *Knickerbocker Broadcasting Co.,* 179 Misc. 787, 38 N. Y. S. 2d 985. But see *Daniell* v. *Voice of New Hampshire, Inc.,* 10 Pike and Fischer Radio Reg. 2045; *Houston Post Co.* v. *United States,* 79 F. Supp. 199.

[4] See *In re Bellingham Broadcasting Co.,* 8 F. C. C. 159, 172.

[5] *In re Port Huron Broadcasting Co.,* 12 F. C. C. 1069; *In re WDSU Broadcasting Corp.,* 7 Pike and Fischer Radio Reg. 769; Public Notice (FCC 54–1155), Use of Broadcast Facilities by Candidates For Public Office, 19 Fed. Reg. 5948, 5951; Public Notice (FCC 58–936), Use of Broadcast Facilities by Candidates For Public Office, 23 Fed. Reg. 7817, 7820–7821.

[6] See S. Rep. No. 1567, 80th Cong., 2d Sess. 13–14 (1948), where, discussing S. 1333, the Committee Report stated:

"The flat prohibition against the licensee of any station exercising any censorship authority over any political or public question discussion is retained and emphasized. This means that the Commission cannot itself or by rule or regulation require the licensee to censor, alter, or in any manner affect or control the subject matter of any such broadcast and the licensee may not in his own discretion exercise any such censorship authority. . . .

"[S]ection 326 of the present act, which deals with the question of censorship of radio communications by the Commission . . . makes clear that the Commission has absolutely no power of censorship over radio communications and that it cannot impose any regulation or condition which would interfere with the right of free speech by radio."

And see, *e. g.,* H. R. Rep. No. 404, 69th Cong., 1st Sess. 17–18 (minority views); S. Rep. No. 772, 69th Cong., 1st Sess. 4; 67 Cong. Rec. 5480, 5484, 12356; 78 Cong. Rec. 10991–10992; Hearings before Senate Committee on Interstate Commerce on S. 1 and S. 1754, 69th Cong., 1st Sess., pt. 2, 121, 125–134; Hearings before Senate Committee on Interstate Commerce on H. R. 7716, 72d Cong., 2d Sess., pt. 2, 9–13; Hearings before Senate Committee on Interstate Commerce on S. 814, 78th Cong., 1st Sess. 59–68, 943–945.

out discrimination, and by insuring that these candidates when broadcasting were not to be hampered by censorship of the issues they could discuss. Thus, expressly applying this country's tradition of free expression to the field of radio broadcasting, Congress has from the first emphatically forbidden the Commission to exercise any power of censorship over radio communication.[7] It is in line with this same tradition that the individual licensee has consistently been denied "power of censorship" in the vital area of political broadcasts.

The decision a broadcasting station would have to make in censoring libelous discussion by a candidate is far from easy. Whether a statement is defamatory is rarely clear. Whether such a statement is actionably libelous is an even more complex question, involving as it does, consideration of various legal defenses such as "truth" and the privilege of fair comment. Such issues have always troubled courts. Yet, under petitioner's view of the statute they would have to be resolved by an individual licensee during the stress of a political campaign, often, necessarily, without adequate consideration or basis for decision. Quite possibly, if a station were held responsible for the broadcast of libelous material, all remarks even faintly objectionable would be excluded out of an excess of caution. Moreover, if any censorship were permissible, a station so inclined could intentionally inhibit a candidate's legitimate presentation under the guise of lawful censorship of libelous matter. Because of the time limitation inherent in a political campaign, erroneous decisions by a station could not be corrected by the courts promptly enough to permit the candidate to bring improperly excluded matter before the public. It follows from all this that allowing censorship, even of the attenuated type advocated here, would almost inevitably force a candidate to avoid controversial issues during political debates over radio and television, and hence restrict the coverage of consideration relevant to intelligent political decision. We cannot believe, and we certainly are unwilling to assume, that Congress intended any such result.

II

Petitioner alternatively argues that § 315 does not grant a station immunity from liability for defamatory statements made during a political broadcast even though the section prohibits the station from censoring allegedly libelous matter. Again, we cannot agree. For under this interpretation, unless a licensee refuses to permit any candidate to talk at all, the section would sanction the unconscionable result of permitting civil and perhaps criminal liability to be imposed for the very conduct the statute demands of the licensee. Accordingly, judicial interpretations reaching the

[7] § 29 of the Radio Act of 1927, 44 Stat. 1172; § 326 of the Communications Act of 1934, 48 Stat. 1091, as amended, 47 U. S. C. § 326.

issue have found an immunity implicit in the section.[8] And in all those cases concluding that a licensee had no immunity, § 315 had been construed— improperly as we hold—to permit a station to censor potentially actionable material.[9] In no case has a court even implied that the licensee would not be rendered immune were it denied the power to censor libelous material.

Petitioner contends, however, that the legislative history of § 315 shows that Congress did not intend to grant an immunity. Some of the history supports such an inference. As it reached the Senate, the provision which became § 18 of the Radio Act of 1927 provided in part that if a station permitted one candidate to use its facilities, it should "be deemed a common carrier in interstate commerce . . ." and could not discriminate against other political candidates or censor material broadcast by them.[10] In the Senate, Senator Dill—the bill's floor manager—introduced an amendment to this provision which, among other things, specifically granted a station immunity from civil and criminal liability for "any uncensored utterances thus broadcast."[11] The amendment was adopted by the Senate, but its provision expressly granting immunity was removed by the Conference Committee without any explanation.[12] Section 18 was incorporated into the Communications Act of 1934 with no explanatory discussion. Subsequently, a great deal of pressure built up for legislation to remove all possible doubt as to broadcasters' liability for libel either by granting them a power to censor libelous statements or by providing an express legislative immunity. Many legislative proposals were made to accomplish these purposes,[13] but no legislation providing either was ever enacted. Thus, whatever adverse inference may be drawn from the failure of Congress to legislate an express immunity is offset by its refusal to permit stations to avoid liability by censoring broadcasts. And more than balancing any adverse inferences drawn from congressional failure to legislate an express immunity is the fact that the Federal Communications Commission—the body entrusted with administering the provisions of the Act—has long interpreted

---

8 *Lamb* v. *Sutton; Yates* v. *Associated Broadcasters, Inc.; Josephson* v. *Knickerbocker Broadcasting Co., supra*, note 3. Cf. *Felix* v. *Westinghouse Radio Stations, Inc.; Charles Parker Co.* v. *Silver City Crystal Co., supra*, note 3.

9 *Houston Post Co.* v. *United States, supra*, note 3; *Sorenson* v. *Wood, supra*, note 2; *Daniell* v. *Voice of New Hampshire, Inc., supra*, note 3.

10 H. R. 9971, 69th Cong., 1st Sess., as reported to the full Senate, May 6, 1926, p. 50, § 4.

11 67 Cong. Rec. 12501.

12 H. R. Rep. No. 1886, 69th Cong., 2d Sess. 10, 18.

13 See, *e. g.*, H. R. 9230, 74th Cong., 1st Sess.; S. 814, 78th Cong., 1st Sess., §§ 7, 9, 10, 11; S. 1333, 80th Cong., 1st Sess., § 15; 98 Cong. Rec. 7401. See also Hearings before the Senate Committee on Interstate Commerce on H. R. 7716, 72d Cong., 2d Sess., pt. 2, 9–11; Hearings before Senate Committee on Interstate Commerce on S. 2910, 73d Cong., 2d Sess. 63–67; Hearings before Senate Committee on Interstate Commerce on S. 814, 78th Cong., 1st Sess. 59–68, 162–163, 362–381, 943–945; Hearings before Select Committee of the House to Investigate the FCC, pursuant to H. Res. No. 691, 80th Cong., 2d Sess. 1–109.

§ 315 as granting stations an immunity.[14] Not only has this interpretation been adhered to despite many subsequent legislative proposals to modify § 315, but with full knowledge of the Commission's interpretation Congress has since made significant additions to that section without amending it to depart from the Commission's view.[15] In light of this contradictory legislative background we do not feel compelled to reach a result which seems so in conflict with traditional concepts of fairness.

Petitioner nevertheless urges that broadcasters do not need a specific immunity to protect themselves from liability for defamation since they may either insure against any loss, or in the alternative, deny all political candidates use of station facilities.[16] We have no means of knowing to what extent insurance is available to broadcasting stations, or what it would cost them. Moreover, since § 315 expressly prohibits stations from charging political candidates higher rates than they charge for comparable time used for other purposes, any cost of insurance would probably have to be absorbed by the stations themselves. Petitioner's reliance on the stations' freedom from obligation "to allow use of its station by any such candidate," seems equally misplaced. While denying all candidates use of stations would protect broadcasters from liability, it would also effectively withdraw political discussion from the air. Instead the thrust of § 315 is to facilitate

---

[14] See note 5, *supra.* In *Port Huron* only two of the five Commissioners participating in the decision expressly concluded that § 315 barred state prosecutions for libel. Two of the others expressed no view on the subject. And one dissented. The Commission's 1948 report to Congress stated, however, that the Commission had interpreted § 315 to grant a federal immunity. 14 F. C. C. Ann. Rep. 28 (1948). And in *WDSU*, released November 26, 1951, a majority of the Commission affirmed the Commission's *Port Huron* decision. 7 Pike and Fischer Radio Reg. 769. See also 24 F. C. C. Ann. Rep. 123 (1958); *Lamb* v. *Sutton, supra*, note 3, at 932–933; *Daniell* v. *Voice of New Hampshire, Inc., supra*, note 3, at 2047; *Charles Parker Co.* v. *Silver City Crystal Co., supra*, note 3, 142 Conn., at 619, 116 A. 2d, at 446.

[15] The Commission's position with respect to § 315 was not only reported to Congress in an Annual Report of the Commission, 14 F. C. C. Ann. Rep. 28 (1948), but it was made the subject of a special investigation by a Select Committee of the House, expressly constituted for that purpose. See H. R. Rep. No. 2461, 80th Cong., 2d Sess. See also *In re WDSU Broadcasting Corp., supra*, note 5, at 772–773. Compare H. R. Rep. No. 2426, 82d Cong., 2d Sess. 20–21. For examples of legislative proposals to modify § 315 see, *e. g.*, S. 2539, 82d Cong., 2d Sess.; H. R. 4814, 84th Cong., 1st Sess.

[16] A dissent here suggests that since WDAY's broadcast was required by federal law, there is a "strong likelihood" that the North Dakota courts might hold that the broadcast was not tortious under state law, or if tortious, was privileged. The North Dakota District Court, however, struck down a state statute which would have granted WDAY an immunity as in violation of a state constitutional provision to "every man" a court remedy for any injury done his "person or reputation." In this situation we do not think that the record justifies the inference that WDAY could have obtained an immunity by calling it a privilege. But whatever North Dakota might hold, the question for us is whether Congress intended to subject a federal licensee to possible liability under the law of some or all of the 49 States for broadcasting in a way required by federal law.

political debate over radio and television. Recognizing this, the Communications Commission considers the carrying of political broadcasts a public service criterion to be considered both in license renewal proceedings, and in comparative contests for a radio or television construction permit.[17] Certainly Congress knew the obvious—that if a licensee could protect himself from liability in no other way but by refusing to broadcast candidates' speeches, the necessary effect would be to hamper the congressional plan to develop broadcasting as a political outlet, rather than to foster it.[18]

We are aware that causes of action for libel are widely recognized throughout the States. But we have not hesitated to abrogate state law where satisfied that its enforcement would stand "as an obstacle to the accomplishment and execution of the full purposes and objectives of Congress."[19] Here, petitioner is asking us to attribute to § 315 a meaning which would either frustrate the underlying purposes for which it was enacted, or alternatively impose unreasonable burdens on the parties governed by that legislation. In the absence of clear expression by Congress we will not assume that it desired such a result. Agreeing with the state courts of North Dakota that § 315 grants a licensee an immunity from liability for libelous material it broadcasts, we merely read § 315 in accordance with what we believe to be its underlying purpose.

Affirmed.

---

17 *In re City of Jacksonville,* 12 Pike and Fischer Radio Reg. 113, 125–126, 180 i-j; *In re Loyola University,* 12 Pike and Fischer Radio Reg. 1017, 1099. See also *In re Homer P. Rainey,* 11 F. C. C. 898. Cf. F. C. C. Report, *In re* Editorializing by Broadcast Licensees, 1 Pike and Fischer Radio Reg., pt. 3, 91:201.

18 See, *e. g.,* statement of Senator Fess, 67 Cong. Rec. 12356.

19 *Bethlehem Steel Co.* v. *New York Labor Board,* 330 U. S. 767, 773; *Hill* v. *Florida,* 325 U. S. 538, 542. See also *San Diego Building Trades Council* v. *Garmon,* 359 U. S. 236; *California* v. *Taylor,* 353 U. S. 553.

8 | THE GREAT DEBATES LAW

Public Law 86-677, 86th Congress
August 24, 1960

This Senate Joint Resolution, which provided the legal basis for the Kennedy-Nixon "Great Debates" of 1960, was passed only after the Democratic and Republican National Conventions were held and the presidential and vice presidential candidates chosen. Many broadcasters hailed the bill's passage as a step toward total elimination of the burdensome equal-time requirements of Section 315 of the Communications Act. It seems unlikely, however, that future suspensions of Section 315 will occur unless neither candidate is an incumbent for the office he seeks.

Resolved by the Senate and House of Representatives of the United States of America in Congress assembled, That that part of section 315(a) of the Communications Act of 1934, as amended, which requires any licensee of a broadcast station who permits any person who is a legally qualified candidate for any public office to use a broadcasting station to afford equal opportunities to all other such candidates for that office in the use of such broadcasting station, is suspended for the period of the 1960 presidential and vice presidential campaigns with respect to nominees for the offices of President and Vice President of the United States. Nothing in the foregoing shall be construed as relieving broadcasters from the obligation imposed upon them under this Act to operate in the public interest.

(2) The Federal Communications Commission shall make a report to the Congress, not later than March 1, 1961, with respect to the effect of the provisions of this joint resolution and any recommendations the Commission may have for amendments to the Communications Act of 1934 as a result of experience under the provisions of this joint resolution.

9 THE SECTION 315 PRIMER

Use of Broadcast Facilities by Candidates for Public Office
31 Fed. Reg. 6660
Adopted April 27, 1966; Printed May 4, 1966

This FCC document provides answers to more than one hundred political broadcasting questions, based on the Commission's interpretations of its own rules and regulations as well as Section 315 of the Communications Act. The complexities inherent in the administration of Section 315 are made apparent, and some particularly fine lines of distinction are drawn.

This Public Notice is a compilation of the Commission's interpretive rulings under section 315 of the Communications Act of 1934, as amended, and the Commission's rules implementing that section of the Act and brings up-to-date and supersedes all prior Public Notices issued by the Commission entitled "Use of Broadcast Facilities by Candidates for Public Office." The Commission has reviewed both its Public Notice (Oct. 9, 1962; FCC 62–1019) and its Supplement thereto (July 31, 1964; FCC 64–733) which contained section 315, as amended, the Commission's rules, additional rulings, and recommended complaint procedures. Significant rulings made subsequent to the 1964 Supplement have been added, and editorial and other revisions have been made with respect to some of the interpretations previously published. Where appropriate, cumulative rulings have been cited. Included herein are the determinations of the Commission with respect to problems which have been presented to it and which appear likely[1] to be involved in future campaigns. While the information contained herein does not purport to be a discussion of every problem that may arise

---

[1] A few of the questions taken up within have been presented to the Commission informally—that is, through telephone conversations or conferences with station representatives. They are set out in this Public Notice because of the likelihood of their recurrence and the fact that no extended Commission discussion is necessary to dispose of them; the answer in each case is clear from the language of section 315.

in the political broadcast field, experience has shown that these documents have been of assistance to candidates and broadcasters in understanding their rights and obligations under section 315.

The purpose of this Notice is to apprise licensees, candidates, and other interested persons of their respective responsibilities and rights under section 315, and the Commission's rules, when situations similar to those discussed herein are encountered. In this way, resort to the Commission may be obviated in many instances and time—which is of great importance in political campaigns—will be saved. We do not mean to preclude inquiry to the Commission when there is a genuine doubt as to licensee obligations and responsibilities to the public interest under section 315. Procedures for filing complaints are set out below. But it is believed that the following document will, in many instances, remove the need for inquiries, and that licensees will be able to take the necessary prompt action in accordance with the interpretations and positions set forth below.

This discussion relates solely to obligations of broadcast licensees towards candidates for public office under section 315 of the Act. It is not intended to include the question of the treatment by broadcast licensees of political or other controversial programs not governed by the "equal opportunities" provisions of that section. As to the responsibilities of broadcast licensees with respect to controversial issues of public importance included in political broadcasts, licensees are referred to the Commission's "fairness doctrine," and the current Public Notice entitled "Applicability of the Fairness Doctrine in the Handling of Controversial Issues of Public Importance."

We have continued the question-and-answer format as an appropriate means of delineating the section 315 problems. Wherever possible, reference to Commission's decisions or rulings are made so that the researcher may, if he desires, review the complete text of the Commission's ruling. Copies of rulings may be found in a "Political Broadcast" folder kept in the Commission's Reference Room. Citations in "R.R." refer to Pike and Fischer, Radio Regulations. . . .

Recommended complaint procedures

Complaints relating to 315 matters are given priority consideration by the Commission. Compliance with the following recommended procedures will further greatly assist in the orderly and expeditious disposition of such compliants. However, we do not mean, of course, to preclude in any way inquiry to the Commission when there is a genuine question as to licensee rights and obligations under section 315. We set out these recommended procedures in order to expedite and permit timely consideration of complaints in this important area. Failure to follow these procedures may result in unnecessary delays in resolution of section 315 complaints.

First, barring unusual circumstances, a complaint should not be made to the Commission until the licensee has denied the candidate's request for time after opportunity for passing on the essential claims raised by the candidate. Further, it has been the Commission's consistent policy to encourage negotiations between licensees and candidates seeking broadcast time or having questions under section 315, looking toward a disposition of the request or questions in a manner which is mutually agreeable to all parties. A complaint relating to a section 315 matter thus should be filed with the Commission after an effort has been made in good faith by the parties concerned to resolve the questions at issue. In this way, resort to the Commission might be obviated in many instances and time—which is of great importance in political campaigns—might be saved.

Where a complaint is filed with the Commission, (i) the complainant should simultaneously send a copy to the licensee, (ii) the licensee should respond, as promptly as possible, and not await Commission inquiry regarding the complaint, and (iii) the complainant and licensee should furnish each other with copies of all correspondence sent to the Commission.

A complaint filed with the Commission should be in written form and should contain: (i) The name and address of the complainant, (ii) the call letters and location (city and State) of the station against whom the complaint is made, and (iii) a detailed statement of the factual basis of the complaint which shall include, but not necessarily be limited to: the public office involved, the date and nature of the election to be held, whether the complainant and his opponent(s) are legally qualified candidates for public office, the date(s) of prior appearances by opponents if any, the time of request for equal opportunities submitted to the licensee, and the licensee's stated reasons for refusing to satisfy the complaint.

If at any time the licensee satisfies the complaint, the licensee should so notify the Commission, setting forth when and how the complaint has been satisfied and furnish a copy of such notification to complainant.

I. The statute

Section 315 of the Communications Act of 1934, as amended, provides as follows:

SEC. 315. (a) If any licensee shall permit any person who is a legally qualified candidate for any public office to use a broadcasting station, he shall afford equal opportunities to all other such candidates for that office in the use of such broadcasting stations: *Provided,* That such licensee shall have no power of censorship over the material broadcast under the provisions of this section. No obligation is hereby imposed upon any licensee to allow the use of its station by any such candidate. Appearance by a legally qualified candidate on any—

(1) Bona fide newscast,

(2) Bona fide news interview,

(3) Bona fide news documentary (if the appearance of the candidate is incidental to the presentation of the subject or subjects covered by the news documentary), or

(4) On-the-spot coverage of bona fide news events (including but not limited to political conventions and activities incidental thereto), shall not be deemed to be use of a broadcasting station within the meaning of this subsection. Nothing in the foregoing sentence shall be construed as relieving broadcasters, in connection with the presentation of newscasts, news interviews, news documentaries, and on-the-spot coverage of news events, from the obligation imposed upon them under this Act to operate in the public interest and to afford reasonable opportunity for the discussion of conflicting views on issues of public importance.

(b) The charges made for the use of any broadcasting station for any of the purposes set forth in this section shall not exceed the charges made for comparable use of such station for other purposes.

(c) The Commission shall prescribe appropriate rules and regulations to carry out the provisions of this section.

II. The Commission's rules and regulations with respect to political broadcasts

The Commission's rules and regulations with respect to political broadcasts coming within section 315 of the Communications Act are set forth in §§ 73.120 (AM), 73.290 (FM), 73.590 (noncommercial Educational FM), and 73.657 (TV), respectively. These provisions are identical (except for elimination of any discussion of charges in § 73.590 relating to noncommercial educational FM stations) and read as follows:

Broadcasts by candidates for public office—(a) *Definitions:* A "legally qualified candidate" means any person who has publicly announced that he is a candidate for nomination by a convention of a political party or for nomination or election in a primary, special, or general election, municipal, county, State or national, and who meets the qualifications prescribed by the applicable laws to hold the office for which he is a candidate, so that he may be voted for by the electorate directly or by means of delegates or electors, and who:

(1) Has qualified for a place on the ballot or

(2) Is eligible under the applicable law to be voted for by sticker, by writing in his name on the ballot, or other method, and (i) has been duly nominated by a political party which is commonly known and regarded as such, or (ii) makes a substantial showing that he is a bona fide candidate for nomination or office, as the case may be.

(b) *General requirements.* No station licensee is required to permit the use of its facilities by any legally qualified candidate for public office, but if any licensee shall permit any such candidate to use its facilities, it shall afford equal opportunities to all such other candidates for that office to use such facilities: *Provided,* That such licensee shall have no power of censorship over the material broadcast by any such candidate.

(c) *Rates and practices.*

(1) The rates, if any, charged all such candidates for the same office shall be uniform and shall not be rebated by any means direct or indirect. A candidate shall, in each case, be charged no more than the rate the station would charge if the candidate were a commercial advertiser whose advertising was directed to promoting its business within the same area as that encompassed by the particular office for which such person is a candidate. All discount privileges otherwise offered by a station to commercial advertisers shall be available upon equal terms to all candidates for public office.

(2) In making time available to candidates for public office no licensee shall make any discrimination between candidates in charges, practices, regulations, facilities, or services for or in connection with the service rendered pursuant to this part, or make or give any preference to any candidate for public office or subject any such candidate to any prejudice or disadvantage; nor shall any licensee make any contract or other agreement which shall have the effect of permitting any legally qualified candidate for any public office to broadcast to the exclusion of other legally qualified candidates for the same public office.

(d) *Records; inspection.* Every licensee shall keep and permit public inspection of a complete record of all requests for broadcast time made by or on behalf of candidates for public office, together with an appropriate notation showing the disposition made by the licensee of such requests, and the charges made, if any, if request is granted. Such records shall be retained for a period of 2 years.

NOTE: See § 1.526 of this chapter.

(e) *Time of request.* A request for equal opportunities must be submitted to the licensee within 1 week of the day on which the prior use occurred.

(f) *Burden of proof.* A candidate requesting such equal opportunities of the licensee, or complaining of noncompliance to the Commission shall have the burden of proving that he and his opponent are legally qualified candidates for the same public office.

In addition, the attention of the licensees is directed to the following provisions of §§ 73.119, 73,289, and 73.654, relating to sponsorship identification which provide in pertinent part:

(a) When a television broadcast station transmits any matter for which money, services, or other valuable consideration is either directly or indirectly paid or promised to, or charged or received by, such station, the station shall broadcast an announcement that such matter is sponsored, paid for, or furnished, either in whole or in part, and by whom or on whose behalf such consideration was supplied: *Provided, however,* That "service or other valuable consideration" shall not include any service or property furnished without charge or at a nominal charge for use on, or in connection with, a broadcast unless it is so furnished in consideration for an identification in a broadcast of any person, product, service, trademark, or brand name beyond an identification which is reasonably related to the use of such service or property on the broadcast.

(b) The licensee of each television broadcast station shall exercise reasonable diligence to obtain from its employees, and from other persons with whom it deals directly in connection with any program matter for broadcast, information to enable such licensee to make the announcement required by this section.

(c) In any case where a report (concerning the providing or accepting of valuable consideration by any person for inclusion of any matter in a program intended for broadcasting) has been made to a television broadcast station, as required by section 508 of the Communications Act of 1934, as amended, of circumstances which would have required an announcement under this section had the consideration been received by such television broadcast station, an appropriate announcement shall be made by such station.

(d) In the case of any political program or any program involving the discussion of public controversial issues for which any films, records, transcriptions, talent, scripts, or other material or services of any kind are furnished, either directly or indirectly, to a station as an inducement to the broadcasting of such program, an announcement shall be made both at the beginning and conclusion of such program on which such material or services are used that such films, records, transcriptions, talent, scripts, or other material or services have been furnished to such station in connection with the broadcasting of such program: *Provided, however,* That only one such announcement need be made in the case of any such program of 5 minutes' duration or less, which announcement may be made either at the beginning or conclusion of the program. . .

(f) The announcement required by this section shall fully and fairly disclose the true identity of the person or persons by whom or in whose behalf such payment is made or promised, or from whom or in whose behalf such services or other valuable consideration is received, or by whom the material or services referred to in paragraph (d) of this section are furnished. Where an agent or other person contracts or otherwise makes arrangements with a station on behalf of another, and such fact is known to the station, the announcement shall disclose the identity of the person or persons in whose behalf such agent is acting instead of the name of such agent.

(g) In the case of any program, other than a program advertising commercial products or services, which is sponsored, paid for, or furnished, either in whole or in part, or for which material or services referred to in paragraph (d) of this section are furnished, by a corporation, committee, association, or other unincorporated group, the announcement required by this section shall disclose the name of such corporation, committee, association, or other unincorporated group. In each such case the station shall require that a list of the chief executive officers or members of the executive committee or of the board of directors of the corporation, committee, association, or other unincorporated group shall be made available for public inspection at the studios or general offices of one of the television broadcast stations carrying the program in each community in which the program is broadcast. . . .

(i) Commission interpretations in connection with the foregoing rules may be found in the Commission's Public Notice entitled "Applicability of Sponsorship Identification Rules" (FCC 63–409; 28 F.R. 4732, May 10, 1963) and such supplements thereto as are issued from time to time.

(Sec. 317, 4 Stat. 1089, as amended; 47 U.S.C. 317)

III. "Uses," in general

In general, any use of broadcast facilities by a legally qualified candidate for public office imposes an obligation on licensees to afford "equal opportunities" to all other such candidates for the same office.

Section 315 of the Act was amended by the Congress in 1959 to provide that appearances by legally qualified candidates on specified news-type programs are deemed not to be a "use" of broadcast facilities within the meaning of that section. In determining whether a particular program is within the scope of one of these specified news-type programs, the basic question is whether the program meets the standard of "bona fides." To establish whether such a program is in fact a "bona fide" program, the following considerations, among others, may be pertinent: (1) The format, nature and content of the programs; (2) whether the format, nature and content of the program has changed since its inception and, if so, in what respects; (3) who initiates the programs; (4) who produces and controls the program; (5) when the program was initiated; (6) is the program regularly scheduled; and (7) if the program is regularly scheduled, specify the time and day of the week when it is broadcast. Questions have also been presented by the appearances on news-type broadcast programs of station employees who are also legally qualified candidates. In such cases, in addition to the above, the following considerations, among others, may be pertinent to a determination of the applicablility of section 315: (1) What is the dominant function of the employee at the station?; (2) what is the content of the program and who prepares the program?; and (3) to what extent is the employee personally identified on the program? In the rulings set forth below, wherein the Commission held that the "equal opportunities" provision was applicable, it should be assumed that the news-type exemptions contained in the 1959 amendments were not involved.

A. Types of uses

1. Q. Does section 315 apply to one speaking for or on behalf of the candidate, as contrasted with the candidate himself?

A. No. The section applies only to legally qualified candidates. Candidate A has no legal right under section 315 to demand time where B, not a candidate, has spoken against A or in behalf of another candidate. (Felix v. Westinghouse Radio Stations, 186 F. 2d 1 (3d Cir. 1950), cert. den. 341 U.S. 909.)

2. Q. Does section 315 confer rights on a political party as such?

A. No. It applies in favor of legally qualified candidates for public office, and is not concerned with the rights of political parties, as such. (Letter to National Laugh Party, May 8, 1957; see also In re WPRO–TV, Letter of Oct. 20, 1964.)

3. Q. Does section 315 require stations to afford "equal opportunities" in the use of their facilities in support of or in opposition to a public question to be voted on in an election?

A. No. Section 315 has no application to the discussion of political issues, as such, but is concerned with the use of broadcast stations by legally qualified candidates for public office. In the 1959 amendment of section 315, relating to certain news-type programs, Congress stated specifically that its action was not to be construed ". . . as relieving broadcasters, in connection with the presentation of newscasts, news interviews, news documentaries, and on-the-spot coverage of news events, from the obligation imposed upon them under this Act to operate in the public interest and to afford reasonable opportunity for the discussion of conflicting views on issues of public importance." The Commission has considered this statement to be an affirmation of its "fairness doctrine," as enunciated in its Report on Editorializing by Broadcast Licensees.

B. What constitutes a "use" of broadcast facilities entitling opposing candidates to "equal opportunities"?

1. Q. If a legally qualified candidate secures air time but does not discuss matters directly related to his candidacy, is this a use of facilities under section 315?

A. Yes. Section 315 does not distinguish between the uses of broadcast time by a candidate, and the licensee is not authorized to pass on requests for time by opposing candidates on the basis of the licensee's evaluation of whether the original use was or was not in aid of a candidacy. (Letter to WMCA, Inc., May 15, 1952, 7 R.R. 1132.)

2. Q. Must a broadcaster give equal time to a candidate whose opponent has broadcast in some other capacity than as a candidate?

A. Yes. For example, a weekly report of a Congressman to his constituents via radio or television is a broadcast by a legally qualified candidate for public office as soon as he becomes a candidate for reelection, and his opponent must be given "equal opportunities" for time on the air. Any "use" of a station by a candidate, in whatever capacity, entitles his opponent to "equal opportunities." (Letter to Station KNGS, May 15, 1952, 7 R.R. 1130; see Q. and A. III.C.1, for a joint Congressional Report; see also letter to Senator Joseph S. Clark, Jan. 31, 1962; and for a Judge's report, see also telegram to Station KSHO–TV, Apr. 24, 1961; see also Q. and A.'s III.B.10, III.C.4; for recent rulings see Q. and A.'s III.B.11, 12, and 13.)

3. Q. If a candidate appears on a variety program for a very brief bow

or statement, are his opponents entitled to "equal opportunities" on the basis of this brief appearance?

A. Yes. All appearances of a candidate, no matter how brief or perfunctory, are a "use" of a station's facilities within section 315.

4. Q. If a candidate is accorded station time for a speech in connection with a ceremonial activity or other public service, is an opposing candidate entitled to equal utilization of the station's facilities?

A. Yes. Section 315 contains no exception with respect to broadcasts by legally qualified candidates carried "in the public interest" or as a "public service." It follows that the station's broadcasts of the candidate's speech was a "use" of the facilities of the station by a legally qualified candidate giving rise to an obligation by the station under section 315 to afford "equal opportunities" to other legally qualified candidates for the same office. (Letter to CBS (WBBM), Oct. 31, 1952; letter to KFI, Oct. 31, 1952.)

5. Q. The United Community Campaigns of America advised the Commission that dating back to the early thirties it had "kicked off" its United Fund and Community Chest Campaigns with a special message broadcast by the President of the United States each fall. For the past several years the broadcast has consisted of a 5 minute program filmed on video-tape in advance at the White House and later carried on the three television networks and the four radio networks. Would the candidate opposing the President be entitled to equal opportunities if the message were carried?

A. The Commission held that section 315 contains no exceptions with respect to broadcasts by legally qualified candidates carried "in the public interest" or as a "public service" and that a candidate's speech in connection with a ceremonial activity is a section 315 "use." It is immaterial whether or not the candidate uses the time to discuss matters related to his candidacy, and the fact that the appearance of the candidate is nonpolitical is not determinative of whether his appearance is a "use." Whether the presentation of the special message in connection with a particular news-type program would meet the criteria for exemption specified in the 1959 amendment is a question initially for the exercise of the good faith judgment of the broadcast licensee. (In re United Community Campaigns, letter of Sept. 2, 1964, 3 R.R. 2d 320; but see Q. and A. III.B.14.)

6. Q. Where a candidate delivers a nonpolitical lecture on a program which is part of a regularly scheduled series of lectures broadcast by an educational FM station, is that station required to grant equal time to opposing candidate?

A. Yes. Unless the candidate's appearance comes within the category of broadcasts exempt from section 315's "equal opportunities" provision, equal time must be granted. The use to which the candidate puts this broadcast time is immaterial. (See Q. and A. III.B.1, supra.) (Telegram to Station WFUV–FM, Oct. 27, 1961.)

7. Q. Are acceptance speeches by successful candidates for nomination for the candidacy of a particular party for a given office, a use by a legally qualified candidate for election to that office?

A. Where the successful candidate for nomination becomes legally qualified as a candidate for election as a result of the nomination, his acceptance speech constitutes a use. (Letter to Progressive Party, July 2, 1952, 7 R.R. 1300.) However, after 1959, acceptance speeches in connection with *political conventions* are governed by section 315(a)(4). (For rulings after the 1959 Amendments see Telegram in re CBS and NBC, July 7, 1960, Q. and A. III.C.22; and letter to Deberry-Shaw Campaign Committee, Sept. 11, 1964, Q. and A. III.C.23.)

8. Q. Does section 315 apply to broadcasts by a legally qualified candidate where such broadcasts originate and are limited to a foreign station whose signals are received in the United States?

A. No. Section 315 applies only to stations licensed by the FCC. (In re CKLW–TV, letter of July 19, 1955.)

9. Q. A candidate for the Democratic nomination for President appeared on a network variety show. A claimant for "equal opportunities" showed that his name had been on the ballots in the Democratic presidential primary elections in two states; that the network had shown him in a film on a program concerned with the various 1960 presidential candidates; and that he was continuing his efforts as a candidate for the Democratic nomination. Would the claimant be entitled to "equal opportunities"?

A. Yes, since the appearance of the first candidate was on a program which was not exempt from the "equal opportunities" requirement of section 315 and the claimant had shown that he was a "legally qualified" candidate for the nomination for the same office. (Telegram to NBC, July 6, 1960.)

10. Q. If a station owner, or a station advertiser, or a person regularly employed as a station announcer were to make appearances over a station after having qualified as a candidate for public office, would section 315 apply?

A. Yes. Such appearances of a candidate are a "use" under section 315. (Letters to KUGN, Apr. 9, 1958; to KTTV, Jan. 23, 1957, 14 R.R. 1227; In re WCVS, letter of Nov. 19, 1956, 14 R.R. 1226b, respectively; and letter to Georgia Assoc. of Broadcasters, May 18, 1962. See also Q. and A.'s III.B. 11, 12, and 13. But cf. letter to KWTX Broadcasting Co., Mar. 16, 1960; Brigham vs. FCC, 276 F. 2d 828 (C.A. 5), Apr. 19, 1960, and Q. and A. III.C.4.)

11. Q. A television station employs an announcer who, "off camera" and unidentified, supplies the audio portion of required station identification announcements, public service announcements, and commercial announcements. The announcer is not authorized to make comments or statements concerning political matters, and he has no control over the format or con-

tent of any program material. In the event that this employee announced his candidacy for the city council, would his opponent be entitled to equal opportunities?

A. No. The employee's appearance for purposes of making commercial, noncommercial, and station identification announcements would not constitute a "use" where the announcer himself was neither shown nor identified in any way. (In re WNEP, letter of March. 16, 1965.)

12. Q. The station employee mentioned in Q. and A.III.B.11, supra, also hosts a weekly dance party on which he is identified but during which he appears or is heard only a portion of the time. He has some discretion with respect to the program's content insofar as he conducts brief conversations with teenagers appearing on the program. In the event he becomes a candidate for the city council, would his opponent be entitled to "equal opportunities"?

A. Yes. The employee's appearance as host of the dance party program would entitle other candidates for the same office to "equal opportunities" for the amount of time he appeared on the program. The deletion of the announcer's identity would not exempt his appearances from the "equal opportunities" provision, since in the case of television it is the appearance itself which constitutes the "use" of the facilities without regard to the format of the program. If an appearance of this nature were made, other candidates would be entitled to free time since the announcer would not have paid for the time he appeared. (In re WNEP, letter of Mar. 16, 1965.)

13. Q. An employee of a radio station who had been for a number of years the station's news director and is responsible for preparing the news material and presenting it on regularly scheduled news programs announced his candidacy for the school board. Prior to becoming a candidate the employee was identified on the news programs he announced, but he will not be identified during his candidacy. Would the appearance of the employee while he was a legally qualified candidate on the particular news-type programs constitute a "use" of the station entitling the employee's opponents to "equal opportunities"?

A. Yes. In cases where the newscaster is identified up to the date of his candidacy and prepares and broadcasts the news, including that of a local nature, the general line of rulings prior to the 1959 amendments to section 315 would be applicable and such appearances would constitute a "use" of the station's facilities. (In re WMAY, letter of Mar. 31, 1965, 4 R.R. 2d 849.)

14. Q. When a station, as part of a newscast, uses film clips showing a legally qualified candidate participating as one of a group in official ceremonies and the newscaster, in commenting on the ceremonies, mentions the candidate and others by name and describes their participation, has there been a "use" under section 315?

A. No. Since the facts clearly showed that the candidate had in no way directly or indirectly initiated either filming or presentation of the event, and that the broadcast was nothing more than a routine newscast by the station in the exercise of its judgment as to newsworthy events. (Letter to Allen Blondy, Feb. 6, 1957, 14 R.R. 1199; cf. CBS, Inc. (Lar Daly case), 26 FCC 715, 18 R.R. 701 [1959] and letter to Lar Daly, Sept. 9, 1959, 18 R.R. 750; see also rulings in III.C., infra, concerning the 1959 Amendments.)

C. What constitutes an appearance exempt from the equal opportunities provisions of section 315?

1. Q. Does an appearance on a program subject to the equal opportunities provision of section 315 such as a Congressman's Weekly Report, attain exempt status when the Weekly Report is broadcast as part of a program not subject to the equal opportunities provisions, such as a bona fide newscast?

A. No. A contrary view would be inconsistent with the legislative intent and recognition of such an exemption would in effect subordinate substance to form. (Letter to Congressman Clark W. Thompson, Feb. 9, 1962, 23 R.R. 178.)

2. Q. Are appearances by an incumbent-candidate in film clips prepared and supplied by him to the stations and broadcast as part of a station's regularly scheduled newscast, "uses" within the meaning of section 315?

A. Yes. Broadcast of such film clips containing appearances by a candidate constitute uses of the station's facilities. Such appearances do not attain exempt status when the film clips are broadcast as part of a program not subject to the equal opportunities provision, for the reasons set forth in Question and Answer III.C.1, above. (Letter to Congressman Clem Miller, June 15, 1962.)

3. Q. A sheriff who was a candidate for nomination for U.S. Representative in Congress conducted a daily program, regularly scheduled since 1958, on which he reported on the activities of his office. He terminated each program with a personal "Thought for the Day." Would his opponent be entitled to "equal opportunities?"

A. Yes. In light of the fact that the format and content of the program were determined by the sheriff and not by the station, the program was not of the type intended by Congress to be exempt from the "equal opportunities" requirement of section 315. (Letter to Station WCLG, Apr. 27, 1960.)

4. Q. A local weathercaster who was a candidate for reelection for Representative in the Texas Legislature was regularly employed by an AM and TV station in Texas. His weathercasts contained no references to po-

litical matters. He was identified over the air while a candidate as the "TX Weatherman." Would his opponent be entitled to "equal opportunities?"

A. No. The Court of Appeals, Fifth Circuit, ruled that the weathercaster's appearance did not involve anything but a bona fide effort to present the news; that he was not identified by name but only as the "TX Weatherman"; that his employment did not arise out of the election campaign but was a regular job; and that the facts did not reveal any favoritism on the part of the stations or any intent to discriminate among candidates. (Letter to KWTX Broadcasting Co., Mar. 16, 1960; Brigham v. FCC, 276 F. 2d 828 (C.A. 5), Apr. 19, 1960; but see Q. and A.'s III.B. 11, 12, and 13.)

5. Q. Where the facts are the same as those set forth in Q. and A. III.B.13, supra, would the appearances of the employee while a legally qualified candidate on news type programs constitute a "use" exempted from the provisions of 315 by reason of the 1959 Amendment?

A. No. The main purpose of the amendment was to allow greater freedom to the broadcaster in reporting *news* to the public, that is to say, in carrying news about and pictures of candidates as part of the contents of news programs. The amendment did not deal with the question of whether the appearance of station employees who have become candidates for office should be exempted on a news-type program where such employees are announcing the news (rather than being a part of the content of the news), any more than it dealt with the general question of such appearances (e.g., on a variety program or as a commercial continuity announcer), and the legislative history indicates that the appearance of the candidate on a news-type program in which he has participated in the "format and production" would not be exempt. (In re WMAY, letter of Mar. 31, 1965, 4 R.R. 2d 849.)

6. Q. A Philadelphia TV station had been presenting a weekly program called "Eye on Philadelphia." This program consisted of personalities being interviewed by a station representative. Three candidates for the office of Mayor of Philadelphia, representing different political parties, appeared on the program. Would a write-in candidate for Mayor be entitled to "equal opportunities"?

A. No, since it was ascertained that the appearances of the three mayoralty candidates were on a bona fide, regularly scheduled news interview program and that such appearances were determined by the station's news director on the basis of newsworthiness. (Telegram In re WCAU-TV, Nov. 2, 1959; see also In re WTMJ–TV, Telegram of Nov. 2, 1964.)

7. Q. A New York television station had been presenting a weekly program called "Search Light." This program consisted of persons, selected by the station on the basis of their newsworthiness, interviewed by a news reporter selected by the station, a member of the Citizens Union (a permanent participant initially selected by the station), and a station newsman who acted as moderator. Two candidates appeared on the program and were interviewed. Is a third opposing candidate entitled to "equal opportunities"?

A. No. The format of the program was such as to constitute a bona fide news interview pursuant to section 315(a)(2), since the program was regularly scheduled, was under the control of the licensee, and the particular program had followed the usual program format. (Telegram in re WNBC, Nov. 1, 1961.)

8. Q. A Washington, D.C., television station had been presenting a weekly program called "City Side." This program consisted of persons being interviewed by a panel of reporters. The panel was selected by the station and the persons interviewed were selected by the station on the basis of newsworthiness. Three candidates for the Democratic nomination for the office of Governor of Maryland were invited to appear on the program and one of them accepted. Would a fourth candidate for the same nomination, not invited by the station to appear, be entitled to "equal opportunities"?

A. No. It was determined that "City Side" was a regularly scheduled, weekly, live, news-interview program on the station for approximately 6 years; that the normal format of the program consisted of the interview of a newsworthy guest or guests by a panel of reporters; that the appearances on the program were determined by the station on the basis of newsworthiness; and that it was on this basis that the three candidates were invited to appear. Such a program constitutes a bona fide news-interview program pursuant to section 315(a)(2). (Telegram to Charles Luthard, Sr., May 12, 1962.)

9. Q. A New York television station had been presenting a weekly half-hour program series for over 2 years. The program, "New York Forum," was presided over by a station moderator and consisted of interviews of currently newsworthy guests by a panel of three lawyers. The guests were selected by the station in the exercise of its bona fide news judgment and not for the political advantage of any candidate for public office. The local bar association suggested the lawyer-interviewers to be used on a particular program but their final selection remained subject to the station's approval. The Democratic and Republican candidates for the office of Governor of New Jersey had appeared on separate programs in the series. Would a third party candidate be entitled to "equal opportunities"?

A. No. Such a program is a bona fide news interview and, as such, appearances on the program are exempt pursuant to section 315(a)(2). (Telegram to Socialist Labor Party of New Jersey, Nov. 2, 1961.)

10. Q. Certain networks had presented over their facilities various candidates for the Democratic nomination for President on the programs "Meet the Press," "Face the Nation," and "College News Conference." Said programs were regularly scheduled and consisted of questions being asked of prominent individuals by newsmen and others. Would a candidate for the same nomination in a State primary be entitled to "equal opportunities"?

A. No. The programs were regularly scheduled, bona fide news interviews and were of the type which Congress intended to exempt from the "equal opportunities" requirement of section 315. (Letter to Andrew J.

Easter, April 28, 1960; In re Lar Daly, letters of May 12 and June 13, 1960; and letter to Congressman Frank Kowalski, July 10, 1962.)

11. Q. On September 30, 1962, one of the networks interviewed two Congressmen, one presenting the Republican Party view and the other presenting the Democratic Party view concerning legislative achievements of the current Congressional session. The program in which the Congressmen appeared, "Direct Line," was initiated in April 1959, and its format, nature, and content had not materially changed since its inception; it was produced and controlled by the network and was regularly scheduled on Sundays as a half-hour program, although the particular program had been expanded to an hour because of preelection interest in the subject matter. The persons interviewed were asked questions submitted by viewers of the program, supplemented by questions prepared in cooperation with the League of Women Voters. The questions to be asked were selected exclusively by employees of the network and propounded by a moderator, also a network employee, although on some occasions, an additional person such as a news reporter assisted the moderator in asking questions. Would the opponent of one of the Congressmen running for re-election be entitled to "equal opportunities"?

A. No. On the basis of the information submitted, the Commission was of the view that the program "Direct Line" was a "bona fide news interview" within the meaning of section 315(a)(2) and, therefore, the Congressmen's appearances were exempt. (Telegram to Martin B. Dworkis, Oct. 10, 1962; see also Telegram to Aaron M. Orange, Nov. 3, 1962; letter to Aaron M. Orange, July 25, 1963, FCC 63–721)

12. Q. One of the networks had been presenting a program called "Issues and Answers" each Sunday since November 27, 1960, and the format, nature, and content of the program had not changed since its inception. The program, originated, produced and controlled by the network in question, consisted of one or more news correspondents interviewing one or more nationally or internationally prominent individuals such as Government officials, U.S. Senators, U.S. Congressmen, foreign ambassadors, etc., on topics of national interest. The Minority Leaders of the Senate and House, one of whom was a candidate for reelection, were interviewed on the program as the official Republican Congressional spokesmen. The following week the official Democratic Congressional spokesmen appeared and were interviewed on the program. Would the opponent of the Republican spokesman who was running for reelection be entitled to "equal opportunities"?

A. No. The Commission ruled that the program "Issues and Answers" was a bona fide news interview program of the type which Congress intended to be exempt from the "equal opportunities" provisions of section 315. (Telegram to Mr. William S. Flanagan, Oct. 23, 1962.)

13. Q. A candidate for the Democratic nomination for President was

interviewed on a network program known as "Today." It was shown that this was a daily program emphasizing news coverage, news documentaries, and on-the-spot coverage of news events; that the determination as to the content and format of the interview and the candidate's participation therein was made by the network in the exercise of its news judgment and not for the candidate's political advantage; that the questions asked of the candidate were determined by the director of the program; and that the candidate was selected because of his newsworthiness and the network's desire to interview him concerning current problems and events. Would the candidate's opponent be entitled to "equal opportunities"?

A. No, since the appearance of the candidate was on a program which was exempt from the "equal opportunities" requirement of section 315. (Telegram to Lar Daly, July 6, 1960.)

14. Q. Does the appearance of a candidate on any of the following programs constitute a "use" under the "equal opportunities" provisions of section 315: "Meet the Press," "Youth Wants to Know," "Capitol Cloakroom," "Tonight," and "PM"?

A. The programs "Meet the Press" and "Youth Wants to Know" were specifically referred to during the Senate debates on the 1959 amendments as being regularly scheduled news interview programs of the type intended to be exempt from the "equal opportunities" provision of section 315. Thus, if the format of these programs is not changed in any material respect, appearances by a candidate on such programs would not constitute a "use" under section 315. (Letter to Senator Russell B. Long, June 13, 1962; see also Q. and A. III.C.10; as to the "Tonight" program, see Q. and A. III.B.9.)

15. Q. A candidate for Governor of the State of New York appeared on "The Barry Gray Show," a nightly news and discussion program which had been broadcast by the station, using the same format, for a period of at least 4 years. The program consisted of a series of interviews of indeterminate length with persons from all walks of life concerning newsworthy events. The show was interrupted five times nightly for 5-minute newscasts, two of which were given by Barry Gray. Barry Gray, an independent contractor, exercised day-to-day control over the program subject to overall and ultimate control by the station. Candidates appearing on the program were selected, not for their own political advantage, but on the basis that they were bona fide candidates and would serve to inform the audience on issues on which the audience would have to make a decision in order to vote. The station allowed Barry Gray the maximum latitude for initiative and editorial freedom. Barry Gray determined, on the basis of the interest value of the guest and the articulate manner in which he expressed himself on the topic under discussion, the amount of time to be allocated to any particular interview, and either actively participated in the discussion, acted as an impartial moderator in the interview, or on occasion, "talked the

show" out if the guest was of little interest value. In some instances, the program consisted of an exchange of views and in other instances, constituted a panel discussion. Would the opponent of the candidate for Governor of New York be entitled to "equal opportunities"?

A. Yes. The Commission held that the definition of a bona fide news interview must be derived from the specific examples of such programs cited in the legislative history of the 1959 amendment to section 315. On the basis of the information submitted, the Commission could not determine that the Barry Gray Show was a bona fide news interview. (Telegram to WMCA, Inc., Oct. 20, 1962, FCC 62–1133.)

16. Q. A New Jersey television station had been presenting for approximately 2½ years a weekly program called "Between the Lines." This program consisted of interviews by a station moderator of persons involved with current public events in New Jersey and New York. The incumbent, candidate for reelection to the State assembly, appeared on the program. Would his opponent be entitled to "equal opportunities"?

A. No. The Commission ruled that ". . . the program in question is the type of program Congress intended to be exempt from the equal time requirements of section 315." (Letter to George A. Katz, Esq., Nov. 2, 1960.)

17. Q. The "Governor's Radio Press Conference" is a weekly 15-minute program which has been broadcast approximately 2 years employing essentially the same format since its inception. In the program, the Governor-candidate is seated in his office and speaks into a microphone; each of the participating stations has selected a newsman, who, while located at his respective station, asks questions of the Governor which the newsman considers to be newsworthy. The questions are communicated to the Governor-candidate by telephone from the respective stations and the questions and the Governor's answers are communicated to the stations by the means of a broadcast line from his office to the stations. The questions and answers are taped both by his office and each of the participating stations, and no tapes are supplied by the Governor to the stations. Questions asked of the Governor and all of the material, including his answers, are not screened, or edited by anyone in his office or on his behalf. The program is unrehearsed and there is no prepared material of any kind used by the Governor or by anyone on his behalf. The newsmen are free to ask any question they wish and each program is under the control of the participating stations. Does the appearance of the Governor-candidate on said program constitute a "use" under the "equal opportunities" provision of section 315?

A. No. Since the program involves the collective participation of the stations' newsmen, is prepared by the stations, is under their sole supervision and control, has been regularly scheduled for a period of time, and was not conceived or designated to further the candidacy of the Governor, it was held to be a bona fide news interview program and, therefore, exempt from the "equal opportunities" provision of section 315. (Letter to Governor Michael DiSalle, June 8, 1962.)

18. Q. The "Governor's Forum" program has been broadcast for approximately 8 months by several participating stations. In this program, the Governor-candidate is seated in his office and speaks into a microphone. The program consist of his answers to and questions submitted by the listening public. Questions asked are either telephoned or written to the stations or directly to his office. The questions which are telephoned or written to the several stations are forwarded to the principal participating station, which then selects the questions, edits the questions, and accumulates them on a tape. The questions telephoned or written to the Governnor's office are likewise selected and edited by his office for taping. The tape or tapes containing the questions are played in his office and the questions and the Governor's answers are then recorded on a master tape prepared by his office. Additional questions are asked of the Governor by the principal station's newsman, present in the Governor's office, to amplify any prior question and answer. On occasion, further editing of the tape has been made by the Governor's office or by the stations. The tape is sent to each of the participating stations by the Governor's office. There is no prepared material or rehearsal by the Governor's office. Would the appearance by the Governor-candidate on the above program constitute a "use" under the "equal opportunities" provision of section 315?

A. Yes. Such a program is not a news-interview program as contemplated by section 315(a)(2). This conclusion has been reached since the selection and compilation of the questions, as well as the production, supervision, control, and editing of the program are not functions exercised exclusively by the stations. (Letter to Governor Michael DiSalle, June 8, 1962.)

19. Q. A Congressman who was a candidate for reelection appeared in a news interview on a station and was interviewed by the station's Public Affairs Department regarding his experiences as a freshman Congressman. The program was described by the licensee as a "bona fide special news interview" and the licensee stated that it had sought the interview on the basis of its news judgment. The interview was conducted by a station employee and the questions asked related to current newsworthy events. The licensee stated further that although the program was a "special news interview" (the station did not broadcast regularly scheduled news interviews but presented special news interviews as the occasion arose and this was deemed by the licensee to be such an occasion), the interview itself and the format and nature of the questions were the same as in news interview programs of other newsworthy individuals and that the program was initiated, produced, and controlled by the licensee. Would the Congressman's opponent be entitled to "equal opportunities"?

A. Yes. The Commission pointed out that the legislative history of the 1959 amendment to section 315 clearly indicated that a basic element of a "bona fide news interview" is that it be regularly scheduled. Accordingly, it held that the Congressman's appearance did not occur in connection with a "bona fide news interview" within the meaning of section 315(a) (2) and that his appearance, therefore, constituted a "use" entitling his opponent to "equal opportunities." (Telegram to Station KFDX-TV, Oct. 26, 1962.)

20. Q. CBS Television Network presented a 1-hour program entitled "The Fifty Faces of '62." The program consisted of a comprehensive news report of the current off-year elections and campaigns. It included a brief review of the history of off-year elections, individual and group interviews, on-the-spot coverage of conventions and campaigns, and flashbacks of currently newsworthy aspects of the current campaigns and elections. In addition to the appearances on the broadcast of private citizens, voters, college students, and candidates, there were approximately 25 political figures, none of whom was on camera for more than approximately 2 or 3 minutes. Some of the candidates appearing on the program mentioned their candidacy; others, including the minority leader of the House of Representatives, who appeared in that capacity and discussed the prospect of his party in the Fall elections, did not discuss their candidacies. The determination as to who was to appear on the program was made solely by CBS News on the basis of its bona fide news judgment that their appearances were in aid of the coverage of the subject of the programs and not to favor or advance the candidacies of any of those who appeared, such appearances being incidental and subordinate to the subject of the documentary. Is the appearance on the program of a candidate, in his capacity as minority leader of the House of Representatives, a "use" within the "equal opportunities" provision of section 315?

A. No. Such a program is a bona fide news documentary pursuant to section 315(a) (3). The appearance of the candidate therein is incidental to the presentation of the subject covered by the documentary and the program is not designed to aid his candidacy. (Telegram to Judge John J. Murray, June 12, 1962.)

21. Q. A television station had been presenting since 1958 a weekly 30 minute program concerning developments in the State legislature with principal Democratic and Republican party leaders of both houses of the legislature participating. At the close of each legislative term, the station televised a one hour summary of the legislature's activities, using film and recordings made during its meetings. Is the appearance, in the latter program, of an officer of the State legislature, who is also a candidate, in which he and others express their views on the accomplishments of the legislative session a "use" under the "equal opportunities" provision of section 315?

A. No. For the reasons stated in Q. and A. III.C.19, supra.

22. Q. A former President expressed his views with respect to a forth-

coming national convention of his party. A candidate for that party's nomination for President called a press conference at the convention site and immediately prior to the convention to comment on said views, which conference was broadcast by two networks. Would said candidate's opponent for the same nomination be entitled to "equal opportunities"?

A. No, since the appearance of the first candidate incidental to a political convention was on a program which constituted "on-the-spot coverage of bona fide news events," pursuant to section 315(a) (4). (Telegram in re CBS and NBC, July 7, 1960; see sec. 315(a) (4), and Q. and A. III.C.23, infra; but see Q. and A. III.B.7, supra.)

23. Q. Are acceptance speeches made at a nominating convention by successful candidates for a political party's nomination for president and vice president uses which entitle other parties' candidates for those offices to "equal opportunities" under section 315?

A. No. Prior to 1959 any use of a station's facilities by a candidate for public office required the station to afford "equal opportunities" to other candidates for the same office. However, one of the specific types of news programs exempted by Congress was "on-the-spot coverage of bona fide news events (including but not limited to political conventions and activities incidental thereto)" in the language of 315(a) (4). The broadcast of an acceptance speech made at a political convention is an aspect of the coverage of the political convention. (Letter to Deberry-Shaw Campaign Committee, Sept. 11, 1964. See also Q. and A. III.C.22., supra; but for a ruling prior to the 1959 Amendments see letter to Progressive Party, July 2, 1952, 7 R.R. 1300, Q. and A. III.B.7.)

24. Q. A Chicago television station covered the annual Saint Patrick Day parade in that city. During the broadcast, the Mayor, a candidate for reelection, appeared for 2 minutes. Would the Mayor's opponent be entitled to "equal opportunities"?

A. No. Broadcast coverage of a parade is the type of bona fide news event contemplated by Congress in enacting the 1959 amendments to section 315. Therefore, such a broadcast would appear to constitute "on-the-spot coverage of bona fide news events" pursuant to section 315(a) (4) and any appearance by a candidate during the course of such a broadcast would not constitute a "use" of broadcast facilities entitling opposing candidates to "equal opportunities." (Letter to Lar Daly, Mar. 28, 1963.)

25. Q. An Indiana station presented the County Court Judge, who was a candidate for the Democratic mayoralty nomination in Gary, Ind., on a program entitled "Gary County Court on the Air." The program had been broadcast live by the station as a public service for the past 14 years, each Monday, Wednesday, Thursday and Friday from 9:05 a.m. to 10 a.m. One of the programs was taped for broadcast 1 day prior to the actual broadcast. The station had met with the presiding Judge some 14 years prior to the election in question to arrange for the broadcasts and each succeeding

judge had agreed to continue the program because of its public interest value. For 7½ years prior to the election in question, the judge who was a candidate for the mayoralty nomination had appeared on the program. Persons appearing in the court had the privilege of declining to have their cases heard during broadcast time to prevent invasion of privacy. If, in the opinion of the presiding judge, certain cases did not lend themselves to broadcast, they were heard at times when the proceedings were not being covered by the station. The court was the usual type of City Court, handling a variety of cases and was not solely a traffic court, and it was, generally, impossible for the judge to control the content and/or persons who did appear. The program could not be by its nature and was not, by licensee insistence, tailored to suit the judge who was a candidate. The format of "Gary County Court on the Air" had remained unchanged since the inception of the program. The station used City Court case decisions on its regularly scheduled newscasts and such decisions also appeared in Gary newspapers. Would the Judge's opponent for the nomination for Mayor be entitled to "equal time"?

A. No. The Commission concluded that the program fell within the "news event" exemption of section 315(a) (4) because the program covered the operation of an official governmental body and because the court proceedings were newsworthy. The Commission held that the program was "bona fide" in view of the fact that it had been presented by the station for 14 years, with this particular judge for 7½ years, and inasmuch as the appearance of the candidate was incidental to the on-the-spot coverage of a news event rather than for the purpose of advancing his candidacy. Therefore, the Commission ruled that "Gary County Court on the Air" fell within the reasonable latitude allowed to licensees for the exercise of good faith news judgment and was exempt from the "equal time" requirement of section 315. (Letter to Thomas R. Fadell, Apr. 10, 1963 (FCC 63–331); affirmed by order entered Apr. 29, 1963, Thomas R. Fadell v. U.S., FCC and WWCA Radio Station, Case No. 14,142 (USCA, 7th).)

26. Q. On September 30, 1962, two candidates for the office of Governor of California held a 1-hour debate which was given coverage on every major television station in California, the time being donated by the stations carrying the debate. The debate was held in San Francisco as part of the annual convention of United Press International which had invited the two candidates to appear and had invited all news media to cover the event. The debate was not arranged by the stations but was broadcast by them as a public service and in the exercise of their bona fide news judgment. No other aspect of the UPI convention was broadcast other than the joint appearance of the two candidates. A third candidate for the same office requested "equal opportunities" and the stations denied the request on the basis that the prior appearances constituted "on-the-spot coverage of a bona fide news event" pursuant to section 315(a) (4) of the Communications Act. Was the third candidate entitled to "equal opportunities"?

A. Yes. The Commission held that neither the language of the amendment, the legislative history nor subsequent Congressional action indicated a Congressional intent to exempt from the "equal opportunities" provision of section 315 a debate qua debate between legally qualified candidates. The Commission pointed out that the bona fides of the licensee's news judgment, while not questioned, was not the sole criterion to be used in determining whether section 315(a) (4) had been properly invoked. It was concluded that where the appearance of the candidates was designed by them to serve their own political advantage and such appearance was ultimately the subject of a broadcast program encompassing only their entire appearance, such program cannot be considered to be on-the-spot coverage of a bona fide news event simply because the broadcaster deems that the candidates' appearance (or speeches) will be of interest to the general public and, therefore, newsworthy. (Telegrams to NBC and KFMB-TV, Oct. 19, 1962; letter to NBC and CBS, Oct. 26, 1962, FCC 62–1132; see also letter to The Goodwill Stations, Inc. (WJR), Oct. 19, 1962.)

27. Q. The Columbia Broadcasting System, Inc., advised the Commission that over the years it had become the practice of the President to hold press conferences; that President Johnson had held such conferences on a periodic, though irregular, basis in the past and would undoubtedly hold press conferences prior to election day, as would his opposing candidate Senator Goldwater. CBS stated that it considered Presidential press conferences important news events, and had given them such broadcast coverage as it in its news judgment had thought was warranted and that it believed it would be in the public interest to continue to cover these press conferences, as well as those of Senator Goldwater, or some of them, in whole or in part, provided this would not require it to afford equal time to all other persons who might also be candidates for the presidency. Would such press conferences be exempt from the requirements of section 315 on the ground that the appearances were considered to be either "bona fide news interviews" or "on the spot coverage" of "bona fide news events"?

A. No. The broadcast of press conferences, such as the one described in the inquiry, would not be exempt from the provisions of section 315 either as "bona fide news interviews" or "on the spot coverage of a bona fide news event." The press conference could not qualify as a "bona fide news interview" exemption inasmuch as it was not a regularly scheduled program, within the recognized and accepted meaning of that term, but rather was one that could be called by the candidates solely in their discretion and at times they themselves specify. Such a press conference could not, in any event, qualify for exemption, since the scheduling and in significant part the content and format of the press conference was not under the control of the network. In addition the broadcast of the press conference could not be deemed to be an "on-the-spot coverage of a bona fide news event," since prior Commission rulings issued on October 19 and 26, 1962 (see Q. and A. III.C.26) pointed out inter alia, ". . . that if the sole test of the on-the-spot coverage exemption is simply whether or not the station's decision to cover the event and put it on a broadcast program constitutes a bona fide news judgment, there would be no meaning to the other three exemptions in section 315(a) since these, too, all involve a bona fide news judgment by the broadcaster." Such a test would, in effect, amount to a repeal of the "equal opportunities" provision of section 315(a)—something Congress clearly did not intend, as shown, for example by the necessity for the suspension of that provision for the 1960 debates between the two major presidential candidates. (Letter to CBS, Sept. 30, 1964, 3 R.R. 2d 623.)

28. Q. The President of the United States during a presidential campaign used 15 minutes of radio and television time to address the Nation with respect to an extraordinary international situation in the Middle East (the so-called Suez crisis). Would the networks carrying this address be obliged to afford "equal opportunities" to the other presidential candidates?

A. No. On the basis of the legislative history of section 315 the Commission concluded that Congress did not intend to grant equal time to all presidential candidates when the President uses the air waves in reporting to the Nation on an international crisis. (Telegram to NBC, CBS, and ABC, Nov. 5, 1956, Public Notice 38387, 14 R.R. 720.)

29. Q. The President of the United States, upon the recommendation of the National Security Council, went on the air to deliver a report to the Nation with respect to an important anouncement by the Soviet Government as to change in its leadership, and the explosion by Communist China of a nuclear device. Would the President's opponents for the Presidency be entitled to "equal opportunities"?

A. No. The networks carrying the report, in determining that such a report by the President on specific, current international events affecting the country's security falls within the "on-the-spot coverage of a bona fide news event" exemption of section 315(a) (4), acted within their "reasonable latitude for the exercise of good faith news judgment." The Commission also discussed its previous ruling of 1956 (Q. and A. III.C.28 supra) and noted that this ruling had been fully reported to the Congress and that Congress had reexamined the concept of "use" in connection with extensive amendments in 1959 to section 315, but did not alter or comment adversely upon the 1956 ruling. The decision was appealed to the U.S. Court of Appeals (D.C. Cir.) and was affirmed by a vote of 3 to 3 without opinion. A petition for certiorari to the Supreme Court was denied. (Letter to Dean Burch, Oct. 21, 1964; cert. denied, 379 U.S. 893 (1964), 3 R.R. 2d 647, 3 R.R. 2d 2025.)

IV. Who is a legally qualified candidate?

1. Q. How can a station know which candidates are "legally qualified"?

A. The determination as to who is a legally qualified candidate for a particular public office within the meaning of section 315 and the Commission's rules must be determined by reference to the law of the State in which the election is being held. In general, a candidate is legally qualified if he can be voted for in the State or district in which the election is being held, and, if elected, is eligible to serve in the office in question.

2. Q. Need a candidate be on the ballot to be legally qualified?

A. Not always. The term "legally qualified candidate" is not restricted to persons whose names appear on the printed ballot; the term may embrace persons not listed on the ballot if such persons are making a bona fide race for the office involved and the names of such persons, or their electors can, under applicable law, be written in by voters so as to result in their valid election. The Commission recognizes, however, that the mere fact that any name may be written in does not entitle all persons who may publicly announce themselves as candidates to demand time under section 315; broadcast stations may make suitable and reasonable requirements with respect to proof of the bona fide nature of any candidacy on the part of applicants for the use of facilities under section 315. (§§ 3.120, 3.290, 3.657, esp. par (f); letters to Socialist Labor Party, Nov. 14, 1951, 7 R.R. 766; CBS Inc., May 28, 1952, 7 R.R. 1189; Press Release of Nov. 26, 1941 (Mimeo 55732); see also Q. and A.'s IV. 11, 12, and 13.)

3. Q. May a person be considered to be a legally qualified candidate where he has made only a public announcement of his candidacy and has not yet filed the required forms or paid the required fees for securing a place on the ballot in either the primary or general elections?

A. The answer depends on applicable State law. In some States persons may be voted for by electorate whether or not they have gone through the procedures required for getting their names placed on the ballot itself. In such a State, the announcement of a person's candidacy—if determined to be bona fide—is sufficient to bring him within the purview of section 315. In other States, however, candidates may not be "legally qualified" until they have fulfilled certain prescribed procedures. The applicable State laws and the particular facts surrounding the announcement of the candidacy are determinatives. (Letter to Senator Earle C. Clements, Feb. 2, 1954; and see also par. (f) of §§ 3.120, 3.290, 3.657.)

4. Q. May a station deny a candidate "equal opportunities" because it believes that the candidate has no possibility of being elected or nominated?

A. No. Section 315 does not permit any such subjective determination by the station with respect to a candidate's chances of nomination or election. (Letter to CBS Inc., May 28, 1952, 7 R.R. 1189.)

5. Q. When is a person a legally qualified candidate for nomination as the candidate of a party for President or Vice President of the United States?

A. In view of the fact that a person may be nominated for these offices by the conventions of his party without having appeared on the ballot of any State having presidential primary elections, or having any pledged votes prior to the convention, or even announcing his willingness to be a candidate, no fixed rule can be promulgated in answer to this question. Whether a person so claiming is in fact a bona fide candidate will depend on the particular facts of each situation, including consideration of what efforts, if any, he has taken to secure delegates or preferential votes in State primaries. It cannot, however, turn on the licensee's evaluation of the claimant's chances for success. (Letter to CBS Inc., May 28, 1952, 7 R.R. 1189; and see also par. (f) of sections 73.120, 73.290, 73,657.)

6. Q. Has a claimant under section 315 sufficiently established his legal qualifications when the facts show that after qualifying for a place on the ballot for a particular office in the primary, he notified State officials of his withdrawal therefrom and then later claimed he had not really intended to withdraw, and where the facts further indicated that he was supporting another candidate for the same office and was seeking the nomination for an office other than the one for which he claimed to be qualified?

A. No. Where a question is raised concerning a claimant's legal qualification, it is incumbent on him to prove that he is in fact legally qualified. The facts here did not constitute an unequivocal showing of legal qualification. (Letter to Lar Daly, Apr. 11, 1956; letter to American Vegetarian Party, Nov. 6, 1956.)

7. Q. If a candidate establishes his legal qualifications only after the date of nomination or election for the office for which he was contending, is he entitled to equal opportunities which would have been available had he timely qualified?

A. No, for once the date of nomination or election for an office has passed, it cannot be said that one who failed timely to qualify therefor is still a "candidate." The holding of the primary or general election terminates the possibility of affording "equal opportunities," thus mooting the question of what rights the claimant might have been entitled to under section 315 before the election. (Letter to Socialist Workers' Party, Dec. 13, 1956; letter to Lar Daly, Oct. 31, 1956, 14 R.R. 713, appeal sub. nom. Daly v. U.S. Case No. 11,946 (C.A. 7th Cir.) dismissed as moot Mar. 7, 1957; cert. den. 355 U.S. 826.)

8. Q. Under the circumstances stated in the preceding question, is any post-election remedy available to the candidate, before the Commission, under section 315?

A. None, insofar as a candidate may desire retroactive "equal opportunities." But this is not to suggest that a station can avoid its statutory obligation under section 315 by waiting until an election has been held and only then disposing of demands for "equal opportunities." (See citations in Q. and A. IV.7.)

9. Q. A, a candidate for the Democratic Party nomination for Pres-

ident, appeared on a variety program prior to the nominating convention because of the prior appearance of B, his opponent. After the closing of the convention, A claimed he was entitled to additional time in order to equalize his appearance with that afforded B. Would A be entitled to additional time?

A. No. A licensee may not be required to furnish the use of its facilities to a candidate for nomination for President after the convention has chosen its nominee. (Telegram to Lar Daly, Nov. 3, 1960.)

10. Q. When a State Attorney General or other appropriate State official having jurisdiction to decide a candidate's legal qualification has ruled that a candidate is not legally qualified under local election laws, can a licensee be required to afford such "candidate" "equal opportunities" under section 315?

A. In such instances, the ruling of the State Attorney General or other official will prevail, absent a judicial determination. (Telegram to Ralph Muncy, Nov. 5, 1954; letter to Socialist Workers' Party, Nov. 23, 1956.)

11. Q. A television station afforded time to the Democratic candidate from the State of California for the U.S. Senate. The station subsequently turned down a request from the Socialist Labor Party for time for their candidate for the same office, on the basis of a telegram which it had received from the Secretary of State of the State of California which declared that he did not consider the Socialist Labor Party candidate a legally qualified candidate under provisions of the California Election Code. The candidate in question was duly nominated and had accepted the nomination at the Party State Convention; the Secretary of State's office was officially notified of his nomination; notification of his candidacy was sent to all news media and was published in the metropolitan newspapers; he had addressed public meetings in four large California cities on behalf of his candidacy. Upon request of the Secretary of State the Deputy Attorney General advised the Commission that under California election law write-in votes may be cast and counted for an individual seeking the office of U.S. Senator and if the individual received a plurality of the votes cast for the office the Secretary of State would certify the individual as having been elected. Would the candidate be considered legally qualified so as to be entitled to "equal opportunities" for the use of the station's facilities?

A. Yes. The Commission's rules define a legally qualified candidate, in part, as any person who has publicly announced that he is a candidate; meets the qualifications prescribed by the applicable laws to hold the office for which he is a candidate so that he may be voted for by the electorate; is eligible under the law to be voted for by writing in his name on the ballot; and makes a substantial showing that he is a bona fide candidate for nomination or office. On the basis of the facts recited it was determined that the candidate was a legally qualified candidate and as such was entitled to "equal opportunities." (Letter to Metromedia, Inc., Oct. 28, 1964.)

12. Q. An incumbent county clerk having publicly announced his intention to run for renomination in an upcoming primary continued to broadcast sports events and otherwise speak on radio. It appeared that he had not filed his notification and declaration papers with the appropriate State official. Is a legally qualified candidate for the same nomination entitled to "equal opportunities" in response to the broadcast by the incumbent?

A. No. The State Attorney General indicated that a person does not become a legally qualified or "bona fide" candidate in the primary until his notification and declaration papers have been received and accepted by the applicable State officer. Since the incumbent county clerk had not filed these required papers, he was not a legally qualified candidate under section 73.120(a) of the Commission rules at the time of his broadcasts. His opponent, therefore, was not entitled to "equal opportunities" to respond to these broadcasts. (In re WDOC; letter of June 4, 1965.)

13. Q. When a State Secretary of State has ruled that an individual has not followed the procedures required by State law for becoming a legally qualified candidate for U.S. Senator from that State, can a licensee be required to afford that individual "equal opportunities" under section 315?

A. No. When it appears that a State Secretary of State has ruled that an individual is not a legally qualified candidate under the State election law and that individual has presented no further information regarding his claimed candidacy, he has failed to meet the burden imposed by section 73.120(f) of the Commission's rules of proving that he is a legally qualified candidate for public office under section 73.120(a) of those rules. (Letter to Socialist Workers Party, in re KNX Oct. 28, 1964.)

14. Q. An individual seeking a U.S. Senate seat requested time from a station equal to that afforded his opponents. The individual's request had been refused by the station on the grounds that he was not a bona fide candidate. The candidate informed the Commission that he had been advised by the local election board that he possessed the necessary requisites to be a write-in candidate and claimed that he was thus entitled to equal time. Would the individual be entitled to equal opportunities under these circumstances?

A. No. The Commission found that the individual had not complied with the Commission's rules for establishing one's self as a legally qualified candidate. He had failed to submit any proof other than his own statements relating to whether he was "eligible under the applicable law to be voted for . . . by writing in his name on the ballot." Therefore, he had not met his burden of proof under section 73.657(f) of the rules. (In re WNHC-TV, letter of Nov. 4, 1964.)

V. When are candidates opposing candidates?

1. Q. What public offices are included within the meaning of section 315?

A. Under the Commission's rules, section 315 is applicable to both primary and general elections, and public offices include all offices filled by special or general election on a municipal, county, state, or national level as well as the nomination by any recognized party of a candidate for such an office.

2. Q. May the station under section 315 make time available to all candidates for one office and refuse all candidates for another office?

A. Yes. The "equal opportunities" requirement of section 315 is limited to all legally qualified candidates for the same office.

3. Q. If the station makes time available to candidates seeking the nomination of one party for a particular office, does section 315 require that it make equal time available to the candidates seeking the nomination of other parties for the same office?

A. No, the Commission has held that while both primary elections or nominating conventions and general elections are comprehended within the terms of section 315, the primary elections or conventions held by one party are to be considered separately from the primary elections or conventions of other parties, and, therefore, insofar as section 315 is concerned, "equal opportunities" need only be afforded legally qualified candidates for nomination for the same office at the same party's primary or nominating convention. The station's actions in this regard, however, would be governed by the public interest standards encompassed within the "fairness doctrine." (Letters to KWFT, Inc., Oct. 22, 1948, 4 R.R. 885; Socialist Labor Party of America, May 13, 1952, 11 R.R. 234; WCDL, Apr. 3, 1953; Senator Joseph S. Clark, Jan. 25 and Apr. 13, 1962; telegram to Dr. Edward J. Leuddeke, Oct. 25, 1961; Letter to E. C. French, Oct. 28, 1964, 3 R.R. 2d 811, Q. and A. V.5; and In re WCBS-TV, Telegram of Oct. 29, 1965.)

4. Q. If the station makes time available to all candidates of one party for nomination for a particular office, including the successful candidate, may candidates of other parties in the general election demand an equal amount of time under section 315?

A. No. For the reason given above, (Letter to KWFT, Inc., Oct. 22, 1948, 4 R.R. 885.)

5. Q. On May 3, 1964, an incumbent Congressman from New York was afforded time to appear on a television program. At that time he was the only person who had been designated by petition under New York law as the Republican nominee for his Congressional seat. The complainant at that date was the only designated Democratic–Liberal nominee. Primaries for both parties were due to be held on June 2, 1964. However, if no fur-

ther nominees were designated by April 28, 1964, and if no petitions for write-in nominees were filed by May 5, 1964, no primary would be held, since the incumbent and the complainant each would have the uncontested nomination of his respective party. In fact, no further petitions, either "designating" or "write-in," were ever filed. Was the licensee correct in refusing "equal opportunities" to the complainant in response to incumbent's May 3 broadcast on the ground that on that date each was merely a candidate for his respective party's nomination, and thus they were not opposing candidates for the same office?

A. Yes. The issue must be determined under the New York State election laws and should be resolved by appropriate State or local authorities. Since neither the complainant nor the Commission was able to obtain an interpretation of that law from the New York authorities, the Commission of necessity interpreted the law. An "uncontested position" as defined by the New York statute is one as to which (1) the number of candidates designated for the particular office does not exceed the number to be nominated or elected thereto by the party in the primary, and (2) no valid petition requesting an opportunity to write-in the name of an undesignated candidate has been filed. If both conditions are fulfilled when the period for filing such petitions is over (May 5), no primary is required. Since condition (2) of this definition could not be fulfilled until May 5, 1964, 2 days after the Republican incumbent's broadcast, neither designated candidate here involved could be considered the nominee of his respective party until May 5, and, therefore, they were not opposing candidates for Congress at the time of incumbent's broadcast. (Letter to E. C. French, Oct. 28, 1964, 3 R.R. 2d 881.)

VI. *What constitutes equal opportunities?*

A. *In general*

1. Q. Generally speaking, what constitutes "equal opportunities"?

A. Under section 315 and §§ 73.120, 73.290, and 73.657 of the Commission's rules, no licensee shall make any discrimination in charges, practices, regulations, facilities, or services rendered to candidates for a particular office.

2. Q. Is a licensee required or allowed to give time free to one candidate where it had sold time to an opposing candidate?

A. The licensee is not permitted to discriminate between the candidates in any way. With respect to any particular election it may adopt a policy of selling time, or of giving time to the candidates free of charge, or of giving them some time and selling them additional time. But whatever policy it adopts it must treat all candidates for the same office alike with respect to the time they may secure free and that for which they must pay.

3. Q. Is it necessary for a station to advise a candidate or a political party that time has been sold to other candidates?

A. No. The law does not require that this be done. If a candidate inquires, however, the facts must be given him. It should be noted here that a station is required to keep a public record of all requests for time by or on behalf of political candidates, together with a record of the disposition and the charges made, if any, for each broadcast. (§§ 73.120(d), 73.-290(d), 73.657(d); and telegram to Norman William Seemann, Esq., May 18, 1962.)

4. Q. If a station desires to make its facilities available on a particular day for political broadcasts to all candidates for the same office, is one of the candidates precluded from requesting "equal opportunities" at a later date if he does not accept the station's initial offer?

A. This depends on all of the circumstances surrounding the station's offer of time and, particularly, whether the station has given adequate advance notice. The Commission has held that a 4-day notice by a Texas station to a Congressman while Congress is in session does not constitute adequate advance notice and the Congressman is not foreclosed from his right to request "equal opportunities." (Letter to Jack Neil, Station KTRM, Apr. 18, 1962.)

5. Q. With respect to a request for time by a candidate for public office where there has been no prior "use" by an opposing candidate, must the station sell the candidate the specific time segment he requests?

A. No. Neither the Act nor the Commission's rules contain any provisions which require a licensee to sell a specific time segment to a candidate for public office. (Letter to Mr. Bill Neil, Station KTRM, Mar. 9, 1962.)

6. Q. Is a station required to sell to a candidate time which is unlimited as to total time and as to the length of each segment?

A. Neither the Act nor the Commission's rules contain provisions requiring stations to sell unlimited periods of time for political broadcasts. Section 315 of the Act imposes no obligation on any licensee to allow the use of its station by any candidate. Commission's programing statement contemplates the use of stations for political broadcasting. Where the station showed that sale of limited time segments to candidates was based on its experience and the interests of viewers in programing diversification, no Commission action was required. (Telegram to J. B. Lahan, May 18, 1962; and telegrams to Grover C. Doggette, Esq., May 22 and 23, 1962. Cf., letter to Station WLBT-TV, Apr. 17, 1962, and letter to Station WROX, May 3, 1962, where the Commission indicated that a public interest question would be raised if the station failed to provide any broadcast time to candidates in a major election being held within the station's coverage area.)

7. Q. If a station offers free time to opposing candidates and one

candidate declines to use the time given him, are other candidates for that office foreclosed from availing themselves of the offer?

A. No. The refusal of one candidate does not foreclose other candidates wishing to use the time offered. However, whether the candidate initially declining the offer could later avail himself of "equal opportunities" would depend on all the facts and circumstances. (Letter on offers of free time, June 13, 1956, 14 R.R. 65.)

8. Q. If one political candidate buys station facilities more heavily than another, is a station required to call a halt to such sales because of the resulting imbalance?

A. No. Section 315 requires only that all candidates be afforded "equal opportunities" to use the facilities of the station. (Letter to Mr. M. R. Oliver, Oct. 23, 1952, 11 R.R. 239.)

9. Q. Can a station contract with the committee of a political party whereby it commits itself in advance of an election to furnish substantial blocks of time to the candidates of that party?

A. Neither section 315 nor the Commission's rules prohibit a licensee from contracting with a party for reservation of time in advance of an election. However, substantial questions as to a possible violation of section 315 would arise if the effect of such prior commitment were to disable a licensee from meeting its "equal opportunities" obligations under section 315. (Letter to Congressman Frank M. Karsten, Nov. 25, 1955.)

10. Q. Where a television station had previously offered certain specified time segments during the last week of the campaign to candidate A, who declined the purchase, and then sold the same segments to A's opponent, was the station obligated under section 315 to accede to A's subsequent request for particular time periods immediately preceding or following the time segments previously offered to him and refused by him and subsequently sold to his opponent?

A. No. But the time offered to candidate A must be generally comparable. The principal factors considered in this situation were: (a) the total amount of time presently scheduled for each candidate; (b) the time segments presently offered to candidate A; (c) the time segments presently scheduled for candidate A's opponent and previously rejected by candidate A; (d) the time segments now scheduled for candidates for other offices, if any, and previously rejected by candidate A; and (e) the station's possible obligations to other candidates for office. (Telegram to Major General Harry Johnson, Nov. 1, 1961.)

11. Q. If a station has a policy of confining political broadcasts to sustaining time, but has so many requests for political time that it cannot handle them all within its sustaining schedule, may it refuse time to a candidate whose opponent has already been granted time, on the basis of its established policy of not canceling commercial programs in favor of political broadcasts?

A. No. The station cannot rely upon its policy if the latter conflicts with the "equal opportunities" requirement of section 315. (Stephens Broadcasting Co., September 4, 1945, 11 F.C.C. 61, 3 R.R. 1.)

12. Q. If one candidate has been nominated by Parties A, B, and C, while a second candidate for the same office is nominated only by Party D, how should time be allocated as between the two candidates?

A. Section 315 has reference only to the use of facilities by persons who are candidates for public office and not to the political parties which may have nominated such candidates. Accordingly, if broadcast time is made available for the use of a candidate for public office, the provisions of section 315 require that "equal opportunities" be afforded each person who is a candidate for the same office, without regard to the number of nominations that any particular candidate may have. (Letter to Thomas W. Wilson, Oct. 31, 1946.)

B. Comparability

1. Q. Is a station's obligation under section 315 met if it offers a candidate the same amount of time an opposing candidate has received, where the time of the day or week afforded the first candidate is superior to that offered his opponent?

A. No. The station in providing "equal opportunities" must consider the desirability of the time segment allotted as well as its length. And while there is no requirement that a station afford candidate B exactly the same time of day on exactly the same day of the week as candidate A, the time segments offered must be comparable as to desirability.

2. Q. If candidate A has been afforded time during early morning, noon and evening hours, does a station comply with section 315 by offering candidate B time only during early morning and noon periods?

A. No. However, the requirements of comparable time do not require a station to make available exactly the same time periods, nor the periods requested by candidate B. (Letter to D. L. Grace, July 3, 1958.)

3. Q. If a station broadcasts a program sponsored by a commercial advertiser which includes one or more qualified candidates as speakers or guests, what are its obligations with respect to affording "equal opportunities" to other candidates for the same office?

A. If candidates are permitted to appear without cost to themselves, on programs sponsored by commercial advertisers, opposing candidates are entitled to receive comparable time also at no cost. (Letter to Senator A. S. Mike Monroney, Oct. 9, 1952, 10 R.R. 451; and telegram to WWIN, May 3, 1962; but see Q. and A. VI.B.4, infra.)

4. Q. When a station broadcasts an appearance by a candidate which constitutes a use and it is paid for by the political campaign committee of a labor union, is an opposing candidate entitled to comparable *free* time?

A. No. Where a political committee of an organization such as a labor union purchases time specifically on behalf of a candidate, opposing candidates are not entitled to *free* time. There is a distinction between this situation and a case where a candidate is permitted to appear on a program which is regularly sponsored. (Telegram to Metromedia in re ILGWU Campaign Committee, Oct. 29, 1964, 3 R.R. 2d 774; but see Q. and A. VI.B.3, supra.)

5. Q. Where a candidate for office in a State or local election appears on a national network program, is an opposing candidate for the same office entitled to equal facilities over stations which carried the original program and serve the area in which the election campaign is occurring?

A. Yes. Under such circumstances an opposing candidate would be entitled to time on such stations. (Letter to Senator A. S. Mike Monroney, Oct. 9, 1952.)

6. Q. Where a candidate appears on a particular program—such as a regular series of forum programs—are opposing candidates entitled to demand to appear on the same program?

A. Not necessarily. The mechanics of the problem of "equal opportunities" must be left to resolution of the parties. And while factors such as the size of the potential audience because of the appearance of the first candidate on an established or popular program might very well be a matter for consideration by the parties, it cannot be said, in the abstract, that "equal opportunities" could only be provided by giving opposing parties time on the same program. (Letter to Harold Oliver, Oct. 31, 1952; letter to CBS, Inc., Oct. 31, 1952; In re WPRO-TV, letter of Oct. 20, 1964.)

7. Q. Where a station asks candidates A and B (opposing candidates in a primary election) to appear on a debate-type program, the format of which is generally acceptable to the candidate, but with no restrictions as to what issues or matters might be discussed, and candidate A accepts the offer and appears on the program and candidate B declines to appear on the program, is candidate B entitled to further "equal opportunities" in the use of the station's facilities within the meaning of section 315 of the act? If so, is any such obligation met by offering candidate B, prior to the primary, an opportunity to appear on a program of comparable format to that on which candidate A appeared, or is the station obligated to grant candidate B time equal to that used by candidate A on the program in question unrestricted as to format?

A. Since the station's format was reasonable in structure and the station put no restrictions on what matters and issues might be discussed by candidate B and others who appeared on the program in question, it offered candidate B "equal opportunities" in the use of its facilities within the meaning of section 315 of the Act. The station's further offer to candidate B, prior to the primary, of its facilities on a "comparable format" was reasonable under the facts of the case, consistent with any continuing obligation to afford caandidate B "equal opportunities" in the use of the station which he may have had. (Letter to Congressman Bob Wilson, Aug. 1, 1958.)

8. Q. A licensee offered broadcast time to all the candidates for a particular office for a joint appearance, the details of which program were determined solely by the licensee. If Candidate "A" rejects the offer and Candidate "B" and/or other candidates accepts and appears, would Candidate "A" be entitled to "equal opportunities" because of the appearance of Candidate "B" and/or other candidates on the program previously offered by the licensee to all of the candidates?

A. Yes, provided the request is made by the candidate within the period specified by the rules. The Commission stated that licensees should negotiate with the affected candidates and that where the offer was mutually agreeable to such candidates, "equal opportunities" were being afforded to the candidates. Where the candidate rejected the proposal, however, and other candidates accepted and appeared, the Commission stated: "Where the licensee permits one candidate to use his facilities, section 315 then—simply by virtue of that use—requires the licensee to 'afford equal opportunities to all other such candidates for that office in the use of such broadcasting station.' This obligation may not be avoided by the licensee's unilateral actions in picking a program format, specifying participants other than and in addition to the candidates, setting the length of the program, the time of taping the time of broadcast, etc., and then offering the package to the candidates on a 'take it or leave it—this is my final offer' basis. For . . . section 315 provides that the station 'shall have no power of censorship over the material broadcast.' (Cf. Port Huron Broadcasting Co., 4 R.R. 1.) Clearly, the 'take it or leave it' basis described above would constitute such prohibited censorship, since it would, in effect, be dictating the very format of the program to the candidate—and thus, an important facet of 'the material broadcast.' We wish to make clear that the Commission is in no way saying that one format is more in the public interest than another. On the contrary, the thrust of our ruling is that the Act bestows upon the candidate the right to choose the format and other similar aspects of 'the material broadcast,' with no right of 'censorship' in the licensee." Cf. Farmers Educational and Cooperative Union of America, North Dakota Division v. WDAY, Inc., 360 U.S. 525. (Letter to Nicholas Zapple, Oct. 5, 1962.)

9. Q. In affording "equal opportunities," may a station limit the use of its facilities solely to the use of a microphone?

A. A station must treat opposing candidates the same with respect to the use of its facilities and if it permits one candidate to use facilities over and beyond the microphone, it must permit a similar usage by other qualified candidates. (Letter to D. L. Grace, July 3, 1958.)

VII. What limitations can be put on the use of facilities by a candidate?

1. Q. May a station delete material in a broadcast under section 315 because it believes the material contained therein is or may be libelous?

A. No. Any such action would entail censorship which is expressly prohibited by section 315 of the Communications Act. (Port Huron Broadcasting Co., 12 FCC 1069, 4 R.R. 1; WDSU Broadcasting Co., 7 R.R. 769.)

2. Q. If a legally qualified candidate broadcasts libelous or slanderous remarks, is the station liable therefor?

A. In Port Huron Broadcasting Co., 12 FCC 1069, 4 R.R. 1, the Commission expressed an opinion that licensees not directly participating in the libel might be absolved from any liability they might otherwise incur under State law, because of the operation of section 315, which precludes them from preventing a candidate's utterances. In a subsequent case, the Commission's ruling in the Port Huron case was, in effect, affirmed, the Supreme Court holding that since a licensee could not censor a broadcast under section 315, Congress could not have intended to compel a station to broadcast libelous statements of a legally qualified candidate and at the same time subject itself to the risk of damage suits. (Read: Farmers Educational & Cooperative Union of America v. WDAY, Inc., 79 S. Ct. 1302 (Oct. 1958) 89 N.W. 2d 102, 164 F. Supp. 928.)

3. Q. Does the same immunity apply in a case where the Chairman of a political party's campaign committee, not himself a candidate, broadcasts a speech in support of a candidate?

A. No, licensees are not entitled to assert the defense that they are not liable since the speeches could have been censored without violating section 315. Accordingly, they were at fault in permitting such speeches to be broadcast. (Felix v. Westinghouse Radio Stations, 186 F. 2d 1, cert. den. 341 U.S. 909.)

4. Q. A candidate prepared a 15-minute video tape which contained the opinions of several private citizens with respect to an issue pertinent to the pending election. If the station broadcast such program in which the candidate did not appear, would the immunity afforded licensees by section 315 from liability for the broadcast of libelous or slanderous remarks by candidates be applicable?

A. No. The provision of section 315 prohibiting censorship by a licensee over material broadcast pursuant to section 315 applies only to broadcasts by candidates themselves. Section 315, therefore, is not a defense to an action for libel or slander arising out of broadcasts by non-candidates speaking in behalf of another's candidacy. Since section 315 does not prohibit the licensee from censoring such a broadcast, the licensee is not entitled to the protection of section 315. (Letter to Mr. William P. Webb, Apr. 24, 1962.)

5. Q. If a candidate secures time under section 315, must he talk about a subject directly related to his candidacy?

A. No. The candidate may use the time as he deems best. To deny a person time on the ground that he was not using it in furtherance of his candidacy would be an exercise of censorship prohibited by section 315. (Letter to WMCA, Inc., May 15, 1952, 7 R.R. 1132.)

6. Q. If a station makes time available to an office holder who is also a legally qualified candidate for reelection and the office holder limits his talks to nonpartisan and informative material, may other legally qualified candidates who obtain time be limited to the same subjects or the same type of broadcast?

A. No. Other qualified candidates may use the facilities as they deem best in their own interest. (Letter to Congressman Allen Oakley Hunter, May 28, 1952, 11 R.R. 234.)

7. Q. May a licensee, as a condition to allowing a candidate the use of its broadcast facilities, require the candidate to submit an advance script of his program?

A. Section 315 expressly provides that licensees "shall have no power of censorship over the material broadcast under the provisions of this section." The licensee may request submission of an advance script, to aid in its presentation of the program (e.g., suggestions as to the amount of time needed to deliver the script). But any requirement of an advance script from a candidate violates section 315. A licensee could not condition permission to broadcast upon receipt of an advance script, because "the Act bestows upon the candidate the right to choose the format and other similar aspects of 'the material broadcast,' with no right of censorship in the licensee." Letter to Nicholas Zapple, October 5, 1962, FCC 62–1031. (See also Farmers Educational and Cooperative Union of America v. WDAY, Inc., 360 U.S. 525 [1958], but cf. letter to H. A. Rosenberg, Louisville, Ky., July 9, 1952, 11 R.R. 236, for a ruling antedating the WDAY decision.)

8. Q. Where a candidate desires to record his proposed broadcast, may a station require him to make the recording at his own expense?

A. Yes. Provided that the procedures adopted are applied without discrimination between candidates for the same office and no censorship is attempted.

VIII. What rates can be charged candidates for programs under Section 315?

1. Q. May a station charge premium rates for political broadcasts?

A. No. Section 315, as amended, provides that the charges made for the use of a station by a candidate "shall not exceed the charges made for comparable use of such stations for other purposes."

2. Q. Does the requirement that the charges to a candidate "shall not exceed the charges for comparable use" of a station for other purposes apply to political broadcasts by persons other than qualified candidates?

A. No. This requirement applies only to candidates for public office. Hence, a station may adopt whatever policy it desires for political broadcasts by organizations or persons who are not candidates for office, consistent with its obligation to operate in the public interest. (Letter to Congressman Charles C. Diggs, Jr., Mar. 16, 1955.)

3. Q. May a station with both "national" and "local" rates charge a candidate for local office its "national" rate?

A. No. Under §§ 73.120, 73.290, and 73.657 of the Commission's rules a station may not charge a candidate more than the rate the station would charge if the candidate were a commercial advertiser whose advertising was directed to promoting its business within the same area as that within which persons may vote for the particular office for which such person is a candidate.

4. Q. Considering the limited geographical area which a member of the House of Representatives serves, must candidates for the House be charged the "local" instead of the "national" rate?

A. This question cannot be answered categorically. To determine the maximum rates which could be charged under section 315, the Commission would have to know the criteria a station uses in classifying "local" versus "national" advertisers before it could determine what are "comparable charges." In making this determination, the Commission does not prescribe rates but merely requires equality of treatment as between 315 broadcasts and commercial advertising. (Letter to Congressman Richard M. Simpson, Feb. 27, 1957.)

5. Q. Is a political candidate entitled to receive discounts?

A. Yes. Under §§ 73.120, 73.290, and 73.657 of the Commission's rules political candidates are entitled to the same discounts that would be accorded persons other than candidates for public office under the conditions specified, as well as to such special discounts for programs coming within section 315 as the station may choose to give on a nondiscriminatory basis.

6. Q. Can a station refuse to sell time at discount rates to a group of candidates for different offices who have pooled their resources to obtain a discount, even though as a matter of commercial practice, the station permits commercial advertisers to buy a block of time at discount rates for use by various businesses owned by them?

A. Yes, section 315 imposes no obligation on a station to allow the use of its facilities by candidates, and neither that section nor the Commission's rules require a station to sell time to a group of candidates on a pooled basis, even though such may be the practice with respect to commercial advertisers. (Letter to WKBT-WKBH, Oct. 14, 1954.)

7. Q. If candidate A purchases 10 time segments over a station which offers a discount rate for purchase of that amount of time, is candidate B entitled to the discount rate if he purchases less time than the minimum to which discounts are applicable?

A. No. A station is under such circumstances only required to make available the discount privileges to each legally qualified candidate on the same basis.

8. Q. If a station has a "spot" rate of 2 dollars per "spot" announcement, with a rate reduction to 1 dollar if 100 or more such "spots" are purchased on a bulk time sales contract, and if one candidate arranges with an advertiser having such a bulk time contract to utilize five of these spots at the 1 dollar rate, is the station obligated to sell the candidates of other parties for the same office time at the same 1 dollar rate?

A. Yes. Other legally qualified candidates are entitled to take advantage of the same reduced rate. (Letter to Senator A. S. Mike Monroney, Oct. 16, 1952.)

9. Q. Where a group of candidates for different offices pool their resources to purchase a block of time at a discount, and an individual candidate opposing one of the group seeks time on the station, to what rate is he entitled?

A. He is entitled to be charged the same rate as his opponent since the provisions of section 315 run to the candidates themselves and they are entitled to be treated equally with their invididual opponents. (Report and order, Docket 11092, 11 R.R. 1501.) (Cf. Q. and A. VI.B.3; and telegram of WWIN, May 3, 1962.)

10. Q. Is there any prohibition against the purchase by a political party of a block of time for several of its candidates, for allocation among such candidates on the basis of personal need, rather than on the amount each candidate has contributed to the party's campaign fund?

A. There is no prohibition in section 315 or the Commission's rules against the above practices. It would be reasonable to assume that the group time used by a candidate is, for the purposes of section 315, time paid for by the candidate through the normal device of a recognized political campaign committee, even though part of the campaign funds was derived from sources other than the candidates' contributions. (Letter on distribution of time among candidates, Oct. 14, 1954.)

11. Q. When a candidate and his immediate family own all the stock in a corporate licensee and the candidate is the president and general manager, can he pay for time to the coroporate licensee from which he derives his income and have the licensee making a similar charge to an opposing candidate?

A. Yes. The fact that a candidate has a financial interest in a corporate licensee does not affect the licensee's obligation under section 315. Thus, the rates which the licensee may charge to other legally qualified candidates will be governed by the rate which the stockholder candidate actually pays to the licensee. If no charge is made to the stockholder candidate, it follows that other legally qualified candidates are entitled to equal time without charge. (Letter to WKOA, Mar. 18, 1957.)

12. Q. A station adopted and maintained a policy under which commissions were not paid to advertising agencies in connection with political advertising although it did pay such commissions in connection with commercial advertising. Further, in the case of commercial advertisers who did not use advertising agencies, the station performed those functions which the advertising agency would normally perform, but in the case of political advertisers, the station performed no such services. An agency which had placed political advertising over the station in a recent election made a demand of the station for payment of the agency commission. Was the station's policy consistent with section 315 of the Communications Act?

A. No. The Commission held that such a policy violated both section 315(b) of the Act and § 73.120(c) of the rules; that the benefits accruing to a candidate from the use of an advertising agency were neither remote, intangible nor insubstantial; and that while under the station's policy, a commercial advertiser would, in addition to broadcast time, receive the services of an advertising agency merely by paying the station's established card rate, the political advertiser, in return for payment of the same card rate, would receive only broadcast time. The Commission held that such a resultant inequality in treatment vis-a-vis commercial advertisers is clearly prohibited by the Act and the rules. (In re KNOE-TV, letter of May 13, 1964, FCC 64–430.)

13. Q. The Commission received a complaint on behalf of a member of the Pennsylvania House of Representatives running for reelection claiming that a local station was charging him more for his political spot announcements than it had charged him for commercial announcements on behalf of his business in the past. The station stated that the rates normally charged to the complainant for his commercial spot announcements on behalf of his business were based on an existing contract between the station and the complainant which had been entered into 8 years previously. The provisions of the contract had apparently been renewed with unchanged rates and the rates set at the time the contract was entered into were less than the present rates the local station charged to other commercial advertisers. The rates being charged to the complainant for his political announcements were the same rates the station currently charged to other commercial advertisers for a comparable use of the station's facilities. Under these circumstances is the station acting in compliance with the provisions of section 315(b) of the Communications Act and of the Commission's rules?

A. Yes. If the station were to allow the complainant to purchase political spot announcements at the rates charged to him for his commercial spot announcements, then the station would either be giving him treatment preferential to that given to his opponents or it would have to charge all candidates this lesser rate. This was not the intent of either section 315(b) of the Communications Act or the Commission's rules. In charging the complainant the rate for a political advertisement that was normally charged other commercial advertisers for a comparable use, the station was acting in compliance with both the Act and the rules. (In re WCBG, letter of Nov. 3, 1964.)

14. Q. The Commission received a complaint alleging that several stations were charging the national rate to a candidate for election to Congress but were charging a candidate for local office a local rate which was less than the national rate. The stations informed the Commission that this classification of national as against local rates for political broadcast purposes paralleled their commercial rate policy which provided that the local retail rate was applicable only to strictly local concerns whose products or services were confined to the immediate metropolitan area and that all other advertisers taking advantage of the station circulation and coverage outside and beyond the metropolitan area must pay the general or national rate. Is the stations' practice with respect to rates charged to political candidates consistent with the Act and the Commission rules?

A. Yes. The stations' action was not inconsistent with either the Act or its rules, since the rates charged to candidates (both for the local office and Congress) were the same as the rates charged to commercial advertisers whose advertising was directed to promoting their businesses within the same area as that encompassed by the political office for which such person is a candidate. (In re WSAV, letter of Sept. 11, 1964.)

IX. Period within which request must be made

1. Q. When must a candidate make a request of the station for opportunities equal to those afforded his opponent?

A. Within 1 week of the day on which the prior use occurred. (Par. (e) of §§ 73.120, 73.290, and 73.657 of the Commission rules; and telegram to WWIN, May 3, 1962.)

2. Q. A U.S. Senator, unopposed candidate in his party's primary had been broadcasting a weekly program entitled "Your Senator Reports." If he becomes opposed in his party's primary, would his opponent be entitled to request "equal opportunities" with respect to all broadcasts of "Your Senator Reports" since the time the incumbent announced his candidacy?

A. No. A legally qualified candidate announcing his candidacy for the above nomination would be required to request "equal opportunities" concerning a particular broadcast of "Your Senator Reports" not later than

1 week after the date of such broadcast. Thus, any of the incumbent's opponents for the nomination who first announced his candidacy on a particular day, would not be in a position to request "equal opportunities" with respect to any showing of "Your Senator Reports" which was broadcast more than 1 week prior to the date of such announcement. (Letter to Senator Joseph S. Clark, Apr. 16, 1962.)

3. Q. A candidate for U.S. Senator in the Democratic primary, who was also the part owner and president of AM and FM stations in the State, wrote to his opponent, the incumbent Senator, and stated, in substance, that he was using a certain amount of time daily on his stations and that the incumbent was "entitled to equal time, at no charge" and was urged to take advantage of the time. A couple of weeks later, the incumbent, by letter, thanked the station owner for advising him "of the accumulation of time" on each station and stated that the station owner would be notified when incumbent decided to start using the accumulated time. The station owner did not respond to the incumbent's letter. About 6 weeks later, incumbent requested equal opportunities. Were the stations correct in advising incumbent that the Commission's 7-day rule was applicable, thereby precluding requests for "equal opportunities" for any broadcasts prior to 7 days before the request?

A. No. The Commission stressed that where, as here, the licensee, or a principal of the licensee, was also the candidate, there is a special obligation upon the licensee to insure fair dealings in such circumstances and held that the licensee was estopped in the circumstances from relying upon the 7-day rule. The Commission held that the incumbent's letter reasonably constituted a notification as required under the rules; that the licensee knew that equal opportunities were requested; and that he could have made, if he wished, reasonable scheduling plans. (Letter in re KLIF, Apr. 22, 1964, FCC 64–363.)

X. Issuance of interpretations of section 315 by the Commission

1. Q. Under what circumstances will the Commission consider issuing declaratory orders, interpretive rulings, or advisory opinions with respect to section 315?

A. Section 5(d) of the Administrative Procedure Act, Title 5, U.S.C.A., provides that "The agency is authorized in its sound discretion, with like effect as in the case of other orders, to issue a declaratory order to terminate a controversy or remove uncertainty." However, agencies are not required to issue such orders merely because a request is made therefor. The grant of authority to agencies to issue declaratory orders is limited, and such orders are authorized only with respect to matters which are required by statute to be determined "on the record after opportunity for an agency hearing." See Attorney General's Manual on the Administrative Procedure

Act, pp. 59, 60; also, In re Goodman, 12 FCC 678, 4 Pike and Fischer R.R. 98. In general, the Commission limits its interpretive rulings or advisory opinions to situations where the critical facts are explicitly stated without the possibility that subsequent events will alter them. It prefers to issue such rulings or opinions where the specific facts of a particular case in controversy are before it for decision. (Letter in re WDSU, June 18, 1958.)

10 FAIR TRIAL VERSUS FREE PRESS

Estes *v*. Texas
381 U.S. 532
June 7, 1965

The conflict between the First, Fifth, Sixth, and Fourteenth Amendments illuminates the weaknesses inherent in a system that places high value both on a free press and trial by jury. The American Bar Association recognized this tangle when it enacted Canon 35 after the notoriously publicized trial of Bruno Hauptmann in the 1930's.

This 5-4 Supreme Court decision, in which the Justices issued six different opinions, holds that when the First and Fourteenth Amendments conflict the latter takes precedence over the former. Furthermore, the Court decided such a conflict results whenever pretrial disclosures create notorious publicity and the proceedings of a courtroom are disrupted by television equipment and personnel. This case constitutes an important precedent for the Court's decision in Sheppard *v.* Maxwell *(384 U.S. 333 (1966)).*

Only the opinion of the Court and the major dissenting opinion appear below.

MR. JUSTICE CLARK delivered the opinion of the Court.

The question presented here is whether the petitioner, who stands convicted in the District Court for the Seventh Judicial District of Texas at Tyler for swindling,[1] was deprived of his right under the Fourteenth Amendment to due process by the televising and broadcasting of his trial. Both the trial court and the Texas Court of Criminal Appeals found against the petitioner. We hold to the contrary and reverse his conviction.

---

[1] The evidence indicated that petitioner, through false pretenses and fraudulent representations, induced certain farmers to purchase fertilizer tanks and accompanying equipment, which in fact did not exist, and to sign and deliver to him chattel mortgages on the fictitious property.

. I

While petitioner recites his claim in the framework of Canon 35 of the Judicial Canons of the American Bar Association he does not contend that we should enshrine Canon 35 in the Fourteenth Amendment, but only that the time-honored principles of a fair trial were not followed in his case and that he was thus convicted without due process of law. Canon 35, of course, has of itself no binding effect on the courts but merely expresses the view of the Association in opposition to the broadcasting, televising and photographing of court proceedings. Likewise, Judicial Canon 28 of the Integrated State Bar of Texas, 27 Tex. B. J. 102 (1964), which leaves to the trial judge's sound discretion the telecasting and photographing of court proceedings, is of itself not law. In short, the question here is not the validity of either Canon 35 of the American Bar Association or Canon 28 of the State Bar of Texas, but only whether petitioner was tried in a manner which comports with the due process requirement of the Fourteenth Amendment.

Petitioner's case was originally called for trial on September 24, 1962, in Smith County after a change of venue from Reeves County, some 500 miles west. Massive pretrial publicity totaling 11 volumes of press clippings, which are on file with the Clerk, had given it national notoriety. All available seats in the courtroom were taken and some 30 persons stood in the aisles. However, at that time a defense motion to prevent telecasting, broadcasting by radio and news photography and a defense motion for continuance were presented, and after a two-day hearing the former was denied and the latter granted.

These initial hearings were carried live by both radio and television, and news photography was permitted throughout. The videotapes of these hearings clearly illustrate that the picture presented was not one of that judicial serenity and calm to which petitioner was entitled. Cf. *Wood* v. *Georgia,* 370 U.S. 375, 383 (1962); *Turner* v. *Louisiana,* 379 U.S. 466, 472 (1965); *Cox* v. *Louisiana,* 379 U.S. 559, 562 (1965). Indeed, at least 12 cameramen were engaged in the courtroom throughout the hearing taking motion and still pictures and televising the proceedings. Cables and wires were snaked across the courtroom floor, three microphones were on the judge's bench and others were beamed at the jury box and the counsel table. It is conceded that the activities of the television crews and news photographers led to considerable disruption of the hearings. Moreover, veniremen had been summoned and were present in the courtroom during the entire hearing but were later released after petitioner's motion for continuance had been granted. The court also had the names of the witnesses called; some answered but the absence of others led to a continuance of the case until October 22, 1962. It is contended that this two-day pretrial hearing cannot be considered in determining the question before us. We cannot agree. Pretrial can create a major problem for the defendant in a criminal case. Indeed, it may be more harmful than publicity during the trial for it may well set the community opinion as to guilt or innocence. Though the September hearings dealt with motions to prohibit television coverage and to postpone the trial, they are unquestionably relevant to the issue before us. All of this two-day affair was highly publicized and could only have impressed those present, and also the community at large, with the notorious character of the petitioner as well as the proceeding. The trial witnesses present at the hearing, as well as the original jury panel, were undoubtedly made aware of the peculiar public importance of the case by the press and television coverage being provided, and by the fact that they themselves were televised live and their pictures rebroadcast on the evening show.

When the case was called for trial on October 22 the scene had been altered. A booth had been constructed at the back of the courtroom which was painted to blend with the permanent structure of the room. It had an aperture to allow the lens of the cameras an unrestricted view of the courtroom. All television cameras and newsreel photographers were restricted to the area of the booth when shooting film or telecasting.

Because of continual objection, the rules governing live telecasting, as well as radio and still photos, were changed as the exigencies of the situation seemed to require. As a result, live telecasting was prohibited during a great portion of the actual trial. Only the opening[2] and closing arguments of the State, the return of the jury's verdict and its receipt by the trial judge were carried live with sound. Although the order allowed videotapes of the entire proceeding without sound, the cameras operated only intermittently, recording various portions of the trial for broadcast on regularly scheduled newscasts later in the day and evening. At the request of the petitioner, the trial judge prohibited coverage of any kind, still or television, of the defense counsel during their summations to the jury.

Because of the varying restrictions placed on sound and live telecasting the telecasts of the trial were confined largely to film clips shown on the stations' regularly scheduled news programs. The news commentators would use the film of a particular part of the day's trial activities as a backdrop for their reports. Their commentary included excerpts from testimony and the usual reportorial remarks. On one occasion the videotapes of the September hearings were rebroadcast in place of the "late movie."

II

In *Rideau* v. *Louisiana,* 373 U.S. 723 (1963), this Court constructed a rule that the televising of a defendant in the act of confessing to a

---

[2] Due to mechanical difficulty there was no picture during the opening argument.

crime was inherently invalid under the Due Process Clause of the Fourteenth Amendment even without a showing of prejudice or a demonstration of the nexus between the televised confession and the trial. See *id.,* at 729 (dissenting opinion of CLARK, J.). Here, although there was nothing so dramatic as a home-viewed confession, there had been a bombardment of the community with the sights and sounds of a two-day hearing during which the original jury panel, the petitioner, the lawyers and the judge were highly publicized. The petitioner was subjected to characterization and minute electronic scrutiny to such an extent that at one point the photographers were found attempting to picture the page of the paper from which he was reading while sitting at the counsel table. The two-day hearing and the order permitting television at the actual trial were widely known throughout the community. This emphasized the notorious character that the trial would take and, therefore, set it apart in the public mind as an extraordinary case or, as Shaw would say, something "not conventionally unconventional." When the new jury was empaneled at the trial four of the jurors selected had seen and heard all or part of the broadcasts of the earlier proceedings.

III

We start with the proposition that it is a "public trial" that the Sixth Amendment guarantees to the "accused." The purpose of the requirement of a public trial was to guarantee that the accused would be fairly dealt with and not unjustly condemned. History had proven that secret tribunals were effective instruments of oppression. As our Brother BLACK so well said in *In re Oliver,* 333 U.S. 257 (1948):

The traditional Anglo-American distrust for secret trials has been variously ascribed to the notorious use of this practice by the Spanish Inquisition, to the excesses of the English Court of Star Chamber, and to the French monarchy's abuse of the *lettre de cachet.* . . . Whatever other benefits the guarantee to an accused that his trial be conducted in public may confer upon our society, the guarantee has always been recognized as a safeguard against any attempt to employ our courts as instruments of persecution. At 268–270. (Footnotes omitted.)

It is said, however, that the freedoms granted in the First Amendment extend a right to the news media to televise from the courtroom, and that to refuse to honor this privilege is to discriminate between the newspapers and television. This is a misconception of the rights of the press.

The free press has been a mighty catalyst in awakening public interest in governmental affairs, exposing corruption among public officers and employees and generally informing the citizenry of public events and occurrences, including court proceedings. While maximum freedom must be allowed the press in carrying on this important function in a democratic society its exercise must necessarily be subject to the maintenance of absolute fairness in the judicial process. While the state and federal courts have differed over what spectators may be excluded from a criminal trial, 6 Wigmore, Evidence § 1834 (3d ed. 1940), the *amici curiae* brief of the National Association of Broadcasters and the Radio Television News Directors Association, says, as indeed it must, that "neither of these two amendments [First and Sixth] speaks of an unlimited right of access to the courtroom on the part of the broadcasting media. . . ." At 7. Moreover, they recognize that the "primary concern of all must be the proper administration of justice"; that "the life or liberty of any individual in this land should not be put in jeopardy because of actions of any news media"; and that "the due process requirements in both the Fifth and Fourteenth Amendments and the provisions of the Sixth Amendment require a procedure that will assure a fair trial. . . ." At 3–4.

Nor can the courts be said to discriminate where they permit the newspaper reporter access to the courtroom. The television and radio reporter has the same privilege. All are entitled to the same rights as the general public. The news reporter is not permitted to bring his typewriter or printing press. When the advances in these arts permit reporting by printing press or by television without their present hazards to a fair trial we will have another case.

IV

Court proceedings are held for the solemn purpose of endeavoring to ascertain the truth which is the *sine qua non* of a fair trial. Over the centuries Anglo-American courts have devised careful safeguards by rule and otherwise to protect and facilitate the performance of this high function. As a result, at this time those safeguards do not permit the televising and photographing of a criminal trial, save in two States and there only under restrictions. The federal courts prohibit it by specific rule. This is weighty evidence that our concepts of a fair trial do not tolerate such an indulgence. We have always held that the atmosphere essential to the preservation of a fair trial—the most fundamental of all freedoms—must be maintained at all costs. Our approach has been through rules, contempt proceedings and reversal of convictions obtained under unfair conditions. Here the remedy is clear and certain of application and its our duty to continue to enforce the principles that from time immemorial have proven efficacious and necessary to a fair trial.

V

The State contends that the televising of portions of a criminal trial does not constitute a denial of due process. Its position is that because no prejudice has been shown by the petitioner as resulting from the televising, it is permissible; that claims of "distractions" during the trial due to the physical presence of television are wholly unfounded; and that physchological considerations are for psychologists, not courts, because they are purely hypothetical. It argues further that the public has a right to know what goes on in the courts; that the court has no power to "suppress, edit, or censor events which transpire in proceedings before it," citing *Craig* v. *Harney,* 331 U.S. 367, 374 (1947); and that the televising of criminal trials would be enlightening to the public and would promote greater respect for the courts.

At the outset the notion should be dispelled that telecasting is dangerous because it is new. It is true that our empirical knowledge of its full effect on the public, the jury or the participants in a trial, including the judge, witnesses and lawyers, is limited. However, the nub of the question is not its newness but, as MR. JUSTICE DOUGLAS says, "the insidious influences which it puts to work in the administration of justice." Douglas, The Public Trial and the Free Press, 33 Rocky Mt. L. Rev. 1 (1960). These influences will be detailed below, but before turning to them the State's argument that the public has a right to know what goes on in the courtroom should be dealt with.

It is true that the public has the right to be informed as to what occurs in its courts, but reporters of all media, including television, are always present if they wish to be and are plainly free to report whatever occurs in open court through their respective media. This was settled in *Bridges* v. *California,* 314 U.S. 252 (1941), and *Pennekamp* v. *Florida,* 328 U.S. 331 (1946), which we reaffirm. These reportorial privileges of the press were stated years ago:

> The law, however, favors publicity in legal proceedings, so far as that object can be attained without injustice to the persons immediately concerned. The public are permitted to attend nearly all judicial inquiries, and there appears to be no sufficient reason why they should not also be allowed to see in print the reports of trials, if they can thus have them presented as fully as they are exhibited in court, or at least all the material portion of the proceedings impartially stated, so that one shall not, by means of them, derive erroneous impressions, which he would not have been likely to receive from hearing the trial itself. (2 Cooley's Constitutional Limitations 931–932; Carrington ed. 1927).

The State, however, says that the use of television in the instant case was "without injustice to the person immediately concerned," basing its position on the fact that the petitioner has established no isolatable prejudice and that this must be shown in order to invalidate a conviction in these circumstances. The State paints too broadly in this contention, for this Court itself has found instances in which a showing of actual prejudice is not a prerequisite to reversal. This is such a case. It is true that in most cases involving claims of due process deprivations we require a showing of identifiable prejudice to the accused. Nevertheless, at times a procedure employed by the State involves such a probability that prejudice will result that it is deemed inherently lacking in due process. Such a case was *In re Murchison,* 349 U.S. 133 (1955), where MR. JUSTICE BLACK for the Court pointed up with his usual clarity and force:

> A fair trial in a fair tribunal is a basic requirement of due process. Fairness of course requires an absence of actual bias in the trial of cases. But our system of law has always endeavored to prevent even the *probability* of unfairness. . . . [T]o perform its high function in the best way "justice must satisfy the appearance of justice." *Offutt* v. *United States,* 348 U.S. 11, 14. At 136. (Emphasis supplied.)

And, as Chief Justice Taft said in *Tumey* v. *Ohio,* 273 U.S. 510, almost 30 years before:

> the requirement of due process of law in judicial procedure is not satisfied by the argument that men of the highest honor and the greatest self-sacrifice could carry it on without danger of injustice. Every procedures which would offer a *possible* temptation to the average man . . . to forget the burden of proof required to convict the defendant, or which might lead him not to hold the balance nice, clear and true between the State and the accused, denies the latter due process of law. At 532. (Emphasis supplied.)

This rule was followed in *Rideau, supra,* and in *Turner* v. *Louisiana,* 379 U.S. 466 (1965). In each of these cases the Court departed from the approach it charted in *Stroble* v. *California,* 343 U.S. 181 (1952), and in *Irvin* v. *Dowd,* 366 U.S. 717 (1961), where we made a careful examination of the facts in order to determine whether prejudice resulted. In *Rideau* and *Turner* the Court did not stop to consider the actual effect of the practice but struck down the conviction on the ground that prejudice was inherent in it. Likewise in *Gideon* v. *Wainwright,* 372 U.S. 335 (1963), and *White* v. *Maryland,* 373 U.S. 59 (1963), we applied the same rule, although in different contexts.

In this case it is even clearer that such a rule must be applied. In *Rideau, Irvin* and *Stroble,* the pretrial publicity occurred outside the courtroom and could not be effectively curtailed. The only recourse other than reversal was by contempt proceedings. In *Turner* the probability of prejudice was present through the use of deputy sheriffs, who were also witnesses in the case, as shepherds for the jury. No prejudice was shown but the circumstances were held to be inherently suspect, and, therefore, such a showing was not held to be a requisite to reversal. Likewise in this case the application of this principle is especially appropriate. Television in its present state and by its very nature, reaches into a variety of areas in which it may cause prejudice to an accused. Still one cannot put his finger on its specific mischief and prove with particularity wherein he was prejudiced. This was found true in *Murchison, Tumey, Rideau* and *Turner*. Such untoward circumstances as were found in those cases are inherently bad and prejudice to the accused was presumed. Forty-eight of our States and the Federal Rules have deemed the use of television improper in the court-room. This fact is most telling in buttressing our conclusion that any change in procedure which would permit its use would be inconsistent with our concepts of due process in this field

VI

As has been said, the chief function of our judicial machinery is to ascertain the truth. The use of television, however, cannot be said to contribute materially to this objective. Rather its use amounts to the injection of an irrelevant factor into court proceedings. In addition experience teaches that there are numerous situations in which it might cause actual unfairness—some so subtle as to defy detection by the accused or control by the judge. We enumerate some in summary:

1. The potential impact of television on the jurors is perhaps of the greatest significance. They are the nerve center of the fact-finding process. It is true that in States like Texas where they are required to be sequestered in trials of this nature the jurors will probably not see any of the proceedings as televised from the courtroom. But the inquiry cannot end there. From the moment the trial judge announces that a case will be televised it becomes a *cause célèbre*. The whole community, including prospective jurors, becomes interested in all the morbid details surrounding it. The approaching trial immediately assumes an important status in the public press and the accused is highly publicized along with the offense with which he is charged. Every juror carries with him into the jury box these solemn facts and thus increases the chance of prejudice that is present in every criminal case. And we must remember that realistically it is only the notorious trial which will be broadcast, because of the necessity for paid sponsorship. The conscious or unconscious effect that this may have on the juror's judgment cannot be evaluated, but experience indicates that it is not only possible but highly probable that it will have a direct bearing on his vote as to guilt or innocence. Where pretrial publicity of all kinds has created intense public feeling which is aggravated by the telecasting or picturing of the trial the televised jurors cannot help but feel the pressures of knowing that friends and neighbors have their eyes upon them. If the community be hostile to an accused a televised juror, realizing that he must return to neighbors who saw the trial themselves, may well be led "not to hold the balance nice, clear and true between the State and the accused. . . ."

Moreover, while it is practically impossible to assess the effect of television on jury attentiveness, those of us who know juries realize the problem of jury "distraction." The State argues this is *de minimis* since the physical disturbances have been eliminated. But we know that distractions are not caused solely by the physical presence of the camera and its telltale red lights. It is the awareness of the fact of telecasting that is felt by the juror throughout the trial. We are all self-conscious and uneasy when being televised. Human nature being what it is, not only will a juror's eyes be fixed on the camera, but also his mind will be preoccupied with the telecasting rather than with the testimony.

Furthermore, in many States the jurors serving in the trial may see the broadcasts of the trial proceedings. Admittedly, the Texas sequestration rule would prevent this occurring there.[3] In other States following no such practice jurors would return home and turn on the TV if only to see how they appeared upon it. They would also be subjected to re-enactment and emphasis of the selected parts of the proceedings which the requirements of the broadcasters determined would be telecast and would be subconsciously influenced the more by that testimony. Moreover, they would be subjected to the broadest commentary and criticism and perhaps the well-meant advice of friends, relatives and inquiring strangers who recognized them on the streets.

Finally, new trials plainly would be jeopardized in that potential jurors will often have seen and heard the original trial when it was telecast. Yet viewers may later be called upon to sit in the jury box during the new trial. These very dangers are illustrated in this case where the court, due to the defendant's objections, permitted only the State's opening and closing arguments to be broadcast with sound to the public.

2. The quality of the testimony in criminal trials will often be impaired. The impact upon a witness of the knowledge that he is being viewed by a vast audience is simply incalculable. Some may be demoralized and frightened, some cocky and given to overstatement; memories may falter, as with anyone speaking publicly, and accuracy of statement may be severely undermined. Embarrassment may impede the search for the truth, as may a natural tendency toward overdramatization. Furthermore, inquisitive strangers and "cranks" might approach witnesses on the street with jibes, advice or demands for explanation of testimony. There is little wonder that the defendant cannot "prove" the existence of such factors. Yet we all know from experience that they exist.

In addition the invocation of the rule against witnesses is frustrated. In most instances witnesses would be able to go to their homes and view broadcasts of the day's trial proceedings, notwithstanding the fact that they had been admonished not to do so. They could view and hear the testimony of preceding witnesses, and so shape their own testimony as to make its im-

---

[3] Only six States, in addition to Texas, require sequestration of the jury prior to its deliberations in a non-capital felony trial. The great majority of jurisdictions leave the matter to the trial judge's discretion, while in at least one State the jury will be kept together in such circumstances only upon a showing of cause by the defendant.

pact crucial. And even in the absence of sound, the influences of such viewing on the attitude of the witness toward testifying, his frame of mind upon taking the stand or his apprehension of withering cross-examination defy objective assessment. Indeed, the mere fact that the trial is to be televised might render witnesses reluctant to appear and thereby impede the trial as well as the discovery of the truth.

While some of the dangers mentioned above are present as well in newspaper coverage of any important trial, the circumstances and extraneous influences intruding upon the solemn decorum of court procedure in the televised trial are far more serious than in cases involving only newspaper coverage.

3. A major aspect of the problem is the additional responsibilities the presence of television places on the trial judge. His job is to make certain that the accused receives a fair trial. This most difficult task requires his undivided attention. Still when television comes into the courtroom he must also supervise it. In this trial, for example, the judge on several different occasions—aside from the two days of pretrial—was obliged to have a hearing or enter an order made necessary solely because of the presence of television. Thus, where telecasting is restricted as it was here, and as even the State concedes it must be, his task is made much more difficult and exacting. And, as happened here, such rulings may unfortunately militate against the fairness of the trial. In addition, laying physical interruptions aside, there is the ever-present distraction that the mere awareness of television's presence prompts. Judges are human beings also and are subject to the same psychological reactions as laymen. Telecasting is particularly bad where the judge is elected, as is the case in all save a half dozen of our States. The telecasting of a trial becomes a political weapon, which, along with other distractions inherent in broadcasting, diverts his attention from the task at hand—the fair trial of the accused.

But this is not all. There is the initial decision that must be made as to whether the use of television will be permitted. This is perhaps an even more crucial consideration. Our judges are high-minded men and women. But it is difficult to remain oblivious to the pressures that the news media can bring to bear on them both directly and through the shaping of public opinion. Moreover, where one judge in a district or even in a State permits telecasting, the requirement that the others do the same is almost mandatory. Especially is this true where the judge is selected at the ballot box.

4. Finally, we cannot ignore the impact of courtroom television on the defendant. Its presence is a form of mental—if not physical—harassment, resembling a police line-up or the third degree. The inevitable close-ups of his gestures and expressions during the ordeal of his trial might well transgress his personal sensibilities, his dignity, and his ability to concentrate on the proceedings before him—sometimes the difference between life and death—dispassionately, freely and without the distraction of wide public

surveillance. A defendant on trial for a specific crime is entitled to his day in court, not in a stadium, or a city or nationwide arena. The heightened public clamor resulting from radio and television coverage will inevitably result in prejudice. Trial by television is, therefore, foreign to our system. Furthermore, telecasting may also deprive an accused of effective counsel. The distractions, intrusions into confidential attorney-client relationships and the temptation offered by television to play to the public audience might often have a direct effect not only upon the lawyers, but the judge, the jury and the witnesses. See Pye, The Lessons of Dallas—Threats to Fair Trial and Free Press, National Civil Liberties Clearing House, 16th Annual Conference.

The television camera is a powerful weapon. Intentionally or inadvertently it can destroy an accused and his case in the eyes of the public. While our telecasters are honorable men, they too are human. The necessity for sponsorship weighs heavily in favor of the televising of only notorious cases, such as this one, and invariably focuses the lens upon the unpopular or infamous accused. Such a selection is necessary in order to obtain a sponsor willing to pay a sufficient fee to cover the costs and return a profit. We have already examined the ways in which public sentiment can affect the trial participants. To the extent that television shapes that sentiment, it can strip the accused of a fair trial.

The State would dispose of all these observations with the simple statement that they are for psychologists because they are purely hypothetical. But we cannot afford the luxury of saying that, because these factors are difficult of ascertainment in particular cases, they must be ignored. Nor are they "purely hypothetical." They are no more hypothetical than were the considerations deemed controlling in *Tumey, Murchison, Rideau* and *Turner*. They are real enough to have convinced the Judicial Conference of the United States, this Court and the Congress that television should be barred in federal trials by the Federal Rules of Criminal Procedure; in addition they have persuaded all but two of our States to prohibit television in the courtroom. They are effects that may, and in some combination almost certainly will, exist in any case in which television is injected into the trial process.

VII

The facts in this case demonstrate clearly the necessity for the application of the rule announced in *Rideau*. The sole issue before the court for two days of pretrial hearing was the question now before us. The hearing was televised live and repeated on tape in the same evening, reaching approximately 100,000 viewers. In addition, the courtroom was a mass of wires, television cameras, microphones and photographers. The petitioner, the panel of prospective jurors, who were sworn the second day, the witnesses and the lawyers were all exposed to this untoward situation. The judge decided that the trial proceedings would be telecast. He announced no restrictions at the time. This emphasized the notorious nature of the coming trial, increased the intensity of the publicity on the petitioner and together with the subsequent televising of the trial beginning 30 days later inherently prevented a sober search for the truth. This is underscored by the fact that the selection of the jury took an entire week. As might be expected, a substantial amount of that time was devoted to ascertaining the impact of the pretrial televising on the prospective jurors. As we have noted, four of the jurors selected had seen all or part of those broadcasts. The trial, on the other hand, lasted only three days.

Moreover, the trial judge was himself harassed. After the initial decision to permit telecasting he apparently decided that a booth should be built at the broadcasters' expense to confine its operations; he then decided to limit the parts of the trial that might be televised live; then he decided to film the testimony of the witnesses without sound in an attempt to protect those under the rule; and finally he ordered that defense counsel and their argument not be televised, in the light of their objection. Plagued by his original error—recurring each day of the trial—his day-to-day orders made the trial more confusing to the jury, the participants and to the viewers. Indeed, it resulted in a public presentation of only the State's side of the case.

As Mr. Justice Holmes said in *Patterson* v. *Colorado,* 205 U. S. 454, 462 (1907):

The theory of our system is that the conclusions to be reached in a case will be induced only by evidence and argument in open court, and not by any outside influence, whether of private talk or public print.

It is said that the ever-advancing techniques of public communication and the adjustment of the public to its presence may bring about a change in the effect of telecasting upon the fairness of criminal trials. But we are not dealing here with future developments in the field of electronics. Our judgment cannot be rested on the hypothesis of tomorrow but must take the facts as they are presented today.

The judgment is therefore reversed.

Mr. Justice Stewart, whom Mr. Justice Black, Mr. Justice Brennan, and Mr. Justice White join, dissenting.

I cannot agree with the Court's decision that the circumstances of this trial led to a denial of the petitioner's Fourteenth Amendment rights. I think that the introduction of television into a courtroom is, at least in the present state of the art, an extremely unwise policy. It invites many constitutional risks, and it detracts from the inherent dignity of a courtroom. But I am unable to escalate this personal view into a *per se* constitutional rule.

And I am unable to find, on the specific record of this case, that the circumstances attending the limited televising of the petitioner's trial resulted in the denial of any right guaranteed to him by the United States Constitution.

On October 22, 1962, the petitioner went to trial in the Seventh Judicial District Court of Smith County, Texas, upon an indictment charging him with the offenses of (1) swindling, (2) theft by false pretenses, and (3) theft by a bailee. After a week spent in selecting a jury, the trial itself lasted some three and a half days. At its conclusion the jury found the petitioner guilty of the offense of swindling under the first count of the indictment. The trial judge permitted portions of the trial proceedings to be televised, under the limitations described below. He also gave news photographers permission to take still pictures in the courtroom under specified conditions.

The Texas Court of Criminal Appeals affirmed the petitioner's conviction, and we granted certiorari, limited to a single question. The question, as phrased by the petitioner, is this:

Whether the action of the trial court, over petitioner's continued objection, denied him due process of law and equal protection of the laws under the Fourteenth Amendment to the Constitution of the United States, in requiring petitioner to submit to live television of his trial, and in refusing to adopt in this all out publicity case, as a rule of trial procedure, Canon 35 of the Canons of Judicial Ethics of the American Bar Association, and instead adopting and following, over defendant's objection, Canon 28 of the Canons of Judicial Ethics, since approved by the Judicial Section of the integrated (State agency) State Bar of Texas.

The two Canons of Judicial Ethics referred to in the petitioner's statement of the question presented are set out in the margin.[1] But, as the Court

[1] Canons of Judicial Ethics. American Bar Association: Judicial Canon 35. Improper publicizing of Court proceedings.

"Proceedings in court should be conducted with fitting dignity and decorum. The taking of photographs in the court room, during sessions of the court or recesses between sessions, and the broadcasting or televising of court proceedings detract from the essential dignity of the proceedings, distract participants and witnesses in giving testimony, and create misconceptions with respect thereto in the mind of the public and should not be permitted.

"Provided that this restriction shall not apply to the broadcasting or televising, under the supervision of the court, of such portions of naturalization proceedings (other than the interrogation of applicants) as are designed and carried out exclusively as a ceremony for the purpose of publicly demonstrating in an impressive manner the essential dignity and the serious nature of naturalization."

Canons of Judicial Ethics, Integrated State Bar of Texas: Judicial Canon 28. Improper Publicizing of Court Proceedings.

"Proceedings in court should be conducted with fitting dignity and decorum. The taking of photographs in the court room, during sessions of the court or recesses between sessions, and the broadcasting or televising of court proceedings unless properly supervised and controlled, may detract from the essential dignity of the proceedings, distract participants and witnesses in giving testimony, and create misconceptions with respect thereto in the mind of the public. The supervision and

rightly says, the problem before us is not one of choosing between the conflicting guidelines reflected in these Canons of Judicial Ethics. It is a problem rooted in the Due Process Clause of the Fourteenth Amendment. We deal here with matters subject to continuous and unforeseeable change—the techniques of public communication. In an area where all the variables may be modified tomorrow, I cannot at this time rest my determination on hypothetical possibilities not present in the record of this case. There is no claim here based upon any right guaranteed by the First Amendment. But it is important to remember that we move in an area touching the realm of free commuication, and for that reason, if for no other, I would be wary of imposing any *per se* rule which, in the light of future technology, might serve to stifle or abridge true First Amendment rights.

I

The indictment was originally returned by a grand jury in Reeves County, Texas, and it engendered widespread publicity. After some preliminary proceedings there, the case was transferred for trial to Smith County, more than 500 miles away. The trial was set for September 24, 1962, but it did not commence on that date. Instead, that day and the next were spent in hearings on two motions filed by defense counsel: a motion to bar television and news cameras from the trial, and a motion to continue the trial to a later date. Those proceedings were themselves telecast "live," and news photographers were permitted to take pictures in the courtroom. The activities of the television crews and news photographers led to considerable disruption of the hearings.[2] At the conclusion of the hearings the motion for

---

control of such trial coverage shall be left to the trial judge who has the inherent power to exclude or control coverage in the proper case in the interest of justice.

"In connection with the control of such coverage the following declaration of principles is adopted:

"(1) There should be no use of flash bulbs or other artificial lighting.

"(2) No witness, over his expressed objection, should be photographed, his voice broadcast or be televised.

"(3) The representatives of news media must obtain permission of the trial judge to cover by photograph, broadcasting or televising, and shall comply with the rules prescribed by the judge for the exercise of the privilege.

"(4) Any violation of the Court's Rules shall be punished as a contempt.

"(5) Where a judge has refused to allow coverage or has regulated it, any attempt, other than argument by representatives of the news media directly with the Court, to bring pressure of any kind on the judge, pending final disposition of the cause in trial, shall be punished as a contempt."

[2] A contemporary newspaper account described the scene as follows:

"A television motor van, big as an intercontinental bus, was parked outside the courthouse and the second-floor courtroom was a forest of equipment. Two television cameras had been set up inside the bar and four more marked cameras were aligned just outside the gates.

"A microphone stuck its 12-inch snout inside the jury box, now occupied by an overflow of reporters from the press table, and three microphones confronted Judge Dunagan on his bench. [C]ables and wires snaked over the floor." The New York Times, September 25, 1962, p. 46, col. 4.

a continuance was granted, and the case reset for trial on October 22. The motion to bar television and news photographers from the trial was denied.[3]

On October 1, the trial judge issued an order delineating what coverage he would permit during the trial.[4] As a result of that order and ensuing con-

[3] In ruling on the motion, the trial judge stated:

"In the past, it has been the policy of this Court to permit televising in the court room under the rules and supervision of the Court. Heretofore, I have not encountered any difficulty with it. I was unable to observe any detraction from the witnesses or the attorneys in those cases. We have watched television, of course, grow up from its infancy and now into its maturity; and it is a news media. So I really do not see any justified reason why it should not be permitted to take its proper seat in the family circle. However, it will be under the strict supervision of the Court. I know there has been pro and con about televising in the court room. I have heard some say that it makes a circus out of the Court. I had the privilege yesterday morning of sitting in my home and viewing a sermon by the First Baptist Church over in Dallas and certainly it wasn't any circus in that church; and I feel that if it is a proper instrument in the house of the Lord, it is not out of place in the court room, if properly supervised.

"Now, television is going to be televising whatever the scene is here. If you want to watch a ball game and that is what they televise, you are going to see a ball game. If you want to see a preacher and hear a sermon, you tune in on that and that is what you are going to get. If the Court permits a circus in this court room, it will be televised, that is true, but they will not be creating a circus.

"Now, the most important point is whether or not it would interfere with a fair and impartial trial of this Defendant. That is the most important point, and that is the purpose, or will be the primary purpose of the Court, to insure that he gets that fair trial.

"There is not anything the Court can do about the interest in this case, but I can control your activities and your conduct here; and I can assure you now that this Court is not going to be turned into a circus with TV or without it. Whatever action is necessary for the Court to take to insure that, the Court will take it.

"There has been one consideration that the Court has given and it is that this is a small court room and there will be hundreds of people trying to get into this court room to witness this trial. I believe we would have less confusion if they would stay at home and stay out of the court room and look in on the trial. With all of those people trying to crowd in and push into this court room, that is another consideration I have given to it."

[4] "In my statement of September 24, 1962, admitting television and other cameras in the court room during the trial of Billie Sol Estes, I said cameras would be allowed under the control and direction of the Court so long as they did not violate the legal rights of the Defendant or the State of Texas.

"In line with my statement of September 24, 1962, I am at this time informing both television and radio that live broadcasting or telecasting by either news media cannot and will not be permitted during the interrogation of jurors in testing their qualifications, or of the testimony given by the witnesses, as to do so would be in violation of Art. 644 of the Code of Criminal Procedure of Texas, which provides as follows: 'At the request of either party, the witnesses on both sides may be sworn and placed in the custody of an officer and removed out of the court room to some place where they can not hear the testimony as delivered by any other witness in the case. This is termed placing witnesses under rule.'

". . . [E]ach television network and the local television station will be allowed one film camera without sound in the court room and the film will be made available to other television stations on a pool basis. Marshall Pengra, manager of Television Station KLTV, Tyler, will be in charge of the independent pool and independent stations may contact him. The same will be true of cameras for the

ferences between the judge and representatives of the news media, the environment for the trial, which began on October 22, was in sharp contrast to that of the September hearings. The actual extent of television and news photography in the courtroom was described by the judge, after the trial had ended, in certifying the petitioner's bill of exceptions. This description is confirmed by my understanding of the entire record and was agreed to and accepted by defense counsel:

Prior to the trial of October 22, 1962, there was a booth constructed and placed in the rear of the courtroom painted the same or near the same color as the courtroom with a small opening across the top for the use of cameras. . . .

Live telecasting and radio broadcasting were not permitted and the only telecasting was on film without sound, and there was not any broadcasting of the trial by radio permitted. Each network, ABC, NBC, CBS and KRLD [KLTV] Television in Tyler was allowed a camera in the courtroom. . . . The telecasting on film of this case was not a continuous camera operation and only pictures being taken at intervals during the day to be used on regular news casts later in the day. There were some days during the trial that the cameras of only one or two stations were in operation, the others not being in attendance upon the Court each and every day. The Court did not permit any cameras other than those that were noiseless nor were flood lights and flash bulbs allowed to be used in the courtroom. The Court permitted one news photographer with Associated Press, United Press International and Tyler Morning Telegraph and Courier Times. However, they were not permitted inside the Bar; and the Court did not permit any telecasting or photographing in the hallways leading into the courtroom or on the second floor of the courthouse where the courtroom is situated, in order that the Defendant and his attorneys would not be hindered, molested or harassed in approaching or leaving the courtroom. The Court did permit live telecasting of the arguments of State's counsel and the returning of the verdict by the Jury and its acceptance by the Court. The opening argument of the District Attorney of Smith County was carried by sound and because of transmission difficulty, there was not any picture. The closing argument for the State by the District Attorney of Reeves County was carried live by both picture and sound. The arguments of attorneys for Defendant, John D. Cofer and Hume Cofer, were not telecast or broadcast as the Court granted their Motion that same not be permitted.

There was not any televising at any time during the trial except from the booth in the rear of the courtroom, and during the argument of counsel to the jury, news photography was required to operate from the booth so that they would not interfere or detract from the attention of either the jurors or the attorneys.

---

press, which will be limited to the local press, Associated Press and United Press.

"I am making this statement at this time in order that the two news media affected may have sufficient notice before the case is called on October 22nd.

"The rules I have set forth above concerning the use of cameras are subject to change if I find that they are too restrictive or not workable, for any reason."

During the trial that began October 22nd, there was never at any time any radio broadcasting equipment in the courtroom. There was some equipment in a room off of the courtroom where there were periodic news reports given; and throughout the trial that began October 22nd, not any witness requested not to be televised or photographed while they were testifying. Neither did any juror, while being interrogated on voir dire or at any other time, make any request of the Court not to be televised.

Thus, except for the closing arguments for the prosecution and the return of the jury's verdict, there was no "live" telecasting of the trial. And, even for the purposes of delayed telecasting on later news programs, no words or other sounds were permitted to be recorded while the members of the jury were being selected or while any witness was testifying. No witnesses and no jurors were televised or photographed over their objection.[5]

Finally, the members of the jury saw no telecasts and no pictures of anything that went on during the trial. In accord with Texas law, the jurors were sequestered, day and night, from the beginning of the trial until it ended.[6] The jurors were lodged each night in quarters provided for that purpose in the courthouse itself. On the evening of November 6, by agreement of counsel and special permission of the court, the members of the jury were permitted to watch the election returns on television for a short period. For this purpose a portable television was brought into the jury's quarters by a court officer, and operated by him. Otherwise the jurors were not permitted to watch television at any time during the trial. The only newspapers permitted the jury were ones from which all coverage of the trial had been physically removed.

II

It is important to bear in mind the precise limits of the question before us in this case. The petition for a writ of certiorari asked us to review four separate constitutional claims. We declined to review three of them, among which was the claim that the members of the jury "had received through the news media damaging and prejudicial evidence. . . ."[7] We thus left undisturbed the determination of the Texas Court of Criminal Appeals that the members of the jury were *not* prejudiced by the widespread publicity which preceded the petitioners' trial. One ingredient of this pretrial publicity was the telecast of the September hearings. Despite the confusion in the courtroom during those hearings, all that a potential juror could have possibly learned from watching them on television was that the petitioner's case had been called for trial, and that motions had been made and acted upon for a continuance, and to exclude cameras and television. At those hearings, there was no discussion whatever of anything bear-

---

[5] There were nine witnesses for the prosecution and no witnesses for the defense.
[6] Arts. 668, 745, and 725, Tex. Code Crim. Proc.
[7] Petition for Writ of Certiorari, Question 3, p. 3.

ing on the petitioner's guilt or innocence. This was conceded by the petitioner's counsel at the trial.[8]

Because of our refusal to review the petitioner's claim that pretrial publicity had a prejudicial effect upon the jurors in this case, and because, insofar as the September hearings were an element of that publicity, the claim is patently without merit, that issue is simply not here. Our decision in *Rideau* v. *Louisiana,* 373 U. S. 723, therefore, has no bearing at all in this case. There the record showed that the inhabitants of the small Louisiana parish where the trial was held had repeatedly been exposed to a television film showing "Rideau, in jail, flanked by the sheriff and two state troopers, admitting in detail the commission of the robbery, kidnapping, and murder, in response to leading questions by the sheriff." 373 U. S., at 725. We found that "[a]ny subsequent court proceedings in a community so pervasively exposed to such a spectacle could be but a hollow formality." *Id.,* at 726. See also *Irvin* v. *Dowd,* 366 U. S. 717.

The *Rideau* case was no more than a contemporary application of enduring principles of procedural due process, principles reflected in such earlier cases as *Moore* v. *Dempsey,* 261 U. S. 86; *Brown* v. *Mississippi,* 297 U. S. 278; and *Chambers* v. *Florida,* 309 U. S. 227, 235–241. "Under our Constitution's guarantee of due process," we said, " a person accused of committing a crime is vouchsafed basic minimal rights. Among these are the right to counsel, the right to plead not guilty, and the right to be tried in a courtroom presided over by a judge." 373 U. S., at 726–727. We had occasion to apply the same basic concepts of procedural due process earlier this Term in *Turner* v. *Louisiana,* 379 U. S. 466. "In the constitutional sense, trial by jury in a criminal case necessarily implies at the very least the 'evidence developed' against a defendant shall come from the witness stand in a public courtroom where there is full judicial protection of the defendant's right of confrontation, of cross-examination, and of counsel." 379 U. S., at 472–473.

But we do not deal here with mob domination of a courtroom, with a kangaroo trial, with a prejudiced judge or a jury inflamed with bias. Under the limited grant of certiorari in this case, the sole question before us is an entirely different one. It concerns only the regulated presence of television and still photography at the trial itself, which began on October 22, 1962. Any discussion of pretrial events can do no more than obscure the important question which is actually before us.

---

[8] "A. [Mr. Hume Cofer, counsel for petitioner] . . . The publicity that was given this trial on the last occasion and the number of cameras here, I think was sufficient to spread the news of the case throughout the county, to every available juror; and it is my opinion that on that occasion, there were so many cameras and so much paraphernalia here that it gave an opportunity for every prospective juror in Smith County to know about this case.
"Q. Not about the facts of the case?
"A. No, sir; not about the facts, nor any of the evidence."

III

It is obvious that the introduction of television and news cameras into a criminal trial invites many serious constitutional hazards. The very presence of photographers and television cameramen plying their trade in a courtroom might be so completely and thoroughly disruptive and distracting as to make a fair trial impossible. Thus, if the scene at the September hearing had been repeated in the courtroom during this jury trial, it is difficult to conceive how a fair trial in the constitutional sense could have been afforded the defendant.[9] And even if, as was true here, the television cameras are so controlled and concealed as to be hardly perceptible in the courtroom itself, there are risks of constitutional dimensions that lurk in the very process of televising court proceedings at all.

Some of those risks are catalogued in the *amicus curiae* brief filed in this case by the American Bar Association: "[P]otential or actual jurors, in the absence of enforceable and effective safeguards, may arrive at certain misconceptions regarding the defendant and his trial by viewing televised pre-trial hearings and motions from which the jury is ordinarily excluded. Evidence otherwise inadmissible may leave an indelible mark. . . . Once the trial begins, exposure to nightly rebroadcasts of selected portions of the day's proceedings will be difficult to guard against, as jurors spend frequent evenings before the television set. The obvious impact of witnessing repeated trial episodes and hearing accompanying commentary, episodes admittedly chosen for their news value and not for evidentiary purposes, can serve only to distort the jurors' perspective. . . . Despite the court's injunction not to discuss the case, it seems undeniable that jurors will be subject to the pressure of television-watching family, friends and, indeed, strangers. . . . It is not too much to imagine a juror being confronted with his wife's television-oriented viewpoint. . . . Additionally, the jurors' daily television appearances may make them recognizable celebrities, likely to be stopped by passing strangers, or perhaps harried by intruding telephone calls. . . ." Constitutional problems of another kind might arise if a witness or juror were subjected to being televised over his objection.

The plain fact of the matter, however, is that none of these things happened or could have happened in this case. The jurors themselves were prevented from seeing any telecasts of the trial, and completely insulated from association with any members of the public who did see such telecasts. This case, therefore, does not remotely resemble *Turner* v. *Louisiana,* 379 U. S. 466, where, during the trial, the jurors were subjected outside the courtroom to unmeasured and unmeasurable influences by key witnesses for the prosecution.

In the courtroom itself, there is nothing to show that the trial pro-

[9] See note 2.

ceeded in any way other than it would have proceeded if cameras and television had not been present. In appearance, the courtroom was practically
unaltered. There was no obtrusiveness and no distraction, no noise and
no special lighting. There is no indication anywhere in the record of any
disturbance whatever of the judicial proceedings. There is no claim that the
conduct of the judge, or that any deed or word of counsel, or of any witness, or of any juror, was influenced in any way by the presence of photographers or by television.

Furthermore, from a reading of the record it is crystal clear that this
was not a trial where the judge was harassed or confused or lacking in command of the proceedings before the jury. Not once, after the first witness
was called, was there any interruption at all of the trial proper to secure a
ruling concerning the presence of cameramen in the courtroom. There was
no occasion, during the entire trial—until after the jury adjourned to reach
its verdict—for any cautionary word to members of the press in the courtroom. The only time a motion was made, the jury was not in the courtroom.
The trial itself was a most mundane affair, totally lacking in the lurid and
completely emotionless. The evidence related solely to the circumstances
in which various documents had been signed and negotiated. It was highly
technical, if not downright dull. The petitioner called no witnesses, and
counsel for petitioner made only a brief closing argument to the jury. There
is nothing to indicate that the issues involved were of the kind where emotion could hold sway. The transcript of the trial belies any notion that frequent interruptions and inconsistent rulings communicated to the jury any
sense that the judge was unable to concentrate on protecting the defendant
and conducting the trial in a fair manner, in accordance with the State and
Federal Constitutions.

IV

What ultimately emerges from this record, therefore, is one bald
question—whether the Fourteenth Amendment of the United States Constitution prohibits all television cameras from a state courtroom whenever
a criminal trial is in progress. In the light of this record and what we now
know about the impact of television on a criminal trial, I can find no such
prohibition in the Fourteenth Amendment or in any other provision of the
Constitution. If what occurred did not deprive the petitioner of his constitutional right to a fair trial, then the fact that the public could view the proceeding on television has no constitutional significance. The Constitution
does not make us arbiters of the image that a televised state criminal trial
projects to the public.

While no First Amendment claim is made in this case, there are intima-
tions in the opinions filed by my Brethren in the majority which strike me
as disturbingly alien to the First and Fourteenth Amendments' guarantees

against federal or state interference with the free communication of information and ideas. The suggestion that there are limits upon the public's right to know what goes on in the courts causes me deep concern. The idea of imposing upon any medium of communications the burden of justifying its presence is contrary to where I had always thought the presumption must lie in the area of First Amendment freedoms. See *Speiser* v. *Randall,* 357 U. S. 513, 525. And the proposition that nonparticipants in a trial might get the "wrong impression" from unfettered reporting and commentary contains an invitation to censorship which I cannot accept. Where there is no disruption of the "essential requirement of the fair and orderly administration of justice," "[f]reedom of discussion should be given the widest range." *Pennekamp* v. *Florida,* 328 U. S. 331, 347; *Bridges* v. *California,* 314 U. S. 252. Cf. *Cox* v. *Louisiana,* 379 U. S. 559, 563.

I do not think that the Constitution denies to the State or to individual trial judges all discretion to conduct criminal trials with television cameras present, no matter how unobtrusive the cameras may be. I cannot say at this time that it is impossible to have a constitutional trial whenever any part of the proceedings is televised or recorded on television film. I cannot now hold that the Constitution absolutely bars television cameras from every criminal courtroom, even if they have no impact upon the jury, no effect upon any witness, and no influence upon the conduct of the judge.

For these reasons I would affirm the judgment.

RELATED READING

ALEXANDER, Herbert E. "Political Broadcasting," *Television Quarterly,* V (Spring, 1966), 65–75.

ARCHER, Gleason L. "Conventions, Campaigns, and Kilocycles in 1924: The First Political Broadcasts," *Journal of Broadcasting,* IV (Spring, 1960), 110–118.

BENJAMIN, Burton. "The Documentary Heritage," *Television Quarterly,* I (February, 1962), 29–34.

BLISS, Edward, Jr., ed. *In Search of Light: The Broadcasts of Edward R. Murrow, 1938–1961.* New York: Knopf, 1967.

BLUEM, A. William. *Documentary in American Television.* New York: Hastings House, 1965.

BRECHNER, Joseph L. "A Statement on the 'Fairness Doctrine,'" *Journal of Broadcasting,* IX (Spring, 1965), 103–112.

————. "News Media and the Courts," *Journal of Broadcasting,* XII (Winter, 1967–68), 3–17.

BRINKLEY, David. "TV News and the Star System," *Television Quarterly,* V (Spring, 1966), 13–18.

BUSH, Warren V. "The Test," *Television Quarterly,* IV (Summer, 1965), 21–27.

CASMIR, Fred L. "Lee Harvey Oswald and Radio and Television," *NAEB Journal,* XXIV (September–October, 1965), 71–83.

CHAFEE, Zechariah, Jr. *Freedom of Speech and Press.* New York: Freedom Agenda, 1955.

CHASE, John. "The TV Editorial Cartoon," *Television Quarterly,* VI (Spring, 1967), 4–16.

CHESTER, Giraud. "The Press-Radio War: 1933–1935," *Public Opinion Quarterly,* XIII (Summer, 1949), 252–264.

CHRISTENSON, Reo M., and Robert O. MCWILLIAMS, eds. *Voice of the People: Readings in Public Opinion and Propaganda.* New York: McGraw-Hill, 1962.

CLARK, David G. "Radio in Presidential Campaigns: The Early Years (1924–1932)," *Journal of Broadcasting,* VI (Summer, 1962), 229–238.

CUSACK, Mary Ann. "The Emergence of Political Editorializing in Broadcasting," *Journal of Broadcasting,* VIII (Winter, 1963–64), 53–62.

DREYER, Edward C. "Political Party Use of Radio and Television in the 1960 Campaign," *Journal of Broadcasting,* VIII (Summer, 1964), 211–217.

DRYER, Sherman H. *Radio in Wartime.* New York: Greenberg, 1942.

EDWARDS, Frank. *My First 10,000 Sponsors.* New York: Ballantine, 1956.

EFRON, Edith. "Television: America's Timid Giant," *TV Guide,* May 18, 1963, 4–11.

Fair Trial vs. A Free Press. Santa Barbara, Cal.: Center for the Study of Democratic Institutions, 1965.

FELLOWS, Harold E. "The Expanding Sphere of Journalism," *Journal of Broadcasting,* I (Summer, 1957), 211–219.

FORD, Frederick W. "The Fairness Doctrine," *Journal of Broadcasting,* VIII (Winter, 1963–64), 3–16.

FRANDSEN, Kenneth D., and James G. BACKES. "Canon Thirty-Five: Televising Courtroom Proceedings," *Quarterly Journal of Speech,* XLIX (December, 1963), 389–394.

FRIENDLY, Alfred, and Ronald L. GOLDFARB. *Crime and Publicity.* New York: Twentieth Century Fund, 1967.

FRIENDLY, Fred W. *Due to Circumstances Beyond Our Control . . .* New York: Random House, 1967.

GILLMOR, Donald M. *Free Press and Fair Trial.* Washington: Public Affairs Press, 1966.

The Great Debates. Santa Barbara, Cal.: Center for the Study of Democratic Institutions, 1962.

HAMILL, Pete. "When the Client Is a Candidate," *New York Times Magazine,* October 25, 1964, 30–31, 128–130.

HARTENBERGER, Werner K. "After Estes, What . . . ?," *Journal of Broadcasting,* XII (Winter, 1967–68), 43–55.

HOLMES, Robert D. "The Broadcaster's Duty to Editorialize," *Journal of Broadcasting,* I (Spring, 1957), 139–145.

HOWELL, Rex G. "Fairness . . . Fact or Fable?," *Journal of Broadcasting,* VIII (Fall, 1964), 321–330.

"Interpreting the FCC Rules and Regulations: Chairman Henry Proposes 'Gordian Knot' to Avert Repeal of Section 315," *Broadcast Management/Engineering,* I (February, 1965), 12, 16.

"Interpreting the FCC Rules and Regulations: Understanding the 'Fairness Doctrine,'" *Broadcast Management/Engineering,* I (August, 1965), 15–18.

JOINER, Charles W., and Garnet R. GARRISON. "ETV Moves into the Courtroom," *NAEB Journal,* XXI (July–August, 1962), 1–5.

KRAUS, Sidney, ed. *The Great Debates.* Bloomington: Indiana University Press, 1962.

KRAUS, Sidney. "Presidential Debates in 1964," *Quarterly Journal of Speech,* L (February, 1964), 19–23.

———. "The Political Use of Television," *Journal of Broadcasting,* VIII (Summer, 1964), 219–228.

KROEGER, Albert R. "News, News, News," *Television,* XXII (February, 1965), 27–33, 50–64.

KURTZ, Robert S. "The Right to Privacy: A Legal Guidepost to Television Programing," *Journal of Broadcasting,* VI (Summer, 1962), 243–254.

LICHTY, Lawrence W., Joseph M. RIPLEY, and Harrison B. SUMMERS. "Political Programs on National Television Networks: 1960 and 1964," *Journal of Broadcasting,* IX (Summer, 1965), 217–229.

LOEVINGER, Lee. "Broadcasting and Religious Liberty," *Journal of Broadcasting,* IX (Winter, 1964–65), 3–23.

MARTIN, Jerry B. "Immunity of Broadcast Stations from Liability for Defamatory Statements by Candidates for Public Office," *Journal of Broadcasting,* IV (Spring, 1960), 140–143.

Mass Communications. Santa Barbara, Cal.: Center for the Study of Democratic Institutions, 1966.

MCMILLIN, John E. "New Voices in a Democracy," *Television Quarterly,* III (Summer, 1964), 27–52.

MESSING, Harold. " 'Defamacasts' and the Supreme Court," *Television Quarterly,* III (Fall, 1964), 43–47.

MILLER, Justin. "The Broadcasters' Stand: A Question of Fair Trial and Free Information," *Journal of Broadcasting,* I (Winter, 1956–57), 3–20.

MORGAN, Edward P. "Who Forgot Radio?," *NAEB Journal,* XXVI (January–February, 1967), 51–61.

NIXON, Richard M. *Six Crises.* New York: Pocket Books, 1962.

OPPENHEIMER, Walter D. "Television and the Right of Privacy," *Journal of Broadcasting,* I (Spring, 1957), 194–201.

PARTAIN, Eugene G. "Use of Broadcast Media in Congressional, Legislative and Quasi-Judicial Proceedings," *Journal of Broadcasting,* IV (Summer, 1960), 123–139.

PERLMUTTER, Alvin H. "TV Takes a Stand," *Television Quarterly,* I (August, 1962), 69–76.

PORTER, Richard D. "Some Values to the Broadcaster of Election Campaign Broadcasting," *Journal of Broadcasting,* VII (Spring, 1963), 145–156.

PRESSMAN, Gabe, Robert Lewis SHAYON, and Robert SCHULMAN. "The Responsible Reporter," *Television Quarterly,* III (Spring, 1964), 8–26.

RIDER, John R. "A Viewer's Guide (Scholarly) to the National Political Conventions," *Journal of Broadcasting,* VIII (Summer, 1964), 229–232.

RIPLEY, Joseph M. "Policies and Practices Concerning Broadcasts of Controversial Issues," *Journal of Broadcasting,* IX (Winter, 1964–65), 25–32.

———. "An Argument for Television in the Civil Courtroom," *Journal of Broadcasting,* XII (Winter, 1967–68), 23–31.

RODELL, Fred. "TV or No TV in Court?," *New York Times Magazine,* April 12, 1964, 16, 101–104.

RONNIE, Art. "First Convention on Radio," *Journal of Broadcasting,* VIII (Summer, 1964), 245–246.

ROSE, Ernest D. "How the U.S. Heard about Pearl Harbor," *Journal of Broadcasting,* V (Fall, 1961), 285–298.

RUBIN, Bernard. *Political Television.* Belmont, Cal.: Wadsworth, 1967.

RYAN, Milo. *History in Sound.* Seattle: University of Washington Press, 1963.

SCHECHTER, A. A. *I Live on Air.* New York: Frederick A. Stokes Company, 1941.

SCHLESINGER, Arthur, Jr. "How Drastically has Television Changed Our Politics?," *TV Guide,* October 22, 1966, 6–10.

SELDES, Gilbert. "The Future of National Debates," *Television Quarterly,* I (August, 1962), 62–68.

SHAYON, Robert Lewis, ed. *The Eighth Art.* New York: Holt, Rinehart and Winston, 1962.

SIEBERT, Frederick S., PETERSON, Theodore, and SCHRAMM, Wilbur. *Four Theories of the Press.* Urbana: University of Illinois Press, 1956.

SMITH, R. Franklin. "The Nature and Development of Commentary," *Journal of Broadcasting,* VI (Winter, 1961–62), 11–22.

SMITH, Robert R. "The Origins of Radio Network News Commentary," *Journal of Broadcasting,* IX (Spring, 1965), 113–122.

SPECIAL COMMITTEE ON RADIO AND TELEVISION OF THE ASSOCIATION OF THE BAR OF THE CITY OF NEW YORK. *Freedom of the Press and Fair Trial: Final Report with Recommendations.* New York: Columbia University Press, 1967.

————. *Radio, Television, and the Administration of Justice: A Documented Survey of Materials.* New York: Columbia University Press, 1965.

"Special Report on Broadcast Editorializing," *Broadcasting,* July 16, 1962, 43–74.

STANTON, Frank. "The Case for Political Debates on TV," *New York Times Magazine,* January 19, 1964, 16, 68–70.

SULLIVAN, John Paul. "Editorials and Controversy: The Broadcasters' Dilemma," *George Washington Law Review,* XXXII (April, 1964), 719–768.

SUTRO, John A. "A Lawyer's View of Courtroom Broadcasting," *Journal of Broadcasting,* XII (Winter, 1967–68), 19–22.

SWING, Raymond. *"Good Evening!,"* New York: Harcourt, Brace & World, 1964.

TEBBEL, John William. *The Compact History of the American Newspaper.* New York: Hawthorn Books, 1963.

TELEVISION INFORMATION OFFICE. *Interaction: Television Public Affairs Programming . . . at the Community Level.* New York: Television Information Office, 1960.

Television Quarterly, V (Winter, 1966). (The entire issue is devoted to political broadcasting.)

THOMSON, Charles A. H. *Television and Presidential Politics.* Washington: The Brookings Institution, 1956.

UNITED STATES CONGRESS, SENATE, COMMITTEE ON COMMERCE. *The FCC's Actions and the Broadcasters' Operations in Connection with the Commission's Fairness Doctrine,* Staff Report for the Subcommittee on Communications [by Robert Lowe], 90th Congress, 2d Session. Washington: Government Printing Office, 1968.

UNITED STATES CONGRESS, SENATE, SUBCOMMITTEE ON FREEDOM OF COMMUNICATIONS OF THE SUBCOMMITTEE ON COMMUNICATIONS OF THE COMMITTEE ON COMMERCE. *Final Report Pursuant to S. Res. 305, 86th Congress,* Parts I–VI, 87th Congress, 1st and 2d Sessions. Washington: Government Printing Office, 1961–1962.

WAPLES, Douglas, ed. *Print, Radio and Film in a Democracy.* Chicago: University of Chicago Press, 1942.

WEEKS, Lewis E. "The Radio Election of 1924," *Journal of Broadcasting,* VIII (Summer, 1964), 233–243.

WHITE, Llewellyn. *The American Radio.* Chicago: University of Chicago Press, 1947.

WHITE, Paul W. *News on the Air.* New York: Harcourt, Brace, 1947.

WHITE, Theodore H. *The Making of the President, 1960.* New York: Atheneum, 1961.

———. *The Making of the President, 1964.* New York: Atheneum, 1965.

WIEBE, Gerhart. "An Historical Setting for Broadcast Journalism," *Journal of Broadcasting,* I (Winter, 1956–57), 35–38.

WOOD, William A. *Electronic Journalism.* New York: Columbia University Press, 1967.

PART FOUR

REGULATION OF COMPETITION

HOW MUCH competition should there be in broadcasting? Despite the apparent physical limitations of the broadcast spectrum and the anti-monopolistic provisions included in the Communications Act of 1934, the answer to this question has been left largely to the discretion of the Federal Communications Commission. In exercising its power to issue broadcast authorizations if the "public interest, convenience, and necessity" will be served, the FCC is free to determine the nature and extent of competition which will best serve the public interest.

This is by no means an easy task. In a broadcasting system almost exclusively supported by advertising revenues, is the public interest best served by licensing as many stations as the spectrum can contain, or by limiting the stations to a number dictated by the available advertising revenues and estimates of capital costs and operating expenses? Is the public interest better served by a large number of competitive stations and services operating on a perhaps flimsy and insecure financial footing, or by a small number of secure, economically protected stations and services? To what extent can the recognized goal of providing diverse services to meet varied tastes and interests be reconciled with the need for a viable means of financing such services through advertising?

The FCC has vacillated between the extremes of "free competition" and "economic protectionism" in facing these difficult questions. Generally, the Commission has sought to avoid direct confrontation with the perplexing issues involved in so-called "economic injury" protests, thereby promoting free competition through the absence of regulation. It has also attempted to discourage anti-competitive network practices and to promote competition among stations and networks through the issuance of rules. But in exercising its questionable jurisdiction over Community Antenna Television (CATV) systems, the Commission has aimed largely to protect the interests of open-circuit TV stations from "unfair competition."

There is the additional question of deciding between competing applicants for a single license. What criteria, if any, should be applied to determine which of several applications for a broadcast facility will be granted? Here, too, the FCC has had difficulty in defining the optimum degree of consistency and flexibility appropriate to comparative broadcast hearings.

The problem of regulating competition in broadcasting will undoubtedly become even more complex, if not perilous, as communication satellites and applications of laser technology are more widely used by radio and television broadcasters. In an industry so dominated by economic considerations, the way in which economic regulation is practiced becomes central in achieving whatever purposes one may assign to the media.

THE SANDERS BROTHERS CASE

1

Federal Communications Commission *v.*
Sanders Brothers Radio Station
309 U.S. 470
March 25, 1940

> *From 1940 to 1958 the FCC interpreted this Supreme Court decision to mean that possible economic injury to an existing licensee was no basis for refusing to license a potential competitor. A careful reading of this document, however, reveals that such was not the sole intent of the Court's decision.*

MR. JUSTICE ROBERTS delivered the opinion of the Court.

We took this case to resolve important issues of substance and procedure arising under the Communications Act of 1934, as amended.[1]

January 20, 1936, the Telegraph Herald, a newspaper published in Dubuque, Iowa, filed with the petitioner an application for a construction permit to erect a broadcasting station in that city. May 14, 1936, the respondent, who had for some years held a broadcasting license for, and had operated, Station WKBB at East Dubuque, Illinois, directly across the Mississippi River from Dubuque, Iowa, applied for a permit to move its transmitter and studios to the last named city and install its station there. August 18, 1936, respondent asked leave to intervene in the Telegraph Herald proceeding, alleging in its petition, *inter alia,* that there was an insufficiency of advertising revenue to support an additional station in Dubuque and insufficient talent to furnish programs for an additional station; that adequate service was being rendered to the community by Station WKBB and there was no need for any additional radio outlet in Dubuque and that the granting of the Telegraph Herald application would not serve the public interest, convenience, and necessity. Intervention was permitted and both applications were set for consolidated hearing.

---

[1] Act of June 19, 1934, c. 652, 48 Stat. 1064; Act of June 5, 1936, c. 511, 49 Stat. 1475; Act of May 20, 1937, c. 229, 50 Stat. 189, 47 U.S.C. 151, *et seq.*

The respondent and the Telegraph Herald offered evidence in support of their respective applications. The respondent's proof showed that its station had operated at a loss; that the area proposed to be served by the Telegraph Herald was substantially the same as that served by the respondent and that, of the advertisers relied on to support the Telegraph Herald station, more than half had used the respondent's station for advertising.

An examiner reported that the application of the Telegraph Herald should be denied and that of the respondent granted. On exceptions of the Telegraph Herald, and after oral argument, the broadcasting division of petitioner made an order granting both applications, reciting that "public interest, convenience, and necessity would be served" by such action. The division promulgated a statement of the facts and of the grounds of decision, reciting that both applicants were legally, technically, and financially qualified to undertake the proposed construction and operation; that there was need in Dubuque and the surrounding territory for the services of both stations, and that no question of electrical interference between the two stations was involved. A rehearing was denied and respondent appealed to the Court of Appeals for the District of Columbia. That court entertained the appeal and held that one of the issues which the Commission should have tried was that of alleged economic injury to the respondent's station by the establishment of an additional station and that the Commission had erred in failing to make findings on that issue. It decided that, in the absence of such findings, the Commission's action in granting the Telegraph Herald permit must be set aside as arbitrary and capricious.[2]

The petitioner's contentions are that under the Communications Act economic injury to a competitor is not a ground for refusing a broadcasting license and that, since this is so, the respondent was not a person aggrieved, or whose interests were adversely affected, by the Commission's action, within the meaning of section 402 (b) of the Act which authorizes appeals from the Commission's orders.

The respondent asserts that the petitioner in argument below contented itself with the contention that the respondent had failed to produce evidence requiring a finding of probable economic injury to it. It is consequently insisted that the petitioner is not in a position here to defend its failure to make such findings on the ground that it is not required by the Act to consider any such issue. By its petition for rehearing in the court below, the Commission made clear its position as now advanced. The decision of the court below, and the challenge made in petition for rehearing and here by the Commission, raise a fundamental question as to the function and power of the Commission and we think that, on the record, it is open here.

First. We hold that resulting economic injury to a rival station is not,

[2] *Sanders Brothers Radio Station* v. *Federal Communications Commission,* 70 App. D.C. 297; 106 F.2d 321.

in and of itself, and apart from considerations of public convenience, interest, or necessity, an element the petitioner must weigh, and as to which it must make findings, in passing on an application for a broadcasting license.

Section 307 (a) of the Communications Act directs that "the Commission, if public convenience, interest, or necessity will be served thereby, subject to the limitations of this Act, shall grant to any applicant therefor a station license provided for by this Act." This mandate is given meaning and contour by the other provisions of the statute and the subject matter with which it deals.[3] The Act contains no express command that in passing upon an application the Commission must consider the effect of competition with an existing station. Whether the Commission should consider the subject must depend upon the purpose of the Act and the specific provisions intended to effectuate that purpose.

The genesis of the Communications Act and the necessity for the adoption of some such regulatory measure is a matter of history. The number of available radio frequencies is limited. The attempt by a broadcaster to use a given frequency in disregard of its prior use by others, thus creating confusion and interference, deprives the public of the full benefit of radio audition. Unless Congress had exercised its power over interstate commerce to bring about allocation of available frequencies and to regulate the employment of transmission equipment the result would have been an impairment of the effective use of these facilities by anyone. The fundamental purpose of Congress in respect of broadcasting was the allocation and regulation of the use of radio frequencies by prohibiting such use except under license.

In contradistinction to communication by telephone and telegraph, which the Communications Act recognizes as a common carrier activity and regulates accordingly in analogy to the regulation of rail and other carriers by the Interstate Commerce Commission,[4] the Act recognizes that broadcasters are not common carriers and are not to be dealt with as such.[5] Thus the Act recognizes that the field of broadcasting is one of free competition. The sections dealing with broadcasting demonstrate that Congress has not, in its regulatory scheme, abandoned the principle of free competition, as it has done in the case of the railroads,[6] in respect of which regulation involves the suppression of wasteful practices due to competition, the regulation of rates charges, and other measures which are unnecessary if free competition is to be permitted.

An important element of public interest and convenience affecting the issue of a license is the ability of the licensee to render the best practicable service to the community reached by his broadcasts. That such ability may

[3] *Radio Commission* v. *Nelson Bros. Co.,* 289 U.S. 266, 285.
[4] See Title II, Sections 201–221, 47 U.S.C. Sections 201–221.
[5] See Section 3 (h), 47 U.S.C. Section 153 (h).
[6] Compare *Texas & Pacific Ry.* v. *Gulf, C. & S.F. Ry. Co.,* 270 U.S. 266, 277; *Chicago Junction Case,* 264 U.S. 258.

be assured the Act contemplates inquiry by the Commission, *inter alia,* into an applicant's financial qualifications to operate the proposed station.[7]

But the Act does not essay to regulate the business of the licensee. The Commission is given no supervisory control of the programs, of business management or of policy. In short, the broadcasting field is open to anyone, provided there be an available frequency over which he can broadcast without interference to others, if he shows his competency, the adequacy of his equipment, and financial ability to make good use of the assigned channel.

The policy of the Act is clear that no person is to have anything in the nature of property right as a result of the granting of a license. Licenses are limited to a maximum of three years' duration, may be revoked, and need not be renewed. Thus the channels presently occupied remain free for a new assignment to another licensee in the interest of the listening public.

Plainly it is not the purpose of the Act to protect a licensee against competition but to protect the public. Congress intended to leave competition in the business of broadcasting where it found it, to permit a licensee who was not interfering electrically with other broadcasters to survive or succumb according to his ability to make his programs attractive to the public.

This is not to say that the question of competition between a proposed station and one operating under an existing license is to be entirely disregarded by the Commission, and, indeed, the Commission's practice shows that it does not disregard that question. In may have a vital and important bearing upon the ability of the applicant adequately to serve his public; it may indicate that both stations—the existing and the proposed—will go under, with the result that a portion of the listening public will be left without adequate service; it may indicate that, by a division of the field, both stations will be compelled to render inadequate service. These matters, however, are distinct from the consideration that, if a license be granted, competition between the licensee and any other existing station may cause economic loss to the latter. If such economic loss were a valid reason for refusing a license this would mean that the Commission's function is to grant a monopoly in the field of broadcasting, a result which the Act itself expressly negatives,[8] which Congress would not have contemplated without granting the Commission powers of control over the rates, programs, and other activities of the business of broadcasting.

We conclude that economic injury to an existing station is not a separate and independent element to be taken into consideration by the Commission in determining whether it shall grant or withhold a license.

Second. It does not follow that, because the licensee of a station can-

[7] See Section 308 (b), 47 U.S.C. Section 308 (b).
[8] See Section 311, 47 U.S.C. Section 311, relating to unfair competition and monopoly.

not resist the grant of a license to another, on the ground that the resulting competition may work economic injury to him, he has no standing to appeal from an order of the Commission granting the application.

Section 402 (b) of the Act provides for an appeal to the Court of Appeals of the District of Columbia (1) by an applicant for a license or permit, or (2) "by any other person aggrieved or whose interests are adversely affected by any decision of the Commission granting or refusing any such application."

The petitioner insists that as economic injury to the respondent was not a proper issue before the Commission it is impossible that Section 402 (b) was intended to give the respondent standing to appeal, since absence of right implies absence of remedy. This view would deprive subsection (2) of any substantial effect.

Congress had some purpose in enacting Section 402 (b) (2). It may have been of the opinion that one likely to be financially injured by the issue of a license would be the only person having a sufficient interest to bring to the attention of the appellate court errors of law in the action of the Commission in granting the license. It is within the power of Congress to confer such standing to prosecute an appeal.[9]

We hold, therefore, that the respondent had the requisite standing to appeal and to raise, in the court below, any relevant question of law in respect of the order of the Commission.

Third. Examination of the findings and grounds of decision set forth by the Commission discloses that the findings were sufficient to comply with the requirements of the Act in respect of the public interest, convenience, or necessity involved in the issue of the permit. In any event, if the findings were not as detailed upon this subject as might be desirable, the attack upon them is not that the public interest is not sufficiently protected but only that the financial interests of the respondent have not been considered. We find no reason for abrogating the Commission's order for lack of adequate findings.

Fourth. The respondent here renews a contention made in the Court of Appeals to the effect that the Commission used as evidence certain data and reports in its files without permitting the respondent, as intervenor before the Commission, the opportunity of inspecting them. The Commission disavows the use of such material as evidence in the cause and the Court of Appeals found the disavowal veracious and sufficient. We are not disposed to disturb its conclusion.

The judgment of the Court of Appeals is *Reversed.*

Mr. Justice McReynolds took no part in the decision of this case.

[9] Compare *Interstate Commerce Commission* v. *Oregon-Washington R. Co.,* 288 U.S. 14, 23–25.

National Broadcasting Co., Inc. et al. *v.* United States et al.
319 U.S. 190
May 10, 1943

This most important Supreme Court decision upheld the FCC's right to issue regulations pertaining to business relationships between broadcasting networks and their affiliated stations. One result of the Court's affirmation of these regulations was the subsequent creation of the American Broadcasting Company network, which arose when NBC was required to divest itself of one of its two networks.

Aside from the central issue of competition, Justice Frankfurter's opinion is particularly noteworthy for its examination of the legislative history of radio regulation and its clarification of the relationship between "public interest, convenience, and necessity" and freedom of speech in broadcasting. Justice Murphy's dissent hints at possible inconsistency between portions of the Court's prior decision in the Sanders Brothers *case and this one.*

MR. JUSTICE FRANKFURTER delivered the opinion of the Court.

In view of our dependence upon regulated private enterprise in discharging the far-reaching rôle which radio plays in our society, a somewhat detailed exposition of the history of the present controversy and the issues which it raises is appropriate.

These suits were brought on October 30, 1941, to enjoin the enforcement of the Chain Broadcasting Regulations promulgated by the Federal Communications Commission on May 2, 1941, and amended on October 11, 1941. We held last Term in *Columbia System v. United States,* 316 U. S. 407, and *National Broadcasting Co. v. United States,* 316 U. S. 447, that the suits could be maintained under § 402 (a) of the Communications Act of 1934, 48 Stat. 1093, 47 U. S. C. § 402 (a) (incorporating by reference the Urgent Deficiencies Act of October 22, 1913, 38 Stat. 219, 28 U. S. C. § 47), and that the decrees of the District Court dismissing the suits for want of jurisdiction should therefore be reversed. On remand the

District Court granted the Government's motions for summary judgment and dismissed the suits on the merits. 47 F. Supp. 940. The cases are now here on appeal. 28 U. S. C. § 47. Since they raise substantially the same issues and were argued together, we shall deal with both cases in a single opinion.

On March 18, 1938, the Commission undertook a comprehensive investigation to determine whether special regulations applicable to radio stations engaged in chain broadcasting[1] were required in the "public interest, convenience, or necessity." The Commission's order directed that inquiry be made, *inter alia,* in the following specific matters: the number of stations licensed to or affiliated with networks, and the amount of station time used or controlled by networks; the contractual rights and obligations of stations under their agreements with networks; the scope of network agreements containing exclusive affiliation provisions and restricting the network from affiliating with other stations in the same area; the rights and obligations of stations with respect to network advertisers; the nature of the program service rendered by stations licensed to networks; the policies of networks with respect to character of programs, diversification, and accommodation to the particular requirements of the areas served by the affiliated stations; the extent to which affiliated stations exercise control over programs, advertising contracts, and related matters; the nature and extent of network program duplication by stations serving the same area; the extent to which particular networks have exclusive coverage in some areas; the competitive practices of stations engaged in chain broadcasting; the effect of chain broadcasting upon stations not licensed to or affiliated with networks; practices or agreements in restraint of trade, or in furtherance of monopoly, in connection with chain broadcasting; and the scope of concentration of control over stations, locally, regionally, or nationally, through contracts, common ownership, or other means.

On April 6, 1938, a committee of three Commissioners was designated to hold hearings and make recommendations to the full Commission. This committee held public hearings for 73 days over a period of six months, from November 14, 1938, to May 19, 1939. Order No. 37, announcing the investigation and specifying the particular matters which would be explored at the hearings, was published in the Federal Register, 3 Fed. Reg. 637, and copies were sent to every station licensee and network organization. Notices of the hearings were also sent to these parties. Station licensees, national and regional networks, and transcription and recording companies were invited to appear and give evidence. Other persons who sought to appear were afforded an opportunity to testify. 96 witnesses were heard by

---

[1] Chain broadcasting is defined in § 3 (p) of the Communications Act of 1934 as the "simultaneous broadcasting of an identical program by two or more connected stations." In actual practice, programs are transmitted by wire, usually leased telephone lines, from their point of origin to each station in the network for simultaneous broadcast over the air.

the committee, 45 of whom were called by the national networks. The evidence covers 27 volumes, including over 8,000 pages of transcript and more than 700 exhibits. The testimony of the witnesses called by the national networks fills more than 6,000 pages, the equivalent of 46 hearing days.

The committee submitted a report to the Commission on June 12, 1940, stating its findings and recommendations. Thereafter, briefs on behalf of the networks and other interested parties were filed before the full Commission, and on November 28, 1940, the Commission issued proposed regulations which the parties were requested to consider in the oral arguments held on December 2 and 3, 1940. These proposed regulations dealt with the same matters as those covered by the regulations eventually adopted by the Commission. On January 2, 1941, each of the national networks filed a supplementary brief discussing at length the questions raised by the committee report and the proposed regulations.

On May 2, 1941, the Commission issued its Report on Chain Broadcasting, setting forth its findings and conclusions upon the matters explored in the investigation, together with an order adopting the Regulations here assailed. Two of the seven members of the Commission dissented from this action. The effective date of the Regulations was deferred for 90 days with respect to existing contracts and arrangements of network-operated stations, and subsequently the effective date was thrice again postponed. On August 14, 1941, the Mutual Broadcasting Company petitioned the Commission to amend two of the Regulations. In considering this petition the Commission invited interested parties to submit their views. Briefs were filed on behalf of all of the national networks, and oral argument was had before the Commission on September 12, 1941. And on October 11, 1941, the Commission (again with two members dissenting) issued a Supplemental Report, together with an order amending three Regulations. Simultaneously, the effective date of the Regulations was postponed until November 15, 1941, and provision was made for further postponements from time to time if necessary to permit the orderly adjustment of existing arrangements. Since October 30, 1941, when the present suits were filed, the enforcement of the Regulations has been stayed either voluntarily by the Commission or by order of court.

Such is the history of the Chain Broadcasting Regulations. We turn now to the Regulations themselves, illumined by the practices in the radio industry disclosed by the Commission's investigation. The Regulations, which the Commission characterized in its Report as "the expression of the general policy we will follow in exercising our licensing power," are addressed in terms to station licensees and applicants for station licenses. They provide, in general, that no licenses shall be granted to stations or applicants having specified relationships with networks. Each Regulation is directed at a particular practice found by the Commission to be detrimental to the "public interest," and we shall consider them *seriatim*. In doing so, however, we do not overlook the admonition of the Commission that the Regulations as well as the network practices at which they are aimed are interrelated:

In considering above the network practices which necessitate the regulations we are adopting, we have taken each practice singly, and have shown that even in isolation each warrants the regulation addressed to it. But the various practices we have considered do not operate in isolation; they form a compact bundle or pattern, and the effect of their joint impact upon licensees necessitates the regulations even more urgently than the effect of each taken singly. (Report, p. 75.)

The Commission found that at the end of 1938 there were 660 commercial stations in the United States, and that 341 of these were affiliated with national networks. 135 stations were affiliated exclusively with the National Broadcasting Company, Inc., known in the industry as NBC, which operated two national networks, the "Red" and the "Blue." NBC was also the licensee of 10 stations, including 7 which operated on so-called clear channels with the maximum power available, 50 kilowatts; in addition, NBC operated 5 other stations, 4 of which had power of 50 kilowatts, under management contracts with their licensees. 102 stations were affiliated exclusively with the Columbia Broadcasting System, Inc., which was also the licensee of 8 stations, 7 of which were clear-channel stations operating with power of 50 kilowatts. 74 stations were under exclusive affiliation with the Mutual Broadcasting System, Inc. In addition, 25 stations were affiliated with both NBC and Mutual, and 5 with both CBS and Mutual. These figures, the Commission noted, did not accurately reflect the relative prominence of the three companies, since the stations affiliated with Mutual were, generally speaking, less desirable in frequency, power, and coverage. It pointed out that the stations affiliated with the national networks utilized more than 97% of the total night-time broadcasting power of all the stations in the country. NBC and CBS together controlled more than 85% of the total night-time wattage, and the broadcast business of the three national network companies amounted to almost half of the total business of all stations in the United States.

The Commission recognized that network broadcasting had played and was continuing to play an important part in the development of radio.

The growth and development of chain broadcasting [it stated], found its impetus in the desire to give widespread coverage to programs which otherwise would not be heard beyond the reception area of a single station. Chain broadcasting makes possible a wider reception for expensive entertainment and cultural programs and also for programs of national or regional significance which would otherwise have coverage only in the locality of origin. Furthermore, the access to greatly enlarged audiences made possible by chain broadcasting has been a strong incentive to advertisers to finance the production of expensive programs. . . . But the fact that the chain broadcasting method brings benefits and advantages to both the listening public and to broadcast station licensees does not mean that the prevailing practices and policies of the networks and their outlets are sound in all respects, or that they should not be altered. The Commission's duty under the Communications Act of 1934 is not only to see that the public receives the advantages and benefits of chain broadcasting, but also, so far as its powers enable it, to see that practices which adversely affect the ability of licensees to operate in the public interest are eliminated. (Report, p. 4.)

The Commission found that eight network abuses were amenable to correction within the powers granted it by Congress:

Regulation 3.101—Exclusive affiliation of station. The Commission found that the network affiliation agreements of NBC and CBS customarily contained a provision which prevented the station from broadcasting the programs of any other network. The effect of this provision was to hinder the growth of new networks, to deprive the listening public in many areas of service to which they were entitled, and to prevent station licensees from exercising their statutory duty of determining which programs would best serve the needs of their community. The Commission observed that in areas where all the stations were under exclusive contract to either NBC or CBS, the public was deprived of the opportunity to hear programs presented by Mutual. To take a case cited in the Report: In the fall of 1939 Mutual obtained the exclusive right to broadcast the World Series baseball games. It offered this program of outstanding national interest to stations throughout the country, including NBC and CBS affiliates in communities having no other stations. CBS and NBC immediately invoked the "exclusive affiliation" clauses of their agreements with these stations, and as a result thousands of persons in many sections of the country were unable to hear the broadcasts of the games.

Restraints having this effect [the Commission observed], are to be condemned as contrary to the public interest irrespective of whether it be assumed that Mutual programs are of equal, superior, or inferior quality. The important consideration is that station licensees are denied freedom to choose the programs which they believe best suited to their needs; in this manner the duty of a station licensee to operate in the public interest is defeated. . . . Our conclusion is that the disadvantages resulting from these exclusive arrangements far outweigh any advantages. A licensee station does not operate in the public interest when it enters into exclusive arrangements which prevent it from giving the public the best service of which it is capable, and which, by closing the door of opportunity in the network field, adversely affects the program structure of the entire industry. (Report, pp. 52, 57.)

Accordingly, the Commission adopted Regulation 3.101, providing as follows:

No license shall be granted to a standard broadcast station having any contract, arrangement, or understanding, express or implied, with a network organization under which the station is prevented or hindered from, or penalized for, broadcasting the programs of any other network organization.

Regulation 3.102—Territorial exclusivity. The Commission found another type of "exclusivity" provision in network affiliation agreements whereby the network bound itself not to sell programs to any other station in the same area. The effect of this provision, designed to protect the affiliate from the competition of other stations serving the same territory, was to deprive the listening public of many programs that might otherwise be available. If an affiliated station rejected a network program, the "territorial exclusivity" clause of its affiliation agreement prevented the network from offering the program to other stations in the area. For example, Mutual presented a popular program, known as "The American Forum of the Air," in which prominent persons discussed topics of general interest. None of the Mutual stations in the Buffalo area decided to carry the program, and a Buffalo station not affiliated with Mutual attempted to obtain the program for its listeners. These efforts failed, however, on account of the "territorial exclusivity" provision in Mutual's agreements with its outlets. The result was that this program was not available to the people of Buffalo.

The Commission concluded that

It is not in the public interest for the listening audience in an area to be deprived of network programs not carried by one station where other stations in that area are ready and willing to broadcast the programs. It is as much against the public interest for a network affiliate to enter into a contractual arrangement which prevents another station from carrying a network program as it would be for it to drown out that program by electrical interference. (Report, p. 59).

Recognizing that the "territorial exclusivity" clause was unobjectionable in so far as it sought to prevent duplication of programs in the same area, the Commission limited itself to the situations in which the clause impaired the ability of the licensee to broadcast available programs. Regulation 3.102, promulgated to remedy this particular evil, provides as follows:

No license shall be granted to a standard broadcast station having any contract, arrangement, or understanding, express or implied, with a network organization which prevents or hinders another station serving substantially the same area from broadcasting the network's programs not taken by the former station, or which prevents or hinders another station serving a substantially different area from broadcasting any program of the network organization. This regulation shall not be construed to prohibit any contract, arrangement, or understanding between a station and a network organization pursuant to which the station is granted the first call in its primary service area upon the programs of the network organization.

Regulation 3.103—Term of affiliation. The standard NBC and CBS affiliation contracts bound the station for a period of five years, with the network having the exclusive right to terminate the contracts upon one year's notice. The Commission, relying upon § 307 (d) of the Communications Act of 1934, under which no license to operate a broadcast station can be granted for a longer term than three years, found the five-year affiliation term to be contrary to the policy of the Act:

Regardless of any changes that may occur in the economic, political, or social life of the Nation or of the community in which the station is located, CBS and NBC affiliates are bound by contract to continue broadcasting the network programs of only one network for 5 years. The licensee is so bound even though the policy and caliber of programs of the network may deteriorate greatly. The future necessities of the station and of the community are not considered. The station licensee is unable to follow his conception of the public interest until the end of the 5-year contract. (Report, p. 61.)

The Commission concluded that under contracts binding the affiliates for five years, "stations become parties to arrangements which deprive the public of the improved service it might otherwise derive from competition in the network field; and that a station is not operating in the public interest when it so limits its freedom of action." (Report, p. 62.) Accordingly, the Commission adopted Regulation 3.103:

No license shall be granted to a standard broadcast station having any contract, arrangement, or understanding, express or implied, with a network organization which provides, by original term, provisions for renewal, or otherwise for the affiliation of the station with the network organization for a period longer than two years:[2] *Provided,* That a contract, arrangement, or understanding for a period up to two years, may be entered into within 120 days prior to the commencement of such period.

Regulation 3.104—Option time. The Commission found that network affiliation contracts unusally contained so-called network optional time clauses. Under these provisions the network could upon 28 days' notice call upon its affiliates to carry a commercial program during any of the hours specified in the agreement as "network optional time." For CBS affiliates "network optional time" meant the entire broadcast day. For 29 outlets of NBC on the Pacific Coast, it also covered the entire broadcast day; for substantially all of the other NBC affiliates, it included 8½ hours on weekdays and 8 hours on Sundays. Mutual's contracts with about half of its affiliates contained such a provision, giving the network optional time for 3 or 4 hours on weekdays and 6 hours on Sundays.

In the Commission's judgment these optional time provisions, in addition to imposing serious obstacles in the path of new networks, hindered stations in developing a local program service. The exercise of networks of

[2] Station licenses issued by the Commission normally last two years. Section 3.34 of the Commission's Rules and Regulations governing Standard and High-Frequency Broadcast Stations, as amended October 14, 1941.

their options over the station's time tended to prevent regular scheduling of local programs at desirable hours. The Commission found that

shifting a local commercial program may seriously interfere with the efforts of a [local] sponsor to build up a regular listening audience at a definite hour, and the long-term advertising contract becomes a highly dubious project. This hampers the efforts of the station to develop local commercial programs and affects adversely its ability to give the public good program service. . . . A station licensee must retain sufficient freedom of action to supply the program and advertising needs of the local community. Local program service is a vital part of community life. A station should be ready, able, and willing to serve the needs of the local community by broadcasting such outstanding local events as community concerts, civic meetings, local sports events, and other programs of local consumer and social interest. We conclude that national network time options have restricted the freedom of station licensees and hampered their efforts to broadcast local commercial programs, the programs of other national networks, and national spot transcriptions. We believe that these considerations far outweigh any supposed advantages from "stability" of network operations under time options. We find that the optioning of time by licensee stations has operated against the public interest. (Report, pp. 63, 65.)

The Commission undertook to preserve the advantages of option time, as a device for "stabilizing" the industry, without unduly impairing the ability of local stations to develop local program service. Regulation 3.104 called for the modification of the option-time provision in three respects: the minimum notice period for exercise of the option could not be less than 56 days; the number of hours which could be optioned was limited; and specific restrictions were placed upon exercise of the option to the disadvantage of other networks. The text of the Regulation follows:

No license shall be granted to a standard broadcast station which options for network programs any time subject to call on less than 56 days' notice, or more time than a total of three hours within each of four segments of the broadcast day, as herein described. The broadcast day is divided into 4 segments, as follows: 8:00 a. m. to 1:00 p. m.; 1:00 p. m. to 6:00 p. m.; 6:00 p. m. to 11:00 p. m.; 11:00 p. m. to 8:00 a. m. Such options may not be exclusive as against other network organizations and may not prevent or hinder the station from optioning or selling any or all of the time covered by the option, or other time, to other network organizations.

Regulation 3.105—Right to reject programs. The Commission found that most network affiliation contracts contained a clause defining the right of the station to reject network commercial programs. The NBC contracts provided simply that the station "may reject a network program the broadcasting of which would not be in the public interest, convenience, and necessity." NBC required a licensee who rejected a program to "be able to support his contention that what he has done has been more in the public interest than had he carried on the network program." Similarly, the CBS contracts provided that if the station had "reasonable objection to any sponsored program or the product advertised thereon as not being in the public interest, the station may, on 3 weeks' prior notice thereof to Columbia, refuse to broadcast such program, unless during such notice period such reasonable objection of the station shall be satisfied."

While seeming in the abstract to be fair, these provisions, according to the Commission's finding, did not sufficiently protect the "public interest." As a practical matter, the licensee could not determine in advance whether the broadcasting of any particular network program would or would not be in the public interest.

It is obvious that from such skeletal information [as the networks submitted to the stations prior to the broadcasts] the station cannot determine in advance whether the program is in the public interest, nor can it ascertain whether or not parts of the program are in one way or another offensive. In practice, if not in theory, stations affiliated with networks have delegated to the networks a large part of their programming functions. In many instances, moreover, the network further delegates the actual production of programs to advertising agencies. These agencies are far more than mere brokers or intermediaries between the network and the advertiser. To an ever-increasing extent, these agencies actually exercise the function of program production. Thus it is frequently neither the station nor the network, but rather the advertising agency, which determines what broadcast programs shall contain. Under such circumstances, it is especially important that individual stations, if they are to operate in the public interest, should have the practical opportunity as well as the contractual right to reject network programs. . . .

It is the station, not the network, which is licensed to serve the public interest. The licensee has the duty of determining what programs shall be broadcast over his station's facilities, and cannot lawfully delegate this duty or transfer the control of his station directly to the network or indirectly to an advertising agency. He cannot lawfully bind himself to accept programs in every case where he cannot sustain the burden of proof that he has a better program. The licensee is obliged to reserve to himself the final decision as to what programs will best serve the public interest. We conclude that a licensee is not fulfilling his obligations to operate in the public interest, and is not operating in accordance with the express requirements of the Communications Act, if he agrees to accept programs on any basis other than his own reasonable decision that the programs are satisfactory. (Report, pp. 39, 66.)

The Commission undertook in Regulation 3.105 to formulate the obligations of licensees with respect to supervision over programs:

No license shall be granted to a standard broadcast station having any contract, arrangement, or understanding, express or implied, with a network organization which (a), with respect to programs offered pursuant to an affiliation contract, prevents or hinders the station from rejecting or refusing network programs which the station reasonably believes to be unsatisfactory or unsuitable; or which (b), with respect to network programs so offered or already contracted for, prevents the station from rejecting or refusing any program which, in its opinion, is contrary to the public interest, or from substituting a program of outstanding local or national importance.

Regulation 3.106—Network ownership of stations. The Commission found that NBC, in addition to its network operations, was the licensee of 10 stations, 2 each in New York, Chicago, Washington, and San Francisco, 1 in Denver, and 1 in Cleveland. CBS was the licensee of 8 stations, 1 in each of these cities: New York, Chicago, Washington, Boston, Minneapolis, St. Louis, Charlotte, and Los Angeles. These 18 stations owned by NBC and CBS, the Commission observed, were among the most powerful and desirable in the country, and were permanently inaccessible to competing networks.

Competition among networks for these facilities is nonexistent, as they are completely removed from the network-station market. It gives the network complete control over its policies. This "bottling-up" of the best facilities has undoubtedly had a discouraging effect upon the creation and growth of new networks. Furthermore, common ownership of network and station places the network in a position where its interest as the owner of certain stations may conflict with its interest as a network organization serving affiliated stations. In dealings with advertisers, the network represents its own stations in a proprietary capacity and the affiliated stations in something akin to an agency capacity. The danger is present that the network organization will give preference to its own stations at the expense of its affiliates. (Report, p. 67.)

The Commission stated that if the question had arisen as an original matter, it might well have concluded that the public interest required severance of the business of station ownership from that of network operation. But since substantial business interests have been formed on the basis of the Commission's continued tolerance of the situation, it was found inadvisable to take such a drastic step. The Commission concluded, however, that the licensing of two stations in the same area to a single network organization is basically unsound and contrary to the public interest," and that it was also against the "public interest" for network organizations to own stations in areas where the available facilities were so few or of such unequal coverage that competition would thereby be substantially restricted. Recognizing that these considerations called for flexibility in their application to particular situations, the Commission provided that "networks will be given full opportunity, on proper application for new facilities or renewal of existing licenses, to call to our attention any reasons why the principle should be modified or held inapplicable." (Report, p. 68.)

Regulation 3.106 reads as follows:

No license shall be granted to a network organization, or to any person directly or indirectly controlled by or under common control with a network organization, for more than one standard broadcast station where one of the stations covers substantially the service area of the other station, or for any standard broadcast station in any locality where the existing standard broadcast stations are so few or of such unequal desirability (in terms of coverage, power, frequency, or other related matters) that competition would be substantially restrained by such licensing.

Regulation 3.107—Dual network operation. This regulation provides that: "No license shall be issued to a standard broadcast station affiliated with a network organization which maintains more than one network: *Provided,* That this regulation shall not be applicable if such networks are not operated simultaneously, or if there is no substantial overlap in the territory served by the group of stations comprising each such network." In its Supplemental Report of October 11, 1941, the Commission announced the indefinite suspension of this regulation. There is no occasion here to consider the validity of Regulation 3.107, since there is no immediate threat of its enforcement by the Commission.

Regulation 3.108—Control by network of station rates. The Commission found that NBC's affiliation contracts contained a provision empowering the network to reduce the station's network rate, and thereby to reduce the compensation received by the station, if the station set a lower rate for non-network national advertising than the rate established by the contract for the network programs. Under this provision the station could not sell time to a national advertiser for less than it would cost the advertiser if he bought the time from NBC. In the words of NBC's vice-president, "This means simply that a national advertiser should pay the same price for the station whether he buys it through one source or another source. It means that we do not believe that our stations should go into competition with ourselves." (Report, p. 73.)

The Commission concluded that "it is against the public interest for a station licensee to enter into a contract with a network which has the effect of decreasing its ability to compete for national business. We believe that the public interest will best be served and listeners supplied with the best programs if stations bargain freely with national advertisers." (Report, p. 75.) Accordingly, the Commission adopted Regulation 3.108, which provides as follows:

No license shall be granted to a standard broadcast station having any contract, arrangement, or understanding, express or implied, with a network organization under which the station is prevented or hindered from, or penalized for, fixing or altering its rates for the sale of broadcast time for other than the network's programs.

The appellants attack the validity of these Regulations along many fronts. They contend that the Commission went beyond the regulatory powers conferred upon it by the Communications Act of 1934; that even if the Commission were authorized by the Act to deal with the matters comprehended by the Regulations, its action is nevertheless invalid because the Commission misconceived the scope of the Act, particularly § 313 which deals with the application of the anti-trust laws to the radio industry; that the Regulations are arbitrary and capricious; that if the Communications Act of 1934 were construed to authorize the promulgation of the Regulations, it would be an unconstitutional delegation of legislative power; and that, in any event, the Regulations abridge the appellants' right of free speech in violation of the First Amendment. We are thus called upon to determine whether Congress has authorized the Commission to exercise the power asserted by the Chain Broadcasting Regulations, and if it has, whether the Constitution forbids the exercise of such authority.

Federal regulation of radio[3] begins with the Wireless Ship Act of June 24, 1910, 36 Stat. 629, which forbade any steamer carrying or licensed to carry fifty or more persons to leave any American port unless equipped with efficient apparatus for radio communication, in charge of a skilled operator. The enforcement of this legislation was entrusted to the Secretary of Commerce and Labor, who was in charge of the administration of the marine navigation laws. But it was not until 1912, when the United States ratified the first international radio treaty, 37 Stat. 1565, that the need for general regulation of radio communication became urgent. In order to fulfill our obligations under the treaty, Congress enacted the Radio Act of August 13, 1912, 37 Stat. 302. This statute forbade the operation of radio apparatus without a license from the Secretary of Commerce and Labor; it also allocated certain frequencies for the use of the Government, and imposed restrictions upon the character of wave emissions, the transmission of distress signals, and the like.

The enforcement of the Radio Act of 1912 presented no serious problems prior to the World War. Questions of interference arose only rarely because there were more than enough frequencies for all the stations then in existence. The war accelerated the development of the art, however, and in 1921 the first standard broadcast stations were established. They grew rapidly in number, and by 1923 there were several hundred such stations throughout the country. The Act of 1912 had not set aside any particular frequencies for the use of private broadcast stations; consequently, the Secretary of Commerce selected two frequencies, 750 and 833 kilocycles, and licensed all stations to operate upon one or the other of these channels. The number of stations increased so rapidly, however, and the situation became so chaotic, that the Secretary, upon the recommendation of the National Radio Conferences which met in Washington in 1923 and 1924,

[3] The history of federal regulation of radio communication is summarized in Herring and Gross, Telecommunications (1936) 239–86; Administrative Procedure in Government Agencies, Monograph of the Attorney General's Committee on Administrative Procedure, Sen. Doc. No. 186, 76th Cong., 3d Sess., Part 3, dealing with the Federal Communications Commission, pp. 82–84; 1 Socolow, Law of Radio Broadcasting (1939) 38–61; Donovan, Origin and Development of Radio Law (1930).

established a policy of assigning specified frequencies to particular stations. The entire radio spectrum was divided into numerous bands, each allocated to a particular kind of service. The frequencies ranging from 550 to 1500 kilocycles (96 channels in all, since the channels were separated from each other by 10 kilocycles) were assigned to the standard broadcast stations. But the problems created by the enormously rapid development of radio were far from solved. The increase in the number of channels was not enough to take care of the constantly growing number of stations. Since there were more stations than available frequencies, the Secretary of Commerce attempted to find room for everybody by limiting the power and hours of operation of stations in order that several stations might use the same channel. The number of stations multiplied so rapidly, however, that by November, 1925, there were almost 600 stations in the country, and there were 175 applications for new stations. Every channel in the standard broadcast band was, by that time, already occupied by at least one station, and many by several. The new stations could be accommodated only by extending the standard broadcast band, at the expense of the other types of services, or by imposing still greater limitations upon time and power. The National Radio Conference which met in November, 1925, opposed both of these methods and called upon Congress to remedy the situation through legislation.

The Secretary of Commerce was powerless to deal with the situation. It had been held that he could not deny a license to an otherwise legally qualified applicant on the ground that the proposed station would interfere with existing private or Government stations. *Hoover* v. *Intercity Radio Co.,* 52 App. D. C. 339, 286 F. 1003. And on April 16, 1926, an Illinois district court held that the Secretary had no power to impose restrictions as to frequency, power, and hours of operation, and that a station's use of a frequency not assigned to it was not a violation of the Radio Act of 1912. *United States* v. *Zenith Radio Corp.,* 12 F. 2d 614. This was followed on July 8, 1926, by an opinion of Acting Attorney General Donovan that the Secretary of Commerce had no power, under the Radio Act of 1912, to regulate the power, frequency or hours of operation of stations. 35 Ops. Atty. Gen. 126. The next day the Secretary of Commerce issued a statement abandoning all his efforts to regulate radio and urging that the stations undertake self-regulation.

But the plea of the Secretary went unheeded. From July, 1926, to February 23, 1927, when Congress enacted the Radio Act of 1927, 44 Stat. 1162, almost 200 new stations went on the air. These new stations used any frequencies they desired, regardless of the interference thereby caused to others. Existing stations changed to other frequencies and increased their power and hours of operation at will. The result was confusion and chaos. With everybody on the air, nobody could be heard. The situation became so intolerable that the President in his message of December 7, 1926, appealed to Congress to enact a comprehensive radio law:

> Due to the decisions of the courts, the authority of the department [of Commerce] under the law of 1912 has broken down; many more stations have been operating than can be accommodated within the limited number of wave lengths available; further stations are in course of construction; many stations have departed from the scheme of allocations set down by the department, and the whole service of this most important public function has drifted into such chaos as seems likely, if not remedied, to destroy its great value. I most urgently recommend that this legislation should be speedily enacted. (H.Doc. 483, 69th Cong., 2d Sess, p. 10.)

The plight into which radio fell prior to 1927 was attributable to certain basic facts about radio as a means of communication—its facilities are limited; they are not available to all who may wish to use them; the radio spectrum simply is not large enough to accommodate everybody. There is a fixed natural limitation upon the number of stations that can operate without interfering with one another.[4] Regulation of radio was therefore as vital to its development as traffic control was to the development of the automobile. In enacting the Radio Act of 1927, the first comprehensive scheme of control over radio communication, Congress acted upon the knowledge that if the potentialities of radio were not to be wasted, regulation was essential.

The Radio Act of 1927 created the Federal Radio Commission, composed of five members, and endowed the Commission with wide licensing and regulatory powers. We do not pause here to enumerate the scope of the Radio Act of 1927 and of the authority entrusted to the Radio Commission, for the basic provisions of that Act are incorporated in the Communications Act of 1934, 48 Stat. 1064, 47 U. S. C. § 151 *et seq.,* the legislation immediately before us. As we noted in *Federal Communications Comm'n* v. *Pottsville Broadcasting Co.,* 309 U. S. 134, 137,

> In its essentials the Communications Act of 1934 [so far as its provisions relating to radio are concerned] derives from the Federal Radio Act of 1927. . . . By this Act Congress, in order to protect the national interest involved in the new and far-reaching science of broadcasting, formulated a unified and comprehensive regulatory system for the industry. The common factors in the administration of the various statutes by which Congress had supervised the different modes of communication led to the creation, in the Act of 1934, of the Communications Commission. But the objectives of the legislation have remained substantially unaltered since 1927.

Section 1 of the Communications Act states its "purpose of regulating interstate and foreign commerce in communication by wire and radio so

---

[4] See Morecroft, Principles of Radio Communication (3d ed. 1933) 355–402; Terman, Radio Engineering (2d ed. 1937) 593–645.

as to make available, so far as possible, to all the people of the United States a rapid, efficient, Nation-wide, and world-wide wire and radio communication service with adequate facilities at reasonable charges." Section 301 particularizes this general purpose with respect to radio:

It is the purpose of this Act, among other things, to maintain the control of the United States over all the channels of interstate and foreign radio transmission; and to provide for the use of such channels, but not the ownership thereof, by persons for limited periods of time, under licenses granted by Federal authority, and no such license shall be construed to create any right, beyond the terms, conditions, and periods of the license.

To that end a Commission composed of seven members was created, with broad licensing and regulatory powers.

Section 303 provides:

Except as otherwise provided in this Act, the Commission from time to time, as public convenience, interest, or necessity requires, shall—
(a) Classify radio stations;
(b) Prescribe the nature of the service to be rendered by each class of licensed stations and each station within any class; . . .
(f) Make such regulations not inconsistent with law as it may deem necessary to prevent interference between stations and to carry out the provisions of this Act . . . ;
(g) Study new uses for radio, provide for experimental uses of frequencies, and generally encourage the larger and more effective use of radio in the public interest; . . .
(i) Have authority to make special regulations applicable to radio stations engaged in chain broadcasting; . . .
(r) Make such rules and regulations and prescribe such restrictions and conditions, not inconsistent with law, as may be necessary to carry out the provisions of this Act. . . .

The criterion governing the exercise of the Commission's licensing power is the "public interest, convenience, or necessity." §§ 307 (a) (d), 309 (a), 310, 312. In addition, § 307 (b) directs the Commission that

In considering applications for licenses, and modifications and renewals thereof, when and insofar as there is demand for the same, the Commission shall make such distribution of licenses, frequencies, hours of operation, and of power among the several States and communities as to provide a fair, efficient, and equitable distribution of radio service to each of the same.

The Act itself establishes that the Commission's powers are not limited to the engineering and technical aspects of regulation of radio communication. Yet we are asked to regard the Commission as a kind of traffic officer, policing the wave lengths to prevent stations from interfering with each other. But the Act does not restrict the Commission merely to supervision of the traffic. It puts upon the Commission the burden of determining the composition of that traffic. The facilities of radio are not large enough to accommodate all who wish to use them. Methods must be devised for choosing from among the many who apply. And since Congress itself could not do this, it committed the task to the Commission.

The Commission was, however, not left at large in performing this duty. The touchstone provided by Congress was the "public interest, convenience, or necessity," a criterion which "is as concrete as the complicated factors for judgment in such a field of delegated authority permit." *Federal Communications Comm'n* v. *Pottsville Broadcasting Co.,* 309 U. S. 134, 138. "This criterion is not to be interpreted as setting up a standard so indefinite as to confer an unlimited power. Compare *New York Central Securities Co.* v. *United States,* 287 U. S. 12, 24. The requirement is to be interpreted by its context, by the nature of radio transmission and reception, by the scope, character and quality of services . . ." *Federal Radio Comm'n* v. *Nelson Bros. Co.,* 289 U. S. 266, 285.

The "public interest" to be served under the Communications Act is thus the interest of the listening public in "the larger and more effective use of radio." § 303 (g). The facilities of radio are limited and therefore precious; they cannot be left to wasteful use without detriment to the public interest. "An important element of public interest and convenience affecting the issue of a license is the ability of the licensee to render the best practicable service to the community reached by his broadcasts." *Federal Communications Comm'n* v. *Sanders Radio Station,* 309 U. S. 470, 475. The Commission's licensing function cannot be discharged, therefore, merely by finding that there are no technological objections to the granting of a license. If the criterion of "public interest" were limited to such matters, how could the Commission choose between two applicants for the same facilities, each of whom is financially and technically qualified to operate a station? Since the very inception of federal regulation by radio, comparative considerations as to the services to be rendered have governed the application of the standard of "public interest, convenience, or necessity." See *Federal Communications Comm'n* v. *Pottsville Broadcasting Co.,* 309 U. S. 134, 138 n. 2.

The avowed aim of the Communications Act of 1934 was to secure the maximum benefits of radio to all the people of the United States. To that end Congress endowed the Communications Commission with comprehensive powers to promote and realize the vast potentialities of radio. Section 303 (g) provides that the Commission shall "generally encourage the larger and more effective use of radio in the public interest"; subsection (i) gives the Commission specific "authority to make special regulations applicable to radio stations engaged in chain broadcasting"; and subsection (r) empowers it to adopt "such rules and regulations and prescribe such restrictions and conditions, not inconsistent with law, as may be necessary to carry out the provisions of this Act."

These provisions, individually and in the aggregate, preclude the notion that the Commission is empowered to deal only with technical and engineering impediments to the "larger and more effective use of radio in the public interest." We cannot find in the Act any such restriction of the Commission's authority. Suppose, for example, that a community can, because of physical limitations, be assigned only two stations. That community might be deprived of effective service in any one of several ways. More powerful stations in nearby cities might blanket out the signals of the local stations so that they could not be heard at all. The stations might interfere with each other so that neither could be clearly heard. One station might dominate the other with the power of its signal. But the community could be deprived of good radio service in ways less crude. One man, financially and technically qualified, might apply for and obtain the licenses of both stations and present a single service over the two stations, thus wasting a frequency otherwise available to the area. The language of the Act does not withdraw such a situation from the licensing and regulatory powers of the Commission, and there is no evidence that Congress did not mean its broad language to carry the authority it expresses.

In essence, the Chain Broadcasting Regulations represent a particularization of the Commission's conception of the "public interest" sought to be safeguarded by Congress in enacting the Commissions Act of 1934. The basic consideration of policy underlying the Regulations is succinctly stated in its Report:

With the number of radio channels limited by natural factors, the public interest demands that those who are entrusted with the available channels shall make the fullest and most effective use of them. If a licensee enters into a contract with a network organization which limits his ability to make the best use of the radio facility assigned him, he is not serving the public interest. . . . The net effect [of the practices disclosed by the investigation] has been that broadcasting service has been maintained at a level below that possible under a system of free competition. Having so found, we would be remiss in our statutory duty of encouraging "the larger and more effective use of radio in the public interest" if we were to grant licenses to persons who persist in these practices. (Report, pp. 81, 82.)

We would be asserting our personal views regarding the effective utilization of radio were we to deny that the Commission was entitled to find that the large public aims of the Communications Act of 1934 comprehend the considerations which moved the Commission in promulgating the Chain Broadcasting Regulations. True enough, the Act does not explicitly say that the Commission shall have power to deal with network practices found inimical to the public interest. But Congress was acting in a field of regulation which was both new and dynamic. "Congress moved under the spur of a widespread fear that in the absence of governmental control the public interest might be subordinated to monopolistic domination in the broadcasting field." *Federal Communications Comm'n v. Potts-ville Broadcasting Co.,* 309 U. S. 134, 137. In the context of the developing problems to which it was directed, the Act gave the Commission not niggardly but expansive powers. It was given a comprehensive mandate to "encourage the larger and more effective use of radio in the public interest," if need be, by making "special regulations applicable to radio stations engaged in chain broadcasting." § 303 (g) (i).

Generalities unrelated to the living problems of radio communication of course cannot justify exercises of power by the Commission. Equally so, generalities empty of all concrete considerations of the actual bearing of regulations promulgated by the Commission to the subject-matter entrusted to it, cannot strike down exercises of power by the Commission. While Congress did not give the Commission unfettered discretion to regulate all phases of the radio industry, it did not frustrate the purposes for which the Communications Act of 1934 was brought into being by attempting an itemized catalogue of the specific manifestations of the general problems for the solution of which it was establishing a regulatory agency. That would have stereotyped the powers of the Commission to specific details in regulating a field of enterprise the dominant characteristic of which was the rapid pace of its unfolding. And so Congress did what experience had taught it in similar attempts at regulation, even in fields where the subject-matter of regulation was far less fluid and dynamic than radio. The essence of that experience was to define broad areas for regulation and to establish standards for judgment adequately related in their application to the problems to be solved.

For the cramping construction of the Act pressed upon us, support cannot be found in its legislative history. The principal argument is that § 303 (i), empowering the Commission "to make special regulations applicable to radio stations engaged in chain broadcasting," intended to restrict the scope of the Commission's powers to the technical and engineering aspects of chain broadcasting. This provision comes from § 4 (h) of the Radio Act of 1927. It was introduced into the legislation as a Senate committee amendment to the House bill (H. R. 9971, 69th Cong., 1st Sess.) This amendment originally read as follows:

(C) The commission, from time to time, as public convenience, interest, or necessity requires, shall— . . .

(j) When stations are connected by wire for chain broadcasting, determine the power each station shall use and the wave lengths to be used during the time stations are so connected and so operated, and make all other regulations necessary in the interest of equitable radio service to the listeners in the communities or areas affected by chain broadcasting.

The report of the Senate Committee on Interstate Commerce, which submitted this amendment, stated that under the bill the Commission was given "complete authority . . . to control chain broadcasting." Sen. Rep. No. 772, 69th Cong., 1st Sess., p. 3. The bill as thus amended was passed by the Senate, and then sent to conference. The bill that emerged from the conference committee, and which became the Radio Act of 1927, phrased the amendment in the general terms now contained in § 303 (i) of the 1934 Act: the Commission was authorized "to make special regulations applicable to radio stations engaged in chain broadcasting." The conference reports do not give any explanation of this particular change in phrasing, but they do state that the jurisdiction conferred upon the Commission by the conference bill was substantially identical with that conferred by the bill passed by the Senate. See Sen. Doc. No. 200, 69th Cong., 2d Sess., p. 17; H. Rep. 1886, 69th Cong., 2d Sess., p. 17. We agree with the District Court that in view of this legislative history, § 303 (i) cannot be construed as no broader than the first clause of the Senate amendment, which limited the Commission's authority to the technical and engineering phases of chain broadcasting. There is no basis for assuming that the conference intended to preserve the first clause, which was of limited scope, by agreeing upon a provision which was broader and more comprehensive than those it supplanted.[5]

A totally different source of attack upon the Regulations is found in § 311 of the Act, which authorizes the Commission to withhold licenses from persons convicted of having violated the anti-trust laws. Two contentions are made—first, that this provision puts considerations relating to competition outside the Commission's concern before an applicant has been convicted of monopoly or other restraints of trade, and second, that, in any event, the Commission misconceived the scope of its powers under § 311 in issuing the Regulations. Both of these contentions are unfounded. Section 311 derives from § 13 of the Radio Act of 1927, which expressly

---

[5] In the course of the Senate debates on the conference report upon the bill that became the Radio Act of 1927, Senator Dill, who was in charge of the bill, said: "While the commission would have the power under the general terms of the bill, the bill specifically sets out as one of the special powers of the commission the right to make specific regulations for governing chain broadcasting. As to creating a monopoly of radio in this country, let me say that this bill absolutely protects the public, so far as it can protect them, by giving the commission full power to refuse a license to anyone who it believes will not serve the public interest, convenience, or necessity. It specifically provides that any corporation guilty of monopoly shall not only not receive a license but that its license may be revoked; and if after a corporation has received its license for a period of three years it is then discovered and found to be guilty of monopoly, its license will be revoked. . . . In addition to that, the bill contains a provision that no license may be transferred from one owner to another without the written consent of the commission, and the commission, of course, having the power to protect against a monopoly, must give such protection. I wish to state further that the only way by which monopolies in the radio business can secure control of radio here, even for a limited period of time, will be by the commission becoming servile to them. Power must be lodged somewhere, and I myself am unwilling to assume in advance that the commission proposed to be created will be servile to the desires and demands of great corporations of this country." 68 Cong. Rec. 2881.

commanded, rather than merely authorized, the Commission to refuse a license to any person judicially found guilty of having violated the anti-trust laws. The change in the 1934 Act was made, in the words of Senator Dill, the manager of the legislation in the Senate, because "it seemed fair to the committee to do that." 78 Cong. Rec. 8825. The Commission was thus permitted to exercise its judgment as to whether violation of the anti-trust laws disqualified an applicant from operating a station in the "public interest." We agree with the District Court that "The necessary implication from this [amendment in 1934] was that the Commission might infer from the fact that the applicant had in the past tried to monopolize radio, or had engaged in unfair methods of competition, that the disposition so manifested would continue and that if it did it would make him an unfit licensee." 47 F. Supp. 940, 944.

That the Commission may refuse to grant a license to persons adjudged guilty in a court of law of conduct in violation of the anti-trust laws certainly does not render irrelevant consideration by the Commission of the effect of such conduct upon the "public interest, convenience, or necessity." A licensee charged with practices in contravention of this standard cannot continue to hold his license merely because his conduct is also in violation of the anti-trust laws and he has not yet been proceeded against and convicted. By clarifying in § 311 the scope of the Commission's authority in dealing with persons convicted of violating the anti-trust laws, Congress can hardly be deemed to have limited the concept of "public interest" so as to exclude all considerations relating to monopoly and unreasonable restraints upon commerce. Nothing in the provisions or history of the Act lends support to the inference that the Commission was denied the power to refuse a license to a station not operating in the "public interest," merely because its misconduct happened to be an unconvicted violation of the anti-trust laws.

Alternatively, it is urged that the Regulations constitute an *ultra vires* attempt by the Commission to enforce the anti-trust laws, and that the enforcement of the anti-trust laws is the province not of the Commission but of the Attorney General and the courts. This contention misconceives the basis of the Commission's action. The Commission's Report indicates plainly enough that the Commission was not attempting to administer the anti-trust laws:

> The prohibitions of the Sherman Act apply to broadcasting. This Commission, although not charged with the duty of enforcing that law, should administer its regulatory powers with respect to broadcasting in the light of the purposes which the Sherman Act was designed to achieve. . . . While many of the network practices raise serious questions under the antitrust laws, our jurisdiction does not depend on a showing that they do in fact constitute a violation of the antitrust laws. It is not our function to apply the antitrust laws as such. It is our duty, however, to refuse licenses or renewals to any person who engages or proposes to engage in practices which will prevent either him-

self or other licensees or both from making the fullest use of radio facilities. This is the standard of public interest, convenience or necessity which we must apply to all applications for licenses and renewals. . . . We do not predicate our jurisdiction to issue the regulations on the ground that the network practices violate the antitrust laws. We are issuing these regulations because we have found that the network practices prevent the maximum utilization of radio facilities in the public interest. (Report, pp. 46, 83, 83 n. 3.)

We conclude, therefore, that the Communications Act of 1934 authorized the Commission to promulgate regulations designed to correct the abuses disclosed by its investigation of chain broadcasting. There remains for consideration the claim that the Commission's exercise of such authority was unlawful.

The Regulations are assailed as "arbitrary and capricious." If this contention means that the Regulations are unwise, that they are not likely to succeed in accomplishing what the Commission intended, we can say only that the appellants have selected the wrong forum for such a plea. What was said in *Board of Trade* v. *United States,* 314 U. S. 534, 548, is relevant here: "We certainly have neither technical competence nor legal authority to pronounce upon the wisdom of the course taken by the Commission." Our duty is at an end when we find that the action of the Commission was based upon findings supported by evidence, and was made pursuant to authority granted by Congress. It is not for us to say that the "public interest" will be furthered or retarded by the Chain Broadcasting Regulations. The responsibility belongs to the Congress for the grant of valid legislative authority and to the Commission for its exercise.

It would be sheer dogmatism to say that the Commission made out no case for its allowable discretion in formulating these Regulations. Its long investigation disclosed the existences of practices which it regarded as contrary to the "public interest." The Commission knew that the wisdom of any action it took would have to be tested by experience:

We are under no illusion that the regulations we are adopting will solve all questions of public interest with respect to the network system of program distribution. . . . The problems in the network field are interdependent, and the steps now taken may perhaps operate as a partial solution of problems not directly dealt with at this time. Such problems may be examined again at some future time after the regulations here adopted have been given a fair trial. (Report, p. 88.)

The problems with which the Commission attempted to deal could not be solved at once and for all time by rigid rules-of-thumb. The Commission therefore did not bind itself inflexibly to the licensing policies expressed in the Regulations. In each case that comes before it the Commission must still exercise an ultimate judgment whether the grant of a license would serve the "public interest, convenience, or necessity." If time and changing circumstances reveal that the "public interest" is not served by application of the Regulations, it must be assumed that the Commission will act in accordance with its statutory obligations.

Since there is no basis for any claim that the Commission failed to observe procedural safeguards required by law, we reach the contention that the Regulations should be denied enforcement on constitutional grounds. Here, as in *New York Central Securities Corp.* v. *United States,* 287 U. S. 12, 24–25, the claim is made that the standard of "public interest" governing the exercise of the powers delegated to the Commission by Congress is so vague and indefinite that, if it be construed as comprehensively as the words alone permit, the delegation of legislative authority is unconstitutional. But, as we held in that case, "It is a mistaken assumption that this is a mere general reference to public welfare without any standard to guide determinations. The purpose of the Act, the requirements it imposes, and the context of the provision in question show the contrary." *Ibid.* See *Federal Radio Comm'n* v. *Nelson Bros. Co.,* 289 U. S. 266, 285; *Federal Communications Comm'n* v. *Pottsville Broadcasting Co.,* 309 U. S. 134, 137–38. Compare *Panama Refining Co.* v. *Ryan,* 293 U. S. 388, 428; *Intermountain Rate Cases,* 234 U. S. 476, 486–89; *United States* v. *Lowden,* 308 U. S. 225.

We come, finally, to an appeal to the First Amendment. The Regulations, even if valid in all other respects, must fall because they abridge, say the appellants, their right of free speech. If that be so, it would follow that every person whose application for a license to operate a station is denied by the Commission is thereby denied his constitutional right of free speech. Freedom of utterance is abridged to many who wish to use the limited facilities of radio. Unlike other modes of expression, radio inherently is not available to all. That is its unique characteristic, and that is why, unlike other modes of expression, it is subject to governmental regulation. Because it cannot be used by all, some who wish to use it must be denied. But Congress did not authorize the Commission to choose among applicants upon the basis of their political, economic or social views, or upon any other capricious basis. If it did, or if the Commission by these Regulations proposed a choice among applicants upon some such basis, the issue before us would be wholly different. The question here is simply whether the Commission, by announcing that it will refuse licenses to persons who engage in specified network practices (a basis for choice which we hold is comprehended within the statutory criterion of "public interest"), is thereby denying such persons the constitutional right of free speech. The right of free speech does not include, however, the right to use the facilities of radio without a license. The licensing system established by Congress in the Communications Act of 1934 was a proper exercise of its power over commerce. The standard it provided for the licensing of stations was the "public interest, convenience, or necessity." Denial of a station license on that ground, if valid under the Act, is not a denial of free speech.

A procedural point calls for just a word. The District Court, by granting the Government's motion for summary judgment, disposed of the case upon the pleadings and upon the record made before the Commission. The court below correctly held that its inquiry was limited to review of the evidence before the Commission. Trial *de novo* of the matters heard by the Commission and dealt with in its Report would have been improper. See *Tagg Bros.* v. *United States,* 280 U. S. 420; *Acker* v. *United States,* 298 U. S. 426.

Affirmed.

MR. JUSTICE BLACK and MR. JUSTICE RUTLEDGE took no part in the consideration or decision of these cases.

MR. JUSTICE MURPHY, dissenting:

I do not question the objectives of the proposed regulations, and it is not my desire by narrow statutory interpretation to weaken the authority of government agencies to deal efficiently with matters committed to their jurisdiction by the Congress. Statutes of this kind should be construed so that the agency concerned may be able to cope effectively with problems which the Congress intended to correct, or may otherwise perform the functions given to it. But we exceed our competence when we gratuitously bestow upon an agency power which the Congress has not granted. Since that is what the Court in substance does today, I dissent.

In the present case we are dealing with a subject of extreme importance in the life of the nation. Although radio broadcasting, like the press, is generally conducted on a commercial basis, it is not an ordinary business activity, like the selling of securities or the marketing of electrical power. In the dissemination of information and opinion, radio has assumed a position of commanding importance, rivalling the press and the pulpit. Owing to its physical characteristics radio, unlike the other methods of conveying information, must be regulated and rationed by the government. Otherwise there would be chaos, and radio's usefulness would be largely destroyed. But because of its vast potentialities as a medium of communication, discussion and propaganda, the character and extent of control that should be exercised over it by the government is a matter of deep and vital concern. Events in Europe show that radio may readily be a weapon of authority and misrepresentation, instead of a means of entertainment and enlightenment. It may even be an instrument of oppression. In pointing out these possibilities I do not mean to intimate in the slightest that they are imminent or probable in this country, but they do suggest that the construction of the instant statute should be approached with more than ordinary restraint and caution, to avoid an interpretation that is not clearly justified by the conditions that brought about its enactment, or that would give the Commission greater powers than the Congress intended to confer.

The Communications Act of 1934 does not in terms give the Commission power to regulate the contractual relations between the stations and the networks. *Columbia System* v. *United States,* 316 U. S. 407, 416. It is only as an incident of the power to grant or withhold licenses to individual stations under §§ 307, 308, 309 and 310 that this authority is claimed,[1] except as it may have been provided by subdivisions (g), (i) and (r) of § 303, and by §§ 311 and 313. But nowhere in these sections, taken singly or collectively, is there to be found by reasonable construction or necessary inference, authority to regulate the broadcasting industry as such, or to control the complex operations of the national networks.

In providing for regulation of the radio, the Congress was under the necessity of vesting a considerable amount of discretionary authority in the Commission. The task of choosing between various claimants for the privilege of using the air waves is essentially an administrative one. Nevertheless, in specifying with some degree of particularity the kind of information to be included in an application for a license, the Congress has indicated what general conditions and considerations are to govern the granting and withholding of station licenses. Thus an applicant is required by § 308 (b) to submit information bearing upon his citizenship, character, and technical, financial and other qualifications to operate the proposed station, as well as data relating to the ownership and location of the proposed station, the power and frequencies desired, operating periods, intended use, and such other information as the Commission may require. Licenses, frequencies, hours of operation and power are to be fairly distributed among the several States and communities to provide efficient service to each. § 307 (b). Explicit provision is made for dealing with applicants and licensees who are found guilty, or who are under the control of persons found guilty of violating the federal anti-trust laws. §§ 311 and 313. Subject to the limitations defined in the Act, the Commission is required to grant a station license to any applicant "if public convenience, interest, or necessity will be served thereby." § 307 (a). Nothing is said, in any of these sections, about network contracts, affiliations, or business arrangements.

The power to control network contracts and affiliations by means of the Commission's licensing powers cannot be derived from implication out of the standard of "public convenience, interest or necessity." We have held that: "the Act does not essay to regulate the business of the licensee. The

---

[1] The regulations as first proposed were not connected with denial of applications for initial or renewal station licenses but provided instead that: "No licensee of a standard broadcast station shall enter into any contractual arrangement, express or implied, with a network organization," which contained any of the disapproved provisions. After a short time, however, the regulations were cast in their present form, making station licensing depend upon conformity with the regulations.

Commission is given no supervisory control of the programs, of business management or of policy. In short, the broadcasting field is open to anyone, provided there be an available frequency over which he can broadcast without interference to others, if he shows his competency, the adequacy of his equipment, and financial ability to make good use of the assigned channel." *Federal Communications Comm'n* v. *Sanders Radio Stations,* 309 U. S. 470, 475. The criterion of "public convenience, interest or necessity" is not an indefinite standard, but one to be "interpreted by its context, by the nature of radio transmission and reception, by the scope, character and quality of services, . . ." *Federal Radio Comm'n* v. *Nelson Bros. Co.,* 289 U. S. 266, 285. Nothing in the context of which the standard is a part refers to network contracts. It is evident from the record that the Commission is making its determination of whether the public interest would be served by renewal of an existing license or licenses, not upon an examination of written applications presented to it, as required by §§ 308 and 309, but upon an investigation of the broadcasting industry as a whole, and general findings made in pursuance thereof which relate to the business methods of the network companies rather than the characteristics of the individual stations and the peculiar needs of the areas served by them. If it had been the intention of the Congress to invest the Commission with the responsibility, through its licensing authority, of exercising far-reaching control—as exemplified by the proposed regulations—over the business operations of chain broadcasting and radio networks as they were then or are now organized and established, it is not likely that the Congress would have left it to mere inference or implication from the test of "public convenience, interest or necessity," or that Congress would have neglected to include it among the considerations expressly made relevant to license applications by § 308 (b). The subject is one of such scope and importance as to warrant explicit mention. To construe the licensing sections (§§ 307, 308, 309, 310) as granting authority to require fundamental and revolutionary changes in the business methods of the broadcasting networks—methods which have been in existence for several years and which have not been adjudged unlawful —would inflate and distort their true meaning and extend them beyond the limited purposes which they were intended to serve.

It is quite possible, of course, that maximum utilization of the radio as an instrument of culture, entertainment, and the diffusion of ideas is inhibited by existing network arrangements. Some of the conditions imposed by the broadcasting chains are possibly not conducive to a freer use of radio facilities, however essential they may be to the maintenance of sustaining programs and the operation of the chain broadcasting business as it is now conducted. But I am unable to agree that it is within the present authority of the Commission to prescribe the remedy for such conditions. It is evident that a correction of these conditions in the manner proposed by the regulations will involve drastic changes in the business of radio broadcasting which the Congress has not clearly and definitely empowered the Commission to undertake.

If this were a case in which a station license had been withheld from an individual applicant or licensee because of special relations or commitments that would seriously compromise or limit his ability to provide adequate service to the listening public, I should be less inclined to make any objection. As an incident of its authority to determine the eligibility of an individual applicant in an isolated case, the Commission might possibly consider such factors. In the present case, however, the Commission has reversed the order of things. Its real objective is to regulate the business practices of the major networks, thus bringing within the range of its regulatory power the chain broadcasting industry as a whole. By means of these regulations and the enforcement program, the Commission would not only extend its authority over business activities which represent interests and investments of a very substantial character, which have not been put under its jurisdiction by the Act, but would greatly enlarge its control over an institution that has now become a rival of the press and pulpit as a purveyor of news and entertainment and a medium of public discussion. To assume a function and responsibility of such wide reach and importance in the life of the nation, as a mere incident of its duty to pass on individual applications for permission to operate a radio station and use a specific wave length, is an assumption of authority to which I am not willing to lend my assent.

Again I do not question the need of regulation in this field, or the authority of the Congress to enact legislation that would vest in the Commission such power as it requires to deal with the problem, which it has defined and analyzed in its report with admirable lucidity. It is possible that the remedy indicated by the proposed regulations is the appropriate one, whatever its effect may be on the sustaining programs, advertising contracts, and other characteristics of chain broadcasting as it is now conducted in this country. I do not believe, however, that the Commission was justified in claiming the responsibility and authority it has assumed to exercise without a clear mandate from the Congress.

An examination of the history of this legislation convinces me that the Congress did not intend by anything in § 303, or any other provision of the Act, to confer on the Commission the authority it has assumed to exercise by the issuance of these regulations. Section 303 is concerned primarily with technical matters, and the subjects of regulation authorized by most of its subdivisions are exceedingly specific—so specific in fact that it is reasonable to infer that, if Congress had intended to cover the subject of network contracts and affiliations, it would not have left it to dubious implications from general clauses, lifted out of context, in subdivisions (g), (i) and (r). I am unable to agree that in authorizing the Commission in § 303 (g) to study new uses for radio, provide for experimental use of frequencies, and "generally encourage the larger and more effective use of radio in the public interest," it was the intention or the purpose of the Congress to confer on the Commission the regulatory powers now being asserted. Manifestly that subdivision dealt with experimental and development work—technical and scientific matters, and the construction of its concluding clause should be accordingly limited to those considerations. Nothing in its legislative history suggests that it had any broader purpose.

It was clearly not the intention of the Congress by the enactment of § 303 (i), authorizing the Commission "to make special regulations applicable to radio stations engaged in chain broadcasting," to invest the Commission with the authority now claimed over network contracts. This section is a verbatim reënactment of § 4 (h) of the Radio Act of 1927, and had its origin in a Senate amendment to the bill which became that Act. In its original form it provided that the Commission, from time to time, as public convenience, interest, or necessity required, should:

> When stations are connected by wire for chain broadcasting, [the Commission should] determine the power each station shall use and the wave lengths to be used during the time stations are so connected and so operated, and make all other regulations necessary in the interest of equitable radio service to the listeners in the communities or areas affected by chain broadcasting.

It was evidently the purpose of this provision to remedy a situation that was described as follows by Senator Dill (who was in charge of the bill in the Senate) in questioning a witness at the hearings of the Senate Committee on Interstate Commerce:

> . . . During the past few months there has grown up a system of chain broadcasting, extending over the United States a great deal of the time. I say a great deal of the time—many nights a month—and the stations that are connected are of such widely varying meter lengths that the ordinary radio set that reaches out any distance is unable to get anything but that one program, and so, in effect, that one program monopolizes the air. I realize it is somewhat of a technical engineering problem, but it has semed to many people, at least many who have written to me, that when stations are carrying on chain programs that they might be limited to the use of wave lengths adjoining or near enough to one another that they would not cover the entire dial. I do not know whether legislation ought to restrict that or whether it had better be done by regulations of the department. I want to get your opinion as to the advisability in some way protecting people who want to hear some other program than the one being broadcasted by chain broadcast. (Report on Hearings Before Senate Committee on Interstate Commerce on S. 1 and S. 1754, 69th Cong., 1st Sess. (1926) p. 123.)

In other words, when the same program was simultaneously broadcast by chain stations, the weaker independent stations were drowned out because of the high power of the chain stations. With the receiving sets then commonly in use, listeners were unable to get any program except the chain program. It was essentially an interference problem. In addition to determining power and wave length for chain stations, it would have been the duty of the Commission, under the amendment, to make other regulations necessary for "equitable radio service to the listeners in the communities or areas affected by chain broadcasting." The last clause should not be interpreted out of context and without relation to the problem at which the amendment was aimed. It is reasonably construed as simply authorizing the Commission to remedy other technical problems of interference involved in chain broadcasting in addition to power and wavelength by requiring special types of equipment, controlling locations, etc. The statement in the Senate Committee Report that this provision gave the Commission "complete authority . . . to control chain broadcasting" (S. Rep. No. 772, 69th Cong., 1st Sess., p. 3) must be taken as meaning that the provision gave complete authority with respect to the specific problem which the Senate intended to meet, a problem of technical interference.

While the form of the amendment was simplified in the Conference Committee so as to authorize the Commission "to make special regulations applicable to radio stations engaged in chain broadcasting," both Houses were assured in the report of the Conference Committee that "the jurisdiction conferred in this paragraph is substantially the same as the jurisdiction conferred upon the Commission by . . . the Senate amendment." (Sen. Doc. No. 200, 69th Cong., 2d Sess., p. 17; H. Rep. No. 1886, 69th Cong., 2d Sess., p. 17). This is further borne out by a statement of Senator Dill in discussing the conference report on the Senate floor:

What is happening to-day is that National Broadcasting Co., which is a part of the great Radio Trust, to say the least, if not a monopoly, is hooking up stations in every community on their various wave lengths with high powered stations and sending one program out, and they are forcing the little stations off the board so that the people cannot hear anything except the one program.

There is no power to-day in the hands of the Department of Commerce to stop that practice. The radio commission will have the power to regulate and prevent it and give the independents a chance. (68 Cong. Rec. 3031.)

Section 303 (r) is certainly no basis for inferring that the Commission is empowered to issue the challenged regulations. This subdivision is not an independent grant of power, but only an authorization to: "Make such rules and regulations and prescribe such restrictions and conditions, not inconsistent with law, as may be necessary to carry out the provisions of this Act." There is no provision in the Act for the control of network contractual arrangements by the Commission, and consequently § 303 (r) is of no consequence here.

To the extent that existing network practices may have run counter to the anti-trust laws, the Congress has expressly provided the means of dealing with the problem. The enforcement of those laws has been committed to the courts and other law enforcement agencies. In addition to the usual penalties prescribed by statute for their violation, however, the Commission has been expressly authorized by § 311 to refuse a station license to any person "finally adjudged guilty by a Federal court" of attempting unlawfully to monopolize radio communication. Anyone under the control of such a person may also be refused a license. And whenever a court has ordered the revocation of an existing license, as expressly provided in § 313, a new license may not be granted by the Commission to the guilty party or to any person under his control. In my opinion these provisions (§§ 311 and 313) clearly do not and were not intended to confer independent authority on the Commission to supervise network contracts or to enforce competition between radio networks by withholding licenses from stations, and do not justify the Commission in refusing a license to an applicant otherwise qualified, because of business arrangements that may constitute an unlawful restraint of trade, when the applicant has not been finally adjudged guilty of violating the anti-trust laws, and is not controlled by one so adjudged.

The conditions disclosed by the Commission's investigation, if they require correction, should be met, not by the invention of authority where none is available or by diverting existing powers out of their true channels and using them for purposes to which they were not addressed, but by invoking the aid of the Congress or the service of agencies that have been entrusted with the enforcement of the anti-trust laws. In other fields of regulation the Congress has made clear its intentions. It has not left to mere inference and guess-work the existence of authority to order broad changes and reforms in the national economy or the structure of business arrangements in the Public Utility Holding Company Act, 49 Stat. 803, the Securities Act of 1933, 48 Stat. 74, the Federal Power Act, 49 Stat. 838, and other measures of similar character. Indeed the Communications Act itself contains cogent internal evidence that Congress did not intend to grant power over network contractual arrangements to the Commission. In § 215 (c) of Title II, dealing with common carriers by wire and radio, Congress provided:

The Commission shall examine all contracts of common carriers subject to this Act which prevent the other party thereto from dealing with another common carrier subject to this Act, and shall report its findings to Congress, together with its recommendations as to whether additional legislation on this subject is desirable.

Congress had no difficulty here in expressing the possible desirability of regulating a type of contract roughly similar to the ones with which we are now concerned, and in reserving to itself the ultimate decision upon the matters of policy involved. Insofar as the Congress deemed it necessary in this legislation to safeguard radio broadcasting against arrangements that are offensive to the anti-trust laws or monopolistic in nature, it made specific provision in §§ 311 and 313. If the existing network contracts are deemed objectionable because of monopolistic or other features, and no remedy is presently available under these provisions, the proper course is to seek amendatory legislation from the Congress, not to fabricate authority by ingenious reasoning based upon provisions that have no true relation to the specific problem.

MR. JUSTICE ROBERTS agrees with these views.

THE CARROLL CASE

Carroll Broadcasting Company *v.*
Federal Communications Commission*
258 F.2d 440 (D.C. Cir.)
July 10, 1958

In this decision the Court of Appeals for the District of Columbia rejected the FCC's interpretation of the Supreme Court's 1940 decision in the Sanders Brothers *case and made it mandatory for the Commission to consider economic injury protests when potential competition seemed likely to affect the public interest adversely. The Commission's request to appeal this decision to the Supreme Court was rejected by the Department of Justice.*

PRETTYMAN, Circuit Judge.

This is an appeal from the Federal Communications Commission and concerns a license for a standard broadcasting station. Carroll, our appellant, is an existing licensee. It unsuccessfully protested the grant of a license to West Georgia, our intervenor.

Carrollton and Bremen are towns in Georgia, twelve miles apart, with populations, respectively, of 8,600 and 2,300. Carroll's main studios are in Carrollton. West Georgia would broadcast from Bremen.

Three issues were prescribed by the Commission for the hearing upon the protest. One of these was upon the request of Carroll and was:

To determine whether a grant of the application would result in such an economic injury to the protestant as would impair the protestant's ability to continue serving the public, and if so, the nature and extent thereof, the areas and populations affected thereby, and the availability of other broadcast service to such areas and populations.

But the Commission ordered "That said issue is not adopted by the Commission and that the burden of proceeding with the introduction of evidence

* Opinion taken with permission from Vol. 258, *Federal Reporter,* second series.

and the burden of proof as to this issue shall be on the protestant." The case was remanded to the examiner for hearings on the added issue and a possible revised decision. The hearings were held, a further initial decision rendered by the examiner, exceptions taken, and oral argument had before the Commission.

On this issue the Commission held that "Congress had determined that free competition shall prevail in the broadcasting industry" and that "The Communications Act does not confer upon the Commission the power to consider the effect of legal competition except perhaps" in Section 307(b) cases. Hence, said the Commission, "it is unnecessary for us to make findings or reach conclusions on this issue." Moreover, the Commission said, pursuant to other decisions by it, as a matter of policy "the possible effects of competition will be disregarded in passing upon applications for new broadcast stations."

It was settled by the Sanders Brothers case[1] that economic injury to an existing station is not a ground for denying a new application. But the Court, it seems to us, made clear the point that economic injury to a licensee and the public interest may be different matters. The Court said, for example:[2]

> *First.* We hold that resulting economic injury to a rival station is not, in and of itself, and apart from considerations of public convenience, interest, or necessity, an element the petitioner must weigh, and as to which it must make findings, in passing on an application for a broadcasting license.

And the Court said:[3]

> This is not to say that the question of competition between a proposed station and one operating under an existing license is to be entirely disregarded by the Commission, and, indeed, the Commission's practice shows that it does not disregard that question. It may have a vital and important bearing upon the ability of the applicant adequately to serve his public; it may indicate that both stations—the existing and the proposed—will go under, with the result that a portion of the listening public will be left without adequate service; it may indicate that, by division of the field, both stations will be compelled to render inadequate service. These matters, however, are distinct from the consideration that, if a license be granted, competition between the licensee and any other existing station may cause economic loss to the latter.

Thus, it seems to us, the question whether a station makes $5,000, or $10,000, or $50,000 is a matter in which the public has no interest so long as service is not adversely affected; service may well be improved by competition. But, if the situation in a given area is such that available revenue will not support good service in more than one station, the public interest

---

[1] *Federal Communications Commission* v. *Sanders Brothers Radio Station,* 309 U.S. 470, 60 S.Ct. 693, 84 L.Ed. 869 (1940).

[2] Id., 309 U.S. at page 473, 60 S.Ct. at page 696.

[3] Id., 309 U.S. at pages 475–476, 60 S.Ct. at pages 697–698.

may well be in the licensing of one rather than two stations. To license two stations where there is revenue for only one may result in no good service at all. So economic injury to an existing station, while not in and of itself a matter of moment, becomes important when on the facts it spells diminution or destruction of service. At that point the element of injury ceases to be a matter of purely private concern.

The basic charter of the Commission is, of course, to act in the public interest. It grants or denies licenses as the public interest, convenience and necessity dictate. Whatever factual elements make up that criterion in any given problem—and the problem may differ from case to case—must be considered. Such is not only the power but the duty of the Commission.

So in the present case the Commission had the power to determine whether the economic effect of a second license in this area would be to damage or destroy service to an extent inconsistent with the public interest. Whether the problem actually exists depends upon the facts, and we have no findings upon the point.

This opinion is not to be construed or applied as a mandate to the Commission to hear and decide the economic effects of every new license grant. It has no such meaning. We hold that, when an existing license offers to prove that the economic effect of another station would be detrimental to the public interest, the Commission should afford an opportunity for the presentation of such proof and, if the evidence is substantial (*i.e.,* if the protestant does not fail entirely to meet his burden), should make a finding or findings.

The Commission says that, if it has authority to consider economic injury as a factor in the public interest, the whole basic concept of a competitive broadcast industry disappears. We think it does not. Certainly the Supreme Court did not think so in the Sanders Brothers case, supra. Private economic injury is by no means always, or even usually, reflected in public detriment. Competitors may severely injure each other to the great benefit of the public. The broadcast industry is a competitive one, but competitive effects may under some sets of circumstances produce detriment to the public interest. When that happens the public interest controls.

The Commission says it lacks the "tools"—meaning specifications of authority from the Congress—with which to make the computations, valuations, schedules, etc., required in public utility regulation. We think no such elaborate equipment is necessary for the task here. As we have just said, we think it is not incumbent upon the Commission to evaluate the probable economic results of every license grant. Of course the public is not concerned whether it gets service from A or from B or from both combined. The public interest is not disturbed if A is destroyed by B, so long as B renders the required service. The public interest is affected when service is affected. We think the problem arises when a protestant offers to prove that the grant of a new license would be detrimental to the public interest. The

Commission is equipped to receive and appraise such evidence. If the protestant fails to bear the burden of proving his point (and it is certainly a heavy burden), there may be an end to the matter. If his showing is substantial, or if there is a genuine issue posed, findings should be made. Perhaps Carroll did not cast its proffer of proof exactly in terms of the public interest, or at least not in terms of the whole public interest. It may be argued that it offered to prove only detriment to its own ability for service. We are inclined to give it the benefit of the most favorable interpretation. In any event, whatever proof Carroll had is already in the record. If it does not support a finding of detriment to the public interest, but merely of a detriment to Carroll, the Commission can readily so find.

The case must be remanded for findings on this point.

Carroll also makes a point about the Commission's findings in respect to West Georgia's basic financial qualifications and about a presumption that a father-in-law, a brother-in-law, and an uncle-in-law form part of the control exercised by a family unit. We find no error in these respects.

Remanded for further findings.

4

IN RE CARTER MOUNTAIN TRANSMISSION CORP.

32 FCC 459

February 14, 1962

The Carter Mountain *decision established that the Commission could deny facilities to serve Community Antenna Television (CATV) systems if existing television stations—and thus the public interest—would be adversely affected by increased competition from such additional CATV facilities. The decision was affirmed by the Court of Appeals (321 F. 2d 359 (D.C. Cir. 1963)) and the Supreme Court refused to review the case (375 U.S. 951 (1963)). This first assumption and ad hoc exercise of regulatory jurisdiction over CATV formed a basis for the FCC's subsequent CATV rulemaking decisions (38 FCC 683 (1965); 31 Fed. Reg. 4540 (1966)). These rules were upheld by the Supreme Court in* United States et al. *v.* Southwestern Cable Co. et al., *decided June 10, 1968.*

By the Commission: COMMISSIONER BARTLEY not participating; COMMISSIONER CROSS dissenting and issuing a statement.

1. This is a protest proceeding under 47 U.S.C. 309(c)[1] and 405, arising out of the application of Carter Mountain Transmission Corp. ("Carter"), for a permit to install microwave radio relay pickup television signals to community antenna systems in Riverton, Lander, and Thermopolis, Wyo. Our grant without hearing was protested by Joseph P. and Mildred V. Ernst, d/b as Chief Washakie TV, licensee of station KWRB–TV, channel 10, Riverton, Wyo. ("KWRB–TV"), protestants alleging, inter alia, that by providing additional service to existing and operating CATV systems located in Thermopolis, Riverton, and Lander, Wyo., the microwave facilities would enhance their competitive standing to the economic detriment of KWRB–TV; and further, that Carter "is not eligible" to hold common carrier authorizations. By memorandum opinion and order of June 29, 1959 (FCC 59–617; 24 F.R. 5402), the effective date of the grant was postponed and the protest was set for oral argument before the Commission, en banc, with the licensee of KWRB–TV, Carter, and the Chief, Com-

[1] The protest was filed under the then provisions of sec. 309(c) of the Communications Act of 1934, 48 Stat. 1085, as amended, 47 U.S.C.A. sec. 309(c).

mon Carrier Bureau, designated as parties. By memorandum opinion and order of May 20, 1960 (FCC 60–564; 25 F.R. 4606), the matter was designated for hearing. On May 25, 1961 (FCC 61D–74), Hearing Examiner Walther W. Guenther released an initial decision looking toward a denial of the protest, a setting aside of the stay of the effectiveness of the grant, and a reinstatement of the grant of the subject application. KWRB–TV filed exception and requested oral argument. The National Association of Broadcasters and Tri-State TV Translator Association sought and were granted leave to file memoranda of law, and the NAB was granted further leave to participate in the oral argument, which was held December 14, 1961.

2. The initial decision sets forth the background and history of the proceeding, which need not be repeated here. Except as modified herein and in the rulings on the exceptions, the Commission is in general agreement with the examiner's findings, which are hereby adopted. Except as modified herein, and in the rulings on the exceptions, the examiner's conclusions not inconsistent with this decision are hereby adopted. For reasons hereinafter stated, the Commission disagrees with the ultimate result reached by the examiner and, as to that portion of the decision reverses the examiner.

3. Two basic questions are presented for determination: (a) whether Carter is in fact a bona fide common carrier eligible for a common carrier microwave facility; and (b) whether, a determination having been made that Carter is a common carrier of a microwave facility to a CATV system, the public interest is inherent and the economic impact is of no legal significance. Each will be discussed in order.

4. KWRB–TV excepts to the examiner's findings and ultimate conclusion that Carter is a bona fide common carrier and to the examiner's failure to find that Carter is the alter ego of Western (a CATV operator). The examiner amply described the situation, adequately discussed the legal proposition, and ultimately concluded correctly. The burden of adducing facts concerning the interlocking ownership between itself and CATV was placed on the applicant, who proved to the examiner's satisfaction that Carter and CATV are separate legal entities, and that the existing degree of common or interlocking ownership would support no contrary inference. KWRB–TV failed to prove anything adverse to this conclusion. In view of the conclusion herein, we do not reach the question of the legal significance of a greater degree of, or a total identity of, ownership, and we refrain from expressing an opinion thereon. The applicant held itself out for hire, invited the public to use its facilities, and indicated its willingness and ability to carry out this hire. As a matter of fact, station KOOK–TV, with which Carter has no affinity of interest, accepted Carter's offer and the examiner rightfully took official notice thereof. Thus, in accordance with the facts gathered pursuant to issues (3) and (4), issue (5) was properly resolved in applicant's favor.

5. After such findings, the examiner stated "[since] a grant of the subject application will serve the public interest [because it is a bona fide common carrier], . . . it is unnecessary to consider, in particular, the nature of the showing made by protestant under issue (2). . . . whatever impact the operations of the CATV systems may have upon protestant's operation of station KWRB–TV, . . . are matters of no legal significance to the ultimate determination made that a grant of the subject application of Carter, a bona fide communications common carrier, will serve the public interest." KWRB–TV urges that the examiner erred in so concluding. The National Association of Broadcasters, Tri-State TV Translator Association, and the Broadcast Bureau join.

6. When this application was designated for hearing, the Commission recognized that the grant of the microwave facility which is to be used to carry CATV into a community could conceivably destroy the only local television service. The Commission retained the right to make a determination on the facts by specifically including issues (1) and (2), which seek respectively to determine the areas and population now being served by KWRB–TV and the nature and type of said service; and to determine the impact which a grant of the instant application would have upon the operation of KWRB–TV, and the resulting injury, if any, to the public now served. Thus, it is clear that the Commission did not consider the impact of no legal significance, but sought facts on which an ultimate conclusion could be predicated. The examiner made adequate findings with respect to these issues, but gave these facts no weight in his conclusions.

7. Carter urges however, that even were the Commission to find an impact and were it to take cognizance of any adverse effect this impact may have on KWRB–TV, it must recognize that the CATV not the carrier (Carter in this instance) is responsible for the impact, and that the two systems are separate legal entities. This argument, appearing meritorious on its face, is set forth by the examiner (initial decision, p. 28, footnote 8). However, the Commission does not construe its responsibilities this narrowly. We find no justification for ignoring our obligations in the field of television simply because it happens to be common carrier activities that are being regulated at the moment. A grant of common carrier radio facilities requires a finding that the public interest will be served thereby; certainly the well-being of existing television facilities is an aspect of this public interest. Thus it is not only appropriate, it is necessary that we determine whether the use of the facility applied for would directly or indirectly bring about the elimination of the only television transmission or reception service to the public. In examining the entire instant situation, we may reasonably assume that the carrier (over which we do have jurisdiction) seeks to improve its present service and add additional services so that it may utilize any customer (i.e., CATV) potential. Carter contends that because we have no jurisdiction over the customer, we cannot consider the activities of the customer in reg-

ulating the carrier. We do not agree. If making the grant enables this customer potential to destroy a basic Commission policy, then even assuming, arguendo, that the applicant is not the direct cause of the impact, the ability to create such a situation in this particular instance is sufficient to warrant an examination into the entire problem. We will not shut our eyes to the impact upon the public service which is our ultimate concern, when it appears that the grant may serve to deprive a substantially large number of the public of a service merely because the common carrier classification is used. The Commission does not operate in a vacuum. We will not permit a subsequent grant to be issued if it be demonstrated that the same would vitiate a prior grant, without weighing the public-interest considerations involved.

8. Carter further urges that considering the use which the common carrier subscriber may make of its facility places the Commission in the position of censoring public communications. Here again we do not agree with this position. As guardian of the public interest, we are entrusted with a wide range of discretionary authority and under that authority we may not only appraise the facts and draw inferences from them, but also bring to bear upon the problem an expert judgment from our analysis of the total situation as to just where the public interest lies.[2] We are not in this instance attempting to do anything more than make a valued judgment in this direction. There is no attempt to examine, limit, or interfere with the actual material to be transmitted. We are merely considering the question of whether the use of the facility is in the public interest, a conclusion which must be reached prior to the issuance of the grant. In seeking this ultimate answer, we must look at the situation in its entirety, and we do not agree that we are acting in any fashion which would constitute "censorship."

9. It would be helpful at this time to set down some of the pertinent facts. KWRB–TV's grade A and B contours include a total of 36,918 persons (1950 U.S. census), in an area of 13,845 square miles, encompassing approximately 10,548 homes.[3] However, only 6 of the towns included in the aforementioned area have a population in excess of 1,000 persons; namely, Lander, Riverton, Thermopolis, Worland, Basin, and Greybull. We are primarily concerned here with the first four towns, having populations of 4,182, 6,845, 3,955, and 5,806 persons, respectively, totaling 20,788 persons, or 5,940 homes. The towns of Lander and Riverton had a relatively small number of subscribers to CATV operations, although from 1958 through 1960 they slowly increased the number of homes placed on

[2] In *Television Corporation of Michigan, Inc.* v. FCC (294 F. 2d 730 (1961)), the Court of Appeals for the District of Columbia Circuit stated, at p. 733, that "[N]either the statutory sections nor the 'priorities' express rigid and inflexible standards: the Commission has a broad measure of discretion in dealing with the many and complicated problems of allocation and distribution of service."

[3] U.S. census national average of approximately 3.5 persons per "household" or "home."

the cable. The towns of Thermopolis and Worland had a large number of CATV subscribers, and these numbers had been decreasing during the years 1958 through 1960 with resultant increased sale of spots for KWRB–TV.

10. KWRB–TV's overall programing serves the public interest. It has permission from each of the three networks with which it is affiliated to carry their entire schedules by deleting the "commercials" and substituting "public service," and it carries public service spots on behalf of the local town and community. It has a good local operating record and programs for the community it serves. If KWRB–TV were no longer to operate, no local programs of this type would be available to persons residing within the grade B contour, and they depend on this station for the airing of this local material.

11. The largest revenue returns are received from the towns of Lander and Riverton. Despite the fact that Worland has approximately 1,600 more persons than does Lander, the revenue from Lander is approximately 6 times that of Worland. This is attributed to the fact that CATV did not make any substantial inroad in Lander, while approximately 75 percent of the homes in Worland are on the cable. A similar type of comparison may be made between the towns of Riverton and Thermopolis.

12. Since its inception, station KWRB–TV has been operating in the "red"; that is, its operating expenses have exceeded its income. However, in each succeeding year of operation the gap between the two has become smaller, and as contended by protestant, should eventually be closed and then changed to "black." KWRB–TV points to a number of contributing factors, some of which are: the closing of the CATV station in Thermopolis (then under another operator) for approximately 6 months during 1960; a decrease in the number of homes carried on the CATV cable in the towns of Thermopolis and Worland where CATV has 44 percent and 75 percent subscriptions; KWRB–TV's being a "family enterprise" with resultant low expense and high productivity; reduction in the amount of syndicated film purchases and the substitution of network programing for which charges are no longer being exacted; but primarily, KWRB–TV's ability to show inroads on the number of cable subscribers together with an increase in its network affiliation status, enabled it to sell its spot advertising more readily, thus increasing its revenue.

13. Duplication of network programing exists not only between the imported programs entering the towns here involved over the cable system, but also with KWRB–TV signal. Network programs carried on KWRB–TV may also appear on one or more of the cable channels, without the local spot advertising. KWRB–TV states that at the present time, however, its picture is clearer and better than the one appearing on the CATV cable in the area. Thus, although a good deal of difficulty is encountered in attempting to sell spots in face of the division of audience, it manages to do so on the basis of better performance. However, it is urged that a grant of

the instant application would permit the CATV to improve its facilities to match that of KWRB–TV, rendering the sale to local advertisers impossible in view of the fact that they would not be able to guarantee any viewing on its channel. Reason and logic cause us to agree with the conclusion that should the CATV system be permitted to expand its services and furnish better technical facilities, KWRB–TV will be placed in the economically disadvantageous position of finding it more difficult to sell its advertising; it would have nothing to point to which would indicate to a potential advertiser that a popular program was being viewed over KWRB–TV vis-a-vis other potential channels. Its one balancing factor of a better picture will have been removed.

14. Licenses are granted by the Commission only if the operations proposed are found to be in the public interest, convenience, and necessity. Hence, when the impact of economic injury is such as to adversely affect the public interest, it is not only within our power, but it is our duty to determine the ultimate effect, study the facts, and act in a manner most advantageous to the public.[4] Although most of the network programs carried by KWRB–TV would continue to be available to the present CATV subscribers in the 6 towns of over 1,000 persons, via translators or CATV's, such programs would not be available to persons not residing in the immediate vicinity of the towns in which the CATV systems and VHF translators operate, nor to persons in the towns unable to pay the CATV charges. Therefore, if KWRB–TV is eventually forced off the air as a result of a grant of the instant application, the public stands to lose its only local outlet, an outlet on which a considerable part of the population in northwestern Wyoming relies.

15. A review of KWRB–TV's revenue for the year 1959 indicates that Lander and Riverton each return $14,191.31 and $17,429.14, respectively, as against a return of $6,457.20 and $2,485.45 from Thermopolis and Worland, respectively, notwithstanding the fact that Worland has a larger population than does Lander. Thus, the four towns made up $40,-563.10 of a total revenue of $66,812.03 for the year 1959. If the CATV pattern is permitted to be altered, and the substantial return from Riverton in particular is reduced, KWRB–TV, despite the fact that it would strive harder, would find it more difficult to sell its advertising in face of the split audience, and this situation, together with facts of record, results in our judgment that the demise of this local operation would result.

16. At the time KWRB–TV was granted its license, the Commission concluded that it was in the public interest to make such a grant. The Commission must now find it in the public interest to grant the instant applica-

---

[4] The courts have held that economic injury to a licensee and public interest may be different matters. However, the former "becomes important when on the facts it spells diminution or destruction of service." *Carroll Broadcasting Company* v. *FCC,* 258 F. 2d 440, 443 (1958).

tion. Standing alone, it might appear that each does in fact serve the public interest, with KWRB–TV showing, inter alia, that it is the only local television outlet for the community, while Carter would show that an increase in its facilities would permit the rendition of better and more efficient service to the CATV serving the community. However, neither stands alone; the effect of one upon the other must be weighed, and the ultimate conclusion must be made to the best interest of the public. True, a grant of the instant application would permit the rendition of better service by the CATV, but at the expense of destroying the local station and its rural coverage. The CATV would permit the urban areas a choice of coverage, but the local station, especially in this case of a single-station market, serves a wider area. A grant of this application will not contemplate an extension of coverage for the entire area included in KWRB–TV's contours, since it is too costly for CATV to enter the rural areas. Thus, the rural people would be left with nothing at all. This is not a true competitive situation where one or the other of the applicants would render the service. In this instance, if KWRB–TV, the local outlet, should be forced to cease operation, the rural people would be left without any service. We do not agree that we are powerless to prevent the demise of the local television station, and the eventual loss of service to a substantial population; nor do we agree that the Commission's expertise may not be invoked in this instance to predict this ultimate situation. Thus, after weighing the public interest involved in Carter's improved facility against the loss of the local station, it must be concluded, beyond peradventure of a doubt, the need for the local outlet and the service which it would provide to outlying areas outweighs the need for the improved service which Carter would furnish under the terms of the instant application. To the extent that this decision departs from our views in the report and order in docket No. 12443, 26 FCC 403 (released April 14, 1959), those views are modified.

17. In view of the foregoing and in light of the evidence adduced, we fail to find that a grant of the instant application would serve the public interest, convenience, and necessity, and therefore the application is denied, without prejudice however, to Carter's refiling when it is able to show that the CATV operation will avoid the duplication of KWRB–TV programing which now exists and that the CATV system will carry the local KWRB–TV signal. Placing of these latter conditions upon the refiling without prejudice is being done with full recognition of the separate corporate entities of Carter and the CATV. The realities of the situation, however, force a recognition of the fact that the conditions we impose upon Carter are a sine qua non to our finding that its operation will be in the public interest. Neither the Commission nor KWRB–TV can bring them about. Carter may accomplish this by a contract relationship between itself and the corporation with which it has some interlocking ownership [Western], or by some less formal means.

Accordingly, *It is ordered,* This 14th day of February 1962, that protest of Joseph P. Ernst and Mildred V. Ernst, d/b as Chief Washakie TV (KWRB–TV), *Is granted;* and the aforementioned application of Carter Mountain Transmission Corp. *Is denied* without prejudice to refiling when a showing can be made that the duplication of programing is adequately avoided and a satisfactory arrangement is arrived at by which the cable system will carry the local KWRB–TV service.

Dissenting statement of Commissioner Cross

I dissent. Even though I sympathize with the plight of station KWRB–TV (channel 10, Riverton, Wyo.) in this instance, I nevertheless consider the relief being granted by the majority sets an undesirable precedent that is against the best overall interests of the broadcasting industry in this country.

In docket No. 12443 (released April 14, 1959), the Commission, after lengthy consideration and deliberation, properly, in my view, determined the rationale for deciding cases like this one. In paragraph 75 of the report and order in docket No. 12443, the Commission stated:

. . . it is neither proper, pertinent, nor necessary for us to consider the specific lawful use which the common carrier subscriber may make of the facilities of the carrier. To take a different view would place the Commission in the anomalous position of acting as censor over public communications, and put us under the burden of policing, not only the use of such facilities but the content of communications transmitted on the facilities. The logical extension of such a philosophy would require us to deny communications facilities of any kind (message telephone, telegraph, etc.) to CATV's and, for example, to deny access to facilities to those acting contrary to our concept of the public welfare. The adjudication of these matters is beyond our province.

Despite this previous statement by the Commission (and the other portions of the report and order in docket No. 12443 on this general subject), the protestant and others have now apparently convinced the majority that the Commission should consider the specific lawful use which the common carrier subscriber may make of the facilities of the carrier. The thrust of their argument in this regard is that the Commission should not, on the one hand, license microwave facilities to a common carrier when part or all of such facilities will be used by a CATV system to the economic detriment of the only television station in the community which has also been licensed by the Commission with its other hand.

Admittedly, this is a hard case, but there is an old saying that hard cases make bad law and, in my opinion, that is what is being done here by the decision of the majority. Having the Commission examine into the specific lawful use which the common carrier subscriber may make of the facilities of the carrier is, in my opinion, not only contrary to common carrier communications law and practice but could open up a veritable Pandora's box which in the end may well redound to the serious detriment of the broadcasting industry itself.

The Commission was aware of these undesirable possibilities at the time it released its report and order in docket No. 12443. Indeed, these factors were significant in persuading the Commission that the best way to protect the broadcaster in situations like this was not through the common carrier licensees but through legislation that would authorize the Commission to have some degree of regulation over the users; i.e., the CATV systems. Such legislation was, in fact, proposed to the Congress by the Commission and is still before the Congress.[5] Accordingly, it is my view that we should not try to correct one isolated situation in the instant case by departing from our previously well-considered and soundly bottomed actions on the subject; i.e., the report and order in docket No. 12443 and our subsequent request to the Congress for the legislation noted above. I would therefore deny the protest and wait for the enactment of the requested legislation to deal with this matter.

[5] S. 1044 and H. R. 6840 were introduced on Feb. 16, 1961, at the Commission's request.

POLICY STATEMENT ON COMPARATIVE BROADCAST HEARINGS

5

FCC 65-689
July 28, 1965

> *The Federal Communications Commission has been confronted with a choice of broad regulatory philosophies since its formation. On one hand is the desire for consistency in administrative law. On the other hand is the need for flexibility in a field of rapid technological innovation, structural change, and managerial ingenuity.*
>
> *The conflict of consistency and flexibility is most evident in the policy statement and concurring and dissenting views below.*

One of the Commission's primary responsibilities is to choose among qualified new applicants for the same broadcast facilities.[1] This commonly requires extended hearings into a number of areas of comparison. The hearing and decision process is inherently complex, and the subject does not lend itself to precise categorization or to the clear making of precedent. The various factors cannot be assigned absolute values, some factors may be present in some cases and not in others, and the differences between applicants with respect to each factor are almost infinitely variable.

Furthermore, membership on the Commission is not static and the views of individual Commissioners on the importance of particular factors may change. For these and other reasons, the Commission is not bound to deal with all cases at all times as it has dealt in the past with some that seem comparable, *Federal Communications Commission* v. *WOKO, Inc.,* 329 U.S. 223, 228,[2] and changes of viewpoint, if reasonable, are recognized as both inescapable and proper. *Pinellas Broadcasting Co.* v. *Federal Communications Commission,* 97 U.S. App. D.C. 236, 230 F. 2d 204, *cert. den.* 350 U.S. 1007.

---

[1] This statement of policy does not attempt to deal with the somewhat different problems raised where an applicant is contesting with a licensee seeking renewal of license.

[2] "[T]he doctrine of *stare decisis* is not generally applicable to the decisions of administrative tribunals," *Kentucky Broadcasting Corp.* v. *Federal Communications Commission,* 84 U.S. App. D.C. 383, 385, 174 F. 2d 38, 40.

All this being so, it is nonetheless important to have a high degree of consistency of decision and of clarity in our basic policies. It is also obviously of great importance to prevent undue delay in the disposition of comparative hearing cases. A general review of the criteria governing the disposition of comparative broadcast hearings will, we believe, be useful to parties appearing before the Commission. It should also be of value to the examiners who initially decide the cases and to the Review Board to which the basic review of examiners' decisions in this area has been delegated. See Section 0.365 of our Rules, 47 CFR O.365.[3]

This statement is issued to serve the purpose of clarity and consistency of decision, and the further purpose of eliminating from the hearing process time-consuming elements not substantially related to the public interest. We recognize, of course, that a general statement cannot dispose of all problems or decide cases in advance. Thus, for example, a case where a party proposes a specialized service will have to be given somewhat different consideration. Difficult cases will remain difficult. Our purpose is to promote stability of judgment without foreclosing the right of every applicant to a full hearing.

We believe that there are two primary objectives toward which the process of comparison should be directed. They are, first, the best practicable service to the public, and, second, a maximum diffusion of control of the media of mass communications. The value of these objectives is clear. Diversification of control is a public good in a free society, and is additionally desirable where a government licensing system limits access by the public to the use of radio and television facilities.[4] Equally basic is a broadcast service which meets the needs of the public in the area to be served, both in terms of those general interests which all areas have in common and those special interests which areas do not share. An important element of such a service is the flexibility to change as local needs and interests change. Since independence and individuality of approach are elements of rendering good program service, the primary goals of good service and diversification of control are also fully compatible.

Several factors are significant in the two areas of comparison mentioned

---

[3] On June 15, 1964 the rule was amended to give the Review Board authority to review initial decisions of hearing examiners in comparative television cases, a function formerly performed only by the Commission itself.

[4] As the Supreme Court has stated, the First Amendment to the Constitution of the United States "rests on the assumption that the widest possible dissemination of information from diverse and antagonistic sources is essential to the welfare of the public," *Associated Press* v. *United States*, 326 U.S. 1, 20. That radio and television broadcast stations play an important role in providing news and opinion is obvious. That it is important in a free society to prevent a concentration of control of the sources of news and opinion and, particularly, that government should not create such a concentration, is equally apparent, and well established. *United States* v. *Storer Broadcasting Co.*, 351 U.S. 192; *Scripps-Howard Radio, Inc.* v. *Federal Communications Commission*, 89 U.S. App. D.C. 13, 189 F. 2d 677, *cert. den.* 342 U.S. 830.

above, and it is important to make clear the manner in which each will be treated.

1. *Diversification of control of the media of mass communications.* Diversification is a factor of primary significance since, as set forth above, it constitutes a primary objective in the licensing scheme.

As in the past, we will consider both common control and less than controlling interests in other broadcast stations and other media of mass communications. The less the degree of interest in other stations or media, the less will be the significance of the factor. Other interests in the principal community proposed to be served will normally be of most significance, followed by other interests in the remainder of the proposed service area[5] and, finally, generally in the United States. However, control of large interests elsewhere in the same state or region may well be more significant than control of a small medium of expression (such as a weekly newspaper) in the same community. The number of other mass communication outlets of the same type in the community proposed to be served will also affect to some extent the importance of this factor in the general comparative scale.

It is not possible, of course, to spell out in advance the relationships between any significant number of the various factual situations which may be presented in actual hearings. It is possible, however, to set forth the elements which we believe significant. Without indicating any order of priority, we will consider interests in existing media of mass communications to be more significant in the degree that they:

(A) are larger, i.e., go towards complete ownership and control;

and to the degree that the existing media:

(B) are in, or close to, the community being applied for;
(C) are significant in terms of numbers and size, i.e., the area covered, circulation, size of audience, etc.;
(D) are significant in terms of regional or national coverage; and
(E) are significant with respect to other media in their respective localities.

2. *Full-time participation in station operation by owners.* We consider this factor to be of substantial importance. It is inherently desirable that legal responsibility and day-to-day performance be closely associated. In addition, there is a likelihood of greater sensitivity to an area's changing needs, and of programming designed to serve these needs, to the extent that

---

[5] Sections 73.35(a), 73.240(a)(1) and 73.636(a)(1) of our rules, 47 CFR 73.35(a), 73.240(a)(1), 73.636(a)(1), prohibit common control of stations in the same service (AM, FM and TV) within prescribed overlap areas. Less than controlling ownership interests and significant managerial positions in stations and other media within and without such areas will be considered when held by persons with any ownership or significant managerial interest in an applicant.

the station's proprietors actively participate in the day-to-day operation of the station. This factor is thus important in securing the best practicable service.[6] It also frequently complements the objective of diversification, since concentrations of control are necessarily achieved at the expense of integrated ownership.

We are primarily interested in full-time participation. To the extent that the time spent moves away from full time, the credit given will drop sharply, and no credit will be given to the participation of any person who will not devote to the station substantial amounts of time on a daily basis. In assessing proposals, we will also look to the positions which the participating owners will occupy, in order to determine the extent of their policy functions and the likelihood of their playing important roles in management. We will accord particular weight to staff positions held by the owners, such as general manager, station manager, program director, business manager, director of news, sports or public service broadcasting, and sales manager. Thus, although positions of less responsibility will be considered, especially if there will be full-time integration by those holding those positions, they cannot be given the decisional significance attributed to the integration of stockholders exercising policy functions. Merely consultative positions will be given no weight.

Attributes of participating owners, such as their experience and local residence, will also be considered in weighing integration of ownership and management. While, for the reasons given above, integration of ownership and management is important *per se,* its value is increased if the participating owners are local residents and if they have experience in the field. Participation in station affairs on the basis described above by a local resident indicates a likelihood of continuing knowledge of changing local interests and needs.[7] Previous broadcast experience, while not so significant as local residence, also has some value when put to use through integration of ownership and management.

Past participation in civic affairs will be considered as a part of a participating owner's local residence background, as will any other local activities indicating a knowledge of and interest in the welfare of the community. Mere diversity of business interests will not be considered. Generally speaking, residence in the principal community to be served will be of primary importance, closely followed by residence outside the community, but within the proposed service area. Proposed future local residence (which is expected to accompany meaningful participation) will also be accorded less weight than present residence of several years' duration.

[6] As with other proposals, it is important that integration proposals be adhered to on a permanent basis. See *Tidewater Teleradio, Inc.,* 24 Pike & Fischer, R.R. 653.
[7] Of course, full-time participation is also necessarily accompanied by residence in the area.

Previous broadcasting experience includes activity which would not qualify as a past broadcast record, i.e., where there was not ownership responsibility for a station's performance. Since emphasis upon this element could discourage qualified newcomers to broadcasting, and since experience generally confers only an initial advantage,[8] it will be deemed of minor significance. It may be examined qualitatively, upon an offer of proof of particularly poor or good previous accomplishment.

The discussion above has assumed full-time, or almost full-time, participation in station operation by those with ownership interests. We recognize that station ownership by those who are local residents and, to a markedly lesser degree, by those who have broadcasting experience, may still be of some value even where there is not the substantial participation to which we will accord weight under this heading. Thus, local residence complements the statutory scheme and Commission allocation policy of licensing a large number of stations throughout the country, in order to provide for attention to local interests, and local ownership also generally accords with the goal of diversifying control of broadcast stations. Therefore, a slight credit will be given for the local residence of those persons with ownership interests who cannot be considered as actively participating in station affairs on a substantially full-time basis but who will devote some time to station affairs, and a very slight credit will similarly be given for experience not accompanied by full-time participation. Both of these factors, it should be emphasized, are of minor significance. No credit will be given either the local residence or experience of any person who will not put his knowledge of the community (or area) or experience to any use in the operation of the station.

3. *Proposed program service.* The United States Court of Appeals for the District of Columbia Circuit has stated that, "in a comparative consideration, it is well recognized that comparative service to the listening public is the vital element, and programs are the essence of that service." *Johnston Broadcasting Co.* v. *Federal Communications Commission,* 85 U.S. App. D.C. 40, 48, 175 F. 2d 351, 359. The importance of program service is obvious. The feasibility of making a comparative evaluation is not so obvious. Hearings take considerable time and precisely formulated program plans may have to be changed not only in details but in substance, to take account of new conditions obtaining at the time a successful applicant commences operation. Thus, minor differences among applicants are apt to prove to be of no significance.

The basic elements of an adequate service have been set forth in our July 29, 1960 "Report and Statement of Policy Re: Commission *en banc*

---

[8] Lack of experience, unlike a high concentration of control, is remediable. *See Sunbeam Television Corp.* v. *Federal Communications Commission,* 100 U.S. App. D.C. 82, 243 F. 2d 26.

Programming Inquiry," 25 F.R. 7291, 20 Pike & Fischer, R.R. 1901, and need not be repeated here.[9] And the applicant has the responsibility for a reasonable knowledge of the community and area, based on surveys or background, which will show that the program proposals are designed to meet the needs and interests of the public in that area. See *Henry* v. *Federal Communications Commission,* 112 U.S. App. D.C. 257, 302 F. 2d 191, *cert. den.* 371 U.S. 821. Contacts with local civic and other groups and individuals are also an important means of formulating proposals to meet an area's needs and interests. Failure to make them will be considered a serious deficiency, whether or not the applicant is familiar with the area.

Decisional significance will be accorded only to material and substantial differences between applicants' proposed program plans. See *Johnston Broadcasting Co.* v. *Federal Communications Commission,* 85 U.S. App. D.C. 40, 175 F. 2d 351. Minor differences in the proportions of time allocated to different types of programs will not be considered. Substantial differences will be considered to the extent that they go beyond ordinary differences in judgment and show a superior devotion to public service. For example, an unusual attention to local community matters for which there is a demonstrated need, may still be urged. We will not assume, however, that an unusually high percentage of time to be devoted to local or other particular types of programs is necessarily to be preferred. Staffing plans and other elements of planning will not be compared in the hearing process except where an inability to carry out proposals is indicated.[10]

In light of the considerations set forth above, and our experience with the similarity of the program plans of competing applicants, taken with the desirability of keeping hearing records free of immaterial clutter, no comparative issue will ordinarily be designated on program plans and policies, or on staffing plans or other program planning elements, and evidence on these matters will not be taken under the standard issues. The Commission will designate an issue where examination of the applications and other information before it makes such action appropriate, and applicants who believe they can demonstrate significant differences upon which the reception of evidence will be useful may petition to amend the issues.

No independent factor of likelihood of effectuation of proposals will be utilized. The Commission expects every licensee to carry out its proposals, subject to factors beyond its control, and subject to reasonable judgment

---

[9] Specialized proposals necessarily have to be considered on a case-to-case basis. We will examine the need for the specialized service as against the need for a general-service station where the question is presented by competing applicants.

[10] We will similarly not give independent consideration to proposed studios or other equipment. These are also elements of a proposed operation which are necessary to carry out the program plans, and which are expected to be adequate. They will be inquired into only upon a petition to amend the issues which indicates a serious deficiency.

that the public's needs and interests require a departure from original plans. If there is a substantial indication that any party will not be able to carry out its proposals to a significant degree, the proposals themselves will be considered deficient.[11]

4. *Past broadcast record.* This factor includes past ownership interest and significant participation in a broadcast station by one with an ownership interest in the applicant. It is a factor of substantial importance upon the terms set forth below.

A past record within the bounds of average performance will be disregarded, since average future performance is expected. Thus, we are not interested in the fact of past ownership *per se,* and will not give a preference because one applicant has owned stations in the past and another has not.

We are interested in records which, because either unusually good or unusually poor, give some indication of unusual performance in the future. Thus, we shall consider past records to determine whether the record shows (i) unusual attention to the public's needs and interests, such as special sensitivity to an area's changing needs through flexibility of local programs designed to meet those needs, or (ii) either a failure to meet the public's needs and interests or a significant failure to carry out representations made to the Commission (the fact that such representations have been carried out, however, does not lead to an affirmative preference for the applicant, since it is expected, as a matter of course, that a licensee will carry out representations made to the Commission).

If a past record warrants consideration, the particular reasons, if any, which may have accounted for that record will be examined to determine whether they will be present in the proposed operation. For example, an extraordinary record compiled while the owner fully participated in operation of the station will not be accorded full credit where the party does not propose similar participation in the operation of the new station for which he is applying.

5. *Efficient use of frequency.*[12] In comparative cases where one of two or more competing applicants proposes an operation which, for one or more engineering reasons, would be more efficient, this fact can and should be considered in determining which of the applicants should be preferred. The nature of an efficient operation may depend upon the nature of the facilities applied for, i.e., whether they are in the television or FM bands where geographical allocations have been made, or in the standard broadcast (AM)

---

[11] It should be noted here that the absence of an issue on program plans and policies will not preclude cross-examination of the parties with respect to their proposals for participation in station operation, i.e., to test the validity of integration proposals.

[12] This factor as discussed here is not to be confused with the determination to be made of which of two communities has the greater need for a new station. See *Federal Communications Commission* v. *Allentown Broadcasting Corp.,* 349 U.S. 358.

band where there are no such fixed allocations. In addition, the possible variations of situations in comparative hearings are numerous. Therefore, it is not feasible here to delineate the outlines of this element, and we merely take this occasion to point out that the element will be considered where the facts warrant.

6. *Character.* The Communications Act makes character a relevant consideration in the issuance of a license. See Section 308(b), 47 U.S.C. 308(b). Significant character deficiencies may warrant disqualification, and an issue will be designated where appropriate. Since substantial demerits may be appropriate in some cases where disqualification is not warranted, petitions to add an issue on conduct relating to character will be entertained. In the absence of a designated issue, character evidence will not be taken. Our intention here is not only to avoid unduly prolonging the hearing process, but also to avoid those situations where an applicant converts the hearing into a search for his opponents' minor blemishes, no matter how remote in the past or how insignificant.

7. *Other Factors.* As we stated at the outset, our interest in the consistency and clarity of decision and in expedition of the hearing process is not intended to preclude the full examination of any relevant and substantial factor. We will thus favorably consider petitions to add issues when, but only when, they demonstrate that significant evidence will be adduced.[13]

We pointed out at the outset that in the normal course there may be changes in the views of individual commissioners as membership on the Commission changes or as commissioners may come to view matters differently with the passage of time. Therefore, it may be well to emphasize that by this attempt to clarify our present policy and our views with respect to the various factors which are considered in comparative hearings, we do not intend to stultify the continuing process of reviewing our judgment on these matters. Where changes in policy are deemed appropriate they will be made, either in individual cases or in further general statements, with an explanation of the reason for the change. In this way, we hope to preserve the advantages of clear policy enunciation without sacrificing necessary flexibility and open-mindedness.

Cases to be decided by either the Review Board or, where the Review Board has not been delegated that function, by the Commission itself, will be decided under the policies here set forth. So too, future designations for hearing will be made in accordance with this statement. Where cases are now in hearing, the hearing examiner will be expected to follow this statement to the extent practicable. Issues already designated will not be changed, but evidence should be adduced only in accordance with this statement. Thus, evidence on issues which we have said will no longer be

---

[13] Where a narrow question is raised, for example on one aspect of financial qualification, a narrowly drawn issue will be appropriate. In other circumstances, a broader inquiry may be required. This is a matter for *ad hoc* determination.

designated in the absence of a petition to add an issue, should not be accepted unless the party wishing to adduce the evidence makes an offer of proof to the examiner which demonstrates that the evidence will be of substantial value under the criteria discussed herein. Since we are not adopting new criteria which would call for the introduction of new evidence, but rather restricting the scope somewhat of existing factors and explaining their importance more clearly, there will be no element of surprise which might affect the fairness of a hearing. It is, of course, traditional judicial practice to decide cases in accordance with principles in effect at the time of decision. Administrative finality is also important. Therefore, cases which have already been decided, either by the Commission or, where appropriate, by the Review Board, will not be reconsidered. We believe that our purpose to improve the hearing and decisional process in the future does not require upsetting decisions already made, particularly in light of the basically clarifying nature of this document.

Dissenting statement of Commissioner Hyde

I dissent to the adoption of the "Policy Statement on Comparative Broadcast Hearings" issued July 28, 1965.

One of the expressed objectives of the Policy Statement is the simplification and the expedition of the Commission's processes with respect to decisions in comparative cases. I agree with the majority that this is a most desirable objective; however, the policy statement as now framed will not achieve expedition. Moreover, to the extent that a degree of simplification of our decisional process may result from its adoption, this result, in my opinion, would be at a price which would be prohibitive and perhaps unlawful. It would press applicants into a mold in order to meet the Commission's preconceived standards, thus deterring perhaps better-qualified applicants from applying; it would preclude significant consideration of material differences among applicants and result in automatic preference of applicants slavishly conforming to the mold, and eventually force the Commission to decide cases on trivial differences among applicants since basically they would all have come out of the same press. I consider this much too high a price to pay to achieve the majority's objective.

I think the initiative in proposing how stations should be owned and operated should remain with the applicants, thus providing opportunities for diversified approaches. Moreover, in the interest of diversity, the initiative for the presentation of program plans should be left with applicants and without undue circumscription as to what should be included or excluded. Then, as a matter of elementary fairness, as well as due process, applicants should be entitled to examination and comparison on the merit of their respective proposals—not merely comparison with previously-adopted positions. It may be that the check-off approach (as argued in the Policy Statement) will be helpful to Examiners and others in making decisions, but even this illusion of facility is certain to disappear as to cases involving competing new applicants who can plan to conform to prescribed formulas.

When competing applications for facilities are filed, the Commission must make an election which involves a comparison of characteristics. As was stated in *Johnston Broadcasting Company* v. *F.C.C.,* U.S.C.A., D.C., May 4, 1949:

> The Commission cannot ignore a material difference between two applicants and make findings in respect to selected characteristics only. Neither can it base its conclusion upon a selection from among its findings of differences and ignore all other findings. It must take into account all the characteristics which indicate differences, and reach an overall relative determination upon an evaluation of all factors, conflicting in many cases. . . .

In this situation, and in order to comply with the directive of the Court, the Commission must consider among other things differences in makeup of applicants and differences in program proposals for the purpose of making the required comparison. But this requirement to consider differences in characteristics does not warrant the Commission to presume to establish—in the abstract—standardized preferences as to how applicants should be organized or as to how programs should be planned. I think that the effort to direct and standardize is incongruous with the basic policy of the Act.

I presume that one of the reasons for the adoption of the Policy Statement is to apprise potential applicants of the views of the Commission (and individual Commissioners) as to the manner in which differences among applicants will be treated. Decisions which have been made are available for this purpose. The views of the Commission and of individual Commissioners as to the effect of differences among applicants in comparative cases are set out in decisions which touch on such differences. Similarly, the specific views of dissenting or of separately-concurring Commissioners are available for analysis.

I know of no two cases where the underlying facts are identical. I know of no two cases where differences among the applicants are identical. Therefore, the significance to be given in each decision to each difference and to each criterion must of necessity vary, and must necessarily be considered in context with the other facts of the individual cases.

If the Commission has been remiss in the past in not spelling out the decisional process in each case as carefully as it should, the obvious remedy is improvement in the preparation of decisions. Moreover, through more carefully written decisions, both the Commission and the applicants can view the weight given to each difference and to each criterion in light of all the facts in a given case. To the extent the other relevant facts in the applicant's case require the same conclusion, an applicant can assume such conclusion will be reached by the Commission. To the extent the other relevant facts require or permit a different conclusion, the Commission will be free to so conclude. However, to attempt to cure what might be considered past omissions in not fully spelling out reasons for decisions by prescribing an arbitrary order and weight to be given to each of such criteria seems to me to be idealizing form over substance, and avoiding statutory and legal requirements in doing so. This is especially true when no need exists for establishing this procedure since a simpler and more adequate solution is at hand.

The proposed fiat as to the weight which will be given to the various criteria—without sound predication of accepted data and when considered only in a vacuum and in the abstract—must necessarily result in a degree of unfairness to some applicants and in the fashioning of an unnecessary straitjacket for the Commission in its decisional process. How can we decide in advance and in a vacuum that a specific broadcaster with a satisfactory record in one community will be less likely to serve the broadcasting needs of a second community than a specific long-time resident of that second community who doesn't have broadcast experience? How can we make this decision without knowing more about each applicant? The majority now says that experience can always be acquired and, therefore, that it is less important than local residence. But the knowledge acquired from such local residence can by the same token be obtained just as easily—if not more easily—than broadcast experience. It seems clear to me that the importance to be given to the element of experience in one case or to the element of local residence in another case will necssarily vary in light of the additional factors involved in each case.

Moreover, the decision by an individual without broadcast experience (or perhaps even without business experience) to take full control of a complicated broadcast venture is held by this proposed Policy to be entitled to a significantly greater preference than a decision by a more prudent applicant who intends to secure competent, experienced and professional management to operate a station under his general direction until he acquires a reasonable degree of experience. It may be reasonable for the Commission to make such a conclusion in the light of all of the facts in a particular case, taking into consideration the specific attributes of the individual concerned, but it is obvious that the same conclusion need not be valid in a second case where the same attributes may not be present. The fact that it may be difficult to explain different decisions in the two cases is taken by the majority as sufficient reason to establish arbitrary preference. This I cannot accept.

The evalution of local needs and how best to provide for them is a highly subjective matter. Is the Commission competent—in advance of a review of all of the pertinent factors in a particular case—to decide that non-professional opinion as to the existence of needs or as to the manner in which the needs can best be fulfilled is automatically entitled to a greater weight than professional opinion based upon prior experience in substantially identical communities? I submit that it is not, and that although the decision might be difficult to make in any one case, and perhaps even more difficult to explain where the decisions differ on this factor in two cases, there can nevertheless be sound bases for different results in cases involving these elements. We should not be foreclosed from exploring them.

The language of the Policy Statement is quite broad in certain areas while, at the same time, the statement tries to be precise and restrictive in its proposed results. For example, terms such as "unusually high percentage of time," "unusual attention to community matters," "minor differences in the proportion of time," "ordinary differences in judgment," etc., are used without definition as to the meaning of the terms. I presume that future decisions will spell out at least some guidelines as to their meaning, but it is obvious that this will be achieved only at great cost to the applicants and after much litigation and then only in connection with the facts of a particular case. Since precise definitions are really not now feasible, why should these terms be employed? And since there appear to be no presently-existing guidelines which can be established in this document, then the ensuing wrangle in comparative cases as to what is ordinary, usual, unusual, high, etc., will take up at least the same time, if not more, than the mere introduction of proof of the basic facts.

I do not believe that the Commission has given sufficient thought to the consequences of establishing the order and weight of preferences in comparative hearing cases. The document says that the policy is to apply to "new" applicants, and that it "does not attempt to deal with the somewhat different problems raised where an applicant is contesting with a licensee seeking renewal of license." I do not believe that a logical or a legal basis can be established for making a distinction between criteria to be applied to renewal applications and criteria applicable to initial applications. The statutory test is exactly the same. The intention of Congress to require the same test was affirmed in the Communications Act Amendments of 1952. Since we must assume that the Commission will find it appropriate or necessary to make uniform application of its statement of preferences, it is essential to consider the consequences of such application. The filing of a new application—organized according to formula—to challenge a renewal applicant could lead to a facile but in many instances unfair and arbitrary decisional process. Is the Commission now ready to read out established broadcasters, not locally owned, but otherwise without blemish in favor of any locally-owned applicants? Is the Commission now ready to read out established broadcasters who are without blemish, except that they utilize competent personnel who do not have an ownership interest, in favor of applicants who propose to operate the facilities personally? Is the Commission ready to accept a new applicant formed to meet this preconceived mold in preference to an existing broadcaster who does not fit into such mold regardless of other circumstances?

I must assume that in the above cases the Commission will not reach its judgments arbitrarily and without giving consideration to all of the significant elements. Upon this assumption, I can foresee the development of case after case where exceptions to the Policy will be found to be necessary in order to reach a decision which a majority will consider to be fair and in the public interest. I can foresee a decisional process which eventually will be substantially similar—if not virtually identical—to the one in existence. Under these circumstances, I cannot believe that the public interest will be served, or the processes of the Commission expedited, by the adoption of the proposed Policy Statement.

No useful purpose would appear to be served by further belaboring these points. While the motives of the majority may be excellent, I do not believe that its objectives can thus be achieved. Moreover, I fear that the degree of uniformity which is being sought will necessarily be detrimental to broadcasting in general and to the public interest.

An overall objection which I think I should state is that the Commission is, in effect, placing legislative-like restrictions upon performance under the responsibility Congress intended it to implement with broad direction. It would appear that we do not trust Commissioners to exercise judgment with as much discretion as Congress intended to repose in the Agency. This restrictive approach not only limits the Agency, but, as has been indicated, threatens to inhibit the development of services which do not conform to preconceived molds.

I think that the Commission should consider—instead of the adoption of this proposed "Policy Statement"—the introduction of such modern and accepted procedural methods as "discovery"—requiring its staff to make a more careful examination of each competing applicant prior to the issuance of hearing orders so as to specify issues which will encompass all material differences among the applicants rather than ordering hearings on generalized, boiler-plate issues and preconceived conclusions; and writing its decisions with such care as to eliminate frivolous and inconsequential matter and in such a manner that applicants would be readily apprised of areas which the Commission considers to be vitally important. I believe that discovery procedure alone will do more to bring light—and to minimize heat—in comparative cases than a general abjuration of trivia. If the parties and, in fact, the Commission can secure factual information about each of the applicants before the hearing, and if thereafter, the Commission will exercise care and discretion in the framing of the issues, more will have been achieved to shorten our hearing procedures than can reasonably be expected from the adoption of this Policy Statement.

Dissenting statement of Commissioner Robert T. Bartley

I believe that our comparative hearings should be expedited by eliminating what has amounted to extensive bickering in the record over minutiae.

As I see it, however, the Commission majority is attempting the impossible here when it prejudges the decisional factors in future cases. My observation is that there are no two cases exactly alike. There are so many varying circumstances in each case that a factor in one may be more important than the same factor in another. Broadcasting—a dynamic force in our society—experiences constant change. I have expressed it differently on occasions by saying, "There's nothing static in radio but the noise." If we are to encourage the larger and more effective use of radio in the public interest, we must avoid becoming static ourselves.

Concurring statement of Commissioner Robert E. Lee

Even though I recognize the Policy Statement adopted by the Commission to be the result of a sincere effort to clarify the historical process of selecting a winner in comparative broadcast hearings, I am concurring with considerable reluctance. I am disappointed that the Commission did not examine alternative methods of "picking a winner" from a group of competing applicants, each of which may be fully qualified but only one of which may be granted. For example, in a recent case involving nine applications where I unqualifiedly concurred with the result arrived at by the majority, I said:

> However, I would much prefer such appropriate changes in the Communications Act and in the Commission's practices and policies as would have permitted, in a case such as this, adoption of a procedure which would, on a comparative basis, eliminate from further consideration several of the applications, and which would have permitted us to direct the remaining applicants to endeavor to work out a satisfactory merger arrangement within a stated reasonable period. In the event that such a merger were thereafter presented to the Commission, an award could have been given to the merged entity. Failing such a merger, the Commission would thereupon proceed to select a winner from among the limited eligibles. *Veterans Broadcasting Company, Inc., et al*, decided January 19, 1965.

Over the years I have participated in decisions in hundreds of "comparative proceedings" and candor compels me to say that our method of selection of the winning applicant has given me grave concern. I realize, of course, that where we have a number of qualified applicants in a consolidated proceeding for a single facility in a given community, it is necessary that we grant one and deny the others. The ultimate choice of the winner generally sustains the Commission's choice despite the recent rash of remands from the Court. Thus, it would appear that we generally grant the "right" application. However, I am not so naive as to believe that granting the "right application" could not, in some cases, be one of several applications.

The criteria that the Commission now says will be decisive—assuming all other things are substantially equal—in choosing among qualified applicants for new broadcast facilities in comparative hearings, are not new. However, the Policy Statement does tend to restrict the scope somewhat of existing factors and if undue delay in the disposition of comparative broadcast hearings is thus prevented, some good will have been accomplished.

I wish to make clear that my concurrance here does not bind me with respect to the weight I might see fit to put upon the various criteria in a given case. For example, while I recognize the problem of diversification of the mass media, I also recognize some counter balancing in the advantages of common ownership of a radio station and a newspaper. I am also persuaded that the public interest may be served by the common ownership of a radio station and a CATV system in the same market. In other words, if it should appear to me in a given proceeding that the owner of a newspaper or of a CATV system would do the better job of serving a particular community, I would not be so concerned with the composition of such an applicant that I would select another that was not "tainted" with the media of mass communication.

Historically, a prospective applicant hires a highly skilled communications attorney, well versed in the procedures of the Commission. This counsel has a long history of Commission decisions to guide him and he puts together an application that meets all of the so-called criteria. There then follows a torturous and expensive hearing wherein each applicant attempts to tear down his adversaries on every conceivable front, while individually presenting that which he thinks the Commission would like to hear. The Examiner then makes a reasoned decision which, at first blush, generally makes a lot of sense—but comes the Oral Argument and all of the losers concentrate their fire on the "potential" winner and the Commission must thereupon examine the claims and counter claims, "weigh" the criteria and pick the winner which, if my recollection serves me correctly, is a different winner in about 50 per cent of the cases.

The real blow, however, comes later when the applicant that emerged as the winner on the basis of our "decisive" criteria sells the station to a multiple owner or someone else that could not possibly have prevailed over other qualified applicants under the criteria in an adversary proceeding. It may be that there is no better selection system than the one being followed. If so, it seems like a "helleva way to run a railroad," and I hope these few comments may inspire the Commission to find that better system even if it requires changes in the Communications Act.

RELATED READING

ARCHER, Gleason L. *Big Business and Radio.* New York: The American Historical Company, 1939.

BALL, F. J. "Economic Injury Theory of Appealable Interest Under the Communications Act," *George Washington Law Review,* VIII (March, 1940), 836–844.

BARBER, Oren G. "Competition, Free Speech, and FCC Radio Network Regulations," *George Washington Law Review,* XII (December, 1943), 34–53.

BERNSTEIN, Marvin H. *Regulating Business by Independent Commission.* Princeton, N.J.: Princeton University Press, 1955.

BROWN, S. M., and J. W. REED. "Regulation of Radio Broadcasting; Competitive Enterprise or Public Utility?," *Cornell Law Quarterly,* XXVII (February, 1942), 249–266.

COLE, John P., Jr. "Community Antenna Television, the Broadcaster Establishment, and the Federal Regulator," *American University Law Review,* XIV (June, 1965), 124–145.

COLLE, Royal D. "Television at the Grassroots: CATV," *Journal of Broadcasting,* VII (Winter, 1962–63), 3–10.

CONRAD, Edwin. "Economic Aspects of Radio Regulation," *Virginia Law Review,* XXXIV (April, 1948), 283–304.

DOERFER, John C. "Community Antenna Television Systems," *Federal Communications Bar Journal,* XIV (1955), 4–14.

EOYANG, Thomas T. *An Economic Study of the Radio Industry in the United States of America.* New York: Columbia University and RCA Institutes, Inc., 1937.

"FCC Disclaims Power to Limit Competition in Broadcasting," *Columbia Law Review,* LVII (November, 1957), 1036–1038.

FEDERAL COMMUNICATIONS COMMISSION. *An Economic Study of Standard Broadcasting.* Washington: Government Printing Office, 1947. (Mimeographed.)

———. *Report on Chain Broadcasting.* Washington: Government Printing Office, 1941.

———. *Report* [to the Broadcast Division of the FCC] *on Social and Economic Data Pursuant to the Informal Hearing on Broadcasting, Docket 4063, Beginning October 5, 1936.* Washington: Government Printing Office, 1938.

FORD, Frederick W. "Economic Considerations in Licensing of Radio Broadcast Stations," *Federal Communications Bar Journal,* XVII (1961), 191–198.

———. "Television: Divided or United?," *Television Quarterly,* III (Fall, 1964), 29–42.

GELMAN, Morris J. "The Future of Television: Will Wire Take Over?," *Television,* XXII (December, 1965), 27–31, 68–77.

GERALD, J. Edward, and George N. ECKLUND. "Probable Effects of Television on Income of Other Media," *Journalism Quarterly,* XXIX (Fall, 1952), 385–395.

GIVENS, Richard A. "Comment: Refusal of Radio and Television Licenses on Economic Grounds," *Virginia Law Review,* XLVI (November, 1960), 1391–1406.

GOLDIN, H. H. "Economic and Regulatory Problems in the Broadcast Field," *Land Economics,* XXX (1954), 223–233.

HALE, G. E., and Rosemary D. HALE. "Competition or Control: Radio and Television Broadcasting," *University of Pennsylvania Law Review,* CVII (March, 1959), 585–620.

HERRING, James M., and Gerald C. GROSS. *Telecommunications: Economics and Regulation.* New York: McGraw-Hill, 1936.

HETTINGER, Herman S. "The Economic Factor in Radio Regulation," *Air Law Review,* IX (April, 1938), 115–128.

"Interpreting the FCC Rules and Regulations: The CATV Rules Reviewed," *Broadcast Management/Engineering,* III (April, 1967), 26–32, 136.

"Interpreting the FCC Rules and Regulations: The CATV Rules Reviewed II," *Broadcast Management/Engineering,* III (May, 1967), 16–18, 24.

"Interpreting the FCC Rules and Regulations: Concentration of Control of Mass Media," *Broadcast Management/Engineering,* II (June, 1966), 13–18.

"Interpreting the FCC Rules and Regulations: The Drive for Diversified Ownership," *Broadcast Management/Engineering,* II (May, 1966), 13–17.

"Interpreting the FCC Rules and Regulations: The Multiple Ownership Philosophy," *Broadcast Management/Engineering,* II (July, 1966), 13–16.

"Interpreting the FCC Rules and Regulations: The Volatile Question of Economic Injury," *Broadcast Management/Engineering,* I (March, 1965), 14–17.

JAMES, Edwin H. "The Growing Snarl in Wired TV," *Television,* XXII (September, 1965), 42–45, 69–70.

KAHN, Frank. "Economic Regulation of Broadcasting as a Utility," *Journal of Broadcasting,* VII (Spring, 1963), 97–112.

KROEGER, Albert R. "Community Antenna Television: Friend or Foe?," *Television,* XIX (June, 1962), 48–51, 76–88.

———. "The Real World of CATV," *Television,* XXII (April, 1965), 37–40, 68–72.

LEVIN, Harvey J. "Broadcast Regulation and Intramedium Competition," *Virginia Law Review,* XLV (November, 1959), 1104–1138.

———. *Broadcast Regulation and Joint Ownership of Media.* New York: New York University Press, 1960.

———. "Competition Among the Mass Media and the Public Interest," *Public Opinion Quarterly,* XVIII (Spring, 1954), 62–79.

———. "Economics in Cross Channel Affiliation of Media," *Journalism Quarterly,* XXXI (Spring, 1954), 167–174.

LOEVINGER, Lee. "The Future of Television," *Television Quarterly,* IV (Fall, 1965), 41–52.

MAYER, Jacob W. "Sanders Brothers Revisited: Protection of Broadcasters from the Consequences of Economic Competition," *Kentucky Law Journal,* XLIX (Spring, 1961), 370–382.

"Note: Economic Injury in FCC Licensing: the Public Interest Ignored," *Yale Law Journal,* LXVII (November, 1957), 135–150.

PALMER, John C., Jr., James R. SMITH, and Edwin L. WADE. "Notes: Community Antenna Television: Survey of a Regulatory Problem," *Georgetown Law Journal,* LII (Fall, 1963), 136–176.

ROBINSON, Thomas P. *Radio Networks and the Federal Government.* New York: Columbia University Press, 1943.

SCHWARTZ, Bernard. "Comparative Television and the Chancellor's Foot," *Georgetown Law Review,* XLVII (Summer, 1959), 655–699.

SEIDEN, Martin H. *An Economic Analysis of Community Antenna Television Systems and the Television Broadcasting Industry.* Washington: Government Printing Office, 1965.

STEINER, Peter O. "Discussion: Goldin's Paper on Economics and Regulatory Problems in the Broadcast Field," *Land Economics,* XXX (1954), 233–236.

UNITED STATES CONGRESS, HOUSE, COMMITTEE ON INTERSTATE AND FOREIGN COMMERCE. *Regulation of Community Antenna Television,* Hearings before Subcommittee, 89th Congress, 1st Session, on H.R. 7715, May 2 and June 2–4, 1965. Washington: Government Printing Office, 1965.

———. *Regulation of Community Antenna Television,* Hearings before Committee, 89th Congress, 2d Session, on H.R. 12914, H.R. 13286, and H.R. 14201, March 22–24 and April 5–7, 1966. Washington: Government Printing Office, 1966.

UNITED STATES CONGRESS, SENATE, COMMITTEE ON INTERSTATE AND FOREIGN COMMERCE. *VHF Booster and Community Antenna Legislation,* Hearings before Subcommittee, 86th Congress, 1st Session, on S. 1739, S. 1741, S. 1801, S. 1886, and S. 2303, Part I, June 30, July 1, 7, 9, 14–16, 1959, Part II on S. 2653, October 27–30, and December 15–16, 1959. Washington: Government Printing Office, 1959, 1960.

PART FIVE

EDUCATIONAL BROADCASTING

EDUCATIONAL institutions were numerous among the earliest radio station experimenters and licensees. Such stations were often operated as adjuncts to departments of physics in colleges and universities. By the time educators became aware of the broader implications of radio for course instruction, many institutions had surrendered their licenses because of the high operational costs, or found themselves saddled with inferior facilities incapable of reaching many people as often as desirable.

Pursuant to Section 307 (c) of the Communications Act of 1934 (see page 69), on January 22, 1935, the FCC recommended to Congress that "no fixed percentages of radio broadcast facilities be allocated by statute to particular types or kinds of non-profit radio programs or to persons identified with particular types or kinds of non-profit activities."[1] This recommendation was based on the Commission's understanding that educational and other non-profit organizations would have ample access to commercial broadcast facilities. To implement its view, the FCC sponsored a conference that began on May 15, 1935, in Washington, D.C., and resulted in the formation of the Federal Radio Education Committee (FREC). The FREC, which first met in 1936, was active through the 1940's, but its enthusiasm for educational programming was not reflected by positive results on the air, and the Committee quietly disbanded.

The FCC followed a different policy with respect to FM broadcasting. Certain FM channels were reserved for educational, non-commercial use. Whenever they felt prepared to do so, educators could apply for licenses without the danger of having all but the least desirable facilities already licensed to commercial interests. Accordingly, twenty channels (88–92 mHz.) in the FM band may be licensed only to non-commercial, educational or-

[1] Quoted in S. E. Frost, Jr., *Education's Own Stations* (Chicago: University of Chicago Press, 1937), p. vi.

ganizations. The FCC further encouraged educational FM broadcasting by permitting low power transmission (as little as ten watts) and reduced hours of operation.

The progress of educational broadcasting since 1950 has been highlighted by reservation of hundreds of TV station assignments for educational use, and by growing awareness that adequate financial support for educational radio and television is needed if these media are to approach the fulfillment of their potentials. The Public Broadcasting Act of 1967 may be viewed as the most recent evidence of the evolutionary development of a dual system of American broadcasting. On one hand is the commercial sector, supported by advertising revenues; on the other, the non-commercial sector with hundreds of FM and TV stations supported by private grants and increasing amounts of governmental funds. Both areas are designed to serve the public interest; neither seems entirely capable of doing so alone.

The continuing development of this dualism is a reaffirmation of the validity of trial-and-error democratic processes; the recognized mistakes of the past encourage struggles toward a more perfect future.

THE FREEZE

From September 30, 1948, to July 1, 1952, no new television sta-tions were authorized. During this "freeze" period, instituted by the FCC because of technical interference problems as well as the insufficient supply of TV channels in light of the burgeoning de-mand for licenses, the Commission established its allocation and assignment goals.

Largely because of the urgings of Commissioner Frieda B. Hennock, the FCC proposed to establish a separate class of educa-tional, noncommercial TV stations in its "Third Notice," issued late in the "freeze." This proposal was formally adopted by the Com-mission in its Sixth Report and Order, *which ended the "freeze," opened the UHF television spectrum, and provided a frequently amended table of assignments for commercial and noncommercial television in which 242 stations were reserved for educational broadcasting.*

A THE THIRD NOTICE

Third Notice of Proposed Rule Making (Appendix A)
16 Fed. Reg. 3072, 3079
Adopted March 21, 1951; Printed April 7, 1951

VI. NON-COMMERCIAL EDUCATIONAL TELEVISION

The existing channel Assignment Table adopted by the Commis-sion in 1945 did not contain any reserved channels for the exclusive use of non-commercial educational television stations, and no changes in this re-spect were proposed by the Commission in its proposed table of July 11, 1949. However, in the Notice of Further Proposed Rule Making issued on the latter date the Commission pointed out that it had "received informal suggestions concerning the possible provision for non-commercial educational broadcast stations in the 470–890 mc. band." Interested parties were afforded the opportunity to file comments in the proceeding concerning these suggestions.

Prior to the hearing on this issue, a number of the parties supporting the reservation of channels for noncommercial educational purposes joined together to form the Joint Committee on Educational Television. This committee offered testimony in support of a request for reservation of channels in both the VHF and UHF portion of the spectrum.

In general, the need for non-commercial educational television stations was based upon the important contributions which noncommercial educational television stations can make in educating the people both in school—at all levels—and also the adult public. The need for such stations was justified upon the high quality type of programming which would be available on such stations—programming of an entirely different character from that available on most commercial stations.

The need for a reservation was based upon the fact that educational institutions of necessity proceed more slowly in applying for broadcast stations than commercial stations. Hence, if there is no reservation, the available channels are all assigned to commercial interests long before the educational institutions are ready to apply for them.

Some opposition to the reservation was presented at the hearing. In general, none of the witnesses opposed the idea of noncommercial educational stations. On the contrary, there was general agreement that such stations would be desirable. Objection was made to the idea of reservation because as stated by some witnesses, the experience of educational institutions in the use of AM and FM radio does not furnish sufficient assurance that the educational institutions would make use of the television channels. However, there was no objection even by these witnesses to a certain form of reservation provided it was for ı reasonably short time.

In the Commission's view, the need for non-commercial educational television stations has been amply demonstrated on this record. The Commission further believes that educational institutions of necessity need a longer period of time to get prepared for television than do the commercial interests. The only way this can be done is by reserving certain channels for the exclusive use of non-commercial educational stations. Obviously, the period of time during which such reservation should exist is very important. The period must be long enough to give educational institutions a reasonable opportunity to do the preparatory work that is necessary to get authorizations for stations. The period must not be so long that frequencies remain unused for excessively long periods of time. The Commission will survey the general situation from time to time in order to insure that these objectives are not lost sight of.

Accordingly, the Commission in its Table of Assignments has indicated the specific assignments which are proposed to be reserved for non-commercial educational stations.[12] Rules concerning eligibility and use of the stations will be substantially the same as those set forth in subpart C of Part III of the Commission's rules and regulations. The reservation of the non-commercial educational stations is not in a single block as in the case of FM since the assignment problems discussed above would sharply curtail the usefulness of a block assignment.

The following method has been employed in making reservations. In all communities having three or more assignments (whether VHF or UHF) one channel has been reserved for a non-commercial educational station. Where a community has fewer than three assignments, no reservation has been made except in those communities which are primarily educational centers, where reservations have been made even where only one or two channels are assigned.[13] As between VHF and UHF, UHF channel has been reserved where there are fewer than three VHF assignments, except for those communities which are primarily educational centers where a VHF channel has been reserved. Where three or more VHF channels are assigned to a community, a VHF channel has been reserved except in those communities where all VHF assignments have been taken up. In those cases, a UHF channel has been reserved.

It is recognized that in many communities the number of educational institutions exceed the reservation which is made. In such instances the various institutions concerned must enter into cooperative arrangements so as to make sure that the facilities are available to all on an equitable basis.

[12] The procedure set forth in paragraphs 12 and 13 of the notice is applicable to any specific assignment proposed to be reserved or to any request that a channel not proposed for reservation should be reserved.

[13] Forty-six communities were considered to be primarily educational centers in accordance with the testimony presented by the Joint Committee on Educational Television. However, this enumeration is not binding and consideration will be given to any proposal filed pursuant to paragraphs 12 and 13 of the notice providing for additions to or deletions from the enumeration.

B | SIXTH REPORT AND ORDER

17 Fed. Reg. 3905, 3908
Adopted April 14, 1952; Printed May 2, 1952

THE EDUCATIONAL RESERVATION

33. Section VI of Appendix A of the Third Notice contained a statement that as a matter of policy certain assignments in the VHF and UHF would be reserved for the exclusive use of non-commercial television stations. Careful consideration has been given to the exceptions taken to this policy proposal in comments filed by several parties[12] pursuant to paragraph 11 of the Third Notice. For the reasons set forth below, the Commission has concluded that the record does support its proposal[13] and it is hereby adopted in the public interest as the decision of the Commission.

34. The only comments directed against the proposal which fulfill the requirements of paragraph 11 of the Third Notice are those filed by NARTB–TV and Allen B. DuMont Laboratories, Inc. The others do not specify their objections nor do they cite the evidence on which their objections are based. It is difficult to ascertain in some cases whether the objection is in fact based upon the view that there is a failure of the record to support the proposal or upon some other general disagreement with the proposal. Since, however, the comments filed by NARTB–TV and DuMont clearly cover all the objections to the proposal made by any of the other parties, a discussion of their exceptions will cover those of the other parties, and it will not be necessary to determine whether the latter comments must be rejected for failure to comply with the provisions of paragraph 11 of the Third Notice.

---

[12] These parties are: NARTB-TV, Allen B. DuMont Laboratories, Inc., Radio Kentucky, Inc., Capitol Broadcasting Co., and the Tribune Co. Some comments were filed which challenged the power of the Commission under the Communications Act to reserve channels for this purpose. Such contentions have been disposed of by the Commission's Memorandum Opinion of July 13, 1951 (FCC 51–709). Other comments objected to the reservation of a channel in a given community. These objections have been considered in another portion of this report. The Joint Committee on Educational Television filed comments in support of the educational reservation, as did many individual educational institutions, and other civic nonprofit organizations.

[13] Communications Measurements Laboratories, Inc., has taken issue with the use of the words "nation wide" in describing the reservation of channels for this purpose. The proposal is self-explanatory in this respect. Although channels have been reserved throughout the nation, the reservation does not set apart any single channel or group of channels on a nation-wide basis.

35. In view of the rather comprehensive and detailed exceptions taken to section VI of Appendix A it is necessary to review the nature and extent of the Commission's proposal in the Third Notice. An extensive hearing was held by the Commission on the issue: whether television channels should be reserved for the exclusive use of noncommercial educational stations. A total of 76 witnesses testified on this issue.[14] Among the subjects upon which the proponents of reservation presented evidence were: the potential of educational television both for in-school and adult education, and as an alternative to commercial programming; the history of education's use of other broadcast media and of visual aids to education; the possibility of immediate or future utilization of television channels by public and private educational organizations and the methods whereby such utilization could be effectuated; the type of program material which could be presented over noncommercial television stations; the history of and prospects for educational organizations' securing broadcast opportunities from commercial broadcasters; and the number of channels, both UHF and VHF, which would be required to satisfy the needs of education throughout the country. The witnesses who opposed the principle of reservation, contending that it was unlikely that educators would make sufficient use of the reserved channels to warrant withholding them from commercial applicants, and that the best results could be achieved by cooperation between educational groups and commercial broadcasters, testified principally about the past record of educators in broadcasting, the cost of a television station, and cooperation between commercial broadcasters and educational institutions.

36. On the basis of the record thus compiled, the Commission concluded, as set forth in the Third Notice, that there is a need for noncommercial educational television stations; that because educational institutions require more time to prepare for television than commercial interests, a reservation of channels is necessary to insure that such stations come into existence; that such reservations should not be for an excessively long period and should be surveyed from time to time; and that channels in both the VHF and UHF bands should be reserved in accordance with the method there set forth.

37. It has been contended that the record in this proceeding fails to support the Commission's proposal in three basic respects; that it has not been shown that educational organizations will, in fact, require a longer period of time to prepare to apply for television stations than commercial broadcasters; that it should have been found that the reservation of channels for this purpose will result in a waste of valuable frequency space because of nonusage and because of the limited audience appeal that educational

---

[14] Of this number, all but five were called by educational organizations or testified in their own behalf in support of the position taken by such organizations in favor of an affirmative resolution of the question. Two other witnesses were in favor of the principle of reservations but differed with witnesses presented on behalf of educational groups with respect to the manner and extent of reservation.

stations will have; and that no feasible plan for stable utilization of channels by educational institutions has been advanced, particularly with respect to the problem of licensee responsibility.

38. None of the commenting parties have contended that the record has failed to support the findings of the Commission in the Third Notice that, based on the important contributions such stations can make in the education of the in-school and adult public, there is a need for noncommercial educational stations. The objections to the Commission's proposal must, therefore, refer to the desire and the ability, as evidenced in the record, of the educational community to construct and operate such stations.[15] We conclude that the record shows the desire and ability of education to make a substantial contribution to the use of television. There is much evidence in the record concerning the activities of educational organizations in AM and FM broadcasting. It is true and was to be expected that education has not utilized these media to the full extent that commercial broadcasters have, in terms of number of stations and number of hours of operation. However, it has also been shown that many of the educational institutions which are engaged in aural broadcasting are doing an outstanding job in the presentation of high quality programming, and have been getting excellent public response. And most important in this connection, it is agreed that the potential of television for education is much greater and more readily apparent than that of aural broadcasting, and that the interest of the educational community in the field is much greater than it was in aural broadcasting. Further, the justification for an educational station should not, in our view, turn simply on account of audience size. The public interest will clearly be served if these stations are used to contribute significantly to the educational process of the nation. The type of programs which have been broadcast by educational organizations, and those which the record indicates can and would be televised by educators, will provide a valuable complement to commercial programming.

39. We do not think there is merit in the contention that the record, with respect to the general phase of the hearing, does not support the general principle of a reservation of channels for educational purposes as set out in the Third Notice because it does not contain detailed information with regard to the desire, ability and qualifications of the educational organizations to construct a noncommercial educational station, or the competing commercial interests which desire to bring television service to the public. In preparing a proposed Assignment Table for the entire nation

---

15 DuMont, in its Comments in Opposition to Comments and Proposals of Other Parties, has submitted the results of a survey which bear upon this question. Insofar as the survey bears upon any specific reservation, DuMont had the opportunity to present it in the portion of the hearing dealing with Appendix C. The Third Notice was not intended to permit the filing of new material on the matters which were already the subject of hearing. DuMont had an opportunity to present this type of evidence in the general phase of the proceeding.

which would provide the framework for the growth of television for many years to come, we could not limit our perspective to immediate demand for educational stations under circumstances where all communities did not have an opportunity to give full consideration to the possibilities of television for educational purposes and to mobilize their resources. Moreover, evidence of specific demand for educational television was submitted for several communities in the general phase of the hearing, and in addition there was presented an estimate of the number of channels required for this purpose for one section of the country based upon the size of the various communities and their general educational requirements. We do not think it unreasonable to believe that general principles of assignment may be derived from such evidence, and that such principles may validly be applied to comparable communities, for the purposes of drawing up a nationwide assignment plan. See, e. g., The New England Divisions Case, 261 U. S. 184, 197–199 (1923).

40. Moreover, the Third Notice provided for the contesting of specific reservations in any community. The Assignment Table adopted below has been prepared after consideration of the specific evidence in support of, as well as in objection to, specific proposed reservations and after consideration of the over-all needs of all communities for television service.

41. The great preponderance of evidence presented to the Commission has been to the effect that the actual process of formulating plans and of enacting necessary legislation or of making adequate financing available is one which will generally require more time for educational organizations than for commercial interests. The record does, of course, show that there are some educational institutions which are now ready to apply for television broadcasting licenses, but this in no wise detracts from the unavoidable conclusion that the great mass of educational institutions must move more slowly and overcome hurdles not present for commercial broadcasters, and that to insure an extensive, rather than a sparse and haphazard development of educational television, channels must be reserved by the Commission at this time. There is moreover, abundant testimony in the record that the very fact of reserving channels would speed the development of educational television. It was pointed out that it is much easier for those seeking to construct educational television stations to raise funds and get other necessary support if the channels are definitely available, than if it is problematical whether a channel may be procured at all.

42. With regard to possible waste of the reserved channels by nonuse, it is contended that evidence offered in the general portion of the hearing, concerning the record of performance of noncommercial educational agencies in aural broadcasting, and their plans and abilities to meet the installation and programming costs of television, can lead only to the conclusion that waste of limited spectrum space through nonusage will result from the reservation of channels for noncommercial educational stations. To

whatever extent the position taken in these exceptions is that any immediate nonuse of channel space available for television constitutes a waste of channels, the Commission cannot agree. The basic nature of a reservation in itself implies some nonuse; to attribute waste of spectrum to the Commission's proposal concerning the use of certain channels by noncommercial educational stations without attributing it to those assignments in the table for smaller cities, which may not be used for some time, is misleading. The very purpose of the Assignment Table is to reserve channels for the communities there listed to forestall a haphazard, inefficient or inequitable distribution of television service in the United States throughout the many years to come. Moreover, as pointed out in another portion of this report, the whole of the Table of Assignments including the reservations of channels for use by noncommercial educational stations is subject to alternation in appropriate rule making proceedings in the future, and any assignment, whether an educational reservation or not, may be modified if it appears in the public interest to do so.

43. We do not believe that in order to support our decision to reserve channels for noncommercial educational stations it is necessary that we be able to find on the basis of the record before us, in the general phase of the hearing, that the educational community of the United States has demonstrated either collectively or individually that it is financially qualified at this time to operate television stations. One of the reasons for having the reservation is that the Commission recognizes that it is of the utmost importance to this nation that a reasonable opportunity be afforded educational institutions to use television as a noncommercial educational medium, and that at the same time it will generally take the educational community longer to prepare for the operation of its own television stations than it would for some commercial broadcasters. This approach is exactly the same as that underlying the Assignment Table as a whole, since reservations of commercial channels have been made in many smaller communities to insure that they not be foreclosed from ever having television stations.

44. Although the record in the general phase of the proceedings does not contain any detailed showing on a community-by-community basis that the educational organizations have made detailed investigation of the costs incident to the construction and operation of television stations and of the exact sources from which such funds could be derived in the near future, nevertheless, the record, as a whole, does indicate that educational organizations in most communities where reservation has finally been made will actually seek the necessary funds. Furthermore, interested persons have had an opportunity to present evidence in the city-by-city portion of the hearings as to whether such funds will be sought or will become available in specific communities. It will admittedly be a difficult and time consuming process in most instances, but the likelihood of ultimate success, and the importance to the public of the objective sought, warrants the action taken. Several educational institutions, it was indicated on the record as early as

the general portion of the hearing, had applied for television stations. The amounts of money spent by other public and private educational groups in aural broadcasting indicates that the acquisition of sufficient funds for television would not be an insurmountable obstacle. It has been shown, for example, that considerable sums have already been spent on visual aids to education. Television is clearly a fertile field for endowment, and it seems probable that sufficient funds can be raised both through this method and through the usual sources of funds for public and private education to enable the construction and operation of many noncommercial educational stations. As concerns the costs of operation there is the possibility of cooperative programming and financing among several educational organizations in large communities. The record indicates that educational institutions will unite in the construction and operation of noncommercial educational television stations. Such cooperative effort will, of course, help to make such stations economically feasible. The fact that somewhat novel problems may arise with respect to the selection and designation of licensees in this field does not—as some have contended—constitute a valid argument against the concept of educational reservations.

45. Several alternative methods for utilizing television in education have been presented to the Commission, but we do not think that any of them is satisfactory. One proposal is to utilize a microwave relay or wired circuit system of television for in-school educational programs. It appears that the cost of a wired circuit for the schools in larger cities might be prohibitive; but the determinative objection to such a proposal is that it would ignore very significant aspects of educational television. It is clear from the record that an important part of the educator's effort in television will be in the field of adult education in the home, as well as the provision of after school programs for children.

46. The NARTB–TV contended that the solution lay in the voluntary cooperation of educators and commercial broadcasters in the presentation of educational programs on commercial facilities. We conclude, however, that this sort of voluntary cooperation cannot be expected to accomplish all the important objectives of educational television. In order for an educational program to achieve its purpose it is necessary that broadcast time be available for educators on a regular basis. An audience cannot be built up if educators are forced to shift their broadcast period from time to time. Moreover, the presentation of a comprehensive schedule of programs comprising a number of courses and subjects which are designed for various age and interest groups may require large periods of the broadcast day which would be difficult if not impossible to obtain on commercial stations.

47. Another alternative was proposed by Senator Edwin C. Johnson of Colorado. This proposal is elaborated in the Senator's statement:

It is my belief as I have repeatedly said that the Commission could and should impose a condition on all television licenses that a certain amount of time be made available for educational purposes in the public interest as a sustaining feature. In this manner, television can become available for educational work now without saddling schools with the enormous burden and expense of constructing and operating a noncommercial educational station. . . . It is my considered opinion that the Commission can best serve the public interest and at the same time extend extremely profitable assistance to the educational processes of this country by imposing a condition in each television license issued which would require the availability of appropriate time for educational purposes.

48. It must be remembered that the provision for noncommercial educational television stations does not relieve commercial licensees from their duty to carry programs which fulfill the educational needs and serve the educational interests of the community in which they operate. This obligation applies with equal force to all commercial licensees whether or not a noncommercial educational channel has been reserved in their community, and similarly will obtain in communities where noncommercial educational stations will be in operation.

49. Aside from the question of the legal basis of a rule which would accomplish Senator Johnson's proposal, the Commission feels it would be impracticable to promulgate a rule requiring that each commercial television licensee devote a specified amount of time to educational programs. A proper determination as to the appropriate amount of time to be set aside is subject to so many different and complex factors, difficult to determine in advance, that the possibility of such a rule is most questionable. Thus, the number of stations in the community, the total hours operated by each station, the number of educational institutions in the community, the size of the community, and countless other factors, each of which will vary from community to community, would make any uniform rule applicable to all TV stations unrealistic. All things considered, it appears to us that the reservation of channels for noncommercial educational stations, together with continued adherence by commercial stations to the mandate of serving the educational needs of the community, is the best method of achieving the aims of educational television.

Who may be licensed to operate noncommercial educational stations

50. While the Third Notice did not specify who would be eligible to own and operate a noncommercial educational station, the Commission has in the past restricted the ownership and operation of such stations to nonprofit educational organizations.

51. The United States Conference of Mayors and the Municipal Broadcasting System, City of New York, have in appropriate comments proposed that eligibility be extended to any municipality operating educational insti-

tutions. The Municipal Broadcasting System states that a "more expeditious management of educational television in the City of New York from an administration standpoint" would result if it were permitted to operate a television station. It further stated that "if the Municipal Broadcasting System is eligible to operate television facilities, the station can be utilized by all of the educational institutions over which it has jurisdiction, rather than having responsibility for the operation placed in a particular school."

52. The Commission is of the opinion that in any community where an independent educational agency is constituted, and is eligible under the Commission's rules to apply for a noncommercial educational television station, there are no compelling reasons for extending eligibility to municipal authorities. The continued operation by the Board of Education of the City of New York since 1939 of noncommercial educational Station WNYE indicates that no insurmountable administrative barriers exist which would preclude the Board of Education as a potential licensee in the television field. Similarly, there is no evidence to indicate that the Board of Education of the City of New York, now eligible under the present rules, would give less access to other educational institutions were it the licensee of a television station than would the Municipal Broadcasting System were it eligible and granted a license. It should be noted that in any community the municipal authorities, or any other group, can take the initiative in constituting a consolidated television authority which would represent municipal educational institutions, private universities and other organizations concerned with education.

53. The Commission has, however, established in its rules an exception providing that where a municipality has no independently constituted educational entity which would be eligible under the rules, the municipality in such case will be eligible to apply for a noncommercial educational station. This exception is designed solely to meet those situations where the municipal authorities do not delegate educational authority but reserve to themselves the management of the municipal educational system.

Partial commercial operation by educational stations

54. In its comments the University of Missouri[16] requests that the Commission authorize ". . . commercial operation on the channels reserved for educational institutions to an amount equal to 50 percent of the broadcast day." It appears from the evidence that funds in the amount of $350,000 are presently available to the University for the construction of a television station, but that no funds are available for the operation of such a station. Accordingly, the University requests that the Commission permit educational institutions to use the reserved assignments to operate stations on a limited

[16] See the discussion, elsewhere in this report, of the assignments in Columbia, Missouri.

commercial non-profit basis. It is urged that if its request is granted the following objectives will be attained:

A. More educational institutions will be in a position to construct and operate television stations throughout the country to the benefit of the public at large without materially affecting the strictly commercial stations;

B. Educational television stations will be able, through income received from commercial programs to better program their stations; and

C. That the commercial programs televised will break the monotony of continuous educational subjects so as to permit the stations to attract and hold audiences.

55. A similar proposal, that the Commission extend the reservation to include all educational institutions which are operated on a nonprofit basis, is made by the Bob Jones University (WMUU) Greenville, South Carolina. The Bob Jones University argues that ". . . the reservation of the privilege of a commercial income commensurate with the operating expense of the educational station . . ." will result in the encouragement and aid to television broadcasting by educational institutions.

56. KFRU, Inc., Columbia, Missouri, opposed the request of the University of Missouri. In its reply to the University, KFRU states that it has no objection to the proposed reservation of Channel 8 for noncommercial educational purposes in Columbia, Missouri. However, it opposes the request of the University for partial commercial operation on the grounds that such an operation would give the educational institution unfair competitive advantages over a commercial licensee.

57. It is our view that the request of the University of Missouri and the Bob Jones University must be denied. In the Third Notice we stated:

In general, the need for noncommercial educational television stations was based upon the important contributions which noncommercial educational television stations can make in educating the people both in school—at all levels—and also the adult public. The need for such stations was justified upon the high quality type of programming which would be available on such stations—programming of an entirely different character from that available on most commercial stations.

A grant of the requests of the University of Missouri and Bob Jones University for partial commercial operation by educational institutions would tend to vitiate the differences between commercial operation and noncommercial educational operation. It is recognized that the type of operation proposed by these Universities may be accomplished by the licensing of educational institutions in the commercial television broadcast service. But in our view achievement of the objective for which special educational reservations have been established—i. e., the establishment of a genuinely educational type of service—would not be furthered by permitting educational institutions to operate in substantially the same manner as commercial applicants though they may choose to call it limited commercial nonprofit operation.

58. The Joint Committee on Educational Television suggests in its final brief that, in communities where only one VHF channel is assigned, and that channel is reserved for use by a noncommercial educational station, the noncommercial educational station should be allowed to broadcast programs which at present are available only from commercial network services. This exception would apply until such time as a commercial Grade A service is available in the area.

59. On January 10, 1952, a Reply and Motion to Strike was filed by Peoria Broadcasting Company, Rock Island Broadcasting Company and Champaign News-Gazette, Inc., with respect to the above described proposal of the Joint Committee. On January 25, 1952, a response to the Joint Motions was filed by the JCET. In view of the fact that the proposal made by the Joint Committee was not previously raised in any of its prior pleadings, the Motion to Strike is granted and the proposal is being given no further consideration.

The use of the VHF for noncommercial educational television

60. The Commission's Third Notice proposed to reserve one of the assigned channels for noncommercial educational television use in all communities having a total of three or more assignments (whether VHF or UHF). Where a community had fewer than three assignments no reservation was proposed except in those communities which were designated as primarily educational centers, where reservations were made although only one or two channels were assigned. Except for educational centers, a UHF channel was proposed in those communities where there were fewer than three VHF assignments. In 26 of the 46 educational centers, the Commission proposed to reserve a VHF channel for educational use. In 23 of these 26 centers a VHF educational reservation was proposed where only one VHF channel was assigned to the community. Where three or more VHF channels were assigned to a community, a VHF channel was proposed to be reserved except in those communities were all VHF assignments had been previously licensed. In those cases, the reservation of a UHF channel was proposed.

61. The Joint Committee on Educational Television in its comment has proposed that a VHF reservation for noncommercial educational institutions in place of a UHF reservation be considered in communities with less than three VHF assignments. On the other hand, some parties have argued that no assignments in the VHF be set aside as educational reservations. The Commission's Third Notice stated that the proposed reservations were not final and that consideration would be given to any specific pro-

posal looking toward additions or deletions. After examining the comments and evidence filed pursuant to the Third Notice, the Commission remains of the view that the bases upon which it determined the apportionment of noncommercial educational assignments by communities are generally sound and should be continued. However, in particular cases the Commission concludes that the evidence warrants deviations from the proposals in the Third Notice, for the reasons stated in the city-by-city portion of this Report.

62. The Joint Committee on Educational Television also proposes that the Commission should specifically state that an educational interest is not to be foreclosed from applying for a VHF channel in the so-called "closed cities" where all VHF assignments have already been made. No properly qualified applicant is ever precluded from applying for any channel in the broadcast field on the expiration of the existing license. Thus, whether educational interests seek a commercial or noncommercial television operation, they are, just as other applicants, eligible to apply for licensed channels upon expiration of the license term of the stations involved.

2 | THE ETV FACILITIES ACT OF 1962

Public Law 87-447, 87th Congress
May 1, 1962

This Act, an amendment to title III of the Communications Act of 1934, constituted the first meaningful cognizance by the Federal Government of the economic difficulties of educational television stations. The Act sought to encourage ETV station construction by making available Federal funds for that purpose on a matching basis.

PART IV—GRANTS FOR EDUCATIONAL TELEVISION BROADCASTING FACILITIES

Declaration of Purpose

SEC. 390. The purpose of this part is to assist (through matching grants) in the construction of educational television broadcasting facilities.

Authorization of appropriations

SEC. 391. There are authorized to be appropriated for the fiscal year ending June 30, 1963, and each of the four succeeding fiscal years such sums, not exceeding $32,000,000 in the aggregate, as may be necessary to carry out the purposes of section 390. Sums appropriated pursuant to this section shall remain available for payment of grants for projects for which applications, approved under section 392, have been submitted under such section prior to July 1, 1968.

Grants for construction

SEC. 392. (a) For each project for the construction of educational television broadcasting facilities there shall be submitted to the Secretary an application for a grant containing such information with respect to such project as the Secretary may by regulation require, including the total cost of such project and the amount of the Federal grant requested for such project, and providing assurance satisfactory to the Secretary—

 (1) that the applicant is (A) an agency or officer responsible for the supervision of public elementary or secondary education or public higher education within that State, or within a political subdivision thereof, (B) the State educational television agency, (C) a college or university deriving its support in whole or in part from tax revenues, or (D) a nonprofit foundation, corporation, or association which is organized primarily to engage in or encourage educational television broadcasting and is eligible to receive a license from the Federal Communications Commission for a noncommercial educational television broadcasting station pursuant to the rules and regulations of the Commission in effect on April 12, 1962;

 (2) that the operation of such educational television broadcasting facilities will be under the control of the applicant or a person qualified under paragraph (1) to be such an applicant;

 (3) that necessary funds to construct, operate, and maintain such educational television broadcasting facilities will be available when needed; and

 (4) that such television broadcasting facilities will be used only for educational purposes.

 (b) The total amount of grants under this part for the construction of educational television broadcasting facilities to be situated in any State shall not exceed $1,000,000.

 (c) In order to assure proper coordination of construction of educational television broadcasting facilities within each State which has established a State educational television agency, each applicant for a grant under this section for a project for construction of such facilities in such State, other than such agency, shall notify such agency of each application for such a grant which is submitted by it to the Secretary, and the Secretary shall advise such agency with respect to the disposition of each such application.

 (d) The Secretary shall base his determinations of whether to approve applications for grants under this section and the amount of such grants on criteria set forth in regulations and designed to achieve (1) prompt and effective use of all educational television channels remaining available, (2) equitable geographical distribution of educational television broadcasting facilities throughout the States, and (3) provision of educational television broadcasting facilities which will serve the greatest number of persons and serve them in as many areas as possible, and which are adaptable to the broadest educational uses.

 (e) Upon approving any application under this section with respect to any project, the Secretary shall make a grant to the applicant in the amount determined by him, but not exceeding (1) 50 per centum of the amount which he determines to be the reasonable and necessary cost of such project, plus (2) 25 per centum of the amount which he determines to be the reasonable and necessary cost of any educational television broadcasting facilities owned by the applicant on the date on which it files such application; except that (A) the total amount of any grant made under this section with respect to any project may not exceed 75 per centum of the amount determined by the Secretary to be the reasonable and necessary cost of such project; and (B) not more than 15 per centum of any such grant may be used for the acquisition and installation of microwave equipment, boosters, translators, and repeaters which are to be used to connect two or more broadcasting stations. The Secretary shall pay such amount, in advance or by way of reimbursement, and in such installments consistent with construction progress, as he may determine.

(f) If, within ten years after completion of any project for construction of educational television broadcasting facilities with respect to which a grant has been made under this section—

(1) the applicant or other owner of such facilities ceases to be an agency, officer, institution, foundation, corporation, or association described in subsection (a)(1), or

(2) such facilities cease to be used for educational television purposes (unless the Secretary determines, in accordance with regulations, that there is good cause for releasing the applicant or other owner from the obligation so to do),

the United States shall be entitled to recover from the applicant or other owner of such facilities the amount bearing the same ratio to the then value (as determined by agreement of the parties or by action brought in the United States district court for the district in which such facilities are situated) of such facilities, as the amount of the Federal participation bore to the cost of construction of such facilities.

Records

SEC. 393. (a) Each recipient of assistance under this part shall keep such records as may be reasonably necessary to enable the Secretary to carry out his functions under this part, including records which fully disclose the amount and the disposition by such recipient of the proceeds of such assistance, the total cost of the project or undertaking in connection with which such assistance is given or used, and the amount and nature of that portion of the cost of the project or undertaking supplied by other sources, and such other records as will facilitate an effective audit.

(b) The Secretary and the Comptroller General of the United States, or any of their duly authorized representatives, shall have access for the purpose of audit and examination to any books, documents, papers, and records of the recipient that are pertinent to assistance received under this part.

Definitions

SEC. 394. For the purposes of this part—

    (1) The term "State" includes the District of Columbia and the Commonwealth of Puerto Rico.

    (2) The term "construction," as applied to educational television broadcasting facilities, means the acquisition and installation of transmission apparatus (including towers, microwave equipment, boosters, translators, repeaters, mobile equipment, and video-recording equipment) necessary for television broadcasting, including apparatus which may incidentally be used for transmitting closed circuit television programs, but does not include the construction or repair of structures to house such apparatus.

    (3) The term "Secretary" means the Secretary of Health, Education, and Welfare.

    (4) The term, "State educational television agency" means (A) a board or commission established by State law for the purpose of promoting educational television within a State, (B) a board or commission appointed by the Governor of a State for such purpose if such appointment is not inconsistent with State law, or (C) a State officer or agency responsible for the supervision of public elementary or secondary education or public higher education within the State which has been designated by the Governor to assume responsibility for the promotion of educational television; and, in the case of the District of Columbia, the term "Governor" means the Board of Commissioners of the District of Columbia.

    (5) The term "nonprofit" as applied to any foundation, corporation, or association, means a foundation, corporation, or association, no part of the net earnings of which inures, or may lawfully inure, to the benefit of any private shareholder or individual.

Provision of assistance by Federal Communications Commission

SEC. 395. The Federal Communications Commission is authorized to provide such assistance in carrying out the provisions of this part as may be requested by the Secretary. The Secretary shall provide for consultation and close cooperation with the Federal Communications Commission in the administration of his functions under this part which are of interest to or affect the functions of the Commission.

Rules and regulations

SEC. 396. The Secretary is authorized to make such rules and regulations as may be necessary to carry out this part, including regulations relating to the order of priority in approving applications for projects under section 392 or to determining the amounts of grants for such projects.

Federal interference or control prohibited

SEC. 397. Nothing contained in this part shall be deemed (1) to amend any other provision of, or requirement under this Act; or (2) to authorize any department, agency, officer, or employee of the United States to exercise any direction, supervision, or control over educational television broadcasting or over the curriculum, program of instruction, or personnel of any educational institution, school system, or educational broadcasting station or system.

FORD FOUNDATION
SATELLITE PROPOSAL

In 1966, as a possible answer to educational television's continuing financial and interconnection problems, the Ford Foundation, ETV's largest single donor, submitted a proposal to the FCC suggesting the establishment of a non-profit satellite system to replace traditional methods of network relay, i.e., microwave and coaxial circuits. The Foundation proposed that the proceeds from such a system be used to support ETV programming.

The following letter which prefaced the proposal, "Comments of the Ford Foundation . . . In the Matter of the Establishment of Domestic Non-Common Carrier Communications-Satellite Facilities by Non-Governmental Entities" (FCC Docket No. 16495), was made available with the kind permission of McGeorge Bundy, President of the Ford Foundation.

THE FORD FOUNDATION
August 1, 1966

The Honorable Rosel H. Hyde
Chairman, Federal Communications Commission
Washington, D.C.

Dear Mr. Chairman:

I have the honor to submit herewith a statement from the Ford Foundation which responds to the invitation of the Federal Communications Commission for "the views and comments of interested parties" on "proposals for the construction and operation of communications satellite facilities" by others than recognized common carriers. I am also addressing this same letter to each of the other Commissioners.

In this covering letter I want to summarize our conclusions—and also to explain informally the deep concern which moved us to make the studies which have led to this submission.

First, I note that the Ford Foundation has no commercial interest and no operating interest in this matter. We exist for the purpose of giving money away—as wisely and constructively as we can. This is the source of our deep interest in the present question.

We have a wider and longer experience of the effort to establish effective non-commercial television than any other single institution in the country. We have been by far the largest single source of funds for this effort. We have fifteen years of experience. We have made grants, directly and indirectly, of more than a hundred million dollars; currently we are making additional grants at the rate of more than ten million dollars a year.

From this experience we have learned three lessons:

(1) The first and most important lesson is that non-commercial television has unlimited potential, for human welfare and for the quality of American life. The best achievements of the best existing stations are proof enough—but there is still more powerful evidence in the best achievements of the best services abroad. And the most powerful evidence of all is the all-but-unanimous conviction of the ablest men in American television today: that nothing is more needed—for television itself as well as for the country—than a first-rate national non-commercial service.

(2) The second lesson is that existing services, and existing means of support, cannot hope to develop more than a fraction of this potential. The existing systems are much better than nothing. Compared to what this country deserves, they are a depressing failure. This is not the fault of the talented and dedicated men who have worked their hearts out for non-commercial television. It is the fault of all of us—in that we have not yet found a way to give this work the resources it needs. It can well be argued that we at the Ford Foundation have contributed to this failure. When we give $6,000,000 a year to the National Educational Television and Radio Center (NET), we seem to have done a lot. And for us it *is* a lot—it is our largest continuing annual grant. But the brutal fact is that our big gift is much too small.

(3) The third lesson follows from the first two: it is that the nation must find a way to a wholly new level of action in this field—one which will release for our whole people all the enlightenment and engagement, all the immediacy and freedom of experience which are inherent in this extraordinary medium and which commercial services—as they freely admit—cannot bring out alone.

These three general conclusions are broadly shared, I believe, among all who have studied this problem—by leaders in the Congress, by the members and staff of your Commission, and by independent experts. They underlie the establishment last year of a distinguished Commission of private citizens to study the future of non-commercial television, under a charge from the Carnegie Corporation and with encouragement from President Johnson. Under the chairmanship of Dr. James Killian that Commission is working hard to produce a prompt and constructive report. It will be good if we can avoid major decisions affecting the future of educational television until we have the benefit of the Carnegie report. A decision limiting the ownership and operation of communications satellites would be such a decision—and *on this ground alone* the Commission would do well to avoid any ruling of this sort at this time.

But there are legitimate and important interests which are pressing for early decisions. The Ford Foundation can well understand the forces that could lead some to argue that great commercial questions should not be delayed for months while everyone waits for "one more report" on the future of educational television. Because the Carnegie Commission is still at work, it is not in a position today to contest this point in detail. Yet it has seemed to us a matter of high importance that the public interest in the future of non-commercial television be fully and properly represented in the pleadings before your Commission. This is what our submission aims to do. Our right to present this view is the right of any element in our society to be heard. Our duty to do it grows from experience, expenditure, and the terms of our Foundation's charter.

This right and this duty are made doubly urgent because of the promise that satellite communications may permit a revolution both in the technology and in the economics of television. Intensive exploratory studies have convinced us at the Ford Foundation that these revolutionary possibilities offer the promise of building a cost-free highway system for multiplied regional and national non-commercial services—and also of providing a large part of the new funds which are desperately needed for non-commercial programming at every level.

The model we present is *one* way, not the *only* way. We are sure it can be improved by public study and comment. The state of the art is changing so fast—and we have had so much to learn since March 2—that we are sure our present design can be improved by criticism. For this reason alone we would welcome hearings on this whole subject. And on wider grounds we are sure that any major restrictive action taken without hearings would be offensive to the public sense of fairness.

While the financial needs of educational television are widely recognized, the sources of the needed funds have been elusive. With the shining exception of the Educational Television Facilities Act of 1962, the Federal Government as a whole has stood to one side (and the Act of 1962, with all its generosity and foresight, carries a total appropriation which is lower than the funds spent by the Ford Foundation alone in the years since the Act was passed). Moreover, Americans are understandably cautious about direct Federal financing of channels of communication to the public. A number of additional remedies have been suggested, and we must hope for more light on this from the Carnegie Commission, but the hard fact is that up to now no remotely adequate solution has been found. We all want educational television to be properly funded. We do not want the Government to "pay the piper and call the tune." We are looking for an answer.

And that is what makes the possibilities of satellites so extraordinarily important. Non-commercial television has two great needs: first, to become a true national network, at a cost it can afford—and second, to have money for programming, at a wholly new level of excellence. Properly used, a television satellite can meet both needs. By its natural economic advantage over long landlines, it can effectively eliminate long-distance charges as a determining element in network choices—commercial and non-commercial alike. And if in the case of commercial networks a major share of these savings is passed on to the non-commercial programmers, then both problems are on the road to solution, and everyone is better off than he was before. This is not magic, or sleight-of-hand. It is a people's dividend earned by the American nation from its enormous investment in space.

We are far from contending that a portion of the savings of the commercial users will pay for every possible program tomorrow. In our formal submission we estimate that such a system might produce $30 million a year for ETV programming almost at once, and perhaps twice that much within ten years. This is more than enough to start the revolution we seek —and there would be still more in the future.

And all this, our analysis suggests, should be accompanied also by a wholly new level of investment—public and private—in the programs of live *instruction* that the satellite system invites. The satellite, used in the right way, can make the desert bloom for whole new areas of television. We do not claim that our way of doing it is the best. We do believe the best way must be found.

One cause of questioning may be the initial human effort of establishing a service of the sort that we suggest. Where can we find the first-rate men for a new nonprofit venture? We have considered this question, and we have asked a number of the best professionals for their opinion. Their verdict is unanimous. We are talking here about a vision of excellence for the life of all Americans. Good men will want to work for it. We are convinced the signal of approval for a system like this one would release a rush of talent for the leaders of the new enterprise.

There is also a question of money. Once it is started, the enterprise will surely pay for itself and for much good besides. But who has the money to get it off the ground? That is a fair question, but we are convinced that there are good answers—in the resources of the commercial networks, in the lending power of those who know a sure success when they see it, and in the resources of those who hold the view that money which helps to turn this corner will be money well used for the quality of American life. Our own commitment to this general purpose is clear.

We fully recognize the legitimate and reasonable needs of others who are concerned with satellite communications. We are convinced that our proposal does no significant harm to the legitimate and recognized interests of Comsat or the common carriers. With or without added responsibility for domestic television, Comsat will remain an unusually privileged commercial enterprise—a prime and protected investment with exclusive chartered rights in international satellite service. Comsat faces international horizons which can engage its full energies for decades to come. The prosperity of *all* does not require for *any* a monopoly of the space communications available to the American people. And for the common carriers the revenue presently at issue is less than 1% of a business which grows by more than that in every season of every year.

For all these reasons, we believe the door to a new and separate broadcast satellite service must not be closed. We do not now present a formal application. We think it right to wait for the report of the Carnegie Commission, and we also believe that the Ford Foundation should not undertake alone the framing of a formal application in a matter which relates to the interests and concerns of all Americans. What we have done initially is to develop one possible model of a solution. We have tested it for technical feasibility with the professional counsel of Dr. Eugene Fubini of the International Business Machines Corporation. We have tested it against the laws with the help of Mr. David Ginsburg of Washington. We have tested its economic validity with the advice of Dr. Paul MacAvoy of the Massachusetts Institute of Technology. We have tested it against the realities of television programming with the help of Mr. Fred Friendly, our Advisor on Television. We have tested it against our own experience in the philanthropic support of non-commercial television. We think this model is sound against all these tests. But our purpose in presenting it is not to ask the Commission to grant a license now, to us or to anyone else. Our immediate purpose is rather to urge the Commission to take no action now that would foreclose these possibilities.

We think the Commission should invite a more formal proposal from the widest possible public. We think such a proposal would be forthcoming. We think it would be compelling. We would be glad to join with others to present it. All that we feel it right to do today is to enter the strongest possible argument against any action that would close the door to this new hope for all Americans.

In summary, our underlying purpose is not to press for a particular solution, and still less to interfere in any way with the legitimate interests of others. Our purpose is to stress four fundamental propositions:

(1) the critical importance to American life of properly designed domestic communications satellite systems;

(2) the very great—and largely unstudied—potential of such systems for non-commercial television and for education in its widest sense;

(3) the possibility that the management of this new national resource and the rates charged for its use can be arranged in such a way as to provide adequate resources for a wholly new level of service to the American people; and

(4) the desirability of most careful deliberation before national decisions

are reached with regard to the assignment of responsibility in this area.

This is a time for due process, and for greatness.

Sincerely,

McGeorge Bundy

THE CARNEGIE COMMISSION'S PUBLIC TELEVISION PROPOSAL*

4

A sweeping proposal to finance and revitalize educational television was made by the Carnegie Commission on Educational Television in 1967. The Commission was headed by James R. Killian, endorsed by President Johnson, and supported by a $500,000 grant from the Carnegie Corporation of New York.

The Commission's report recommended creation of a "Corporation for Public Television" to be financed through a Federal levy on sales of television sets. According to the Commission's definition, "Public Television" included those programs unsuited for commercial TV presentation, but not instructional programming.

The Carnegie Commission on Educational Television has reached the conclusion that a well-financed and well-directed educational television system, substantially larger and far more pervasive and effective than that which now exists in the United States, must be brought into being if the full needs of the American public are to be served. This is the central conclusion of the Commission and all of its recommendations are designed accordingly.

Although our Report deals primarily with what the Commission has chosen to call Public Television rather than with instructional television, we believe it to be urgently in the public interest that both categories be extended and strengthened. We concentrate on Public Television in the conviction that this service both requires and is ready for immediate action. Instructional television, which we consider no less significant, needs intensive further study in the total context of the educational enterprise, and is the subject of a major recommendation to this end.

The programs we conceive to be the essence of Public Television are in general not economic for commercial sponsorship, are not designed for the classroom, and are directed at audiences ranging from the tens of thou-

* "A Proposal to Extend and Strengthen Educational Television: A Summary of the Commission's Report," from *Public Television: A Program for Action* (January 25, 1967), pp. 3–9. Copyright © 1967 by the Carnegie Corporation of New York. Reprinted by permission of Harper & Row, Publishers.

sands to the occasional tens of millions. No such system now exists to serve us as model, and hence we have been obliged to develop a suitable new arrangement to bring this kind of television to the country. The Commission's proposal deals primarily with that new arrangement.

Although it provides for immediate assistance to existing stations, this is a proposal not for small adjustments or patchwork changes, but for a comprehensive system that will ultimately bring Public Television to all the people of the United States: a system that in its totality will become a new and fundamental institution in American culture.

This institution is different from any now in existence. It is not the educational television that we now know; it is not patterned after the commercial system or the British system or the Japanese system. In the course of our study, we examined all those and others: members of the staff visited Canada, England, Italy, Germany, and Sweden, and papers were commissioned on the Japanese and Russian systems. We found in many countries serious and skillful attempts to provide superior television programming, and in some countries highly successful attempts. But when such a system was successful it met the special needs of society in terms of that society's culture and tradition, and there was little or nothing we could expect to import. We propose an indigenous American system arising out of our own traditions and responsive to our own needs.

Accordingly, the Commission submits the following recommendations for the consideration of the people of the United States, their government, and those who for two decades have created and sustained the various institutions that constitute educational television.

THE COMMISSION URGES IMMEDIATE ACTION TO EXTEND AND STRENGTHEN EDUCATIONAL TELEVISION

1

We recommend concerted efforts at the federal, state, and local levels to improve the facilities and to provide for the adequate support of the individual educational television stations and to increase their number.

An effective national educational television system must consist in its very essence of vigorous and independent local stations, adequate in number and well equipped. They should reach all parts of the country. They should be individually responsive to the needs of the local communities and collectively strong enough to meet the needs of a national audience. Each must be a product of local initiative and local support.

Many good stations exist; they must be made better. Weak stations must be provided with the kind of support which will cure and not perpetuate their weakness. All educational television stations require greatly increased resources.

THE COMMISSION PROPOSES A NEW INSTITUTION FOR PUBLIC
TELEVISION

2

*We recommend that Congress act promptly to authorize and to establish a
federally chartered, nonprofit, nongovernmental corporation, to be known
as the "Corporation for Public Television." The Corporation should be
empowered to receive and disburse governmental and private funds in order
to extend and improve Public Television programming. The Commission
considers the creation of the Corporation fundamental to its proposal and
would be most reluctant to recommend the other parts of its plan unless the
corporate entity is brought into being.*

The Corporation will exist to serve the local station but will neither
operate it nor control it. Its primary mission will be to extend and improve
Public Television programming. Programs financed by the Corporation will
be made available to all stations, but each station will decide whether and
when it will use the program. We stress the critical importance of having
private funds available to the Corporation; such funds should be available
at the outset.

3

*We recommend that the Corporation support at least two national produc-
tion centers, and that it be free to contract with independent producers to
prepare Public Television programs for educational television stations.*

One center now in being is National Educational Television, which
should at once be strengthened.

4

*We recommend that the Corporation support, by appropriate grants and
contracts, the production of Public Television programs by local stations
for more-than-local use.*

The greatest practical diversity of program production sources is essential to the health of the system. Stations exist which now produce programs of interest outside their own areas, but which are in need of further
financial assistance. Other stations should be encouraged to develop comparable talent and capacity.

5

*We recommend that the Corporation on appropriate occasions help support
local programming by local stations.*

These would be low-cost programs prepared to meet the direct needs of the local community.

6

We recommend that the Corporation provide the educational television system as expeditiously as possible with facilities for live interconnection by conventional means, and that it be enabled to benefit from advances in technology as domestic communications satellites are brought into being. The Commission further recommends that Congress act to permit the granting of preferential rates for educational television for the use of interconnection facilities, or to permit their free use, to the extent that this may not be possible under existing law.

The Corporation has the responsibility for the distribution of programs. Public Television can never be a national enterprise until effective interconnection has been provided both in order to distribute programs to educational television stations promptly and economically and to provide for live regional or national broadcasts when the occasion demands. The interconnection of stations should make the best of each community available to all communities.

7

We recommend that the Corporation encourage and support research and development leading to the improvement of programming and program production.

Public Television should be free to experiment and should sponsor research centers where persons of high talent can engage in experimentation. The kind of experimentation once sponsored by the Ford Foundation TV-Radio Workshop is an example of what we are reaching for.

8

We recommend that the Corporation support technical experimentation designed to improve the present television technology.

Intensive research and development could make possible significant improvements in picture quality or savings in frequency spectrum.

9

We recommend that the Corporation undertake to provide means by which technical, artistic, and specialized personnel may be recruited and trained.

The Corporation should sponsor fellowship programs designed to attract talented persons into in-service training programs and into its research centers. In addition, it should provide stipends for senior fellows—men and women of talent and experience—to enable them to spend periods of residence at the various centers.

THE COMMISSION PROPOSES ENLARGED FEDERAL SUPPORT FOR TELEVISION

10

We recommend that Congress provide the federal funds required by the Corporation through a manufacturer's excise tax on television sets (beginning at 2 percent and rising to a ceiling of 5 percent). The revenues should be made available to the Corporation through a trust fund.

In this manner a stable source of financial support would be assured. We would free the Corporation to the highest degree from the annual governmental budgeting and appropriations procedures: the goal we seek is an instrument for the free communication of ideas in a free society.

The excise tax will provide the Corporation with approximately $40 million of federal funds during its first year of operation, rising gradually to a level of $100 million a year. We propose that the rate be raised to 3 percent, bringing in $60 million, after the first year. The Commission intends these revenues to be added to those available from other federal, local, and private sources to be used primarily for the support of programming for Public Television. We recommend that federal agencies continue to make grants to educational television stations for special purposes.

11

We recommend new legislation to enable the Department of Health, Education, and Welfare to provide adequate facilities for stations now in existence, to assist in increasing the number of stations to achieve nationwide coverage, to help support the basic operations of all stations, and to enlarge the support of instructional television programming.

The Commission views the responsibility of the Department of Health, Education, and Welfare as that of providing the basic facilities and operating funds for a national system of educational television stations. The Corporation, in contrast, will direct its attention to programming and related activities delineated in previous recommendations which are aimed to provide a new kind of Public Television for national and local audiences. The responsibility for instructional television for formal classroom use does not lie within the purview of the Corporation, but rather with state and local educational systems and the Department of Health, Education, and

Welfare. The Commission urges, as an interim measure, extension and amplification of the Educational Television Facilities Act of 1962, which has been of critical assistance in expanding educational television.

THE COMMISSION PROPOSES CONTINUING STUDY TO IMPROVE INSTRUCTIONAL TELEVISION

12

We recommend that federal, state, local, and private educational agencies sponsor extensive and innovative studies intended to develop better insights into the use of television in formal and informal education.

The Commission believes that the Public Television system it proposes will benefit the content of instructional television. But the Commission also believes that instructional television must be studied in the full context of education, and that further major investments in instructional television must benefit from the discovery of ways in which television can best contribute to the educational process. In addition to universities, nonprofit corporations, and the stations themselves, some of the Regional Educational Laboratories contemplated in Title IV of the Elementary and Secondary Education Act of 1965 might be appropriate agencies to conduct the necessary programs of research and development.

President Lyndon B. Johnson, in his comprehensive "Message on Education and Health in America" of February 28, 1967, requested legislation incorporating major aspects of the Carnegie Commission's Public Television proposal. The President left the question of long-term financing for Public Television for future determination, and included radio as well as television in his legislative recommendation. Only the portion of the message treating Public and Instructional broadcasting is included here.

Building for tomorrow

Public television

In 1951, the Federal Communications Commission set aside the first 242 television channels for non-commercial broadcasting, declaring: "The public interest will be clearly served if these stations contribute significantly to the educational process of the Nation."

The first educational television station went on the air in May 1953. Today, there are 178 non-commercial television stations on the air or under construction. Since 1963 the Federal Government has provided $32 million under the Educational Television Facilities Act to help build towers, transmitters and other facilities. These funds have helped stations with an estimated potential audience of close to 150 million citizens.

Yet we have only begun to grasp the great promise of this medium, which, in the words of one critic, has the power to "arouse our dreams, satisfy our hunger for beauty, take us on journeys, enable us to participate in events, present great drama and music, explore the sea and the sky and the winds and the hills."

Non-commercial television can bring its audience the excitement of excellence in every field. I am convinced that a vital and self-sufficient non-commercial television system will not only instruct, but inspire and uplift our people.

Practically all non-commercial stations have serious shortages of the

582

facilities, equipment, money and staff which they need to present programs of high quality. There are not enough stations. Interconnections between stations are inadequate and seldom permit the timely scheduling of current programs.

Non-commercial television today is reaching only a fraction of its potential audience—and achieving only a fraction of its potential worth.

Clearly, the time has come to build on the experience of the past fourteen years, the important studies that have been made, and the beginnings we have made.

> *I recommend that Congress enact the Public Television Act of 1967 to:*
>
> —*Increase federal funds for television and radio facility construction to $10.5 million in fiscal 1968, more than three times this year's appropriations.*
>
> —*Create a Corporation for Public Television authorized to provide support to non-commercial television and radio.*
>
> —*Provide $9 million in fiscal 1968 as initial funding for the Corporation.*

Next year, after careful review, I will make further proposals for the Corporation's long-term financing.

Non-commercial television and radio in America, even though supported by federal funds, must be absolutely free from any federal government interference over programming. As I said in the State of the Union Message, "we should insist that the public interest be fully served through the public's airwaves."

The board of directors of the Corporation for public television should include American leaders in education, communications and the creative arts. I recommend that the board be comprised of fifteen members, appointed by the President and confirmed by the Senate.

The Corporation would provide support to establish production centers and to help local stations improve their proficiency. It would be authorized to accept funds from other sources, public and private.

The strength of public television should lie in its diversity. Every region and community should be challenged to contribute its best.

Other opportunities for the Corporation exist to support vocational training for young people who desire careers in public television, to foster research and development, and to explore new ways to serve the viewing public.

One of the Corporation's first tasks should be to study the practicality and the economic advantages of using communication satellites to establish an educational television and radio network. To assist the Corporation, I am directing the Administrator of the National Aeronautics and Space Administration and the Secretary of Health, Education, and Welfare to conduct experiments on the requirements for such a system, and for instructional television, in cooperation with other interested agencies of the government and private sector.

Formulation of long-range policies concerning the future of satellite communications requires the most detailed and comprehensive study by the Executive Branch and the Congress. I anticipate that the appropriate committees of Congress will hold hearings to consider these complex issues of public policy. The Executive Branch will carefully study these hearings as we shape our recommendations.

Instructional television

I recommend legislation to authorize the Secretary of Health, Education, and Welfare to launch a major study of the value and promise of instructional television which is being used more and more widely in our classrooms, but whose potential has not been fully developed.

THE PUBLIC BROADCASTING ACT OF 1967

6

$Go \leftarrow to\ 550$

Public Law 90-129, 90th Congress
November 7, 1967 (Amended to April 26, 1968)

An outgrowth of the Carnegie Commission's proposal and President Johnson's request for legislation to implement that proposal, this Act extends the provisions of the ETV Facilities Act of 1962, authorizes a study of instructional broadcasting, and creates a Corporation for Public Broadcasting. The Corporation is empowered to receive and disburse funds for the production and distribution of educational programs.

It remains to be seen whether and how sufficient financial support for educational radio and television will be generated as a result of this legislation.

TITLE I—CONSTRUCTION OF FACILITIES

Extension of duration of construction grants for educational broadcasting

Sec. 101. (a) Section 391 of the Communications Act of 1934 (47 U.S.C. 391) is amended by inserting after the first sentence the following new sentence: "There are also authorized to be appropriated for carrying out the purposes of such section, $10,500,000 for the fiscal year ending June 30, 1968, $12,500,000 for the fiscal year ending June 30, 1969, and $15,000,000 for the fiscal year ending June 30, 1970."

(b) The last sentence of such section is amended by striking out "July 1, 1968" and inserting in lieu thereof "July 1, 1971."

Maximum on grants in any State

Sec. 102. Effective with respect to grants made from appropriations for any fiscal year beginning after June 30, 1967, subsection (b) of section 392 of the Communications Act of 1934 (47 U.S.C. 392(b)) is amended to read as follows:

"(b) The total of the grants made under this part from the appropriation for any fiscal year for the construction of noncommercial educational television broadcasting facilities and noncommercial educational radio broadcasting facilities in any State may not exceed 8½ per centum of such appropriation."

Noncommercial educational radio broadcasting facilities

Sec. 103. (a) Section 390 of the Communications Act of 1934 (47 U.S.C. 390) is amended by inserting "noncommercial" before "educational" and by inserting "or radio" after "television."

(b) Subsection (a) of section 392 of the Communications Act of 1934 (47 U.S.C. 392(a)) is amended by—

(1) inserting "noncommercial" before "educational" and by inserting "or radio" after "television" in so much thereof as precedes paragraph (1);

(2) striking out clause (B) of such paragraph and inserting in lieu thereof "(B) in the case of a project for television facilities, the State noncommercial educational television agency or, in the case of a project for radio facilities, the State educational radio agency";

(3) inserting "(i) in the case of a project for television facilities," after "(D)" and "noncommercial" before "educational" in paragraph (1) (D) and by inserting before the semicolon at the end of such paragraph ", or (ii) in the case of a project for radio facilities, a nonprofit foundation, corporation, or association which is organized primarily to engage in or encourage non-commercial educational radio broadcasting and is eligible to receive a license from the Federal Communications Commission; or meets the requirements of clause (i) and is also organized to engage in or encourage such radio broadcasting and is eligible for such a license for such a radio station";

(4) striking out "or" immediately preceding "(D)" in paragraph (1), and by striking out the semicolon at the end of such paragraph and inserting in lieu thereof the following: ", or (E) a municipality which owns and operates a broadcasting facility transmitting only noncommercial programs;";

(5) striking out "television" in paragraphs (2), (3), and (4) of such subsection;

(6) striking out "and" at the end of paragraph (3), striking out the period at the end of paragraph (4) and inserting in lieu thereof "; and", and inserting after paragraph (4) the following new paragraph:

"(5) that, in the case of an application with respect to radio broadcasting facilities, there has been comprehensive planning for educational broadcasting facilities and services in the area the applicant proposes to serve and the applicant has participated in such planning, and the applicant will make the most efficient use of the frequency assignment."

(c) Subsection (c) of such section is amended by inserting "(1)" after "(c)" and "noncommercial" before "educational television broadcasting facilities", and by inserting at the end thereof the following new paragraph:

"(2) In order to assure proper coordination of construction of noncommercial educational radio broadcasting facilities within each State which has established a State educational radio agency, each applicant for a grant under this section for a project for construction of such facilities in such State, other than such agency, shall notify such agency of each application for such a grant which is submitted by it to the Secretary, and the Secretary shall advise such agency with respect to the disposition of each such application."

(d) Subsection (d) of such section is amended by inserting "noncommercial" before "educational television" and inserting "or noncommercial educational radio broadcasting facilities, as the case may be," after "educational television broadcasting facilities" in clauses (2) and (3).

(e) Subsection (f) of such section is amended by inserting "or radio" after "television" in the part thereof which precedes paragraph (1), by inserting "noncommercial" before "educational television purposes" in paragraph (2) thereof, and by inserting "or noncommercial educational radio purposes, as the case may be" after "educational television purposes" in such paragraph (2).

(f) (1) Paragraph (2) of section 394 of such Act (47 U.S.C. 394) is amended by inserting "or educational radio broadcasting facilities" after "educational television broadcasting facilities," and by inserting "or radio broadcasting, as the case may be" after "necessary for television broadcasting."

(2) Paragraph (4) of such section is amended by striking out "The term 'State educational television agency' means" and inserting in lieu thereof "The terms 'State educational television agency' and 'State educational radio agency' mean, with respect to television broadcasting and radio broadcasting, respectively," and by striking out "educational television" in clauses (A) and (C) and inserting in lieu thereof "such broadcasting".

(g) Section 397 of such Act (47 U.S.C. 397) is amended by inserting "or radio" after "television" in clause (2).

Federal share of cost of construction

Sec. 104. Subsection (e) of section 392 of the Communications Act of 1934 (47 U.S.C. 392(e)) is amended to read as follows:

"(e) Upon approving any application under this section with respect to any project, the Secretary shall make a grant to the applicant in the amount determined by him, but not exceeding 75 per centum of the amount determined by the Secretary to be the reasonable and necessary cost of such project. The Secretary shall pay such amount from the sum available therefor, in advance or by way of reimbursement, and in such installments consistent with construction progress, as he may determine."

Inclusion of territories

Sec. 105. (a) Paragraph (1) of section 394 of the Communications Act of 1934 is amended by striking out "and" and inserting a comma in lieu thereof, and by inserting before the period at the end thereof ", the Virgin Islands, Guam, American Samoa, and the Trust Territory of the Pacific Islands."

(b) Paragraph (4) of such section is amended by inserting "and, in the case of the Trust Territory of the Pacific Islands, means the High Commissioner thereof" before the period at the end thereof.

Inclusion of costs of planning

Sec. 106. Paragraph (2) of section 394 of the Communications Act of 1934 is further amended by inserting at the end thereof the following: "In the case of apparatus the acquisition and installation of which is so included, such term also includes planning therefor."

TITLE II—ESTABLISHMENT OF NONPROFIT EDUCATIONAL BROADCASTING CORPORATION

Sec. 201. Part IV of title III of the Communications Act of 1934 is further amended by—

(1) inserting

"Subpart A—Grants for Facilities"

immediately above the heading of section 390;

(2) striking out "part" and inserting in lieu thereof "subpart" in sections 390, 393, 395, and 396;

(3) redesignating section 397 as section 398, and redesignating section 394 as section 397 and inserting it before such section 398, and inserting immediately above its heading the following:

"Subpart C—General"

(4) redesignating section 396 as section 394 and inserting it immediately after section 393;

(5) inserting after "broadcasting" the first time it appears in clause (2) of the section of such part IV redesignated herein as section 398 ", or

over the Corporation or any of its grantees or contractors, or over the charter or bylaws of the Corporation,".

(6) inserting in the section of such part IV herein redesignated as section 397 the following new paragraphs:

"(6) The term 'Corporation' means the Corporation authorized to be established by subpart B of this part.

"(7) The term 'noncommercial educational broadcast station' means a television or radio broadcast station, which (A) under the rules and regulations of the Federal Communications Commission in effect on the date of enactment of the Public Broadcasting Act of 1967, is eligible to be licensed or is licensed by the Commission as a noncommercial educational radio or television broadcast station and which is owned and operated by a public agency or nonprofit foundation, corporation, or association or (B) is owned and operated by a municipality and which transmits only noncommercial programs for educational purposes.

"(8) The term 'interconnection' means the use of microwave equipment, boosters, translators, repeaters, communication space satellites, or other apparatus or equipment for the transmission and distribution of television or radio programs to noncommercial educational television or radio broadcast stations.

"(9) The term 'educational television or radio programs' means programs which are primarily designed for educational or cultural purposes."

(7) striking out the heading of such part IV and inserting in lieu thereof the following:

"PART IV—GRANTS FOR NONCOMMERCIAL EDUCATIONAL BROADCASTING FACILITIES; CORPORATION FOR PUBLIC BROADCASTING"

(8) inserting immediately after the section herein redesignated as section 398 the following:

"Editorializing and support of political candidates prohibited

"Sec. 399. No noncommercial educational broadcasting station may engage in editorializing or may support or oppose any candidate for political office."

(9) inserting after section 395 the following new subpart:

"Subpart B—Corporation for Public Broadcasting

"Congressional Declaration of Policy

"Sec. 396. (a) The Congress hereby finds and declares—

"(1) that it is in the public interest to encourage the growth and development of noncommercial educational radio and television broadcasting, including the use of such media for instructional purposes;

"(2) that expansion and development of noncommercial educational radio and television broadcasting and of diversity of its programing depend on freedom, imagination, and initiative on both the local and national levels;

"(3) that the encouragement and support of noncommercial educational radio and television broadcasting, while matters of importance for private and local development, are also of appropriate and important concern to the Federal Government;

"(4) that it furthers the general welfare to encourage noncommercial educational radio and television broadcast programing which will be responsive to the interests of people both in particular localities and throughout the United States, and which will constitute an expression of diversity and excellence;

"(5) that it is necessary and appropriate for the Federal Government to complement, assist, and support a national policy that will most effectively make noncommercial educational radio and television service available to all the citizens of the United States;

"(6) that a private corporation should be created to facilitate the development of educational radio and television broadcasting and to afford maximum protection to such broadcasting from extraneous interference and control.

"Corporation Established

"(b) There is authorized to be established a nonprofit corporation, to be known as the 'Corporation for Public Broadcasting,' which will not be an agency or establishment of the United States Government. The Corporation shall be subject to the provisions of this section, and, to the extent consistent with this section, to the District of Columbia Nonprofit Corporation Act.

"Board of Directors

"(c) (1) The Corporation shall have a Board of Directors (hereinafter in this section referred to as the 'Board'), consisting of fifteen members appointed by the President, by and with the advice and consent of the Senate. Not more than eight members of the Board may be members of the same political party.

"(2) The members of the Board (A) shall be selected from among citizens of the United States (not regular fulltime employees of the United States) who are eminent in such fields as education, cultural and civic affairs, or the arts, including radio and television; (B) shall be selected so as to provide as nearly as practicable a broad representation of various regions of the country, various professions and occupations, and various kinds of talent and experience appropriate to the functions and responsibilities of the Corporation.

"(3) The members of the initial Board of Directors shall serve as incorporators and shall take whatever actions are necessary to establish the Corporation under the District of Columbia Nonprofit Corporation Act.

"(4) The term of office of each member of the Board shall be six years; except that (A) any member appointed to fill a vacancy occurring prior to the expiration of the term for which his predecessor was appointed shall be appointed for the remainder of such term; and (B) the terms of office of members first taking office shall begin on the date of incorporation and shall expire, as designated at the time of their appointment, five at the end of two years, five at the end of four years, and five at the end of six years. No member shall be eligible to serve in excess of two consecutive terms of six years each. Notwithstanding the preceding provisions of this paragraph, a member whose term has expired may serve until his successor has qualified.

"(5) Any vacancy in the Board shall not affect its power, but shall be filled in the manner in which the original appointments were made.

"Election of Chairman; Compensation

"(d) (1) The President shall designate one of the members first appointed to the Board as Chairman; thereafter the members of the Board shall annually elect one of their number as Chairman. The members of the Board shall also elect one or more of them as a Vice Chairman or Vice Chairmen.

"(2) The members of the Board shall not, by reason of such membership, be deemed to be employees of the United States. They shall, while attending meetings of the Board or while engaged in duties related to such meetings or in other activities of the Board pursuant to this subpart be entitled to receive compensation at the rate of $100 per day including travel time, and while away from their homes or regular places of business they may be allowed travel expenses, including per diem in lieu of subsistence, equal to that authorized by law (5 U.S.C. 5703) for persons in the Government service employed intermittently.

"Officers and Employees

"(e) (1) The Corporation shall have a President, and such other officers as may be named and appointed by the Board for terms and at rates of compensation fixed by the Board. No individual other than a citizen of the United States may be an officer of the Corporation. No officer of the Corporation, other than the Chairman and any Vice Chairman, may receive any salary or other compensation from any source other than the Corporation during the period of his employment by the Corporation. All officers shall serve at the pleasure of the Board.

"(2) Except as provided in the second sentence of subsection (c) (1) of this section, no political test or qualification shall be used in selecting, appointing, promoting, or taking other personnel actions with respect to officers, agents, and employees of the Corporation.

"Nonprofit and Nonpolitical Nature of the Corporation

"(f) (1) The Corporation shall have no power to issue any shares of stock, or to declare or pay any dividends.

"(2) No part of the income or assets of the Corporation shall inure to the benefit of any director, officer, employee, or any other individual except as salary or reasonable compensation for services.

"(3) The Corporation may not contribute to or otherwise support any political party or candidate for elective public office.

"Purposes and Activities of the Corporation

"(g) (1) In order to achieve the objectives and to carry out the purposes of this subpart, as set out in subsection (a), the Corporation is authorized to—

"(A) facilitate the full development of educational broadcasting in which programs of high quality, obtained from diverse sources, will be made available to noncommercial educational television or radio broadcast stations, with strict adherence to objectivity and balance in all programs or series of programs of a controversial nature;

"(B) assist in the establishment and development of one or more systems of interconnection to be used for the distribution of educational television or radio programs so that all noncommercial educational television or radio broadcast stations that wish to may broadcast the programs at times chosen by the stations;

"(C) assist in the establishment and development of one or more systems of noncommercial educational television or radio broadcast stations throughout the United States;

"(D) carry out its purposes and functions and engage in its activities in ways that will most effectively assure the maximum freedom of the noncommercial educational television or radio broadcast systems and local stations from interference with or control of program content or other activities.

"(2) Included in the activities of the Corporation authorized for accomplishment of the purposes set forth in subsection (a) of this section, are, among others not specifically named—

"(A) to obtain grants from and to make contracts with individuals and with private, State, and Federal agencies, organizations, and institutions;

"(B) to contract with or make grants to program production entities, individuals, and selected noncommercial educational broadcast stations for the production of, and otherwise to procure, educational television or radio programs for national or regional distribution to noncommercial educational broadcast stations;

"(C) to make payments to existing and new noncommercial educational broadcast stations to aid in financing local educational television or radio programing costs of such stations, particularly innovative approaches thereto, and other costs of operation of such stations;

"(D) to establish and maintain a library and archives of noncommercial educational television or radio programs and related materials and develop public awareness of and disseminate information about noncommercial educational television or radio broadcasting by various means, including the publication of a journal;

"(E) to arrange, by grant or contract with appropriate public or private agencies, organizations, or institutions, for interconnection facilities suitable for distribution and transmission of educational television or radio programs to noncommercial educational broadcast stations;

"(F) to hire or accept the voluntary services of consultants, experts, advisory boards, and panels to aid the Corporation in carrying out the purposes of this section;

"(G) to encourage the creation of new noncommercial educational broadcast stations in order to enhance such service on a local, State, regional, and national basis;

"(H) conduct (directly or through grants or contracts) research, demonstrations, or training in matters related to noncommercial educational television or radio broadcasting.

"(3) To carry out the foregoing purposes and engage in the foregoing activities, the Corporation shall have the usual powers conferred upon a nonprofit corporation by the District of Columbia Nonprofit Corporation Act, except that the Corporation may not own or operate any television or radio broadcast station, system, or network, community antenna television system, or interconnection or program production facility.

"Authorization for Free or Reduced Rate Interconnection Service

"(h) Nothing in the Communications Act of 1934, as amended, or in any other provision of law shall be construed to prevent United States communications common carriers from rendering free or reduced rate communications interconnection services for noncommercial educational television or radio services, subject to such rules and regulations as the Federal Communications Commission may prescribe.

"Report to Congress

"(i) The Corporation shall submit an annual report for the preceding fiscal year ending June 30 to the President for transmittal to the Congress on or before the 31st day of December of each year. The report shall include a comprehensive and detailed report of the Corporation's operations, activities, financial condition, and accomplishments under this section and may include such recommendations as the Corporation deems appropriate.

"Right to Repeal, Alter, or Amend

"(j) The right to repeal, alter, or amend this section at any time is expressly reserved.

"Financing

"(k) (1) There are authorized to be appropriated for expenses of the Corporation for the fiscal year ending June 30, 1969, the sum of $9,000,000, to remain available until expended.

"(2) Notwithstanding the preceding provisions of this section, no grant or contract pursuant to this section may provide for payment from the appropriation for the fiscal year ending June 30, 1969, for any one project or to any one station of more than $250,000.

"Records and Audit

"(l) (1) (A) The accounts of the Corporation shall be audited annually in accordance with generally accepted auditing standards by independent certified public accountants or independent licensed public accountants certified or licensed by a regulatory authority of a State or other political subdivision of the United States. The audits shall be conducted at the place or places where the accounts of the Corporation are normally kept. All books, accounts, financial records, reports, files, and all other papers, things, or property belonging to or in use by the Corporation and necessary to facilitate the audits shall be made available to the person or persons conducting the audits; and full facilities for verifying transactions with the balances or securities held by depositories, fiscal agents and custodians shall be afforded to such person or persons.

"(B) The report of each such independent audit shall be included in the annual report required by subsection (i) of this section. The audit report shall set forth the scope of the audit and include such statements as are necessary to present fairly the Corporation's assets and liabilities, surplus or deficit, with an analysis of the changes therein during the year, supplemented in reasonable detail by a statement of the Corporation's income and expenses during the year, and a statement of the sources and application of funds, together with the independent auditor's opinion of those statements.

"(2) (A) The financial transactions of the Corporation for any fiscal year during which Federal funds are available to finance any portion of its operations may be audited by the General Accounting Office in accordance with the principles and procedures applicable to commercial corporate transactions and under such rules and regulations as may be prescribed by the Comptroller General of the United States. Any such audit shall be conducted at the place or places where accounts of the Corporation are normally kept. The representative of the General Accounting Office shall have access to all books, accounts, records, reports, files, and all other papers, things, or property belonging to or in use by the Corporation pertaining to its financial transactions and necessary to facilitate the audit, and they shall be afforded full facilities for verifying transactions with the balances or securities held by depositories, fiscal agents, and custodians. All such books, accounts, records, reports, files, papers and property of the Corporation shall remain in possesssion and custody of the Corporation.

"(B) A report of each such audit shall be made by the Comptroller General to the Congress. The report to the Congress shall contain such comments and information as the Comptroller General may deem necessary to inform Congress of the financial operations and condition of the Corporation, together with such recommendations with respect thereto as he may deem advisable. The report shall also show specifically any program, expenditure, or other financial transaction or undertaking observed in the course of the audit, which, in the opinion of the Comptroller General, has been carried on or made without authority of law. A copy of each report shall be furnished to the President, to the Secretary, and to the Corporation at the time submitted to the Congress.

"(3) (A) Each recipient of assistance by grant or contract, other than a fixed price contract awarded pursuant to competitive bidding procedures, under this section shall keep such records as may be reasonably necessary to fully disclose the amount and the disposition by such recipient of the proceeds of such assistance, the total cost of the project or undertaking in connection with which such assistance is given or used, and the amount and nature of that portion of the cost of the project or undertaking supplied by other sources, and such other records as will facilitate an effective audit.

"(B) The Corporation or any of its duly authorized representatives, shall have access for the purpose of audit and examination to any books, documents, papers, and records of the recipient that are pertinent to assistance received under this section. The Comptroller General of the United States or any of his duly authorized representatives shall also have access thereto for such purpose during any fiscal year for which Federal funds are available to the Corporation."

TITLE III—STUDY OF EDUCATIONAL AND INSTRUCTIONAL BROADCASTING

Study authorized

Sec. 301. The Secretary of Health, Education, and Welfare is authorized to conduct, directly or by contract, and in consultation with other interested

Federal agencies, a comprehensive study of instructional television and radio (including broadcast, closed circuit, community antenna television, and instructional television fixed services and two-way communication of data links and computers) and their relationship to each other and to instructional materials such as videotapes, films, discs, computers, and other educational materials or devices, and such other aspects thereof as may be of assistance in determining whether and what Federal aid should be provided for instructional radio and television and the form that aid should take, and which may aid communities, institutions, or agencies in determining whether and to what extent such activities should be used.

Duration of study

Sec. 302. The study authorized by this title shall be submitted to the President for transmittal to the Congress on or before June 30, 1969.

Appropriation

Sec. 303. There are authorized to be appropriated for the study authorized by this title such sums, not exceeding $500,000, as may be necessary.

RELATED READING

BRONSON, Vernon. "ETV: A Proper Home," *Television Quarterly,* II (Summer, 1963), 74–78.

———. "Implications of Communications Satellites for Educational Television," *NAEB Journal,* XXII (November–December, 1963), 54–59.

BUNDY, McGeorge. "Educational TV: A National Awakening," *NAEB Journal,* XXVI (May–June, 1967), 3–8.

CARLSON, Robert A. "1951: A Pivotal Year for ETV," *Educational Broadcasting Review,* I (December, 1967), 47–54.

COSTELLO, Lawrence F., and George N. GORDON. *Teach With Television,* 2nd ed. New York: Hastings House, 1965.

DONNELLY, Richard. "The Ford Foundation: Where the Giving is Easy," *Television,* XXIV (February, 1967), 24–27, 49–51.

Educational Television: The Next Ten Years. Stanford, Cal.: Institute for Communication Research, 1962.

Education on the Air (Yearbook of the Institute for Education by Radio [and Television]). Columbus: Ohio State University Press, 1930–1953, and irregularly thereafter.

EMERY, Walter B. "Is There a Constitutional Flaw in the Public Broadcasting Act of 1967?," *Educational Broadcasting Review,* II (February, 1968), 17–21.

ESHELMAN, David. "About College FM Stations," *NAEB Journal,* XXIV (September–October, 1965), 33–42.

———. "The Emergence of Educational FM Broadcasting," *NAEB Journal,* XXVI (March–April, 1967), 53–64.

FROST, S. E., Jr. *Education's Own Stations.* Chicago: University of Chicago Press, 1937.

GLICK, Edwin L. "Trial by Fire: The First 10 Years of WGBH-TV," *NAEB Journal,* XXV (September–October, 1966), 10–17.

GOULD, Samuel B. "ETV—Neither Separate Nor Equal," *Television Quarterly,* I (November, 1962), 33–39.

HANEY, John B. "Public Opinion on Tax-Supported Television," *Journal of Broadcasting,* V (Fall, 1961), 315–324.

HERLINGER, Paul. "ETV and the All-Channel Law," *NAEB Journal,* XXII (July–August, 1963), 11–16.

HILL, Harold E. *The National Association of Educational Broadcasters. A History.* Urbana, Ill.: National Association of Educational Broadcasters, 1954. (Mimeographed.)

KOENIG, Allen E., and Ruane B. HILL, eds. *The Farther Vision: Educational Television Today.* Madison: University of Wisconsin Press, 1967.

JOHNSON, Nicholas. "The Why of Public Broadcasting," *Educational Broadcasting Review,* I (December, 1967), 5–10.

JORGENSEN, Norman E., Louis SCHWARTZ, and Robert A. WOODS. "The Misunderstood Media: A Legal Look at Educational Broadcasting," *Educational Broadcasting Review,* I (October, 1967), 7–14.

MARSH, C. S., ed. *Educational Broadcasting, 1936: Proceedings of the First National Conference on Educational Broadcasting.* Chicago: University of Chicago Press, 1937.

MURPHY, Judith, and Ronald GROSS. *Learning by Television.* New York: Fund for the Advancement of Education, 1966.

NEWSOM, Carroll V., ed. *A Television Policy for Education.* Washington: American Council on Education, 1952.

PIERSON, W. Theodore. "What Is the American System of Broadcasting?," *Journal of Broadcasting,* X (Summer, 1966), 191–198.

POWELL, John Walker. *Channels of Learning.* Washington: Public Affairs Press, 1962.

SCHRAMM, Wilbur. *The Impact of Educational Television.* Urbana, University of Illinois Press, 1960.

————, Jack LYLE, and Ithiel De Sola POOL. *The People Look at Educational Television.* Stanford, Cal.: Stanford University Press, 1963.

SIEPMANN, Charles A. *TV and Our School Crisis.* New York: Dodd, Mead, 1958.

SKORNIA, Harry J. "The NAEB: Past and Future," *NAEB Journal,* XX (January–February, 1961), 55–64.

SMITH, R. Franklin. "A Look at the Wagner-Hatfield Amendment," *NAEB Journal,* XXIII (March–April, 1964), 64–72.

————. "Madame Commissioner," *Journal of Broadcasting,* XII (Winter, 1967–68), 69–81.

SMITH, Robert R. "Duopoly and ETV," *NAEB Journal,* XXV (May–June, 1966), 40–48.

STODDARD, Alexander J. *Schools for Tomorrow: An Educator's Blueprint.* New York: Fund for the Advancement of Education, 1957.

Teaching by Television. New York: Ford Foundation and Fund for the Advancement of Education, 1961.

Television Quarterly, VII (Winter, 1968). (The entire issue deals with public television.)

TYSON, Levering, ed. *Radio and Education.* Chicago: University of Chicago *Press,* 1931–1935.

UNITED STATES CONGRESS, SENATE, COMMITTEE ON COMMERCE. *The Public Television Act of 1967,* Hearings before the Subcommittee on Communications, 90th Congress, 1st Session, on S. 1160, April 11–14, 25–28, 1967. Washington: Government Printing Office, 1967.

"Untapped Financial Resources for Educational Broadcasting" (a series of four articles on the subject), *NAEB Journal,* XXIV (March–April, 1965), 26–45.

WYLIE, Donald G. "Twenty Years of Airborne TV," *NAEB Journal,* XXIII (November–December, 1964), 70–76.